RONALD COLMAN

Ronald Colman and Jane Wyatt are beautifully dressed for paradise in this publicity shot for *Lost Horizon* (1937). From the author's collection.

RONALD COLMAN

A *Bio-Bibliography*

SAM FRANK

Foreword by Robert E. Morsberger

Bio-Bibliographies in the Performing Arts,
Number 74
James Robert Parish, Series Adviser

GREENWOOD PRESS
Westport, Connecticut • London

PN
2287
.C57
F73
1997

Library of Congress Cataloging-in-Publication Data

Frank, Sam.
    Ronald Colman : a bio-bibliography / Sam Frank : foreword by
Robert E. Morsberger.
       p.   cm.—(Bio-bibliographies in the performing arts, ISSN
0892–5550 ; no. 74)
  Filmography: p.
  Discography: p.
  Includes biliographical references and index.
  ISBN 0–313–26433–3 (alk. paper)
  1. Colman, Ronald, 1891–1958. 2. Colman, Ronald, 1891–1958—
Bibliography. 3. Motion picture actors and actresses—United
States—Biography. I. Title. II. Series.
PN2287.C57F73 1997
791.43′028′092—dc21
  [B]   96–50240

British Library Cataloguing in Publication Data is available

Copyright © 1997 by Sam Frank

All rights reserved. No portion of this book may be
reproduced, by any process or technique, without the
express written consent of the publisher.

Library of Congress Catalog Card Number: 96–50240
ISBN: 0–313–26433–3
ISSN: 0892–5550

First published in 1997

Greenwood Press, 88 Post Road West, Westport, CT 06881
An imprint of Greenwood Publishing Group, Inc.

Printed in the United States of America

The paper used in this book complies with the
Permanent Paper Standard issued by the National
Information Standards Organization (Z39.48–1984).

10 9 8 7 6 5 4 3 2 1

The author and publisher gratefully acknowledge permission for use of the following material:

Lyrics for "The Halls of Ivy" theme song by Vick Night, Sr. Courtesy of Vick Night, Jr.

Excerpts from a review of the premiere of "The Halls of Ivy" in *Weekly Variety,* October 27, 1954.
Courtesy of *Variety.*

Excerpt from a letter from Joan Benny to Sam Frank, dated January 14, 1992, and permission to
reprint the winning entry from the "I Can't Stand Jack Benny Because" contest. Courtesy of Joan
Benny.

Every reasonable effort has been made to trace the owners of copyright materials in this book, but in
some instances this has proven impossible. The author and publisher will be glad to receive information leading to more complete acknowledgments in subsequent printings of the book and in the
meantime extend their apologies for any omissions.

Dedicated with love to my trio of Ronald Colman soulmates
without whom this book could not have been written:

Kendall Miller

Robert E. Morsberger

George Evans Schatz

To Dr. Robert Knutson,
Cinema Librarian Emeritus of USC, for
teaching me much of what I know about researching film history.

To Hans Conried,
one of the greatest actors of this century
and one of Colman's frequent radio co-stars.
I knew him the last two years of his life and miss him dearly.

And to my mother,
Sarah "Mickey" Frank,
for supporting and encouraging my obsession
with Ronald Colman since it began in 1965.

CONTENTS

ACKNOWLEDGMENTS

This book is the product of 29 years of obsessive love and research. Though I compiled much of the material through books and articles and my own interviews, I also had help from a lot of people before and after I started this project:

Stage: Herbert G. Goldman; Miles Krueger; Julia Law of London's Theatre Museum; the Los Angeles Central Library for rare copies of plays; Richard Mangan of the Mander & Mitchenson theater archive in Kent, England; and Marilyn Rovner.

Filmography: Julian Allen of the BFI's Library Services Dept. and Olwen Terris and Jane Hockings of their National Film Archive; Eileen Bowser of MOMA; John Cocchi for proofing and adding to cast lists; James Cozart and David Parker of the Library of Congress's (LC) film preservation department; Ben Brewster, Donald Crafton and Maxine Fleckner Ducey of the Wisconsin Center for Film and Theater Research; Bob Dickson.

The late John Hampton of Silent Movie in Hollywood and its current owner, Larry Austin, for screening Colman movies over the years; Jack Hardy of Grapevine Video; the late Ron Haver of LACMA's film department for including Colman movies in various series during his 21-year tenure; Charles Hopkins and Eric Jerstad of the UCLA Film Archives; ex-Cinecon Vice-President Ed Hulse for obtaining *$20 a Week* for screening at Cinecon 28; Katharine Loughney and Madeline Matz of LC's film division.

Radiography: CBS librarian John Behrens for press releases; Frank Bresee; Ned Comstock of USC's Cinema Library; Norman Corwin; Nena Couch of the Lawrence & Lee Theatre Research Institute at Ohio State University for *Favorite Story* cast lists; John Dunning; Randy Eidemiller; Milton Ferguson for his *Halls of Ivy* database and copies of shows; Ken Greenwald for voice IDs; Dan Haefele; Charles Henry; Jay Hickerson; Jerome Lawrence for material on *Favorite Story*; Chris Lembesis, Jr.; Edwin Matthias of LC; Milton and Barbara Merlin for background on *Everything for the Boys* and *The Halls of Ivy*; the National Archives; the late Walter Brown Newman; Radio Yesteryear; Kim Scharf of the Santa Barbara branch of United Way; ex-Cinecon Vice-President Mike Schlesinger for obtaining *Her Night of Romance* for Cinecon 30; David Siegel; *The Nostalgia Entertainment Sourcebook* by Randy Skretvedt and Jordan R. Young; the late Ray Stanich; Willard Waterman; Ron Wolf of Pacific Pioneer Broadcasters in Hollywood for access to scores of radio shows and PPB's invaluable reference library; and Jeff Walden of BBC archives.

TV Shows: CBS librarian John Behrens for *Ivy* and *G.E. Theater* press releases; Valerie Bisson-Goldberg of ITC for *Ivy* syndication releases; Milton Ferguson and Milton

Merlin for *Ivy* data, but Ferguson especially for episode soundtracks; *Ivy* producer William Frye; and UCLA's Powell Library for videotape access to the *Four Star* shows.

Bibliography: The gracious and friendly staff of the Academy's Margaret Herrick Library for their help; and UCLA's microfilm and Dickson Art Center libraries. Also Stacey Behlmer, John Cocchi, Ken Greenwald, Mike Jittlov and Dana Snow. And Michael Gray of Voice of America for copyright searches.

Discography: Steven Lasker of Decca Records and Bernadette Moore of BMG, the latter for RCA records.

Special thanks: Leigh Strother-Vien for proofing, indexing and computer expertise resulting in a professional print-out that's a joy to read.

Joe Zeff for computer expertise that helped Leigh with special typography and time-saving techniques. Also for index formatting and final proofing before printout.

The Los Angeles Science Fantasy Society, Inc. (LASFS), of which I am a member, for the generous use of the club's library computer and printer for final production.

Ray Briem of KABC Los Angeles for his enthusiastic support in giving me a forum for my Colman crusade on late-night radio shows in October 1987, April 1989, and on December 1, 1994, two weeks before his retirement.

In addition to the above, a trio of Colman soul mates who have not only given me valuable material but have guided and advised me and sharpened my thoughts and insights on Ronald Colman's uniqueness and impact as a movie and radio star. They are Kendall Miller, George Schatz and Robert Morsberger.

Ken has been a one-man cheering squad, motivator and collaborator, and the lightning rod for my insights. George and Bob began their love affairs with Colman when they first saw *Lost Horizon* in 1937. Bob, a one-man historical essay team in his own right, has assiduously sent me clippings I might have overlooked and pointed out motifs in Colman movies I hadn't considered. George gave me a base list of 150-plus articles, a base list of stage work, undying support, a masterfully written personal monograph on Colman's career in 1982 that was later published in *Classic Images*, and copies of several radio shows I needed to hear.

Then there are the delightful Gassman twins, John and Larry, who copied 140 radio shows for me for the cost of blank tape and who provided additional details (especially on Jack Benny) and voice IDs. The radio chapter could not have been finished without them. Just as important, they have given me an outlet on their KPCC Pasadena vintage radio show and once on their Christmas marathon to revive some of Colman's best radio work, some of it not heard since it first aired. Their brotherly friendship, whimsical humor, humanity, graciousness and support is valued not only by me but by the thousands of listeners to whom they are also warmly cherished friends.

I must also thank former KPCC host Ian Whitcomb for song credits and for being the only public radio host in Los Angeles besides the Gassmans to have me on his show to celebrate Colman's 100th birthday in 1991. His show, which ran from 1990-96, was an oasis of musical bliss in a rock and roll desert.

Also, my grateful thanks to Jim Parish for helping me get the contract to write this book, for advising me on various details, and for steering me to research outlets I wouldn't otherwise have known about. And to my editors, Lynn Taylor and George Butler, for their support and encouragement.

FOREWORD

by Robert E. Morsberger
Professor of English
California Polytechnic University
Pomona, CA

Of all the movie stars in the 1920s, '30s and '40s, few shone more brightly than Ronald Colman. A consummate, spellbinding actor, Colman was nominated four times for the Academy Award, winning it for a spectacular performance in *A Double Life* that was praised by Laurence Olivier. Olivier, generally considered the greatest actor of the century, was such an admirer that in his early twenties he deliberately modeled himself on Colman, though he thought he was "nothing as handsome or attractive" as Colman and lacked "his magic and magnetism."[1] In the 1930s, the two actors became such close friends that Colman arranged for Olivier and Vivien Leigh to be married secretly at his San Ysidro Ranch in Santa Barbara, and lent them his yacht for their honeymoon.

Several times Colman was voted the handsomest actor in Hollywood, once when he was in his late fifties; and William Wellman, though he quarreled with Colman on the set of *The Light that Failed*, told the astonished actor that his voice was the most beautiful he had ever heard. Indeed, Colman's cultured, poetically modulated voice—which could be romantic, whimsical, commanding, or tragic—was one of the most famous among film stars.

Colman's speech had perfect timing; he never used the wise-cracking, machine-gun delivery that was so common in movies of the 1930s. One admirer said he would walk miles just to hear Colman recite the alphabet. When Benita Hume married him in 1938, she beamed "I not only have that beautiful man, but that voice!"[2] A top star in the silent era, when he and Vilma Banky rivalled Garbo and Gilbert as a great love team, Colman became more popular, even legendary in his day, in talkies.

Colman liked to call his screen persona a "gentleman adventurer," and Joe Franklin writes that Colman "was without question the leader of the small but select band of 'gentleman' heroes."[3] Though less athletic than Errol Flynn, Colman could be as dashing a swashbuckler. His *The Prisoner of Zenda* vies with *The Adventures of Robin Hood* as the most beloved swashbuckler of all time. He was as skilled a light, urbane comedian as his friend William Powell, or as Cary Grant, who was afraid to be cast with him in *The Talk of the Town* lest Colman walk off with the top acting honors, which he did. Colman could express suffering as well as Fredric March; he could play tragedy and comedy with equal aplomb. No one excelled Colman in noblesse oblige. No actor seemed more intelligent, more scholarly or philosophical, more thoughtful and sensitive, more idealistic, more gallant in self-sacrifice. Jeffrey Richards writes that "The camera caught and conveyed that blend of inner sensitivity and inner strength that gave such depth and feeling to Colman's best performances."[4]

When Frank Capra wanted to cast the role of the idealistic yet philosophical adventurer chosen to succeed the High Lama at the utopia of Shangri-La, he said he would not make *Lost Horizon* unless he could get Ronald Colman. Wanting to remake *The Prisoner of Zenda*, David O. Selznick said he would film it only if Colman would agree to play the dual roles of the nobly romantic Englishman and the kidnapped king he impersonates only to relinquish the princess he comes to love in order to rescue the king from being murdered in his dungeon and restore him to the throne.

If I Were King, the swashbuckling romantic comedy about François Villon—thief, king of vagabonds, and the greatest poet of medieval France, was designed specifically for Colman. If a director wanted an actor to play an idealistic lawyer who unbends from his rigidity while falling in love, saving an innocent man (Cary Grant) from a murder charge, and becoming an enlightened Supreme Court Justice, who else but Ronald Colman? To play a sensitive World War I veteran suffering twice from amnesia and trying to find the woman he loves who is lost in a forgotten corner of his mind, who else but Colman? For an idealistic doctor trying to research preventive medicine, who else but Colman? For the scholarly and humanistic president of Ivy College, who else but Colman? For a witty, high-minded intellectual who worked with Einstein and really does know everything on a TV quiz program, who else but Colman? Certainly no other actor could plausibly play the Spirit of Mankind, pitting creativity and idealism against the destructive cynicism of Satan.

Colman was literate offscreen as well. He was a dedicated reader, the owner of an impressive library, the friend of writers like John Galsworthy (who finished *The Forsyte Saga* as a guest at Colman's ranch), and William Faulkner, of musicians like Arthur Rubinstein. He worked with most of the best directors, including Ernst Lubitsch, King Vidor, Henry King, John Cromwell, Frank Lloyd, Frank Capra, George Stevens, Lewis Milestone, William Wellman, George Cukor, Joseph Mankiewicz, and John Ford. The latter called him at the time the best actor he had ever directed.

Colman was the first and best Beau Geste (both F. Scott Fitzgerald—in *Tender is the Night*—and Charles Schultz's Snoopy say so), the best of many Bulldog Drummonds, the noblest of all Sydney Cartons sacrificing his live to save the husband of the woman he loves. "Nobody," writes John Baxter, "has captured so accurately Carton's melancholy fatalism or the moral necessities which can drive a man to self-destruction. If only for the scene where Carton waits in the snow at Christmas time and watches the carollers and church-goers hurry past to the warmth of the home which he does not possess [Colman's 1935] *A Tale of Two Cities* must be considered one of the most successful films of the period."[5]

No actor projected more intelligence; Colman could actually convey the process of thinking. George Cukor, who directed Colman's Oscar-winning performance in *A Double Life*, said "Colman had so much equipment for a screen actor: he was photogenic, he could move, he could give the impression of movement and yet remain perfectly still, he had this plastic quality, he'd studied Chaplin and Fairbanks. For the death scene, I was shooting from a high angle, and I told him, 'When you die, all your life, everything that's happened, should come into your eyes for a brief moment.' Well, he did it—told me he did it—but I couldn't see it when we shot it. Next day, in the rushes, it was there. He knew how to let the quality of thought come out."[6]

Yet for all his sensitivity, intellectuality and urbanity, Colman could and did play rogues, a circus clown, a Gypsy, a Devil's Island convict, criminals, drunks, a drug-addicted Member of Parliament, a scruffy Arab beggar, and the ultimate Boston Brahmin. He played characters in literature by Shakespeare, George Eliot, Oscar Wilde, Joseph Conrad, Sinclair Lewis, Charles Dickens, Anthony Hope, Ouida, Rudyard Kipling, James Hilton, and John P. Marquand. Had he been willing to shave his trademark moustache (the most admired and imitated in films) more often and taken a few more chances on roles offered to him that departed from his image, he might have had an even more impressive career.

And had he made more films, he might be better remembered today. "See me less often, but see me at my best," he told his audiences. As an unfortunate consequence, he made far fewer films than most of his contemporaries. James Stewart, for instance, made more films from 1938 to 1940 than Colman did from 1938 to 1950. Twenty of Colman's American films are silent (four of them lost or destroyed), and only one of those (*Lady Windermere's Fan*) is available on videotape, though several have been resurrected for theatrical screenings in the last decade; and many of his talking films are vintage ones from the early 1930s. From 1932 on, Colman rarely made more than one movie a year. After 1942, there were intervals of several years between his movies.

Though so many of Colman's films are classics that 11 of them have been remade, some several times—certainly a record—Colman did not always choose the best scripts. Among movies he turned down were *Anna Karenina* opposite Garbo, *Julius Caesar*, *Gone with the Wind* and *Jane Eyre*. In 1940, he turned down *Rebecca* in order to do a limp screwball comedy, which he followed with an even limper one before making a spectacular comeback with *Random Harvest* and *The Talk of the Town*, both in 1942. Except for a cameo in *Around the World in 80 Days* and his dignified, literate role in the otherwise disastrous *The Story of Mankind*, Colman's last starring film, *Champagne for Caesar*, was released in 1950, so that people who saw his films when they came out are now all elderly. "I like old broads like you," Walter Matthau says to Glenda Jackson in *House Calls*. "I don't have to explain things, like who Ronald Colman is."

Those film stars who have become cult figures are usually the ones whose lives were marred by scandal and excess, suffered breakdowns, and died tragically and usually young, like Judy Garland, Errol Flynn, Vivien Leigh, James Dean and Montgomery Clift. Colman did none of these. A very private person, as his daughter Juliet called him, he was as gracious in person as on screen, according to practically everyone who knew him. Joe Franklin writes that he could never find anyone inclined to malign Colman. "He conducted his personal life via a code of honor and chivalry that seems to have forestalled the making of any enemies....Now that he's gone, and his old films are reappearing on television, it's suddenly apparent how vital a part of the movie scene were his courtly manners and graceful good humor, and how very much he'll be missed."[7]

For the sake of moviegoers, of stage, television and radio buffs who want all the facts about Colman, Sam Frank's bio-bibliography is invaluable. An indefatigable researcher, Frank has been studying Ronald Colman for 27 years. Among his contributions is a record of Colman's stage work as complete as records permit; a guide to short films never before documented; a complete guide to Colman's TV work; a thorough discography; a list of awards, honors and nominations; and an astonishingly comprehensive radiography that establishes Colman as a major radio player, who hosted or acted in hundreds of shows. He and his wife, Benita, became enormously popular as repeat guest stars on the *Jack Benny* show, in which Colman spoofed his cultured image as a foil for Benny's supposed vulgarity. And the award-winning *The Halls of Ivy* counted Fredric March as one of its devoted fans. Now thanks to Sam Frank, we have a reliable record of all of Colman's work in all media. If anything has been left out, it is only because no record survives.

NOTES

1. Juliet Benita Colman. **Ronald Colman, A Very Private Person** (New York: Morrow, 1975), p. 158.

2. *Ibid*, p. 166.

3. Joe Franklin. **Classics of the Silent Screen, A Pictorial Treasury** (New York: Bramhall, 1959) p. 148.

4. Jeffrey Richards. **Swordsmen of the Screen** (London: Routledge and Kegan Paul, 1977), p. 157.

5. John Baxter. **Hollywood in the Thirties** (New York: Paperback Library, 1970), p. 34.

6. Gavin Lambert. **On Cukor** (New York: G.P. Putnam's Sons, 1972), pp. 197-199.

7. Franklin, p. 149.

PREFACE

This book is about giving a major movie star the critical recognition largely denied him since his death in 1958. In the first ten years following death in 1958, there were no Colman biographies, and scant mention of him in books on other movie stars, or in most of the few film history books written to that time. Here was a superstar who had made scores of movies and been critically acclaimed in most of them, but you wouldn't have known it from the movie books being published in the 1960s.

Many of these references misspelled his last name as Coleman, and many reference book writers since the 1960s have continued to misspell it. This despite the fact that his name on screen is spelled Colman. A 1943 *Current Biography* Colman biographical sketch had more information than most other reference volumes and that was just three pages.

Beyond that, the men writing the film history books in the 1960s seemed reluctant to acknowledge that Ronald Colman had even existed. He was certainly not a household name among children and young adults at the time, as were Bogart, Cagney, Flynn, Gable and Grant, all of whose movies were shown on local television far more often than Colman's.

It was in 1965, after discovering and being excited by a few of his movies on television, that I became an ardent fan of Ronald Colman. I wanted to know not only who he was, but why TV showings and revival theater screenings of his movies were so rare, why he was being overlooked in the American film history to which he had so richly contributed.

Thirty years later, I have the answers to all of my questions, and Colman is, by happy coincidence, finally better known to film buffs through cable TV and home video. Yet, he is still neglected by film historians, and excluded from Golden Age star roundups in Entertainment Weekly, Film Comment and other magazines. This book is designed to show that he deserves greater attention.

This is not to say that Colman is alone in being consigned to film history limbo. Contemporaries such as William Powell, Fredric March, Ray Milland, Melvyn Douglas, Wallace Beery, Robert Donat, Robert Montgomery, Rosalind Russell, Jean Arthur, Irene Dunne, Claudette Colbert, Kay Francis and Loretta Young have also been slighted in film journals and legendary star roundups. Most don't have one biography to their name. All the same, Colman's star qualities and the influence of those qualities on a generation of sophisticated stars has rarely been explored, and never at length.

The reasons for this are many. For one, Colman made only 12 movies after 1937, usually only one a year. In contrast, Bogart made seven films in 1939 alone, Tyrone Power made nine movies from 1938-39 and a legion more by 1950, and Gable churned them out for MGM before and after his war service.

Add to this that all but a two-reel fragment of his British silent film work is lost, that several of his American silent movies are also lost or incomplete at best, and that few of the complete ones are shown at film festivals.

Nevertheless, Colman had a profound impact on two generations of moviegoers and a generation of radio listeners from the late 1940s to early 1950s. The time is long overdue for that work to be documented.

In this book you will find the entirety of Colman's career in all media, all of it put in perspective and relief. In tracking his evolution as an actor and star, I have discovered a man who had a thematic agenda: he wanted his movies, once he became a star, to impart a system of humane values, beliefs and ideals that would make them a richly ennobling experience, not only for those who first saw them, but for subsequent generations.

In addition to giving Colman his due as a gifted actor, I have corrected scores of factual errors and a mountain of misinformation in dozens of other books.

My corrections come from documentary source materials and the scores of interviews I have conducted since 1977 with the goal of publishing a definitive Ronald Colman biography. With a few exceptions, the stars, directors and craftsmen to whom I have spoken all remembered the man with warm regard and professional esteem. At a classic radio show convention in November of 1992, I scurried around with my pocket recorder getting brief reminiscences from the veteran actors there who had worked with him on *The Halls of Ivy*, *Favorite Story* and other shows.

Among these alumni, actor Peter Leeds was the most succinctly personal: "Talk about class, talk about elegance, talk about professionalism, talk about style. Ronald Colman personified these qualities better than any almost any other star I have worked with. It was a joy and a privilege to share a mike with him."

In short, the thousands of hours of research that went into compiling this book enable me to guarantee it as a wholly reliable source of accurate information about the entirety of Ronald Colman's career.

This book is divided into 12 chapters:

1. A biographical sketch which precisely tracks Colman's life and career, and which includes a step-by-step chronology of his famous libel suit against producer Samuel Goldwyn. Includes selective quotes from interviews I did over a period of 15 years, from 1977 to 1992.

2. A chronology of all of Colman's professional stage work, all of his movies, radio highlights, and all of his TV shows.

3. A thesis chapter charting and analyzing Colman's growth as an actor from his stage origins to his American silent movie stardom to the sound films of the late 1920s through late 1940s that gave us the Colman persona. I also discuss why it was that he allowed this persona to limit his talent.

4. A bibliographical essay examining what was written about Colman during his career and why, why so little has been written about Colman since his death, and why *this* book is only the fourth about him while many of his contemporaries have dozens. This and the thesis chapter provide the contextual key to the rest of the book.

5. A listing of Colman's amateur stage and music hall work in England, and all of his

professional stage work in England and the United States. With as complete cast and credits as could be assembled, plot summaries, review quotes, background and comments.

6. A complete listing of all of Colman's work in movies, including several short subjects and newsreels never before documented. The silents through 1925 are listed in chronological order for the first time, with shorts and newsreels interspersed throughout. Each film has the most complete and accurate listing of cast and credits obtainable, New York and Los Angeles release dates for the American films because they didn't always open in New York first, an accurate timing (noting where footage and whole reels are missing), plot summary, quotes from reviews, anecdotes and comments and the making of the movie, Academy Award nominations and awards, and cross references to radio and commercial record versions.

   Also included are video, theatrical and archival sources for the surviving films, and a source guide at chapter's end to the archives and independent film and home video sources.

7. Colman's complete and remarkably prolific radio career, listed in mostly chronological order, with as complete cast and credits as could be assembled, synopses or summarized contents, excerpts from a few *Variety* reviews, and cross reference to those shows based on Colman movies. The exceptions to chronology are the syndicated *Favorite Story* and *The Halls of Ivy*, the latter so that the reader can chart its evolution as a series.

   This chapter concludes with archival and commercial sources for the shows.

8. Colman's complete but limited television career, most of which was the TV version of *The Halls of Ivy*, with nearly complete casts and complete credits for all episodes. The *Ivy* shows are cross referenced to their radio originals. Also including three TV shows about him after his death.

9. A discography that includes the seven albums Colman recorded, commercial printings of his radio shows, and recordings of music from his movies. Cross referenced to the movies and radio shows.

10. A listing of awards, honors and nominations, including his Golden Globe and Oscar for *A Double Life*, the numerous awards for the radio version of *The Halls of Ivy*, and his two posthumous stars on the Hollywood Walk of Fame, including their exact locations. All cross referenced to the film and radio shows.

11. An annotated bibliography divided into books about Colman or with chapters on him, newspaper and magazine articles, and program notes for revivals of his film and radio work. Selectively cross referenced to various sections to save space.

12. A comprehensive index of nearly 1000 names, titles and radio generics throughout the book. The generics are to help the reader locate Christmas shows, variety shows, war relief shows, interviews, fantasy shows and so on.

INTRODUCTION

For three generations, Ronald Colman was the gentleman adventurer non pareil, his name synonymous with old world charm, elegance and savoir faire. A Colman movie from the late 1920s on was a major event, because by then he was usually making only one or two a year, having established his charismatic screen presence with 15 pictures released between September 1923 and January 1927.

When sound was taking its toll on dozens of silent stars in the late 1920s, Colman's warmly modulated, beautifully cultured British voice, and playful sense of humor enlarged his personality, making him the international idol of millions. Add to this that he had the singular distinction of being the only male star for an entire studio, Samuel Goldwyn Productions, from 1925 to early 1930. Aside from a few *Potash and Perlmutter* comedies in the early to late 1920s, Goldwyn made nothing but Ronald Colman movies until he started making Eddie Cantor musicals in 1930.

For all of his silent movie success, it was sound that gave Colman his true screen personality. The early sound era freed Colman from the heavy melodramas in which he had been trapped during the late 1920s, so that he could display the lighter side that was his real forte. He was a gaily charming gentleman adventurer outwitting dastardly villains in *Bulldog Drummond* (1929), a roguish Devil's Island convict magnetically attracting his warden's love-starved wife in *Condemned* (1929), a gentleman thief in *Raffles* (1930), and a whimsical upper class black sheep in *The Devil to Pay* (1930). These and other variations on the adventuresome man-about-town with upper-crust breeding and an easygoing air made him internationally famous. He was instantly likeable, trustworthy and romantically vulnerable. Men round the world sought to emulate his style, voice and moustache. Women yearned to marry him to lighten the tragic burden they saw in his eyes beneath the smiling charm.

From 1929 on, Colman influenced scores of other male stars—Laurence Olivier, Gary Cooper*, David Niven, Brian Aherne, Melvyn Douglas, Don Ameche, Rex Harrison, etc.—with his debonair manner, distinctive voice and pencil moustache. His keen eye for scripts failed him when he formed a production partnership in 1939 with a group of friends and colleagues, but he made far fewer mediocre pictures than other stars making four or five movies a year.

However, his was only one of several heroic types flourishing in that first decade of sound. Cowboys, gangsters, detectives, monsters, swashbucklers (of whom Colman was one in the late 1920s and again in the late 1930s), and other archetypes drew fans by the tens of millions to movie theaters every day of the week. There was an escapist hero for every vicarious fantasy, every noble dream of good vs. evil.

Therein lies one of the three major reasons Colman could remain a star for more than three decades, yet become largely forgotten when he died in 1958. His heroic type largely vanished after World War Two, replaced first by the film noir heroics of Humphrey Bogart, Robert Mitchum and others, then by the surly rebelliousness of Marlon Brando, James Dean and others of that breed. The gentleman was out, the rebel or anti-hero was and still is king. This emphasis on the anti-hero in books and at revival screenings gives the impression that the gentleman adventurer types were a minor heroic breed when in fact they were just as dominant as the gangsters and other macho types.

The second major reason for Colman's being neglected is that he left far fewer movies to be remembered by than Bogart, Grant et al. (See Preface.) The third, and possibly most important, reason is that his private life was free of the scandals, sex and sensationalism for which Sinatra, Monroe, Brando, Flynn and other, more public stars, are infamous. The dirt that sells movie star books isn't there.

Ironically, while Colman is receiving little contemporary attention in books and magazines, his movies are continuously shown on American Movie Classics, Turner Classic Movies and Turner Network Television. They are also being shown more frequently at revival theaters and film festivals. And 16 of his 28 sound features are for rent or sale on videotape and laser disc. For a man being neglected or ignored in print, the visual media are working overtime to restore his name to public consciousness.

Thus, today's film buffs and scholars who happen on Colman's movies on cable TV and home video may find themselves as thrilled by his personality, voice, integrity and idealism as were the worldwide millions who grew up with those films. This book is for those buffs and scholars who want to know more about the man, the niche he made for himself and how that niche relates to the larger overview of American film history.

* While making *The Winning of Barbara Worth* in 1926, Cooper both studied Colman's style of underplaying and was advised by Colman on same. Cooper later unsuccessfully lobbied Paramount to play Sydney Carton, and Frank Capra for the lead in *Lost Horizon*. In 1939, he played the Colman lead in a remake of *Beau Geste*.

BIOGRAPHY

For two generations of moviegoers, Ronald Colman personified the ideal British gentleman. His expressive face, beautifully cultured voice, easygoing elegance, charming wit with a dash or two of whimsy, warm dignity, old school integrity, and gentle, soft-spoken humanity were his trademarks. Audiences felt warmed and ennobled by his charismatic screen presence, his unique magic as a star. If you walked out of a Colman movie starring him between 1923 and 1950, you felt good for having spent time with this man, that for an hour-and-a-half or two you had escaped your problems by having Ronald Colman act as your gentlemanly surrogate in a problematic world.

Such was Colman's urbane impact that many of his movie star contemporaries emulated his style or moustache or both. Laurence Olivier, William Powell, Douglas Fairbanks Jr., David Niven, Brian Aherne, Warner Baxter, Rex Harrison and others freely borrowed from him. Whether in silent or sound films, Colman underplayed to profound effect, conveying an aura of thoughtful tranquility, of supreme aplomb. He was romantic yet down-to-earth, intellectual yet transcendent. He gave good value for the price of admission, rarely letting audiences down.

Though he trained and disciplined himself to create an indelible screen character, Ronald Colman had some genetic help as well. He was a descendant of the renowned 18th century actor and playwright, George Colman the Elder (1732-1794), and his son, George Colman the Younger (1762-1836). However, he didn't discover his family's theatrical roots until he became a movie star, when his belief in reincarnation finally prompted him to ask his Aunt Constance to investigate the family tree. As a child, there was no reason for him to suspect anything of the kind in his lineage because he was raised in a proper and conventional Victorian household by parents who were solidly respectable family-oriented members of the British middle class.

Ronald's father, Charles, was an upright businessman in the silk-importing trade. His mother, Marjory (née Fraser), was an industrious and devoted housewife. Marrying in 1881 after a whirlwind courtship when she was 30 and he was 33, they immediately started raising a large family, which was typical of the time. However, their first-born, a boy, died in infancy in 1882. Ronald was the third son and fourth in line of birth. The other four were Gladys (born 1883), Edith (1886), Eric (1889), and Frieda (1895).

Ronald Charles was born on February 9, 1891, in a house called Woodville at 156 Sandycombe Road in the fashionable suburb of Richmond, Surrey. However, it wasn't until

45 days after his birth that he was christened and Marjory officially registered the birth at Somerset House in Richmond. The clerk, George Bensted, must have been hard of hearing because he got the name wrong on the birth certificate, registering the child as Roland Charles. It remains a mystery as to why Marjory didn't make him redo the certificate with the right name. Ronald was also born into the Christian religion—specifically the Church of England.

Ronnie, as he came to be known, wasn't a lonely child because the Colman household was always bustling with activity and relatives, but he wasn't an outgoing one either. His father tended to be a quietly disciplined man, so, as a boy, Ronnie cultivated a liking for privacy, keeping his thoughts to himself and insisting on saying his bedtime prayers alone.

A product of an age in which people were not typically demonstrative, his acquired need for privacy grew partly out of a few childhood incidents, such as accidentally pulling up one of his father's cherished flower bulbs while working in the garden. (See B191) After events like that, he determined it was best to keep to himself and not get in anybody's way. The result was that he became more inhibited emotionally than most other children. (See B191) This held true for him into adulthood.

Though Ronnie was closer to Marjory than to Charles—she was his dearest friend and companion, giving him a sense of humor—he was nevertheless devoted to his father, though admittedly a little frightened of him. Not without warmth and humor—otherwise Marjory never would have married him—Charles was generally a practical-minded man. When his two sons reached grade school age, he started taking them to his London office, where he would show them a few things about his silk importing trade. Charles wanted to expose his sons to the world, while getting one or both of them interested in his business. Ronnie would later recall those early London trips with vivid fondness:

> I enjoyed those trips to father's office tremendously. They stimulated my imagination as nothing else did. And my imagination needed stimulating, for I was not a very imaginative child. I didn't care to read fairy tales. I didn't believe in fairies, or indeed anything I couldn't see, touch, hear or taste.[1]

In addition to giving his son a taste for the exotic, Charles also introduced him to a new sideshow novelty called moving pictures on his 11th birthday, February 9, 1902. He took Ronnie to the Earls Court exhibitions, which were catchpenny shows with bands, whirligigs, fortune tellers and shell games. It was a dreamland and a "sucker trap." Ronnie loved it.

After Charles paid their admissions, they went into a darkened tent where Ronnie saw his first movie: An express train speeding out of a tunnel and heading straight for the bench on which he and his father were sitting:

> The sensation it gave me of narrowly escaping a violent death did not seem to me to come under the heading of amusement. Father laughed when, safely out in the open air again, I told him what I thought of this divertissement. Then he said, "This invention has a future, son, watch it. Animated pictures are going to make the fortunes of a great many people."[2]

Ronnie found the theater far more appealing, seeing a good deal of it as a child. Charles apparently liked to take his family to various professional productions in London and to local amateur shows, as much because he admired fine acting for its own sake as because he wanted to broaden his family's interests. He was also smitten with the acting bug, joining the Thames Valley Shakespeare Society in the fall of 1902. In February of 1903, he was cast as Borachio in Shakespeare's *Much Ado About Nothing*. This role, a drunken villain, was far removed from his normal temperament, which was precisely why Charles enjoyed it. When Charles was interviewed about the production in Twickenham by a reporter from the *Thames Valley Times*, who inquired about Ronnie's presence at the rehearsal, he remarked that, "The kid's mad on acting."[3] Indeed he was, watching spellbound as his normally staid father took on a new dimension in a comic role, while getting caught up himself in the rhythm and poetry of Shakespeare's language, beginning a lifelong love affair with the Bard.

Also in 1902, the Colmans moved from Richmond to Ealing, an upscale suburb close to London. Charles's business was thriving, and his daughters needed parlor and porch space to entertain their beaux, so it was time for a change. At the same time, Ronnie was enrolled at a nearby public school (private school to Americans) within easy bicycling distance. It was at this school, run by a German headmaster, that Ronnie received a thorough educational drilling and developed his lifelong zest for reading.

Never an athletic child—though he did regular exercises to keep fit—or part of any gang of chums, Ronnie was soon plundering the school's library, discovering and taking to heart the works of Byron, Keats, Shelley, Dickens, Melville, Stevenson and Carroll. His greatest love, though, was for Shakespeare, for the vitality, passion and imagination of his verses, themes and insights. The more he read of these and many other writers, the more he was inspired to read, as many pages per day and volumes per week for which he could find time.

His one concession to non-academic life was taking part in school plays because that was where he could draw himself out without feeling foolish. He overacted with gusto as he imagined himself to be the nobly swashbuckling heroes he was reading about.

After four years at the private school, Ronnie, now 15, was sent to a boarding school at Littlehampton, Hadley, on the Sussex coast. It was there that he began planning a career in engineering, inspired by the books he had read about great engineers and their accomplishments. He now studied to go to Cambridge, where his academic and personal worlds would be opened wide.

Cambridge and a career in engineering were not meant to be. On February 23, 1907, at age 56, Charles became ill with pneumonia. Ronnie sped home to Ealing just in time to be with his father when he died. Suddenly, the family's life changed radically. Charles's business had collapsed along with his health. Not thinking of the future, Charles had not saved very much in his last few years, so that after funeral expenses, there was only a meager annual stipend for Marjory and the children. Ronnie and Eric were now adults by default, forced to leave school at term's end to find work to help support the family.

For the next seven years, Ronnie toiled as an underpaid accountant for the British Steamship Company, his working conditions right out of a Dickens novel. For diversion after working hours, he joined a theatrical club called The Bancroft Amateur Dramatic Society and became part of a teenage music hall troupe called The Mad Medicos (later The Popinjays). He also joined a military drilling brigade for the noise and excitement of it.

Life might have gone on indefinitely in this directionless mode if it hadn't been for the outbreak of World War I in the summer of 1914. Ronnie enlisted at once on August 5, but less out of patriotic fervor—neither he nor most of his peers had any idea what the war was about—than to get out of his dull and mundane office routine. After only a few weeks of boot camp training (experienced recruits were in short supply), he and his fellow troops were shipped to active duty in France as part of a larger group of soldiers known as "Kitchener's Contemptibles", after their Irish-born commander-in-chief, who was a hero of the Sudan campaign. Even less formally, they were known as "The Ladies From Hell" for their kilts.

Ronnie saw frightening carnage on the battlefields at Messines and Ypres, watching in horror as his fighting comrades had their faces and limbs blown off. Then, during one chaotic battle, he was wounded by shrapnel in his left knee and fractured his ankle stumbling over a stone when a bomb exploded nearby. He was immediately sent to a field hospital, where the shrapnel was removed by a nurse and his leg put in a cast. When his wounds failed to heal properly after several months at a desk job, he was invalided from the war on May 6, 1915 with an honorable discharge and the Mons Bar for distinguished service.

It was also in the field that he contracted pneumonia. This illness, combined with the smoking habit he acquired as a soldier, left him with a permanent case of lung fibrosis or emphysema; permanent because he never gave up smoking. The shrapnel wounds also left him with a limp that took him several years to get rid of.

Upon his return to England in May, Ronnie was beside himself with indecision over what to do next with his life. Returning to work as a clerk was out of the question, nor could he see himself in any of several solid professions such as law or medicine because he had no aptitude or gift for them. By the end of the year, he was personally and professionally adrift. At that time, he ran into an uncle who was with the Foreign Office. With no other prospects in sight, he asked his uncle if an appointment could be arranged for him with a consulate in the Orient. The uncle said he would see what he could do.

Then Ronnie, in his own words, "collided with the theater."

In early 1916, he briefly joined a tour with The Scallywags, a pierrot concert party revue staged by showman George Denby. After leaving the troupe when Denby couldn't pay him the £6 a week he felt he deserved, he became reacquainted with some old amateur acting friends, taking the advice of one of them to audition for a small role in a play that actress Lena Ashwell was staging at the London Coliseum in late June. Ashwell liked his dark young looks, so she cast him as an Indian herald in a playlet by Sir Rabindranath Tagore called "The Maharani of Arakan."

Ashwell took such a liking to Ronnie that she invited him to several theatrical luncheon parties, where he mingled with theater royalty such as Sir Gerald DuMaurier, Charles Wyndham and others. Ashwell always introduced him by saying, "Here is a boy who will do great things in the theater."

It was at one of these parties that Ashwell introduced Ronnie to actress Gladys Cooper. Cooper was so impressed with his soft-spoken demeanor that she cast him in a supporting role in her new play, *The Misleading Lady.*

The play opened August 28, 1916 at the Gaiety in Manchester, moving to the Playhouse in London on September 6, where it ran for seven months, garnering Ronnie his first favorable reviews. (These despite a war wound limp which caused him to be rather clumsy walking down a staircase about two minutes into the first act each night). And yet, he still hadn't decided on a career in theater.

That decision was made one night when he was sitting alone in his flat,

> "...reading an encouraging review of my performance in the play. Word came that my uncle had obtained the promise of a position for me in an Oriental consulate. I held the review in one hand, my uncle's note in the other. What to do? I knew that I had to decide, then. No flashlight exploded in my brain leaving there an illuminated answer to my problem. I remember that a mere drop of the hand, a reflex action, decided it for me. For automatically, I dropped the note on my desk and went on reading the review. And my choice was made."[4]

Ronnie sent his uncle a note thanking him, and that was that. He was smitten with acting and the praise that came with a good performance. More than that, acting was a way of freeing himself from his normally shy and inhibited manner, just as it had been for his father. With a script, he could be as playful, scheming, wicked, witty, charming, adventurous and profound as he pleased.

During the last month of *The Misleading Lady*, in March 1917, he was loaned to the Court Theatre in London for two matinée performances of a comedy called *Partnership*. Once *Lady* ended, he was cast as the understudy to Reginald Bach in the plum role of a young syphilitic in a translated French play called *Damaged Goods*. When Bach left one month into what had become a cause célèbre hit, Ronnie took over on April 17.

Venereal disease was a scandalous topic in the late 1910s, so naturally any play about it—especially a candidly written and well-acted one—was going to have a theater packed for months, in this case several theaters: the main company at the St. Martin's in London, and the road company in June and July 1917. Other young actors had avoided auditioning for the juvenile lead in this play for fear of the perceived stigma attached to it, but Ronnie saw it as a found opportunity to showcase himself and he made the most of it, earning his best notices up to that time. He also earned more money as the juvenile lead.

During the run of *Damaged Goods*, he was talked into making his first movie by a man named George Dewhurst. Because he hadn't had any camera experience and Dewhurst (who apparently had none, either) didn't bother coaching him on the considerable differences between movie and stage acting, the job resulted in an awful two-reel drama (title unknown, though possibly called *The Live Wire*) that was never released, much to Ronnie's relief. He went to a preview of the film, took a brief look at himself on screen, and fled.

Awful as that first camera experience was, it didn't deter him from acting in more movies. Screen work paid much-needed money when stage roles were scarce.

Stage work, however, kept Ronnie almost as busy as he wished until the end of 1918. Two months after the run of *Damaged Goods*, he was cast in two Jewish roles. The first a melodrama about religious bigotry called *The Little Brother*, the second a comedy of Jewish life called *The Bubble*. He was also hired in November 1918 for the touring company of a spy play called *The Live Wire*, having understudied the lead for the London run.

It was *The Live Wire* that introduced him to an actress named Thelma Raye (née Thelma Victoria Maud), who bedazzled him with her seemingly brittle sophistication. He, in turn, captivated her with his low-key charm and good-humored intelligence. They became romantically involved and lived together once the touring company ended. (In the late 1910s, an unmarried couple living together was considered sexually scandalous, so this was certainly a bold move for a proper gentleman like Ronnie.)

After the run of *The Bubble*, in November of 1918, Ronnie accepted a part in a feature film called *The Toilers*, again produced by George Dewhurst, but with a director named Tom Watts. It was partly shot on location at a beautiful but cold Cornish fishing village. Colman played a Cornish fisherman seeking fame and fortune in London. The role was a melodramatically shallow one (worse, he still knew nothing about screen acting), but it did pay some badly needed money, as did five other films he made in 1919: *A Daughter of Eve*, *Sheba*, *Anna the Adventuress*, *Snow in the Desert* and *A Son of David* (released in 1920). Without those roles, however small, he would have starved since he worked in only one play that year, a failed comedy called *Skittles*.

By late summer of 1919, Thelma was pressuring him to marry her—they were now living solely on his acting wages and he was named in a divorce proceeding by the husband he learned Thelma had left. Having his hand forced in this manner, Ronnie did what he felt was the noble thing by marrying Thelma as soon as her divorce decree was final. If he hadn't been manipulated, he wouldn't have signed a London marriage registry on September 18, 1919; aside from the theater, Ronnie had nothing in common with Thelma and would have parted from her. But now he had a wife, whom he would quickly discover was shrewishly demanding and could be dangerously jealous of him professionally.

In December, Ronnie was hired for the touring company of *The Great Day* beginning in January, followed by one more movie called *The Black Spider*. After that, everything dried up as the London theater went into a post-war slump caused by returning soldiers and stage theaters being turned into movie houses.

Despite his long runs in *The Misleading Lady* and *Damaged Goods*, his three months in *The Little Brother*, and the critical praise he had gotten for all three, he was not an in-demand stage actor. Moreover, his film work had mostly been minor, quick-cash jobs. Despite an offer to join film producer Cecil Hepworth's stock company, Ronnie used his remaining funds to travel by ship to New York City in the late summer of 1920, as much to flee Thelma as to find work on the American stage, and maybe even in American movies.

He booked second-class passage on the *Zealand* with only one change of clothing, three clean collars, and a small amount of money. (Colman and other sources cite the amount as anywhere from $20 to $57.) When he arrived at Ellis Island, he showed a customs officer his passport, identifying him as an "artiste".

Like most young actors trying to establish themselves in Manhattan, then as now, Ronnie had to wash dishes and live on little food before landing two walk-on bits in *The Dauntless Three* in Atlantic City. The play closed after a one-week trial run in late October.

That was followed by the bit part of a high priest opposite George Arliss's suavely heathenish Raja of Rukh in *The Green Goddess*. Rehearsals began November 29, 1920 for a three-week Philadelphia trial run starting December 27. On January 18, 1921, the play premiered at the Booth Theatre in Manhattan, earning Ronnie a line of praise in the January 29 *Billboard*, but he had been replaced a week before the review appeared. Why he was fired after eight weeks with the *Green Goddess* company is a mystery, begging the question of what caused the show's producer/director Winthrop Ames to get rid of him during opening week rather than in Philadelphia.

After another try-out part in *The Silver Fox* in May of 1922 in Washington, D.C., he was singled out for praise on August 16 by New York Times theater critic Alexander Woollcott for his butler role in a murder comedy called *The Nightcap*. He left *that* play after two weeks when he got the lucky break of being offered the second juvenile lead in the seven-and-a-half-month road company of a hugely popular romantic comedy starring Fay Bainter called *East is West*.

Los Angeles was a one-week tour stop during Thanksgiving week 1921 (which was partly why he accepted the role), where Ronnie quickly learned he wasn't welcome at the movie studios despite a letter of introduction to D.W. Griffith. He was naturally dispirited by the rejections, but the $150 a week he was making on tour surely made up for the turn-downs.

Since he got free room and board on the tour, Ronnie accumulated $4950 (33 weeks times $150 per), part of which was eaten by American and resident alien taxes, part of which he doubtless sent to Thelma, because he could finally afford to, and to share his success with his wife. When the tour ended in New York City on April 29, 1922, Ronnie used part of what was left (probably $2000 after the above expenses) to bring Thelma to live with him in a decent Manhattan flat. After spending a week or two getting reacquainted with his wife because the summer audition season had not begun, Ronnie was off on a quest for more work; this time with a reservoir of cash and self-confidence to see him through.

After two months of auditions, he was hired by producer Al Woods for the second lead in the late August Atlantic City trial run of a Somerset Maugham play called *East Of Suez*. Fired by Woods at week's end, he was immediately hired by Ruth Chatterton for her touring company of *La Tendresse* at $450 a week. She had been introduced to Ronnie by Fay Bainter, saw him in *East is West*, and was so impressed with his performance that when she had to replace her second lead, he was her first choice for the plum role of an adulterer, starting with the New York run. *La Tendresse* opened at the Empire Theatre on September 25, 1922, ironically four days after *East of Suez* opened at the Eltinge.

After getting favorable critical attention in this play, especially from Woollcott again, he was seen one night by movie director Henry King on the recommendation of famed New York photographer James Abbé, who may have read the Woollcott review. King was scouting Broadway plays for a handsome and talented unknown to play the male lead in a picture he and Lillian Gish were co-producing called *The White Sister*, based on a popular novel by Frances Marion Crawford.

Both King and Gish—after she too saw the play at King's behest—agreed that the sensitive young English actor would be ideal as a sensitive young Italian lover. Their good judgment was confirmed after making a screen test, in which King slicked down the actor's hair, then drew a pencil moustache on him with a marking pen to make him look older, more dashing *and* Italian.

When Ronnie learned he had been cast in a Hollywood movie being produced by a renowned director and a renowned actress, he secured his release from *La Tendresse* on October 21, 1922, never dreaming it was his farewell to the stage and the turning point in his life and career. Not only had he been offered a choice film role at $500 a week with expenses paid, but his director and leading lady were rehearsing the movie's cast during the sea trip to Italy (where the movie would be shot on location) and coaching him individually on the art of movie acting, which was then the art of pantomime. King had ordered Ronnie to grow a moustache along the pencil line he had drawn on the young man's lip during the screen test, an order he dutifully obeyed.

By the time the cast and crew reached Italy, Ronnie had grown his first moustache at King's request, making him more photogenic—especially with his now slicked-down hair—and mature-looking at age 31. He also now had the sort of grounding in camera acting he had not received for any of his other movie roles, making him forever grateful to King and Gish for their unstinting professional generosity, though the lessons had clearly been necessary.

Throughout much of the *The White Sister* shoot, Ronnie was accompanied and hounded by Thelma. He had sent for her to be with him in his moment of professional breakthrough, but instead of basking in and being supportive of her husband's newfound limelight, Thelma was bitterly jealous. She was a vicious person, characterized by Lillian Gish, Henry King, Colman friend Alvin Weingand, and a few others who knew her later on during the early years of Ronnie's Hollywood stardom, as an evil and vindictive woman.

She was certainly an abusive one, according to Gish (TV49), having long and angry fights with Ronnie in their hotel room in Italy, one night giving him a black eye. He endured these humiliations, covering for his wife's foul temper and physical assaults because he wasn't the sort to lose his temper with or fight a woman.

Returning to New York in the June of 1923 after finishing *The White Sister* and playing a bit role in Samuel Goldwyn's *The Eternal City* while in Italy, Ronnie now had an impeccable entree into movies. His first role after a heady lead was a minor secondary one, but it was opposite George Arliss again, playing his son in a drama called *$20 a Week*. The two men became fast friends.

After a month of shooting at the Biograph Studios, Ronnie sailed for Italy in August to play opposite Gish once more in *Romola* (1924), again under Henry King's direction. It was on this movie that he met and became lasting friends with William Powell, who had been cast in the lead role of a politically ambitious fugitive in 1490s Florence.

While Ronnie was busy filming *Romola, The White Sister* premiered in New York on September 5, 1923 as a single theater attraction. Critical and public acclaim for his performance as an ill-fated lover made Ronald Colman an overnight sensation.

Just as important, the accolades for *The White Sister* enabled King and Gish to find a studio buyer for the movie, which they couldn't before the premiere because pictures at that time with a religious theme were considered box office poison. When it was sold to Metro and put into general release in February of 1924, *The White Sister* was cut by 50 minutes by Gish herself to tighten the story and pacing (including several convent scenes showing Gish's character becoming a nun), but with all of Colman's footage intact.

What Colman brought to his role as an Italian army captain that electrified audiences was sheer screen presence combined with several personal qualities: Sincerity, warm vulnerability, innate gentleness, a quiet dignity, and tender humor. It was a natural, earthy performance in a moviemaking era often characterized by melodramatic acting. The screen lit up when Ronald Colman walked into the frame in *The White Sister*, making women the world over fall madly in love with him. He also became a hero to male moviegoers for his quiet force and tender manners.

(Ironically, his portrayal of an Italian was so convincing that he received several letters from Italian men asking why he was so ashamed of his heritage that he felt compelled to change his last name to Colman.)

For all the acclaim he was now receiving, what mattered most to Ronnie was divorcing Thelma. After being slapped by her in public in Italy in March of 1923 while they were dancing at a masquerade party (B3), or in Italy in March of 1924 while watching an opera (B7), he left her for good on the spot. Separation notwithstanding, Thelma continued to make life miserable for him until July 31, 1934 when he finally forced her to divorce him after he had backed out of other divorce suits in 1925 and 1932.

When he left Italy that May, Ronnie returned to Manhattan to retrieve the rest of his belongings, then headed for Hollywood, where Samuel Goldwyn had hired him for a movie called *Tarnish* on the strength of his *White Sister* performance. When *Tarnish* was finished, Goldwyn offered him a four-year contract with a starting salary of $1250 a week, escalating to $4000 a week in 1928. The producer had found the debonair leading man of his dreams and did not want to lose him to another, bigger studio. Though he could easily have signed with MGM or Paramount, Ronnie accepted the offer for the money and star grooming and because the contract implied solid confidence in his talent.

This joining of producer and star was both opportune and a mismatch. Opportune because Goldwyn was an instinctive showman in need of a handsome leading man—his first—for his young studio; a mismatch because they were temperamental opposites. Goldwyn was an obsessive, vulgar, publicity-conscious producer, while Colman was a quiet and undemonstrative sort who preferred to do his work and keep to himself at home, shying from publicity. Goldwyn did have a keen eye for good commercial vehicles, but he was also prone to publicity gimmicks that exasperated Colman, such as linking him romantically with his leading ladies. Nevertheless, they made each other rich and famous.

At first, Goldwyn used Colman in a trio of profitable romantic melodramas, loaning him to producer Joseph Schenck, who cast him in three comedies with the Talmadge sisters. A few of these movies were forgettable, but as a group they boosted Colman's reputation because most of them were released in rapid succession: the aforementioned *Tarnish, Her Night of Romance* (both 1924), *A Thief in Paradise*, the steamy sensation, *His Supreme*

Moment, and *The Sporting Venus* (the latter two with Blanche Sweet), all released in 1925.

What made him stand out? He was as handsome, suave and debonair as many other leading men of that time, but his playful humor, effortless gallantry and consummate underplaying set him apart from hammier stars like John Barrymore, Antonio Moreno, and Francis X. Bushman. There was something uniquely charismatic and vulnerable yet warmly dignified about Ronald Colman, even in mediocre pictures, that made audiences pack theaters to watch him regardless of the overall quality of the current vehicle.

Though he wasn't getting the kinds of full-bodied roles he wanted and merited, Ronnie *was* fitting into the Hollywood social scene, deepening his established friendships with William Powell and Warner Baxter, carousing with them now and then. They were quickly dubbed The Three Musketeers of Hollywood, with a fourth star, Richard Barthelmess, as their D'Artagnan. They weren't nearly as wild as John Barrymore and *his* alcoholic cronies, but they did their share of social drinking and discreet womanizing.

He also became lasting and intimate friends with cowboy star Tim McCoy, a gentlemanly, reserved fellow like himself, but one with a gift for telling wild and tall but true tales of the West that enthralled his British companion.

In the summer of 1925, Ronnie was given his most important role since *The White Sister.* Goldwyn cast him opposite a golden-haired Hungarian sensation named Vilma Banky in *The Dark Angel,* a melodrama of *nearly* ill-fated love. Once again, his career was moving ahead. He now had a leading lady with whom he was striking on-screen sparks (though he had made an excellent team with Sweet), whose meltingly sensual beauty and earthy humor perfectly complemented his own tender, urbane demeanor and dark good looks. And he finally had a role in which he could demonstrate his range and depth as an actor. As did *The White Sister, The Dark Angel* hinged on a theme of self-sacrifice, this time set against a World War I and post-war backdrop.

The Colman-Banky team was a hugely popular one, predating the even more popular team of John Gilbert and Greta Garbo by two years. While they lasted, Colman-Banky were idolized by the moviegoing public in *The Winning of Barbara Worth* (1926, a western about the irrigation of the Colorado desert and the movie that made Gary Cooper a star), *The Night of Love, The Magic Flame* (both 1927) and *Two Lovers* (1928). In these last three, Colman was cast, respectively, as a Spanish gypsy, an evil count and his circus clown lookalike, and a Flemish patriot a la the Scarlet Pimpernel. He felt miscast as a swashbuckling Valentino type (which was what Goldwyn and other producers wanted at the time after Valentino's untimely death in October of 1926) because it was far from his image of himself as a British gentleman.

For her part, Vilma didn't think these costume dramas made the most of her talent either, but there was nothing she or Ronnie could do about it; they were under contract and not big enough stars to say no to their boss, even if they had been so inclined. What bothered them more than the scripts were Goldwyn's contrived "news" stories that they were a romantic pair offscreen as well. That ended in 1928 when Vilma married actor Rod LaRoque.

In between films with Banky, Colman made his best and most popular silent movie, *Beau Geste* (1926), a haunting adventure saga and the prototype for all Foreign Legion movies thereafter. It was in *Beau Geste* that Colman found his ideal persona, which he would repeat with variations through the 1930s: a middle or upper-class Englishman who nobly sacrifices his happiness and sometimes his life for someone or some ideal, or both, he values more than himself.

Noblesse oblige wasn't new to movies in 1926, but Colman elevated it to an art, relying on debonair humor and gracious likability instead of corn and pathos. The huge commercial successes of *Beau Geste* and the Banky films made him an international movie star. Not wanting other studios to benefit from his star power any more or grab him once his contract was up in mid-1928, Goldwyn offered Ronnie a new and irresistible contract in mid to late 1927: $5000 a week for seven years whether he was working or not, otherwise known as pay or play; he would make two movies a year at most; and he would have the right to turn down any properties Goldwyn offered. The trade-off? No more loanouts, even if they were movies he was dying to make. He would be exclusive to and synonymous with Goldwyn.

The next turning point for Ronnie came in 1929 with the advent of talkies. By that time, sound had ended the silent era, ruining or demoting the careers of scores of stars for their foreign accents or for having voices that were too flat, too bass, too nasal, or which simply did not match their silent screen personalities. John Gilbert was the most famous of those sound film casualties, but not because his voice was high or squeaky, because it wasn't. He failed because he became melodramatically leaden in a string of bad movies. Otherwise, Gilbert had a non-distinctive but perfectly acceptable tenor voice.

Colman was not only one of the few male stars whose careers were enhanced by sound, he was one of the few silent stars to bridge the technical gap between silence and sound. Others were Gary Cooper, William Powell and Norma Shearer. For Colman, the early carbon mike revealed a warmly intimate, beautifully cultured, superbly modulated Anglo-American accent that perfectly complemented his handsome features and debonair image. He sounded the way audiences thought he would. His stage training also made him easy and natural before the mike, as though he had been making talkies for years.

After a final silent in 1929—a commercial failure called *The Rescue*, from the Joseph Conrad novel—Colman was cast in carefully crafted talking vehicles such as *Bulldog Drummond*, *Raffles*, and *The Devil to Pay*. These and other early sound films, though mostly mediocre, made him a talking picture superstar, crystallizing his new dual persona as an amiably cultivated and gallant worldly hero or rogue.

Ironically, Colman was opposed to making sound movies at first, partly because he thought the intrusion of the microphone would destroy the art of screen pantomime that was the hallmark of the silent era (which it did for the most part, Colman's characteristically understated portrayals being a notable exception), partly because he was a naturally conservative man resistant to change.

(However, *Bulldog Drummond* was *not* his first sound film appearance. In late 1928, a newsreel crew filmed him and newly elected California Governor Clement C. Young in Colman's Beverly Hills backyard for a two-strip Technicolor movie industry commercial. See F31.)

Reluctant as he was at first to make sound movies, Colman caused such a sensation with his voice and his casually sophisticated manner in his first two talkies, *Bulldog Drummond* and *Condemned* (both 1929), that he became one of the few actors—before the rules were changed—to be doubly nominated for an Academy Award as Best Actor, losing to George Arliss for *Disraeli*. (Arliss's presence and shadow seemed to be almost everywhere in the early stages of Colman's career, yet today it is Arliss who is even more forgotten by all but hardcore film buffs. On a personal level, Colman and Arliss were friends.)

Seen today, *Bulldog Drummond*, a detective spoof, is painfully slow and static at times, but Colman's dash and whimsy are fun, especially in the first reel, which moves a lot faster than the rest of the movie. That had almost everything to do with the fact that the noisy sound camera was imprisoned in a sound booth, as were nearly all the other early talkies. Actors not used to sound were wooden at best, pacing was leaden, and movement was painfully constricted during the first two years of talking feature production.

These same deficiencies also marred *Condemned*, a Devil's Island melodrama about a love affair between Colman and warden's wife Ann Harding. But, audiences didn't mind the technical and plot deficiencies as long as they got to see *and* hear Ronald Colman being charming and heroically carefree as often as possible.

Since the public had loved Colman as a debonair rogue in *Condemned*, Goldwyn followed it with *Raffles* (1930), a slick but thin tale of a gentleman thief by that name who mingles with the upper class by day so he can steal their jewels by night. Sidney Howard crafted an expert script from E.W. Hornung's play (filmed twice before with John Barrymore and House Peters), but the movie's production did not flow as smoothly as the writing.

Goldwyn was profoundly dissatisfied with Harry D'Arrast's direction, finding it too fast for his taste and its quick pacing not in keeping with Colman's urbanity. He went to the set after seeing the first few day's rushes and had an argument with D'Arrast about the pacing.

"You and I don't speak the same language, Mr. Goldwyn," D'Arrast haughtily told the producer. "I'm sorry, Mr. D'Arrast, but it's my money that's buying the language," Goldwyn pointedly replied.[5]

D'Arrast was replaced by George Fitzmaurice, who had previously directed Colman in *The Dark Angel* and *The Night of Love*. His continental touch was more to Goldwyn's liking, although the brisk pacing remained the same. In the end, neither director received screen credit, making it the only Colman movie officially not directed by anyone. Which was of no consequence to moviegoers, who flocked to *Raffles*; it was just the sort of gentleman thief nonsense audiences enjoyed seeing Ronald Colman play.

The follow-up to *Raffles*, *The Devil to Pay*, was even better. A fast-paced, exuberant, hilariously witty drawing room romp, it is easily the best of the Colman talkies for Goldwyn. Yet, for all its obvious skill and pleasure, *The Devil to Pay* didn't make a profit until it was marketed worldwide in 1931, according to Goldwyn biographer A. Scott Berg. It also made money in re-release during WWII and when it was sold to TV in the early 1960s.

While he was garnering critical and public acclaim as a witty and adventurous man of the world onscreen, offscreen Ronnie was leading a carefully guarded private life. He drank with his Musketeer buddies and played tennis with them at his Beverly Hills home; maintained friendships with Tim McCoy and Adolphe Menjou (both extreme right wingers, though Ronnie was a moderate conservative at most); and enjoyed brief, discreet affairs with various female stars, including Thelma Todd and the later notorious Mary Astor, to whom he proposed in the early 30s, but who turned him down.

His affairs with actresses were among the best-kept secrets in a town ever-abuzz with gossip. Few outside his closest friends knew he even had these romances until they were over. Fewer still knew he was married to Thelma Raye, technically making him an adulterer. All Thelma cared about however, when she made herself known, was badgering him for money.

The late 1920s through early 1930s were the years when Ronald Colman became firmly established as a pre-eminent and international sound movie star, and as the unofficial leader of Hollywood's British colony of actors. Away from the studio and the colony, he indulged his love of literature with first editions of Dickens, Stevenson (his first love as a boy next to Shakespeare), Kipling, Galsworthy, Lewis Carroll and Shaw, and with handsome leatherbound editions of the Bard's plays and sonnets. He also greatly enjoyed the work of F. Scott Fitzgerald, an extra kick being that Fitzgerald mentioned him in two novels—*Tender is the Night* and *The Last Tycoon*—and made him a cameo character in *The Pat Hobby Stories*. Colman was Fitzgerald's favorite star while Ronnie, in turn, was flattered by all the mentions and the supporting role. Fitzgerald also wrote a few treatments for proposed Colman movies, none of which were produced.

Ronnie's biggest purchase in the late 1920s was a large and splendid squire-like house on Mound Street in Beverly Hills. He later moved in 1934 to one on Summit Drive up the road from Benedict Canyon. Whether entertaining friends or retreating from the world after work, Ronnie had the privacy he cherished, aided by two Filipino houseboys and his faithful valet, Tommy Turner, a soft-spoken Britisher and former Goldwyn prop man (which is how they met) who worked for him for 30 years.

Colman's first movie of the 1930s was also one of his worst, through no fault of his or that of director George Fitzmaurice. Sam Goldwyn was tricked by the writing team of Ben Hecht and Charles MacArthur into buying a gentleman thief story a la *Raffles*, set in the North African desert. Goldwyn paid $25,000 and 3 percent of the gross profits, thinking he had the best of the bargain. In return, the two writers gave him nothing for several weeks; they were busy cranking out scripts for other studios. Furious at this cavalier breach of contract, Goldwyn demanded a script, so Hecht reportedly spent one day almost round-the-clock dictating an absurd script to his secretary, a scenario filled with unbelievable scenes, vapid characters and dumb dialogue, all of it made up as he went along.

Instead of admitting he'd been tricked and throwing out the script, Goldwyn went ahead and produced it as written under the title *The Unholy Garden* (1931), casting a pre-*King Kong* Fay Wray as the female lead. He was determined to get his money's worth no matter what it cost him (coining a Goldwynism). For his part, despite his understandable but repressed anger with an inferior script (which he had the right to reject), Ronnie nevertheless gave a crisply professional performance. Predictably, *The Unholy Garden* was a commercial failure, losing Goldwyn $200,000, for which he had no one but himself to blame.

While *The Unholy Garden* was in pre-production, Goldwyn bought the film rights to Sinclair Lewis's *Arrowsmith*. Lewis had just won the 1930 Nobel Prize for literature, and the novel won the 1926 Pulitzer Prize, which Lewis declined because he felt he should have won for *Main Street*. It was certainly a prestigious property, but Goldwyn bought it for its story of a self-sacrificingly idealistic research scientist who finds a cure for bubonic plague; a seemingly ideal role for the selfless Colman image the star and his producer wanted to build.

The role of Martin Arrowsmith was certainly more substantial than the carefree rogues and charmers Colman had played in five straight movies. Aiming for the utmost quality for this production, Goldwyn signed Sidney Howard (who had written three of those five) for the adaptation, while John Ford was borrowed from Fox to direct (at a hefty price to Goldwyn), and Helen Hayes was cast as Arrowsmith's supportively earthy wife, Leora.

The only screen version of *Arrowsmith* was mostly a critical success and certainly a commercial hit, ranking among the top 30 money makers of the 1931-32 season. It was also Oscar-nominated for Best Picture of 1931-32, losing to *Grand Hotel*. Colman turned out to be miscast as a midwesterner, but it *was* the most serious-minded of his early talkies.

After finishing work on *Arrowsmith*, Ronnie took a long and well-earned vacation, going on a world tour with a friend named Alvin Weingand. Weingand was a young hotel manager he had met in 1928 through a mutual actor friend named Charles Lane. They became fast friends at once, Weingand recalled, "because we were both soft-spoken gentlemen with a love of tennis and scotch whiskey. When you have those two things in common, you have the basis for a lasting friendship."[6]

Al abhorred the Hollywood social scene, which suited Ronnie just fine because he needed a close friend who had no interest in and nothing to do with show business. So, with Ronnie paying all expenses, Al became his round-the-world traveling companion for seven months, a journey that finally took Ronnie to the various ports of call with which his father had done business as a silk merchant.

When Ronnie returned to Hollywood in the spring of 1932, relaxed, refreshed and with vivid memories of life in other countries, he was ready for a new movie, but had to bide his time till mid-summer to begin work on *Cynara*, a drama of adultery directed by King Vidor. Both Ronnie and Sam Goldwyn were appalled by the idea of Ronald Colman playing an adulterer, but they were desperate for material since finishing *Arrowsmith* the previous October, so Frances Marion and King Vidor were hired to write and direct. Just before *Cynara* began shooting, Goldwyn also acquired the rights to *The Masquerader*, a proven stage hit more congenial to the Colman persona.

It was while he was working on *Cynara* that Ronnie's career was fatefully upended by a single newspaper column by Sidney Skolsky of New York's *Daily News*. The story of this incident has been told several times, but never accurately and in sequence. Using the Skolsky column itself, newspaper, *Variety* and magazine stories that followed, and film production dates, here is what probably happened and why.

On Tuesday August 16, during the second week of filming, Skolsky visited the *Cynara* set (now called *I Have Been Faithful* because Goldwyn thought it was a more easily pronounced title), hoping to get an interview with Colman. He was turned down through Goldwyn publicist Lynn Farnol because Colman did not like his columns. Instead, Skolsky watched a scene being filmed. Being in Ronnie's line of sight, Skolsky made him blow his lines. An assistant was sent to ask Skolsky to step behind the camera, out of the actor's line-of-sight.

During a break in filming, Skolsky talked with Farnol, who gave the columnist a press release and let slip that Colman often took a shot of liquor before playing his love scenes. "He believes that by getting more than slightly drunk, he plays love scenes—well, more in love," Farnol gushed.[7]

(Colman leading-lady Blanche Sweet attested to Berg about Ronnie's drinking habit, and a *Variety* column of September 20, 1932 referred to a fan magazine interview with Helen Hayes in which she also mentioned his drinking problem. This habit had inadvertently begun with *The White Sister* in 1923, when Henry King and Lillian Gish got him drunk to do an emotionally charged scene.)

That afternoon, Skolsky filed a story to the *Daily News* that not only embellished this tidbit—"He feels that he looks better for pictures when moderately dissipated than when completely fit"—but blatantly and snidely libeled the actor's professional competence by putting a distortive spin on the press release's description of his daily regimen for dressing, makeup and acting:

"He doesn't memorize his entire part. He merely memorizes the scene he is to play that day—and then he has a difficult time remembering his lines. The screen is a great medium for such actors. When he forgets, they merely re-shoot. Imagine playing a scene over on stage because an actor forgot his lines!...

"Colman walks on the set in his street clothes, unless it is a costume picture or a tuxedo is required, and he doesn't use make-up. His tan is the exact shade required for the screen. His dark brown hair is streaked with gray. This handsome juvenile is no youngster."

This and more, all of it specious and disingenuous since Skolsky's beat was actors playing for a camera, not a theater audience. It would have infuriated any screen actor, let alone one of Colman's caliber and stature.

When the column appeared on August 17 (B393), a friend of Ronnie's called it to his attention. Wasting no time, he went to see Farnol, who sheepishly apologized for the liquor remarks, offering to do whatever he could to repair the damage. Ronnie later went to Goldwyn's office, demanding that Goldwyn fire Farnol and issue a retraction to the press. Goldwyn admitted the man had made a mistake but saw no reason to fire him, and refused the retraction. Knowing that Farnol had apologized to Ronnie, Goldwyn surely wondered what his star really wanted. Ronnie left Goldwyn's office to continue work on *Cynara* and ponder his next move.

On Monday September 12, the start of *Cynara*'s last two weeks of filming, a lawyer named Neil S. McCarthy filed a $2,000,000 lawsuit for Colman against Goldwyn in Los Angeles Superior Court, claiming defamation of the star's character resulting from a press release and the Skolsky column. The lawsuit became a blaring banner headline in the *Los Angeles Evening Express* on September 13: **RONALD COLMAN SUES GOLDWYN FOR MILLIONS**. For a man to whom publicity was anathema, Colman now had a mountain of it, especially since it was unheard of for a star to sue his producer. The shock of the suit rippled through the movie industry.

The time lag between publication of the column and the filing of the suit begs the question of that lag, why Colman waited so long. The answer, according to an interview Colman gave Rosalind Shaffer for the December 1932 *Motion Picture* magazine, was that a newspaperwoman he knew who was writing a story on him called to ask about details in the Skolsky story and a press release the columnist had drawn on for it. That was when he decided to take action, as a means of a protest. Though it was Skolsky who had libeled him, Colman did not hold him to blame.

This, of course, was disingenuous and had to be. Had he admitted the real reason for the suit, Colman's integrity would have been damaged and he would have been liable for perjury. He was playing a bluff, with his career as the high stakes poker chip.

What was really behind the lawsuit was that Ronnie was hurting professionally from Goldwyn's vulgarity, of being cast in ludicrous melodramas that demeaned his talent and image and cheapened his name value, though his contract did give him the right of rejection on stories. Most of all, he had had his fill of being denigrated by the people who wrote the press books (in those books, he was depicted as a stuffy and aloof martinet), and of publicity stories and gimmicks that were cheap, trashy and false, such as linking him and Vilma Banky as real lovers.

Goldwyn saw Colman as an erudite cash machine while Ronnie knew he was capable of more masterful work. Had Goldwyn given him a better choice of stories or loaned him for parts he was being asked to play, Ronnie might have been content to stay. As it was, the Skolsky column, in combination with Farnol's remarks, were the last straws. He believed that a lawsuit, publicly embarrassing Goldwyn, would scare the producer into voiding the remainder of his contract.

The ploy didn't work. Ronnie had made it clear months earlier that he would not be signing a new contract in 1934, so Goldwyn was determined to make his star abide by the old one no matter what.

Nearly two months after Colman's suit was filed, Goldwyn's lawyers filed an answer in Los Angeles Superior Court on November 10, saying in effect that the libelous remarks had been made, but by an individual, not by the company. In his Goldwyn book, Berg states that Colman dropped his suit following production of *The Masquerader* and never worked for Goldwyn again because of a contract stalemate. In fact, Colman did not drop the suit until the following October.

The Masquerader began filming November 14, 1932, four days after Goldwyn answered the libel suit, and finished production in mid-January. At a farewell Christmas party at his home, Ronnie told his friends he would be packing for a trip to England within the month.

A month after *The Masquerader* finished, on February 12, 1933, Goldwyn hedged his commercial bet by sneak previewing it to critical and audience applause. Believing he had a winner, Goldwyn shelved it till August 25.

Ronnie held true to his Christmas pledge. After *Masquerader* finished in mid-January

1933, he went on a second, longer world tour, again with Al Weingand as his valet, this time for the purpose of finding a perfect place for a resort hotel with Ronnie as a silent partner. They were away for ten months, returning in mid-November 1933.

After combing the world for the utopia they had in mind (on this voyage, as for the previous one, Ronnie paid both their expenses), they found what they were looking for in Santa Barbara: A garden spot called San Ysidro Ranch. They wanted to buy it at once, but had to wait until April 30, 1935 to take over. Over the 23 years they co-owned the ranch (the partnership ending with Ronnie's death in 1958), it became *the* guest resort for the rich and famous from all over the world because they were the only ones who could afford to stay there.

While on vacation, Ronnie had a brief change of heart about returning to Goldwyn, according to a wire service report on August 22, 1933 (B313). However, back in Los Angeles the following month, he was again resolved not to make another movie for Goldwyn. The reason was that he had been contacted by producer Joseph Schenck, who had just formed Twentieth Century Pictures with Darryl F. Zanuck on the United Artists lot where Goldwyn also had his studios.

The two producers needed a male superstar to kick off their first year of production, and they were also in sync with the kinds of stories Ronnie wanted to film, so they began negotiating with Goldwyn to end the Colman contract. A deal was finally struck on October 16, 1933 whereby Goldwyn would void Ronnie's contract as the price for Ronnie dropping his suit and remaining on the United Artists lot. No money changed hands. The ordeal was over.

Louella Parsons in the *Los Angeles Herald Express* made the "surprise" announcement on October 17 (B323) that Goldwyn had decided to waive the remainder of Colman's contract, bowing to the inevitable. That same day in the *Los Angeles Times* (B369), Edwin Schallert printed a more cautious report, calling the deal a rumor.

Whatever Ronnie initially felt about Skolsky's verbal assault, what the infamous column really accomplished in the end was yanking a languishing star out of a succession of forgettable potboiler melodramas and thrusting him into his classic period in sound films. It was the wrong story at the right time.

As for the commercial fates of *Cynara* and *The Masquerader*, the public rejected both. Colman fans didn't accept him as an adulterous husband in the first or as a drug addict in the second. They were also thin star vehicles.

Ironically, Goldwyn felt that *The Masquerader* would make more money than *Cynara* because Colman's performance as a drug-addicted Member of Parliament was offset by his portrayal of the MP's nobler lookalike journalist cousin who becomes the MP's professional double. Goldwyn's idea was that two Ronald Colmans would give the public double value for its money, while Ronnie felt that a dual role did nothing to enhance his reputation, even in proven material like this.

(Because Goldwyn refused to loan Colman to other studios after *Beau Geste*, Ronnie could not accept plum roles in movies that would have been naturals for him, such as Rouben Mamoulian's *Queen Christina* opposite Greta Garbo, and Lubitsch's *Design for Living*. It is well documented in several Garbo biographies that Colman was sought for the role of the Spanish ambassador after she turned down Olivier, and would only accept John Gilbert. According to Lubitsch biographer Scott Eyman, Colman and Leslie Howard were wanted to co-star in *Design for Living*, but the idea was scotched because their fees were too high, though Colman was not contractually free to accept the role even had he lowered his fee.)

Just as important for Ronnie as freedom from Goldwyn and finding San Ysidro, was finally getting Thelma to divorce him in a British court. He and Weingand had faked an adulterous weekend with two women Ronnie asked to help him in order to force Thelma's hand. (See B3) The legalities were over quickly on July 31, 1934, giving Thelma an annuity for life (she outlived him), but at last Ronnie was free and single again.

Just as happily, his first movie for 20th Century was a very good comedy-mystery sequel to *Bulldog Drummond*, called *Bulldog Drummond Strikes Back* (1934). The idea was suggested by writer Nunnally Johnson, who had screened *Bulldog Drummond* on the United Artists lot while searching for an ideal Colman vehicle. Johnson proposed the sequel to Zanuck, who pitched it to Ronnie, and the movie was on.

Bulldog Drummond Strikes Back was a commercial success because it was a fun and inventive mystery spoof, re-establishing Ronald Colman as a light romantic star after three consecutive melodramas for Goldwyn, and teaming him for the second time with Loretta Young.

In early 1935, Ronnie met and began courting British actress Benita Hume, his opposite in many ways. Where he was reserved and introspective, she was gregarious and loved being the life of any party. He was moody, she was gay. They fell in love almost at once, but for all his attachment to Benita, Ronnie resisted marriage, his bad experience with Thelma having taken its toll.

Now that he had left Goldwyn, Ronnie was playing increasingly flamboyant or demanding roles, sometimes a bit of both. *Bulldog Drummond Strikes Back* was followed by the title role in the dull biographical movie *Clive of India* (1935), a tale of the obsessive soldier who helped secure India for the British empire in the late 18th century.

His second movie for 1935 was a forgettable bit of fluff called *The Man Who Broke the Bank at Monte Carlo* (1935) under the new banner of 20th Century-Fox because 20th Century had merged with Fox. It was also a commercial flop. Audiences would not accept Colman as an exiled Russian nobleman turned cab driver, especially with a vacuous script and Joan Bennett as a wooden romantic interest. Either Colman thought he could pull off this kind of inane light comedy through sheer urbane verve or Zanuck wanted to vary his roles or a little of both.

His third and best role of the year (filmed before *Monte Carlo*) was also his best and most personally rewarding since sound took over. It was also a part he had coveted for years: Sydney Carton in *A Tale of Two Cities*. Preparing for this complex role, Colman went through more meticulous at-home rehearsals than ever before so that the character who finally emerged would be the cynical yet sympathetic ne'er-do-well Dickens envisioned.

Audiences and critics alike were awestruck by this new, mature Ronald Colman. The stylized mannerisms that had been an integral part of his acting repertoire for so long had largely vanished. In their place was a reflective and earthy performance displaying Colman's previously untapped talent to disappear into a character, showing him from the inside out.

A Tale of Two Cities was made by Colman on loan to MGM for David O. Selznick, with whom he would work again two years later. In fact, his performance as Carton earned him the best reviews of his career to date. It also had the critics and the public speculating on what he might do next now that he had expanded his range. At this point, they were speculating in vain because Colman still had one more movie to make under his Fox contract: *Under Two Flags* (1936), an entertaining Foreign Legion saga in the *Beau Geste* mold, but nowhere near the level of that classic. It made money as a popular springtime attraction because Colman's charismatic presence and romantic technique made a typical adventure script look better than it was.

With the completion of *Under Two Flags* on March 5, 1936, Colman's contract with Zanuck ended. He decided not to renew it in favor of freelancing his talent among the other major studios. He found he was greatly in demand, his per picture fee averaging $150,000. As he once told his then-agent, Bill Hawks, "Before God, I'm worth $35 a week. Before the film industry, I'm worth whatever you can get."[8]

Before and after his Fox contract expired, Colman was offered or suggested for numerous roles. He felt unsuited to some, was afraid of the dramatic risks posed by others, didn't want to break with the debonair romantic type he had established, or he was simply part of the studio casting musical chairs game withoout knowing it. The movies he rejected, were planned for him or for which he was suggested from the late 1920s through late 1930s included *The Brothers Karamazov* (for Goldwyn, B22), Bringing Up Baby[9], The Rains Came[10], *The Dawn Patrol* (1930 version, B20a), *Captain Blood* (B20a) *Intermezzo* (B19) *Rebecca* (B19), Jane Eyre[11], and the ultimate Technicolor epic of the 1930s, *Gone With the Wind* (B94 and B190), as Rhett Butler. Undoubtedly he would have been superb in some of these movies and miscast in others. Had he made just a few of them, he would certainly have been better remembered by film historians, and his work would have been more frequently revived than was the case until the cable TV and home video boom.

While he was busy choosing from some of Hollywood's best scripts, Ronnie was also busy courting Benita Hume while establishing San Ysidro Ranch, and devoting more time to his hobbies, such as astronomy, gardening and painting still lifes. And he played poker on Friday nights through the early 1950s with Arthur Rubinstein, Jascha Heifetz, Tim McCoy, and Clark Gable, naming a few friends.

It wasn't until the summer of 1936, however, that he was able to take these rests on a regular basis. Following a two-week rest after *Under Two Flags*, Ronnie was at Columbia beginning March 23, 1936, making his best-remembered movie, *Lost Horizon* (1937). That and his next two, *The Prisoner of Zenda* (1937) and *If I Were King* (1938) formed a heroic trilogy, more fully discussed in the "Art and Influence of Ronald Colman" chapter.

The irony of these three fine movies in a row was that Ronnie had now limited himself to making only one or two films a year so that another half dozen great pictures were not immediately forthcoming. He didn't want to overexpose himself, his income gave him the life he wanted, and the investments he made using that income let him be more selective about his roles. Yet he kept far less of his weekly acting paychecks than one would think.

Because of high federal tax rates from 1934 on, more than half of all his earnings—and those of every other highly paid star—went to the U.S. income tax; another portion went to British taxes because he never became an American citizen; he paid Thelma monthly alimony; and he occasionally donated to charities, more so during WWII when 28% of his net income went to war bonds and war relief. From an average weekly income of $7000, including investments, he kept about $1800. For example, of the $362,500 he made in 1937, $267,000 or 74% went to taxes. Still, he had enough money after all of these deductions to keep himself in comparative luxury.

Heavy taxes and alimony were also among the reasons he never returned to the stage. His name alone would have guaranteed sold-out theaters in any play he chose to star, but there was more to be earned in movies. He was also afraid of going back on stage after so many years away. So he became a star type, staying with what worked best and paid most.

While he was busy making *If I Were King*, Ronnie was deeply involved with Benita, but fearfully reluctant to propose marriage because of the psychological residue from Thelma. Benita, however, was determined to marry the man she loved, so in late September of 1938, she packed her belongings, moved out of the room she was using in Ronnie's house and took a train out of town. She wanted to force Ronnie's hand by compelling him to make up his mind about marriage. The ruse worked. Ronnie wired her at her first train stop to come home and exchange vows. A few days later, on September 30, they were quietly married at San Ysidro Ranch with a few close friends present, including Al Weingand and Tim McCoy. As an amusing sidelight, Ronnie called the two main gossip columnists, Hedda Hopper and Louella Parsons, with the news minutes after the ceremony, but it was Hopper who broke the news first since she was about to go on the air with her weekly broadcast. After the calls, the newlyweds went on their honeymoon.

Fortified with the emotional security of a good marriage, Ronnie now felt like taking a risk or two with his next screen role, so his second movie for Paramount was a break from the noblesse oblige types he had been playing for years, an adaptation of Rudyard Kipling's first novel, *The Light That Failed* (1939). Kipling was a big box office name that year because of the huge success of *Gunga Din*, but the two movies couldn't have been more opposite in theme, tone and temperament.

Whereas *Gunga Din* is a schoolboyish comedy-adventure, *The Light That Failed* is an introspective drama about a brilliant but arrogant artist who goes blind from a battle wound just as he is finishing his masterpiece, Melancholia.

The Light That Failed is one of the best movies Colman ever made, with thoughtful, leisurely writing, direction and pacing. The making of it, though, was a chore because Ronnie was constantly clashing with director William "Wild Bill" Wellman, who was as fiery and bullheaded as Ronnie was reserved and quietly adamant (B3, B89). Their biggest confrontation was over Wellman casting a then minor actress named Ida Lupino as Bessie, the prostitute who poses for Melancholia. Ronnie had wanted actress friend Vivien Leigh, who was then comparatively unknown to American audiences.

Despite this clash of wills and temperaments, *The Light That Failed* was an artistic and fair commercial success, showing that Colman could veer from his established heroic type without losing audience sympathy.

Also in 1939, on January 15, Ronnie made his radio debut as a series regular on the Kellogg-sponsored show *The Circle* on NBC. He had done a few other radio shows to promote his movies, but had held back on regular appearances for fear of seeming undignified. He left *The Circle* (for which he was paid $5000 per broadcast), a forerunner of today's talk/variety shows, after just four weeks because Noel Coward goaded him into demanding better scripts or he would quit (B421). He was President, Cary Grant was Vice President, Carole Lombard was the Resident Feminist, Groucho Marx was the heckling Treasurer, and Chico Marx was the Assistant Heckler. The series lasted only 26 weeks, ending that July. For more details see pages 133-34.

That June, Ronnie started another chapter in his radio career by making his first appearance on *Lux Radio Theater* in a fair truncation of *The Prisoner of Zenda*. Audiences loved listening to the Colman voice on the radio—he was a natural for the medium.

After turning down the leads in *Rebecca* and *Jane Eyre* (the former because he felt it was too much of a woman's picture while failing to realize the vast new movie audience it would have given him), Ronnie joined forces with friends Charles Boyer, Anatole Litvak and Bill Hawks to form a production company called United Producers, which would distribute a series of hand-picked movies through RKO. The result was two flat, minor comedies titled *Lucky Partners* (1940) and *My Life With Caroline* (1941). The first was largely a critical hit, but made little money, while the latter met with mostly critical and public indifference.

After years of excessive caution in choosing his roles, the one time he took a chance by co-producing his own movies, Colman misjudged what he needed to be playing, what audiences wanted to see him do. It also hurt that Lewis Milestone, who directed both movies, had no flair for this kind of light comedy.

Had Colman starred in *Rebecca* or *Jane Eyre* or a few of the other, more qualitative, movies he was offered, he would have had an incredible string of commercial and artistic successes, running almost unbroken from *Bulldog Drummond Strikes Back* in 1934 to *Random Harvest* in 1942. Ironically, he played the Maxim de Winter role in *Rebecca* for a *Lux Radio Theater* role in 1941, opposite Ida Lupino, another irony.

When *Lucky Partners* was released and before production began on *My Life with Caroline*, Colman began another production partnership for movies to be partly financed by and released through Fox. This time his partners included Boyer, Litvak, Milestone and Irene Dunne. But, despite a contract signed by all, nothing ever came of the deal.

After *Caroline* was released in the fall of 1941, a clash of star egos over billing resulted in Colman accepting third billing after Cary Grant and Jean Arthur in an excellent social comedy drama for Columbia titled *The Talk of the Town* (1942). The movie was a big summer/fall hit because it delighted audiences with its star trio (billing aside, Colman stole the show) in a comedy of ideas about the theory and practice of the law, directed with wit, depth and flair by George Stevens.

Following it in December was the even more popular *Random Harvest*, in which Colman played an amnesiac WW1 soldier who marries a music hall performer played by Greer Garson. The elegant and charming star chemistry in *Random Harvest* netted the movie more than $4 million in domestic rentals (on a budget of $2 million), broke attendance records at Radio City Music Hall, and won Colman his third Oscar nomination for Best Actor. He lost to James Cagney's more flamboyant performance as George M. Cohan in *Yankee Doodle Dandy*.

Just as he was cresting once more in movies, the kinds of roles at which he excelled were disappearing and the few that were being written were offered to younger stars in the Colman mold like David Niven, Douglas Fairbanks, Jr. and Don Ameche. Furthermore, the kinds of dramas and comedies he specialized in had largely fallen out of vogue in favor of war movies starring Humphrey Bogart, Errol Flynn, Cary Grant and Tyrone Power. Ronnie didn't want to chase Nazi and Japanese spies and soldiers in war adventures, so he didn't make any, though he would have been fine in such British war movies as *In Which We Serve* and *The Invaders*.

Seemingly desperate for escapist material, Colman's last movie during the war years was a fairly entertaining remake of the Arabian Nights play, *Kismet* (1944), co-starring Marlene Dietrich. It was his first Technicolor movie and made a small profit on a reported $3 million budget, largely because audiences got a kick from the roguish charm and vocal magic he brought to another beggar king role.

Though only three new Ronald Colman movies were released during the war, Colman was nevertheless all over the place in allied movie theaters the world over. Several of his movies from the 1930s were re-issued by Fox, Goldwyn and Columbia, mostly to take advantage of a new generation of moviegoers who had never seen them and because they were from a more escapist era. Columbia, in particular, re-released *Lost Horizon* as *Lost Horizon of Shangri-La* to exploit President Roosevelt's famous remark that General Doolittle's headline-making bombing raid over Tokyo had been launched from Shangri-La.

(In January 1948, Ronnie remarked to Louella Parsons on her gossip radio show that every soldier he met while visiting stateside army and navy hospitals had seen *Lost Horizon* and *The Prisoner of Zenda*.)

As Colman's contemporary movie career declined, his radio career exploded, of his own choosing. He was a frequent guest on dramatic series like *Lux Radio Theater* and *Screen Guild Players*, and performed on numerous war bond, war relief, and variety shows.

His first longish stint as a radio host came about in mid-1943 when the ad agency of Ruthrauff and Ryan, at the behest of the head of the Electric AutoLite spark plug company (a man named Armstrong), teamed him with famed radio writer/director Arch Oboler for a series to be called *Everything for the Boys*. See pages 144-46 for the complete story.

In the fall of 1943, Ronnie's personal life took on added meaning and joy when Benita became pregnant for the first and only time. The prospect of becoming a father in middle-age both delighted and alarmed him, the latter because he was concerned with what the rest of his show business peers would think of his becoming a father at the age of 53. That concern vanished at once when Juliet Benita Colman was born on July 24, 1944. From then on, Ronnie and Benita were two beamingly proud parents. The birth of Juliet was another reason Ronnie kept mostly to radio work for the rest of his career. He wanted to be with his only child as much as possible, taking photos of her every day for a complete visual record of her childhood.

So it was that his radio career accelerated in 1945 with appearances on *Suspense*, *Lux*, *The Doctor Fights*, *Columbia Presents Corwin*, *Command Performance*, *The Radio Reader's Digest*, and two hilarious performances with Benita on the *Jack Benny Program* as Benny's long-suffering next-door neighbors; performances that led to their becoming Benny show regulars. For complete details, see pages 156-58.

In the middle of his run on the Benny show, Ronnie began hosting another long-running radio series: *Favorite Story*, produced, directed and mostly written by his good friends, Jerome Lawrence and Robert E. Lee, for syndication starting in the fall of 1948. For complete details, see pages 163-65.

A year before he started recording *Favorite Story*, Ronnie played the title role in the movie version of the John P. Marquand social satire and Broadway hit *The Late George Apley* (1947), about a stuffy and priggish Boston patriarch in 1912-13. Scripted by Philip Dunne and directed by Joseph L. Mankiewicz, it was a modest commercial success.

Less than two weeks after *The Late George Apley* finished shooting, Ronnie became deathly ill. He was admitted to St. John's Hospital in Santa Monica on Friday September 6, 1946 with a head infection and temperature of 105. Under the care of his personal doctor, Robert J. Kositchek, Ronnie's temperature dropped to near normal by Monday, September 9, and he was home a week later. Had he died from the infection, a good part of his life's work would have remained undone or done by someone else. He would also have missed out on the role that finally won him the Oscar.

Several months after this life-threatening illness, in the spring of 1947, he took on his most challenging screen role and one he had to be talked into: a schizophrenic stage star playing Othello who lets the character take over his off-stage life to the point of committing murder and suicide in *A Double Life*. The original script was by Ruth Gordon and Garson Kanin. The murder victim was a young and sexy Shelley Winters.

However, the characterization of the seemingly charming Anthony John was not an easy one for Ronnie to develop; the *Othello* scenes scared him. For all his love of Shakespeare, he had been afraid to act in a movie version of one of the Bard's plays. So producer Michael Kanin hired stage actor Walter Hampden to tutor Ronnie. Beyond that, director George Cukor aggressively prodded Ronnie out of his shell of British reserve to get a more expansive and demonic performance than he had ever given.

For this bravura departure role, Ronnie deservedly won two awards. The first was a Golden Globe Award for Best Actor on March 10, 1948. The second was his long-coveted Academy Award as Best Actor. However, what won him the Oscar had as much to do with the lobbying campaign he waged in the trade papers to get his fellow Academy members to vote for him as with the sentiment of those voters that he had been a star too long *not* to have won. The statuette was as much a lifetime achievement award as it was sincere applause for a fine job of acting. Whatever the reasons for the award, Ronnie was in a state of exhilarated shock the night of March 20, 1948, when his name was finally called out. Accepting the

Oscar, he said:

"Ladies and Gentlemen, I am very happy and very proud and very lucky. Lucky because I know I wouldn't be standing on this stage tonight without the grand contributions of so many others. Of a great script and a great part, from Ruth Gordon and Garson Kanin. Of the wonderful help of George Cukor, Michael Kanin and Bill Goetz.

"And I'm not forgetting a splendid cast, and all the departments that gave their skill and talents to making this picture. So, to all of them, especially, my deepest gratitude. And to you, ladies and gentlemen, my warmest thanks."

Choking back tears, he then went backstage with Olivia de Havilland where hundreds of press photos were taken, at least one of them showing his British reserve momentarily abandoned for a look of sheer jubilation. Other shots were taken as he posed with former co-star Loretta Young (who had won for Best Actress for *The Farmer's Daughter*) and former producer Darryl F. Zanuck, who had won for his production of *Gentleman's Agreement*. It seemed fitting that they should share the Oscar spotlight that night.

Intuitively sensing that Ronnie would win, Jack Benny had his writers conjure a series of scripts based on the Oscar win. The second script, airing on March 28, featured the ultimate borrowing gag: Benny was borrowing everything else from the Colmans' house, so why not borrow the Oscar as well? The twist was that it would be stolen by a mugger and Jack would then spend the next several weeks trying to retrieve the Oscar or replace it.

With his Oscar win fresh at hand, Ronnie set out on a European tour with Benita on May 10, 1948 to promote the movie in England and Belgium. During this three-month professional holiday, he did two radio interviews on the BBC. Back home, there was also the prospect of acting in and narrating a series of low-budget TV shows based on stories by Dickens and O. Henry. The series was never made.

Despite his hard-earned Oscar, his radio stardom, his beautiful little daughter, Juliet, and all the other people and things he had come to prize, Ronnie found himself experiencing acute bouts of depression due to middle age and a lack of scripts (see B3, B7 and B78) to fit the image he once had; an image no longer in vogue in American movies. He was unwilling to let go of his gentleman adventurer persona, *A Double Life* notwithstanding. Nor would he dye his hair or shave his moustache for some of the roles being offered, although he had, in fact, been dying his hair for movie roles from 1934 to 1942 and dyed it for *A Double Life*. He was afraid or unwilling to become a reputable character star now that the peak of his romantic stardom had passed. His vanity or ego or both wouldn't allow it.

In a last attempt to regain his stature as a debonair star, Colman starred in a funny but flawed TV quiz show satire called *Champagne for Caesar* (1950). It lasted only a month in first run before being sold to television by its unscrupulous producer, Harry Popkin.

Champagne for Caesar became a late show cult classic, but its stars—including Art Linkletter, as quiz host Happy Hogan—never got any money for their work in it after receiving their first paychecks from Popkin, who had also just produced *D.O.A.* (1949). Popkin had promised all five stars that they would receive supplemental checks when filming ended, but those checks were never sent. Ronnie received $25,000, but was cheated out of another $75,000 and a part of the profits guaranteed by contract. Furious over this deception, he sued Popkin for his money, but in October of 1952, sold his case to a professional litigator for a few cents on the dollar to be rid of the legal aggravations (B133).

Before *Champagne for Caesar* was briefly released starting in late April of 1950, Ronnie and Benita began their final and best-remembered venture into series radio: *The Halls of Ivy*. For the story of this series, see pages 181-83.

When *Ivy* left the air in June of 1952, Ronnie took another risk he had long been avoiding: TV guest roles, but all filmed and none live. Milton Merlin from the *Ivy* shows coaxed him into starring in a series of *Four Star Playhouse* productions as a favor to Ronnie's friend and *Four Star* co-producer, David Niven. Ronnie agreed, providing that Merlin, who had become a friend through their shared love of classic literature and classical and jazz music, wrote or co-wrote all the scripts.

So Milton and Ronnie began by adapting Lord Dunsany's short story, *The Lost Silk Hat* as Ronald Colman's television debut on October 23, 1952. This comedy of a debonair gentleman who loses his top hat earned such good ratings that Ronnie filmed three more shows for *Four Star*, one of them indirectly.

The fourth show, *A String of Beads*, was produced by Ronnie as the pilot for a series of Maugham adaptations under the aegis of his own company, Everest Productions. The pilot aired on *Four Star*, but before it could be sold, CBS offered the Colmans the TV version of *Ivy* as a series.

The offer to film *Ivy* couldn't have come at a better time. Ronnie had moved his family to Santa Barbara as their permanent home, and middle age was taking its toll. The individual TV shows were a morale booster, but they weren't regular work. Ronnie was still doing radio shows a few times a year, but he really wanted another movie role. It wasn't that there weren't any scripts, but the ones he did accept either didn't get made because the financing dropped out—this happened three times in 1953—or he kept turning down scripts, citing ill health or a reluctance to spend several months at a foreign location or that he wasn't right for the part being offered.

For example, in 1953, he was offered the role of Captain Vere in a low-budget production of *Billy Budd* to be shot off Catalina Island, but reportedly turned it down on doctor's orders because of the amount of time that would have been spent at sea, even though he was used to long yacht trips[12]. In 1956, according to film historian Barry Norman, he was offered the plum part of martinet Colonel Nicholson in David Lean's *The Bridge on the River Kwai*.

Kwai would have been a magnificent opportunity for one final, great performance, but he turned down that one because he didn't want to spend six months in Ceylon, a tough location no matter his health. In the end, Alec Guinness took the role and won an Oscar as Best Actor for it. These and other rejected or missed chances are the sort that cause endless speculation as to the kinds of performances Colman might have given in his last years had he not been overly cautious or just plain scared of dropping his star persona in favor of playing a variety of character roles as his friend, Charles Boyer, was doing on *Four Star* and in movies. Ironically, Boyer accepted a pirate role in a remake of DeMille's *The Buccaneer* (1958) after Ronnie turned it down (B16).

With all of that missed work, TV *Ivy* was a godsend. It was familiar, Barbara Merlin would be adapting 35 of the radio scripts, and he would be working steadily for nine months, starting on June 5, 1954. TV *Ivy* would also be Benita's first on-screen acting since marrying Ronnie in 1938, with the exception of the *Four Star* show, "Ladies on His Mind." Ironically, there was some trepidation on the part of CBS executives about casting her for that reason; she wasn't known to the TV audience. See pages 208-9 for the complete story.

In between all this TV work, Ronnie was asked to narrate a one-hour radio show of highlights from Handel's *Messiah*. He turned to Milton Merlin to select the highlights and oversee the production. The program got good ratings when it was first heard on ABC on Christmas Eve 1953, so it was broadcast a second time the following Christmas Eve.

Back in television, *Ivy* finished production on March 9, 1955. A few months later, CBS canceled the show due to low ratings. Even if the show and its ratings had been better, Ronnie could not have continued. He badly needed a rest and he wanted, in his own time, to pursue producing movies. He was hoping to acquire the rights to two plays by Shaw, *Back to Methuselah* and *Man and Superman* (B3), but these productions, discussed for European production, never got past the talking stage. All he managed to do for the rest of 1955 was appear on Santa Barbara radio on October 18 to help support their local Community Chest drive. He also took part in a silent movie star reunion held by the George Eastman House in Rochester, New York on December 7.

Otherwise, Ronnie's professional life was at a virtual standstill and he was turning morose (B3, B7). No one, it seemed, wanted the old Ronald Colman anymore. Milton Merlin offered to conjure an original screenplay depicting the Colman character as an elder statesman, but it never came to be. Worse than that, in Ronnie's view, he was passed over for knighthood in the mid-1950s when those honors were being passed out to his peers (he had never become an American citizen, so he was eligible). More personally, when he attended a celebrity golf tournament being held at the Beverly Hills Hotel, no one recognized him, though they did recognize Bing Crosby, Frank Sinatra and other stars (B7). He was hurt that after more than 30 years of international stardom, he was a ghost figure to the crowd.

Concerned as he was with being recognized for his life's work, he had many other things to keep him busy. Indeed, his private life was always richly rewarding. His screen character was obsolete, but he had a splendid home life. He played golf a good deal, was an amateur astronomer and photographer (he won awards for the latter), painted several still lifes (winning awards for those, too), read a great deal, and made the most of country life at San Ysidro Ranch's Random House, named for the movie *Random Harvest*. He was the very image of the noble British squire he had cultivated in his movies. He was also a proud and devoted father, although Juliet did have what was for him an annoying California accent.

During the summer of 1956, Ronnie filmed three TV shows. He appeared one time each on the syndicated *Studio 57* and *General Electric Theater*, and paid a visit to the *Jack Benny* TV show with Benita.

His next-to-last film role was a cameo in the Mike Todd production of *Around the World in 80 Days* (1956). He played the part of an Indian railroad official with the old panache, a fitting farewell to the brand of British nobility he had personified onscreen so well for so long.

His last movie was also the worst of his sound film career: Irwin Allen's *The Story of Mankind* (1957). He was signed by Allen to play the Spirit of Mankind, defending humanity's strong points against the accusations of a smug Devil (Vincent Price) in order to dissuade a heavenly tribunal from letting mankind blow itself up with the hydrogen bomb.

Ronnie couldn't have made a worse choice for his screen swan song. Thinking it would be a serious cinema of historical milestones based on the famous book by Willem Hendrik Van Loon, he was appalled to see at the rushes that he had been duped into being part of a fiasco. The parts of Allen's script not involving him were a tiresomely ludicrous hash of drama and comedy, with dozens of cameo stars horribly miscast. When asked by a reporter in his dressing room what the movie was based on, Ronnie witheringly replied, "I believe they took it from the liner notes of the book."[13]

During a break in filming his *Mankind* role, he went to New York City in December to narrate an abridgement of *A Christmas Carol* for NBC's *Monitor* and to be interviewed for that show about the movie. Not an outwardly religious man, Ronnie loved Christmas and the Christmas spirit, so he was always amenable to doing these seasonal shows. This one turned out to be his last, airing on December 23, 1956.

Professionally idle for over a year, death came quickly for Ronald Colman. On the night of May 19, 1958, he was rushed to Santa Barbara Memorial Hospital with severe respiratory problems, chiefly pneumonia. The next morning he was dead. Pneumonia complicated by his long-standing lung fibrosis or emphysema due to smoking had claimed his life at 67. He was buried on May 22 at Santa Barbara Cemetery by his family and friends, including William Powell and Richard Barthelmess. He also received a handsome pictorial tribute the following week in *Life* magazine, a piece titled "Departure of a Debonair Star" (B232).

The following chapters provide a detailed inventory and analysis of Colman's work in all media, from the famous to the forgotten. The sum total shows a body of work long overdue for historical and critical recognition.

NOTES

1. Gladys Hall. "Romantic Recluse: The Private Life of a Public Hero: Part 1." *Photoplay.* January 1939. B191.

2. *Ibid.*

3. Ronald Colman obituary. *Thames Valley Times.* May 21, 1958. B409.

4. Gladys Hall. "Romantic Recluse: Part 2." *Photoplay.* February 1939. B192.

5. A. Scott Berg. *Goldwyn: A Biography.* pg. 192. Knopf, 1988. B22.

6. Author interview with Al Weingand in February of 1977.

7. Sidney Skolsky. *Daily News* column, August 17, 1932. B393.

8. Various print sources, but no specific attribution.

9. Mentioned in *Cary Grant: A Touch of Elegance* by Warren G. Harris. New York: Doubleday, 1987. Page 88.

10. Mentioned in *Halliwell's Film Guide, 7th Edition.* New York: Scribners, 1989. Page 835 in his entry for *The Rains Came.*

11. Discussed in a 1982 letter to the author by *Jane Eyre* screenwriter, DeWitt Bodeen.

12. Same as for 11.

13. Author interview with Vincent Price in January of 1992.

CHRONOLOGY

1891   February 9: Ronald Charles Colman is born in Richmond, Surrey, England to Charles and Marjory Colman.

1902   February 9: Sees first motion picture on 11th birthday at Earls Court Exhibition. Family moves from Richmond to Ealing. Is enrolled at a nearby public (i.e., private) school.

1903   February: Watches father perform role of drunken villain in *Much Ado About Nothing*, an amateur production staged by the Thames Valley Shakespeare Society.

1905   Fall: Is enrolled at Hadley boarding school, Littlehampton, Sussex. Acts in school plays.

1907   February 23: Higher education cut short by Charles's death from pneumonia. Goes to work for British Steamship Company that summer starting at $2.50 a week. Plays banjo and sings drinking songs in Masonic smoker for extra money. Joins Bancroft Amateur Dramatic Society to act in productions of popular plays.

1911   Plays banjo and does monologues at London's Clavier Hall for extra money.

1912   Joins musical hall troupe called The Mad Medicos, playing banjo and doing readings and impressions.

1914   August 5: Joins British army when World War I starts.

1915   May 6: Invalided out of army with honorable discharge due to war wounds. Has no idea what to do professionally.

1916   January(?): Tours with Denby's Pierrot Troupe.
        June 19: "The Maharani of Arakan" opens in London.
        August 28: *The Misleading Lady* opens in Manchester.

September 6: *The Misleading Lady* opens in London.

1917   April 17: Takes over juvenile lead in controversial venereal disease play, *Damaged Goods*, in London.
Late summer or early fall: First movie role in unreleased short, title unknown.

1918   February 6: *The Little Brother* opens in London.
April 29: *The Little Brother* opens in Manchester.
September 9: *The Bubble* opens in Manchester.
October 28: *The Bubble* opens in Wimbledon.
December 2: *The Live Wire* begins tour with one-week run in Manchester. Meets future first wife, Thelma Raye, who is the play's female lead.

1919   March: *The Toilers*, first feature film, opens.
May 26: *Skittles* opens in Westcliff-on-Sea.
August: *A Daughter of Eve* (feature film) opens.
September 18: Marries Thelma.
October: *Sheba* (feature film) opens.
December?: *Snow in the Desert* (feature film) opens.

1920   January-February?: Touring company of *The Great Day*.
February: *Anna the Adventuress* (feature film) opens.
April: *A Son of David* (feature film) opens.
May: *The Black Spider* (feature film) opens.
Late summer: Sails to U.S. for better job opportunities.
October 25: *The Dauntless Three* opens trial run in Atlantic City.
December 27: *The Green Goddess* opens trial run in Philadelphia.

1921   January 18: *The Green Goddess* opens in New York, but he is fired after first week.
May 2: *The Silver Fox* opens trial run in D.C.
Summer: Acts in first American film, *Handcuffs or Kisses?*, which plays a few theaters that October.
August 15: *The Nightcap* opens in New York. He is singled out in reviews.
September 11-April 29, 1922: Role of James Potter in touring company of hit Fay Bainter play, *East is West*.

1922   August 28: *East of Suez* opens trial run in Atlantic City.
September 25: *La Tendresse* opens on Broadway.
October 21: Leaves play and stage career for male lead in Henry King movie *The White Sister*, starring Lillian Gish.

1923   September 5: New York premiere of *The White Sister*.

1924   February 18: National release of *The White Sister*.
Summer: Signs four-year contract with Samuel Goldwyn after making *Tarnish* for him.
June 4: *$20 a Week* opens.
October 12: *Tarnish* opens.

October 25: *Her Night of Romance* opens.
December 1: *Romola* opens.

1925 January 24: *A Thief in Paradise* opens.
April 12: *His Supreme Moment* opens.
May 10: *The Sporting Venus* opens.
August 23: *Her Sister From Paris* opens.
September 25: *The Dark Angel* opens. First of five teamings with Hungarian actress Vilma Banky.
November 16: *Stella Dallas* opens.
December 26: *Lady Windermere's Fan* opens.

1926 April 4: *Kiki* opens.
August 5: *Beau Geste* opens.
October 14: *The Winning of Barbara Worth* opens, reteaming him with Banky.

1927 January 24: *The Night of Love* with Banky opens.
Mid-year: is offered and signs exclusive seven-year contract with Goldwyn following successes of *Beau Geste* and *Barbara Worth*.
August 26: *The Magic Flame* with Banky opens.

1928 March 22: *Two Lovers*, final film with Banky opens.

1929 January 2: Final silent *The Rescue*, opens, commercial failure mainly due to advent of sound, but the movie is also leaden.
May 2: *Bulldog Drummond*, first talkie, premieres in New York City.
November 11: *Condemned* opens.

1930 July 24: *Raffles* opens.
Best Actor Oscar nominations for first two talkies.
December 18: *The Devil to Pay* opens.

1931 October 28: *The Unholy Garden* opens.
December 7: *Arrowsmith* opens.

1932 August 15: *Cynara* starts filming.
August 17: Sidney Skolsky column in New York's Daily News states that Colman drinks on the set to do his love scenes.
September 12: Libel suit against Goldwyn for $2 million over Skolsky column, hoping for public retraction by Goldwyn. Goldwyn refuses, filing denial response on November 10.
November 14: *The Masquerader* starts filming.
December 24: *Cynara* opens.

1933 Mid-January: *The Masquerader* finishes. Goes on world tour with friend, Al Weingand.
August 25: *The Masquerader* opens.
October 16: Drops lawsuit in exchange for moving from Goldwyn to newly formed 20th Century Pictures, both on United Artists lot.

Mid-November: Returns to Los Angeles.

1934   July 31: Thelma divorces him in British court.
August 15: *Bulldog Drummond Strikes Back*, first film for 20th Century, opens, teaming him with Loretta Young for first time since *Devil to Pay*.

1935   January 17: *Clive of India*, third and final film with Loretta Young, opens.
March(?): Meets and falls in love with British actress Benita Hume, whom he starts courting.
April 30: Becomes co-owner with Weingand of San Ysidro Ranch in Santa Barbara, CA.
November 14: *The Man Who Broke the Bank at Monte Carlo* opens.
December 15: *A Tale of Two Cities* opens.

1936   March 5: Finishes filming *Under Two Flags* for Fox.
March 23: Starts filming *Lost Horizon* for Capra.
April 30: *Under Two Flags* opens.
May 27: Is offered the role of Rhett Butler in *Gone With the Wind* by David O. Selznick. After several months of indecision, turns it down.

1937   March 2: *Lost Horizon* premieres in San Francisco.
September 2: *The Prisoner of Zenda* opens.

1938   September 28: *If I Were King* opens.
September 30: Marries Benita Hume at San Ysidro Ranch.

1939   January 15: Radio debut as a series regular on *The Circle* (NBC).
June 5: First *Lux Radio Theater* (CBS) in "The Prisoner of Zenda".
Is offered roles in a score of A movies, including *Intermezzo*, *The Rains Came* and *Rebecca*, but makes only *The Light That Failed*. Forms production partnership with Charles Boyer, Anatole Litvak and his business manager, Bill Hawks, to make a series of movies for distribution through RKO.
December 24: *The Light that Failed* opens.

1940   September 5: First movie of partnership, *Lucky Partners*, co-starring Ginger Rogers, opens and falls flat commercially. Does more radio shows.
November: Begins second partnership with Boyer, Litvak, Charles Feldman, Irene Dunne and Lewis Milestone in conjunction with 20th Century-Fox. Nothing comes of it.

1941   Appears on a number of radio shows to keep working while looking for good scripts.
August 29: *My Life With Caroline*, co-starring Anna Lee, is released and fails commercially.

1942   August 21: *The Talk of the Town* premieres in Washington, D.C., re-establishing him as a top romantic lead.
Meanwhile, he is all over radio on war bond, war relief, drama and variety shows.
September 1: Starts cross-country war bond tour with several female stars,

including Irene Dunne, Greer Garson and Hedy Lamarr.
December 15: *Random Harvest* opens.

1943   June: Is teamed with radio dramatist Arch Oboler by ad agency for Electric
Auto-Lite to produce war-related drama/variety series called *Everything for the
Boys*. Personal chemistry lacking in teaming.

1944   January 18: *Boys* debuts amid producer-star hostility.
June 13: After nearly six months of mostly bad plays and poor ratings, Colman
version of *Boys* canceled. Replaced by variety show with singers Helen Forrest
and Dick Haymes.
July 24: Juliet Benita Colman, only child, is born.
August 22: First Technicolor movie, *Kismet*, opens.

1945   December 9 and 23: Ronnie and Benita cause comedic sensation on *Jack Benny*
show on NBC radio. Benny signs them to appear three times per season starting
in 1946.

1946   Benny shows continue to be audience hit as Colman spoofs his public image.
September 6: Checks into hospital with pneumonia. Is released 10 days later.
October 20: Rare villainous role in "The Green Goddess" on *Theater Guild on the
Air*.

1947   March 20: *The Late George Apley* opens.
April: Starts recording episodes for syndicated radio series, *Favorite Story*.
December 25: *A Double Life* opens in Los Angeles only, to qualify for Academy
Awards.

1948   February 19: *A Double Life* opens in a few big cities.
March 10: Wins Golden Globe as Best Actor for *A Double Life*.
March 20: Wins Academy Award for same.
March 22: *A Double Life* begins staggered national release.
March 28: Oscar is "borrowed" by Jack Benny for start of famous running gag on
Benny show.
September: *Favorite Story* begins first season in national syndication except for
Los Angeles.

1949   Continues radio career while turning down several movie roles, mostly character
parts. He and Benita are offered husband-and-wife leads in radio sitcom about
college life called *The Halls of Ivy*. They happily accept.
November 17: Last *Favorite Story* recording session.

1950   January 6: *The Halls of Ivy* debuts on NBC, sponsored by Schlitz Beer.
April 26: *Champagne for Caesar* opens. Ties with Laurence Olivier as the second
best movie actor of the half century in a *Weekly Variety* poll. Chaplin takes first
place.

1951   *The Halls of Ivy* achieves high ratings and wins several awards, including the
Peabody Award, April 26, for Best Dramatic Radio Show of the Year.

1952   June 25: *Ivy* ends after three seasons when Schlitz beer drops sponsorship.
Summer: Moves family from Beverly Hills to Santa Barbara.
October 23: TV debut on *Four Star Playhouse* in "The Lost Silk Hat" (CBS).

1953   March 19: Presenter on first televised Oscar show.
March 26: "The Man Who Walked Out on Himself", on *Four Star Playhouse* (CBS).
May 21: "Ladies on His Mind", on *Four Star Playhouse* (CBS).
Fall: Produces and stars in *A String of Beads*, pilot for Somerset Maugham anthology.
December 24: Narrates bridge segments for abridgement of Handel's "Messiah" on ABC radio network.

1954   January 21: Pilot for Maugham anthology airs on *Four Star*, but he abandons series when CBS offers him and Benita TV version of *The Halls of Ivy*.
June 5: Production begins on *The Halls of Ivy*.
October 19: *The Halls of Ivy* debuts on CBS.

1955   March 9: Production ends on TV *Ivy*.
October 13: TV *Ivy* ends with final rerun.
October 18: Radio appeal with Benita for the Santa Barbara Community Chest Drive.
December 7: One of 19 guests of honor at silent movie movie star reunion in Rochester, NY sponsored by George Eastman House.

1956   Turns down Alec Guinness role in *The Bridge on the River Kwai*, then plays Spirit of Man role in Irwin Allen's *The Story of Mankind*.
October 11:"Perfect Likeness" airs on syndicated *Studio 57*.
October 17: Premiere of *Around the World in 80 Days*, in which he plays cameo role as Indian railroad official.
November 5: He and Benita make their only appearance on Jack Benny's TV show (CBS).
December 16: "The Chess Game" airs on *General Electric Theater* (CBS).
December 23: Abridged reading of *A Christmas Carol* for NBC radio's weekend cultural show, *Monitor*.

1957   Toys with producing movies on his own, but nothing comes of it. Turns down pirate role in *The Buccaneer*, which friend Charles Boyer accepts.
October 23/November 8/November 13: *The Story of Mankind* opens in Philadelphia, New York and Los Angeles to critical drubbing, horrible word-of-mouth and Colman's personal scorn.

1958   May 19: Dies of pneumonia at age 67. Buried at Santa Barbara Cemetery.
August 15: Honored posthumously as one of first six stars inducted into Walk of Fame on Hollywood Blvd.

1960   February 9: Unveiling of 1538 stars on Walk of Fame. Receives second, posthumous, star for TV *Ivy*.

THE ART AND INFLUENCE
OF RONALD COLMAN

This chapter is intended as a brief examination of Colman's artistic evolution, the strengths and shortcomings of his physicality and acting technique, the thematic patterns of his best known movies, the treatment of women in his films, and his influence and impact on several generations of actors, writers and audiences. My purpose is to provide the reader with a contextual key to his work. All references to screen directions are from the audience's viewpoint.

PHASES, FACETS AND TRAINING

When we speak of the resourcefully debonair Ronald Colman character, we are thinking of that character as it evolved from *Bulldog Drummond* (1929) on. Yet, like any other movie star, Colman's career had several distinct phases and phases that overlapped, so that the Colman we know from sound films is much different from the Colman of American silent movies, and the Colman of British silents and British and American theater is far different still.

Ronald Colman stage actor was a man learning his craft while struggling to establish himself and pay his bills. In his American silent period, he played a rich variety of roles, nearly always sympathetic, but even when he was playing a rogue or a cad or a thief, he was almost always redeemed in the last reel by the influence of a good woman. Heroic self-sacrifice became his primary theme, most memorably in *Beau Geste*, but there were many more facets to his career.

When Colman fans who know him only from his movies hear him singing on radio shows, they are astonished because they are unaware that he got his professional start in British music hall. For the same reason, hearing him calling a square dance on an episode of *The Halls of Ivy* (R361) sounds odd until you learn that from 1948 to about 1952, he was part of a celebrity square dance craze in Beverly Hills.

If you read the play *Damaged Goods*, you discover an even greater dimension of his talent because he had to perform an hysterical breakdown on stage for 250+ shows when his syphilitic character is confronted with the fact that he has infected his own daughter. The closest he ever came to that sort of rigorously disciplined outburst on film were scenes in *A*

Double Life when he jealously rages at his ex-wife and slugs his press agent over a newspaper story.

If you read the play *East is West*, you find that, as the dilettante reformer, Jimmy Potter, he had to teach coquettish Ming Toy to dance the shimmy eight or nine times a week for seven-and-a-half months. And yet for all his evident ability as a singer and mild hoofer, he never made a musical comedy.

Thus, there was far more to Colman's range than the gentleman adventurer persona he crafted, but which he would only occasionally hint at in movies, more so on radio. Calling attention to this talent, however, begs the question of whence it came. He never had what we think of as classical training, instead learning his craft mainly from experience, keen observation of stage stars like Gerald duMaurier and George Arliss, and repeatedly watching the movies of Charlie Chaplin and Douglas Fairbanks to study and emulate their pantomimic grace and agility. No doubt he practiced what he observed both in private and with his fellow actors.

Colman also believed in reincarnation and when he discovered that he was indeed descended from George Colman the Elder and Younger, who were 18th century actors and playwrights, that belief appeared confirmed. He told magazine writer Gladys Hall in one interview (B193) that on one return trip to England, he had stood on the very stage where these men had performed and sensed he had been there before.

Beyond what he felt was an inherited gift for acting, Colman was also coached by a British stage and screen actor named Robert Vallis, with whom he worked in a British movie called *A Son of David* (1920). And he received extensive training in screen acting from Henry King and Lillian Gish en route to Italy in 1922 for *The White Sister*.

THE FACE

Laurence Olivier in his book *On Acting* (B75) says of his budding film ambition in the late 1920s, "I knew even then, I think, that no one, not even Douglas Fairbanks, could match Ronald Colman's screen close-ups. They were marvelous because he had a beautiful face, and because he had a deep but gentle masculinity: the ideal of the dark Englishman." More than that, he had a trustworthy face radiating warmth, kindness and compassion. The moustache adds definition to his star quality by making him the archetypal British gentleman, but he does look more open without it, especially as Sydney Carton.

However, his classic face had flaws resulting in a "bad" right side and the need to cover up blemishes (moles and a scar above his right eye caused by a childhood accident) through make-up and artful lighting. The bad side was due to the right eyelid having a diagonal slant while the left one was rounded and more pleasing in profile. Facial flaws were not unique to Colman, but the way they were handled *was* part of the Hollywood myth of physically near-perfect matinée idols.

TECHNIQUE: THE VOICE

The distinctive voice for which Colman is best remembered, and which has never ceased being widely imitated—especially in a multitude of cartoons and commercials since his death—was a result of stage training, personal discipline and chain smoking. The training gave his voice melody, resonance and a range of about one octave, while the smoking, over time, gave him a rasp in his upper register. When he speaks love to Jane Wyatt in *Lost Horizon*, Madeleine Carroll in *The Prisoner of Zenda*, and Frances Dee in *If I Were King*, there is no voice in the world more thrillingly romantic. Yet, when he raises his voice in command or anger, as in *Clive of India*, or pushes it for the dramatic radio monologue "The Jervis Bay Goes Down" (R24), his mellow inflection turns raspy. This was due to the lung fibrosis or emphysema that plagued him from World War One on, but about which he never did anything, like seeing a doctor or quitting smoking, even after he was hospitalized in 1946 and 1957 for pneumonia. He was strangely cavalier about his health.

According to Los Angeles pathologist Griffith D. Thomas, "People who are chronic smokers develop what is known as chronic obstructive pulmonary disease or so-called chronic bronchitis. Scar tissue forms in the lung, which diminishes the amount of lung tissue to exchange oxygen. It's a progressive disease and can sometimes stop when a person gives up smoking, but the scarred lung tissue can never grow back.

"The raspiness of Colman's voice in the upper register was clearly caused by the fibrosis. He would have had difficulty exhaling because as the air traveled up the spinal tree or bronchi, he had to make sounds. The more he exhaled, the more he had to strain to get the air out of his lungs. If you listen carefully, but not to the voice, I'm willing to bet that you can hear him straining to get the air out of his lungs."

This did not prevent Colman from having a resounding effect when exhorting a mob in *If I Were King* or *The Talk of the Town*, yet his voice in that range did acquire a harsher tone over the years. It is certainly at its worst in his reading of Bible quotations for Handel's "Messiah" (R401).

On the other hand, he could do an expert cockney, which he did for a few seconds in *A Double Life*; East and West coast American, as he did on stage for *The Misleading Lady* and *East is West* respectively; and a pleasant Scottish, which he used once on radio for "The Ghost Goes West" on *Everything For the Boys* (R61). Yet, when playing an American doctor of pioneer stock in *Arrowsmith*, he is resolutely British. Conversely, as a stuffy law professor in *The Talk of the Town* and *The Late George Apley*, his cultured accent is right at home for a well-bred New Englander. In the long, run, however, sticking with the stage-trained voice and cadence that made him rich and famous, he limited the parts he could play.

On radio, that beautifully distinctive voice was all that mattered. With a first-rate script, Colman could lift the listener with a transcendence few other actors could match. His narrations of "Blood for a Hero" on *Unlimited Horizons* (R36) and the 1944 version of "Juggler of Our Lady" (R85) are superb, caressing every word in the first so that we feel the plight of the dying gunner pilot, while making us sympathize with the hapless juggler Barnaby in the latter. He can also make you share his righteous indignation on the "Leslie Hoff Painting" (R296) episode of *The Halls of Ivy*, or as Jean Valjean in "Les Miserables" (R396) on *Lux Radio Theater*, or chill you with his suave heathen in "The Green Goddess" (R108) on *Theater Guild on the Air*.

When it came to comedy, he could make an audience roar when playing "himself" on the *Jack Benny* show, or when being eruditely witty on *The Halls of Ivy*, beautifully playing off his wife Benita in both. Radio allowed a wider range of characterizations, which is why nearly every movie star loved doing radio shows: they could play against type.

On the other hand, Colman walked through many a radio role just for the money, often letting listeners know his disinterest in the part with a patented, often annoying chuckle. Examples of these mechanical performances are "Rebecca", "The Petrified Forest", "The Browning Version" and other roles on *Lux Radio Theater*. One wonders if the listening audience ever felt cheated by this clockwork acting.

TECHNIQUE: THE EYES

Next to his voice were his eyes, the expressiveness of which he developed in silent movies. Let us examine this pantomimic skill in detail, using scenes in *A Tale of Two Cities*, *Lost Horizon* and *A Double Life*.

In the Christmas sequence of the first, Colman as Sydney Carton is first seen drunkenly bemused, leaning against a lamppost as snow is falling. After he accepts Elizabeth Allan's invitation to Christmas Eve mass, we next see him beside her in a church pew. As she lights a candle and says a prayer for him, we cut to a close-up in which he shifts his eyes to the left for a second to avoid looking at Allan, then looks straight at her. Cut to a close-up of her, framed to look angelic. Cut back to him in close-up as his eyes begin to tear with shame over being dissipated in her presence. In the background, a choir is singing "O Come, All Ye Faithful."

In the next scene, Allan invites him into the warm hospitality of her home for a family Christmas. With his face in right profile, he begs off because of his drunkenness, but when she tells him she wants to be his friend despite his obvious shortcomings, the barest movement of his head and right eye show that he is stunned by this remark. After she warmly bids him goodnight, the camera slowly tracks into his face as he shifts his eyes to the left, giving serious thought to this unexpected offer of the hearth and home he doesn't have.

Cut to a medium long shot as he slumps against another lamppost as snow falls, his hands in his coat pockets. A group of boy carolers pass by singing "O Come, All Ye Faithful" as the camera again tracks into him. Now he is gravely contemplating his loneliness, yet how he might now be redeemed because a woman he worships yet barely knows has told him she likes and cares for him. Just as the carolers finish passing, he straightens up, gives a bemused look and starts walking away as we fade out.

In just a few, mostly wordless minutes, as though we are watching a silent movie, Colman has shown and made us feel Carton's emotional conflict. For all of his carefree air, the man is heartsick over how he has fallen. He shows even greater visual depth in the first High Lama sequence of *Lost Horizon*, playing opposite Sam Jaffe.

In this sequence, Colman is shown mostly in tight close-up as the two men discuss the purpose of Shangri-La and the benefits of near immortality. As Colman arises when Jaffe finishes his speech, there is the most incredible look in his eyes—that of a man who has found his spiritual home and father. A door has opened wide for a glimpse into his contemplative soul. When I discussed this shot with the movie's director, Frank Capra, in 1984, he said: "It was the most remarkable thing I have ever seen. I wasn't watching an actor acting, but showing me who he really was inside. I'm still astonished when I see it."

Two other, bookend, scenes in *Lost Horizon* also bear discussion. When Colman first arrives at Shangri-La, we feel deja vu because of his own haunted look as he stares at the utopian landscape before him, glances back at the stormy portal through which he has just come, then back at Shangri-La. "He had a feeling, half mystical, half-visual, that he had arrived at a final destination," says Hilton of Conway in the novel.

When he is compelled to leave Shangri-La for the sake of his restless brother, he stands at the portal once more, this time with a look of deep anguish, his eyes tearing, just as they implosively teared in the *Two Cities* church scene.

My final examples are from the murder and suicide scenes in *A Double Life*. In the first, he is sitting in Shelley Winter's apartment in a trance-like state of delusion. When she asks him to turn out the light and come to bed, he turns his head slowly from left to right, a frighteningly vacant look in his eyes; she has said the wrong thing at the wrong time, causing him to leap over the edge into murderous insanity. He gets up, plays with a lamp while reciting lines by rote from *Othello* about the difference between extinguishing a light and a life, then steps menacingly toward her, continuing to babble. As she tries to escape, he grabs her left arm, pulling her toward him and to her death by a suffocating kiss. He is terrifying. So much so that Winters recalls in her autobiography (B98) being scared by the realism of his acting as they were shooting the scene.

In the movie's next-to-last scene, he is lying on his stage bed, bleeding to death from stabbing himself. He is finally being released from an inner storm of emotions: agony, anguish, madness, and consuming obsession, then peace. As Edmond O'Brien peels away the actor's beard and wig, Colman as Anthony John recalls an old-time thespian named Kirby, famous for his death scenes:

"They'd shout, 'Die again, Kirby, die again,' and he'd, he'd get up and bow and—die again...Suddenly, I thought, no one should shout 'Die again' 'cause—I couldn't have. The things that go through one's head. Doesn't feel bad now. Peaceful, really."

As he dies, uttering his ex-wife Brita's name, his entire life is illuminated in his eyes for a few seconds, then those eyes are still as a shadow passes gently over his face. The conflicts he has endured on and off stage are at an end. He has missed his final curtain call to meet his tragic fate.

What is especially remarkable about his performance in *A Double Life*, and why, I think, it won him a long overdue Oscar, is that he abandoned much of his customary restraint for it while retaining his affective use of physical understatement, plunging into a netherworld of maddening obsession. Although George Cukor, the movie's director, didn't feel Colman had a real grasp of the demonic because the straight *Othello* scenes were beyond him, his transformation from a charming, talented heel to a murdering schizoid clearly shows otherwise. It is a masterful performance.

In each of these films, Colman displays an acting range that includes a gay and charming side, but which goes well beyond it to show conflicting needs, desires and passions. Had he taken on more such roles, shaved his moustache more often to play others (as he should have for Anthony John), and adopted other accents, the scope of his achievements would have rivaled those of Olivier, who himself sought to emulate the silent and early sound Colman.

TECHNIQUE: MANNERISMS

For all of the uplifting artistry of his voice and eyes and affective economy of movement, Colman also brought to his work a number of physical mannerisms—some charmingly distinctive, some theatrically stylized—though he always denied it. Some of these are evident starting with *The White Sister*, while others are linked to the advent of sound.

When showing anger whether standing or sitting, he will usually lift his right arm and clench his fist. When walking, he will sometimes do so with a stiff or heavy gait. When he's telling off someone, he will back away to his left, then come forward as though to say "And another thing." An example of this trick is in *The Masquerader* when good boy Loder runs into bad boy Chilcote.

He also had particular *ways* of walking. When ambling along, he will walk with a jaunty gait. When hastening to action, he will hunch his shoulders, then dart forward. When playing period characters like François Villon and Sydney Carton, his body language is almost entirely different because he is playing outside a contemporary mode. For Carton, he adopts a casual saunter and an occasional tilt to convey a seemingly carefree attitude. For Villon, his movements are those of a mischievous rascal, loose and easy, a grand use of silent movie pantomime to convey character.

The one romantic act at which he was sometimes awkward was embracing his leading women for a kiss. He will put his arms around the woman in a literally heavy-handed clutch, then give her a brief sideways brush on the lips, which was all that was allowed by the Hays censorship code. And yet, his kissing scenes with Lillian Gish in *The White Sister* and Jane Wyatt in *Lost Horizon* are as smoothly natural and sigh-inducing as can be.

There is also his worried look, used to convey tragedy or a heavy emotional burden. Depending on the script and direction, this could be powerfully effective, as in *Lost Horizon* when he is repressing tears over leaving Shangri-La; blatantly mechanical, as in *The Masquerader* when he is divided over making love to Elissa Landi; or strained, as in *The Rescue*, when he is torn between temptress Lily Damita and his friends.

Asked about working with Colman on *Random Harvest* for a *Films in Review* profile of himself in the early 1980s, Alan Napier recalled Colman telling him that whenever he wanted to look worried, he would think of his household accounts. When I interviewed Jane Wyatt in 1983, she said that "Whenever he wanted to get that faraway look, he would use a sideways glance. He knew exactly what he was doing every second."

The most frequent mannerism is the head-bobbing routine. When he is laughing, he will bob his head to the right, then back and to the left. However, he indulged in the head bobbing mainly when he was making a mediocre comedy like *The Man Who Broke the Bank at Monte Carlo*. Yet there it is, briefly, in *A Tale of Two Cities*, as he bobs from side to side for emphasis while pouring out his heart to Elizabeth Allan. Much of this was undoubtedly unconscious, but since he saw all the rushes of his daily work, you would think he would have wanted to retake a few scenes now and then. In later classics like *Lost Horizon*, *If I Were King*, *The Talk of the Town* and *A Double Life*, nearly all of these mannerisms are absent, so he clearly kept training himself through the years to rid his performances of them.

The best use of the head bob is what I call the half-bob, when he cocks his head to his right, as though deep in thought or contemplation. This technique was unique to Colman, and is part of what makes watching him so affecting: You can see him thinking his way through a dilemma, using his intellect in a way that is quietly exciting.

Some of these mannerisms are annoying if you watch several of his lesser movies in a row, while others are always a charming part of the fun of watching Ronald Colman. But this is also true of most other great stars, what makes them distinctive and memorable.

MOTIFS: THEMES

The themes of honor, duty, self-sacrifice and idealistic integrity that characterize the Colman character began with the silent *Beau Geste*, but achieved their greatest expression in a consecutive heroic trilogy: *Lost Horizon*, *The Prisoner of Zenda* and *If I Were King*. Colman didn't plan it that way, but they do make a convenient straight line. These three and *Beau Geste* each focus on a different level of heroism.

For *Beau Geste*, it is a brotherly or Three Musketeers heroism. The next three are cultural heroism in *Lost Horizon*; kingly or mensch heroism in *Zenda* (mensch is Yiddish for "a responsible person"); and populist heroism in *King*. The heroism exemplified in *Lost Horizon* is the most rarified since it deals with saving mankind's cultural legacy from its own worst, warring impulses. The heroism in *Zenda* is more psychological since the two Rudolfs can easily be seen as a metaphor for a divided self: the indulgently immature half taking lessons from the grown-up, wiser half.

The populist heroism in *If I Were King* is in a league with that of *The Adventures of Robin Hood*: daringly adventurous leadership to pull the common people together in their own best interests. The difference between the two is that instead of a beleaguered peasantry driven to criminality by a brutalizing royal usurper in *Robin Hood*, the mob in *King* are a criminal lot already, made so by generations of poverty and royal corruption and neglect. Instead of motivating his fellow thieves to action through rousing sentiment as does Errol Flynn's Robin Hood, Colman's Villon hits them where they live in a refreshingly unsentimental crowd scene, Preston Sturges at his trenchant best:

"We all know there is no honor among thieves," he declares, "so I'm not going to talk to you about honor. And I'm not appealing to any patch of decency I know you never had. Now, as you stand there, the city is falling, falling to thieves like ourselves; cutthroats who have come all the way from Burgundy to take what belongs to us. Cutthroats to cut our purses. Macs to mash our women. Are we going to let these poachers move in on *our* preserve? These country louts show *us* how it's done? Are they going to starve us to death? Then I tell you this: there is no city that cannot be conquered unless it wants to be. And whether they like it or not, *we are part of the city*, the part that knows how to *fight! Or don't we?*"

These four films exemplify the sum total of Colman's image as a gentleman hero, showing by the selection and consistency of that work the star's authorial stamp on the scripts. The trilogy were also part of an adventure movie cycle running from 1934 to 1942, mirroring and paralleling the Depression and the imminence of world war.

In all of these movies, the Colman character valiantly fights to save lives and preserve the values of decency, honesty, fair play, integrity, and moral strength and conviction his enemies seek to desecrate and abolish. (In *Lost Horizon*, the struggle is an internal one, but no less affecting). They are the world of the adventure classics Colman devoured and loved as a boy. A milieu in which chivalrous virtue triumphs because one resourcefully mature, innately decent man battles or leads a battle against the moral corruption and territorial greed of other men.

MOTIFS: WOMEN

The women in Colman's movies are usually his adored and adoring partners; seldom less intelligent than he, but also seldom by his side fighting for the old school values I have defined. Furthermore, in several films, both silent and sound, Colman chooses the virtuous or non-sexual good girl over the sexy gamine. However, these motifs were not unique to Colman nor always by choice, since women in Hollywood films of the 1920s through '40s usually functioned as window dressing for the adventurous male.

Though there were rambunctious bad girls you wish he could have chosen instead, there were also good girls just as sexually appealing because of the women playing them. His partner in five silent films, Vilma Banky, was a radiant beauty whose sensual charm and warmth both complemented his own darkly handsome screen presence and compellingly spurred his valiant heroics. For her love, he made a desert bloom in *The Winning of Barbara Worth* and vanquished his wicked double in *The Magic Flame*.

His other screen partners were either alluring good girls or a mixture of naughty and nice. Unintellectual as she is, Ellen Drew's Huguette in *If I Were King* makes a far spicier partner than Frances Dee's vapidly decorative Katherine; Claudette Colbert's lusting spitfire, Cigarette, in *Under Two Flags,* is far more colorful than Rosalind Russell's white bread aristocrat; Elissa Landi's quiet sexuality in *The Masquerader* is far more attractive than Juliette Compton's vamp turn as the ill-tempered mistress; and Blanche Sweet's warmly sexual cabaret star in *His Supreme Moment* is far preferable to Kathleen Myers's coldly scheming socialite. On the other hand, Celeste Holm's intellectual vamp in *Champagne for Caesar* gives him the best of both worlds.

The good woman can also be a powerful influence, helping Colman's character define who he is and what he stands for. Examples are Helen Hayes' feisty helpmate wife in *Arrowsmith*; Loretta Young's socialite soulmate in *The Devil to Pay* and dutifully supportive wife in *Clive of India*; Jean Arthur's spunky landlady dragging him from an ivory tower to the real world in *The Talk of the Town*; Greer Garson's music hall queen first wife turned dutiful secretary second wife patiently walking him through his amnesia in *Random Harvest*; and Jane Wyatt's utopian soulmate guiding him to his destiny in *Lost Horizon*. In most of these pictures, the movie star millions of women wanted to marry was partnered with a woman whom many men would have wanted to marry.

GENERATIONS OF INFLUENCE

When Colman became a silent movie star in 1924, the reigning romantic idols were Rudolph Valentino, John Gilbert, Douglas Fairbanks, John Barrymore, Ramon Novarro, Antonio Moreno, and Lewis Stone. Except for Stone, who was low-key, dignified and gentlemanly, they were all flamboyantly dashing, given to melodramatic color and flair. Fairbanks and Gilbert, in particular, were exuberantly animated, with flashing eyes that gave each a robust sex appeal.

Colman became Stone's successor with his equally low-key style and subtle underplaying, of which some film historians, such as William K. Everson, are critical, seeing it as a lack of animation. Everson finds Colman's performances dull in several of his dramatic silents for this reason. In some cases, such as his gypsy king role in *The Night of Love*, he is indeed stiff because his heart doesn't appear to be in it. But there is also the quiet dignity of his Stephen Dallas in *Stella Dallas*, providing a relieving contrast to the boorish antics of Jean Hersholt's Ed Munn. Such criticism, however, becomes moot starting with *Bulldog Drummond*, when Colman's voice freed him for lighter portrayals, whereas John Gilbert got heavier with sound because of laughable romantic dialogue and leaden pacing.

Colman's influence on his peers began with Laurence Olivier, who modeled his 1927 stage performance as Beau Geste on Colman's; disastrously, since the play flopped. The real influence began with the early talkies, when his beautifully cultured voice, playfully suave manner, dashing heroics and pencil moustache became the style to emulate and imitate.

Charles Boyer, David Niven, Brian Aherne, Warner Baxter, Douglas Fairbanks, Jr., John Howard, Ray Milland, and William Powell all patterned at least part of their screen images on the Colman model. Boyer, with his bedroom eyes and seductive voice, became the French Ronald Colman, while Howard imitated him in several *Bulldog Drummond* films, and Niven carried on the Colman style after Colman's death.

What made Colman the role model was not just that he became the first romantic talking film star, but that his brand of finesse, elegant elan and gentle humanity left audiences with a feeling of tranquility, an internal glow. These other stars had their own followings, but Colman led them, in voice, style, tone and humanist personality. Niven, Powell, Boyer, Niven et.al. had distinctive styles, yet it was Colman who became the worldwide symbol of cultured erudition, largely because of his memorable voice.

Examples abound:

Katharine Hepburn as a road company actress in *Sylvia Scarlett* (1936) mimics the voice to Brian Aherne.

Dennis Morgan imitates him into a transcription machine in *Kitty Foyle* (1940).

A Colman imitator whispers love to Jeanne Crain in *State Fair* (1945) as she sings "It Might As Well Be Spring".

In the Disney cartoon, *Donald's Double Trouble* (1946), Donald Duck has a suave Ronald Colman-sounding lookalike duck woo Daisy for him. In *Donald's Dream Voice* (1948), Donald is a door-to-door salesman getting nowhere with his unintelligible quack when he buys a bottle of Ajax voice pills that make him sound like guess who.

Paul Frees imitated Colman for Toucan Sam in the Froot Loops TV ads of the 1960s-80s, and for Ape in the Jay Ward series *George of the Jungle* (1967-70).

Allan Swift as Odie Cologne in the TV cartoon series *The King & Odie* (1960-63) used a Colman accent.

Don Adams paid homage to and imitated him in *Prisoner of Zenda* parody episodes of *Get Smart* in 1968.

Charlton Heston imitated his voice and mannerisms for the first few minutes of his portrayal of the Earl of Essex in *Elizabeth the Queen* on *Hallmark Hall of Fame* in 1968, and imitated the voice for his 1980 Los Angeles stage performance as Sherlock Holmes in *The Crucifer of Blood*.

A 1992 episode of the cable TV cartoon series *Opus and Bill* used a Colman-accented character.

The May 17, 1993 episode of the hit TV series *Northern Exposure* was about dubbing *Zenda* into an Indian language to preserve that language.

More subtly, his restrained style is echoed by Anthony Hopkins in *Howard's End*, *The Remains of the Day* and *Shadowlands*, and by Daniel Day-Lewis in *The Age of Innocence*. Their Colman-like performances had audiences flocking to these movies by the millions.

There are scores more examples—verbal, literary and performance—I have compiled over the years, what I call Colmania, but this handful will suffice to make my point: That Colman's voice and style endure whether or not his name recognition does.

WHAT WAS VS. WHAT MIGHT HAVE BEEN

Throughout much of his career, Colman liked to play it safe with proven material or material similar to what he had already done, or a little of both. Most of his movies were derived from popular novels or plays, with an occasional original. *Bulldog Drummond Strikes Back*, though an original, was a follow-up to his first sound film; *The Light That Failed* and *Random Harvest* recalled *The Dark Angel*; *Under Two Flags* was a reworking of *Beau Geste*; and *Kismet* was a faint carbon of *If I Were King*.

He wasn't afraid of original material, but as a businessman, he generally wanted to go with pre-sold stories, especially if they were tailored to his personality and his limitations as he saw them. And yet, playing with proven material was not without its risks. Popular as the movie was, he was clearly miscast in *Arrowsmith*; audiences did not accept or like him in *Cynara* or *The Masquerader*; *Clive of India* lost money by giving the public talk instead of action; and *Lucky Partners* and *My Life of Caroline* failed because the scripts were out of touch with a contemporary audience, badly written and tailored to Colman's star ego instead of good storytelling.

Colman was clearly at his best with plays that mixed witty, sardonic and romantic dialogue; in which he played characters with moral strength and dimension; in which he was championing a righteous populist or humanist cause or the preservation of western culture; in which he adhered to values playing on themes of honor, duty, valor, self-sacrifice, romantic love, integrity, reliability and trust. He wanted his screen character to stand for the things he stood for, but without being pompous or rigid about it. He had dignity with both elegant and whimsical humor. He was handsome, but he used his handsomeness to cast a spell of enchantment, not merely to attract and charm. Perhaps most important, he imbued his characters with an inner majesty and tender compassion that made Ronald Colman not just a star name, but a symbol for all that was good and decent and humane and warmly civilized about mankind as a whole. He could presume to play the Spirit of Mankind in an otherwise awful movie because he had personified that spirit in dozens of good to excellent movies.

What he failed to do was extend himself very often beyond noblesse oblige into more varied character types who could also reflect shades of being human. He could have electrified audiences as the bum turned butler in *My Man Godfrey*, as Maxim de Winter in *Rebecca*, as the romantically torn pianist in *Intermezzo*, as the arrogantly ambitious Earl of Essex in *Elizabeth and Essex*, as the comic strip detective magician Mandrake the Magician, as the bridge-building martinet colonel in *The Bridge on the River Kwai* and so many other parts he either foolishly rejected or for which he would have been incomparable. Shaving his moustache and quitting smoking would also have helped immensely. As noted earlier, the first would have extended his range by making him more facially flexible, while the second would have given him a more elastic vocal range. There was so much more he could have given us in addition to the celluloid dreams he left that one can't help feeling as exasperated for what he passed up and the mediocre movies he made by contract or choice as grateful for what he did.

A BIBLIOGRAPHICAL ESSAY

This chapter discusses the kind of interview Colman gave most writers, the Colman myth, what he revealed to the few journalists he trusted, the fan magazine obsession with his love life, why so little has been written about him in movie magazines and books since his death, and why there have been only three other books about him besides this one. All numbers refer to the bibliography.

Ronald Colman was written about as much as any other star, but he rarely gave in-person interviews. Those writers who did manage to nab him for a few minutes on a movie set (B274, 401) got nothing but charmingly polite rhetoric for their trouble. He hated publicity with a passion, but he also knew that keeping in the public eye so that that public would continue paying to see his movies was part of his job. So he perfected the art of answering questions by saying a lot of nothing.

This left magazine and newspaper writers with the task of writing around the lack of interview quotes, so they came up with the Ronald Colman Myth. Writers like Dan Camp (B115), Richard Hosic (B207) and Mark Milton (B285) took pains to debunk the myth that Colman was a Man of Mystery or a Sphinx. And yet in none of the hundreds of newspaper and magazine articles I read while researching this book did I come across even one in which a writer actually created this so-called myth. The real myth was that there was a myth so that these writers could debunk it to fill space to justify their paychecks.

Although Colman often stated that he was indifferent to these stories, letting the Hollywood gossip mongers think about him what they wished, he nevertheless gave an interview to Gladys Hall (B385, writing as Faith Service) in 1931, dismissing the Man of Mystery image as so much nonsense by writers who had nothing better to write about. He felt that his private life was his own and if the Hollywood gossip mill didn't like his being such bad copy, that was just too bad. He again felt the need to debunk the gossipers in 1941 to James Carson of *Modern Screen*, (B118).

Another interview he felt the need to give was to Rosalind Shaffer of *Motion Picture*, B389, about his libel suit against Goldwyn. This because he believed his motive for the suit was seen as a publicity stunt. It wasn't, but he wasn't being entirely truthful, either, when he said it was his means of protesting the Goldwyn publicity department's long-standing habit of telling lies about him. He did it to scare Goldwyn into voiding his contract.

Next to creating a myth, the fan magazines were endlessly preoccupied from the late 1920s to late 1930s with whom he was dating; his marriage to and divorce from his first wife, Thelma; what it would be like to be his wife; and who might be the lucky next Mrs.

Ronald Colman. Love life puff pieces were written by Elinor Glynn (B182), Arline Merton (B283), A.L. Woolridge (B429), and Sheila Worth (B430).

Also repeatedly over the years, newspapers and magazines were filled with endless inventories of his hobbies, friends, travels, daily routine and habits (B115, 118, 274, 405), all written as though adding them up would tell his fans about the man behind the image.

The best of the articles about his private life was written by Hedda Hopper for the *Los Angeles Times* (B204). She tells wonderful stories about poker nights at his house, his whimsical sense of humor, and what he did at home when he wasn't making movies.

And yet for all his aversion to interviews, scores of them were published in hundreds of papers. The truth was that nearly all of these interviews came directly from studio press books. Colman preferred that journalists take their quotes from the publicity handouts rather than sit down for lengthy in-person chats. This meant that writers like Grace Kingsley and Marquis Busby of the *Los Angeles Times* had to contrive stories around these press book quotes (not included in the bibliography for this reason), occasionally saying in print that that was exactly what they were doing.

On the other hand, he did give interviews to *Los Angeles Times* writers Mary Mayer (B280), Arthur Millier (B284), Edwin Schallert (B371, career piece), Elza Schallert (B374), and Alma Whitaker (B425, career piece) when it suited his needs for publicity and dispelling gossip and rumors.

Which brings us to the question of how many in-person and in-depth interviews Colman gave. Of the 333 newspaper and magazine items listed in the bibliography for this book, only 24 are face-to-face interviews, including the five above. Of these 24 stories, 17 are what I would consider in-depth profiles giving insight to Colman's background, views on a variety of subjects and acting technique in general.

The writer who got the most out of him because she apparently gained his complete trust was Gladys Hall, who also went by the name Faith Service. (Magazine writers, then as now, often used several pseudonyms so it wouldn't look as though one person wrote half of each issue, which they often did.) From 1930 to 1939, she published eight stories about him (B188-93, 385-86) in which he revealed how he came to be the kind of man and actor he was. It was to Hall he told the story of the first woman he ever loved (B189). It was to Hall he revealed his belief in reincarnation (B193). It was Hall who, in the January and February 1939 issues of *Photoplay* (B191-92), got him to talk at length about his obsession with privacy, his innate shyness, and his need to act to overcome that shyness, which, of course, is true for many actors. On the latter point, she made this observation and quoted these remarks in the January issue:

"It has always seemed, to those of us who know Ronald Colman well, that half of the complete explanation of the enigma of him lies in the discrepancy between the characters he plays on the screen and the character he is in private life. There is something significant in the fact that, wishing to avoid all exhibitionism in his private life, he plays such swashbuckling characters on the screen. For, if you think back over a couple of the Colman pictures—'Bulldog Drummond', 'Beau Geste', 'Under Two Flags', 'Clive of India', 'The Prisoner of Zenda', and most recently 'If I Were King'—you cannot but realize that Ronald Colman always plays the parts of spectacular, adventurous men. As he is a freelance—which means that he himself chooses the stories he wants to make for the screen—it is fairly obvious that he deliberately chooses to play exhibitionistic characters.

"This is, Mr. Colman agrees, a point well taken. He said, 'Perhaps the contradiction can be further explained by my admitting that if ever I am called upon to make a speech at some affair which I am attending in a private capacity, I am sunk, miserably self-conscious, regrettably inadequate. If, on the other hand, a script calls for me to do a scene in which I must stand up and harangue a thousand extras, I can harangue away for hours and think nothing of it. Which simply means, I think, that as an actor, I am neither inhibited nor self-conscious, whereas in my own capacity as a man, I am both.

"I'm not much of a hand at analyzing myself, but I have heard of split personalities. Perhaps, in my case, the split comes between my screen self and my real self. I've never thought of this before, but it now occurs to me that I may have become an actor so that I could pretend to be the kind of fellow I cannot be in real life. Trying to explain why the sword-swallowing hero I like to play on the screen is so different from my unexciting self is, for me, a task almost too difficult to attend. *I* is a subject about which I know very little. I am not given to introspection. The majority of my interests, apart from my work, are active interests, such as tennis, gardening, sailing. Which indicates, if I understand correctly my cursory readings of psychology, that I would be classified as an extrovert. My way of living, then,' concluded Mr. Colman, 'probably does date back to my childhood. Certainly I learned, very early in life, that to make myself as unobtrusive as possible was to make myself as popular as possible.'"

These remarks are not entirely ingenuous. He was indeed a reflective and psychologically self-aware man, as a 1926 interview with Ruth Waterbury (B417) shows. For her, he gave a deeper look into his emotional and intellectual perceptions than he gave even Gladys Hall or ever showed on screen.

What he had no reluctance to talk about with writers was his need for privacy, journalists treating stars as Gods, and his own lack of star ego. He was consistent on the privacy issue and told W.H. Mooring of *Film Weekly* (B290) that he felt stars were over-rated as people. For the third, Colman never accepted less than first billing after *The Talk of the Town*, which is one reason he turned down a lot of scripts. Moreover, as Richard Hosic points out in "Exploding the Colman Myths" (B207), Colman's agents saw to it that his contracts specified the size of his name above the title on screen. He once told one of those agents, "Before God, I'm worth $35 a week. Before the studios, I'm worth whatever you can get." He knew exactly his commercial value.

As for the man behind the image, people I have interviewed who knew him well, like Al Weingand and Douglas Fairbanks, Jr., have said that he was very much offscreen as he was on. As he made clear to Gladys Hall above, no he wasn't. Furthermore, as John Russell Taylor observes in his book *Strangers in Paradise* (B92), the dreamy idealist image Colman created had little to do with the everyday man who spent more time with his huge library than he did socializing.

Colman also stated several times in interviews that although he considered himself an artist, for him acting was mainly a means to an end, that end being the splendid home life and rich variety of hobbies his star salaries afforded him. Which is partly why his screen output dwindled after 1942 and partly why it ceased altogether between *Champagne for Caesar* (1950) and *Around the World in 80 Days* (1956).

What I have discovered in reading all of the interviews he did give is that their sum total paints a nearly definitive portrait of him as a man and actor, and that the sum total of quotes combined with the articles he himself wrote (B122-23) could easily be lifted en masse for a semi-autobiographical biography. And yet, his daughter Juliet's book about him is the only Colman biography since his death in 1958. Moreover, with a handful of exceptions, he has been consistently ignored, overlooked and forgotten by movie magazines of all kinds, especially when they do cover stories on the 10 or 20 or 30 greatest Hollywood stars of the 1920s through 50s.

Why is this?

The answer has to do with the archetypal character he created: the nobly adventurous British gentleman, a screen type that largely disappeared after WWII, though the tradition was continued by the likes of Stewart Granger and David Niven. Because he didn't fit the prevailing anti-heroic screen type of the 1950s to the present, embodied by Dean and Bogart and the current spate of action idols, he was and is ignored, at least in print. But then, so are dozens of other stars of the 1930s and 40s, such as William Powell, Robert Donat, Irene Dunne, Claudette Colbert and Robert Montgomery. They and Colman do not have the same mystique or endless caché as Bogart, Flynn, Cagney, Bette Davis, Dean, Monroe, and Wayne. The first five have in common that they were Warner stars and that they all had impudent or rebellious and largely anti-intellectual personae. They fit in with a contemporary culture geared to anti-heroes.

Thus, when *Entertainment Weekly* published its August 15, 1993 cover story on the 30 greatest stars of all time, Bogart was the cover boy because he was deemed by that magazine's writers and editors to be Movie Star #1 Of All Time, period, no argument. Colman was not included in the line-up. When *Playgirl* chose five Golden Age stars for their December 1993 cover story on great male stars of the past (Grant, Gable, Flynn, Cooper, Power) and three potentials for the future (Brosnan, Dalton, Satterfield), Colman was omitted. With few film historians or critics championing him since his death, his omission from these magazines is no surprise, but no less a shame.

The few who have tried to revive Colman as a name to reckon with are Steven R. Bird (B114, shelved for three years until there was space to fill), J.V. Cottom (B127), Julian Fox (B159-60), myself (B163, 165, 176), Jeffrey Richards (B361), and George Evans Schatz (B375-77). Eleven articles published between 1970 and 1990 compared to how many hundreds each for any one of the above-named cult stars? Editors see either no urgency to publish articles about Colman or no reader interest if they do feel he merits attention.

The main theme of most of the articles that *have* been published is precisely this, each analyzing what made Colman magically unique and why he has largely been omitted from film history in print.

Jeffrey Richards in *Focus on Film* presents a thesis that Colman has been ignored because he fits the model of the imperial archetype:

"Physically, the imperial archetype resembles the classic western (sic): tall, thin, phlegmatic, but also moustached. The moustache is, above all, the badge of the imperialist... With the moustache comes a serenity, a belief in oneself and one's duty, a feeling of solid reliability, which is reinforced by the other key icons of the genre, the pipe and the pith helmet.

"Spiritually, the imperial archetype is quiet, dignified, dependable and unemotional...Colman embodies all of these characteristics, both physical and spiritual..."

Colman is a mismatch for this definition. Except for playing empire builder Robert Clive (for which he shaved his moustache), because the man's megalomania fascinated him, Colman turned down all scripts offered him afterward that gloried in and glorified British imperialism, including *Gunga Din* (1939). The mythical kingdom of *The Prisoner of Zenda* is the backdrop for a metaphoric fable of honor, duty and responsibility, values that are certainly not limited to the British empire. Likewise, the battle with the Fuzzy Wuzzies in *The Light That Failed* is the backdrop for a tale of artistic corruption leading to spiritual and literal blindness.

As for Richards's spiritual definition, Colman is hardly a phlegmatic sort. Look to the renunciation and love scenes in *Zenda*, his love scene in *Lost Horizon*, and his departure and return scenes in same, citing a few examples.

Furthermore, Richards contradicts his imperial archetype thesis in his summation, saying that "it is the star personality rather than the actor which is the stuff of cinematic myth. The two need not be mutually exclusive. But the truly great stars had something more than simply acting skill and Colman had it." He then notes the lunatic cameo casting for *The Story of Mankind*, concluding that "it was somehow fitting that Colman should have been chosen to play the Spirit of Man, for, in his screen characters, he had shown the heights to which man could rise, the fulfillment he could achieve by giving his life a purpose and a meaning." Ideals which are consonant with becoming a whole, decent, compassionate, civilized and loving person, *not* an imperialist.

While Richards has several valid points to make about the essence of Colman's stardom, his reasoning about the imperialist aspect is off because Colman was always looking for characters who were at odds with their milieu, but who could rise under embattled circumstances to reach the Ronald Colman standard.

Compare this with Colman fan George Schatz's personalized reflections on the actor's career and impact in *Classic Film Collector*, B375; reflections having nothing to do with academic notions, but rooted instead in Schatz's emotional and intellectual responses to Colman since first seeing *Lost Horizon* in 1937.

At first Schatz laments that writing about Colman is fruitless in the late 1960s:

"What would be the purpose of reviving comment on a man whose name falls limp on the ears of a generation born since his years of success and over a decade past his death? He won no real battles, conveyed no heritage, solved no human problems."

He then answers this question, happily contradicting himself:

"What was it, then, that Colman offered that allowed us to leave that darkened theater suddenly realizing that there was existence of a fuller life for ourselves than we had anticipated or envisioned when we entered? Did he in fact demonstrate a heritage of utilizing the accumulated fruits of civilized conduct and knowledge that we have either overlooked or forgotten?

"There seemed to be some indefinable quality, some unique combination of appearance, voice, quiet humor or personal projection that made us pay, by the millions, to spend some time with him, not to be preached at or instructed by, but simply to be complimented by his example of what qualities the human species is capable, even the least of us. Perhaps this is the heritage that Colman offered: that it is most important to not only reveal what man is, but what man can be."

R. Dixon Smith complements this insight with his own in his book *Ronald Colman, Gentleman of the Cinema* (B12):

"What, then, is the cake? Restraint, understatement, and subtlety, in conjunction with personal charisma. It was the light and unself-conscious way he carried himself that made him so appealing and which made his conflicts so much more deeply felt by the his public. It was easy for men to feel that he was within their reach as a model—smooth and suave, yet able to suffer the same self-doubts and pangs of love that every sensitive man experiences. And for women, he represented the best of all possible lovers: physically devastating and adroit, yet revealing a sense of romantic incompleteness, that sad but uncomplaining look in his eyes which made every female on the block want to protect him."

All of these men, and myself, are saying in our various ways that Ronald Colman created a character emblematic of humanity as a whole, speaking to each person individually of the emotional and intellectual fulfillment awaiting us if we but have the ambition and the heart to journey beyond the horizon. Which is precisely what *Lost Horizon* is about, and why that movie has had a resounding impact for nearly 60 years.

So, with all of these wonderful qualities going for him and all of these great movies to his name, why is it that Colman is perennially rejected for biographical treatment by book publishers? Because his private life was comparatively free from scandal; he was discreet about his girlfriends while still married to his first wife, Thelma; for all his carousing with his Musketeer friends, he was not a colorful character in the Hollywood scene; he was a charitable, kind, decent, talented man who gave his audiences every kind of wish fulfillment they could want while zealously keeping his home life to himself; he shunned publicity; and he was professionally generous to his co-stars, giving them advice and guidance when asked. There are few negative anecdotes about him.

On top of all of which, his name has not been continuously revived in any of the glamorous movie magazines and prestigious film journals. Disregarding its several faults, this is precisely why Juliet Colman's 1975 biography was not a big seller despite a well-mounted publicity push by its publisher, William Morrow. Young moviegoers didn't know who he was. Ironically, just five years later, the home video and cable television markets began to give Colman and scores of other forgotten Golden Age stars the attention and respect due them because their classic movies were suddenly rich fodder for those markets. Colman's pictures are film festival favorites and steady sellers on home video, yet no one in print has remarked on this multi-media revival of his work.

Even without a slew of magazine features or a major biography, Colman's reputation has steadily grown. Not for nothing did TNT film programmer Lisa Matteas schedule *Lost Horizon* as part of a *Favorite Movies* series in November 1993. Not for nothing did AMC pay tribute to Colman on his birthday in 1991-93. Not for nothing have AMC and TMC played his movies on a regular basis year after year.

(The only major print work in the midst of all this was the Smith book, published in 1991 to take advantage of the actor's 100th birthday.)

Veteran and younger film buffs who are continuously checking out all the good old movies on the above stations and TMC (Turner Movie Classics) are running into Ronald Colman over and over again. Fans of silent movies are also rediscovering his work at conventions like Cinecon and Cinefest. All that remains is a long overdue rediscovery in print, to which this book is a contribution.

STAGE WORK

This chapter marks the first time that Ronald Colman's professional stage work in England and the United States has been, as far as possible, fully and accurately documented using original sources: playbills, trade papers and newspapers, and several of the plays for synopses instead of reviews. His work before June 1916 cannot be wholly traced.

Though Juliet Colman and Ronald himself paint a bleak picture of much of his stage career in the U.S., the truth was not nearly that bad. Colman did have little to live on when he first came to New York in the late summer of 1920. And prior to his first stage role, he did wash dishes to pay for a cheap room and a diet consisting mainly of soup and rice pudding. However, struggling actors could often slide on their weekly rent for up to two months since the cost of living was low. Actors also saw themselves as an informal professional fraternity and were obliged to take full advantage of this esprit de corps to borrow money, especially since they were not paid for rehearsals.

Colman's most difficult periods were before *The Dauntless Three* (1920) and the total of four months following *The Green Goddess* (1920-21) and *The Silver Fox* (1921), when he barely kept from starving. While he did work for most of the 1921-22 season, it was all on tour so that his name was not in demand the following season.

His stage work can be divided into four periods: (1) high school plays; 2) amateur theatricals and paying music hall-type work in England, (3) professional work on the British stage, and (4) professional work on the American stage. All professional roles are in boldface for ease of finding them.

The musical selections listed for British dramas were played by a pit band as overture, intermission and exit music.

1905-1907

S1 HADLEY SCHOOL: LITTLEHAMPTON, SUSSEX
He performed in such plays as *The Admirable Crichton* and *Fanny's First Play*. According to the 1943 edition of *Current Biography* (B4), "At one time he contrived to get a member of Sir George Alexander's company to come and look him over. 'He did,' Colman recalls, 'and looked right over me.'" Alexander was a famous director and actor.

1907-1911

S2 Banjo player at a Masonic smoker at age 17.

S3 BANCROFT AMATEUR DRAMATIC SOCIETY.

He appeared in such plays as *The Admirable Crichton*, *Sowing the Wind*, *The Private Secretary*, *Charley's Aunt*, and works by Oscar Wilde and Gilbert and Sullivan, in the latter of which he sang and danced. These productions were staged as part of a vanity theater trend popular in England at the time, meaning that Colman and his fellow amateurs had to pay to rent a theater and director for the privilege of hamming before a paying audience to get the money to recoup their costs. There is no way to know if they made a profit. They also did revue shows in which Colman sang British drinking songs while playing guitar and banjo.

S4 Monologue and banjo performances at Clavier Hall in London in 1911 for extra income.

1912-1914(?)

S5 Member of concert party group of friends calling themselves The Mad Medicos, earning money performing in salons, Masonic smokers etc. He played banjo, read short story and novel excerpts and, with friend Jack Buckbarrow, did impressions; of whom is not known. Later known as The Popinjays for summertime work, according to Juliet Colman.

1916

S6 THE SCALLYWAGS or THE POPINJAYS(?).

Early 1916. A touring Pierrot concert party organized by showman George Denby.

This touring party was Colman's first professional work since he was part of a paid company. According to writers P.L. Mannock (B277) and Wilson D'Arne (B135), both of whom saw the show in Derby (pronounced Darby), Colman was the light comedian of the troupe. A photo of him in this revue in *Modern Screen* (B286) and *Photoplay* (B191) shows him in clown costume sans clown make-up. He sang a duet by Paul A. Rubens (music) and Percy Greenbank (lyrics) from the show *Tonight's the Night* (1914), played songs on his banjo, and recited a monologue called "Spotty—A Tale of the Trenches."

According to Mannock, Colman left the troupe when Denby could not pay him the £6 a week he was asking. *Modern Screen* says the troupe was called The Scallywags, while Mannock recalled it as The Popinjays, which supposedly was the summer version of The Mad Medicos before the war.

S7 THE MAHARANI OF ARAKAN.
A one-act romantic Indian comedy adapted by George Calderon (1868-1915) and Sir Rabindranath Tagore (1861-1941) from Tagore's short story. Directed by Arthur Weigall. Costumes by Edith Craig. Music by Inyat Khan's Indian musicians. Part of a variety bill including violinist Marie Hall, a sketch called "Her Lonely Soldier", and T.C. Fairbairn's naval songs. See B123.

Playdates: London Coliseum, Monday June 19 to Saturday July 1 at 2:30 and 8 p.m. daily.

Cast: Lena Ashwell (Amina, a Mogul Maharani or Princess), Austin Leigh (King Dazia of Arakan), Esmé Beringer (Roshanara, Amina's sister), **Ronald Colman** (Rahmat Sheikh, Indian Herald).

Synopsis: Disguised as a peasant, the King of Arakan woos Mogul princess Amina, who is secretly living in a fisherman's hut. He then sends her a message as himself saying that he intends to marry her. Roshanara reminds her that the king's father killed theirs, Shah Shuja, so she must avenge that death. When Amina discovers that the king and her peasant lover are the same, she changes her mind about killing him, ending the feud between the two families.

Notes: Colman played his first professional London role in blackface. He had no lines and only had to wave a flag and toot a horn for Ashwell's entrance. She had hired him for the part at £2 a week. Ashwell, by the way, was 45, making her a middle-aged princess.

S8 THE MISLEADING LADY. A three-act drama by Charles Goddard and Paul Dickey. Produced by George Grossmith and Edward Laurillard in conjunction with Frank Curzon. Directed by Felix Edwardes. Scenery by Walter Hann. Musical selections from the Gaiety Production of *Theodore & Co*. Intermission music by Kendal Grimston's Quartette with solo violin by Paul Brunet. See B123.

Playdates: Theatre Royal in Manchester, August 28-September 2 for 7 performances. The Playhouse in London, Wednesday September 6 to Saturday March 24, 1917 for 229 performances.

Cast: Gladys Cooper (Helen Steele), Malcolm Cherry (Jack Craigen), Edith Saville (Jane Wentworth), Edgar Payne (Sidney Parker), Sarah Benedict (Grace Buchanan), Violet Winter (Amy Foster), **Ronald Colman** (Stephen Weatherbee), Cecil Sully (Spider Sanborn), Lambert Terry (Babe Merrill), Mrs. Leslie Faber (Mrs. John W. Cannell), Wilfred Draycott (John W. Cannell), Allan Jeayes (Henry Tracey), Arthur Finn (Keen Fitzpatrick), Weedon Grossmith (Boney), Sidney C. Sinclair (Tim Macmahon), George Hewitson (Bill Fagan).

Note: Sarah Benedict and George Hewitson were replacements for Mabel Hicks and Herbert James in Manchester.

Synopsis: At a house party on the Upper Hudson in New York, actress Helen Steele seduces famed explorer Jack Craigen into proposing marriage to convince producer Sidney Parker that she is right for the vamp lead in his new play. When Craigen learns he has been duped and why, he is so furious he kidnaps Steele from the party to his bungalow in the Adirondacks. There, he chains her to a wall and lectures her on the sexual ploys of women in general and herself in particular. When he finally frees her, she accidentally knocks him out with his own telephone. She bandages him, goes looking for help, comes back, and confesses her love for him. The play ends with Stephen Weatherbee, a friend of Steele's, coming to rescue her.

Notes: Weatherbee—acts one and three—is a genial young man with no distinctive character. Colman was paid £6 a week to give him one. The play itself is a rather nasty spin on the theme of feminine wiles entrapping men, concluding that women secretly love macho brutes. It originally opened at the Apollo in Atlantic City on November 17, 1913 with Inez Buck and Lewis Stone as Helen and Jack, followed by the New York premiere at the Fulton on November 25, 1913. A 1932 film version stars Claudette Colbert and Edmund Lowe.

1917

S9 PARTNERSHIP. A light comedy in three acts by Elizabeth Baker. Presented by London Repertory Theatre. Produced by A. E. Drinkwater. No director listed on the playbill.

Playdates: Court Theatre in London on Monday and Tuesday March 5 and 6 at 2:30 p.m.

Cast: Agnes Thomas (Miss Blagg), Dorothy Holmes Gore (Miss Tracey), Dulce Musgrave (Lady Smith Carr Smith), Laura Cowie (Kate Rolling), **Ronald Colman**

(Webber), Nigel Playfair (Goodrich), Alix Grein (Maisie Glow), Dawson Milward (George Pillatt), Richard Lambart (Lawrence Fawcett), F.W. Woodward (Elliman).

Notes: Colman played these matinees toward the close of *The Misleading Lady*. Drinkwater apparently saw him in *Lady* and asked its producers to borrow him. It meant extra money for Colman and didn't interfere with the mid-week matinee of *Lady*, so the deal was made. Though the files at Mander & Mitchenson have no record of the London Repertory Theatre, M&M's director, Richard Mangan, says that "they were probably one of the many small societies which existed at the time and used to put on matinee or Sunday performances."

S10 DAMAGED GOODS. (French title: *Les Avaries*.) A 1902 drama by Eugéne Brieux, translated from the French by John Pollock. Produced by The Society for the Production of Damaged Goods, by arrangement with Charles B. Cochran. Directed by James Bernard Fagan for the St. Martin's and road companies. See B30, B123, B392.

Music: "Le Calif de Bagdad" overture by Boieldie; Fantasia from "Sylvia" by Delibes; "Valse Triste" by Sibelius; "None But the Lonely Heart" by Tchaikovsky; "Mignette Suite" by Missa; "I'm Going Back to Dear Old England" march by Ball.

Playdates: St. Martin's Theatre, London, Thursday March 15 through Saturday October 27 for 283 performances, including 27 extra matinees. June 4-9 at the Liverpool Olympia.

Reginald Bach played the role of George Dupont for the first month. He was replaced by Colman (who was understudying him) beginning April 17. Moreover, there were two casts with Colman, the original and a touring company, though I wasn't able to learn where it went after the Liverpool Olympia. Bach rejoined the St. Martin's production during the road company run, but was replaced by Colman once again by July 9.

Cast (St. Martin's Theatre): J. Fisher White (The Doctor), **Ronald Colman** (George Dupont), Nona Wynne (Henriette Dupont, George's wife), Mary Grey (Madame Dupont, George's Mother), Edith Lester Jones (The Nurse), Sybil Hammerling (The Maid), S. Newberry (The Student), Bassett Roe (M. Loches, the Father-in-Law), Margaret Omar (A Woman), Corney Grain (A Man), Joan Vivian-Rees (A Girl).

Cast (Liverpool Olympia): Charles V. France (The Doctor), **Ronald Colman** (George Dupont), Irene Barnett (Henriette Dupont), Molly Tremaine (Madame Dupont), Beryl Brodie (The Nurse), St. Barbe West (M. Loches), Gladys Jesson (A Woman), Geoffrey Campion (A Student), Bert Ratcliffe (A Man), Frances Kendal (A Girl). No actress listed for The Maid.

Synopsis: In 1902 Paris, a hypocritically moralistic social-climbing notary named George Dupont contracts syphilis from a prostitute, but ignores his doctor's advice to wait four years to be certified cured before marrying. Instead, he takes a fake cure, marries for money, social position and children, and gives the disease to his newborn daughter, who then transmits it to her nurse. Madame Dupont then tries to trick the nurse into accepting 1000 francs to stay on, but when the nurse learns the truth from the doctor, she demands the money to keep quiet. When Henriette overhears this, she leaves George at once, taking the baby with her.

Dupont's deputy father-in-law, M. Loches, then asks George's doctor for a certificate of disease for Henriette Dupont as a basis for compelling divorce. The doctor refuses, lecturing Loches on stigma, scandal, and the sexual ignorance born of hypocritical prudery that breeds syphilis in the first place. He then shows Loches two female patients and a distraught father whose lives have been maimed by syphilis and double standards. His purpose in showing Loches the tragic fruits of same is to convince him of the need for sex education and health certificates for marriage.

Review: *The Stage*, 6-6-17: "Ronald Colman very skillfully judges the limits and necessities of the young husband and uses them with most commendable style and feeling."

Commentary: This was the first British play—though from a French source—dealing with the scandalously taboo topic of venereal disease. For that reason, and because it was an electrifyingly dramatic tour de force in its own right, it was a theatrical cause célèbre, playing to packed houses for more than seven months despite negative reviews calling it a lecture in the guise of a play. The *Manchester Guardian* critic complained that it lacked Shavian wit to make the message palatable, but Pollock's translation was striving for directness, honesty and candor, not cleverness. Pollock was right, the critics were wrong.

Reading the play today, I find it remarkable that it has not been revived and revised to fit the AIDS epidemic. With only a minor amount of updating for current medical reality and to get rid of the notion that prostitutes are the main means of transmission, it could easily galvanize contemporary audiences just as it did those in 1917.

Despite giving an acclaimed performance for nearly seven months, Colman was not cast in Alexander Butler's 1919 British film of the play, but J. Fisher White, Bassett Roe and Joan Vivian-Rees were. Stage star Campbell Gullan played Dupont because he was a bigger commercial draw. Richard Bennett had previously produced and starred in a 1914 five-reel American film version as Dupont (expanding it to seven reels in 1915 according to *Variety*) after staging it on Broadway. The British film exists, but not the Bennett. A 1937 American version stars Pedro de Cordoba as the Doctor.

1918

S11 THE LITTLE BROTHER. A play in prologue and three acts by Benedict James, based on the novel "The Rabbi and the Priest" by Milton Goldsmith. Presented by Walter Hast and Leon Zeitlin. Produced by Leon M. Lion. Directed by Douglas Gordon. Scenery: Pullinger. Costumes: H & L Nathan. Musical director: J.B. Hastings. Stage manager: Henry Scatchard.

Music, Ambassadors run: "Yelva" overture by Reissiger; Russian Melodies by Yakov Krein; "Prelude" by Rachmaninoff; "None but the Lonely Heart" by Tchaikovsky; Hebrew melodies arranged by J.B. Hastings; "Barcarolle" by Tchaikovsky; "Kol Nidre" by Max Bruch; "Slavonic Rhapsody" by Friedermann; "Carminetta" by Lassailly.

Music, Gaiety run: Overture, "Russian Folk Songs", arranged by H. Higgs; "The Arcadians" by Lionel Monckton and Howard Talbot; "Longing" and "It is Only a Tiny Garden" by Haydn Wood; "Wonder Eyes" by Percy Fletcher; "The Violin Song" from "Tina" by Paul A. Rubens; "Musette" by Neil Moret.

Playdates: Ambassadors Theatre in London, Wednesday February 6 to Saturday April 13 for 78 performances. Gaiety Theatre in Manchester, Monday April 29 to Saturday May 11 for 16 performances.

Note: Although the Manchester playbill gives the opening night as April 22, the play is not listed in the Guardian for that week, but for the week after.

Cast for Ambassadors run:

Prologue (Russia, a Sabbath afternoon, Winter of 1876): Mary Grey (Marie, Elkantrovitch's servant), A. Corney Grain (Thaddeus Vinogradof, the Village Baker), Helen Temple (Blume, Elkantrovitch's Wife), Kathleen Cope (Mordecai Elkantrovitch, the Elder Son), Roy Byford (Uncle Tulpen, Wealthy Merchant of Kieff), Sydney Paxton (Isaac Elkantrovitch, the Village Ironmonger), Howard Brenan (Shmul), Henry Scatchard (Shlomke), Lilian Mason (Rivkah), Constance Backner (Freme), Joan Byford (Hinda),

Arthur Ewart (Moshe), Erbe Hayman (Cheskal), Gertrude Harrison (Reuchel), Beatrice Drury (Yetta), Alfred Woods (Komarof, Leader of Rioters), Tom Nye (Ivan, a Rioter).

The Play (New York, 1916-1917): Mignon O'Doherty (Bridget), Cecily Byrne (Judith), **Ronald Colman** (George Lubin), Sydney Paxton (Vanderlinde), J. Fisher White (Rabbi Elkan), Ben Nathan (Shinovitch), Roy Byfard (Rube Samuels), Lyn Harding (Father Petrovich of the Greek Church), Hilda Davies (Mrs. Lomas), Mary Grey (Marie).

Cast for Gaiety run (some roles not listed on playbill):

Prologue: Evelyn Walsh Hall (Elkantrovitch's Servant), Mignon O'Doherty (Elkantrovitch's Wife), Joan Vivian-Rees (Mordecai Elkantrovitch), Frank Arlton (Uncle Tulpen), H. Hodges (Isaac Elkantrovitch), Henry Scatchard (Shlomke), Irve Hayward (Moshe), Joan Byford (Hinda), Henry Taft (Komarof), Tom Dare (Ivan).

The Play: Mignon O'Doherty (Bridget), Cecily Byrne (Judith), **Ronald Colman** (George Lubin), Henry Reddan (Vanderlinde), J. Fisher White (Rabbi Elkan), Ben Nathan (Shinovitch), Frank Arlton (Rube Samuels), Lyn Harding (Father Petrovich), Joan Vivian-Rees (Mrs. Thomas), Evelyn Walsh Hall (Marie).

Synopsis: A story of religious bigotry spanning 40 years in which a Russian Jew (Father Petrovich) becomes an antisemitic, pogrom-instigating Russian priest, not knowing that he was born Jewish. In the end, he is reconciled with his brother, Rabbi Elkan, when their children intermarry.

Reviews: *The Stage*, 2-11-18: "Ronald Colman is fresh and earnest."

London Times, 2-8-18: "If the author had been content to confine his Jewish Rabbi and Russian Priest to their legitimate dramatic use as characters in violent contrast and conflict, he might have produced a real work of art...unfortunately, our Frankenstein loses control of his monster.

"Neither Rabbi nor Priest can forget that he is a preacher, and each indulges in verbose tirades, proclaiming his faith, just at the moment when, for dramatic purposes, silence would be golden."

Note: Colman played a young Jewish man who marries a "shiksa" or gentile.

S12 THE LIVE WIRE. A spy play by Sidney Blow and Douglas Hoare. Presented by André Charlot by arrangement with C.B. Cochran. Colman understudied Donald Calthrop, then was hired for *The Bubble* before *The Live Wire* opened. See S13 and S14.

Cast: George Skelton (Mulligan), Hilda Trevelyan (Betty Byrne), C.M. Hallard (Sir Hartley Meristham), Helen Morris (Christina Anderson), Alex Scott-Gatty (Mervyn Chester), Henry Drag (Inspector Woods), Albert Sims (P.C. Waldon), Donald Calthrop (Wilfred Carpenter).

Playdates: St. Martin's Theatre, Tuesday August 27 to Saturday November 2 for 79 performances.

S13 THE BUBBLE. A comedy of Jewish life in four acts by Edward Locke.

Playdates: Gaiety Theatre in Manchester, Monday September 9 to Saturday September 21. Wimbledon Theatre in Wimbledon, Monday October 28 to (?). Yearbooks for *The Stage* and *The Era* show only these two runs.

Cast: Ben Nathan (Jacob Cohen), Lauderdale Maitland (Joseph Marks), **Ronald Colman** (David Goldsmith, reporter for a financial paper), Joan Pereira (Mrs. Cohen), Eva Embury (Rosa).

Review: *The Stage*, 10-31-18: "Ronald Colman is convincingly and suitably rough."

S14 THE LIVE WIRE. Touring company in December.

Playdates: Included the Theatre Royal in Manchester, December 2-8.

Cast: Ronald Colman (Wilfred Carpenter), Thelma Raye (Betty Byrne), Jack Fortescue (Mervyn Chester). No other names or credits were available.

Synopsis: The editor of a newspaper called *The Live Wire* discovers he has a German spy in his midst even as his paper is obsessed with the subject. After several plot twists, the spy is revealed to be a staff writer whose weakness is sending coded messages peppered with French phrases.

Review: N.C., *Manchester Guardian*, 12-3-18: "Mr. Jack Fortescue has carefully studied the methods of the German agent as revealed in the manuscript, and not less successful is Mr. Ronald Colman's exegesis of an officer in the British army."

Note: It was during this tour that Colman met Thelma Raye (née Thelma Victoria Maud), his future first wife.

1919

S15 SKITTLES. A comedy by Lechmere Worrall and Arthur Rose, based on a scenario by the late Paul A. Rubens.

Playdates: Palace Theatre at Westcliff-on-Sea, Monday May 26 to (?)

Cast: Edmund Gwenn (William Wiggleshaw), **Ronald Colman** (Lord Roftus), Danell Greene (Lawrie Cately), Lester Warren (Adam Beazley), Huntley Gifford (Tom Whiteley), Gertrude Sterroll (Lady Roftus), Alisa Grahame (Hon. Margaret Atherton), Frances White (Mrs. Toffin), Muriel Martin Harvey (Skittles).

1920

S16 THE GREAT DAY. A drama by Louis N. Parker and R. Sims. Colman played the juvenile lead in the touring company in January-February(?) 1920. The London premiere was at Drury Lane Theatre on September 12, 1919.

AMERICAN STAGE WORK

1920

S17 THE DAUNTLESS THREE. A mystery by Horace Annesley Vachell and Walter Hackett. See B1, B123.

Playdates: Trial run at the Globe Theatre in Atlantic City, October 25-30.

Cast: Starring Robert Warwick and Estelle Winwood, with **Colman** in two walk-on bits: Act 1, as a Turkish Chief of Police dressed in white except for a red fez; Act 2, as a Bearded Russian Spy.

Synopsis: A detective recovers a missing diamond.

Review: Charles Scheuer, *Variety*, 10-29-20: "Despite an evidently noticeable premiere premiere, the authors must still stand the responsibility for the lack of applause and the chilly attitude of the audience toward the detective hero who has so frequently won their admiration on screen...'The Dauntless Three' was not ready...It looked as if Mr. Warwick's superior abilities were being exhibited on the same par as those of Theda Bara."

Note: Colman stated in several magazine interviews in the 1920s and 30s that the play closed after a two-week run, during which he received $75 a week, yet neither *Variety* or

Billboard list a second week after the Globe.

S18   THE GREEN GODDESS. A drama in four acts by British theater critic William Archer (1856-1924). Produced and directed by Winthrop Ames. See R109, B123.

Playdates: Trial run opening the newly reconstructed Walnut Street Theatre in Philadelphia, December 27, 1920-January 15, 1921. New York City premiere: Booth Theatre, January 18, 1921.

Cast for first week only of New York run: George Arliss (Raja of Rukh), Ivan F. Simpson (Watkins), Herbert Waring (Major Antony Crespin), Olive Wyndham (Lucilla Traherne), Cyril Keightley (Dr. Basil Traherne), Herbert Ranson (Lt. Denis Cardew), **Ronald Colman** (High Priest), David A. Leonard (Temple Priest), Helen Nowell (An Ayah).

Synopsis: When a plane crash lands in a remote region of the Himalayas, its passengers—Crespin and the Trahernes—are kidnapped by the suave but heathen Raja who rules there. He holds them hostage in exchange for the release from prison of his three brothers, who are to be executed in London for murder. When the British government rejects the swap, the Raja plans the ritual sacrifice of his captives, offering to spare Lucilla if she will marry him once her husband is dead. A telegraphed message to the outside gets Crespin murdered by the Raja, but it also brings a bomber squadron to the rescue. The Green Goddess of the title is a green, three-armed idol.

Review: Patterson James, *Billboard*, 1-29-21: "Ronald Colman is very good as the temple (sic) priest."

Commentary: The successful Philadelphia run notwithstanding, Colman was replaced as the High Priest (who has two scenes totaling about 4 or 5 minutes) in New York after the first week by Guilo Bacchia. Why he was fired will forever remain unknown.

The play is part anti-British imperialist satire, part melodramatic claptrap. The latter is mostly about Lucilla's affair with Crespin, partly a nod to anti-Asian sentiment of the time. For all of that, it was Arliss's suavely cultivated star turn with an undertone of creepy menace that made the play a lot of fun and thus a resounding commercial success.

Arliss also played the Raja in a 1923 silent and a 1930 sound remake. Colman played the Raja on radio in 1946.

1921

S19   THE SILVER FOX: An Exposure of Five Egotists in three acts by Cosmo Hamilton from the Austrian play by Ferenc Herezeg. Presented by William Faversham and Lee Shubert. Directed by Faversham.

Playdates: The Sam S. Shubert-Belasco in Washington, D.C. May 2-7. New York premiere minus Colman: Maxine Elliott Theater on September 5, 1921.

Cast: Lawrence Grossmith (Edmund Quilter, a popular novelist), Dorothy Cumming (Helen, his Wife), Flora Sheffield (Frankie Turner, her cousin), Claude King (Major Christopher Stanley, a poet), **Ronald Colman** (Captain Douglas Belgrave, a flying man).

Synopsis: The socialite wife of a wealthy novelist contrives to make him divorce her so she can marry their best friend, a poet. Her bait is a dashing, womanizing aviator. At the same time, her cousin, a conniving sexpot, contrives to take the author away from his wife so *she* can marry him. In the end, both women get what they want.

Review: Meakin, *Variety*, 5-6-21: "In his brief moment, Ronald Colman was most convincing as the flying man."

Commentary: Not convincing enough for the producers, who replaced him after the trial run with Ian Keith. They also replaced Cumming, Sheffield and King with Violet

Kemble Cooper, Vivienne Osborne and Faversham himself, respectively.

Colman's firing was fortuitous since he went from this play to *The Nightcap*. As it was, he had only two scenes totaling about 12 minutes in a boringly repetitive, implausibly awful play. None of the characters are real, especially the male leads, who are dimensionless emotional masochists. Quilter is complacent, oblivious to reality and easily manipulated, while Stanley has the world's worst case of madonna/whore complex, making you wonder why Helen married the first and falls in love with the second.

S20 THE NIGHTCAP. A mystery comedy in three acts written and directed by Max Marcin and Guy Boltin.

Playdates: 39th Street Theatre in New York. August 15-October 1 for 56 performances.

Cast (in order of appearance): **Ronald Colman** (Charles, a butler), John Wray (Officer Shannon), John Daly Murphy (Jerry Hammond), Jack Raffael (Col. James Constance), H. Dudley Hawley (Lester Knowles), Elisabeth Risdon (Mrs. Lester Knowles), Flora Sheffield (Anne Maynard), Grant Mills (Fred Hammond), Jerome Patrick (Robert Andrews), Walter Horton (George Rainsford), Wilson Day (Rev. Dr. Forbes), Halbert Brown (Coroner Watrous), W.W. Shuttleworth (Detective Seldon).

Synopsis: Embezzling bank president Robert Andrews contrives to be murdered by one of his cohorts in the embezzlement so that his insurance policies will repay the stolen money. When co-conspirator Lester Knowles is murdered instead, the Coroner accuses Andrews. In desperation, Andrews makes an offer to Charles the butler, an ex-convict: Take $10,000 to shoot Bob or take the fall for the murder. Before Charles or one of his crooked cronies can shoot Bob, it's learned that the bank has been robbed (removing evidence of Bob's crime) and that Officer Shannon shot Knowles, thinking him to be a burglar. Bob and his new wife, Anne (they married 30 minutes before the murder) thus have a fresh start and a new motto: "If you're afraid of being found out, don't do it!"

Reviews: Alexander Woollcott, *New York Times*, 8-16-21: "The authors have contrived a rough and ready entertainment, most of which is robustly amusing...Ronald Colman and John Wray make two small parts tell."

Theater Magazine: "Ronald Colman and John Wray succeed in making much of two smaller parts."

Commentary: For a play billed as a mystery comedy, there isn't any comedy until the middle of act two, which has amusing but standard twists. However, the Butler role did give Colman a grand opportunity for dry and wry vocal and physical humor, which is what appealed to Woollcott and then to *East is West* producer William Harris, Jr. Harris most likely approached *Nightcap*'s producer to get Colman released after August 27 in return for a replacement actor, Cameron Matthews. Coincidentally, *Nightcap*'s run slumped commercially after those first two weeks, switching to the smaller Bijou Theatre in early October to cut expenses.

S21 EAST IS WEST. A comedy in three acts and a prologue by Samuel Shipman and John B. Hymer. Producer: William Harris, Jr. Staged by Clifford Brooke. Musical Director: Fred A. Baker. Overture and Chinese songs by Robert Hood Bowers. Main song: "Chinese Lullaby." See B1, B123.

Musical Program: Overture ("East is West"), Frederic Norton (Selections from "Chu Chin Chow"), Hugo Frey ("Cho-Cho San", adapted from "Madame Butterfly"), Exit Music ("Smiling" by Richard Coburn and Vincent Rose).

Cast in order of appearance: Harry Belmont (Attendant on Love Boat), Albert Berg

(Proprietor of Love Boat), Frederick Howard (Billy Benson), Robert Harrison (Lo Sang
Kee), William Kline (Customer), William Tennyson (Hop Toy), Fay Bainter (Ming Toy),
Harry Maitland (Chang Lee), Arthur Ginson (Servant), **Ronald Colman** (James Potter),
Ralph Locke (Charlie Yang), Maria Namara (Mildred Benson), Leonora Von Ottinger (Mrs.
Benson), Harry Maitland (Thomas, a Butler), George Fitzgerald (Andrew Benson), Gordon
Stables (Mr. Armstrong), Dorothy Burgess (Miss Fountain), Zena Bear (Miss Davis),
George Valin (Mr. Davis), Grace Burgess, Helen Joseffy, Zena Bear, Margaret Norton,
Dorothy Burgess (Sing Song Girls), William Kline, Harry Belmont (Tong Men).

Broadway run at the Astor Theatre: Starring Fay Bainter, directed by Clifford
Brooke. December 25, 1918 to June 19, 1920 for approximately 600 performances, except
for August 6 to September 6, 1919 when only one performance was given due to a
stagehands' walkout in sympathy with an Actor's Equity strike.

Touring company with Ronald Colman: September 11, 1921 to April 29, 1922.

Note: There are several gaps in the itinerary for lack of access to papers in tour cities
where they would have played, but this is still more than has ever been reconstructed.

Itinerary: Metropolitan in Minneapolis (September 11-17); Metropolitan in St. Paul
(September 18-24); Lyceum in Rochester (October 6-8); Heilig in Portland (October 17-22);
Century in San Francisco (October 24-November 12); Mason Opera House in Los Angeles
(November 21-26); Broadway in Denver (December 12-17); Berchel in Des Moines
(December 22-24); Sam S. Shubert in Kansas City, MO (December 26-31); Jefferson in St.
Louis (January 9-14); Sam S. Shubert in Cincinnati (January 16-22); Hartman in Columbus
(January 23-25); Murat in Indianapolis (January 26-28); Sam S. Shubert in Louisville
(January 30-February 1); Garrick in Detroit (February 6-11); Hanna in Cleveland (February
13-18); Alvin in Pittsburgh (February 20-25); Sam S. Shubert-Garrick in Washington, D.C.
(February 27-March 4); Auditorium in Baltimore (April 3-8); Poli's in Washington, D.C.
(April 16-22); Sam S. Shubert-Riviera in New York City (April 24-29).

Synopsis: The time is 1910-11. The settings are a Chinese Love Boat (euphemism for
slave ship) on the Yangtse River in China, and San Francisco. When feisty young Ming Toy
is sold into slavery aboard the Love Boat by her father, Hop Toy, Chinese shop owner Lo
Sang Kee buys her at the behest of his young American friend, Billy Benson, to save her
from the clutches of a brutal mandarin. Kee then takes her to live at his dry goods shop in
the Chinese quarter of San Francisco.

A year later, playboy and dilettante reformer James Potter visits Kee to check on a
Missionary Society rumor that Kee is living with a Chinese woman who sits in his shop
window all day making "goo-goo eyes" at passing men. When Kee tells Potter about the
Love Boat, Jimmy tells him to get rid of Ming Toy or she will be deported back to China.
Potter than tries to convert Ming Toy to Christianity, but finds she is already a confirmed
Christian. Instead, he teaches her to dance the "shimmy."

To prevent deportation, Kee sells her to Chinatown's thuggishly narcissistic chop suey
king, Charlie Yang, but Billy, son of a former ambassador, intervenes to hie her to his
family's home as their new maid without Yang knowing. Billy falls in love with her and is
willing to risk social disgrace through miscegenation until Ming Toy learns three minutes
before curtain that Hop Toy had stolen her as a baby from her white missionary father. This
clears the way for her marriage to Billy and stops Yang from having his tong men murdering
him for taking Ming Toy.

Reviews: Paul Bliss, *Minneapolis Journal*, 9-12-21: "Ronald Colman was personable
as James Potter."

Marjorie C. Driscoll, *San Francisco Chronicle*, 10-25-21: "An excellent company
(Bainter) has brought with her...Ronald Colman as the reforming Jimmy Potter—grand job,

reforming, when one can have all the fun of flirting with a Ming Toy without the fear of being reformed oneself."

Edwin Schallert, *Los Angeles Times*, 11-22-21: "The list of excellent players is too long to mention here. A few (include) Ronald Colman."

Guy Price, *Los Angeles Evening Herald*, 11-22-21: "Ronald Colman and Frederick Howard are each splendid, the former a trifle more convincing perhaps."

Unsigned, *Washington Post*, 2-28-22: "Frederick Howard as Billy Benson and Ronald Colman as James Potter are juveniles of more than usual ability, and happily lacking in the nasal whine that so often characterizes youth on stage."

T.M.C., *Baltimore Sun*, 4-4-22: "Ronald Colman is passable, but several of the minor roles are rather clumsily played."

Commentary: The second and most commercially successful of the racist plays in which Colman performed. A Broadway hit, it was a vehicle for Fay Bainter that catered happily to the white American chauvinism of the time. The Chinese characters are all stock stereotypes and the dialogue is peppered with "Chink" jokes. For all of that, it was the last-minute revelation that Ming Toy is really "one of us" that made the play a hit. However, that begs an important question: If Ming Toy is white, why doesn't anyone ever notice that she doesn't have Oriental eyes?

None of this mattered to Colman, who grabbed the part because it was a splendid professional break, paid $150 a week plus room and board, and took him on a free grand tour of the United States, landing him in Hollywood to visit the movie studios, where he could finally use his letters of introduction. He got nowhere during his one precious week in Los Angeles. Far worse, despite the tour with *East is West*, he could only get a try-out role in his next play.

Two film versions were made of this play: 1922 (First National) with Constance Talmadge; and 1930 (Universal) with Mexican actress Lupe Velez, Edward G. Robinson and Lew Ayres.

1922

S22 EAST OF SUEZ. A play in five scenes by W. Somerset Maugham. Produced by A.H. Woods. Directed by Lester Lonergan.

Playdates: Trial run at Woods' Theatre in Atlantic City, NJ, August 28-September 2. New York premiere minus Colman at the Eltinge Theatre on September 21, 1922.

Cast: Florence Eldridge (Daisy), John Halliday (George Conway), **Ronald Colman** (Henry Anderson), Lucille La Verne (Amah), Geoffrey Kerr (Harold Knox), Gypsy O'Brien (Sylvia Knox), Nathaniel Sack (Wu, Harry's Servant), Howard Lang (Lee Tai Chang), Herbert Haywood (A Coolie Barber), Baby Tang (Herself), Baby Ming (Herself).

Synopsis: In Peking, China, 30-year-old British consul Henry "Harry" Anderson marries a treacherous 27-year-old Eurasian named Daisy. Treacherous because she has not only hidden her sordid sexual past from him and lied to him about her age, she has married him only so she can be near his diplomatic service colleague, George Conway, her ex-lover.

After Daisy's Amah or governess (her mother, it turns out) unsuccessfully tries to have Harry killed to free Daisy from her loveless marriage (George is attacked by a hired thug instead), Harry's new assignment to Chung-King is postponed and he leaves for a few months on another mission. Left alone and crazy with lust for George, Daisy sends his love letters to her to Harry out of spite. Learning this and fearing ruination, George blows out his brains. At just that moment, Harry returns in a frenzy, carrying Daisy's incriminating letters.

Comments: Maugham's rabid melodrama shamelessly catered to anti-Asian racism and was thus a commercial success. For Colman, it was a much-needed job. However, he was fired after the trial run, which is when Ruth Chatterton came to his rescue, offering him a plum role as the "other man" in *La Tendresse* at $450 a week. He gladly seized the offer. He was replaced in *East of Suez* by Leonard Mudie, who would later show up in several Colman movies in bit parts.

S23 LA TENDRESSE (*Adulteress*). A drama of adultery by Henry Bataille, translated and adapted by Ruth Chatterton. Produced, directed by and starring Henry Miller. See B123.

    Cast: Henry Miller (Paul Barnac), Ruth Chatterton (Martha Dellieres), Elmer Brown (Monseigneur de Cabriac), Marguerite St. John (Mademoiselle Louise), Louise Le Bay (Aubin), Elfin Finn (Colette), William Pearce (Jacques), Norma Havey (the Governess), H. Cooper-Cliffe (Fernal), Edward McKay (Legardier), Mary Fowler (Mlle Tigraine), Sidney Riggs (Carlos Jarry), Jean de la Cruz (Count de Jadigny), William Hanley (Julian d'Ablincourt), **Ronald Colman** (Alain Sergyll), A.G. Andrews (Guerin), Florence Fair (Mlle. Morel).

    Playdates: Empire Theatre, September 25-November 18 for 64 performances as part of a cross-country tour.

    Synopsis: When a middle-aged actor named Paul Barnac discovers that his mistress, Martha Dellieres, is having an affair with a young man named Alain Sergyll, he plots to sabotage their liaison.

    Review: Alexander Woollcott, *New York Times*, 9-26-22: "...one fine, direct and authentic performance is given by an actor named Ronald Colman."

    This was Colman's final stage work. Though the trade paper *Cast* lists him as being with *La Tendresse* till November 18, he and Henry King and Lillian Gish all stated in interviews over the years that he left the show after four weeks, on October 21, to play the romantic lead in the movie *The White Sister*.

    A few times during his Hollywood career, Colman toyed with the idea of returning to the stage, this time as a star, but it was never more than talk. This was partly because he had found his star niche, partly because he made more money in movies and radio than anything the stage could have offered, though he was worth $2 million by 1932. The larger truth may have been that it scared him to think of going back on stage after so many years in front of the camera. The closest he ever came to a return were the play scenes in *A Double Life*, which were staged at Universal. The lobby scenes for that movie were filmed, as a sweet irony, where Colman was discovered nearly 25 years earlier, at the Empire Theatre.

    The Empire Theatre opened on January 25, 1893 with *The Girl I Left Behind Me* by David Belasco and Franklin Fyles. It closed on May 30, 1953 with a final performance of *The Time of the Cuckoo* by Arthur Laurents, starring Shirley Booth. It was demolished that summer to make way for an office building.

FILMOGRAPHY

This chapter documents features, shorts, newsreels and other films starring, narrated by or including Ronald Colman, providing production credits, casts, plot synopses, reviews of the time and my own commentaries. However, several things require explanation.

1) Several running times for sound films differ from the studio timings—which are rarely accurate—and those in other reference books. I have timed these movies in theaters, on cable TV and on home video, or I have done a precise footage count on Steenbecks at UCLA and the Library of Congress (LC). Timings are mostly given to the minute and second for the record rather than rounded to the nearest minute.

2) For silent movie timings, please note again that studio footage counts are rarely, if ever, accurate. Also that in the 1920s, silent speeds could vary within a feature from 20 to 24 frames per second (fps) in concert with the action on screen. Even so, a few of these movies should not be shown at sound speed because it makes human activity look jerky and unnatural. "Keep in mind," says LC curator Madeline Matz, "that if that's how movies looked back then, the industry would have died a quick and early death."

For silents where my timing differs from the studio's, I will give both. I have timed these movies at revival theaters and Cinecon and on home video.

3) I have corrected the chronology of British silents using release dates and reviews, and the chronology of American silents using Los Angeles and New York dates.

4) Where reviews for British films are absent, I either could not find any or the ones I have did not mention Colman.

5) Colman's name is in bold for those British silents in which he had minor or unbilled roles, and for F9 and F11, for ease of finding those parts.

6) Credits for the English films and some of the American ones are incomplete because they were all I could find.

7) Cross reference is limited to radio and records for reasons of space. Everything else is in the index by title.

8) An archival print listed as a composite negative means that the picture and soundtrack are on separate reels. A composite positive comprises reels from two or more prints.

Please also note that titles held by MOMA may not be available for loan to other film institutions or festivals.

9) Addresses and phone numbers for archives and a few video sources are given at the

the end of this chapter.

Though most of Colman's sound movies are now shown more often on commercial and cable TV, especially AMC and TNT, the one that has never aired is *Bulldog Drummond Strikes Back*, the rights to which are owned by Janus Films. The literary rights expired in 1987 and complete 35mm archival safety and fine grain prints do exist, so there is no reason this movie cannot be shown in theaters or on television.

As for the silents, most of the extant ones made in America have been withheld from video release and TV showings, even though many other silent movies are on home video and have been shown on PBS and cable TV. The one exception is *Lady Windermere's Fan*, which is in the public domain. I hope that listing all the archival and theatrical sources for 35mm prints of these movies will hasten their video release. If the silent classics of other stars can be sold on tape, why not those of Ronald Colman?

What this filmography makes clear is that although Colman made far fewer movies in the 1930s and 40s than his peers, he left a body of work that includes at least 20 good to excellent silent and sound pictures.

All Colman quotes are from a Gladys Hall two-part series on Colman in the January and February 1939 issues of *Photoplay*.

GLOSSARY
NE: Non-extant, does not exist.
GEH: George Eastman House.
LC: Library of Congress.
MOMA: Museum of Modern Art.
BFI: British Film Institute in England.
UCLA: University of California at Los Angeles.
AAN: Academy Award Nomination.
AA: Academy Award.
BA: Best Actor.
BSA: Best Supporting Actor or Actress.

THE BRITISH SILENTS

All seven of Colman's British features were presumed destroyed in the London Blitz of WWII, along with thousands of other movies when the warehouses they were in were destroyed by German bombers. Amazingly, a fragment of *The Toilers* was obtained by the BFI in 1990. No other prints, whole or partial, are known to survive.

F1 THE LIVE WIRE (?) Dewhurst, 1917.
Producer, Director, Screenwriter and Photographer: George Dewhurst. Production crew: Ronald Colman.
Cast: Ronald Colman (The Young Man), Phyllis Titmuss (The Young Girl).
Story details and title unknown. Latter often given as *The Live Wire*, but no one knows for sure. Never released. Two reels. NE.
Note: Colman's first movie was shot in one day in a vacant room in an old house set up as a studio. He was paid £1 to act, shift scenes as the sole crew member, and set up lights. To his relief, the film was never released after a sneak preview that had the audience walking out.

F2 THE TOILERS Diamond Super for Neville Bruce, 1919.

Producer: George Dewhurst. Director: Tom Watts. Screenplay: Eliot Stannard, R.C. Sheriff, from the novel *The Toilers of the Sea* by Victor Hugo. Photographer: Egrot.

Cast: Manora Thew (Rose), George Dewhurst (Jack), Gwynne Herbert (Mother), Ronald Colman (Bob), Eric Barker (Jack as a child), John Corrie (Lighthouse Keeper), Mollie Teraine (Merchant's Daughter).

Release date and length: Late March 1919. Five reels. Re-released September 5, 1920.

Synopsis: A young Cornish fisherman (Colman) deserts his widowed foster mother and brother (Herbert and Dewhurst) to seek his fortune in London. Once there, he romances but is rejected by the daughter of his employer, and is fired for his effort. Other disillusioning experiences follow, after which the young man returns to his fishing village, where he finds that another man has married his former sweetheart.

Note: Location shooting was done at Covent Garden Market, London Bridge, Petticoat Lane and a Cornish fishing village.

Reviews: *Bioscope*, March 1919: "The human interest of the tale is depreciated by the vague and inconsistent characterization of the hero, who commences as an ambitious, determined, and capable, if egotistical, young man, and, later, shows himself to be merely a rather foolish weakling, quite lacking in the qualities with which one is at first led to credit him...It is not Ronald Coleman's (sic) fault that one can feel very little interest in Bob."

Kinematograph Weekly: 7-1-20: "It is a pleasure to state that, of its kind, and according to its aim, 'The Toilers' is a practically perfect photoplay...Gwynne Herbert, as the mother, is the embodiment of uncomplaining toil, and the rest of the cast, including...Ronald Colman...is thoroughly good."

Note: Still without training as a film actor and still limping from his war injury, Colman's acting style in his first released awkwardly theatrical by his own account. Despite his previous experience with Dewhurst, he took the part because he badly needed the money. He later recalled that "My hands and arms went round and round like windmills, and I was all over the place like a jumping jack, giving highly 'nervous' accounts of myself."

Archival Source: BFI. 35mm safety viewing prints of two reels running a combined 1429 feet (15:52 at 24 fps, 17:46 at 20 fps) copied from 35mm nitrate reels donated in 1990.

F3 A DAUGHTER OF EVE Broadwest for Walturdaw, 1919.

Producer and Director: Walter West.

Cast: Violet Hopson (Jessica Bond), Stewart Rome (Sidney Strangeway), Cameron Carr (Charles Strangeway), Ralph Forster (John Bond), Edward Borfield (Sir Hugh Strangeway), Vesta Silva (Jessica as a child), **Ronald Colman** (unbilled character role).

Release date and length: August 1919. Five reels.

Synopsis: Murder drama involving a young lady (Hopson) who wakes up to find it was all a dream.

F4 SHEBA Sutherland for Kinemagraphic Distributors, 1919.

Producer and Director: Cecil M. Hepworth. Screenplay: Blanche McIntosh, from the novel *Rita*.

Cast: Alma Taylor (Sheba Ormatroyd), Gerald Ames (Paul Meredith), James Carew (Levison), Lionel Howard (Count Pharamonde), Eileen Dennes (Bessie Saxton), Mary Dibley (Rhoda Meredith), Diana Carey (Mrs. Ormatroyd), Eric Barker (Rex Ormatroyd), **Ronald Colman** (unbilled character role).

Release date and length: October 1919. 5,475 feet.

Synopsis: A girl named Sheba marries the son of a famous opera singer, then learns he is already married. She then tries to make a new life for herself.

Notes: Colman was still using theatrical mannerisms, but taking cues from his last two movies, he started toning down a bit for his work in *Sheba*. Hepworth, a distinguished director of the 1910s who had made some successful Dickens adaptations, cast him in an unimportant part because he was available. However, he did take note of Colman "for another and better part as soon as there was an opportunity...I must have thought well of him for I remember inviting him to join our company, but he said that he was determined to go to America. I do not suppose he has ever regretted that determination, but I have—often." (B51)

F5 SNOW IN THE DESERT Broadwest for Walturdaw, 1919.

Producer and Director: Walter West. Screenplay: Benedict James, from the novel by Andrew Soutar.

Cast: Violet Hopson (Felice Beste), Stewart Rome (William B. Jackson), Sir Simeon Stuart (Sir Michael Beste), **Ronald Colman** (Rupert Sylvester), Mary Masters, A.B. Caldwell, and Poppy Wyndham (unbilled).

Release date and length: December ? 1919. 7,000 feet.

Synopsis: Romantic melodrama about a business tycoon's wife (Hopson) who leaves her staid husband (Beste) for a poet (Rome). She later goes back to her husband when she learns he is seriously ill and helps save his business and his health.

F6 ANNA THE ADVENTURESS Sutherland for National Photoplay Distributors, 1920.

Producer and Director: Cecil M. Hepworth. Screenplay: Blanche McIntosh, from the novel by E. Philips Oppenheim.

Cast: Alma Taylor (Anna and Annabel Pelissier), James Carew (Montague Hill), Gerald Ames (Nigel Ennison), Gwynne Herbert (Aunt), Christine Rayner (Mrs. Elicote), **Ronald Colman** (Brendan), James Armand (Sir John Ferringhall), Jean Cadell (Mrs. White).

Release date and length: February 1920. 6,280 feet.

Synopsis: Convoluted romantic melodrama about twin sisters (Taylor), one of whom marries a man (Carew) she believes to have died in an accident on their honeymoon, but who later reappears to reclaim his bride.

Review: *Kinematograph Weekly*, 2-12-20: "Gerald James is good as Nigel Ennison, as is James Armand as Sir John Ferringhall, and also Ronald Colman as Brendan."

Note: Colman was getting better at underplaying, earning good notices for this performance, but he was still having difficulty with his war limp. When he saw this movie with a paying audience, he overheard one woman remark on his awkward walking.

F7 A SON OF DAVID Broadwest for Walturdaw, 1920. See B287.

Producer: Walter West. Director: E. Hay Plumb. Screenplay: Benedict James, based on a story by Charles Barnett.

Cast: Poppy Wyndham (Esther Raphael), Ronald Colman (Maurice Phillips), Arthur Walcott (Louis Raphael), Constance Blackner (Miriam Myers), Robert Vallis (Sam Myers), Joseph Pacey (Maurice as a child), Vesta Sylva (Esther as a child).

Release date and length: April 1920. 4,700 feet.

Synopsis: A Jewish boy in Whitechapel named Maurice Phillips trains to be a boxer to get revenge on the man he believes murdered his father in the ring. When he finally gets his chance for the match, he learns that the veteran boxer is innocent, that his father actually died of a heart attack after the bout. Maurice then marries his fiancée, Esther, a rabbi's daughter.

Review: *Bioscope*, 4-5-20: "An interesting study of Jewish life and character...Ronald Coleman (sic), Poppy Wyndham and Robert Vallis all act very cleverly, but it would have been wiser to cast players of a distinctively Jewish type for these roles...It strikes an original note and should prove very attractive to a majority of audiences."

Note: Director E. Hay Plumb was a genial ex-vaudevillian who worked with Colman to tone down his theatricality. Veteran character actor Vallis, however, apparently was even more instrumental in coaching Colman since he was equally at home on stage and screen. The result was, reportedly, his most natural performance to date in the most critically and commercially popular of his British features. Even so, Colman felt he had badly overdone his performance:

"My screen shadow seemed to me terrible, unspeakably dreadful. In the big moment I had to knock out a man, an ex-professional, who could have killed and eaten me."

F8 THE BLACK SPIDER B & C Shows for Butcher's Kinemagraphic Distributors, 1920.

Director and Screenplay: William J. Humphrey, from the novel by Carlton Dawe. No other production details are known.

Cast: Lydia Kyasht (Angela Carfour), Sam Livesey (Reginald Conway), Ronald Colman (Vicomte de Beauvais), Bertram Burleigh (Archie Lowndes), Mary Claire (Coralie Mount), Dorothy Cecil (Marjorie West), C. Hayden Coffin (Lord Carfour), Adeline Hayden Coffin (Lady Carfour), Betty Hall.

Release date and length: May 1920. 5,800 feet.

Synopsis: At Monte Carlo, Angela Carfour becomes engaged to the Vicomte de Beauvais while in love with a man named Archie Lowndes. Suddenly, Monte Carlo is plagued by a series of jewel robberies committed by a man known as the Black Spider. In the end, it is revealed that the Vicomte is the Black Spider, freeing Angela to marry Archie.

Reviews: *Bioscope*, 5-13-20: "Ronald Colman makes the bold, bad Vicomte a romantic figure in the short glimpses we have of him."

Kinematograph Weekly, 5-13-20: "Ronald Colman as Beauvais and Bertram Burleigh as Archie Lowndes have small opportunities to shine in their unreal parts."

Notes: *The Black Spider* was a precursor to Colman's gentleman thief role in *Raffles* (F34). He had greatly improved his screen acting by this time, but was still regarded by most producers as a pleasant but unmemorable second lead. He agreed with them, years later remarking, "I persevered in those English films, and persevere is the word, though I am the first to admit that I was a very bad actor in them."

The most these seven features did for him professionally was to earn him some badly needed money between scarce stage jobs. Actor John Howard told me in 1979 that when he was filming *Lost Horizon* in 1936, he saw one of them—he couldn't recall which one but remembered it being interesting—at Colman's house when he was invited there for dinner one night. Regrettably, that print in Colman's private collection decomposed decades ago.

THE AMERICAN SILENTS

Of the 21 American silent movies Ronald Colman made, before and after he became a star, 16 have survived: 9 complete, 7 incomplete.

F9 HANDCUFFS OR KISSES? Lewis J. Selznick Pictures Company for Select Motion Pictures Corporation, 1921.

Producer: Lewis J. Selznick. Director: George Archainbaud. Screenplay: Lewis Allen

Browne, from the short story "Handcuffs and Kisses" by Thomas Edgelow. Photographer: Jules Cronjager.

Cast: Elaine Hammerstein (Lois Walton), Julia Swayne Gordon (Mrs. Walton); Dorothy Chappell (Violet), Robert Ellis (Peter Madison), Alison Skipworth (Miss Strodd), Florence Billings (Miss Dell), Ronald Schabel (Leo Carstairs), George Lessey (Elias Pratt), **Ronald Colman** (Lodyard, a playboy).

Release date and length: New York, October 1921. 6 reels. No evidence of Los Angeles screenings.

Synopsis: Melodrama about a young woman named Lois Walton who is cheated out of her father's estate by a conniving aunt who wants the money for her own daughter, then sent to a reformatory when she rebels. After various tribulations at the reformatory, Lois marries a young and handsome trial lawyer. Colman plays a rich, shallow playboy whom she knows for a short time.

Reviews: Jolo, *Variety*, October 14: "Interesting production—interesting as entertainment. It tells the public a lot of things about reformatories and should have a good effect upon young girls headed in that direction."

Exhibitors Herald: "Too much like anti-reformatory propaganda...It is steeped in gloom without a bit of comedy relief." (Review quote taken from B159.)

Notes: Colman made this movie during the summer of 1921 between stage rehearsals for *The Nightcap* to make up for the money he wasn't getting for those rehearsals. Very little money since this was a low-budget film that played on the bottom half of a few double bills in New York—but not advertised in the New York Times—and a few other cities. It lost money. Colman later recalled that "I was offered a very insignificant part in a very insignificant picture. All they wanted was a sharp-looking dress suit and someone to fill it."

In 1978, Killiam Films, which owns a 4-reel print, presented a rare screening of it. Film historian William K. Everson attended that screening, found the picture entertaining and says that "Colman was dapper as ever in his brief appearances in three of the reels. It was clear, though, that the mid-section was missing."

F10 THE WHITE SISTER   Inspiration Pictures, Inc. Distribution: Metro Pictures Corporation, 1923.

Producers: Henry King and Lillian Gish. Charles H. Duell, President of Inspiration. Director: Henry King. Screenplay: George V. Hobart and Charles V. Whittaker, from the novel by Frances Marion Crawford. Photographers: Roy Overbaugh, Ferdinand Ris. Art Director: Robert M. Haas. Stills Photographer: James Abbé. Titles: Will M. Richey, Don Bartlett. Film Editors: Duncan Mansfield and Lillian Gish (the latter cut five reels for general release). Musical Score: Carl Breil.

Cast: Lillian Gish (Angela Chiaromonte), Ronald Colman (Captain Giovanni Severi), Gail Kane (Marchesa di Mola), J. Barney Sherry (Monsignor Saracinesca), Charles Lane (Prince Chiaromonte), Juliette La Violette (Madame Bernard), Sig Serena (Prof. Ugo Severi), Alfredo Bertone (Filmore Durand), Ramon Ibanez (Count del Ferice), Alfredo Martinelli (Alfredo del Ferice), Carloni Talli (Mother Superior), Giovanni Viccola (General Mazzini), Antonio Barda (Alfredo's Tutor), Giacomo D'Attino (Solicitor to the Prince), Michele Gualdi (Solicitor to the Count), Giuseppe Pavoni (Archbishop), Francesco Socinus D'Attino (Solicitor to the Prince), Michele Gualdi (Solicitor to the Count), Giuseppe Pavoni (Archbishop), Francesco Socinus (Prof. Torricelli), Sheik Mahomet (Bedouin Chief), James Abbé (Lt. Rossini), Duncan Mansfield (Commander Donato), Thelma Colman (Extra).

Release dates and timings: New York at the 44th Street Theater as an Inspiration Picture, September 5. Variety timing: 161 minutes. National release as a Metro Picture,

February 18, 1924. 110½ minutes.

Gish states a premiere timing of 160 minutes in B3. Second timing from tape of bootleg print.

Synopsis: Angela Chiaromonte, an aristocratic Italian, is cheated out of her half of her late father's estate by her evil sister, Marchesa de Mola. She also loses her soldier fiance, Giovanni Severi, when he is captured by Arabs in a desert attack during an engineering expedition. Believing him dead, Angela becomes a nun, taking her final vows just before Giovanni escapes from the Arabs (after being held prisoner for two years), and returns to Italy. After running into him at the convent, she refuses to see him, so he abducts her in hope of persuading her to petition the Pope for a release from her vows. She refuses. Just when he gives up hope of getting her back, Vesuvius erupts and the sky opens up with a powerful storm. Giovanni then drowns while trying to save people from the ensuing flood. His death moves Angela to dedicate her life as a nun to his memory.

Reviews: Harriette Underhill, *New York Tribune*, 9-6-23: "Unless we are mistaken, we heard that this was his first appearance on the screen or his first lead...and if this is true, we advise him not to do any more pictures. He can never be any better than he is now, for we consider him the perfect leading man, and he might get worse. He puts a tenderness and a sincerity in his love scenes that rob them of all mawkishness."

Variety, 9-13-23: "The heroic figure is played by Ronald Colman, a most convincing characterization of the dashing Italian army officer. He is a comer for the screen."

Motion Picture Classic, December 1923: "A newcomer is Ronald Colman, who plays the broken-hearted lover, and he gives a performance of quiet force and dignity. He never seems to be acting, which makes his expressions all the more natural and genuine."

Edwin Schallert, *Los Angeles Times*, 2-19-24: "The supporting cast contains many names, but none that will shine any brighter than Ronald Colman. There is a Latin fire in his playing, but it is splendidly tempered."

Commentary: Colman electrified audiences with his newly acquired screen presence and naturalness and the personal qualities all the critics observed. (However, King had to get him drunk to do his impassioned confrontation scene with Gish.) The screen lit up when Ronald Colman walked into the frame in *The White Sister*, making women the world over fall madly in love with him and becoming a hero to men for his courtliness, conviction and fortitude.

The excellence of his performance is powered by the chemistry of his romance with Gish, magically conveyed in one glowing image in the first reel. As they kiss, she swoons, as though melting into him. Though the script sets up Angela as a sexually unobtainable saint through a madonna-like portrait of her by a worshipful artist, she is clearly a woman with normal desires. Yet, from that kissing scene on, events are contrived to rob her of her lover in exchange for a life of devotion to the church.

This exchange sets up the film's central emotional conflict when she runs into Giovanni in the church. She reacts with horror upon discovering he is alive because she now has to choose between him and her vows. Since their love was foreshadowed to be doomed by the portrait in the first reel, we know she won't break her vows, and yet the basis for those vows was her presumption of his death. Even worse, Giovanni has to die for the "sin" of trying to get Angela to leave the church for him. A death that made it easy for the writers since it avoided a realistic resolution, but which is a dramatic dodge all the same, letting Angela and the church off the hook. Several critics made this very complaint.

In a 1973 photo book (B41), Gish explained the decision to change the happy ending of the original novel: "Our story had, I thought, an impossible situation for a successful film...You can't care about a character you see taking solemn vows before God at eight o'clock and then by nine o'clock changing her mind. We decided we would have to kill one of them. Since the nun's life was secure, we killed Ronnie."

That is rationalizing a bogus ending. The seeming reverence for church dogma over reality the movie conveys is what earned it the Vatican's enthusiastic endorsement. An endorsement which was probably of little or no consequence to moviegoers. They lined up by the millions to see a beautifully made tragic love story that gave them a handsome new matinee idol named Ronald Colman. *The White Sister* was *the* big romantic hit of the 1923-24 season, proving once again, as DeMille also showed that season with *The Ten Commandments*, that religion is always big box office with a compelling love story and charismatic leads.

The White Sister was #12 on the New York Times 15 Best list for 1923. It was re-released in 1928, by which time Colman was internationally famous so that it was profitable for MGM to reacquaint his public with the movie that made him a star in the first place. A 1915 version starred Viola Allen and Richard Travers. It was remade by MGM in 1933, starring Clark Gable and Helen Hayes.

Theatrical Source: Turner Entertainment.

Print Source for this book: 16mm transfer to videotape.

F11 THE ETERNAL CITY Samuel Goldwyn for First National, 1924. See page 116 of B22.

Producer: Samuel Goldwyn. Director: George Fitzmaurice. Screenplay: Ouida Bergere, from the 1901 novel and 1903 play by Hall Caine. Photographer: Arthur Miller. No other production credits are available.

Cast: Barbara La Marr (Donna Roma Valonna), Bert Lytell (David Rossi), Lionel Barrymore (Baron Bonelli), Richard Bennett (Beuno Rocco), Montagu Love (Charles Minghelli, Leader of the Reds), Betty Bronson, Joan Bennett (Pages), **Ronald Colman** (uncredited bit part), Benito Mussolini and King Victor Emmanuel (in newsreel shots).

Release dates and timings: New York at the Strand, January 20. Los Angeles at the Million Dollar, January 28. Length: 7,800 feet (86 minutes, 40 seconds.) Variety timing: 81 minutes. NE.

Synopsis: Childhood sweethearts Donna Roma Valonna and David Rossi are separated when David goes off to war. Believing him killed in battle, Roma becomes a renowned sculptress who is patronized by Baron Bonelli, secret leader of the Bolsheviks. When David returns after WWI ends, he joins Mussolini's Fascist movement, leading the Blackshirts against the Reds. Running into an astonished Roma, he denounces her for being Bonelli's mistress, kills Bonelli in a duel, learns Roma was not his mistress, and they are happily reunited.

Notes: Colman played an extra part as a soldier in crowd scenes before returning to New York after filming *The White Sister*. It was found money and gave him his first contact with the Goldwyn company and Fitzmaurice, who would later direct him in eight movies. Pauline Frederick played Roma in a 1915 film version.

F12 $20 A WEEK Selznick for Distinctive Pictures, 1924, Tinted.

Producer: Lewis J. Selznick. Director: Harmon F. Weight. Screenplay: Forrest Halsey, from the short story "The Adopted Father" by Edgar Franklin. Photographer: Harry A. Fischbeck. Art Director: Clark Robinson.

Cast: George Arliss (John Reeves), Taylor Holmes (William Hart), Edith Roberts (Muriel Hart), Walter Howe (Henry Sloane), Redfield Clarke (George Blair), *Ronald Colman* (Chester Reeves), Ivan Simpson (James Pettison), Joseph Donohue (Little Arthur),

William Sellery (Clancy, Restaurant Keeper), George Henry (Hart's Butler).

Release date and timings: New York at the Strand, June 8. No evidence of Los Angeles screenings. 5,990 feet (66 minutes.) Variety timing: 68 minutes. Preservation print runs 63 minutes, 38 seconds due to decomposition.

Synopsis: Spoiled Chester Reeves makes a bet with his millionaire father, John, that the old man cannot live on $20 a week. John accepts the challenge by getting a job at a steel plant. Meanwhile, Chester marries Muriel Hart, daughter of the plant's owner. In a twist of fate, John saves the plant from financial ruin by uncovering an in-house embezzler, exposing him at a board of directors meeting. He is then made a partner in the plant and reunited with his family.

Review: Harriette Underhill, *New York Herald Tribune*, 6-10-24: "Mr. Coleman (*sic*)...is quiet and attractive."

Variety, 6-11-24: "The unimportant role of the hero is well handled by Ronald Coleman (sic)."

Commentary: This is Arliss's show all the way, commanding the screen with his quietly thoughtful presence. In fact, one can see that Colman picked up a lot of his own understated technique from studying Arliss. Which is why he leaped at the chance to make the movie; to work again with a master he had idolized since his brief stint with Arliss in *The Green Goddess*, S18.

Several critics dismissed *$20* as a lesser Arliss vehicle because he wasn't playing a cunning character from one of his stage hits, yet it turns out to be an enjoyably well-crafted example of a vanished genre, dramatizing the romance of capitalism as opposed to its corruptive power. Arliss portrays Reeves as a charmingly wise and level-headed force for capitalistic integrity, a model of business sagacity and personal warmth.

Arliss remade *$20 a Week* in 1933 as *The Working Man*.

Archival Source: LC. Tinted nitrate print less reel two due to decomposition, preservation dupe negative and 35mm safety print.

F13 TARNISH Samuel Goldwyn for First National, 1924.

Producer: Samuel Goldwyn. Director: George Fitzmaurice. Screenplay: Frances Marion, from the play by Gilbert Emery. Photographers: William Tuers, Arthur Miller. Art Director: Ben Carré. Film Editor: Stuart Heisler.

Cast: May McAvoy (Letitia Tevis), Ronald Colman (Emmett Carr), Marie Prevost (Nettie Dark), Albert Gran (Adolf Tevis), Mrs. Russ Whytall (Josephine Tevis), Priscilla Bonner (Aggie), Harry Myers (Barber), Kay Deslys (Mrs. Stutts), Lydia Yeamans (Mrs. Healy), William Boyd (Bill), Snitz Edwards (Mr. Stutts), Norman Kerry (John Graves.)

Release dates and timing: New York at the Strand, October 12. Los Angeles at the Rialto, November 21. 6,831 feet (76 minutes). Variety timing: 73 minutes. NE.

Synopsis: Good-hearted, hard-working stenographer Letitia Tevis is in love with her boss, Emmett Carr, until she learns that he and her profligate father, Adolf, have both had affairs with gold-digging manicurist Nettie Dark. Despite this sexual "tarnish" on Emmett's past, she loves him enough to forgive him.

Reviews: Edwin Schallert, *Los Angeles Times*, 8-27-24: "(The director and screenwriter) have given the screen a work of quality, and one that should be popular because of its extremely direct and intimate appeal...Ronald Colman is the young business man who feels the taint of 'tarnish,' and he has made sentiment manifest in his portrayal with dignity."

Variety, 10-15-24: "Ronald Colman, as Emmett Carr, is the best thing in the film...The direction is fair enough, but the terrific punch expected when Nettie and Tishy meet (and on the stage it was a smash) is absent. In fact, what should have been an inspired production seems strangely uninspired and workmanlike."

Notes: The first of three pictures for Goldwyn on a good girl/bad girl or madonna/whore theme. Colman's critically acclaimed performance and the profit *Tarnish* accrued from it convinced Goldwyn he had found his ideal leading man, so he signed Colman to a non-exclusive four-year contract; meaning that other producers could borrow the actor for a handsome loan-out fee to Goldwyn.

F14 HER NIGHT OF ROMANCE Constance Talmadge for First National, 1924.

Producer: Joseph M. Schenck. Director: Sidney Franklin. Original Screenplay: Hans Kräly. Photographers: Ray Binger, Victor Milner. Film Editor: Hal Kern.

Cast: Constance Talmadge (Dorothy Adams), Ronald Colman (Lord Paul Menford), Jean Hersholt (Joe Diamond), Albert Gran (Samuel C. Adams, Dorothy's father), Robert Rendel (Prince George), Sidney Bracey (Butler), Joseph Dowling (Professor Gregg), Templar Saxe (Dr. Wellington), Eric Mayne (Dr. Scott), Emily Fitzroy (Nurse), Clara Bracey (Housekeeper), James Barrows (Old Butler), Claire De Lorez (Paul's Artist Friend).

Release dates and timing: Los Angeles at Loew's State, October 25, 1924. New York at the Capitol, January 11, 1925. 7,211 feet (80 minutes). My timing: 78 minutes.

Synopsis: While posing as a homely spinster to deter fortune hunters, American heiress Dorothy Adams (Talmadge) meets a charming young English lord named Paul Menford (Colman). However, she doesn't know he is a lord or that he is bankrupt and living on borrowed money. To raise more money, Menford sells her father his family's mansion without them knowing it's his. He then pretends to be a doctor to cure Dorothy's lethargy as a means to establish a friendship.

When Paul stays the night at his former home after a drunken night on the town, he and Dorothy are forced to become pretend newlyweds lest anyone think they had a night of unmarried sex. In this manner, they fall in love and she learns who he really is. A real wedding of the two is briefly endangered by Dorothy's mistaken impression that Paul had conspired with his real estate agent, Joe Diamond, to get her to marry Paul so the two could divide her estate. After a series of farcical machinations to convince her of his love, Paul and Dorothy kiss and make up.

Reviews: Grace Kingsley, *Los Angeles Times*, 10-27-24: "Constance and Ronald Colman (are) a most intriguing pair of lovers...Their teamwork is great...(Colman) remains a thoroughly accomplished and magnetic actor."

Harriette Underhill, *New York Herald Tribune*, 1-12-25: "Miss Talmadge and that attractive Ronald Colman are quite wasted on such drivel."

Mordaunt Hall, *New York Times*, 1-13-25: "Ronald Colman...gives an easy and natural performance as a young English lord."

Commentary: In his first co-starring role as a light leading man, Colman is charmingly polished, borrowing from the dapper style of Max Linder and the comic repertoire of Charlie Chaplin. The latter influence is evident in a scene where he drunkenly tries to hang his top hat on a chandelier shadow, recalling Chaplin's *One A.M.* His romantic chemistry with Talmadge is a delight, with business and close-ups that invite the audience to share their feelings and root for a happy ending to the misunderstandings driving the plot. The funniest scene by far is when Colman as the pretend doctor gingerly applies a stethoscope to Talmadge's bosom, afraid of seeming forward.

The one, big plot snag is that in the sixth reel, when Talmadge confronts Colman over his seeming pact with Hersholt, the script won't let Colman explain, to keep the story going for two more reels. Audiences overlooked this blatant contrivance, but it *is* bothersome all the same.

After a series of stolid leading men, like Tulio Carminati, who made her movies less appealing, Colman's ingratiating presence and humorous charm made Talmadge an audience favorite once more, while adding to Colman's reputation. *Her Night of Romance's* commercial success prompted Schenck to reteam the stars the following year in *Her Sister From Paris.* Colman and Schenck also became good personal friends.

Archival Source: LC: 35mm nitrate and preservation negatives and 35mm print.

F15 ROMOLA Inspiration Pictures for Metro-Goldwyn Pictures, 1924. Tinted.

Producer/Director: Henry King. Screenplay: Will M. Ritchey from the novel by George Eliot. Photographers: Roy Overbaugh, William Schurr, assisted by Ferdinand Risi. Art director: Robert M. Haas. Assistant director: Joseph C. Boyle. Technical advisor: Dr. Guido Biagi. Shipbuilder: Tito Neri. Titles: Jules Furthman, Don Bartlett. Film editor: Duncan Mansfield. Lab work: Gustav Dietz. Musical score and theme: Louis H. Gottschalk. Shot on location in Italy.

Cast: Lillian Gish (Romola Bardi), Dorothy Gish (Tessa), William H. Powell (Tito Melema aka Naldo), Ronald Colman (Carlo Buccellini), Charles Lane (Baldasarre Calvo), Herbert Grimwood (Father Girolamo Savonarola), Bonaventure Ibanez (Bardo Bardi), Frank Puglia (Adolfo Spini), Amelia Summerville (Brigida), Tina Ceccaccci Renaldi (Monna Ghita), Edulilo Mucci (Nello), Angelo Scatigna (Bratti), Alfredo Bertone (Piero de Medici), Ugo Uccellini (Bishop of Nemours), Alfredo Martinelli (Tournabuoni), Gino Boursi (Capt. of the Barque), Pietro Nistri (Pirate Captain), Alfredo Fossi (Pirate Galley Master), Attilio Diodati (Tomaso), Pietro Betti (Fra Sylvestro), Ferdinando Chianese (Archbishop), Toto Lo Bue (Fra Benaducci), Carlo Duse (Bargello), Guiseppe Zocchi (Executioner), Eugenio Mattioli, Guiseppe Becattini (Papal Legates), Rinaldo Rinaldi, Enrico Monti, Baron Guiseppe Winspere, Francesco Ciancamerla, Baron Alfredo Del Judici, Baron Serrge Kopfe, Gastone Barnardi, Giovanni Salvini (Council of Eight), Countess Tolombi, Marchese Imperiale, Princess Isabella Romanoff, Countess Tambourini, Princess Bianca Rafaello, Marchese Fabrizio, Prince Alexander Talone, Baron Alfredo Del Judici, Baron Guiseppe Winspere (Banquet Members).

Release dates and timings: New York at the George M. Cohan, December 1. Los Angeles at Grauman's Egyptian, December 6. 12,974 feet (144 minutes at 20 fps). Cut to 11 reels or 129 minutes at 20 fps for general release in February 1925. In the 1930s, cut to 8,685 feet or 96½ minutes for general release.

Synopsis: In 1492 Florence, Italy, profligate ruler Piero de Medici flees the city, leaving it to mob rule angrily inspired by the reform gospel of the evangelist Savonarola. At just this moment, a shipwrecked Greek named Tito Melema arrives. Taking advantage of a leaderless government and ingratiating himself with blind scholar Bardo Bardi, Tito schemes his way up the Italian political ladder. He does this with the help of another schemer, Adolfo Spini, and by virtue of a ring from the sacred college of Pythagoras given him by his foster father, Baldasarre Calvo, to ransom Calvo from a pirate slave camp. Instead, Tito uses the ring to pass himself as a scholarly genius.

In quick order, Tito has a bastard child by a peasant girl named Tessa, marries socially influential Romola Bardi (who is secretly loved by artist Carlo Buccellini) after promising to finish her now late father's work, and becomes Chief Magistrate. When Calvo suddenly shows up at Tito and Romola's wedding, Tito at first brushes him off as a madman. Calvo tells his tale to Carlo, who then brings Calvo to a banquet in Tito's honor, where Calvo denounces him, then is jailed. Tito then becomes head of the Council of Eight so he can decree a death penalty for political dissenters, especially Savonarola. He also sells the Bardi library, revealing his treachery to Romola. When Tito's death decree backfires on him so that he too is accused of treason, he has to flee an angry mob. In the end, the sweetly innocent Tessa drowns while fleeing the mob with Tito, Calvo drowns Tito, Savonarola is burned at the stake, and Carlo is reunited with Romola, with who m he adopts Tessa's baby.

Review: Harriette Underhill, *New York Herald Tribune*, 12-8-24: "Ronald Colman, who plays the hero, has no chance at all to show what he can do as a lover."

Commentary: King's budget for *Romola* was $2 million, a tremendous sum for the early 1920s, even for an historical epic. However, when King and his company arrived in Florence, they found the city to be so modern that King was forced to reconstruct 15th century Florence on a 17-acre set several miles outside the city. In the end, he became obsessed with art direction at the expense of telling a compelling story.

Indeed, most critics were captivated by *Romola's* lavish production values while complaining about its deliberate or static pacing and choppy editing. Though the movie wasn't as big a hit as King's previous movie, *The White Sister*, enough people flocked to see it that several big cities played it first run for two months, followed by a good second run.

Seen today in the 129-minute version with tinting restored, *Romola* is mainly a static bore. Whereas Lillian Gish recut *The White Sister* to remove extraneous convent scenes to give the story swifter pacing, King adhered to a procession of lingering tableaux in *Romola*, making the viewer want to shout, "Get a move on." Although the movie is ostensibly about its title character, the story is really about Tito's rise to power, a rise that is constantly talked about but never seen. Instead, the script dwells on his treacherous marriage to Romola, while keeping Tessa as his simple-minded mistress. Both the cut and restored versions give the impression that Tito rises to God-like power within two years when the story spans seven years. The restored half-hour includes two scenes of Colman sardonically confronting Powell about not being what he claims, and a portion of the banquet sequence where Lillian Gish demands that Charles Lane prove his allegations by finding the passage in Homer's Odyssey quoted on Tito's ring.

Small though it was, Colman took the part for the chance to work with King and Gish again. By the time the picture was released, he was busy in Hollywood making a string of movies for Goldwyn and Schenck. His momentary highlight is chastising a mob for trampling Romola for defending Savonarola.

Archival Sources: UCLA. 16mm prints reserved for preservation in the Stanford Theatre Foundation Collection, originally owned by John Hampton. These prints and others were used for a 35mm blow-up restoration supervised by Robert Gitt, with the assistance of Rosa Castro and Eric Aijala, and financed by David and Lucille Packard.

MOMA: One 16mm reel only.

F16 A THIEF IN PARADISE George Fitzmaurice for Samuel Goldwyn. Released by First National, 1925.

Producer: Samuel Goldwyn. Director: George Fitzmaurice. Screenplay: Frances Marion, from the novel "The Worldlings" by Leonard Merrick. Photographer: Arthur Miller, ASC. Art Director: Ben Carré. Film Editor: Stuart Heisler.

Cast: Doris Kenyon (Helen Saville), Ronald Colman (Maurice Blake), Aileen Pringle (Rosa Carmino), Claude Gillingwater (Noel Jardine), Alec B. Francis (Bishop Saville), John Patrick (Ned Whalen), Charles Yourée (Philip Jardine), Etta Lee (Rosa's Maid), Lon Poff (Jardine's Secretary).

Release dates and timing: Los Angeles at the Alhambra, January 24. New York at the Strand, January 25. 7,355 feet (81 minutes, 45 seconds). Variety timing: 71 minutes. NE, except for copies of the trailer owned by several collectors.

Synopsis: When millionaire's son Philip Jardine drowns in an undersea struggle over a pearl with derelict beachcomber Maurice Blake, Blake's scheming lady friend, Rosa, talks him into posing as Jardine to collect an inheritance from Jardine's estranged family in San Francisco. The plan goes awry when Blake falls for Helen Saville, the daughter of the Jardine's neighbor; his conscience starts nagging him. Then Rosa shows up to ensure the scheme works out and she doesn't lose Blake. In the end Blake confesses, Helen decides she loves him after all and the story ends happily.

Reviews: Harriette Underhill, *New York Herald Tribune*, 1-27-25: "It also has the most provocative love scene we have ever seen on the screen. So palpitatingly intimate was it that we were covered with confusion and looked away. Other people laughed. They had to do something!"

Florence Lawrence, *Los Angeles Examiner*, 1-26-25: "The shadings of emotion, the assumption of a varied and brilliant range of characterizations and sincerity and conviction in every move place Colman high in the list of dramatic figures in the cinema world."

Guy Price, *Los Angeles Evening Herald*, 1-26-25: "The entire cast does well, Ronald Colman especially, as the thief who steals the old father's love, and the girl's."

F17 SCREEN SNAPSHOTS Columbia, 1925. See F18.

Production credits unavailable. Released in May(?) Timing: 9 minutes, 42 seconds. Colman segment (top of reel): 1 minute, 40 seconds. Grapevine Video from original 35mm nitrate print. Missing opening title and credits, if any.

One of a weekly newsreel series showing movie stars at play or doing promotional gags or making their movies, etc. The series ran from 1920 to 1958. This may have been the first featuring Colman. I have been able to track down only two other reels in this series with him, for which see F46 and F60.

Segment: Blanche Sweet has trouble getting her new French roadster moving, so Ronald Colman and director George Fitzmaurice come by to see if they can get it moving. Stalling the engine is a poster that is unreadable without freeze-framing shots of the poster on a big TV screen. It looks to be an ad for a charity ball.

Silent stars in other segments include Anna May Wong, Anna Q. Nilsson and Mary Philbin.

F18 HIS SUPREME MOMENT Samuel Goldwyn for First National, 1925. Part Two-strip Technicolor. See F17.

Producer: Samuel Goldwyn. Director: George Fitzmaurice. Screenplay: Frances Marion, from the novel "World Without End" by May Edginton. Photographer: Arthur Miller. Art director: Ben Carré. Film Editor: Stuart Heisler.

Cast: Blanche Sweet (Carla King), Ronald Colman (John Douglas), Kathleen Myers (Sara Deeping), Belle Bennett (Carla Light), Cyril Chadwick (Harry Avon), Ned Sparks (Adrian), Nick de Ruiz (Mueva), Anna May Wong (Harem Girl in play), Kalla Pasha (Pasha in play), Jane Winton.

Release dates and timing: New York at the Strand, April 12. Los Angeles at Loew's State, June 13. 6,565 feet (73 minutes). Variety timing: 75 minutes. NE.

Synopsis: Wealthy socialite Sara Deeping and stage star Carla King vie for the love of mining engineer John Douglas. Deeping schemes to win Douglas's love by having a friend finance his next venture in South America, believing that without Carla around, she will succeed. She doesn't reckon with Carla spending a platonic year with John at the mine as his sister to test their love. On the other hand, Carla's plan doesn't anticipate her loneliness at the mine and John's troubles with his men. When Carla is stricken with a fever after rescuing

John from a mine fire, Sara shows up to cause more trouble between them. Back in New York, Carla's mother sends for John on the pretext that Carla is deathly ill. She tells him that Carla is marrying a millionaire, who will back John financially. John is angry at first but when Carla confesses her love for him, they plan to go back to the mine to make it a success, this time as husband and wife.

Reviews: Mordaunt Hall, *New York Times*, 4-13-25: "He is careful in his make-up and looks every inch a man, rugged and good-looking and thoroughly at his ease."

Harriette Underhill, *New York Herald Tribune*, 4-13-25: "Blanche Sweet and Ronald Colman played with a simplicity and sincerity worthy of a better cause."

Variety, 4-15-25: "It is safe to predict that wherever the picture is shown, the women are going to go wild over the love making Ronald Colman does on the screen. He is out for the matinee idol honors and bids fair to receive them."

Whitney Williams, *Los Angeles Times*, 6-14-25: "His work shines bright and clear, enabling him to give the impression of being absolute master of every situation."

Guy Price, *Los Angeles Evening Herald*, 6-15-25: "...it is done in such a way that one forgets the time-old plot and revels in the very beauty of the production, the adroitness which Colman, the lover, employs in the numerous love scenes, and the radiance of Blanche Sweet, who seems to remain ever charmingly young and fresh."

Notes: The third and last of the Goldwyn good girl/bad girl cycle, it got a lot of critical applause for its Technicolor cabaret scenes and steamy love scenes. Depending on which reviews you read, these love scenes were either very proper or so sultry the critic wondered how they got past the censors. Decades later, Sweet told Goldwyn biographer A. Scott Berg that Colman took swigs of liquor before doing their love scenes, a habit begun on *The White Sister*.

F19 THE SPORTING VENUS Metro-Goldwyn-Mayer, 1925.

Producer/Director: Marshall Neilan. Screenplay: Thomas J. Geraghty, from the short story by Gerald Beaumont. Photographer: David Kesson. Art Director: Cedric Gibbons. Assistant Director: Thomas Held. Wardrobe: Ethel P. Chaffin.

Filmed in England, France, Scotland, Spain and America.

Cast: Blanche Sweet (Lady Gwendolyn Grayle), Ronald Colman (Donald MacAllan), Lew Cody (Prince Carlo Marno), Josephine Crowell (Countess Van Alstyne), Edward Martindel (Sir Alfred Grayle), Kate Price (Housekeeper), Hank Mann (Marno's Valet), Arthur Hoyt (Detective), George Fawcett (Sandy MacAllan).

Release dates and timings: New York at the Capitol, May 10. Los Angeles at Loew's State, June 27. 5,938 feet (66 minutes). My timing: 65 minutes.

Synopsis: Because Lady Gwen was not born a boy and her mother died after giving birth, Sir Alfred, the last of his line, leaves her to the care of nurses and governesses until she grows up. When she reaches 18, a headstrong tomboy horseman, she falls for commoner medical student Donald McAllan. They are parted when he goes to serve in WWI. When he returns on leave two years later, fortune hunter Prince Carlo Marno deceives him into believing that Gwen has left him for Marno. Meeting two weeks later at a military ball, Donald doesn't tell her what Marno has said, and she doesn't press him on why he's been avoiding her since his return.

Gwen then becomes Marno's fiancée on the rebound from Donald, attaining a debauched reputation as the Sporting Venus. When she discovers after two years of being thus engaged that Marno is a debt-ridden phony, she leaves him to recover her health on the coast of France before returning to Scotland. Now a wealthy surgeon and the owner of Crayle castle, Donald rescues her from suicide during a stormy night. They end up getting married on the same day Marno is forced by his creditors to marry an ugly rich woman.

Reviews: Harriette Underhill, *New York Herald Tribune*, 5-12-25: "Ronald Colman is the hero, and he is so splendid and human and likable!"

Mordaunt Hall, *New York Times*, 5-11-25: "Mr. Colman is quite effective in many of the scenes, but his performance is not as sincere and thorough as the one he gave in 'His Supreme Moment'."

Sisk, *Variety*, 5-13-25: "The flaw is that Marno, obviously a roué, should have been accepted by Lady Gwen without knowing him, and that Donald should have let Gwen go without questioning her on the night of their meeting...The cast is perfect with Miss Sweet and Colman taking the laurels."

Commentary: An entertaining movie despite its absurd second half. It was made because Neilan was a hot director. He was also Sweet's husband, so they also got a European trip at MGM's expense. The company traveled to foreign locales to make a minor soap opera with offbeat comic touches.

Its importance today is the powerful romantic chemistry between Colman and Sweet, making you wonder why they weren't teamed for more movies despite the commercial failure of this one. Compared physically, Sweet and Vilma Banky, Colman's partner in five films, have much in common. Both are beautiful blondes with similarly perfect and sensual star quality faces the camera adores. They also have humor, vulnerability and radiant elan, beautifully playing off of Colman's humor, vulnerability and reserved charm.

One of the most affecting scenes in *Venus* exemplifies this chemistry. Leaving for a WWI battlefront, Colman's face lights with the excitement of Sweet's love for him (she has come 100 miles to say goodbye) while Sweet smiles as she tearfully shakes with fear that her boyfriend may be killed. You feel her agony.

The badly contrived romantic misunderstanding that drives the story's second half is probably what killed the movie commercially since it played only one week in cities like Los Angeles and New York. The commercial heat engendered by *His Supreme Moment* was cooled, but doubtless the public would have come to see Colman and Sweet in another, better vehicle.

Theatrical Source: Turner Entertainment.

F20 HER SISTER FROM PARIS Schenck for First National, 1925. Tinted.

Producer: Joseph M. Schenck. Director: Sidney Franklin. Screenplay: Hans Kräly, from the play by Ludwig Fulda. Photographer: Arthur Edeson. Art Director: William Cameron Menzies. Wardrobe: Adrian. Assistant Director: Scott R. Beal. Score includes Strauss's "The Blue Danube" for a dance number in a flashback sequence.

Cast: Constance Talmadge (Helen Weyringer alias Lola La Perry), Ronald Colman (Joseph Weyringer), George K. Arthur (Robert Well), Margaret Mann (Bertha), Gertrude Claire (Anna, Housekeeper), Mario Carillo (The King).

Release dates and timing: New York at the Alhambra, August 23. Los Angeles at the Boulevard, October 3. 7,255 feet (80 minutes, 40 seconds). Variety timing: 74 minutes.

Synopsis: The neglected mousy wife of a Viennese author determines to put the sparkle back in their marriage by seducing him as her own sexy twin sister.

Reviews: Harriette Underhill, *New York Herald Tribune*, 8-25-25: "Ronald Colman is most attractive as the husband of the other twin."

Sumner Smith, *Motion Picture World*, 9-17-25: "The husband, played by Colman, is very much the butt of the comedy and he provides a fine foil to Constance's genius."

Skig, *Variety*, 8-26-25: "Ronald Colman...gives an excellent performance...(He) won consistent laughs for himself with pantomiming."

Notes: After being considered lost for more than 50 years, *Her Sister From Paris* was recovered and preserved by LC in 1987. The revival premiere was at Cinefest in Syracuse on March 6, 1993. Film historian Bill Everson says that he and the audience found it a very funny movie. "Talmadge and Colman sparked each other in a way that Talmadge's other leading men in her other comedies at the time had not. Colman clearly was having a good time with his light comedy role. Indeed, he is much more animated than in several of his other silents. There are lapses in logic and plausibility, but it's a delightfully entertaining film, so that none of that matters in the end".

Archival Source: LC. 35mm dupe negative and safety preservation print.

Remade in 1941 with Greta Garbo as *Two-Faced Woman*.

F21 THE DARK ANGEL Samuel Goldwyn for First National, 1925.

Producer: Samuel Goldwyn. Director: George Fitzmaurice. Screenplay: Frances Marion, from the play by H.B. Trevelyan. Photographer: George S. Barnes, ASC. Art Director: Ben Carré. Film Editor: Stuart Heisler.

Cast: Ronald Colman (Alan Trent), Vilma Banky (Kitty Vane), Wyndham Standing (Captain Gerald Shannon), Frank Elliott (Lord Beaumont), Charles Lane (Sir Hubert Vane), Helen Jerome Eddy (Miss Bottles), Florence Turner (Roma), Billy Butts (Boy).

Release dates and timing: Los Angeles at Loew's State, September 25. San Francisco at the Warfield, October 3. New York at the Strand, October 11. 7,311 feet (81 minutes). Variety timing: 75 minutes. NE.

Colman and Banky showed for the Los Angeles premiere, Banky went solo to the San Francisco opening, and Colman was alone at the New York premiere.

Synopsis: Alan Trent goes to war after spending an unmarried night of love with his fiancée, Kitty Vane. He is then blinded in battle and discharged. However, he doesn't want Kitty to know he's still alive for fear she would marry him out of pity, so he disappears to the North of England where he makes a career writing children's books. Believing him dead, Kitty becomes engaged to Gerald Shannon. When she learns Alan is alive and where on the eve of her wedding, she goes to him at once. He pretends he can still see, putting off her romantic advances, pretending he doesn't love her anymore. When he gives himself away, she professes her love for him despite his blindness, so they become engaged anew.

Reviews: Florence Lawrence, *Los Angeles Examiner*, 9-28-25: "Ronald Colman...is denied opportunity for that fervid love-making which has put him in top row of matinée screen idols, but his handling of the difficult role is interesting and impressive, and he makes his naturally reserved style count in every second of his work for the camera."

San Francisco Chronicle, 10-5-25: "Trent...is the finest thing he has done since 'The White Sister,' and is nearly as good as his work in that beautiful film, and because of his excellence in the part, revives an interest in him that was slowly dying like a fire that lacks fuel. He looks handsome as a slender, starved soldier and plays his blind scenes with wonderful restraint and naturalness."

Mordaunt Hall, *New York Times*, 10-12-25: "Ronald Colman, who acts Trent, is most sympathetic and capable. A strong man might well be excused for weeping at some of the scenes in this delightful romance, especially when Trent decides to end it all and changes his mind through the cheerful note of a youngster's voice."

Richard Watts Jr., *New York Herald Tribune*, 10-12-25: "Ronald Colman plays the blinded hero with suavity and skill, and in that splendid scene at the close of the picture, he rises to the opportunity splendidly."

Note: *The Dark Angel* was one of the biggest commercial and artistic successes of 1925, creating a new and internationally famous romantic team, yet neither Goldwyn nor any archive have even one print. A collector somewhere may. It was #6 on the New York Times 10 Best list for 1925.

Fredric March (in the Colman role), Merle Oberon and Herbert Marshall starred in the 1935 Goldwyn remake.

F22 STELLA DALLAS Samuel Goldwyn for United Artists, 1925.

Producer: Samuel Goldwyn. Director: Henry King. Screenplay: Frances Marion from the novel by Olive Higgins Prouty. Director of Photography: Arthur Edeson, ASC. Art Director: Arthur Stibolt. Costumes: Sophie Wachner. Film Editor: Stuart Heisler.

Cast: Ronald Colman (Stephen Dallas), Belle Bennett (Stella Dallas), Alice Joyce (Helen Dane), Lois Moran (Laurel Dallas), Jean Hersholt (Ed Munn), Douglas Fairbanks, Jr. (Richard Grosvenor), Charles Lane (Stephen Dallas, Sr.), Vera Lewis (Matilda Philiburn), Beatrix Pryor (Mrs. Grosvenor), Maurice Murphy, Newton Hall, Jack Murphy (Morrison Children), Robert Gillette, Winston Miller, Charles Hatten (Morrison Children, Ten Years Later).

Release dates and timing: New York at the Apollo, November 16. Los Angeles at the Forum, April 2, 1926. 10,237 feet (113 minutes). MOMA archival print runs 107 minutes, 45 seconds, which appears to be the complete movie.

Synopsis: The suicide of his embezzler father causes Stephen Dallas to break his engagement to socialite Helen Dane and leave town in disgrace for a job in the legal department of a cotton mill. Out of loneliness, he marries a young lower class woman named Stella Martin, with whom he has a daughter named Laurel. When Stephen is relocated to the mill's New York office, Stella refuses to leave her friends or to part with Laurel. For the next 15 years, Laurel is raised by Stella, who is vulgar and uncouth and wears clothes that are 30 years out of fashion, yet who is a warm and good-hearted mother for all that.

Easing her loneliness without Stephen, Stella becomes friends with uncouth kindred spirit Ed Munn, an alcoholic horse trainer whose obnoxiously vulgar manner and sense of humor repel Laurel and shock Stephen on one of his rare visits to Stella. The final humiliation for Laurel comes when Stella makes a spectacle of herself at a posh country club, after which both women overhear the cruel remarks of two of the country club women about Stella on the train ride home.

Stella then visits the widowed Helen Dane Morrison, agreeing to let Stephen divorce her if he and the new Mrs. Dallas will make a better home life for Laurel. When Laurel learns what her mother has done, she goes back to Stella, who then shocks Laurel back into Stephen's and Helen's home by pretending to be engaged to loathsome Ed Munn. In the end, Laurel marries country club socialite Richard Grosvenor as Stella watches from outside the Dallas house in the rain.

Review: Gregory Goss, *Los Angeles Examiner*, 4-3-26: "With that rare sensitiveness that has made him one of the screen's most popular players, Ronald Colman endows the role of Stephen Dallas with unusual charm."

Commentary: For all of its reputation as a silent classic, *Stella Dallas* is rarely screened and rarely mentioned when the Barbara Stanwyck remake is discussed. Indeed, when the Bette Midler remake, *Stella* was released in 1989, the Colman version was never even alluded to in the reviews.

For all of its present day popularity, the 1937 version is inferior to the silent original, largely because of casting. Colman, Bennett and Moran have a believability and dimension that Stanwyck, John Boles and Anne Shirley fail to match in the remake. Stanwyck has too much of a pre-image as a brassy lady to be convincing as a vulgarian; Boles plays Stephen as a snobbish stiff, and Shirley lacks Moran's warmly affecting emotional range. In the original, our sympathy for Stephen and excitement over his rare appearances after he leaves Stella stem entirely from Colman's personal warmth and quiet dignity in contrast to the embarrassing vulgarity of Bennett's Stella. He almost makes the viewer forget that Stephen has abandoned his child during her formative years. For all of his professed love for her on her tenth birthday in the form of a gift, why does he stay away for thirteen years, waiting until Laurel is 14 to take her away for a two-week visit to New York? Because he hates being with Stella? That is not a good reason.

This gaping narrative hole aside, *Stella Dallas* is a powerfully affecting movie because Henry King's mature and invisible direction dramatizes unchanging class conflicts and gives us two sympathetic women who could just as easily be living today as in 1925. It's a timeless universal tragedy.

Stella Dallas was #9 on the New York Times 10 Best list for 1925.

Theatrical Source: Samuel Goldwyn Company.

Archival Source: MOMA: 35mm safety projection print and 16mm viewing print.

F23 LADY WINDERMERE'S FAN Warner Bros., 1925. Blue tinted. Film Festival, Grapevine Video, Video Yesteryear.

Producer: Jack L. Warner. Director: Ernst Lubitsch. Screenplay: Julien Josephson, from the play by Oscar Wilde. Photographer: Charles Van Enger, ASC. Assistant Cameraman: Willard Van Enger. Assistant Directors: George Hippard, Ernst Laemmle. Art Director: Harold Grieve. Costumes: Sophie Wachner. Electrical Effects: H.W. Murphy. Art Titles: Victor Vance. Titles: Maude Fulton, Eric Locke.

Cast: Ronald Colman (Lord Darlington), May McAvoy (Lady Margaret Edith Windermere), Bert Lytell (Lord Windermere), Irene Rich (Mrs. Edith Erlynne), Edward Martindel (Lord Augustus Lorton), Carrie Daumery (Duchess of Berwick), Helen Dunbar (Gossipy Duchess Mrs. Cowper-Cowper), Billie Bennett (Gossipy Duchess Lady Plymdale), Larry Steers (Party Guest), Wilson Benge (Butler).

Release dates and timing: New York at the Warner, December 26. Los Angeles at the Forum, January 30, 1926. 7,740 feet (87 minutes). MOMA timing: 81 minutes, 52 seconds. See notes below.

Synopsis: Edith Erlynne blackmails Lord Windermere into paying her money on a regular basis or she will tell his wife that she is her presumed dead mother. Years earlier, she had left her husband for another man and could not return because of the scandal. Hoping to seduce Lady Windermere, caddish Lord Darlington makes her believe Lord Windermere is having an affair with Edith when she is really being romanced by Lord Lorton. After a party at which Edith ingratiates herself with the female social snobs, the two women have a confrontation at Darlington's apartment suite, Edith begging Margaret not to act rashly as she once did. When Margaret accidentally leaves her fan on a couch, discovered by Lorton when Darlington returns with him and some other men, Edith takes the blame to avert scandal for Margaret. When Augustus confronts Edith with the fan incident, she "forgives" him, thereby charming him into resuming his pursuit of her. Margaret never does learn that Edith is her mother.

Reviews: Harriette Underhill, *New York Herald Tribune*, 12-29-25: "It is difficult to conceive of Mr. Colman's being an unsuccessful lover."

Mae Tinée, *Chicago Tribune*, 1-5-26: "As Lord Darlington ...Ronald Colman is a sweet, sweet thing. Naughty, O, yes—but nice—O, Yes!"

Katherine Lipke, *Los Angeles Times*, 12-27-25: "As Lord Darlington, he promises to create a new and interesting place for himself. It is a role filled with subtleties, of thought projected without much, if any, forceful action."

Florence Lawrence, *Los Angeles Examiner*, 2-1-26: "Ronald Colman and Bert Lytell are worldly wise and self-restrained after the manner of men of social position in continental life."

Commentary: For all the visual touches Lubitsch added to compensate for his decision not to use Wilde's epigrams for the intertitles, and for all the lavish production values, this is no more than an above-average drama about high society snobbery and hypocrisy, with an occasional laugh. Its strengths are Colman's low-key presence and bemused humor as a mildly caddish fellow, and Rich's shrewd sophistication. Its weakest link is Lytell's stolid performance. Surprisingly, Colman walks with a lumbering gait in a few scenes, a rare reminder of his war limp.

A British version was made in 1916. Madeleine Carroll and George Sanders starred in a 1949 Technicolor remake called *The Fan*.

Video Source Note: Video Yesteryear's uncut 16mm print plays in slow motion at 16 fps, while Grapevine Video's fair-looking 16mm print runs 65 minutes at sound speed, as do most prints except MOMA's and Yesteryear's.

Theatrical Sources: Turner Entertainment. Fair-looking 16mm Kodascope print.

Archival Sources: GEH. 16mm print.

MOMA: 35mm dupe negative, nitrate and safety preservation prints and 16mm viewing print, all running 81 minutes, 52 seconds, which former curator Eileen Bowser says is complete. MOMA's restoration premiere was held January 17, 1992.

UCLA: 35mm nitrate print of first reel only and wretched-looking 16mm print running 65 minutes.

F24 KIKI First National, 1926.

Producer: Joseph M. Schenck. Director: Clarence Brown. Screenplay: Hans Kräly, from the play by David Belasco as adapted from the French play by André Picard. Photographer: Oliver T. Marsh, ASC.

Cast: Norma Talmadge (Kiki), Ronald Colman (Victor Renal), Gertrude Astor (Paulette), Marc MacDermott (Baron Rapp), George K. Arthur (Adolphe), William Orlamond (Brule), Erwin Connelly (Joly), Frankie Darro (Pierre), Mack Swain (Pastryman).

Release dates and timing: New York at the Capitol, April 4. Los Angeles at the Million Dollar, May 20. 8,299 feet (92 minutes).

Synopsis: A street girl named Kiki rises from newspaper peddler to chorus girl, then steals the affections of the theater manager, Victor Renal, from his sweetheart, Paulette.

Reviews: *Picture Play*, 7-26: "Ronald Colman is unusually good playing opposite Miss Talmadge. Her softer wiles seem to suit him better than the frantic ambitions of Constance Talmadge."

Hollywood Life, 3-26: "Ronald Colman as Renal gives his usual flawless performance."

Guy Price, *Los Angeles Evening Herald*, 5-21-26: "You are impatient with Renal, played by Ronald Colman, for not falling in love with Kiki at their first meeting instead of hesitating through innumerable reels. Colman once again gives an excellent account of himself as Kiki's lover."

Commentary: I've only seen the heavily cut 16mm MOMA print, so I can't offer a thorough assessment. Still, it's easy to see why *Kiki* was *the* comedy sensation of 1926. Audiences thoroughly enjoyed watching Talmadge cut loose with playful mischievousness after years of watching her in heavy dramas. She is clearly having a ball with her part, as is Colman with his. His Renal is a cad who forces himself on Kiki after their first kiss, but who redeems himself at the end with gallantry when he is won over by Kiki.

Even more surprising than the caddishness is a slapstick scene he has with Talmadge. While she is feigning a cataleptic fit, he tries to keep her propped in a standing position as he reaches for the phone. This is the only instance I know where Colman shows a knack for knockabout, making one wish he had done more.

For all the raves and four months of packed houses, this was Talmadge's only comedy. She went right back to drama with *Camille* (1927). Also ironically, this was Colman's last silent comedy. When *The Dark Angel* and *Stella Dallas* became colossal dramatic hits, *Kiki's* success notwithstanding, he was thereafter cast in six successive dramatic leads, starting with *Beau Geste*, his biggest silent success.

Kiki was remade in 1931 with Mary Pickford.

Archival Sources: LC. 35mm nitrate negative, nitrate print, preservation dupe negative, preservation fine grain print, and 35mm safety viewing copy.

MOMA: 35mm safety print, dupe negative and fuzzy-looking 16mm safety print, with Czechoslovakian intertitles, but missing the 40-minute theatrical middle section showing Kiki becoming a chorus girl.

UCLA: 35mm nitrate print of first reel and amber tinted 35mm nitrate print of the trailer. Latter runs 2 minutes, 46 seconds.

F25 BEAU GESTE Herbert Brenon for Paramount, 1926.

Producers: Adolph Zukor and Jesse L. Lasky. Director: Herbert Brenon. Screenplay: Paul Schofield. Adaptation: John Russell, from the novel by Percival Christopher Wren. Photographer: J. Roy Hunt, ASC. Art Director: Julian Boone Fleming. Supervising Film Editor: Julian Johnson. Musical Score: Dr. Hugo Riesenfeld. March theme: "Song of the Legion." Music by Frank Tours, James Bradford and Hans Spialek. Lyrics by Edward Lockton. Associate Producer: William LeBaron. Assistant Director: Ray Lissner. Production Superintendent: Frank Blount.

Cast: Ronald Colman (Michael "Beau" Geste), Neil Hamilton (Digby Geste), Ralph Forbes (John Geste), Norman Trevor (Major Henri de Beaujolais), Noah Beery (Sergeant-Major Lejaune), Alice Joyce (Lady Patricia Brandon), Mary Brian (Isobel Rivers), William Powell (Boldini), Victor McLaglen (Hank), Donald Stuart (Buddy), George Regas (Maris), Bernard Siegel (Schwartz), Paul McAllister (St. Andre, bearded Legionnaire), Redmond Finlay (Cordere), Ram Singh (Prince Ram Singh), Maurice Murphy (Young "Beau"), Philippe De Lacey (Young Digby), Mickey McBan (Young John).

Release dates and timing: New York at the Criterion, August 25. Los Angeles at the Forum, November 23. 10,600 feet (129 minutes at 20 fps). Most prints run 102 minutes, 47 seconds at sound speed. See archival notes below.

Synopsis: The three Geste brothers—Michael (nicknamed Beau), John and Digby—join the French Foreign Legion to save their aunt, Lady Patricia Brandon, from disgrace over the sale of a rare diamond called the Blue Water. Just as she was about to sell a paste fake (having sold the real one years earlier for money to raise her nephews to manhood), Beau stole it, but John and Digby claimed guilt as well. In the legion, they are faced with a martinet sergeant named Lejaune, a weaselly Judas named Boldini, and hordes of marauding Arabs. In the end, Beau and Digby die with valor, leaving John to return to his aunt when his term is over.

Reviews: Mordaunt Hall, *New York Times*, 8-26-26: "Ronald Colman is easy and sympathetic in the title role. His acting in this production is only equaled by his impersonations in 'The White Sister' and 'The Dark Angel.'"

Variety, 9-1-26: "When all is said and done, Colman, in the title role, hasn't so very much to do. Hamilton equals him for footage and Forbes exceeds him...Colman's work invariably being even, he makes no deviation here, but with the limited footage and action, it serves to throw Hamilton and Forbes to the fore."

Guy Price, *Los Angeles Evening Herald*, 11-24-26: "It must be admitted that Messrs. Colman, Hamilton and Forbes are given very little opportunity, in comparison with Mr. Beery, to display any fine acting. It is in the later scenes of the picture, when each makes a sacrifice for the other, that their intrinsic ability is brought to the fore."

Edwin Schallert, *Los Angeles Times*, 11-25-26: "Colman attains a perfection of sympathetic feeling in his portrayal. It is a nobly done interpretation."

Commentary: *Beau Geste* established the prototype for Foreign Legion pictures, telling a valiant story of honor, duty, and self-sacrificial brother love against a backdrop of war and brutality, doing so with unobtrusive flair, pithy humor and a hauntingly timeless quality. And there is Ronald Colman—who does indeed have less footage than his co-stars—upholding a code of honor and decency with his gracefully selfless panache, charm and humor.

Beau Geste was a labor-of-love film for director Herbert Brenon, who loved the novel's action, heroism and romantic idealist title character. His zeal persuaded Zukor to buy the rights, borrow Colman from Sam Goldwyn for a handsome fee, and scout a desert location in Yuma. Location shooting took three months, beginning in March of 1926. Among the 2000 extras cast as marauding Arabs and as legionnaires defending Fort Zinderneuf against those Arabs were real ex-legionnaires. The sweltering heat didn't make it an easy shoot, but it did produce an authentic-looking movie.

Beau Geste cost $900,000 to make, grossing several times that in domestic and foreign release. Its 1927 sequel, *Beau Sabreur*, with Gary Cooper, was a commercial failure. It has been remade several times, most notably in 1939 with a miscast Gary Cooper as Beau, and a chillingly evil Brian Donlevy stealing the show, outdoing Noah Beery's vicious commanding officer in the original. Yet the original has never been equalled or topped for its sheer hypnotic power or its haunting opening scenes of Fort Zinderneuf being defended literally in spirit. There is something about those scenes with only an organ backdrop that the 1939 version doesn't quite recapture.

Most important of all to this study, *Beau Geste* gave Colman a new image as a self-sacrificing gentleman adventurer, a persona that would see its full fruition in the late 1930s.

Beau Geste was #2 on the New York Times 10 Best list and was chosen Picture of the Year by Photoplay readers, see A2.

Theatrical Source: MCA.

Archival Sources: GEH. 16mm print.

LC: 35mm nitrate composite print, preservation dupe negative, and viewing copy running 9,358 feet (104 minutes).

MOMA: 35mm safety print, dupe negative and 16mm circulating library copies, all running 102:47.

UCLA: 35mm nitrate reels 1-4, but with footage removed to stop deterioration. Not for viewing.

Notes: Paramount's footage count is probably inaccurate and LC's Madeline Matz says there is no assurance that their print is complete. At 22 fps, their timing is 113 minutes; at 20 fps, it is 125.

Colman books by Quirk and Smith cite Technicolor scenes, but none of the reviews mention them, nor do the Paramount production files on this movie or the program book for it. It may have been that Zukor touted color photography when he announced production, then changed his mind.

The 1965 remake stars Guy Stockwell, Doug McClure and Telly Savalas. A 1977 parody called *The Last Remake of Beau Geste* stars Marty Feldman, Michael York and Trevor Howard.

F26   THE WINNING OF BARBARA WORTH   Samuel Goldwyn for United Artists, 1926.

Producer: Samuel Goldwyn. Director: Henry King. Screenplay: Frances Marion, from the novel by Harold Bell Wright. Photographer: George S. Barnes, ASC. Assistant Cameraman: Gregg Toland. Special Effects: Ned Mann. Art Director: Carl Oscar Borg. Film Editor: Viola Lawrence. Titles: Rupert Hughes. Musical Score: Ted Henkel. Location Manager: Ray Moore.

Cast: Ronald Colman (Willard Holmes), Vilma Banky (Barbara Worth/Emigrant woman), Charles Lane (Jefferson Worth), Paul McAllister (Lee, the Seer), E.J. Ratcliffe (James Greenfield), Gary Cooper (Abe Lee), Clyde Cook (Tex), Erwin Connelly (Pat Mooney), Sam Blum (Horace Blanton), Edwin J. Brady (McDonald), William Patton), Little Rosebud), Fred Esmelton (George Cartwright), Carmencita Johnson (Barbara Worth as a child).

Release dates and timings: Los Angeles at the Forum, October 14. New York at the Strand, November 28. 8,757 feet (97 minutes, 18 seconds). My timing: 89 minutes.

Colman and Banky showed up for the Los Angeles premiere.

Synopsis: In 1910s Northern California, landowner Jefferson Worth forms an alliance with a group of Eastern money men to finance a desert reclamation project by damming the Colorado River. He hires as his chief Engineer a New Yorker named Willard Holmes, who is accompanied by his financier foster father, James Greenfield. Adapting himself to the West, the debonair Willard courts Worth's adopted daughter, Barbara, while his chief rival, shy ranch hand Abe Lee, looks on in inarticulate frustration.

When Willard discovers that Greenfield is making the dam with inferior materials, Greenfield tries to discredit his engineering, but Holmes is able to persuade Worth to finance a rival dam. When Abe discovers that the first dam is about to burst, he rides to warn the settlers of the impending flood, but is pinned down in a canyon by Greenfield's hired gunmen. Willard, who is bringing the settlers' pay money to them, rescues Abe and both men ride to give the alarm. Lee and Greenfield are both killed in the ensuing flood. Willard then completes his dam, irrigates the valley and marries Barbara.

Reviews: Herbert Moulton, *Los Angeles Times*, 10-15-26: "Colman's performance as the young engineer is handled with the easy poise that stamps all of his work."

Ung, *Variety*: 10-20-26: "Colman in his nonchalant manner interpreted the Holmes role most satisfactory (sic) and did a smart thing in playing in a straightaway manner, instead of the egotistical, which another player might have done, and in this way could have lost the sympathy of the audience."

Mordaunt Hall, *New York Times*, 11-29-26: "Ronald Colman ...acquits himself competently, and to the casual observer there is no reason why his love for Barbara should not have been reciprocated long before it is."

Commentary: Notable today as the movie that made a star of Gary Cooper, *Barbara Worth* is an epic minus the epic. The background story of the dam and town being built is potentially more thrilling than the cliched foreground story of a romantic triangle, but we are deprived of a montage conveying the excitement of history in the making. The climactic desert flood sequence is undeniably sensational, but the movie as a whole lacks dimension.

Despite all that, *Barbara Worth* was a smash hit. The two stars felt ill-suited to a western, but didn't show it. Banky is alluring and Colman gives his usual finely crafted performance, this time as a man of ambition and action, though he does look incongruous in a cowboy suit. Ironically, he was playing what he had dreamed of becoming in high school: A civil engineer.

For his part, Cooper was so awed by working with Colman that he dreamed of playing roles Colman had made or would make his own, including Sydney Carton and Beau Geste. Regrettably, some of his scenes, including his death in Colman's arms, were cut at Goldwyn's command, according to director King, after a sneak preview that made Goldwyn feel Cooper was stealing the show. This is why Cooper disappears when the flood ends. The cut scenes may have been erroneously included in the studio's footage count.

Veteran organist Gaylord Carter toured with this movie from March through May of 1971 when Goldwyn reissued it as a roadshow event. It is also the best known of the Colman-Banky films because it is still frequently revived while their other two surviving complete movies never are.

Theatrical Source: Samuel Goldwyn Company.

Archival Sources: LC. Unused Nevada desert footage only. Nitrate print, preservation dupe negative and viewing copy, each 3 reels.

UCLA: 35mm safety print of first reel excerpt only.

F27 THE NIGHT OF LOVE Samuel Goldwyn for United Artists, 1927.

Producer: Samuel Goldwyn. Director: George Fitzmaurice. Screenplay: Lenore J. Coffee, from a Spanish poem by Pedro Calderon de la Barca (1600-1681). Photographer: George S. Barnes, ASC. Assistant Cameraman: Thomas E. Brannigan. Art Director: Carl Oscar Borg. Technical Director: John K. Holden. Film Editor: Grant Whytock. Titles: Edwin Justus Mayer.

Cast: Ronald Colman (Montero), Vilma Banky (Princess Marie), Montagu Love (Bernardo, Duke de la Garda), Natalie Kingston (Dame Beatriz), Laska Winter (Gypsy Bride), Sally Rand (Gypsy Dancer), John George (Jester), Bynunsky Hyman, Gibson Gowland (Gypsy Bandits), William Tooker (Spanish Ambassador), Charles Holt (Grandee).

Release dates and timing: New York at the Strand, January 24. Los Angeles at the Criterion, February 21. 7,462 feet (82 minutes, 55 seconds).

Colman and Banky showed up for the Los Angeles premiere.

Synopsis: A gypsy king gets revenge on a duke for causing his bride to kill herself on their wedding night rather than submit to sex with the duke according to feudal law.

Reviews: Harriette Underhill, *New York Herald Tribune*, 1-24-27: "'The Night of Love' is only a frenzied tale of the seventeenth century. So they lived and so they died."

Variety, 1-26-27: "Colman's performance is bound on all sides by the mechanics of pantomiming before the camera. He plays a gypsy Robin Hood and screens as being too well aware of the fact to merge into the role."

Mordaunt Hall, *New York Times*, 1-25-27: "Mr. Colman, with a shock of curly hair, gives a fine performance as the gypsy chieftain."

Commentary: Beautifully made romantic trash that made a hit with the public as Colman became Goldwyn's answer to Valentino. That Banky had previously been partner to both men was commercial frosting. Colman's performance, however, is marked by humorless machismo as the nostril flaring gypsy. The only scene with any emotional depth is the last, when the two stars pray for salvation.

Archival Source: MOMA. 35mm nitrate print, dupe negative and 16mm viewing print, the latter 78 minutes.

F28 THE MAGIC FLAME Samuel Goldwyn for United Artists, 1927.

Producer: Samuel Goldwyn. Director: Henry King. Screenplay: Bess Meredyth, from the play *King Harlequin* by Rudolf Lothar. Continuity: June Mathis. Photographer: George S. Barnes, ASC. Art Director: Carl Oscar Borg. Titles: George Marion, Jr., Nellie Revelle. Film Editor: Viola Lawrence. Theme song: Sigmund Spaeth. Assistant Director: Robert Florey. Technical Advisor: Captain Marco Elter.

Cast: Ronald Colman (Tito, the Clown/Cassati, the Count), Vilma Banky (Bianca, the Aerial Artist), Agostino Borgato (Ringmaster), Gustav von Seyffertitz (Duke Umberto, the Chancellor), William Bakewell (Italian Prince), Harvey Clark (de Bono, the Aide), Shirley Palmer (the Wife), Cosmo Kyrle Bellew (the Husband), George Davis (Utility Man), André Cheron (Manager), Vadim Uraneff (Visitor), Meunier-Surcouf (Sword Swallower), Paoli (Weight Thrower), David Mir (Manicurist).

Release date and timing: Los Angeles opening at the Million Dollar, August 26. New York at the Rialto, September 17. 8,308 feet (92 minutes). Variety timing: 100 minutes.

Synopsis: A circus clown takes the place of his evil count lookalike, winning the love of a beautiful aerialist.

Reviews: Harriette Underhill, *New York Herald Tribune*, 9-19-27: "He made the two characters so different that one found it difficult that the one man could be mistaken for the other."

Rush, *Variety*, 9-21-27: "Romantic novelty splendidly produced and capitally acted by these two highly satisfactory screen players, again in partnership in a graceful story that fits them trimly...at first glance it's all sugary and sweet, perfect for the flaps who just love the handsome Colman and the ravishing Vilma."

Note: The second in the pseudo-Valentino cycle (costing $642,912) sounds like the most fun for its circus backdrop and the rare opportunity to watch Colman playing a clown and a villain, yet it has not been revived for decades.

Archival Source: GEH. 35mm and 16mm safety prints of first five reels only.

F29 TWO LOVERS Samuel Goldwyn for United Artists, 1928. Synchronized music and sound effects.

Producer: Samuel Goldwyn. Director: Fred Niblo. Screenplay: Alice D.G. Miller, from the novel "Leatherface: A Tale of Old Flanders" by Baroness Emmuska Orczy. Photographer: George S. Barnes, ASC. Art Director: Carl Oscar Borg. Titles: John Colton. Film Editor: Viola Lawrence. Musical Score: Hugo Riesenfeld. Songs: "Grieving" by Wayland Axtell and "Lenora" by Abner Silver. Assistant Director: H. Bruce Humberstone.

Cast: Ronald Colman (Mark Van Rycke), Vilma Banky (Lenora De Vargas), Noah Beery (the Duke of Azar), Nigel de Brulier (William, Prince of Orange), Virginia Bradford (Gretel, the Tavern Girl), Helen Jerome Eddy (Donna Inez, the Duenna), Paul Lukas (Dom Ramon De Linea, the Spanish Captain), Fred Esmelton (Meinherr Charles Van Rycke, the High Bailiff of Ghent), Eugenie Besserer (Madame Clemence Van Rycke, his wife), Harry Allen (Jean), Marcella Daly (Marda), Scotty Mattraw (Innkeeper), Lydia Yeamans Titus (Innkeeper's Wife).

Release dates and timings: New York at the Embassy, March 22. Los Angeles at the United Artists, August 29, Silent: 8,706 (96 minutes, 43 seconds). With score and sound effects: 8,817 feet (98 minutes).

Note: Differing negatives for the silent and sound versions may account for the difference in timings for this movie and *The Rescue*.

Synopsis: In 1572 Flanders, Lenora De Vargas is forced by her ruthless uncle, the Duke of Azar, into marriage with Mark Van Rycke, son of the High Bailiff; ostensibly to cement an alliance between Spain and the subjugated Flemings, but really to have Lenora spy on Mark to learn the whereabouts of William of Orange and the Flemish Robin Hood, "Leatherface." Discovering that Mark *is* Leatherface when she overhears him at a secret meeting with his followers, Lenora tries to betray him to the Duke, but Mark waylays her message. Meanwhile, having discovered Van Rycke's secret himself after Mark has killed another vicious Spaniard, Don Ramon, the Duke has Mark captured and brought in for torturing. Switching sides, Lenora aids the rebels coming to Mark's rescue by lowering the castle's drawbridge. William of Orange then arrives to tell Mark that Lenora, who now loves her swashbuckling husband, made the victory possible.

Reviews: Harriette Underhill, *New York Herald Tribune*, 3-23-28: "Mr. Colman proves conclusively that he is an infallible artist, for in this role he has no aids to romanticism...Mr. Colman used no make-up and his hair was rumpled. So, when his young wife learned to love him, it was for himself."

Mori, *Variety*, 3-28-28: "Bedroom scenes are enticing, especially since the leading players register high power sex appeal in photography. Miss Banky gets the men and Colman is surefire with the women, though each scores strongly with both sexes...All the producers got for their money is the period costume setting. Nothing in the picture warrants the title, which, though weak, will draw attention."

Notes: Orzcy's novel was one of 40,000 entries in a contest offering a $2,500 prize to whoever came up with the idea for the final Colman-Banky vehicle. Goldwyn made some lofty pronouncements that he was reteaming them with other actors for their own artistic good, but the truth was that he had run out of ideas, their pictures were costing a fortune to make because of their high salaries—*Two Lovers* cost $714,046—the stars were tired of making costume charades and public interest was waning, in part because Banky's marriage to actor Rod LaRoque hampered their image as a romantic team.

The plot of *Two Lovers* sounds hilariously absurd, but enjoyable all the same for Colman's athletic swashbuckling.

Banky made one more barely profitable silent, *The Awakening*, as the sole star, then flopped in the Goldwyn part-talkie, *This is Heaven* (1929) and the MGM all-talkie *Lady to Love* (1930). Her Hungarian-accented English was awful and her acting stilted. Goldwyn never used her again, telling her to collect her weekly $5000 paycheck for the last two years of her contract. After making one final film in Germany, *Der Rebell/The Rebel* (1932), she retired wealthy and happily married to LaRoque until his death in 1969.

Archival Source: MOMA: 35mm nitrate print and 16mm viewing print, each missing reels 3, 7 and 8 out of 10. Not considered preserved until the missing reels are found.

F30 MOVIE INDUSTRY COMMERCIAL Samuel Goldwyn(?) 1928. Two-strip Technicolor and sound.

Production credits unknown. Three minutes.

Synopsis: Standing in his Beverly Hills backyard, Ronald Colman introduces California Governor Clement C. Young, who makes some general remarks about the movie industry and its importance to families and individual moviegoers.

Comment: Historically notable as Colman's first appearance on sound film, and in color. For the record, his opening remarks are:

"Governor Young, on behalf of the motion picture industry, I would like to greet you and your charming family."

Turns to the camera: "Ladies and Gentlemen! I am very proud to have been selected to introduce Governor Young to our vast motion picture audience. He is well-known to the entire motion picture industry as a man sincerely interested in human progress and the

development of talking pictures into this world-wide product. Governor Young."
Print Source: Anonymous private collector.

F31 THE RESCUE Samuel Goldwyn for United Artists, 1929. Synchronized music and sound effects.

Producer: Samuel Goldwyn. Director: Herbert Brenon. Screenplay: Elizabeth Meehan, from the novel by Joseph Conrad. Photographer: George S. Barnes, ASC. Art Director: William Cameron Menzies. Titles: Katherine Hilliker, H. H. Caldwell. Film Editors: Marie Halvey, Katherine Hilliker, H.H. Caldwell. Musical Score: Dr. Hugo Riesenfeld. Assistant Director: Ray Lissner. Filmed partly in Santa Cruz, California.

Cast: Ronald Colman (Captain Tom Lingard), Lily Damita (Lady Edith Travers), Alfred Hickman (Mr. Travers), Theodore von Eltz (Carter), John Davidson (Rajah Pata Hassim), Philip Strange (d'Alcacer), Bernard Siegel (Jorgensen), Sojin (Daman), Harry Cording (Belarab), Laska Winter (Immada), Duke Kahanamoku (Jaffir), Louis Morrison (Shaw), George Regas (Wasub), Christopher Martin (Tenga).

Release dates and timings: Los Angeles at the United Artists, January 2. New York at the Rialto, January 12. Silent print: 7,910 feet (87 minutes, 53 seconds). With score and sound effects: 7,980 feet (88 minutes, 40 seconds). Variety timing of sound version: 96 minutes. Incomplete Eastman House print: 78 minutes.

Synopsis: Captain Tom Lingard, a social outcast, is a gun runner to warring tribes in the South Seas. He owes his life to Pata Hassim, the Rajah of Wajo, who once saved his life, an action that alienated the Rajah's tribesmen. Just as Lingard and Hassim are planning an assault to restore the Rajah to his throne, Lady Edith Travers shows up with her bombastic wealthy husband, who takes an instant dislike to Lingard. Edith, though, is attracted to Tom's animal magnetism. When Travers and one of his party are captured and held captive by the Wajo natives, Tom is torn between saving them and ruining his business and keeping faith with Hassim.

Tom hatches a plan to have it both ways that involves Edith bringing him a ring as the signal to rescue her husband. However, when Edith shows up at Tom's tent on the beach, she doesn't give him the ring, but spends the night making love to him. The result is that Travers and friend are rescued while Tom's ship blows up with Hassim and his friends. Though the tragedy is clearly Edith's fault, Tom blames himself. His affair with Edith over, their ships sail in opposite directions.

Reviews: Edwin Schallert, *Los Angeles Times*, 1-3-29: "Colman has a role of seriousness and sacrifice which fits him very admirably. His portrayal is creditable and interesting, though perhaps not equalling his finest."

Mordaunt Hall, *New York Times*, 1-13-29: "Even though Ronald Colman may not answer Conrad's description of Tom Lingard, his performance is so earnest and sensitive that, in spite of his coal-black hair, his clean-shaven chin and small mustache, he is not only far from disappointing, but he reflects the spirits of 'King Tom.'"

Photoplay, 3-29: "Ronald Colman...is right out of the Conrad pattern, one that suffers deeply without any flamboyant emotion...The repressed acting of Colman makes the figure very real...It isn't another 'Beau Geste,' but director Herbert Brenon has brought out in Colman the same quality that characterized him in that earlier work."

Notes: When Goldwyn signed Lily Damita, his first vehicle for her and Colman was *A Tale of Two Cities*, with Danita as Lucie Manette (B218). When Damita balked, Goldwyn bought the rights to the Conrad novel for its theme of self-sacrifice, though Lingard is described as a tall, burly, bearded man with a dark disposition. The critics felt that Colman overcame his miscasting, but that the film as a whole was a downbeat let-down. Seeing *The*

Rescue today, the reasons for both its commercial and artistic failures are obvious.

Brenon's heart was not in the production; his pacing is a ponderous bore. Beyond that, Colman is physically and temperamentally miscast (when Damita describes him as "primitive and dangerous," you have to laugh), while Damita has no screen presence despite a multitude of close-ups meant to give her a sultry sex appeal. On top of which, Colman's near-constant tortured expressions look forced.

Because a reel is missing from the lone preservation print, the plot becomes confusing. Even if it weren't, it's still a drag. The best thing about it is the gorgeously sharp and textured photography. What killed it commercially was that when it was released, audiences didn't want movies with only synchronized sound. They wanted all-talking films or nothing. So, *The Rescue* was pulled after a few weeks and never seen again in its entirety. The negative was destroyed in the mid-1970s after Goldwyn died, along with negatives and prints of other Goldwyn silents. Only this incomplete archival print survives as far as anyone knows.

Archival Source: GEH. 35mm safety print of 8 of the 9 reels. Missing reel 6 or 7.

THE SOUND MOVIES

Until late 1930, many sound movies were also released in silent versions for those theaters that hadn't yet installed sound equipment. Colman's first three talkies were released both sound and silent.

F32 BULLDOG DRUMMOND Howard Productions for United Artists, 1929. Embassy Video 3032, Pioneer Video LD 90751.

Producer: Samuel Goldwyn, **AAN** for BP. Director: F. Richard Jones. Screenplay: Sidney Howard, from the 1921 play by Herman Cyril "Sapper" McNeile and Gerald duMaurier and the novel by "Sapper." Continuity: Wallace Smith. Photographers: George S. Barnes, Gregg Toland. Art Director: William Cameron Menzies, **AAN**. Film Editors: Frank and Viola Lawrence. Songs: "Wine Inspires Me" and "I Says to Meself Says I" by Jack Yellen and Harry Akst. Assistant Director: Paul Jones. Associate Director: A. Leslie Pearce.

Cast: Ronald Colman, **AAN** for BA (Capt. Hugh Drummond), Claud Allister (Algy Longworth), Joan Bennett (Phyllis Benton), Montagu Love (Carl Peterson), Lilyan Tashman (Irma Peterson), Lawrence Grant (Dr. Lakington), Wilson Benge (Danny, Drummond's valet)), Charles Sellon (John Travers), Adolph Milar (Marcovitch), Tetsu Komai (Chong), Gertrude Short (Barmaid), Donald Novis (Singer), Tom Ricketts (Colonel, a Club Member).

Release dates and timing: New York premiere at George White's Apollo Theater, May 2 (R1). Los Angeles premiere at Grauman's Chinese, August 14. San Francisco premiere at the California, August 29. 89 minutes.

Colman made personal appearances at all three premieres.

Synopsis: Independently wealthy, retired and bored army officer Hugh Drummond advertises for adventure. The adventure he gets is helping a young woman named Phyllis Benton free her uncle, John Travers, from a gang of crooks who are keeping him imprisoned and drugged at a nearby phony sanitorium till he signs over his fortune to them. Despite the interference of his silly ass companion, Algy Longworth, Drummond saves the day, outwitting the crooks to save Travers, who then outwit him to make their escape. But, no matter, because Phyllis has fallen for Drummond and he for her.

Reviews: Irene Thirer, *New York News*, 5-3-29: "A peach of a happy, snappy, thrilling picture that will endear Ronald Colman more than ever to the hearts of his public. You'll simply adore him in this role."

Mordaunt Hall, *New York Times*, 5-3-29: "Mr. Colman is as ingratiating when he talks as when he was silent. He has served his time on the stage and therefore the microphone holds no terrors for him. His performance in this part is matchless so far as talking pictures are concerned."

Richard Watts Jr., *New York Herald Tribune*, 5-3-29: "Mr. Colman is the fortunate man whose stature is increased about 900 times by the coming of speech. The possessor of a pleasant, cultured voice and an easy manner, he plays with such charm, gaiety, ease and resource that his portrayal is one of the distinct achievements of the talking photoplay."

Edwin Schallert, *Los Angeles Times*, 8-15-29: "'Bulldog Drummond' gives him a new personality...He loses nothing by the transition but rather gains a great deal. He has a cultivated and resonant voice, and an ability to color words which will probably permit him a long range in his future career."

George C. Warren, *San Francisco Chronicle*, 8-30-29: "Colman is a joy as Drummond. Nonchalant, daring, handsome, he suggests the brave man bored with the comforts of a too easy life...His voice is pleasant, his diction excellent and his action that of a gentleman."

Samuel Goldwyn in *Film Weekly*, 6-10-29: "What Chaplin is to the silent film, Colman will be to sound."

Commentary: Colman's first talkie was a commercial triumph. It showcased his beautifully cultured, warmly modulated voice, while giving him a new screen image as a playfully gallant and urbane gentleman adventurer with a light comic touch in the face of his enemies. His voice matched his appearance and audiences loved it. Just as important, the low-key acting style that had been his silent movie trademark, combined with his stage training, made his transition to sound deceptively effortless. His voice revealed his real personality while his pantomimic expressiveness showed an actor in complete command of the sound medium. Otherwise, the movie as a whole is horribly dated, with severe faults.

Despite two weeks' rehearsal, after the masterfully directed and edited first reel, it slows to a static crawl, beginning the moment the inexperienced 19-year-old Bennett opens her mouth in a melodramatic whine. Except for the delightfully silly ass Alister, the veteran supporting cast is wooden. That can partly be attributed to their lack of ease with sound compounded by having to huddle awkwardly around obviously planted microphones as in most other 1929 talkies. The other part is that this is mostly a stiff play transcription, with one gruesome lapse: Drummond kills the phony doctor merely for trying to kiss Phyllis.

Bulldog Drummond set the pattern for all future Drummond films, the opposite of "Sapper's" Drummond, who is a rough-hewn thug. It cost $618,032, netting $750,000 profit from worldwide rentals. Director Jones developed tuberculosis shortly after filming, dying on December 14, 1930 at age 36.

Followed five years later by a sequel, *Bulldog Drummond Strikes Back*. Fox followed the Goldwyn hit with *Temple Tower* (1930) with Kenneth McKenna. The first two Drummond movies were *Bulldog Drummond* (British, 1922) with Carlyle Blackwell, and *The Third Round* (British, 1925) with Jack Buchanan.

Theatrical Source: Samuel Goldwyn Company.

Archival Sources: LC. Nitrate composite print, composite dupe negative, and 35mm composite viewing print.

BFI: 35mm nitrate print and 35mm safety viewing print running 87 minutes.

UCLA: 16mm projection print and VHS copy of same (PVA8105).

F33 CONDEMNED Howard Productions for United Artists, 1929. See R2.

Producer: Samuel Goldwyn, **AAN** for BP. Director: Wesley Ruggles. Screenplay:

Sidney Howard, from the book *Condemned to Devil's Island* by Blair Niles. Dialogue Director: Dudley Digges. Photographers: George S. Barnes, Gregg Toland, ASC. Art Director: William Cameron Menzies. Film Editor: Stuart Heisler. Song: "Song of the Condemned" by Jack Meskill and Peter Wendling.

Cast: Ronald Colman, **AAN** for BA (Michel Oban), Ann Harding (Madame Vidal, the Warden's Wife), Louis Wolheim (Jacques Duval), Dudley Digges (Jean Vidal, the Warden), William Elmer (Pierre Ledoux), Albert Kingsley (Felix), William Vaughan (Vidal's Orderly), Constantine Romanoff (Brute convict), John George (Hunchbacked convict), Harry Semels (Guard in Solitary), Elizabeth "Tiny" Jones (Gossip), Stephen Selznick, Harry Ginsberg, Baldy Biddle, John George, Arturo Kobe, Emile Schwartz, John Schwartz, Bud Somers (Convicts).

Release dates and timing: New York at the Selwyn, November 3. Los Angeles at Grauman's Chinese, December 5 (R2). 86 ½ minutes. Colman showed up for the Los Angeles premiere. Re-issued in 1944 by Film Classics as *Condemned to Devil's Island.*

Synopsis: Imprisoned on Devil's Island, debonair thief Michel Auban becomes houseboy to the warden's wife. They fall in love and plot to escape even as her bullying husband grows suspicious. Michel finally does escape through the jungle with fellow convict Jacques Duval. When Michel meets Madame Vidal on a ship bound for France, he is caught in her stateroom by the pursuing posse, headed by the warden. Jacques deliberately falls overboard with Jean Vidal, drowning him while getting shot to death himself. Michel then returns to Devil's Island to finish his sentence. On his release, he is happily reunited with the widow Vidal.

Reviews: Louella Parsons, *Los Angeles Examiner*, 12-6-29: "You may wonder how a prisoner can be as blithe and gay as Ronald Colman. But you only wonder briefly, for Mr. Colman has so much charm you forget to be logical. His gaiety, his absolute indifference to danger, and his happy insouciance are merely attractive, and who cares about common sense when there is an actor with Colman's appeal in the offing?"

Edwin Schallert, *Los Angeles Times*, 12-6-29: "Colman assumes a difficult character because there is almost a constant indication that he cannot shake off the old life of deception and take on the new one of love and devotion to an ideal of woman-hood...Certainly Colman gives a clean-cut effort in the portrayal that all but justifies the character."

Variety, 11-6-29: "Film has too many false notes to make it a standout effort...Unnecessary tender touches as Colman repeatedly returns for a last caress with pursuers milling all around him...But Colman plays well, at times is outstanding in his pantomime and has his already established ability to handle lines. If ever given a chance, he will probably scintillate in a light comedy theme."

Commentary: For the first reel, *Condemned* has a primal excitement. The opening scenes aboard the convict ship evoke the primitive conditions of the voyage and the dread of prison those conditions instill. The direction, camera work and editing are hair-raisingly stylish until the ship reaches Devil's Island. Dramatic interest is held for another reel, then the picture bogs into slow motion.

Colman is impeccably charming as always and that's another problem: You just can't believe that anyone so polished and debonair would get caught in the first place. However, that wouldn't matter if one could believe that he and Harding are in love, which one can't because they have no chemistry. They are only attracted because the script says so.

The best thing about *Condemned* next to Colman is neanderthal-looking Louis Wolheim, whose roguish charm matches Colman's, belying his ugly looks. The two of *them* make a better pair than Colman-Harding. Digges, on the other hand, seems to be dazed or sleepwalking most of the time and *he* was the dialogue director.

Condemned was a hit for Colman's vocal charm (earning him a tandem Best Actor Oscar nomination with *Bulldog Drummond*) and because it enacted the female fantasy of the sexy thief who's far more exciting than her dullard husband. It cost $753,320. Profit figures are unavailable.

Theatrical Source: Samuel Goldwyn Pictures.

F34 RAFFLES Howard Productions for United Artists, 1930.

Producer: Samuel Goldwyn. Directors (neither credited): Harry d'Arrast and George Fitzmaurice. Screenplay: Sidney Howard, from the play *Raffles, the Amateur Cracksman* by E.W. Hornung and Eugene Wiley Presbrey. Photographers: George S. Barnes, Gregg Toland, ASC. Art Directors: William Cameron Menzies, Park French. Film Editor: Stuart Heisler. Sound: Oscar Lagerstrom, **AAN**. Music: Piano rendition of "The Blue Danube" by Strauss. Assistant Director: H. Bruce Humberstone. Technical Directors: John Howell, Gerald Grove.

Cast: Ronald Colman (A.J. Raffles), Kay Francis (Lady Gwen), David Torrence (Inspector MacKenzie), Frederick Kerr (Lord Harry Melrose), Alison Skipworth (Lady Kitty Melrose), Bramwell Fletcher (Bunny Manders), John Rogers (Crawshay), Wilson Benge (Barraclough), Frances Dade (Ethel Crowley), Virginia Bruce (Debutante).

Release date and timing: Los Angeles at the United Artists and New York at the Rialto, July 24. 70 minutes, 40 seconds.

Synopsis: Debonair jewel thief A.J. Raffles quits his thieving for love of Lady Gwen, then decides to steal a necklace from Lady Melrose to raise £1000 to help his friend, Bunny, pay a gambling debt. He also matches wits with wily Inspector MacKenzie. When the necklace is returned by Bunny in exchange for a £1000 reward by Lord Melrose, followed by Gwen returning her stolen bracelet to MacKenzie, Raffles escapes. He gives the inspector the dodge on a foggy London street, to MacKenzie's bemused admiration.

Reviews: Rush, *Variety*, 7-30-30: "'Raffles' still remains the best romantic crook to date....Moreover, in the hands of the bland Colman, it gets a persuasive reading that makes it fresh, even after an over-supply of stories of similar import."

Richard Watts Jr., *New York Herald Tribune*, 7-25-30: "Mr. Colman, whose ironic, bantering nonchalance has become one of the most satisfying institutions of the talking cinema, offers one of his most engaging performances as the romantic society bandit."

Commentary: The character of Raffles is a Victorian fantasy: a debonair, charming and witty sophisticate who acts as our larcenous surrogate. Hornung conceived him in 1899 as an opposite to his brother-in-law Sir Arthur Conan Doyle's Sherlock Holmes. This fourth film version of the story was a well-played matinee diversion in 1930 that today holds up as a briskly paced antique version of a hit stage play. However, it has no memorable dialogue and a parched feel for lack of music aside from snatches of "The Blue Danube." Yet, even with witty banter and badly needed music, *Raffles* would not have been a classic. It was made purely as a star vehicle to showcase Colman's poise and charm. But, unlike Joan Bennett and Fay Wray in *Bulldog Drummond* and *The Unholy Garden*, respectively, Francis's warm acting is a match for Colman's. You can believe they're in love.

Raffles netted $200,000 domestic profit against a cost of $719,758. Colman's talkies were making a fortune.

When Goldwyn remade *Raffles* in 1940 with David Niven, Olivia de Havilland and Dudley Digges, the script was revised and updated by John van Druten. He made Raffles a thief who steals to aid the poor (how, then, does he make his money?), using about a third of Sidney Howard's original shot for shot. By then, sound production had greatly improved so that the pacing is swift, and scoring is added, but it still isn't a good movie. Niven's bland charm and weak facial nuances are no match for Colman's charisma and expert expressions in close-ups. And Digges makes a plodding detective compared to Torrence's memorably crafty MacKenzie. On the other hand, de Havilland matches Francis's affectionate approach with a sexy one.

However, because of the Hays Code, Raffles could no longer blithely get away with his crimes. So, a final scene was tacked on showing Niven giving de Havilland one last kiss before implausibly giving himself up to Digges.

Silent versions, all titled *Raffles, the Amateur Cracksman*, star J. Barney Sherry (Vitagraph one-reeler, 1905), John Barrymore (1917), and House Peters (1919). *Raffles*-like movies include *To Catch a Thief* (1955) with Cary Grant; *The Pink Panther* (1964) with David Niven; and *Final Cut* (1980) with Burt Reynolds.

Theatrical Source: Samuel Goldwyn Company.

Archival Source: UCLA. 35mm safety print of first 3 reels, ca. 55 minutes.

F35 THE DEVIL TO PAY Samuel Goldwyn for United Artists, 1930. Pioneer Video LD 90751.

Producer: Samuel Goldwyn. Director: George Fitzmaurice. Story and dialogue: Frederick Lonsdale. Adaptation: Benjamin Glazer.Dialogue Director: Ivan Simpson. Photographers: George S. Barnes, Gregg Toland, ASC. Music: Alfred Newman. Art Director: Richard Day. Film Editor: Grant Whytock. Assistant Director: H. Bruce Humberstone. Technical Advisors: Lady Maureen Stanley, Lt. Col. G.I. McDonnell.

Cast: Ronald Colman (Willie Hale), Loretta Young (Dorothy Hope), Florence Britton (Susan Leeland), Frederick Kerr (Lord Leeland), David Torrence (Mr. Hope), Mary Forbes (Mrs. Hope), Paul Cavanagh (Grand Duke Paul), Crawford Kent (Arthur Hale), Myrna Loy (Mary Crayle), Ivan Simpson (Owner of Pet Shop), Forrester Harvey.

Release dates and timing: New York at the Gaiety, December 18, 1930. Los Angeles at the United Artists, February 5, 1931. 72 minutes, 15 seconds.

Synopsis: After selling his belongings in East Africa, upper-class black sheep Willie Hale returns home to England, where he buys a dog and charms his rich father, Lord Leeland, into giving him more money. After reuniting with his old girlfriend, actress Mary Crayle, he meets and falls in love with heiress Dorothy Hope. Dorothy then breaks her engagement to Grand Duke Paul because she finds bankrupt Willie far more irresistibly charming. She also makes Willie agree to stop seeing Mary.

Mistakenly thinking he has breached this agreement, Dorothy pays Willie off. He sends the money to destitute Paul, who gladly accepts it, showing Willie's true character to Dorothy. When they make up, Lord Leeland laughingly informs them that Dorothy's father is making them a wedding present of a sheep farm in Australia. At least if Willie goes broke this time, Dorothy's father is footing the bill, not him.

Reviews: Mordaunt Hall *New York Times*, 12-19-30: "This latest Samuel Goldwyn production is a wholesome, carefree picture with bright lines and one in which a cheery mood is sustained from the opening scene to the final fade-out...It gives Mr. Colman even a better opportunity than he had in 'Bulldog Drummond' and he takes full advantage of his witty lines."

Richard Watts Jr., *New York Herald Tribune*, 12-19-30: "'The Devil to Pay' is six reels of Ronald Colman being charming, but since it happens that Mr. Colman can be charming without offense, ostentation or self-consciousness, and that Frederick Lonsdale, who wrote the photoplay, is an expert at making something out of nothing, the result is a polished, tasteful and entirely likeable screen comedy."

Bige, *Variety*, 12-24-30: "Ronald Colman starred, impresses as having a good time sailing through this naughty boy part. He plays it well, and it should do well by him."

Commentary: *The Devil to Pay* is Colman's light comedy masterpiece, with a nonpareil command of comic pantomime and expertly stylish delivery of witty dialogue galore. He practically dances the role of Willie Hale, making everyone in his path except Torrence and Cavanagh feel better for having met him. Which is the point of the story: That a self-confident, upbeat attitude is infectious. There is also the radiant chemistry between Colman and 17-year-old Loretta Young, and the show-stopping comic rapport between Colman and George the dog. The scene in which Colman buys George at a pet shop is a masterpiece of comic timing.

Parenthetically, why Willie's last name isn't Leeland is never explained for American audiences who aren't familiar with the naming customs of the English aristocracy - Leeland is the family title.

Just a bit longer than *Raffles*, *The Devil to Pay* seems much shorter because Fitzmaurice's ebullient direction keeps Lonsdale's inventive script happily on the move. When it's over, one aches to see Colman as Jack Worthing in Oscar Wilde's *The Importance of Being Earnest*. *The Devil to Pay* was #5 on the New York Times Ten Best list for 1930 and made a neat profit (figure unavailable) on a negative, print and distribution cost of $687,179.

Theatrical Source: Samuel Goldwyn Company.

Archival Source: UCLA. 35mm nitrate studio print.

F36 THE UNHOLY GARDEN Samuel Goldwyn for United Artists, 1931.

Producer: Samuel Goldwyn. Director: George Fitzmaurice. Story: Ben Hecht and Charles MacArthur. Screenplay: Ben Hecht. Photography: George S. Barnes, ASC. Musical Score: Alfred Newman. Art Directors: Richard Day, Willy Pogany. Sound: Frank Grenzbach. Film Editor: Grant Whytock.

Cast: Ronald Colman (Barrington Hunt), Fay Wray (Camille de Jonghe), Estelle Taylor (Elize Mowbry), Warren Hymer (Smiley Corbin), Tully Marshall (Baron Louis de Jonghe), Lawrence Grant (Dr. Shayne), Ullrich Haupt (Colonel von Axt), Kit Guard (Kid Twist), Henry Armetta (Nick the Goose), Lucille La Verne (Mme. Lucie Villars), Mischa Auer (Prince Nicolai Poliakoff), Henry Kolker (Police Inspector), A.E. Anson (Inspector Onbray, sic?), Charles H. Mailes (Alfred de Jonghe), Morgan Wallace (Captain Kruger), Arnold Korff (Louis Lautrac), Nadja (Native Dancer), William von Brincken.

Release dates and timing: New York at the Rialto, October 28. Los Angeles at the United Artists, October 30. 74 minutes.

Synopsis: Fleeing from Marseilles to Algeria, British bank robber Barrington Hunt hijacks the car of prostitute Elize Mowbry (hired by the local police chief to snare him). He hies them both to a broken down Saharan hotel inhabited by other thieves. Hunt then joins a scheme with his fellow crooks and former partner Smiley Corbin to locate and steal the hidden fortune of Baron de Jonghe, a fugitive embezzler. But Hunt doesn't count on falling in love with de Jonghe's pretty daughter, Camille. Eluding the other crooks after finding the cache, he gives Camille the money, tells her he must leave her to pay for his crimes to be worthy of her, then makes off in Elize's car with Smiley.

Reviews: Philip K. Scheuer, *Los Angeles Times*, 10-31-31: "Swashbuckling Ronald enters into the spirit of make-believe with his old dash and humor, always (and quite properly) assured that everything will come out all right in the end."

Richard Watts Jr., *New York Herald Tribune*, 10-29-31: "'The Unholy Garden' is a confused and ineffective photoplay which never manages to be successful as either melodrama or comedy...Colman is as suave and debonair as usual."

Mordaunt Hall, *New York Times*, 10-29-31: "In this picture, Ronald Colman...does his one good deed before he speeds off in somebody else's car with a thug who would probably like to put a bullet through him...Mr. Colman performs with his usual savoir faire."

Sid, *Variety*, 11-3-31: "Splendid presentation of an ordinary story...(Colman) is particularly good here, neither over or under-playing, and lending the whole thing a touch of humor which is very enjoyable."

Display ad: "..a symphony of emotion..a maelstrom of action..a typhoon of joyous abandon!" Tag line: "Where there ain't no Ten Commandments."

Commentary: The ad is the best part of the picture. Allegedly written in one round-the-clock day by Hecht, *The Unholy Garden* is mildly spoofy matinee trash with soundstage atmosphere. Third-rate crooks holing up in a desert outpost with seemingly no money to pay their rent is an absurd idea, but more important, it is impossible to believe that Hunt would nobly give up his ignoble calling for love of any woman. Certainly not when the woman is badly played by a misdirected and bland Fay Wray, best known for her far superior work in King Kong. Colman does his usual polished work with material far beneath him, but for once his public recognized junk for what it was and did him a favor by staying away. It cost $634,609.

Theatrical Source: Samuel Goldwyn Company.

F37 ARROWSMITH Howard Productions for United Artists, 1931. Embassy Video 3026. Pioneer Home Video LD PSE 94-35. Same print as for Embassy.

Producer: Samuel Goldwyn, **AAN** for BP. Director: John Ford. Screenplay: Sidney Howard, **AAN**, from the 1925 novel, which won the Pulitzer Prize, by 1930 Nobel Prize-winner Sinclair Lewis. Director of Photography: Ray June, ASC, **AAN**. Musical Score: Alfred Newman. Art Director: Richard Day, **AAN**. Sound: Jack Noyes. Film Editor: Hugh Bennett. Assistant Director: H. Bruce Humberstone.

Cast: Ronald Colman (Dr. Martin Arrowsmith), Helen Hayes (Leora Tozer Arrowsmith), Richard Bennett (Dr. Gustav Sondelius), A.E. Anson (Professor Max Gottlieb), Clarence Brooks (Dr. Oliver Marchand), Alec B. Francis (Cecil Twyford), Claude King (Dr. A. DeWitt Tubbs), Bert Roach (Bert Tozer), Myrna Loy (Joyce Lanyon), Russell Hopton (Dr. Terry Wickett), David Landau (State Veterinarian), Lumsden Hare (Sir Robert Fairland, Island Governor), Charlotte Henry (Pioneer Girl), James Marcus (Doc Vickerson), DeWitt Jennings (Mr. Tozer), Beulah Bondi (Mrs. Tozer), John Qualen (Henry Novak), Adele Watson (Mrs. Novak), Sidney DeGrey (Dr. Hesselink), Florence Britton (Miss Twyford), Ward Bond (Policeman), Pat Somerset, Eric Wilton (Ship's Officers), Erville Alderson (Pioneer), George Humbert (Italian Uncle), Raymond Hatton (Drunk), Theresa Harris (Native Mother), Kendall McComas (Johnny), Walter Downing (City Clerk), Edmund Mortimer (Ship passenger), and Bobby Watson.

Release dates and timings: New York at the Gaiety, December 7. Los Angeles at the United Artists, February 4, 1932. 108 minutes. Censored 1937 re-release: 95 minutes.

Synopsis: Research scientist Martin Arrowsmith seeks a cure for bubonic plague. Finding it, he forsakes traditional scientific methodology to save lives in Haiti in grief over his wife Leora dying of the plague. In tribute to her death, Martin forsakes the commercial institute funding his work for a life of pure research with the aid of colleague Terry Wickett.

Reviews: Richard Watts Jr., *New York Herald Tribune*, 12-8-31: "...he is too definitely British for the part and, in addition to that, he is perhaps a bit too dashing and romantic looking for his role of an eager-eyed zealot with a religious passion for scientific research."

Sid, *Variety*, 12-15-31: "Colman either lacks the depth to portray such a part or has been permitted by his supervisors to seem to be in over his head. At no time does he impart the unquenchable thirst for research, the sense of humility, futility, and idolatry for another and older scientist which the author wrote into the character."

Edwin Schallert, *Los Angeles Times*, 2-5-32: "He has seldom, if ever, given the screen a better (performance)....Only here and there does a certain acting consciousness invade his presentation...but the elements of the portrayal are so fine that this is scarcely distracting."

Louella O. Parsons, *Los Angeles Examiner*: 2-5-32: "Mr. Colman conveys the idea of the well-bred, suave young Englishman more at home in a drawing room than in a laboratory."

Commentary: A commercial success, *Arrowsmith* holds up as a creaky antique, plagued by a miscast Colman in his first serious talking role. He had the temperament for the part, but lacked the American temperament and physicality to make it believable. He could not get past looking and sounding like a debonair gentleman instead of an obsessed doctor and scientist. He is a Britisher playing an American with a pioneer past. There are scenes in which he is believable and sympathetic, especially when he is grief-stricken over Hayes's death, but for the most part, he is way out of his depth. On the set, he was in such turmoil one day getting a grip on the character that Goldwyn had to pay a visit to calm and reassure him, something that had never happened before.

Other problems include Howard's episodic script, stagy and stereotypical perform-ances by Bennett and Anson, a lack of music until the last few reels when the action switches to Haiti, and Ford's uneven direction and pacing. He wasn't at home with the material and it shows. Best of all is Helen Hayes as Leora. Her earthy performance steals the show; it also clashes with Colman's mannered acting.

Costing $721,579 (negative, prints, ads, etc.), *Arrowsmith*, was one of the 15 top-grossing movies of 1932 (profit figure unavailable), and was Oscar-nominated for Best Picture. It was also #4 on the New York Times Ten Best list and #3 on Film Daily's list.

Theatrical Source: Samuel Goldwyn Company.

Archival Sources: LC. 101-minute 35mm nitrate composite print, nitrate composite negative, preservation composite dupe negative, and composite viewing print. Plus 35mm composite safety viewing print of 10-minute screen test with Colman and Hayes.

BFI: Master nitrate tinted print of the trailer running 2 minutes, not yet duplicated for preservation and viewing.

Notes: The only known complete print in the U.S. is a 16mm copy owned by film historian William K. Everson. The cable TV and home video version runs 98 ½ minutes, 3 of which are blown-up footage from the Everson print restoring part of Myrna Loy's nearly deleted role, reduced for implied adultery. Goldwyn knew about the longer LC print—which includes what they took from Everson—and had the remaining 7 missing minutes in the Everson print, so there was no reason they couldn't have made a complete TV and home video print using sparkling footage for what they did restore and 16mm for the rest.

F38 CYNARA   Samuel Goldwyn for United Artists, 1932. Working title: *I Have Been Faithful*.

Producer: Samuel Goldwyn. Director: King Vidor. Screenplay: Lynn Starling and Frances Marion from the play by H.M. Harwood and Robert Gore Browne and Browne's novel *An Imperfect Lover*. Film title taken from the Ernest Dowson poem, "Non sum qualis eram" (1896). Photography: Ray June, ASC. Art Director: Richard Day. Film Editor: Hugh Bennett. Musical Score: Alfred Newman. Assistant director: Sherry Shourds. Sound: C. Noyer. Sound: Frank Maher. Song: "Blue Skies" by Irving Berlin (1926), sung by Phyllis Barry. Charlie Chaplin footage from *A Dog's Life* (1918).

Cast: Ronald Colman (Jim Warlock), Kay Francis (Clemency Warlock), Phyllis Barry (Doris Emily Lea), Henry Stephenson (Sir John Tring), Viva Tattersall (Milly Miles), Florine McKinney (Gorla Keutich, Clemency's sister), Clarissa Selwynne (Onslow), Paul Porcasi (Joseph), George Kirby (Mr. Boots), Donald Stuart (Henry), Wilson Benge (Merton, Warlock's valet), C. Montague Shaw (Constable), Halliwell Hobbes (Coroner), George Humbert (Angry slot machine player in restaurant), Marquis of Annandale (Himself).

Release dates and timings: New York at the Rivoli, December 24. Los Angeles at the United Artists, December 29. 78 minutes, 45 seconds. Reissued in 1945 at 72 minutes by Film Classics as *I Was Faithful*. TV prints as *Cynara* are 72 minutes.

Timings given in reviews range from 72 to 80 minutes. Original release timing taken from BFI print, which may be a longer British version.

Synopsis: Happily married and renowned barrister Jim Warlock has an affair with a young shopgirl named Doris while his wife, Clemency, is away in Venice. When he ends the affair, Doris kills herself. Her suicide prompts an official investigation, at which Jim refuses to soil her reputation further by acknowledging she had had previous affairs. The resulting scandal forces him to flee to Naples, then to South Africa, joined at the last minute for the latter trip by the forgiving Clemency.

Reviews: Mordaunt Hall, *New York Times*, 12-26-32: "Mr. Colman gives an ingratiating portrayal...There is a pleasing sincerity about his acting, which evidently has been helped by Mr. Vidor's imaginative direction."

Motion Picture Herald, 11-5-32: "Regardless of what kind of stage show 'Cynara' was, it is now a motion picture depending on familiar but fine romance and drama, with Ronald Colman's artistic acting always predominant."

Rush, *Variety*, 1-3-33: "Stage play has been put on screen with beautiful balance of directness and simplicity. It finds Ronald Colman in probably the best clean-cut acting he has done since 'Raffles', not excepting 'Arrowsmith'."

Commentary: Well-made but dry, thin and unexciting story seeming to take place in 1932, yet with a movie theater showing 1918 Chaplin at a time when silent pictures had vanished from British cinemas. Vidor added a few cinematic flourishes, such as bits of paper flung out a cab window turning into birds flying over Venice, missing from the other stage plays Goldwyn bought for Colman. But there is no getting around the lack of scenes showing the evolution of the affair, which may be due to cut re-issue prints. For all of Colman's customary fine underplaying, the story lacks emotional fire and character development to make the suicide and ensuing scandal involving and thus tragically affecting. The movie really only jolts to life in the last minute when Colman beams with joy and embraces Francis as she joins him in exile.

Even with a richer script, *Cynara*, costing $697,958, might still have been the commercial failure it was because audiences didn't want to see Colman as an adulterer, however gallant at the end. He and Goldwyn were talked into making it against their better judgment by Goldwyn publicist Arthur Hornblow Jr. because it had been a hit British play.

Newcomer Dorothy Hale tested for and was cast as Clemency, but either quit or was fired the first week. Kay Francis was then borrowed from Warners.

Theatrical Source: Samuel Goldwyn Company.

Archival Source: BFI. 35mm nitrate and 35mm safety viewing prints running 78:45, both without a soundtrack.

F39 THE MASQUERADER Samuel Goldwyn for United Artists, 1933.

Producer: Samuel Goldwyn. Director: Richard Wallace. Adaptation and Screenplay: Howard Estabrook, from the novel by Katherine Cecil Thurston (1904) and the play by John

Hunter Booth (1917). Additional Dialogue: Moss Hart. Dialogue director: A. Leslie Pearce. Assistant director: Sherry Shourds. Photographer: Gregg Toland, ASC. Art director: Richard Day. Sound: Oscar Lagerstrom. Film editor: Stuart Heisler. Musical score: Alfred Newman. Incidental piano music: Elissa Landi.

Cast: Ronald Colman (John Chilcote/John Loder), Elissa Landi (Eve Chilcote), Juliette Compton (Lady Diana Joyce), David Torrence (Fraser), Claude King (Lakely), Halliwell Hobbes (Brock), Helen Jerome Eddy (Robbins, Clifford's Inn maid), Eric Wilton (Alston), Creighton Hale (Bobby Blessington), Montagu Shaw (Speaker of the House), Buddy Roosevelt (Colman's double).

Release dates and timing: Los Angeles at the Criterion, August 25. New York at the Rivoli, September 3. 74 minutes.

Synopsis: After collapsing in Parliament while making a speech about an anti-machinery strike, drug-addicted MP John Chilcote runs into his lookalike cousin, John Loder, a freelance journalist. Loder chastises him for failing his party and his country in its "hour of crisis", facetiously telling Chilcote he's available to double for him at weddings and receptions. When Chilcote becomes gravely ill, Loder takes over for him in Parliament and falls in love with his wife, Eve. She then falls in love with the new man she believes her husband has become. Loder then rids himself of Chilcote's mistress, Lady Diana Joyce. When Chilcote dies, Loder continues the deception with Eve's knowledge and happy complicity.

Note: Goldwyn previewed *The Masquerader* at the Ritz Theater in New York City on February 12, 1933. Some further work may have been done, but it was shelved till August. Not knowing if Colman would return to him, he didn't want to release it so soon after *Cynara*.

Reviews: Bige, *Variety*, 2-17-33: "It will be no disappointment to Colman fans. On the contrary, the star's excellent performance will land him further laurels."

Harrison Carroll, *Los Angeles Herald*, 8-26-33: "Colman's trick of underplaying never stood him in better stead than in this story, so full of dangerous opportunities for heroics."

Edwin Schallert, *Los Angeles Times*, 8-26-33: "...the central character of Loder ideally suits Colman, while he lends enough of conviction to Chilcote. He has range for acting in the picture, and the situations intrigue."

Louella O. Parsons, *Los Angeles Examiner*, 8-26-33: "Perhaps you and I are gullible when we believe that any man can have a double who is such a perfect replica of himself that his own wife is fooled. Still, we don't mind being gullible when it's all in the cause of good clean entertainment and Ronald Colman."

Commentary: *The Masquerader* was as much a commercial failure as *Cynara* and it's easy to see why. It's a thin melodrama with no dimension and no background on the ugly character of Chilcote: how and why he came to prominence in the presumably Tory party, why he is a drug addict and what drug precisely beyond alcohol he is taking, why his party's leaders depend on him for a Churchillian speech in Parliament, and why they don't simply kick him out of the party for instability and incompetence. When Loder finally does make a speech in his place, it is a string of platitudes. Cliches are going to save England in this "Hour of Crisis"? In this movie they do.

You also wonder what Chilcote's mistress sees in him personally beyond his political station and why she doesn't leave him when it's clear he's out of control. Yet, reversing the usual madonna/whore pattern, Landi's long-suffering wife is prettier and has far more sex appeal than Compton's mercenary mistress. She has a sensual allure, her bedroom eyes beckoning Colman, who is torn between making love to her and keeping up his pretense.

For all of Landi's sex appeal, it is Hobbes who steals the show as the loyal but exasperated servant who is appalled by Chilcote's self-destruction and who is frankly just as glad to have Loder take his place forever. The scene in which he explodes at Chilcote is a gem of accumulated anger.

When filming began, Colman was preoccupied with breaching his contract the minute it ended, so he gave mechanical performances. He invested Chilcote with a mannered heavy delivery, while playing Loder with all the stock mannerisms he knew: His famous worried expression when beckoned to bed by Landi; his habit of backing away to the left, then coming forward as though to say "And another thing" when berating Chilcote for betraying his party; and his trademark jauntiness when he wants to rely on surface charm rather than internal fortitude. Audiences were not enchanted.

After a months-delayed start, shooting—which cost $678, 983—was held up midway through in December 1932 because Landi fell ill. Goldwyn auditioned several women to replace her, including Benita Hume (who did a reading with Colman) but waited for Landi's return in the end. Thankfully, this was the end of a string of mostly minor and mediocre stage and book adaptations that kept Colman's larger talents reined by a producer obsessed with words at the expense of rich and memorably moving cinematic imagery.

Theatrical Source: Samuel Goldwyn Company.

Guy Bates Post made a career of this show in several stage runs from 1917 to 1929, in between which he made a 1922 film version for First National. The story's basic idea was reused for *Moon Over Parador* (1988) and *Dave* (1993).

F40 BULLDOG DRUMMOND STRIKES BACK Twentieth Century Pictures for United Artists, 1934.

Producers: Joseph M. Schenck and Darryl F. Zanuck. Director: Roy Del Ruth. Original screenplay: Nunnally Johnson, from characters created by H.C. "Sapper" McNeile. Adaptation: Henry Lehrman. Photographer: Peverell Marley, ASC. Art Director: Richard Day. Costumes: Gwen Wakeling. Musical Score: Alfred Newman. Film Editor: Allen McNeil. Associate Producers: William Goetz and Raymond Griffith.

Cast: Ronald Colman (Capt. Hugh Drummond), Loretta Young (Lola Field), Warner Oland (Prince Achmed), Charles Butterworth (Algy Longworth), Una Merkel (Gwen Longworth), C. Aubrey Smith (Inspector Alfred Reginald Nielson), Kathleen Burke (Lady Jane Sothern), Arthur Hohl (Dr. Owen Sothern), George Regas (Singh), Ethel Griffies (Mrs. Field), H.N. Clugston (Mr. Field), Mischa Auer (Hassan), Douglas Gerrard (Parker), Halliwell Hobbes, E.E. Clive, Yorke Sherwood (Policemen), William O'Brien (Banquet Servant), Pat Somerset, Vernon Steele, Creighton Hale (Wedding Guests), Gunnis Davis (Harsh-Voiced Man), Charles Irwin (Drunk), Wilson Benge (Nielson's Valet), Olaf Hytten (Hotel Clerk), Charles McNaughton (Hotel Manager), Bob Kortman (Henchman), Doreen Monroe (Woman in Hotel Room), Billy Bevan (Man in Hotel Room).

Release dates and timing: New York at the Rivoli, August 15. Los Angeles at the United Artists, September 19. 83 minutes.

Synopsis: With the aid of his newly married friend, Algy, and a pretty young woman named Lola, Bulldog Drummond foils a gang of fur dealers, headed by Prince Achmed, trying to smuggle cholera-infected furs into England.

Reviews: Land, *Weekly Variety*, 8-21-34: "Colman is attractively Colmanesque throughout. He is the gay blade, the debonair adventurer never long without a counter-move and escaping death or failure innumerable times."

Mordaunt Hall, *New York Times*, 8-16-34: "Mr. Colman gives an admirable portrayal, conjuring adroitly with the various phases of the story."

Louella O. Parsons, *Los Angeles Examiner*, 9-20-34: "The Ronald Colman that you like and that I like is back again with us, with the old fire in his eyes, the charm and personality that makes him so valuable as a star."

Commentary: Parsons was right. *Bulldog Drummond Strikes Back* (*BDSB*) put Colman back in top form in a familiar role, the only time he played a character twice. Inventive writing, the vast improvements in sound filming since the first Drummond movie, and a superior supporting cast all add up to a honey of a mystery spoof. Johnson's crackerjack script pokes genial fun at murder mystery cliches: The sinister Oriental villain and his equally sinister gang of thugs, the pretty girl in the middle, a witness who faints on the verge of revealing what the mystery is about, the hero and his sidekick saving the day while trapped inside a locked room, etc.

Through it all, Colman is at his charming and whimsically humorous best, romantically smitten with Young, constantly yanking Butterworth away from his marriage bed with Merkel, and verbally thumbing his nose at the villains while admitting occasional defeat. The pacing is slow at times and there are story holes due to post-production cuts, but it's all an enjoyable lark, with an excitingly fiery climax. The production cost of $542,128 was handily recouped.

Most important of all, *BDSB* re-established Colman as a light comic hero who is instantly likeable, infinitely trustworthy and resourceful, and unafraid to take chances in the face of reluctant authority. His style utterly influenced every actor playing Drummond thereafter.

A series of eight B-film Drummonds were made by Paramount from 1937 to 1939. The first starred Ray Milland, the rest John Howard. Other Drummonds from 1939 on were Jack Buchanan (British, 1939), Ron Randell (1947), Tom Conway (1948), Walter Pidgeon (British, 1951), and Richard Johnson (British, one each in 1967 and 1970), Drummond was also spoofed in *Bullshot Crummond* (1987).

There were also three British Drummond films in 1934: *The Return of Bulldog Drummond* (Ralph Richardson), *Bulldog Jack* (Jack Hulbert) and *Bulldog at Bay* (Hulbert).

Theatrical Source: Janus Films in New York City.

Archival Sources: MOMA. 35mm nitrate print running 56:45, fine-grain print from nitrate negative, and 16mm viewing print running 83 minutes.

UCLA: 35mm nitrate studio prints of reels 8 and 9, running about 19 minutes.

F41   CLIVE OF INDIA Twentieth Century Pictures for United Artists, 1935. See R3.

Producer: Darryl F. Zanuck. Presented by Joseph M. Schenck. Director: Richard Boleslawski. Screenplay: W.P. Lipscomb and R.J. Minney from their play, **Clive**, and Minney's biography **Clive**. Director of Photography: Peverell Marley, ASC. Film Editor: Barbara McLean. Musical Score: Alfred Newman. Art Director: Richard Day. Sound: Vinton Vernon, Roger Heman. Costumes: Omar Kiam. Songs as background motifs: "Drink to Me Only with Thine Eyes", "Rule Britannia" (Thomas Arne, 1741) and "God Save the King". Associate Producers: William Goetz and Raymond Griffith. Assistant Director: Ben Silvey.

Cast: Ronald Colman (Robert Clive), Loretta Young (Margaret Maskeleyne Clive), Colin Clive (Capt. Johnstone), Francis Lister (Edmund Maskeleyne), C. Aubrey Smith (Prime Minister), Cesar Romero (Mir Jaffar), Montagu Love (Governor Pigot), Lumsden Hare (Sgt. Clark), Ferdinand Munier (Adm. Charles Watson), Gilbert Emery (Sullivan, Speaker at House of Commons), Leo G. Carroll (Manning), Etienne Girardot (Warburton), Robert Greig (Mr. Pemberton), Mischa Auer (Suraj Ud Dowlah), Leonard Mudie (Gen. Burgoyne), Phillip Dare (Capt. George), Wyndham Standing (Col. Townsend), Ian Wolfe (Kent), Alex Pollard (St. Aubyn and Footman), Ferdinand Gottschalk (Old Member, House of Commons), Doris Lloyd (Mrs. Nixon), Edward Cooper (Cooper, Clive's Butler), Eily Malyon (Mrs. Clifford, Clive's Housekeeper), Joseph Tozer (Sir Frith, a Doctor), Phyllis Clare (Miss Smythe, Margaret's Friend), Ann Shaw (Lady Lindley), Vernon P. Downing (Stringer, clerk), Neville Clark (Vincent), Peter Shaw (Miller), Douglas Gerrard (Lt. Walsh), Connie Leon (Ayah), Charles Evans (Surveyor), Vesey O'Davoren (Assistant Surveyor), Lila Lance (Native Indian Woman selling pomegranates), Lionel Belmore (Official at Reception), Lumsden Hare (Messenger at Husting), Olaf Hytten (Parson at Husting), Pat Somerset (Lt. Walsh, official in Margaret's room), Bruce Cooke (Boy Bugler), Edward Cooke (Boy Drummer), Tommy Martin (Robert Clive Jr.), Nadine Beresford (Governess), Mary MacLaren (Nurse), Phyllis Coghlan (Betty, the Maid).

Release dates and timing: New York at the Rivoli, January 17. Los Angeles at Loew's State and Grauman's Chinese, February 22. 93½ minutes.

Synopsis: The story of Robert Clive, founder of the British empire in India. In 1748, when the French, Dutch, Portuguese and British are in fierce competition to establish trade in India, Clive, a clerk for the East India Company, becomes a soldier in the Company's army. He then saves the siege of Trichinopoly by attacking the Indian ruler at Arcot, destroying his army piecemeal. However, much of the story centers on his marriage to fellow clerk Edmund Maskeleyne's sister, Margaret. His most acclaimed victory is the Battle of Plassey in 1757 against Suraj Ud Dowlah, the King of Bengal. This in retaliation for smothering to death 146 British subjects in a guard house at Fort McWilliam, thenceforth known as the Black Hole of Calcutta. And yet, after securing Indian trade exclusively for England, East India and the British army dismantle his work, while Members of Parliament libel and slander his good name in the press and the House of Commons. As the story ends, he has cleared his name in the House with a speech defending his actions and honor.

Reviews: Andre Sennwald, *New York Times*, 1-18-35: "Ronald Colman, suppressing the debonair manner which has made him one of our finest light comedians, enacts the title role with vigor and conviction, providing a touching portrait of a man with a consuming passion for power. Certainly this is one of his best screen achievements."

Richard Watts Jr., *New York Herald Tribune*, 1-18-35: "'Clive of India' is more interested in the domestic adventures of the great conqueror than in his victories and it is vastly concerned with the ingratitude of nations toward their heroes...Mr. Colman, without his mustache, manages to impersonate Clive attractively, although he has been more at home in earlier and more hirsute dramas."

Abel, *Weekly Variety*, 1-22-35: "Colman is an excellent Clive sans his familiar moustache. The powder wigs of the day do their bit to maintaining romantic illusion."

Commentary: For all the money and effort that went into it, *Clive* is a misfired slice of history. Instead of excitingly dramatizing Clive's step-by-step seizure of India for England, Zanuck budgeted a production that allowed one horribly staged and badly edited battle sequence (the Battle of Plassey) while spending inordinate time on Clive's married life and his talky machinations with self-interested bureaucrats. Most of the big events are glossed over in silent movie fashion using title cards.

The best sequence is when Clive is changing clothes in front of the East India Company's directors, arrogantly informing them of the tactics he will use to get his job done with their support. This is followed by Clive barking at his motley troops to stand to attention and forward march. Only in this segment do we get a hint of the megalomaniac risk taker Clive was. Otherwise, the script gives Clive little chance to catch fire as more than an especially ambitious soldier. The most contrived sequence is when he crosses the river to Plassey in a downpour, looking for all the world like Washington crossing the Delaware. There is also a failure of nerve to end the film with Clive's suicide after a final public disgrace.

Colman is also to blame with a performance that vacillates between being Clive and playing Ronald Colman, compromising credibility to please his fans. Nevertheless, sans moustache, Colman is handsomer than ever, his face open to a wider range of expression. But, he would have to wait until *A Tale of Two Cities* to take full advantage of that range.

Theatrical Source: Twentieth Century Fox Pictures.

Archival Sources: BFI. 35mm nitrate preservation print and 35mm nitrate preservation reel of 2:45 trailer, neither yet duped for viewing prints.

UCLA: 35mm nitrate studio print.

F42   THE MAN WHO BROKE THE BANK AT MONTE CARLO   Twentieth Century-Fox, 1935.

Producers: Nunnally Johnson and Darryl F. Zanuck. Director: Stephen Roberts. Screenplay: Nunnally Johnson and Howard Smith from the play *Monsieur Alexandre, Igra, Lepy and the Gamble* by Illie Surgutchoff and Frederick Albert Swann. Director of Photography: Ernest Palmer, ASC. Musical Director: Oscar Bradley. Incidental Music: Bert Kalmar and Harry Ruby. Song: "I'm The Man Who Broke the Bank at Monte Carlo" by Fred Gilbert (1892).

Cast: Ronald Colman (Paul Gallard), Joan Bennett (Helen Berkeley), Nigel Bruce (Ivan), Colin Clive (Bertrand Berkeley), Montagu Love (Casino Director), Frank Reicher, Lionel Pape (Assistant Directors), Ferdinand Gottschalk (Office Manager), Charles Fallon (Croupier), Leonid Snegoff (Nick the Chef), Georgette Rhodes (Check Room Girl), Alphonse DuBois (Taxi Driver), Andre Cheron (Dealer), Ramsay Hill, Milton Royce, (Ushers), Bruce Wyndham (Excited Man), John Carradine (Despondent Man), Rudolf Myzet (Changeur), Anya Taranda (Girl at Bar), Alphonse Martell (Chasseur), William Stack, John Spacey (Directors), Don Brodie (Photographer), John Miltern (First Assistant Director), Leonard Carey, Theodore Lodi, Jacques Venaire (Captains of Waiters), E.E. Clive, Bob De Coudic, Joseph De Stefani (Waiters), Gino Corrado (Desk Clerk), Ferdinand Munier (Maitre d'Hotel), Maurice Cass (Assistant Maitre d'Hotel), George Davis, Louis Mercier (Taxi Drivers), John George (Hunchback), Lynn Bari (Flower Girl), Georges Sorel (Hotel Clerk), Frank Dunn (Stewart), Shirley Aaronson (Telephone Girl), Charles Coleman (Head Waiter), Will Stanton (Drunk Waiter), Vladimir Bykoff (Helen's Guide), Christian Rub (Gallard's Guide), I. Miraeva (Singing & Dancing Cook), Joseph Marievsky, Noiman Stengel (Singers), J. Vlaskin, W. Sabot, N. Mohoff (Dancers).

Release date and timing: New York at Radio City Music Hall, November 14. Los Angeles at the Four Star, December 7. 66 minutes. The British version runs 67 minutes.

Synopsis: Using money given him by his fellow Russian refugees, Prince turned cab driver Paul Gallard breaks the bank at a Monte Carlo casino playing baccarat. Prize money for all. The casino's directors retaliate by hiring a blonde vamp named Helen to seduce Gallard back to the gaming table to lose the winnings. But, Helen falls in love with Paul, so she doesn't carry through the scheme with her conniving brother, Bertrand. Nevertheless, Paul does go back and loses everything. In the end, discovering that he is a taxi driver and not a millionaire as she had supposed, Helen decides to marry him. The story ends with Paul proposing a toast with his fellow refugees at a Russian cafe.

Reviews: Chic, *Weekly Variety*, 11-20-35: "Ronald Colman does not quite inject the dash which he probably was expected to contribute, so it's not a 'Bulldog Drummond', though it should do well enough with the public. Colman at times seems to be playing under wraps...looking a bit old, (he) plays a little too seriously in most scenes and never gives his action the flair which would possibly have pulled this to the top."

Los Angeles Times, 12-9-35: "Ronald Colman, the debonair, continues on his easy, cheerful and nonchalant way...A kind of romantic intrigue constitutes its plot, with dialogue that often assumes a very fantastic air, but which the star handles with jauntiness that does him credit."

Commentary: After a glittery opening reel in which Gallard breaks the bank simply by taking the cards as they come, the movie falls apart, settling into a banal, boring and unbelievable plot device; the same one used 15 years later in *Champagne for Caesar* (F62) and with the same inherent flaw: If the vamp is in love with Colman's character, why take the money she is offered to ruin him when the money he has won is so much greater?

But, since there is no chemistry between Colman and Bennett, why care? Six years after their first teaming in *Bulldog Drummond*, Bennett had progressed from overdone to wooden. She didn't come into her own until she dyed her hair black for film noirs in the 1940s. For his part, Colman indulges his stylized matinee idol mannerisms—bobbing his head a lot and exaggerating his vocal cadence, for example—in a vain effort to pump life into a flat farce. So much is made of so little that the short running time seems endless. *Monte Carlo* died a quick commercial death.

Theatrical Source: Twentieth Century Fox.

Archival Sources: BFI. 35mm safety print.

UCLA: 35mm nitrate studio print.

F43 A TALE OF TWO CITIES Metro-Goldwyn-Mayer, 1935. MGM/UA Video for VHS (MV600078) and LD (MLS1008). See R5, R6, R32, R102, R186, D5, D9.

Producer: David O. Selznick, **AAN** for BP. Director: Jack Conway. Screenplay: W.P. Lipscomb and S.N. Behrman from the novel by Charles Dickens. Bibliography: Thomas Carlyle's **The French Revolution**, M. Clery's **Journal of the Temple**, Mlle. des Escherolles' **Memoirs**, and M. Nicolas's **Memoirs**. Revolutionary Sequence Directors: Val Lewton and Jacques Tourneur. Additional Uncredited Directors for Various Scenes: Robert Z. Leonard and W.S. Van Dyke. Director of Photography: Oliver T. Marsh, ASC. Art Director: Cedric Gibbons. Associate Art Directors: Fredric Hope, Edwin B. Willis. Wardrobe: Dolly Tree. Recording Director: Douglas Shearer. Film Editor: Conrad A. Nervig, **AAN**. Music: Herbert Stothart. Christmas Carols: "God Rest Ye, Merry Gentlemen," "Hark, the Herald Angels Sing" and "O Come, All Ye Faithful" (John Francis Wade), the latter sung in Latin and English. Sung by: Father Finn's Paulist Choristers.

Cast: Ronald Colman (Sydney Carton), Elizabeth Allan (Lucie Manette), Edna May Oliver (Miss Pross), Reginald Owen (C.V. Stryver), Basil Rathbone (Marquis St. Evremonde), Blanche Yurka (Madame Therese Defarge), Henry B. Walthall (Dr. Alexander Manette), Donald Woods (Charles Darnay), Walter Catlett (Barsad), Fritz Leiber (Gaspard), H.B. Warner (Gabelle), Mitchell Lewis (Ernest Defarge), Claude Gillingwater (Jarvis Lorry), Billy Bevan (Jerry Cruncher), Isabel Jewell (Mlle. Fontaine, Seamstress), Lucille La Verne (The Vengeance), Tully Marshall (Woodcutter), Fay Chaldecott (Lucie, the Child), Eily Malyon (Mrs. Cruncher), E.E. Clive (Judge in Old Bailey), Lawrence Grant (Prosecuting Attorney in Old Bailey), Robert Warwick (Tribunal Judge), Ralf Harolde (Tribunal Prosecutor), John Davidson (Morveau), Tom Ricketts (Tellson, Jr.), Donald Haines (Jerry Cruncher, Jr.), Barlowe Borland (Jacques 116), Ed Peil, Sr. (Cartwright), Edward Hearn (Leader), Richard Alexander (Executioner), Cyril McLaglen (Headsman), Frank Mayo (Jailer), Walter Kingsford (Victor the Jailer), Rolfe Sedan (Condemned Dandy), C. Montague Shaw (Chief Registrar), Chappell Dossett (English Priest), Forrester Harvey (Joe, Coach Guard), Billy House (Border Guard), Shirley McDonald (Jacques #2), Elsa Buchanan (Candy Clerk), Yorke Sherwood (Old Crony), Joseph Tozer (Inspector), Judith Vosselli

(Wife of Count), Burr Carruth (Guillotine Seller), Torben Meyer (Lackey #1).

Release dates and timing: New York at the Capitol, December 15. Los Angeles at Grauman's Chinese and Loew's State, January 8, 1936. 126 minutes.

Synopsis: The lives and fates of several people in England and France are intertwined with and determined by the French Revolution. At the center of all this fateful activity is an alcoholic but gifted British lawyer named Sydney Carton who sacrifices his life to the guillotine so that the women he secretly loves can smuggle her ex-aristocrat husband to safety.

Reviews: Chic, *Weekly Variety*, 1-1-36: "Gone are his drawing room mannerisms, shaved along with his moustache. He makes the figure likeable, pathetic and intensely sad while going through most of the picture with a smile on his face."

Edwin Schallert, *Los Angeles Times*, 1-9-36: "It embellishes with new luster the career of Ronald Colman...One knows on seeing this actor in 'Tale of Two Cities' that many of his finer talents for drama have neglected. They are here brilliantly disclosed."

Commentary: For years, Colman had told interviewers of his longing to play Sydney Carton, while vainly trying to get Goldwyn to film the book. He finally got his wish when Selznick offered him the role. However, because of a 1937 dinner speech by Selznick, a Selznick book by Ron Haver, and a story by Brian Aherne in his book on George Sanders that Aherne himself was in the running to play Carton, false stories persist that Colman at first refused the role because he didn't want to play Darnay as well (Selznick). Moreover, that he didn't want the part at all (B50) and that he was reluctant to shave his moustache (B16).

For the first, Haver was wrong. Colman disliked dual roles and felt audiences would not believe Colman sacrificing himself for Colman, so Selznick had the script revised. Instead of making Carton and Darnay improbably identical twins, it gives them only a vague resemblance (Donald Woods does slightly resemble Colman). A scene not in the book showing Carton setting up Barsad for courtroom blackmail was written, making the trial far more plausible. Furthermore, one of the film's most memorable sequences, Christmas Eve. is not in the book, either. Haver took Selznick's speech at face value instead of reading the Colman interviews, which include B106 and B218. For the third, Colman had shaved for Clive, so he had no problem shaving to play his dream role. On top of which, Aherne had only been in Hollywood since 1933 as a Colman look and soundalike, so he would not have been given the lead in a Selznick spectacular.

Colman's performance as Carton marked the first time since *Beau Geste* in 1926 that he was a superb dramatic actor at work, dropping most of his trademark mannerisms and living the part. He imbues the character with warmth, sardonic humor, off-hand worldliness, and an implosive poignancy so that we feel for a man who is bleeding from the inside from years of self-destructive behavior while presenting a blithe front. And yet, Carton never explains why he gave up on life in his 20s. What Dickens left out, the screenwriters could and should have filled in.

Far more so than in *Clive* because he has a greater affinity for Carton, Colman's face lends itself to character rather than character type. He is not only handsomer without the moustache, he is more emotionally naked, as his close-ups in the Christmas sequence and guillotine finale powerfully show.

So why wasn't he nominated for a Best Actor Oscar for his brilliant work? Perhaps because he was on the nominating committee for the 1936 awards and felt it would be immodest to suggest his own nomination. If so, he did himself a grave injustice after finally playing the one role he had coveted. His Carton is the definitive portrayal of the part, more richly shaded and powerfully moving than Dirk Bogarde's melancholy turn in 1958, and far more sympathetic than Chris Sarandon's pompously cynical portrayal in a 1980 TV movie.

The first film version of this story, made in 1911 with Maurice Costello as Carton, survives at UCLA.

Video Source note: The print used is gray and grainy and speeded by 1 fps to save tape. It runs 121 minutes. The LD version is at normal speed.

Theatrical Source: Turner Entertainment. Their colorized version ranges from muddy to lovely, but generally is a vivid improvement because of the color.

Archival Sources: LC. 35mm nitrate picture negative, nitrate soundtrack negative, and preservation composite fine grain masters of first five reels. Also 35mm safety viewing print of the complete movie.

BFI: 35mm nitrate print.

UCLA: 35mm nitrate print, 35mm safety projection print, 16mm safety print, 16mm safety conservation print.

F44 UNDER TWO FLAGS Twentieth Century-Fox, 1936.

Producer: Darryl F. Zanuck. Presented by Joseph M. Schenck. Associate Producer: Raymond Griffith. Director: Frank Lloyd. Screenplay: W.P. Lipscomb and Walter Ferris from the 1867 novel by Ouida (Maria Louise de la Ramée). Photography: Ernest Palmer, ASC. Director of Battle Sequences: Otto Brower. Battle Photography: Sidney Wagner, ASC. Art Director: William Darling. Settings: Thomas Little. Film Editor: Ralph Dietrich. Musical Score: Louis Silvers. Additional music: "Pale Hands I Love Beside the Shalimar" (background motif), "The Blue Danube," and "La Marseillaise" (Claude de Lisle). Costumes: Gwen Wakeling. Sound; Joseph Aiken, Roger Heman. Technical Advisors: Douglas Baxter, Jamiel Hasson and Otto Steiger. Ballistics Expert: Lou Witte. Assistant Directors: Ad Schaumer, A.F. Erickson.

Cast: Ronald Colman (Sergeant Victor aka Rafe Brett), Claudette Colbert (Cigarette), Victor McLaglen (Major J.C. Doyle), Rosalind Russell (Lady Venetia Cunningham), Gregory Ratoff (Ivan), Nigel Bruce (Captain Menzies), C. Henry Gordon (Lt. Petaine), Herbert Mundin (Rake), John Carradine (Cafard, cut from reissue prints), Lumsden Hare (Lord Seraph), J. Edward Bromberg (Col. Ferol), Onslow Stevens (Sidi Ben-Youssiff), Fritz Leiber (French Governor), Thomas Beck (Pierre), William Ricciardi (Cigarette's Father), Frank Reicher (French General), Francis McDonald (Husson), Harry Semels (Sgt. Malinas), Nicholas Soussanin (Levine), Douglas Gerrard (Col. Farley), Louis Mercier (Barron), Frank Lackteen (Ben Hamidon), Jamiel Hasson (Arab Liaison Officer), Gwendolyn Logan (Lady Cairn), Hans Von Morhart (Hans), Tor Johnson (Bidou), Marc Lawrence (Grivon), George Regas (Keskerdit), Ronald J. Pennick (Cpl. Vaux), Rolfe Sedan (Mouche), Eugene Borden (Villon), Tony Merlo (Cartouche), Harry Worth (Dinant), Alex Palasthy (Hotel Manager), Rosita Harlan (Ivan's Girl).

Release dates and timings: New York at Radio City Music Hall, April 30. Los Angeles at Loew's State and Grauman's Chinese, May 15. 110 minutes. Cut to 98 minutes for World War II re-release and subsequently released to TV at that length.

Synopsis: The setting is late 19th century Abeshé, a Foreign Legion outpost in Southern Algeria. Sergeant Victor falls for patrician Lady Venetia not knowing he is being pursued by sexy cafe owner and Legion mascot, Cigarette, who in turn is lusted after by Major Doyle. Meanwhile, believing that Victor has stolen his girl, jealous Doyle keeps sending him on missions from Fort Ain Seraf to protect Fort Giardia, hoping he'll be killed. As a ruse, Victor lets himself be held prisoner by warring Arab chieftain Sidi Ben-Youssiff to give the Legion time to find and attack Youssif's soldiers. In the nick of time, Cigarette leads the Legion's charge against Youssif, dying for her bravery, for which she earns a

Legion funeral. At the funeral, Victor is again an honorable civilian—having learned his now-dead brother confessed the crime, whatever it was, for which Victor joined the Legion to take the fall—and reunited with Venetia.

Reviews: Abel, *Weekly Variety*, 5-6-36: "Ronald Colman does all right on the romance interest...If the kid were really turned loose in a civilized community, one wonders about his Donjuanish progress."

Edwin Schallert, *Los Angeles Times*, 5-16-36: "Colman has a rather thankless role, to which he brings an acceptable light touch that relieves...Colman's jauntiness exemplified in other less imposing films remains pleasing and his personality carries, but this is for him no 'Tale of Two Cities.'"

Louella O. Parsons, *Los Angeles Examiner*, 5-16-36: "Ronald Colman never gives a bad performance, but some ways did not seem to me to create as much sympathy as he should in a character so undeniably heroic...I thought he was a little too restrained for an officer who could fall in love so quickly."

Commentary: Typical Hollywood product of its time. An impeccably produced, smoothly entertaining star vehicle cashing in on Colman's gentleman adventurer image and the adventure movie cycle of the period with a story similar to *Beau Geste* (F25), Ouida having published her novel 58 years before Wren's.

Colman's Victor is scruffy and earthy yet debonair, reserved when he needs to be, and romantic. Above all, he is loyal to the legion and willing to sacrifice himself to save the troops. He has sex in the desert with the lusty Cigarette, but prefers the refinement of Venetia. Watch the scene in which Colman first meets Russell for his subtle facial pantomime and body language: burgeoning interest in her, confounded by resigned or bemused exasperation with McLaglen's blustering vulgarity.

The worst thing about *Under Two Flags* is that Colman turned down *My Man Godfrey* to make it. It was also filmed in 1916 with Theda Bara, Herbert Heye and Stuart Holmes, re-issued in 1919; and in 1922 with Priscilla Dean, James Kirkwood and Stuart Holmes (different role from 1916).

Theatrical Source: Twentieth Century Fox Pictures.

Archival Sources: MOMA. 35mm safety print running 99 minutes 42 seconds, but unavailable for viewing until the missing 10+ minutes are restored.

UCLA: Scratchy and dirty nitrate print running 96 minutes because of splices and missing footage at the end of reel 5 or beginning of reel 6, according to UCLA's Orion database.

F45   LOST HORIZON   Columbia, 1937. Released overseas as *Les Horizons Perdus* (France), *Orizzonte Perduro* (Italy), *Das Verlorene Paradies* (Germany). Columbia/TriStar Video on VHS, 60763. Laser disc withdrawn in 1993 for remastering. Trailer on Rush Video. See R27, R54, R110, R173, D3, D10, D15-17.

Executive Producer: Harry Cohn. Producer and Director: Frank Capra, **AAN** for BP. Screenplay: Robert Riskin from the 1933 novel by James Hilton. Additional uncredited writers: Sidney Buchman (rewrite of first High Lama scene), Frank Capra, Frances Marion (various). Plus improvisations by main cast members. Director of Photography: Joseph Walker, ASC. Assistant Cameramen: Alfred S. Keller, William Jolly, Irving Klein, Roy Babbit, Sam Rosen, ASC. Second Unit Photography: Henry Freulich, ASC. (Ojai footage and other scenes). Aerial Photographer: Elmer G. Dyer. Assistant Aerial Camera: Rod Tolmie. Special Camera Effects and Matte Paintings: E. Roy Davidson and Ganahl Carson. Art Director: Stephen Goosson, **AA**. Assistants to Goosson: Lionel Banks and Paul Murphy. Set Designer: Cary Odell. Interior Decorations: Babs Johnstone. Set Photographer: Schuyler

Crail. Costume Designs: Dan Groesbeck. Costumes: Ernest Dryden. High Lama Make-up: Jack Dawn. Sound: Edward Bernds, but **AAN** for John Livadary, head of Columbia's sound department. Film Editors: Gene Milford and Gene Havlick, **AA**. Musical Score: Dimitri Tiomkin. Musical Director: Max Steiner. Choral Voices: Hall Johnson Choir. Choral Director: Jester Hairston. Orchestrations: Charles Maxwell, Herman Hand, Max Reese, William Grant Still, Bernhard Kaun, Hugo Friedhofer, George Parrish, Robert Russell Bennett, Peter Brunelli. Musical Advisor: Max Rabinowitsch. Song: "Brahms' Lullaby". Technical Advisors: Harrison Forman and John Tettener. Dialogue director: Harold Winston. Assistant Directors: C.C. Coleman, Milton Carter. Ice House Technician: Regis Gubser. Microphones: Buster Libbott. Dialogue Director: Harold Winston. Script Clerk: Eleanor Hall. Make-up: Charles Huber, Johnny Wallace. Wardrobe: William Bridgehouse, Daisy Robinson. Hairdressers: Helen Hunt, Rhoda Donaldson. Dog trainers: Charles J. deSoria, Rennie Reniro. Bird trainer: Archie Beckingsale. Tibetan musical instruments: Henry Eichheim (misspelled by Capra as Eichman). Stills: Alfredo Valenti, Irving Lippman. Poster Artist: James Montgomery Flagg. Himalayan footage: Arnold Fanck's *Stürme außer dem Mountblanc* (*Storm Over Mont Blanc*, 1930, aka *Avalanche*) and Andrew Marton's *Der Dämon des Himalaya* (*Demon of the Himalayas*, 1934).

    Cast: Ronald Colman (Robert Conway), Jane Wyatt (Sondra Bizet), Edward Everett Horton (Alexander P. Lovett), John Howard (George Conway), Thomas Mitchell (Henry Barnard/Chalmers Bryant), Margo (Maria), Isabel Jewell (Gloria Stone), H.B. Warner, **AAN** for BSA (Chang), Sam Jaffe (Father Perrault, High Lama), Margo (Maria), Hugh Buckler (Lord Gainsford), David Torrence (Prime Minister), Val Duran (Talu, plane hijacker), Milton Owen (Fenner, pilot knocked out by Talu), Richard Loo (Shanghai Airport official), Noble Johnson (Leader of porters), Leonard Mudie (Roberts, Foreign Secretary), Boyd Irwin, Sr. (Assistant Foreign Secretary), John Tettener (Montaigne, white-haired man at piano with Sondra), John Miltern (Carstairs), John Burton (Wynant), John T. Murray (Meeker), Max Rabinowitz (Sieveking, Pianist): these last four in deleted shipboard prologue), Dennis D'Auburn (Aviator), George Chan (Chinese Priest), Norman Ainsley, David Clyde (Stewards), Eric Wilton (Englishman), Lawrence Grant (Robertson, Clubman), Neil Fitzgerald, Derby Clark (Radio operators), Willie Fung, Victor Wong (Bandit Leaders), Matthew Carlton (Pottery maker), Joe Herrera (Candle maker), Mary Wiggins (nude double for Jane Wyatt), Buddy Roosevelt (horseback double for Ronald Colman).

    Release dates and timing: San Francisco at the Geary, March 2. New York at the Globe, March 3. Los Angeles at the Four Star, March 10. London at the Tivoli, April 19. 132 minutes.

    Ending and timing changed to 131 minutes, 15 seconds in mid-March starting with the New York run. Running time about six weeks after American premieres: 123 minutes. General release timing for Los Angeles and New York second runs starting September 29 and 30, 1937, respectively: 116 minutes, 9 seconds.

    Re-release title and timing in the fall of 1942: *Lost Horizon of Shangri-La*. 108 minutes, 45 seconds. Television release title and timing from the early 1950s to mid-1960s: *Lost Horizon of Shangri-La*, 95 minutes. It started being shown on TV at 108:45 in 1966. Cable TV title and timing in 1983: *Lost Horizon*, 116:09. Roadshow restoration timing in 1986: 131:10. In 1992, a five-second shot from the first High Lama scene was added to UCLA's restoration print.

    None of the 16mm rental prints in the 1960s and 70s ran longer than 108:45, but film rental companies advertised it at 118 minutes because they never questioned Columbia's erroneous timing by counting the footage themselves.

    American Film Institute restoration, 1977-1986: Head preservationist: Robert Gitt.

Supervisor and print locater: Lawrence F. Karr. Assistants: Audrey E. Kupferberg, Joe Empsuch. Restoration includes 16½ minutes of restored footage—some of it from the BFI—plus 6 minutes of stills and freeze frames in lieu of still missing footage.

Longest restored scenes: Conway's drunken pacifist monologue aboard the hijacked plane, 2:30; pigeon house sequence with Conway and Sondra, 2:15; portions of first High Lama scene, 1:45; Chang trying to comfort Gloria as she contemplates suicide, 1:05. Longest sequence still missing: Barnard and Lovett visiting the Valley of the Blue Moon, 3:20.

Synopsis: Four men and one woman are hijacked from a Chinese rebellion in Baskul to a mysterious utopia called Shangri-La in the farthest reaches of the Tibetan mountains. One of the hijacked passengers, a British diplomat named Robert Conway, learns that he was deliberately kidnapped and brought to Shangri-La to replace the dying High Lama. He also learns that the purpose of Shangri-La is to preserve mankind's cultural treasures against the ravages of war while giving meaning to near-immortal life, since Shangri-La's environment slows the aging process.

Meanwhile, Robert's hot-tempered brother, George, is itching to return to England as soon as possible. With the help of a seemingly young Russian woman named Maria, George persuades his brother to leave Shangri-La. During the return mountain trek, George and Maria die, leaving Robert to struggle back to England as best he can. He does make it back, but flees shortly after, trekking through treacherously snowy Tibetan mountains to return to Shangri-La to fulfill his destiny as a man of learning, vision, and action.

Reviews: Howard Barnes, *San Francisco Chronicle*, 3-4-37: "Ronald Colman, as Conway, also has the power to unleash one's imagination while he stamps the direct drama with power and authority. His is a brilliant and sensitively felt characterization."

Abel, *Weekly Variety*, 3-10-37: "Colman, with fine restraint, conveys the metamorphosis of the foreign diplomat falling in with the Arcadian idyll that he beholds in the Valley of the Blue Moon."

Edwin Schallert, *Los Angeles Times*, 3-11-37: "The whole idea is very romantic, and it has an undercurrent of deep spirituality. Utopian the Tibetan city may be, but it is a Utopia of logic...Colman is the force in the picture that truly gives it conviction."

Mordaunt Hall *New York Times*, 3-3-37: "Grand adventure, magnificently staged, beautifully photographed and capitally played. Mr. Capra was guilty of a few editorial cliches, but otherwise, it was a perfect job."

London Times, 4-19-37: "(Capra) has overstepped the boundary between comedy and fantasy and found himself not quite at home on either side of it."

Newspaper ad copy: "Stunning In Its Sweep, Tremendous In Its Power, Towering in its Magnitude. A Story So New, So Miraculous, So Thrilling, So Beautiful That All Mankind will Acclaim this the Greatest Picture Ever Made."

Commentary: *Lost Horizon* had a 2½-year gestation. Capra had to wait over a year for Colman to finish with his Fox and MGM commitments; Capra ran 34 days and $776,337 over a 66-day schedule and a $1.25 million budget; Colman was paid either $125,000 or $165,000, depending on the source, including post-production scenes and retakes; the script was continuously revised, added to on the set, and scenes rewritten; there was the nightmare of finding both *an* actor and the *right* actor to play the High Lama; nearly an hour had to be removed after a failed sneak preview in Santa Barbara on November 22, 1936; and retakes and new scenes were shot into January 1937.

The final cost, including prints, advertising, and distribution was $2,626,337. Gross rentals through October 1985, according to Joseph McBride (B65), were $5,295,546, with a net profit of $1,048,337. However, McBride doesn't say if these figures include foreign and TV rentals, and he doesn't include these rentals plus cable rentals and home video sales through 1991, when his book went to press.

Despite all of above-mentioned problems, and much more, it was a happy if challenging shoot for the cast and crew, and editors Havlick and Milford were able to carve a remarkable picture from what was originally a 5-hour-plus rough cut. A movie that garnered a lot of praise on initial release, but reportedly only turned a profit in subsequent reissues throughout the 1940s. Although McBride claims that the movie lost money on first release, it played for months on end in first and second release throughout the U.S. and throughout the world; *Weekly Variety* listed it as one of the 38 top-grossing movies of 1936-37; it ranked #10 on the *New York Times* list for 1937 and was #4 on *Film Daily*'s list.

The movie's reputation is largely due to the personal traits Colman brought to his performance. He not only makes us believe in Shangri-La, but that he himself has the attributes to be its leader and savior: nobly adventurous idealism tempered by a mature and questioning intellect and a diplomat's skill in dealing with the real world. *Lost Horizon* is a haunting movie because Colman is haunted by the universal quest for inner peace and a sanctuary—spiritually and literally.

It was badly remade as a musical in 1973, starring Peter Finch and Charles Boyer. An earlier and different musical version by Jerome Lawrence, Robert E. Lee and James Hilton opened at New York City's Winter Garden on June 13, 1956 for 21 performances. It was later staged live in color on *Hallmark Hall of Fame* on October 24, 1960, with Richard Basehart as Conway and Claude Rains as the High Lama.

Home Video Notes: Neither the VHS or LD versions (running 131:10) fully capture the pictorial quality of the original 1937 release because the transfers were made from the restoration print. But that can be rectified if Columbia/TriStar video ever produces an ultra deluxe version from a composite transfer using the last remaining nitrate prints and the restoration footage.

Archival Sources: LC. 116-minute nitrate 1937 general release print; nitrate composite fine grain master and negative; preservation composite fine grain master; nitrate and safety soundtrack negatives; preservation positive soundtrack; theatrical projection print; composite viewing copy. All of the above except the first are the results and by-products of the restoration and preservation project.

Plus a nitrate print of the 34-minute exhibitor's trailer from 1936 minus soundtrack. This trailer was shown dual projector, so the soundtrack reels are lost. It consists of takes used in the released version plus alternate takes and outtakes, including a scene between Wyatt and Jewell.

BFI: 35mm nitrate viewing print running 115 minutes. No preservation material. It's all at LC.

UCLA: 35mm safety print of the restored version, and nitrate print of the original trailer.

F46 SCREEN SNAPSHOTS: #9 FOR 1937 Columbia Pictures. See F45.

Production credits unavailable.

Three sequences: 1) Behind-the-scenes during the shooting of *Lost Horizon* at Malibu Beach; 2) the homes of Anna Sten, Ann Sothern and Virginia Sale; 3) and the San Juan Capistrano handicap at Santa Anita, with shots of dozens of stars at the races.

Release date and timing: May 22. 10 minutes.

F47 THE PRISONER OF ZENDA Selznick International Pictures for United Artists, 1937. MGM/UA Home Video VHS 301644, LD 103968. See R12, R254, D18.

Producer: David O. Selznick. Director: John Cromwell. Uncredited additional directors: W.S. Van Dyke (dueling scenes), George Cukor (renunciation scene). Screenplay: John L. Balderston. Adaptation: Wells Root, based on Edward Rose's adaptation of Anthony Hope's novel. Additional Dialogue: Donald Ogden Stewart. Rewrite of renunciation scene: Sidney Howard (uncredited). Director of Photography: James Wong Howe, ASC. Musical Score: Alfred Newman. Coronation March: "Hail the Conquering Hero Comes" from Handel's *Judas Maccabeus*. Post-Coronation Waltz: "An Artist's Life" by Johann Strauss, Jr. Art Director: Lyle Wheeler, AAN. Set Decoration: Casey Roberts. Special effects: Jack Cosgrove. Costumes: Ernest Dryden. Supervising Film Editor: Hal C. Kern Film Editor: James E. Newcom. Sound: Oscar Lagerstrom. Fencing Master: Ralph Faulkner. Sword fight choreographer: Fred Cravens. Technical advisors: Prince Sigvard Bernadotte and Colonel Ivar Enhorning. Assistant to Producer: William H. Wright. Assistant to Director: Frederick Spencer.

Cast: Ronald Colman (Rudolf Rassendyll/King Rudolf), Madeleine Carroll (Princess Flavia), Douglas Fairbanks, Jr. (Rupert of Hentzau), Mary Astor (Antoinette de Mauban), C. Aubrey Smith (Col. Zapt), Raymond Massey (Black Michael), David Niven (Fritz von Tarlenheim), Montagu Love (Detchard), William von Brincken (Kraftstein), Philip Sleeman (Lauengram), Eleanor Wesselhoeft (Cook), Florence Roberts (Duenna), Torben Meyer (Black Michael's Butler), Lawrence Grant (Marshal Strakcncz), Charles K. French (Bishop), Ian MacLaren (Cardinal), Ralph Faulkner (Bersonin), Byron Foulger (Master Johann), Howard Lang (Josef), Ben Webster (British Ambassador), Evelyn Beresford (British Ambassador's Wife), Boyd Irwin (Master of Ceremonies), Emmett King (von Haugwitz, Lord High Chamberlain), Al Shean (Orchestra Leader), Charles Halton (Passport Officer), Alexander D'Arcy (De Gautet), Spencer Charters (Porter), Nigel Bruce, Halliwell Hobbes (Club Members in deleted prologue and epilogue).

Release dates and timing: New York at Radio City Music Hall, September 2. Los Angeles at Grauman's Chinese and Loew's State, October 6. 101 minutes. Some prints were made with sepia-tone, which is a brownish wash.

Synopsis: While on holiday in Ruritania, British squire Rudolf Rassendyll takes the place of the drugged and kidnapped king, his lookalike cousin Rudolf. He then foils the plan of Michael, the king's half-brother, and Rupert of Hentzau, to steal the throne, while falling in love with Princess Flavia, who is duty-bound to marry the king. After Rassendyll rescues the king, he and Flavia part, placing honor and duty to king and country above personal passion for each other.

Reviews: Abel, *Weekly Variety*, 9-1-37: "Colman has the ability to make a full dress court uniform appear as comfortable as a suit of pajamas. He never trips over his sword, or loosens his collar for air. No matter how ridiculous the costume, he can make love in a moonlit garden as though he means it."

Gould Cassal, *Brooklyn Daily Eagle*, 9-3-37: "In the dual role of King and commoner, Ronald Colman gives his best performance; he puts on an excellent show, shading the two personalities deftly and running from drama to humor with singular ease."

Hollywood Reporter, 8-28-37: "The cast, headed by Ronald Colman (et al.), delivered as fine a group of performances as has ever been seen on the screen...Mr. Colman...added more laurels to his exceptional screen contributions."

New York News, 9-2-37: "The picture is superbly acted by a fine cast, and it has been directed with verve and distinction by John Cromwell. Its star, Ronald Colman, has never been better."

Commentary: Like *Lost Horizon*, *The Prisoner of Zenda* went through a good deal of post-production reshooting and re-cutting. Production began March 8, 1937, finishing in mid-May. It was previewed in late May at 135 minutes, including a prologue and epilogue framing device showing the elderly Rassendyl at his men's club getting word that Flavia has died. He then recalls his adventure in Zenda to two fellow club members.

According to Ronald Haver, Selznick was far from satisfied with this version, ordering 31 shots retaken and/or rewritten beginning in early July, including the renunciation scene, which was directed by George Cukor because John Cromwell was busy on another movie. The framing device was removed as a narrative hindrance, as it was on *Lost Horizon*. The final cost, including 400 prints, was either $1.25 million (B94) or $1.3 million (B50), grossing $2.8 million, earning a profit of $182,000 (B94) or $665,000 (B50). Whether this is just domestic or worldwide isn't mentioned by David Thomson or Haver.

Either way, *Zenda* was a popular and influential movie. Colman is at his zenith playing the reluctant but valiant gentleman adventurer who displays the qualities and virtues it takes to be a mature and temperate ruler while saving a kingdom from the clutches of a jealous sibling and an amoral opportunist. The film remains a model of storytelling, a beautifully crafted fable on the favorite Colman themes of honor, duty and self-sacrifice in a just cause. The story has been endlessly remade and copied, but this remains the definitive version, with an ideal cast.

All it lacks is the Technicolor for which it screams and for which it was originally planned. Selznick went with black-and-white because cameraman James Wong Howe determined that Colman's head on another actor's body for the two hand-shaking scenes would look obvious in color. When I asked Howe at a late 1970 LACMA tribute to him why he didn't make a screen test to see if he was right, he replied that it hadn't occurred to him. The movie *was* colorized in 1989, but it's not the same as being filmed in three-strip Technicolor.

Theatrical Source: Turner Entertainment.

Archival Sources: BFI. 35mm nitrate preservation print and 35mm safety viewing print of a 4:45 segment.

UCLA: Grainy and muddy-sounding 16mm print of complete film, and original trailer on VHS from 16mm reel of several movie trailers. Also nitrate print of the trailer.

Previously filmed in 1913 with James K. Hackett and Beatrice Beckley, in England in 1915 with G.L. Tucker, and in 1922 with Lewis Stone and Phyllis Terry. Remade by MGM in Technicolor in 1952 using the 1937 script (almost shot for shot), with Stewart Granger, Deborah Kerr and James Mason. Remade in 1977 as a comedy vehicle for Peter Sellers. Contemporary variations include *Moon over Parador* (1988) with Richard Dreyfuss and Sonia Braga, and *Dave* (1993) with Kevin Kline and Sigourney Weaver, though these movies owe equally as much to *The Masquerader*. Spoofed by Blake Edwards in his 1965 comedy *The Great Race* and by Don Adams in his TV series *Get Smart*. This is clearly a popular story or plot device.

F48 IF I WERE KING Frank Lloyd for Paramount, 1938. See R105, R147.

Producer and Director: Frank Lloyd. Screenplay: Preston Sturges, based on the play by Justin Huntly McCarthy. Director of Photography: Theodor Sparkuhl, ASC. Special Photographic Effects: Gordon Jennings. Film Editor: Hugh Bennett. Sound: Harold C. Lewis and John Cope, but **AAN** for L.L. Ryder, head of Paramount sound department. Musical Score: Richard Hageman, **AAN**. Musical Director: Boris Morros. Art Directors: Hans Dreier and John Goodman, **AAN**. Set Decorations: A.E. Freudeman. Costumes: Edith Head. Poem excerpts: "If I Were King" by McCarthy, "Ballad of the Hanged" and "Where Are the Snows of Yesteryear?" by Villon. Poem recited in the tavern sequence is by Sturges. Associate Producer: Lou Smith. Assistant Directors: William Tummel and Harry Scott.

Cast: Ronald Colman (François Villon), Basil Rathbone (King Louis XI), Frances Dee

(Katherine dc Vaucelles), Ellen Drew (Huguette du Hamel), C.V. France (Father Villon), Henry Wilcoxon (Captain of the Watch), Heather Thatcher (The Queen), Stanley Ridges (René de Montigny), Bruce Lester (Noël de Jolys), Walter Kingsford (Tristan l'Hermite), Alma Lloyd (Colette), Sidney Toler (Robin Turgis), Colin Tapley (Jehan le Loup), Ralph Forbes (Oliver le Dain), John Miljan (Thibaut d'Aussigny), William Haade (Guy Tabarie), Adrian Morris (Colin de Cayleux), Montagu Love (General Dudon), Lester Matthews (General Saliere), William Farnum (General Barbezier), Paul Harvey (Burgundian Herald), May Beatty (Anna), Francis McDonald (Casin Cholet), Ann Evers, Jean Fenwick (Ladies-in-Waiting), Pat West (Storehouse Keeper), John George (Ugly Dwarf Beggar), Henry Brandon (Soldier).

Release dates and timing: New York at the Paramount, September 28. Los Angeles at the Paramount, November 17. 101 minutes.

Synopsis: The time and place are 1460s Paris. After foiling a treacherous plan by King Louis's XI's grand constable, poet/beggar/rogue François Villon is appointed by Louis to take the dead constable's place; Louis wants to see if he will dispense the king's justice any better. Not only does Villon temper justice with mercy, he opens the king's storehouses to the poor and wretched of Paris, who are being starved by Burgundian soldiers surrounding the city. In this, he has the support of Katherine de Vaucelles, lady-in-waiting to the Queen, who secretly loves him. When the king's generals refuse to fight the Burgundians, François leads his fellow beggars and thieves to victory over the Burgundians by appealing to their criminal self-interests. Rewarding and punishing him at the same time, Louis spares Villon's life while exiling him from Paris. As François is leaving the city limits, Katherine follows him in her carriage.

Reviews: *Hollywood Reporter*, 9-14-38: "Then, too, it is an ideal part for Ronald Colman, that of Villon. His delivery of poetry and wit is one to keep him high favorite among the 'fem fans.'"

Daily Variety, 9-14-38: "'If I Were King' provides Ronald Colman with the broadest opportunity of his long reign as a thespian, and he makes the most of it...(He) is as beloved by the customers at the fadeout as he was by the people of Paris after he rallied them to rout the Duke of Burgundy's invading forces."

Abel, *Weekly Variety*, 9-21-38: "Colman's delineation of the adventurous poet-philosopher, Villon, is excellent, carrying through it a verve and spontaneity for an outstanding performance."

Frank S. Nugent, *New York Times*, 9-29-38: "His confession that he has been the associate of cutthroats and wantons carries no conviction at all. Secretly he knows, and we know, that he always dresses for dinner."

Commentary: For its first 50 minutes, *If I Were King* is one of the greatest American movies ever made, due to a wickedly witty and unsentimental script by Sturges; fast, fun, intelligent pacing and direction by Lloyd; and Colman's most flamboyantly colorful and roguish performance to date as a French Robin Hood. The differences between his previous two roles and this one are phenomenal. He is earthy yet debonair, intellectual yet low-down, idealistic but practical, and a champion of the underprivileged.

Matching him almost move for move, and nearly stealing the show, is Basil Rathbone, cackling his way through an astonishingly spidery performance. He is a king who means well and knows he has enemies within, but who is simultaneously out of touch with the people he rules and at a loss for a strategy for dealing with the Burgundians. Both men are in top form, with Dee and Drew mainly peripheral to their machinations.

The second half suffers from the script and direction running out of steam, verve and inventiveness. It flags for most of half an hour while Colman romances Dee and deals with the stubborn generals, then switches to high gear again for the final routing of the Burgundians. The ending is a let-down as Katherine merely follows Villon in a carriage as he leaves Paris. The radio version, R105, tops it.

Sturges intended the show as a thinking man's Robin Hood and nearly succeeded in matching the same year Errol Flynn film. What the script lacks are more outdoor scenes, more of Villon's charismatic leadership of his fellow thieves, more of his relationship with Huguette, competition between the two women for him, and Technicolor. (Huguette dies only because she has to be out of the way as Katherine's rival). Since the story had almost nothing to do with the real Villon (who disappeared around 1463 his early 30s), Sturges could have dared even more in matching the competition.

Other movies about Villon include *If I Were King* with William Farnum and Betty Ross Clarke (1920), *The Beloved Rogue* (1927) with John Barrymore, and two versions of *The Vagabond King*: One with Dennis King and Jeanette MacDonald (1930, two-strip Technicolor), the other with Oreste and Kathryn Grayson (1956).

Theatrical Source: MCA Pictures.

Archival Source: UCLA. 35mm nitrate studio print, scratchy 16mm safety trailer on compilation reel.

F49 THE LIGHT THAT FAILED Paramount, 1939. Trailer on Rush Video. See R15, R160.

Producer and Director: William A. Wellman. Screenplay: Robert Carson, from the 1890 novel (his first) by Rudyard Kipling. Director of Photography: Theodore Sparkuhl, ASC. Art Directors: Hans Dreier and Robert Odell. Set Decorations: A.E. Freudeman. Second Unit Director: Joseph O. Youngerman (battle scenes). Second Unit Cameraman: Guy Bennett. Unit Manager: Sidney Street. Sound: Hugo Grenzlock and Walter Oberst. Film Editor: Thomas Scott. Musical Score: Victor Young. (Interpolation of Hindu music supposedly "Yankee Doodle Dandy" played backwards.) Technical Advisors: Captain Jack R. Durham-Mathews, Alf Nicholson. Assistant Directors: Fritz Collings, Stanley Goldsmith. Battle scenes shot at Black Mesa and Santa Fe, New Mexico.

Cast: Ronald Colman (Dick Heldar), Walter Huston (Torpenhow), Muriel Angelus (Maisie), Ida Lupino (Bessie Broke), Dudley Digges (The Nilghai), Mr. Whiskers (Mr. Binkle, the Scotch Terrier), Ernest Cossart (Beeton), Ferike Boros (Madame Celeste Binat), Pedro de Cordoba (Monsieur Binat), Colin Tapley (Gardner), Fay Helm (Red-haired girl), Ronald Sinclair (Dick at 12), Sarita Wooton (Maisie at 11), Halliwell Hobbes (Eye Doctor), Colin Tapley (Gardner), Charles Irwin (Soldier Model), Francis McDonald (George), George Regas (Cassavetti), Wilfred Roberts (Barton), Colin Kenny (Doctor), Joe Collings (Thackeray), Ted Deputy (Johnnie, Officer), Major Sam Harris (Wells), Larry Lawson (Andy, Officer), Clive Morgan (Slim), Robert Perry (Hoke, Officer), Carl Voss (Chaps, Officer), Benjamin Watson (Manny), Pat O'Malley (Bullock), Barbara Denny (Waitress), Clara M. Blore (Mother), Leslie Francis (Man with Bandaged Eyes), George Chandler, George H. Melford, Cyril Ring, Hayden Stevenson (War Correspondents), Barry Downing (Little Boy), Harold Entwistle (Old Man with Dark Glasses).

Release dates and timing: New York at the Rivoli, December 24. Los Angeles at the Paramount, March 7, 1940. 97 minutes.

Synopsis: In 1890s England, artist Dick Heldar is catching the public's fancy with his realistic paintings of war scenes from the Sudan, but quickly turns to romanticized portraits for more money. This to the disgust of his close friends, war correspondents Torpenhow and Nilghai. When Dick starts going blind from a cut received in battle, he resolves to paint his masterpiece, "Melancholia." Desperate to finish it, he drinks heavily to keep his eyesight going, driving his model, a prostitute named Bessie, to hysteria. In revenge, Bessie destroys the painting. When Dick shows the painting to his childhood playmate and fellow painter, Maisie, she thinks he has gone mad. After Bessie tells Dick the truth, he journeys straightaway back to the Sudan to be with Torp, and to die in the battle of Ondurman (1895). Reaching the British war camp, Dick has Torp put him on a horse. He immediately rides into battle with the soldiers, dying a quick death from an enemy bullet.

Reviews: Frank Nugent, *New York Times*, 12-25-39: "Mr. Colman has rarely handled a role with greater authority or charm, manfully underplaying even the surefire melodramatics of the sequence in which he goes blind—a heaven-sent infirmity for 99 out of 100 hard-pressed actors."

Harry Friedman, *Los Angeles Examiner*, 3-8-40: "This role will probably not be one of Colman's most popular...As an acting job, though, it is among Colman's best. The restraint, shading of moods, and the climax when he learns he will lose his sight, are dramatic acting at its best."

Philip K. Scheuer, *Los Angeles Times*, 3-8-40: "Self-centered, mockingly egotistical (Heldar) is, yes, and insatiably hungry for material success; yet through Colman's illuminating characterization, these flaws become readily forgivable. We recognize them for what they are: but a single side of the sensitive and complex Heldar."

Commentary: After five years of playing noble characters, Colman finally extended his range as the gifted but arrogant and selfish Dick Heldar. He can paint realistically for impact, but he makes more money selling the "romance" of war to magazines. He also has three types of relationships going: his male bond with Torpenhow, his selfish wooing of the untalented Maisie, and his callous treatment of Bessie. His literal loss of sight is also a metaphor for being blinded by his prideful arrogance and materialism.

Colman's emotional range as Heldar shows an instinctive grasp of characterization beyond his usual work. He also has an excellent male co-star in Walter Huston, who was a last-minute replacement for Thomas Mitchell, who changed his mind in favor of the role of Doc Boone in Stagecoach. Huston is strongly affecting as a man whose grief over his friend's blindness is stronger than his scorn for his sellout. However, as happened with Basil Rathbone in *If I Were King*, Huston almost steals the show with an easygoing American manner contrasted with Colman's more accented British style.

Apparently, enough Colman fans were put off by his risky performance and the story's emphasis on introspection and emotional darkness that the movie made only a small profit. Nevertheless, it features some of his finest work.

Previously filmed in 1916 with Robert Edeson and José Collins, and 1923 with Percy Marmont and Jacqueline Logan.

Theatrical Source: MCA, which has safety and nitrate prints and a nitrate trailer.

Archival Source: UCLA. 35mm nitrate prints of reels 1, 3 and 4, running about 58 minutes total.

F50 LUCKY PARTNERS United Producers for RKO, 1940. RKO Video 2014.

Producer: George Haight. Director: Lewis Milestone. Screenplay: Allan Scott and John van Druten from the short story "Bonne Chance." Director of Photography: Robert de Grasse, ASC. Special Photographic Effects: Vernon L. Walker. Art Director: Van Nest Polglase. Associate Art Director: Carroll Clark. Set Decorations: Darrell Silvera. Sound: John E. Tribby. Film Editor: Henry Berman. Musical Score: Dimitri Tiomkin. Tune being whistled at top of first reel: "Comin' Through the Rye". Miss Rogers's Gowns: Irene. Executive Producer: Harry E. Edington. Assistant Director: Argyle Nelson.

Cast: Ronald Colman (David Grant/Paul Knight Somerset), Ginger Rogers (Jean

Newton), Jack Carson (Freddie Harper), Spring Byington (Aunt Lucy), Cecilia Loftus (Mrs. Sylvester), Harry Davenport (Judge), Walter Kingsford (Wendell), Lucile Gleason (Ethel's Mother), Helen Lynd (Ethel), Hugh O'Connell (Niagara Clerk), Brandon Tynan (Mr. Sylvester), Leon Belasco (Nick #1), Eddy Conrad (Nick #2), Benny Rubin, Tom Dugan (Spielers), Billy Gilbert (Charles, waiter), Otto Hoffman (Clerk), Douglas Spencer (Well-Wisher), Alex Melesh (Art Salesman), Dorothy Adams (Maid), Frank Mills (Bus Driver), Billy Benedict (Delivery Boy), Dorothy Vernon (Woman on Bus), Allen Wood, Dick Hogan (Bell Boys), Murray Alper (Bellboy, Orchestra Leader), Max Wagner (Waiter), Tommy Mack (Joseph), Al Hill (Motor Cop), Robert Dudley (Bailiff), Charles Halton (Newspaperman), Grady Sutton (Reporter), Nora Cecil (Club Woman), Harlan Briggs (Mayor), George Watts (Plainclothesman), Olin Howland (Tourist), Fern Emmett (Hotel Maid), Lloyd Ingraham (Chamber of Commerce Member), Edgar Dearing (Desk Sergeant), Jane Patten (Bride), Bruce Hale (Bridegroom), Gayne Whitman (Announcer's Voice).

Release dates and timing: New York at Radio City Music Hall, September 5. Los Angeles at the Pantages and the Hillstreet, September 7. 99 minutes. The British version is two minutes shorter.

Synopsis: A Greenwich Village artist (Colman) and a bookshop errand girl (Rogers) share a winning lottery ticket, go on a fake honeymoon with their winnings, fall in love, wind up in court over some farcical complications, and end up planning to marry and go on a real honeymoon—all to the consternation of her dimwitted fiance (Carson).

Reviews: Abel, *Daily Variety*, 8-14-40: "Colman and Miss Rogers work together with smooth blending of talents and romantic warmth. He is at his debonair best in the whimsical situations. She confirms her right to stand amongst the most resourceful of the screen's comediennes."

Hollywood Reporter, 8-14-40: "Ronald Colman displays his usual dapper, debonair and at times, insouciant personality, which invariably causes women to sigh softly and make comparative mental notes."

Bosley Crowther, *New York Times*, 9-6-40: "Ronald Colman and Ginger Rogers in the leads are still two of Hollywood's most pleasant people...(They) play with an easy and infectious zest."

John L. Scott, *Los Angeles Times*, 9-7-40: "(Colman) again reveals that subtlety in performance which marks his every appearance on screen."

Background and Commentary: When he finally became an independent producer in league with longtime friends, Colman disastrously misread the public's appetite both for screwball farces and what they wanted to see him playing after *The Light That Failed*. He also miscast his friend Milestone to direct two poor scripts. Milestone could do comedy, but not the screwball kind.

Nor did he get the hint when every female comedy star in town turned down the female lead after reading Alan Scott's dismal script. Colman finally got Ginger Rogers because she was his box office equal, under contract to RKO, a guaranteed draw and she wanted to work with him, turning down the Rosalind Russell role in *His Girl Friday* for the chance. And yet when production began in the spring of 1940 because there was a start date commitment, the script was incomplete. Production had to be halted for three weeks midway through while Milestone dragooned John van Druten to rewrite the dreadful second half, which originally had Byington and Winninger at the hotel as part of a farcical free-for-all. The above information comes from Milestone biographer David Parker.

For all the attempts to salvage a bad package, *Lucky Partners* misfires almost from the start. After an excitingly promising opening reel, beginning with shots of two pairs of feet walking down a street to the whistled tune of "Comin' Through the Rye," the story settles into being a flatly written and directed farce, rave reviews notwithstanding. The best scene is a split screen showing Colman on the phone with Rogers reciting poetry to her.

Also bothersome is Hays Office censorship of potentially sexy scenes. Every time Colman and Rogers are on the verge of emotional ignition, they are forced to pull back, to refrain from some witty flirting (the dialogue throughout is largely as flat as the direction) and more than one brief, mild kiss. With a witty and clever script by someone like Robert Riskin, Samson Raphaelson or Sidney Buchman, and more adept handling by a skilled farceur like Capra or Lubitsch, this could have been a briskly risqué farce getting away with murder. But Colman satisfied himself with second-best, disappointing his public for the first time in years. Worse still, he turned down *Rebecca* to make it.

Archival Sources: LC. 35mm nitrate picture negative, nitrate soundtrack negative, preservation composite fine-grain master print, and 3/4" video viewing copy.

BFI: 97-minute nitrate master print.

F51 MY LIFE WITH CAROLINE United Producers for RKO, 1941.

Producer and Director: Lewis Milestone. Screenplay: John van Druten and Arnold Belgard, from the play *Train to Venice* by Louis Verneuil and Georges Berr. Director of Photography: Victor Milner, ASC. Special Photographic Effects: Vernon L. Walker. Art Director: Nicholai Remisoff. Set Decorations: Darrell Silvera. Sound: John L. Cass. Film Editor: Henry Berman. Musical Score: Werner Heymann. Gowns: Edward Stevenson. Executive Producer: William Hawks. Assistant Director: Edward Donahue.

Cast: Ronald Colman (Tony Mason), Anna Lee (Caroline Bliss Mason), Charles Winninger (Mr. Bliss), Reginald Gardiner (Paul Martindale), Gilbert Roland (Paco del Valle), Katherine Leslie (Helen), Hugh O'Connell (Muirhead), Murray Alper (Jenkins, chauffeur), Matt Moore (Walters, the Butler), Robert Greig (Albert, the Maitre d'), Richard Carle (Dr. Curtis), Clarence Straight (Bill, the Pilot), Dorothy Adams (Rodwell), Nicholas Soussanin (Pinnock, butler), Jeanine Crispin (Delta), James Farley (Railroad Conductor), Billy Mitchell (Railroad Porter), Gar Smith (Radio Announcer), Feodor Chaliapin (Sky Man).

Release dates and timing: Los Angeles at the Pantages and the Hillstreet, August 29. New York at Loew's Criterion, October 29. 81 minutes.

Synopsis: Just as bubbleheaded Caroline Mason is on the verge of being smitten with a new man, her husband, publisher Tony Mason, relates to the audience her last two flirtations, both of which he effortlessly quashed before they turned serious.

Note: *My Life with Caroline* was sneak previewed at the Alexander Theater in Glendale, CA on July 15, 1941.

Reviews: *Look*, 7-29-41: "...is scarcely recognizable as the directorial handiwork of Lewis Milestone...This is a drawing-room farce, no less. It is frothy, light-headed, inconsequential. It is delicate to the point of being anemic. Yet Milestone admirers hail it as exemplifying the director's hitherto unexploited comedy touch."

Hollywood Reporter, 7-16-41: "Colman's understanding husband role is out of this world, but he invests it with his accustomed suave polish, quietly making the show his own... the best scenes occurring when Colman's voice speaks for his wife when he is explaining what she is explaining."

America, 9-6-41: "Ronald Colman plays the patient husband with his usual talent for making trifles romantically amusing, and Anna Lee is too convincing as the erratic spouse... This is superficially amusing entertainment for *adults*."

Bosley Crowther, *New York Times*, 10-30-41: "Things have come to a pretty pass, certainly, when Ronald Colman, that old debonair dog, has to work to hold onto his lady as laboriously as he does (here)...Either Mr. Colman is slipping or his writers are."

Commentary: The *Look* critic either forgot or had never seen Milestone's highly regarded comedies *Two Arabian Knights* (1928, Oscar winner for Best Comedy Direction, 1928-29) and *The Front Page* (1931). But this was farce, at which Milestone was indeed flat-footed. A sexist, chauvinist farce at that, with Colman on debonair automatic pilot and two inherent narrative flaws: Why such a well-educated man is married to such a bubblehead except for sex, and why she remains married to him since he obviously doesn't care about her except when she strays. There has to be a better reason for an audience to root for a man manipulating his errant wife into coming back to him other than that he is played by Ronald Colman. For all his well-spoken refinement, Tony Mason is a louse.

When I interviewed Anna Lee in February of 1977, she told me that playing Caroline was difficult because there was no character for her to grab hold. So, she had Ronnie devise bits of business for her to compensate. When John Ford happened to see *Caroline* at an RKO screening room during a break in filming *How Green Was My Valley*, he immediately cast Lee in it during the last weeks of shooting. "To this day," Lee remarks, "I have no idea what he saw in me as Caroline that made him cast me, but I will always be very glad he did. Ronnie, of course, was a joy to work with, but I do wish the script and my character had been better developed."

Archival Sources: LC. 35mm nitrate picture negative, nitrate soundtrack negative, preservation composite fine grain master print, and 3/4" viewing copy.

BFI: 35mm safety preservation print and viewing prints.

UCLA: 16mm print.

F52 IT HAPPENED ONE NOON Columbia, 1942. See F53.

Trailer for Columbia's Canadian release of the British movie *The Invaders* (British title: *The 49th Parallel*). No production credits but as the title says, it was likely shot during a lunch break by the photographer for *The Talk of the Town*. Running time: 5 minutes, 15 seconds. Star/director segments: 1 minute, 50 seconds.

Featuring: Ronald Colman, Cary Grant, Jean Arthur, George Stevens.

Synopsis: The stars of Columbia's *The Talk of the Town* return to the cottage set after a two-hour lunch break, enthusing to their director, George Stevens, about the dramatic qualities of a new British war movie they have just finished watching called *The Invaders* (1941).

Print Source: UCLA. Worn-out 16mm print on a tape with a 16mm print of *The Invaders*, PVA8003.

F53 THE TALK OF THE TOWN Columbia, 1942. Columbia/TriStar Video on VHS 60780 and LD 30780. LD withdrawn 12-31-93 for redo. Production title: *Three's a Crowd*. Aka *Mr. Twilight* and *The Gentleman Misbehaves*. See F52.

Producer and Director: George Stevens. Screenplay: Irwin Shaw and Sidney Buchman, **AAN**, from a story by Sidney Harmon, **AAN**. Adaptation: Dale Van Every. Director of Photography: Ted Tetzlaff, ASC, **AAN** for B&W. Montage Effects: Donald Starling. Film Editor: Otto Mayer, **AAN**. Musical Score: Frederick Hollander, **AAN**. Musical Director: Morris Stoloff. Art Director: Lionel Banks, **AAN**. Set Decoration: Rudolph Sternad, Fay Babcock, **AAN**. Associate Producer: Fred Guiol. Assistant Director: Norman Deming.

Cast: Cary Grant (Leopold Dilg), Jean Arthur (Nora Shelley), Ronald Colman (Professor Michael Lightcap), Edgar Buchanan (Sam Yates), Glenda Farrell (Regina Bush), Charles Dingle (Andrew Holmes), Emma Dunn (Mrs. Shelley), Rex Ingram (Tilney), Leonid Kinskey (Jan Pulaski), Tom Tyler (Clyde Bracken), Don Beddoe (Chief of Police), George

Watts (Judge Grunstadt), Clyde Fillmore (Senator James Boyd), Frank M. Thomas (District Attorney), Lloyd Bridges (Donald Forrester, Reporter), Ferike Boros (Mrs. Pulaski), Eddie Laughton (Henry), Billy Benedict (Western Union Boy), Pat McVey (First Cop), Ralph Peters (First Moving Man), Max Wagner (Second Moving Man), Harold "Stubby" Kruger (Ball Player), Maynard Holmes (Ballpark Vendor), Jack Carr (Ballpark Usher), Lee "Lasses" White (Hound Keeper), William Gould (Sheriff), Edward Hearn, Bill Lally, Ralph Dunn (Sergeants), Dewey Robinson (Jake), Mabel Todd (Operator), Dan Seymour (Headwaiter), Frank Sully (Road Cop), Lee Prather (Sergeant at Arms), Clarence Muse (Doorkeeper), Leslie Brooks (Secretary), Alan Bridge (Desk Sergeant), Robert Walker (Deputy), Joe Cunningham (McGuire), Jack Gardner (Cameraman), Roberta Smith, Dorothy Babb (School Girls), Lee Phelps (Detective), Edward Coke, Jack Shay, Eddie Bruce (Reporters), Joe McGuinn (Jailer), Georgia Backus and Lelah Tyler (Bit women).

Release dates and timing: Washington, D.C. at the Earle, August 21. New York at Radio City Music Hall, August 27. Los Angeles premiere and personal appearance by Colman, August 29 at the Four Star as a benefit for the Hollywood Canteen. Los Angeles opening at the Pantages and the Hillstreet, September 7. 118 minutes.

Synopsis: Framed for burning down a factory, New England radical Leopold Dilg escapes jail. He hides in the cottage of longtime friend Nora Shelley at just the moment her summer boarder, stuffy law professor Michael Lightcap, prematurely arrives during the night. They then work to soften Lightcap's ivory tower view of the law to get him to use his prestige to ask for a new trial for Dilg. Michael not only goes through mental and emotional changes—he is also nominated to the Supreme Court—he discovers and apprehends the real arsonist, freeing Dilg. Furthermore, because of her own changed feelings, Nora has to choose between Justice Lightcap and Leopold as the man she loves and wants to marry. After some indecision, she chooses Dilg.

Reviews: *Hollywood Reporter*, 7-27-42: "Ronald Colman, wearing a beard to cause him to seem older, is a joy as the legal light. He is grand when he decides to shave off the beard during the plot development. None of these fine performers have ever been presented more advantageously."

Nelson B. Bell, *Washington Post*, 8-22-42: "It has substance, warmth, humor and excited, all interpreted by a *ne plus ultra* cast that never misses a trick...Ronald Colman, as Lightcap, manages a smooth gradation from the suavely austere, legal theorist to a man of action and 'one of the people.'"

Background and Commentary: Though they had worked together on radio in *The Circle*, and would do so again on *Lux Radio Theater* in 1943 and *Command Performance* in 1944, Colman and Grant were not friends and did not get along. This according to Colman's later friend and television producer, William Frye. According to Grant biographers Higham and Moseley (B52), Grant felt insecure about matching his light comedy talent with Colman's, so he had his agent beat out Colman's for top billing. Which is why the script title was changed from the more evocative *Mr. Twilight*, so that Colman was no longer the title character.

As it turned out, Colman handily stole the show from Grant in this excellent social comedy about the theory of law vs. its practice. Potentially dark material, especially with a would-be lynching thrown in, is handled with seasoned finesse by George Stevens, a master at light perspective.

But then, he had a first-rate script and the ensemble chemistry of three fine stars, who are a joy to watch as they each go through a series of changes. However, there was one big hitch in the ending. The two men were of equal romantic stature so that it became a toss-up as to which one would end up with Arthur. So, two endings were filmed, with sneak preview audiences choosing Grant as the lucky man by a slight margin. But Colman was also a winner. He lost the girl for the first time, but he won the audience with his expert portrayal of an ivory tower jurist forced to adapt to a real world he's been avoiding for twenty years. The movie's critical and commercial success made him a top-billed star again, paving the way for the even bigger success of *Random Harvest*.

Theatrical Source: Turner Entertainment.

Archival Sources: LC. Nitrate composite fine grain master, nitrate composite print, preservation dupe negative, preservation soundtrack negative, and composite viewing copy.

BFI: 117-minute 35mm nitrate and safety viewing prints.

UCLA: 35mm nitrate studio print, viewing with archive staff approval, 16mm print, and VHS viewing copy from same.

F54 HEARST METROTONE NEWS FOOTAGE 1942 See B302.

Filmed August 27, 1942 for September release. No credits available. Colman segment runs 2 minutes, 40 seconds.

Second item on reel of unedited and mostly silent newsreel footage. Series of silent shots of Colman and several female stars en route to Washington to start the Stars Over America war bond campaign. The women with him are Greer Garson, Irene Dunne, Hedy Lamarr, Ann Rutherford, Lynn Bari, and Virginia Gilmore. Segment as released is not on file.

Print Source: UCLA, PVA3944.

F55 RANDOM HARVEST MGM, 1942. MGM/UA Video VHS M300961, LD 1009616. See R53, R121.

Producer: Sidney Franklin, **AAN** for BP. Director: Mervyn LeRoy, **AAN**. Screenplay: Claudine West, George Froeschel and Arthur Wimperis, **AAN**, from the novel by James Hilton. Director of Photography: Joseph Ruttenberg, ASC. Art Director: Cedric Gibbons. Associate Art Director: Randall Duell. Set Decorations: Edwin B. Willis. Set Decorations Associate: Jack Moore. Sound: Douglas Shearer. Film Editor: Harold F. Kress. Musical Score: Herbert Stothart. Production Number: "She's Ma Daisy" (1905) by Harry Lauder (Co-lyrics and music) and J.D. Harper (co-lyrics). Staged by Ernst Matray. Runs 2½ minutes. Performed by Greer Garson. Wedding hymn: "O Perfect Love." Ballet music from *Swan Lake* by Tchaikovsky. Gowns: Kalloch. Make-up: Jack Dawn. Hair Styles: Sydney Guilaroff.

Cast: Ronald Colman, **AAN** for BA (Smithy/Charles Rainier), Greer Garson (Paula Ridgeway/Paula Hanson), Philip Dorn (Dr. Jonathan Benét), Susan Peters, **AAN** for BSA (Kitty), Reginald Owen ("Biffer" Briggs), Henry Travers (Dr. Sims), Margaret Wycherly (Mrs. Deventer), Bramwell Fletcher (Harrison), Rhys Williams (Sam), Una O'Connor (Tobacconist), Aubrey Mather (Sheldon), Arthur Margetson (Chetwynd), Jill Esmond (Lydia), Marta Linden (Jill), Melville Cooper (George), Alan Napier (Julian), David Cavendish (Henry Chilcotte), Norma Varden (Julia), Ann Richards (Bridget), Elisabeth Risdon (Mrs. Lloyd), Charles Waldron (Mr. Lloyd), Ivan Simpson (Vicar), Marie de Becker (Vicar's Wife), Clement May (Beddoes), Arthur Shields (Chemist), John Burton (Pearson), Alec Craig (Comedian), Henry Daniell (Heavy Man), Mrs. Gardner Crane (Mrs. Sims), C. Montague Shaw (Julia's Husband), Lumsden Hare (Sir John), Frederic Worlock (Paula's Attorney), Wallis Clark (Jonys), Harry T. Shannon (Badgeley), Arthur Space (Trempitt, Sanitorium Patient), Ian Wolfe (Registrar), Helena Phillips Evans (Ella, Charwoman), Aubrey Mather (Sheldon), Clement May (Beddoes), Harry T. Shannon (Badgeley), Hilda Plowright, Rita Page (Nurses), Keith Hitchcock (Commissionaire), Terry Kilburn (Boy),

Matthew Boulton, Cyril McLaglen (Policeman), David Clyde (Lodge Keeper), Pax Walker (Sheila), Forrester Harvey (Taxi Driver), Reginald Sheffield (Judge), Boyd Irwin (Party Whip), Major Sam Harris (Member, House of Commons), Clifford Severn (Albert), Walter Tetley (Call Boy), Leonard Mudie (Old Man), Peter Lawford (Soldier).

Release dates and timing: New York at Radio City Music Hall, December 17. Los Angeles at four theaters, December 31. 124 minutes, 15 seconds. British version runs 2½ minutes longer. Then record run of six weeks at Radio City.

Synopsis: On November 11, 1918, the day World War One ends, John Smith, a shell-shocked soldier at a British sanitorium, meets and runs away with a music hall queen named Paula Ridgeway. They marry and have a son, but their happiness is interrupted when he recovers his memory in London after being struck by a taxi. Resuming his place as Charles Rainier, heir to a British industrial family, he has no memory of Paula. A few years later, he becomes engaged to his cousin, Kitty.

The engagement ends when Kitty realizes he isn't all there for her emotionally. Meanwhile, Paula re-enters his life as his secretary, Paula Hanson, and they marry again. (Their son has died in the interim.) In the end, Charles finally regains his memory and the Paula he really loves.

Reviews: James Agee, *The Nation*, 12-26-42: "I would also like to recommend 'Random Harvest' to those who can stay interested in Ronald Colman's amnesia for two hours and who could with pleasure eat a bowl of Yardley's shaving soap for breakfast."

John T. McManus, *PM*, 12-18-42: "The obvious flaw in all this, which it is probably not cricket to mention, is that all the forgotten wife needed to do at any point, as far as I can see, was to walk up to the guy with a pleasant 'Hey! Remember me?' and *Random Harvest* would have been all over but the fadeout."

Bosley Crowther, *New York Times*, 12-18-42: "Miss Garson and Mr. Colman are charming; they act perfectly. But they never seem real...One might also inquire mildly why it is that the wife in this case never persuaded her aberrant husband to consult a doctor in an effort to regain his lost life."

Daily Variety, 11-25-42: "Colman does a masterly job, never at a loss for the exact suggestion of bewilderment or alternating assurance of the officer who escapes a convalescent institution to marry the showgirl who befriends him and who alternates between two half-real worlds of work and affection before final restoration comes."

Commentary: Half elegant romantic fantasy, half preposterous and dreary soap opera, *Random Harvest* made money because Colman and Garson clicked as a romantic team, not because it was a good story. McManus's assessment is dead-on, that Garson need only tell her amnesiac husband who she is and we have a 75-minute movie.

To prevent her from doing so, psychiatrist Philip Dorn blocks her with the psychological nonsense that if she does remind him, he will resent her for it. Why would he, or any man, resent being woken to the fact that he left a pretty wife behind whom he cherishes?

The truth is the story lacks suspense and a point. As in *Les Miserables*, the Hilton novel's plot device keeps us guessing for a while as to whether the protagonist at the beginning and the middle is the same man. Seeing him on screen kills that device, so all we have left is our inherent interest in Ronald Colman as a star personality. Without that interest, the story cannot work. A man loses his memory twice, regains it twice and in between marries the same woman twice. Why should we care?

Furthermore, Colman is far too old for the part. He ages in appearance over a period of 17 years from 48 to 50, and yet he is supposed to have been a private in the trenches of WWI. Had he shaved his moustache and dyed his hair for the first half, he would have shed at least 10 years, looking more believable.

What makes the role a good one for him anyway is that he shows a good deal of dramatic range: from shell-shocked, stammering amnesia to married bliss to exuberant fatherhood to groping within his mind for the last, plodding hour for the psychological and literal keys that will unlock his past.

Today as when it was new, Colman's elegant finesse and subtle acting, his wonderful teaming with Garson, and the moving final scenes are what enchant audiences, reminding them of a gentler though artificial brand of moviemaking.

Theatrical Source: Turner Entertainment.

Archival Sources: BFI. Restricted access 35mm safety viewing print running 126:08 and 35mm nitrate preservation print running 126:42. Prints acquired from separate sources.

UCLA: VHS viewing copy, PVA1458, taken from 16mm print.

F56 KISMET MGM, 1944, Three-strip Technicolor.

Producer: Everett Riskin. Director: William Dieterle. Screenplay: John Meehan, from the play by Edward Knoblock. Director of Photography: Charles Rosher ASC, **AAN** for Color. Technicolor Advisors: Natalie Kalmus, Henri Jaffa. Music: Herbert Stothart, **AAN**. Orchestrations: Murray Cutter. Songs: "Tell Me, Tell Me, Evening Star" (sung by Marlene Dietrich, then by Joy Ann Page), "Willow in the Wind" (sung by Page) by Harold Arlen and E.Y. Harburg. Recording Director: Douglas Shearer, **AAN**. Art Direction: Cedric Gibbons, Daniel B. Cathcart, **AAN**. Set Decorations: Edwin B. Willis, Richard Pefferle, **AAN**. Special Effects: Warren Newcombe. Costume Supervision: Irene. Costumes Executed By: Karinska. Make-up: Jack Dawn. Hair Styles: Sydney Guilaroff. Film Editor: Ben Lewis. Dance director: Jack Cole. Assistant Director: Marvin Stuart.

Cast: Ronald Colman (Hafiz), Marlene Dietrich (Princess Jamilla), James Craig (Caliph), Edward Arnold (Mansur, the Grand Vizier), Joy Ann Page (Marsina), Florence Bates (Karsha), Harry Davenport (Agha), Hugh Herbert (Feisal), Hobart Cavanaugh (Moolah), Robert Warwick (Alfife), Beatrice and Evelyne Kraft (Dancers), Barry Macollum (Amu), Victor Kilian (Jehan), Charles Middleton (Vatuk Rista), Harry Humphrey (Royal Gardener), Nestor Paiva (Captain of Police), Roque Ybarra (Miser's Son), Minerva Urecal (Retainer), Jimmy Ames (Major Domo), Cy Kendall (Herald), Charles La Torre (Alwah, Sign maker), Marek Windheim (Sapu), Noble Blake (Hassan, Nubian slave), Anna Demetrio (Cafe Proprietress), Dan Seymour (Fat Turk), Mitchell Lewis (Sheik), Phiroz Nazir, Asit Ghosh (Nabout Fighters), Carmen D'Antonio (Specialty Dancer in Cafe), Eve Whitney, Joyce Gates, Jessie Tai Sing, Zedra Conde, Barbara Glenz, Frances Ramsden (Cafe Girls), Charles Judels (Rich Merchant), Dale Van Sickel (Assassin), Gabriel Gonzales (Monkey Man), Bruno Weise (Pole Act), Zack Williams (Executioner), Paul Singh (Caliph's Valet), Eddie Abdo (Voice Prayer in Arabic), Pedro De Cordoba (Muezin), Paul Bradley (Magician), Louis Manley (Fire Eater), John Schaller, Ramiro Rivas, William Rivas (Juggling Trio), Yvonne De Carlo (Member of Queen's Retinue), Morris Ankrum (Caliph's Messenger), Leatrice Joy Gilbert (Dancing Girl), Frank Morgan (Unbilled Opening Narrator).

Release dates and timing: New York at the Astor, August 22. Los Angeles at three theaters, September 19. 100 minutes.

Synopsis: Bagdad beggar/magician Hafiz masquerades as a prince by night to woo the princess Jamilla, while keeping his virgin daughter Marsina cooped up at home as he searches for a prince to marry her. Meanwhile, the Caliph, disguised as a gardener, starts a romance with Marsina. Hoaxing his way into the palace to manipulate the Vizier into marrying Marsina, Hafiz gets away with the ruse until he is arrested for stealing his fine clothes from the local merchants. Talking his way out of having his hands chopped off for the theft, Hafiz promises the Vizier to murder the Caliph in exchange for the Vizier deposing Jamilla to marry Marsina. When the Caliph thwarts Hafiz's murder attempt then reveals that he is the "gardener's son" his daughter loves, Hafiz escapes capture to kill the Vizier. For the attempted murder, the Caliph banishes Hafiz to Hassir. For saving his life, he makes Hafiz the Prince of Hassir for real. In the end, Hafiz is joined on his journey to Hassir by Jamilla as the Caliph and Marsina prepare to marry.

Reviews: Ed Sullivan, *Citizen News*, 8-29-44: "He glides through with the greatest of ease, alternately a consummate rascal and a gentle, adoring father. He falters only when he attempts broad comedy such as stuttering to denote confusion or by an extra bit of heavy mugging here and there. On the whole, however, he turns in one of his more excellent performances."

New Yorker, 8-26-44: "(Colman) agitates his full share of rich Persian costume, does sleight of hand tricks with handkerchiefs and knives, smiles mockingly but gaily, and, in short, gives you practically everything in the second drawer of his repertory."

Hollywood Reporter, 8-22-44: "As the beggar king, Ronald Colman gives a superb performance, one of the best of his entire career. He gives the flamboyant role the perfect touch of restraint which makes the beggar warmly human, always likeable and convincingly real, no mean feat."

Daily Variety, 8-22-44: "Colman plays his role with dash and the kind of gymnastic bravado which reflects the elder Douglas Fairbanks heritage and which underscores the rich humor of the character with distinctive Colman suavity."

Commentary: Not wanting to make war movies, Colman retreated to a past persona: A beggar/thief/rogue a la François Villon. The punishment/reward ending even recalls *If I Were King*. While it's always a pleasure watching Colman in a scruffy role, *Kismet* has nowhere near the heart, depth, romance and risky wit of the earlier Preston Sturges script.

The teaming with Dietrich has a light comedy quality to it, belieing their coldness to each other off-camera (B34). But notice that except for one scene in the palace when Colman is escaping Craig, she never looks at him. The worst part of Dietrich's role is her vaunted dance with her legs painted gold. Though the critics called attention to the gilding, the choreography and music that go with it are laborious.

As for Page, who was Jack Warner's stepdaughter, she didn't register with audiences. Usually billed as Joy Page, she is best remembered for a short, sympathetic role in **Casablanca** as a young wife whom Claude Rains tries to blackmail into having sex with him. She lacked screen presence to go beyond this and other minor roles.

In all, *Kismet* is amusing but forgettable, crying out to be a full-blown musical, as it was on Broadway in the 1953-54 season with Alfred Drake as Hafiz. This version has just two songs, both mediocre. Could Colman have passed muster as a singing star? With some brush-up coaching, no question. After all, he had begun his career in British music hall. He also sang twice on *Command Performance* (R79, R80) the month *Kismet* was released.

William Dieterle had previously filmed a German version of *Kismet* in 1920. An American silent version was also made in 1920, followed by a sound version in 1930, both starring Otis Skinner, who had starred in the American stage version in 1911. The Colman version was released to television in 1955 in black-and-white as *Oriental Dream* so as not to confuse it with the MGM musical *Kismet*, starring Howard Keel, released that same year. In the mid-1970s, color prints were finally leased to TV stations, still titled *Oriental Dream*.

Theatrical Source: Turner Entertainment.

Archival Sources: GEH. 16mm color print.

LC: Original nitrate 3-strip Technicolor picture negatives, a total of 30 reels; nitrate soundtrack negatives, 10 reels; nitrate composite Technicolor print; and 3/4" video viewing copy made from the nitrate Technicolor print.

F57 THE LATE GEORGE APLEY Twentieth Century-Fox, 1947. See R118.
Producer: Fred Kohlmar. Directors: Joseph L. Mankiewicz, Ernst Lubitsch (the latter for scenes added in post-production). Screenplay: Philip Dunne, from the play by John P. Marquand and George S. Kaufman based on Marquand's novel. Director of Photography: Joseph La Shelle, ASC. Post-production Photography: Joe McDonald. Special Effects: Fred Sersen. Art Directors: James Basevi, J. Russell Spencer. Set Decorations: Thomas Little, Paul S. Fox. Sound: Bernard Freericks, Roger Heman. Film Editor: James B. Clark. Musical Score: Cyril J. Mockridge. Musical Director: Alfred Newman. Songs: "Sweet Little Marigold" (composer uncredited, solo by Vanessa Brown, accompanied by main cast), "Every Little Movement Has a Meaning All Its Own" (1912) by Carl Hoschner, and "I'll Take You Home Again, Kathleen" (1871) by Thomas Westendorf (background motif). Orchestral Arrangements: Maurice de Packh. Costumes: René Hubert. Makeup: Ben Nye. Assistant Director: F.E. Johnson.
Cast: Ronald Colman (George Apley), Peggy Cummins (Eleanor Apley), Edna Best (Catherine Apley), Vanessa Brown (Agnes Willing), Richard Haydn (Horatio Willing), Charles Russell (Howard Boulder), Richard Ney (John Apley), Percy Waram (Roger Newcombe), Mildred Natwick (Amelia Newcombe), Nydia Westman (Jane Willing), Francis Pierlot (Wilson), Kathleen Howard (Margaret, the Apley's Maid), Helen Freeman (Lydia), Paul Harvey (Julian H. Dole), Helen Dickson (Governess), J. Pat Moriarty (Policeman), Theresa Lyon (Chestnut Vendor), William Moran (Henry Apley), Clifford Brooke (Charles), David Bond (Manager of Modiste Shop), Ottola Nesmith (Madame at Modiste Shop), Diana Douglas (Sarah), Wyndham Standing (Bit Gentleman), Mae Marsh (Bit Maid), Thomas Leffingwell (Servant), Vesey O'Davoren (Minister), Cordelia Campbell (Child Skater).
Release dates and timing: New York at Radio City Music Hall, March 20. Los Angeles at four theaters, April 16. 98½ minutes.
Synopsis: In 1912 Boston, Emerson-quoting patriarch and priggish stuffed shirt conservative George Apley has his provincial and familial complacency turned upside down. He is aghast to learn on Thanksgiving Day that his son, John, does not want to marry his cousin, Agnes, and that his free-thinking daughter, Eleanor, wants to marry an English professor with radical views, named Howard Boulder. Apley finds himself a 19th century man who believes that Boston is the "hub of the universe" coping with 20th century ideas stating otherwise.
Ironically, after George accepts his son's choice, John is rejected by his prospective father-in-law because of class differences: he is Bostonian while his fiancée is rooted in Worcester. As for Eleanor, George finally reconciles himself to his daughter's needs over rigid provincial traditions. In the end, in June of 1913, Eleanor and Howard head off to be married with George's blessing while Agnes happily marches down a church aisle to marry John.
Reviews: Bosley Crowther, *New York Times*, 3-21-47: "'The Late George Apley' has been botched on the screen—but good! ...For one thing Mr. Colman doesn't speak his lines, he sings—and he accompanies them with such gestures, such nods and flourishes, as a Brahmin would despise."
Edwin Schallert, *Los Angeles Times*, 4-17-47: "Colman's comedy, of synthetic flavor, gets laughs because it is well accepted, for he knows his technique. But one does not feel that even he himself ever dreamt that he was actually Apley. Certainly there is no subconscious—let us say—realization of the character on his part. And without Apley, there

is no 'Late George Apley."

Virginia Wright, *Daily News*, 4-17-47: "Ronald Colman makes Apley a pleasant stuffed shirt. With his natural charm, he avoids caricature, and creates in the Bostonian a real, if ultra-conservative person."

Jack D. Grant, *Hollywood Reporter*, 1-31-47: "Colman's performance, unlike any he has previously delivered, sparks the fun, gives it overtones that are by turns riotous and delicate."

Commentary: When Colman made *Apley*, he had become a complacent and rusty film actor from nearly three years' absence and a dependence on radio. He also had a director who didn't push him and a script softened from the novel and play to accomodate him.

The character is the same as Michael Lightcap in *The Talk of the Town*: both begin with backward beliefs and stuffy temperaments, both end with those beliefs and temperaments liberalized and more attuned to reality. However, the quality of the characterizations is markedly different.

Colman's Lightcap convincingly evolves in subtle degrees because his material is sharp and his performance is compelling; he is submerged in the role. Colman's Apley evolves in leaps but is not convincing because the source material has been weakened and we can see the actor acting, going through the motions as his eyes betray him. We can see the wheels turning as he pretends to be something he isn't in real life. Colman seems to be acting in one movie while the other actors are performing in another.

Another reason for this autopilot performance may be that Mankiewicz was so grateful Colman chose him to direct based on his direction of *Dragonwyck* and was so in awe of the star that he made no attempt to ground him more firmly in his character. Whatever the reason, Colman's performance is mostly a technically proficient one. He quickly establishes the one-note, selfish level that pleases him, seldom budging from it.

There are two scenes, however, that stand out for their sharp writing and the way one character in each confronts Apley over his priggishness: Roger Newcombe gently and warmly chiding his lifelong friend and brother-in-law George for his stuffy attitudes and forgetting his own youth, reflecting the author's view and therefore the audience's; and Howard Boulder angrily telling off Apley in front of his, Boulder's, friends and Agnes on a street in New York.

As for Lubitsch, he directed scenes written to build up Cummins's role, including one in which she encourages Brown's Agnes to stand up for herself. This according to Brown.

Apley is a fairly entertaining mockery of social snobbery and elitist mores, but far from the first-rate satiric tragedy it could have been. Yet, after skating through it, Colman next gave the most daring performance of his career.

Theatrical Source: Twentieth Century-Fox Pictures.

Archival Sources: LC. 16mm viewing copy.

MOMA: 35mm 16mm safety prints running 79 minutes, missing reel 3.

BFI: 35mm nitrate preservation and 35mm safety viewing prints.

UCLA: Grainy 35mm safety print with scratches at top and bottom of reels. Missing end titles and a few opening ones from splices. Runs 97 minutes, 50 seconds.

F58 A DOUBLE LIFE Kanin Productions for Universal-International Pictures, 1947. Republic Pictures Video (5518, includes theatrical trailer), taken from UCLA archival print. Production title: *The Art of Murder*. French title: *Une Double Vie*. See F59, D19, D20, D21.

Producer: Michael Kanin. Director: George Cukor, **AAN**. Screenplay: Ruth Gordon and Garson Kanin, **AAN**. Director of Photography: Milton Krasner, ASC. Production Design: Harry Horner. Art Directors: Bernard Herzbrun, Harvey Gillett. Film Editor: Robert

Parish. Sound: Leslie I. Carey, Joe Lapis. Set Decorations: Russell A. Gausman, John Austin. Special Photography: David S. Horsley, ASC. Music: Miklos Rozsa, **AA**. Dramatic Coach for *Othello* sequences: Walter Hampden. Miss Hasso's Gowns: Yvonne Wood, Travis Banton. Hair Stylist: Carmen Dirigo. Make-up: Bud Westmore. Portrait Artist: William Shulgold. Colman bust and face mask: Bernhard Sopher. Assistant Director: Frank Shaw. Production Assistants: George Yohalem, Jack Murton. Plays: "A Gentleman's Gentleman" snippet by Robert Sherwood, and *Othello* by William Shakespeare.

Cast: Ronald Colman, **AA** for BA (Anthony John), Signe Hasso (Brita Kaurin), Edmond O'Brien (Bill Friend), Shelley Winters (Pat Kroll), Ray Collins (Victor Donlan), Philip Loeb (Max Lasker), Millard Mitchell (Al Cooley), Joe Sawyer (Captain Ray Bonner, but listed as Pete in end credits), Charles La Torre (Vito Stellini, Venezia Restaurant owner), Whit Bissell (Dr. Roland F. Stauffer, Coroner), John Drew Colt (Stage Manager), Peter Thompson (Assistant Stage Manager), Elizabeth Dunne (Gladys), Alan Edmiston (Rex), Art Smith, Sid Tomack (Wigmakers), Wilton Graff (Dr. Mervin), Harlan Briggs (Oscar Bernard), Claire Carleton (Waitress), Betsy Blair, Janet Warren, Marjory Woodworth (Actresses in Wig Shop), Curt Conway (Reporter), Robert E. Kean (2nd Photographer), Kay Lavello (Large Woman), Sarah Selby (Anna, Lasker's Secretary), Alexander Clark (Barry), Harry Bannister (2nd Actor), Joann Dolan (Ellen), Joyce Matthews (Ellen's friend), Harry Oldridge, Nick Dennis, Barry Macollum, Frank Richards (Stagehands), Janet Manson, Augusta Roeland (Giggly fans in Empire Theatre lobby), Angela Clarke (Lucy), Paddy Chayefsky (1st Photographer), Russ Conway (1st Reporter), Reginald Billado (3rd Reporter), Fernanda Eliscu (Landlady), Joe Bernard (Husband), Charles Jordan (Bartender), Walter McGrail (Steve), Joey Ray (Boyer), Hal Melone (Head Usher), Elmo Lincoln (Detective), Howard Mitchell, Pete Sosso (Tailors), Albert Pollett (Costume Designer), Laura Kasley Brooks (Dowager), George Manning (Usher).

Actors in *Othello* sequences: Guy Bates Post (Lodovico), David Bond, Leslie Denison, Virginia Patton, Thayer Roberts, Fay Kanin (Amelia), Arthur Gould-Porter, Frederic Worlock, Boyd Irwin, Percival Vivian.

Actors in "A Gentleman's Gentleman" Sequence: Elliott Reid, Georgia Caine, Mary Young, Percival Vivian.

Release dates and timing: Oscar-qualifying run at the Guild Theater in Hollywood, December 25, 1947 to January 7, 1948. National release in major cities like New York and San Francisco: February 19, 1948. Staggered post-Oscar national release beginning March 22, 1948. London premiere and personal appearance by Colman: Leicester Square Theatre, May 20, 1948. 104 minutes, 20 seconds.

Synopsis: Brilliant but schizophrenic stage star Anthony John plays Othello to public and critical acclaim, but starts confusing his performance with his real life. Going over the edge into jealous madness—believing his actress ex-wife, Brita, to be having an affair with their press agent, Bill—he murders his sometime lover, a waitress named Pat. When his crime is discovered, he stabs himself on stage during a performance, dying just before his curtain call.

Reviews: Ruth Waterbury, *Los Angeles Examiner*, 12-25-47: "...you will see the always charming, persuasive and very handsome Ronald Colman suddenly become dynamic, arrogant and touching. Never in his distinguished career has Colman ever done anything that even touched the magnificence of his work here. I don't see how he can ever surpass it."

Howard Barnes *New York Herald Tribune*, 2-20-48: "There can be no gainsaying the power and variety of the Colman portrayal...He has always been a steady and winning actor, but he demonstrates at the Music Hall that he has a remarkable perception of the 'emotional disease' which must afflict most of the great artists of the theater."

Bosley Crowther, *New York Times*, 2-20-48: "They have handed the veteran actor the role of his lengthy career. The only question is whether Mr. Colman is more spectacular as the mentally distressed star of Broadway or the bearded Venetian Moor. In either case, he plays an actor cocked and primed for romantic tragedy...Now, what does Mr. Colman do for an encore?"

London Times, 5-21-48: "Mr. Colman tries hard. He is successful in establishing that Tony into Othello equals a murderer who does not confine his activities to the footlights, but, as Othello played seriously and at some length, he fails. As an exercise in the art of keeping his fingers pressed on Desdemona's windpipe, it is a triumph, but something more is expected of Othello than that, and Mr. Colman, for all his air of being perplexed in the extreme, cannot supply it."

Commentary: *A Double Life* was first offered to Laurence Olivier, who was then preparing his *Hamlet*. Nor was it easy to talk Colman into it once the Kanins decided they would cast against type. However, once he had committed to dramatizing the dark side of his profession, Colman was constantly prodded and challenged by Cukor, going way past his accustomed persona into sick obsession, explosive anger, jealous paranoia, and murderous dementia. An actor who had spent most of his film career being kind and gentle suddenly showed he could chill an audience with a terrifying transformation into a schizoid demon.

A few critics felt the premise to be a false one, that any actor this unstable could not be a good actor, while conceding that they were mesmerized all the same. Tony John is indeed unhinged at the end—you have to be to kill yourself on stage—but since this *is* fiction, we are watching an extreme of the obsessiveness of acting.

For all the finely honed craft he called upon, Colman's performance is hampered by his inability to get under the skin of Othello. He lacks strength and conviction. His dynamic portrayal of John would also have been enhanced by shaving his moustache and dying his hair to look more plastic and less like Ronald Colman and closer to Hasso's age. Speaking of which, she is far too young to have been with him for the 20 years the script implies. More important, they have no sexual chemistry, whereas Colman and Winters do.

Despite the Oscar win, *A Double Life* made only a small profit. For all the risk he took, Colman apparently scared the public by *being* scary. Yet, he never regretted it. He had done some of his finest work and won his coveted award.

Garson Kanin today recalls that he and his wife, Ruth, were not inspired by Paul Robeson's famous Broadway run as Othello, and yet Robeson's Desdemona was also played by a Swedish actress, Uta Hagen. Kanin also says that they had never seen two British movies with strikingly similar plots: *Men Are Not Gods* (1937), in which Rex Harrison is a stage star who takes his Othello too seriously, and *The Brighton Strangler* (1945), about a murderous stage actor.

Alcoa Hour on NBC remade *A Double Life* as a live one-hour TV show on January 6, 1957, starring Eric Portman and Shelley Winters.

Archival Sources: BFI. 35mm nitrate preservation print and 35mm safety viewing print.

UCLA: 35mm nitrate master positive, preservation dupe negative, safety projection print, French-dubbed 16mm master positive. The original negative is lost to decomposition.

F59 20 YEARS OF ACADEMY AWARDS RKO release of an Academy of Motion Picture Arts and Sciences production, 1948. See F58, R121, R122.

No production credits. Narrated by Carey Wilson. Released the first week in April. Running time: 18 minutes.

Rapid-fire montage of scenes from all 20 Best Picture winners and Oscar-winning performances, including scenes from *A Double Life*. Clips are silent but with scoring. First shown at the Academy Awards on March 20, 1948, minus the final segment, of course, which was added a few days later for theatrical release.

Print Source: UCLA: 35mm nitrate print, which will revert to the Academy by 1996.

F60 A FILM RECORD OF THE 21ST ANNUAL ACADEMY AWARDS 1949. Produced by the Academy of Motion Picture Arts and Sciences. Directed by G. Carleton Hunt. Opening narrator: Walter Winchell. Photography: Frank King and Charles E. Burke. Film Editor: Philip Martin. Sound: John Aalberg.

A 72-minute film of the March 24, 1949 show. See F59.

MC Robert Montgomery introduces Colman 65 minutes in. Colman segment runs 2 minutes, 45 seconds. He presents Jane Wyman with an Oscar for Best Actress for *Johnny Belinda*.

Print Sources: AMPAS. 35mm nitrate print of 1 reel, 16mm viewing print. UCLA: VHS copy of 16mm print, PVA7953.

F61 SCREEN SNAPSHOTS: HEART THROBS OF YESTERDAY Columbia, Series 30, 1950. See F17, F46.

Includes clips of Colman at the peak of his stardom.

Print Source: LC. 35mm nitrate composite print, dupe negative and safety print.

F62 CHAMPAGNE FOR CAESAR Cardinal Pictures for United Artists, 1950. VCI Video 4502, taken from a scratchy 16mm TV print with a few splices.

Executive Producer: Harry M. Popkin. Producer: George Moskov. Director: Richard Whorf. Screenplay: Hans Jacoby and Fred Brady. Director of Photography: Paul Ivano, ASC. Art Director: George van Marter. Set Decorations: Jacques Mapes. Costumes: Maria Donovan. Furs: Al Teitelbaum. Sound: Hugh McDowell, Mac Dagleish. Film Editor: Hugh Bennett. Musical score: Dimitri Tiomkin. Make-up Artists: William Knight, Ted Larsen. Hair Stylist: Scotty Rackin. Technical Assistants: John Claar and Robert H. Forward (by arrangement with CBS and KTTV for the *Masquerade for Money* scenes). Associate Producer: Joseph H. Nadel. Assistant Directors: Ralph Slosser and Leon Chooluck.

Cast: Ronald Colman (Beauregard Bottomley), Celeste Holm (Flame O'Neil), Vincent Price (Burnbridge Waters), Barbara Britton (Gwen Bottomley), Art Linkletter ("Happy" Hogan), Ellye Marshall (Frosty), Byron Foulger (Gerald), Gabriel Heatter, George Fisher (Announcers), Vici Raaf (Waters's Secretary), Douglas Evans (Radio Announcer), John Eldredge (Executive #1), Lyle Talbot (Executive #2), George Leigh (Executive #3), John Hart (Executive #4), Mel Blanc (Caesar's Voice), Peter Brocco (Fortune Teller), Brian O'Hara (T-Man Buck), Jack Daly (T-Man Scratch), Gordon Nelson (TV Science Lecturer), Herbert Lytton (Chuck Johnson), George Meader (Brown).

Release dates and timing: New York benefit premiere for New York Heart Fund at the Mark Hellinger, February 5. Los Angeles opening at seven theaters, April 26. New York at the Capitol, May 11 (previewed May 10). 99 minutes, 15 seconds.

Synopsis: When chronically unemployed intellectual Beauregard Bottomley is rejected for a job by Burnbridge Waters, the lunatic head of the Milady soap company, he schemes to bankrupt the tycoon with an uninterrupted winning streak on the TV/radio quiz show Waters sponsors, *Masquerade for Money*. In retaliation, Waters hires an intellectual vamp named Flame O'Neil to distract Bottomley into giving a wrong answer. When the scheme backfires, Waters goes literally for broke with a final show broadcast from the

Hollywood Bowl. To Waters's relief, Bottomley cannot answer the final question—"What is your social security number?"—but it turns out that the two men have struck a deal in exchange for a wrong answer *whatever* the question. The movie ends with Bottomley's sister, Gwen, marrying quiz host Happy Hogan, Waters drinking champagne with Caesar—Bottomley's alcoholic parrot—and Beauregard eloping to Las Vegas with Flame.

Notes: When this movie was made in 1949, KTTV channel 11 was the CBS station for Los Angeles, co-owned by the Los Angeles Times. *Champagne for Caesar* was trade screened in Hollywood on January 27, 1950 for a February 7 opening following the February 5 benefit premiere. I have no idea why or when the release date was pushed back nearly three months.

Reviews: *Independent Film Journal*, 2-11-50: "Ronald Colman, in a wisely cast role which permits his flair for comedy, is properly and archly wise as a genius who can furnish answers ranging from Einstein's theories to how to say farewell in Japanese."

Red Kann, *Motion Picture Herald*, 2-11-50: "...generally an amusing film, punctuated by many chuckles and occasionally substantial belly laughs. It also is spotty and just dull.... Some of the business is silly and far-fetched beyond all reason, even allowing for the satire and the burlesque consciously intended. Performances are led by Colman and Miss Holm. Price is made to exaggerate outlandishly throughout."

Hollywood Reporter, 2-7-50: "Ronald Colman is his charming debonair self in the part of the mental giant, and his persuasive underplaying is a big factor in the success of the show."

Lowell E. Redelings, *Hollywood Citizen-News*, 4-27-50: "The audience with this reviewer at the Hawaii Music Hall...had itself a gay evening laughing and chuckling at Colman's ability to answer any and all questions put to him on a Hollywood radio quiz program...The acting by the principals is top-notch. Colman is excellent, as always, and so is Vincent Price."

John McCarten, *New Yorker*, 5-20-50: "The idea would be a good one, perhaps, for a short film, but here it goes on and on, with all kinds of complications dragged in by the ears, until sleep comes dropping slow upon the audience."

National Legion of Decency: Adults only rating.

Commentary: A commercial flop despite a big ad push by Westinghouse, this is the one Colman movie to become a cult favorite thanks to its frequent late show airings over the last 40-plus years. Taken as a satiric fantasy about television—the first of its kind—it's a funny jab at the lowest common denominator quality that would later characterize most TV game shows forever. Taken literally, the plot has numerous holes and a romantic subplot that stops the story cold midway through:

1) For all his chronic unemployment, Beauregard manages to live in a nice middle class house with his sister, Gwen. The flip side is that they look like father and daughter.

2) For all the national celebrity he accrues from *Masquerade for Money*, not one television executive offers Beauregard the chance to host his own quiz show. Not only is this unreal, but what a wonderful comic opportunity is missed by *not* showing him in direct competition with *Masquerade for Money*.

3) If Beauregard did win the $40 million, the 78% upper tax bracket at the time would force him to sell the company to pay the taxes. Moreover, the two IRS agents would not be trailing him like gangsters.

4) The Hollywood Bowl sequence. Wouldn't Waters schedule Bottomley last instead of first, building the suspense? Whether or not he wins, the show is over in five minutes, so what do they do for the other 20 after commercials? There should also have been a few lines explaining why the sudden deal between Waters and Bottomley.

5) Flame O'Neil. Who is she, where does she come from, what has she done before, how much is Waters paying her, and why doesn't she turn her back on Waters once she falls for Bottomley in favor of Beauregard's game show winnings? This is *The Man Who Broke the Bank at Monte Carlo* all over again. Same idea, different backdrop, but this time the romance stops the momentum for a half-hour.

All of these holes surely bothered Colman when he signed, but he clearly felt the premise had enough potential, especially with some re-writing (which never happened), that he said yes. In the end, both he and the movie were losers. *Caesar* was not only a commercial failure, Colman had to sue producer Harry Popkin for $75,000 of salary never paid him. (See B290.) Price, Holm and Linkletter all told me that Popkin also breached contract payments with them, but that they didn't join Colman in his lawsuit because of the time and expense.

For all its flaws, *Caesar* is still a delicious poke at early commercial television, with Colman in top form as a witty intellectual charmer. His verbal sparrings with Price and Linkletter are a delight, and he does have a sexual chemistry with Holm. My favorite bit is Albert Einstein calling the show to tell "Happy" Hogan on the air that Bottomley's explanation of his "space-time continuum" theory is correct, counterpointed by Waters's hilarious reactions in his viewing booth.

Trade paper reports since 1980 have touted a remake with either Richard Dreyfuss or John Travolta, but nothing ever came of them. Nor could it unless *Caesar* was remade as a period piece. The story could not happen on contemporary television.

Archival Sources: BFI. 35mm safety print.

UCLA: 16mm print in which the sound for the last 400 feet is from an earlier reel. VHS viewing copy, RA10121.

F63 THE 24TH ANNUAL ACADEMY AWARDS March 20, 1952. Color 16mm print of 90-minute show. See R395.

Print Sources: Academy office building in Beverly Hills.

UCLA: Award show clips in color on 3/4" tape, RA266434.

F64 HEARST METROTONE NEWS Late March 1952.

March 20, 1952. 24th Annual Academy Awards. Vol. 23 #260. See R395. Commentary by Peter Roberts. 90-second segment with a clip of Colman giving Vivien Leigh's Best Actress Oscar for *A Streetcar Named Desire* to his former co-star, Greer Garson, who was accepting for Leigh.

Print Source: UCLA VHS copy, PVA4040M.

F65 THE 25TH ANNUAL ACADEMY AWARDS March 19, 1953. 16mm kinescope of two-hour show. See R396 and TV2.

Print Source: Academy office building in Beverly Hills.

F66 HEARST METROTONE NEWS Late March 1953.

Vol. 24 #260. 25th Annual Academy Awards. See R396 and TV2. Commentary by Kani Evans. One-minute item at top of 18-minute reel for late March release to theaters. Last segment is 15-second clip of Shirley Booth on huge TV screen receiving her Oscar as Colman onstage looks on in lower foreground. Third item is raw footage of live ceremony, with Colman announcing Booth as a winner in the last 20 seconds of a 7½-minute segment.

Print Source: UCLA VHS copy, PVA5477.

F67 THE GLOBE PLAYHOUSE Circa 1953, 16mm.
Direction, Script, Photography, Production Design and Editing by William E. and Mildred R. Jordan. Acknowledgements: James E. Phillips, Ph.D. for research guidance. Richard Jones for "Greensleeves" adaptation. J. Arthur Rank for *Henry V* sequence. Based on Shakespearian scholarship, particularly the work of John Crawford Adams, Ph.D. Narration by Mr. Ronald Colman. Timing: 17½ minutes.
Synopsis: What looks to be a UCLA Theater Arts Dept. thesis film about the architecture of the Globe Theatre and its various facets, using a wooden model. The final sequence comprises scenes from *Macbeth*, using voice-over actors and physically performed by pieces of balsa wood shifted about the "theatre" floor by magnets.
Commentary: Simultaneously boring and laughable, this educational short is patronizingly written, assuming that the viewer has no idea of stage craft. Colman's straight narration of an obviously awful script begs the question of why he let himself get talked into doing it. Moreover, watching balsa wood characters voiced by wooden-sounding actors is as ludicrous as it sounds. The *Henry V* footage is a pan shot of the Thames at the top after the credits.
Print Source: Film collector Bob Dickson.

F68 AROUND THE WORLD IN 80 DAYS Michael Todd for United Artists, 1956. Todd-AO EastmanColor in 70mm. Aspect ratio: 2:1. Two versions were made: one at 30 fps for roadshow, one at 24 fps for regular runs. A few scenes are differently staged because of this. Warner Bros. Video VHS 11321 from 35mm print, LD 70926. Timing taken from tape. See R226, R378, D22.
Producer: Michael Todd, **AA** for BP. Director: Michael Anderson, **AAN**. Screenplay: S.J. Perelman, James Poe and John Farrow, **AAN**, from the novel by Jules Verne. Director of Photography: Lionel Lindon, ASC, **AA** for Color. Todd-AO Consultant: Schuyler A. Sanford. Special Effects: Lee Zavitz Musical Score: Victor Young, **AA**. Art Directors: James W. Sullivan, Ken Adam and Julio Molina, **AAN**. Set Decorations: Ross Dowd **AAN**. Costumes: Miles White, **AAN** for Color, Anna Duse, M. Cottin, Mme. Rey. Choreographer: Paul Godkin. Sound: Joseph Kane. Film Editor: Paul Weatherwax, **AA**. End Credits Sequence: Saul Bass. Associate Producers: William Cameron Menzies and Kevin O'Donovan McClory. Documentary Unit Director: Sidney Smith. Parisian, Middle Eastern and Asian Unit Director: Kevin O'Donovan McClory. Prologue features scenes from the 1902 George Méliès version of Jules Verne's *A Trip to the Moon*, footage of a rocket being launched from White Sands, New Mexico, and space footage showing the receding shape of the earth.
Cast: David Niven (Phileas Fogg), Cantinflas (Passepartout), Shirley MacLaine (Princess Aouda), Robert Newton (Inspector Fix). Cameo players: Charles Boyer (M. Gasse, clerk, Thomas Cook, Paris), Joe E. Brown (Station Master, Fort Kearney), Martine Carol (Girl in Railroad Station, Paris), John Carradine (Col. Proctor, San Francisco Politico), Charles Coburn (Clerk, Hong Kong Steamship office), **Ronald Colman** (Official, Great Indian Peninsular Railway), Melville Cooper (Steward, H.M.S. Mongolia), Noel Coward (Roland Hesketh-Baggott, Manager, London employment agency), Finlay Currie (Reform Club Member), Reginald Denny (Inspector, Bombay police), Andy Devine (First Mate, S.S. Henrietta), Marlene Dietrich (Owner, Barbary Coast saloon), Luis Miguel Dominguin (Bullfighter, Spain), Fernandel (Coachman, Paris), Ava Gardner (Bullfight Spectator), Sir John Gielgud (Foster, Ex-employee of Fogg), Hermione Gingold (Tart, London), Josæe Greco (Flamenco Dancer, Cave of the Seven Winds), Sir Cedric Hardwicke (Sir Francis Cromarty, Bombay-Calcutta Train), Trevor Howard (Fallentin, Reform Club Member),

Glynis Johns (Tart, London), Buster Keaton (Train Conductor, San Francisco to Fort Kearney), Evelyn Keyes (Tart, London), Beatrice Lillie (Revivalist Leader, London), Peter Lorre (Japanese Steward, S.S. Carnatic), Edmund Lowe (Chief Engineer, S.S. Henrietta), A.E. Matthews (Billiard Player, Reform Club), Mike Mazurki (Drunk, Hong Kong dive), Col. Tim McCoy (Commander, U.S. Cavalry, Fort Kearney), Victor McLaglen (Helmsman, S.S. Henrietta), John Mills (London Cabby), Robert Morley (Ralph, a Governor of the Bank of England), Alan Mowbray (British Consul, Suez), Edward R. Murrow (Prologue Commentator), Jack Oakie (Captain, S.S. Henrietta), George Raft (Bouncer, Barbary Coast saloon), Gilbert Roland (Achmed Abdullah), Cesar Romero (Henchman of Achmed Abdullah), Frank Sinatra (Piano Player, Barbary Coast saloon), Red Skelton (Drunk, Barbary Coast saloon), Ronald Squire (Reform Club Member), Basil Sydney (Reform Club Member), Harcourt Williams (Hinshaw, Aged steward, Reform Club).

Veteran actors in bit or extra parts: Philip Ahn, Walter Kingsford, Richard Loo, Philip Van Zandt (bits), Gertrude Astor, Anita Louise Dano (Dano was married name), Minta Durfee, Ruth Gordon, Major Sam Harris, Stuart Holmes, Buddy Roosevelt, Dick Ryan, James Van Horn (extras).

Release dates and timing: New York at the Rivoli. October 17. Los Angeles at the Carthay Circle, December 22. 182 minutes, including 11½ minutes of overture and exit music.

Part one runs 112:40. Part two runs 57:50 for a total of 170½ minutes. The opening Edward R. Murrow prologue runs 6½ minutes, of which 3½ is excerpts from *A Trip to the Moon*. The entertainingly semi-animated closing credits by Saul Bass run 6 minutes, 35 seconds. Colman appears 76:45 into part one for a segment running 1:35. His footage runs 56 seconds.

Synopsis: Independently wealthy British clubman Phileas Fogg bets the other members of his club that he can traverse the globe in exactly 80 days. In the course of his almost non-stop journey with his servant, Passepartout, Fogg travels by hot air balloon, ships, trains, an elephant and an ostrich, and rescues an Indian princess from ritual sacrifice. He is also followed by a Scotland Yard detective who believes he has robbed the Bank of England. Through all of this, Phileas discovers how lonely he really is for a woman's presence and touch for all his rigidly masculine adherence to daily routine. He wins the bet, but more important, the princess wins his heart.

Reviews: Critical praise was nearly unanimous. *80 Days* was cited as a combination of grand adventure film and beautifully photographed travelogue. A few pointed out that some of the travelogue scenes could have been cut to speed up the story, but otherwise they all had a grand time, though most of the reviews read like so much puffery. Colman is mentioned in passing in a few of them.

Commentary: Colman shows up as an Indian railway official to tell Niven and company that the Indian railway line they are on isn't quite finished, so they have to somehow find an elephant to make it through the dense brushland. Onscreen for less than a minute, Colman nevertheless stands out for his trademark panache and humor, making one wish he had not been resistant to other character roles. Film historian Laurence J. Quirk remarks that Colman's scene can be taken as a metaphor for the end of the British empire, at least in movies, but that is taking the scene and the movie as a whole too seriously. The scene is simply a good gag, though it does beg the question of how train passengers are expected to carry on through thick brushland when only an elephant can do the trick.

One marvelous thing *80 Days* did as a whole was to put Colman and five of his personal friends in the same movie, four of them for the first and only time: Charles Boyer, Noel Coward, Cedric Hardwicke and Tim McCoy. The fifth is David Niven.

Theatrical Source: Warner Bros.

Archival Sources: LC: 70mm picture and track elements; 70mm Todd-AO print; 35mm magnetic track print, reels 1, 3-6, 8-20; and 35mm magnetic track print, reels 3-4, 8-14, 16-19.

UCLA: 35mm anamorphic general release print with optical track running 148 minutes.

F69   THE STORY OF MANKIND Cambridge Productions for Warner Bros., 1957. Widescreen (1.85:1) and Technicolor. See R406.

Producer and Director: Irwin Allen. Screenplay: Irwin Allen and Charles Bennett from the book by Hendrik Willem van Loon. Director of Photography: Nick Musuraca, ASC. Technicolor Consultant: Robert Brower. Art Director: Art Loel. Set Decorations: Arthur Krams. Costumes: Marjorie Best. Musical Score: Paul Sawtell. Sound: Stanley Jones. Supervising Film Editor: Roland Gross. Film Editor: Gene Palmer, ACE. Research: Jean McChesney. Technical Advisor: Ruth K. Greenfield. Associate Producer: George E. Swink. Assistant Director: Joseph Don Page.

Cast: Ronald Colman (The Spirit of Man), Vincent Price (Mr. Scratch), Sir Cedric Hardwicke (High Judge), Hedy Lamarr (Joan of Arc), Groucho Marx (Peter Minuit), Harpo Marx (Isaac Newton), Chico Marx (Italian Monk), Virginia Mayo (Cleopatra), Agnes Moorehead (Queen Elizabeth), Peter Lorre (Nero), Charles Coburn (Hippocrates), Cesar Romero (Spanish Envoy), John Carradine (Khufu), Dennis Hopper (Napoleon), Marie Wilson (Marie Antoinette), Helmut Dantine (Antony), Edward Everett Horton (Sir Walter Raleigh), Reginald Gardiner (William Shakespeare), Marie Windsor (Josephine), George E. Stone (Waiter), Cathy O'Donnell (Early Christian Woman), Melville Cooper (Major Domo), Henry Daniell (Bishop of Beauvais), Francis X. Bushman (Moses), Franklin Pangborn (Marquis de Varennes), Jim Ameche (Alexander Graham Bell), Nick Cravat (Mr. Scratch's Assistant), Dani Crayne (Helen of Troy), Anthony Dexter (Christopher Columbus), Austin Green (Abraham Lincoln), Leonard Mudie (Chief Inquisitor), Reginald Sheffield (Julius Caesar), Abraham Sofaer (Indian Chief), Melinda Marx (Early Christian Child), Alexander Lockwood (Promoter), Bart Mattson (Cleopatra's Brother), Don Megowan (Early Man), Marvin Miller (Armana), Nancy Miller (Early Woman), Robert Watson (Adolf Hitler), Major Sam Harris (Nobleman in Queen Elizabeth's Court), David Bond (Early Christian), Richard Cutting (Court Attendant), Toni Gerry (Wife), Eden Hartford (Laughing Water, an Indian Maiden), Burt Nelson (Early Second Man), Tudor Owen (Court Clerk), Ziva Rodann (Concubine), Harry Ruby (Indian Brave), William Schallert (Earl of Warwick).

Release dates and timing: Philadelphia, October 23. New York at the Paramount, November 8. Los Angeles at 11 theaters, November 13. 100 minutes. A rough cut running three hours was sneak previewed in March 1957.

Synopsis: When mankind prematurely invents the hydrogen bomb, a heavenly tribunal debates whether man should be allowed to continue existing or blow himself up. The Spirit of Man argues the pros and cons of mankind with the Devil in a series of scenes from history. In the end, the tribunal decides that mankind's virtues are equal to its faults, leaving a final decision to a future time.

Reviews: *New Yorker*, 10-16-57: "Ronald Colman has the suave and sanguine air of a D.A.R. lecturer booked solid for the season."

Kap, *Weekly Variety*, 10-23-57: "Ronald Colman, as always, is a dignified personification of the Spirit of Man."

Hollywood Reporter, 10-23-57: "The most serious criticism...is that it does not live up to its title. How could it be a presentation of mankind, which means the human race, and omit Christ, Mohammed, Buddha, Plato, Galileo, Luther, Marx and Lenin? This 'Story of Mankind' is a Sunday supplement story in which the characters have been chosen for their superficial glamour rather than any other value."

Philip K. Scheuer, *Los Angeles Times*, 11-14-57: "All that we get, unhappily, is a mishmash of Technicolor 'cameos,' amateurishly conceived and acted, interspersed with stock shots from better Warner movies than this one...These three, by the way (Colman, Price, Hardwicke), don't fall into the amateurishly acted generalization above. With what they have, they play with wit and humor."

Commentary: When Irwin Allen optioned the Van Loon book, he had made a name for himself producing nature and animal documentaries, including *The Sea Around Us* (1953, Oscar winner) and *The Animal World*. Mike Todd's cameo star idea for *Around the World in 80 Days* inspired him to make his own cameo star epic. But whereas Todd was careful to cast stars in bit parts that fit them, Allen cast for weird novelty and the offbeat, hence the Marx Brothers, Hedy Lamarr and so on. The viewer is both fascinated and repelled by all these stars, most of whom give the worst performances of their lives.

The exceptions to all the bad acting are Colman, Price and Hardwicke, all of whom Allen wisely cast to type. Who else but Colman could be said to have consistently personified the Spirit of Man in his role as a romantic movie star? Yet having cast these men, Allen misused them as backdrop for a series of insufferable tableaus. The idea of a heavenly tribunal deciding man's fate is pretentious enough without a star parade for its own sake. When the focus is on Colman and Price, they almost manage to make this nonsense compelling. As always, Colman carries himself impeccably, but Allen's script, direction and constant intercutting of stock footage from other, better Warner movies (even the mediocre ones), keep mocking him.

The worst aspect of this mess is that Colman said yes to it after turning down the role of Colonel Nicholson (Alec Guinness) in *The Bridge on the River Kwai*, according to film historian Barry Norman. He didn't want to spend six months filming in Ceylon, but just as important, he would have had to take second billing to William Holden. So he turned down a great script that might have won him another Oscar and certainly would have revived his career.

With all the other scripts being offered Colman at the time, most of them for character parts, what a shame that he let Allen, a professional schlockmeister for the rest of his career, con him into bowing out with this one.

Theatrical Source: Warner Bros.

Archival Sources: LC. 35mm Technicolor viewing print.

UCLA: 35mm Technicolor print of reels 3 and 4.

ARCHIVES AND SPECIAL COLLECTIONS

George Eastman House. 900 East Ave., Rochester, NY 14607-2298.

(716) 271-3361. Fax: (716) 271-3970. Paolo Cherchi Usäi, Senior Curator, Film Collections. Large collection of stills from 41 of his American films.

Library of Congress. Motion Picture and Recorded Sound Division. Washington, DC 20540. (202) 707-8572. David Francis, Director. You must write for viewing appointments several weeks or months in advance.

Margaret Herrick Library of the Academy of Motion Picture Arts and Sciences.
333 S. La Cienega Blvd. in Beverly Hills. (310) 247-3000 for special collections. Clippings and microfiches for most of Colman's American movies, plus hundreds of stills for them, and chronological microfiches on the man dating from 1925.

Museum of Modern Art. 11 W. 53 St., New York, NY 10019-5498.
Film Study Center: (212) 708-9613 or (212) 708-9614. Mary Lee Bandy, Curator. Large collection of stills from his American films.

National Film and Television Archives and British Film Film Library Services.
Both housed at the BFI, 21 Stephen St., London W1P 1PL, England. Olwen Terris, film curator. Phone: 011-44-71-255-1444. Fax: 011-44-71-436-7950.

UCLA. Media Lab of the Archive Research and Study Center (ARSC). ARSC is at 180 Powell Library, Monday-Friday 8 a.m.-5 p.m. to hand in written requests for movies and TV shows. 270 Powell Library to see them. 35mm prints can only be seen off campus by appointment at 1015 N. Cahuenga in Hollywood. (310) 206-5388.
Trimester viewing hours: Monday-Thursday: 8 a.m.-8:45 p.m. Friday: 8-4:45. Saturday: Noon-4:45. Sunday: Noon-6:45. Summer hours: Monday-Friday: Noon-4:45.

Wisconsin Center for Film and Theater Research. Film and Photo Archive: 816 State Street, Madison, WI 53706. (608) 264-6466, Fax (608) 264-6472. Archive director: Donald Crafton. Hours: Monday to Friday 8:30 a.m.-4:30 p.m. In addition to 16mm prints of a few Colman films, Wisconsin has a collection of *3400* stills from all of his American movies, and a file of 98 portrait shots. This is probably the largest archival collection of Colman movie stills in the U.S.

INDEPENDENT HOME VIDEO AND FILM SOURCES

Festival Films. Ron Hall, owner. 2841 Irving Ave. S., Minneapolis, MN 55408. (612) 870-4744. *Lady Windermere's Fan.*

Grapevine Video. Jack Hardy, owner. POB 46161, Phoenix, AZ 85063. (602) 245-0210.
Silent *Screen Snapshots* and *Lady Windermere's Fan.*

Killiam Shows. Sandra Bernhack, owner. 500 Greenwich St. #501A, New York, NY 10013. (212) 925-4291. 4-reel print of *Handcuffs or Kisses?*.

SF Rush Video. Bill Longen, Owner. 1576 Feel St. #1, San Francisco, CA 94117.
(415) 921-TAPE. Trailer tapes. Trailers for *Lost Horizon*, F45 (Adventure tape TA-1) and *The Light That Failed*, F49 (1939 tape, T-1939-1).

Video Yesteryear. Box C, Sandy Hook, CT 06482. 800-243-0987.
All silent titles are transferred at 16 fps, which puts most of them into slow motion. *Lady Windermere's Fan* looks and plays awful.

A rare still from the lost British movie *Anna the Adventuress* (1920) with Alma Taylor and a moustacheless 29-year-old Ronald Colman. Note his bedroom eyes. Courtesy of British Film Institute.

On the set of *Kiki* (1926), director Clarence Brown, Ronald Colman, and Norma Talmadge pose for a publicity shot with, of all things, a baby goat. From the author's collection.

Ralph Forbes, Ronald Colman, and Neil Hamilton are the devoted Geste brothers in the definitive version of the classic French foreign saga, *Beau Geste* (1926). From the author's collection.

The NBC radio premiere of "Bulldog Drummond" at George White's Apollo Theater in New York City, May 2, 1929. Left to right: Samuel Goldwyn, Rudy Vallee, radio emcee Graham McNamee, movie censor Will Hays, Constance Bennett, Ronald Colman, Bank of Italy (later Bank of America) founder A. H. Giannini, boxer Jack Dempsey, D. W. Griffith. Courtesy of Kendall Miller.

Ronald Colman as Sydney Carton, Elizabeth Allen as Lucie Manette, and Edna May Oliver as Miss Pross in church on Christmas Eve in *A Tale of Two Cities* (1935). From the author's collection.

Claudette Colbert as Foreign Legionnaire mascot, Cigarette, is furious with Colman, as Corporal Victor, for spurning her in *Under Two Flags* (1936). From the author's collection.

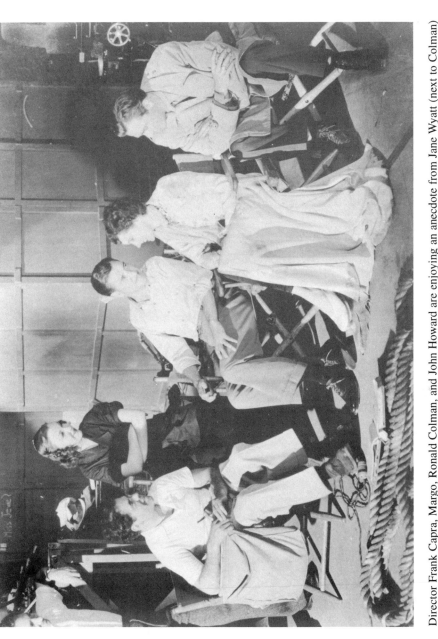

Director Frank Capra, Margo, Ronald Colman, and John Howard are enjoying an anecdote from Jane Wyatt (next to Colman) while waiting for the next set-up for *Lost Horizon* in 1936. From the author's collection.

Ronald Colman as French rogue/poet/thief Francois Villon tries to seduce Frances Dee as Katherine de Voucelles with a poem he has written titled "If I Were King" in the movie of the same name (1938). From the author's collection.

Ronald Colman (far right) prepares to turn in arsonist Tom Tyler (far left) while Cary Grant and Jean Arthur ponder his decision in *The Talk of the Town* (1942). From the author's collection.

Greer Garson couldn't be happier that husband Ronald Colman has regained his memory for the romantic climax of *Random Harvest* (1942), Colman's biggest hit movie of the 1940s. From the author's collection.

Thanksgiving dinner in 1912 with the Apley family circle in *The Late George Apley* (1947). Richard Ney, Richard Haydn, Mildred Natwick, Francis Pierlot, Ronald Colman, Nydia Westman, Percy Waram, Kathleen Howard (as the maid, behind Waram), Vanessa Brown, Edna Best (back to camera). From the author's collection.

Ronald Colman as schizoid actor Anthony John playing Othello in *A Double Life* (1947). The bearded actor to his right is Guy Bates Post as Ludovico. From the author's collection. Copyright © 1947 Universal Pictures Co., Inc.

Benita and Ronald Colman in a publicity shot for the television version of *The Halls of Ivy* (1954). From the author's collection.

RADIOGRAPHY

Ronald Colman's radio work was incredibly prolific: Over 400 shows, on more than half of which he was host or star of four series. Most of these shows were either on NBC or the syndicated series *Favorite Story*. And most of them survive at various archives, on commercial recordings and in private collections. Their ready accessibility makes an evaluation of Colman's radio career both easy and mostly a pleasure.

This is the first detailed listing of Colman's radio work, and its completeness is due mostly to tapes and information provided by several radio buffs, Colman fans, archivists and CBS librarian John Behrens. Discovering the sheer volume and variety of these shows compels a profound re-evaluation of Colman's range as an actor. They certainly attest that he became a major radio star in between the few movies he made during the 1940s.

There were two main reasons Colman did so many shows, especially during the war years. One was his zeal to boost GI and public morale through programs aimed at a wartime audience. Another was simply to keep busy, since he didn't want to make movies with a wartime plot and good star roles for a man of his age and screen type became scarce, which held into the late 1940s and 1950s.

His close friend and agent, Nat Wolff (who was also his first director on *The Halls of Ivy*) was the mastermind behind much of this output. Wolff was also married to actress Edna Best, another dear friend, which was why she was one of Colman's most frequent radio co-stars.

From 1941 on, when his performances became more frequent, Ronald Colman's beautifully familiar voice was a regular, welcome presence in millions of American homes. This auditory omnipresence, combined with his rich movie legacy, makes it all the more remarkable that Colman became a practically forgotten star for more than 25 years after his death. Indeed, the frequent broadcasts of his movies and radio shows in the last decade should have resulted in more attention from film and radio historians than has been the case.

Most of what follows is a chronological listing of Colman's radio shows from 1929 to 1956. There are two exceptions: *Favorite Story*, which was syndicated, and *The Halls of Ivy*, his longest running network series. In the case of *Ivy*, keeping the episodes together enables the reader to track the series' evolution straight through. For those series for which Colman was the host, star or semi-regular, the numbering begins with the first show, not with the exposition so that the reader can more easily locate the first show or appearance.

Some shows have odd timings because they were odd-length specials, or ran overtime (a rarity) or were followed by a news break.

For most series other than his own on which Colman performed several times through the years, I will give personnel and sponsorship credits in the first listing only. For all-star benefit, promotional and memorial shows, Colman's name is in boldface for ease of finding it.

Stories Colman did more than once are cross-referenced. Types of programs such as War Bond and War Relief shows, Variety and Christmas shows, etc., are listed in the index.

Regarding radio versions of *Lost Horizon*, it was the second most adapted Colman picture, both for him and other actors, yet none of those shows were based on the 1937 movie, only on the James Hilton novel. Columbia Pictures either would not or could not grant radio rights to Robert Riskin's screenplay for the Frank Capra picture, though they readily granted rights for every other Columbia movie.

You will find archival and commercial sources for these programs at the end of this chapter.

NETWORKS AND GLOSSARY

ABC, CBS, NBC, NBC Blue and Red[*], Mutual Broadcasting System (Mutual), Armed Forces Radio Service (AFRS), British Broadcasting Corporation (BBC), and Canadian Broadcasting Corporation (CBC).

CTC = coast-to-coast live. Sus = sustaining or no commercials. All war bond, war relief, specialty and charity shows were sustaining.

R1 MOVIE PREMIERE: BULLDOG DRUMMOND
May 2, 1929. WJZ New York for a 15-station NBC Blue network. 15 minutes. 8:15-8:30 p.m. EST. See F31, R2, R79, R125.

From George White's Apollo Theatre in New York City. MC: Graham McNamee. Brief remarks by: Ronald Colman, Samuel Goldwyn, Constance Bennett, D.W. Griffith, Douglas Fairbanks, Mary Pickford, Fanny Brice, Rudy Vallee and others.

This premiere marked Colman's radio debut. No discs are known to survive, if they were made at all. The ad hoc network included WJR Detroit, WBBA Boston, KFRC Houston, and WDAR San Antonio, but did not extend further west than Texas.

R2 MOVIE PREMIERE: CONDEMNED
December 5, 1929. MC: Harry Richman. WABC New York for CBS, but originating in Hollywood. 8:30 p.m. PST, CTC, sus. 30 minutes. See F32, R1, R125.

From Grauman's Chinese Theater in Hollywood. Brief remarks by Ronald Colman, Ann Harding, Charlie Chaplin, Gary Cooper, Jack Benny and other stars in the theater's lobby.   No discs are known to survive, if they were made at all.

R3 GENERAL MILLS AND 20TH CENTURY PICTURES SHOW
April 14, 1934. MC: Rupert Hughes. Music: Abe Lyman and Alfred Newman Orchestras.

------

[*] In 1941, the FCC decreed that NBC's Blue and Red networks constituted a monopoly, ordering NBC to sell one of them. Lifesaver king Edward J. Noble, who owned ABS (American Broadcasting System) bought Blue for $8 million on October 12, 1943. ABS with Blue became ABC in 1945.

Sponsors: General Mills and 20th Century Pictures. KFI Hollywood and WEAF New York for NBC Red, and Radio Normandy for England, 4 p.m. PST, CTC. 60 minutes.

Cast: (Hollywood) George Arliss, **Ronald Colman**, Constance Bennett, Tullio Carminati, Fredric March, Jack Oakie, Vivienne Segal, Beatrice Selvira (beauty consultant to United Artists). (New York) Tess Gardella (Aunt Jemima), Armida, Senator Royal S. Copeland, David Percy, Betty Crocker, Donald E. Davis (President of General Mills), Howard Claney.

Promotional broadcast for General Mills and the newly formed 20th Century Pictures company headed by Darryl F. Zanuck and Joseph M. Schenck. Alternating between Hollywood and New York, with an international hook-up to England and South America, one of the first of its kind. Program includes monologues, a dramatic sketch and songs.

Review: Land, *Weekly Variety*, April 17: "Outstanding was Ronald Colman, whose splendid voice sprayed a million parlors with the same sort of appeal he exercises from the screen. He combined chattiness with dignity and addressed himself specifically to Great Britain and South America, where international hook-ups were also bringing the program."

R4 HOLLYWOOD HOTEL
October 12, 1934. Host: Louella Parsons. Regulars: Dick Powell, Rowene Williams, Ted Fio-Rito's Entertainers, William O'Neal and El Brendel. Announcer: Ken Niles. Music: Raymond Paige Orchestra. Theme song: "Blue Moon" by Richard Rodgers and Lorenz Hart. Sponsor: Campbell Soups. CBS. 30 minutes. See F41.

Ronald Colman and Loretta Young play a scene from their forthcoming movie *Clive of India*. Second show of series and Colman's dramatic radio debut.

R5 HOLLYWOOD HOTEL
September 6, 1935. Colman and Elizabeth Allan play a scene from their forthcoming movie, *A Tale of Two Cities*. CBS. 30 minutes. See below.

R6 A TALE OF TWO CITIES
December 21, 1935. Guest speaker: Author Hugh Walpole. Music: Harry Stockwelly, a male octet and St. Luke's Choristers of Long Beach. KFI Hollywood for NBC Red. 4 p.m. PST, CTC, sus. 30 minutes. See above and F43, R32, R102, R186, D5, D9.

Cast: Ronald Colman (Sydney Carton), Benita Hume (Lucie Manette), Edna May Oliver (Miss Pross), Walter Catlett (Barsad), Reginald Owen (Stryver), Donald Haines (Jerry Cruncher, Jr.) and others from the movie's cast.

Special broadcast of scenes from the movie, which had premiered in New York, but not in Los Angeles. Also the first radio tandem of Colman and Hume (who wasn't in the movie), who had been dating for about nine months.

R7 BRITISH STARS SALUTE KING GEORGE VI
May 11, 1937. Host: Douglas Fairbanks, Jr. Announcer: Clinton Teviss. Plus His Majesty's Consul, Francis Ewan. Musical director: Ray Noble. KECA Hollywood for NBC Blue and Radio Normandy for England. 11 a.m. PST, CTC, sus. 30 minutes. See F46, R12, R13, R254, D17.

Ronald Colman, Madeleine Carroll, C. Aubrey Smith, Raymond Massey and David Niven, all on the set of *The Prisoner of Zenda* in Culver City, give brief messages of congratulations to George VI in honor of his coronation on May 12.

THE CIRCLE (January 15-February 5 for Colman)

Producer: J. Walter Thompson Co. Announcer: Jack Frazer. Script supervisor: Dick Mack. Marx Brothers writers: Tiffany Thayer, Robert Colwell, John Whedon, Dick Chevillat, Stanley Davis, Manny Mannheim. Musical director: Robert Emmett Dolan. Singers: The Foursome Quartet. Sponsor: Kellogg Co. WEAF New York for NBC Red on a 52-station network, but originating from Hollywood. Broadcast day and time: Sunday, 7 p.m. PST, CTC. 60 minutes. See B52, B64, B220, B419-22.

Regulars: Ronald Colman (President), Carole Lombard (Vice President), Cary Grant (Beadle, Devil's Advocate), Groucho Marx (Heckler), Chico Marx (Assistant Heckler), Lawrence Tibbett, Basil Rathbone (replaced Colman Feb. 12), Madeleine Carroll (replaced Lombard March 12).

Heralded as a breakthrough talk/variety grabbag show, *The Circle* was Colman's first radio venture as a series regular. The regular cast comprised the first six names above. The series had a huge budget, including $28,000 total for the regulars ($5000 each for Colman and opera star Tibbett), a large (for radio) orchestra, and a chorus.

Colman quit the show after only four weeks of a 12-week contract, goaded by his good friend, Noel Coward, who advised him to assert himself on scripts and guest stars. In a rare fit of pique, Ronnie angrily confronted John Reber (head of J. Walter Thompson, the ad agency for Kellogg), who then threatened to tear up Colman's contract. Colman dared him to, Reber did and that was the end of Colman's brief tenure with the show. Grant and Lombard quit after the February 19 and March 5 shows respectively, both complaining about inferior scripts. Colman was succeeded by Basil Rathbone, who stayed with the show till it was canceled. Problem was that there was one writer for Colman, Lombard and Grant at $350 a week, but several writers hired independently by the Marxes. (For documentation of the above, see B395.)

The show reportedly tried to be low, middle and highbrow all at once, dooming it to commercial failure. It ended after 26 weeks on July 9, 1939, costing NBC and Kellogg a combined $2 million, according to radio historian John Dunning. Though the premiere show doesn't seem to exist—or the last two with Colman—the second show does, but minus the first minute.

R8 THE CIRCLE
January 15, 1939. Premiere show. Tibbett almost didn't make it to the Hollywood studio because of a New York City storm, delaying his plane flight. No one at NBC or the ad agency thought to have him simply go to WEAF instead of making weekly round trips. Show includes sketch of Rudyard Kipling's "The Phantom Rickshaw." See also R151.

Review: Bob Landry, *Weekly Variety*, January 18, 1939: "A strange contrast is the smartness of the production in general and the extreme corniness of the Kellogg commercials, which are fired point blank out of a slightly rusty 1926 howitzer...Program is rather suggestive of one of the casual English what-ho gatherings with an Oxfordian chairman. It's a reverse on the usual complaint. They may admit it's art this time, and say instead, 'But is it commercial?'"

R9 THE CIRCLE
January 22, 1939. NBC. 62 minutes.

Colman plays a doctor in a Civil War ghost story skit and performs a monologue as Socrates; guest José Iturbi plays a Chopin Nocturne; Grant sings Noel Coward's "Mad Dogs and Englishmen" and an FCC regulation about station IDs; Groucho and Chico do a comic song routine called "Fifteen Bucks"; and Lombard makes an electrifying (especially considering the time) feminist speech about why she thinks women would rule the world better than men.

Seemingly the only extant show, so I have no idea what there was in this script and the two that followed that made Colman discontented. Best segments here are Grant singing, the ghost story, and Lombard's remarkable diatribe.

This episode ran overtime because of Groucho's and Chico's ad libs, for which they were doubtless chastised.

R10 THE CIRCLE
January 29, 1939. NBC. 60 minutes.

R11 THE CIRCLE
February 5, 1939. NBC. 60 minutes.
Noel Coward is the guest. A *Weekly Variety* article of February 15 (See B395) states that if Coward hadn't done the show, Colman might have remained content to stay with it. See page 134 for capsule version of Colman's walk-out.

R12 LUX RADIO THEATER (CBS, 1939-1953, 16 shows)
June 5, 1939. "The Prisoner of Zenda", from the 1937 movie of Anthony Hope's novel. Producer/Host: Cecil B. DeMille (till 1-22-45). Announcers: Melville Ruick (till 7-13-42), John Milton Kennedy (9-14-42 through mid-1952), Ken Carpenter (9-52 on). Writers: George Wells, Harry Kerr and others. Music director: Louis Silvers. Sound effects: Charlie Forsyth. KNX Hollywood for CBS. 60 minutes. 63 stations plus 29 on the CBC at the time. See F46, R7, R254, D17, B177.
   Broadcast day and time: Monday, 6 p.m. PST, CTC, except for R27, 5 p.m.
   Cast: Ronald Colman (Rudolf Rassendyll, Prince Rudolf), Benita Hume (Princess Flavia), Douglas Fairbanks Jr. (Rupert of Hentzau), C. Aubrey Smith (Colonel Zapt), Ralph Forbes (Black Michael), Paula Winslowe (Antoinette de Mauban), Peter Wills (Fritz von Tarlenheim), Eric Snowden (Joseph), Ian McLaren (the Cardinal), Lou Merrill (Detchard), Frank Nelson (Krafstein), Ross Forrester, Bob Burleson, Gaughan Burke, James Eagles, Bob Payton, Noreen Gammill, Charles Emerson, Ethel Sykes, Gabon Galt.
   Stale, sluggish read-through (except for Fairbanks, who steals the show by having a fine time) until midway through act two, when everyone stops sleepwalking and starts acting.

R13 TRIBUTE TO KING GEORGE VI AND QUEEN ELIZABETH
June 11, 1939. Hostess: Gertrude Lawrence. Music: Ray Noble Orchestra and Sir Adrian Boult conducting the NBC Symphony. KFI Hollywood for NBC Red. 11 a.m. PST, CTC. 60 minutes. See R7.
   Partial Program: Ray Noble Orchestra ("Charlie is My Darling" and "Bonnie Mary of Argyle"); Vivien Leigh and Basil Rathbone (poems by Robert Browning and Elizabeth Barrett Browning respectively. "Let's Contend No More Love" and "How Do I Love Thee"); Nigel Bruce, Sir Cedric Hardwicke and C. Aubrey Smith ("Three Little Fishies"); Greer Garson and Leslie Howard (a scene from *Goodbye Mr. Chips*); Lawrence ("Limehouse Blues", "Do, Do, Do What You Done Once More, Baby", and "A Cup of Coffee, a Sandwich and You", songs she introduced on stage); Brian Aherne (Rupert Brooks's poem "A Soldier"); Dennis King ("Annie Laurie"); George M. Cohan (farewell toast), and **Ronald Colman** (passage from *Henry V*). Also performing (but I don't know what): Laurence Olivier, David Niven, Freddie Bartholomew, Anna Neagle, George Sanders, Reginald

Gardiner, Roland Young, Edna Best, Herbert Marshall, Judith Anderson, and Madeleine Carroll.

All-star tribute to King George VI and Queen Elizabeth, who were visiting the United States. Someone at NBC had the bright idea for Hollywood's British colony of actors to broadcast a show for the royal couple's amusement during a hot dog picnic at Hyde Park hosted by President Roosevelt. Program order, except for Colman, taken from edited NBC retrospective broadcast.

R14 GULF SCREEN GUILD THEATER (1939-1950, 10 shows under two series titles)
October 15, 1939. "None Shall Part Us" by Leonard Spiegelgas. Director/Host: Roger Pryor. Sponsor: Gulf Oil. Pitchman: John Conte. Theme: Opening of Tchaikovsky's Piano Concerto #1. Music: Oscar Bradley and his Gulf Orchestra. Actors' salaries donated to the Motion Picture Relief Fund. CBS. 30 minutes.

On October 19, 1942, this series became *Screen Guild Players*, with a new director, host, conductor and sponsor.

Cast: Ronald Colman (Capt. Alan Harcourt), Joan Crawford (Sarah Farrington), Lew Ayres (Michael Farrington), Montagu Love (Sir George Packman).

In 1937, Scotland Yard detective Harcourt tracks down career criminal Michael Farrington, only to end up marrying his widow, Sarah, and shielding her from the sordid truth about her first husband's profession.

Maudlin soap opera that sinks its valiant cast. Best part is at the end when the three stars play a forfeit quiz game with Pryor. When Colman misses his question, he has to recite "Mary Had a Little Lamb" as Orson Welles would do it. The listener can picture him doing a double take as the audience roars with laughter when he is told his penalty.

R15 GOOD NEWS OF 1940
February 8, 1940. Host: Edward Arnold. Regulars: Fanny Brice and Hanley Stafford as Baby Snooks and Daddy. Music: Meredith Willson and his Orchestra. Sponsor: Maxwell House Coffee. Pitchman: Warren Hull. CBS. 60 minutes. See F49, R161.

Ronald Colman (Dick Heldar), Ida Lupino (Bessie Broke), Muriel Angelus (Maisie) and Frank Nelson (Torpenhow) perform a 24-minute, one-act abridgement of *The Light That Failed* to plug the movie. Colman gives a strong performance, improving on his screen portrayal.

R16 ARCH OBOLER'S PLAYS
March 16, 1940. "The Most Dangerous Game" by Richard Connell. Adapted, produced and directed by Oboler. Music: Gordon Jenkins. NBC Red, sus. 30½ minutes. See R22, R31, R52 for other Oboler-directed shows.

Cast: Ronald Colman (Sangor Rainsford), Sophie Stewart (Mrs. Rainsford), Jay Novello (Count Zarkoff and shipboard passenger).

One of many radio versions of this famous short story about a mad game hunter (Novello) who chases human prey, in this case Colman. Stewart's role is not in the original story. Above-average script with a solid performance by Colman and eerie music to convey a psychological mood, but with a gratuitous anti-isolationist speech for Rainsford that makes the show run 1½ minutes overtime.

Colman did the program because he was a fan of Oboler's show. When Oboler relocated to Hollywood from Chicago, Colman insisted on playing in "The Most Dangerous Game" for free to increase Oboler's audience. In the end he accepted only the union minimum of $17.50, according to radio historian John Dunning.

There have been several movie versions of this story, arguably the best of which was made in 1932, starring Joel McCrea, Fay Wray, Leslie Banks and Robert Armstrong.

R17   CANADIAN RED CROSS EMERGENCY APPEAL
September 29, 1940. Program coordinator: C.P. McGregor. MC: Alan Mowbray. Music: The Don Lee Orchestra, conducted by David Rose. Performed before an audience of 3000 at a Warner Bros. sound stage. Mutual, CBC and the Associated Broadcasting Stations of Southern California. 60 minutes.

Program: Canadian Prime Minister W.L. MacKenzie-King (opening address from Ottawa); Gloria Jean with The Meglin Kiddies and Charles Previn's Orchestra ("What Did We Learn at School?" by Vivien Ellis); Reginald Gardiner (imitating a train); Anna Neagle ("Prayer of the Red Cross Nurse"); Maxine Gray ("Goodnight Sweetheart" and "The Very Thought of You" by Ray Noble); Herbert Marshall (ode to London to the "Westminster Movement" from the *London Suite* by Eric Coates); Mary Pickford ("Do You Hear the Children Weeping?" by Elizabeth Barrett Browning and appeal); Betty Jane Rhodes ("Danny Boy" aka "Londonderry Air"); the Dionne quintuplets—Marie, Yvonne, Cecile, Emily and Annette—with their doctor, Alan Roy Dafoe, in Calendar, Ontario, (the quints sing "Oh, Canada"); **Ronald Colman** (20-second poem, "To Britain"); Canadian opera star Ann Jamison, ("The Lass with the Delicate Air"); Madeleine Carroll ("Twelve O'Clock", a July 1940 *New York Times* editorial about England's will to survive); "This Other Eden," air raid shelter playlet by Gene Lockhart, with Lockhart (Air Raid Warden), Sir Cedric Hardwicke (Herbert Boggs), Binnie Barnes (Matilda Boggs), George Sanders (Mr. Mannering), Freddie Bartholomew (Alan Barclay), June Lockhart (Marjorie Barclay); Gloria Jean ("After Every Rainstorm a Rainbow Appears"); C. Aubrey Smith (Kipling's "Ballad of the Clamperdown"); Merle Oberon (appeal); Laurence Olivier ("Once More Unto the Breach, Dear Friends" from Shakespeare's "Henry V"); Vivien Leigh (speech "Let Us Drink" from Noel Coward's play "Cavalcade"); closing with "God Save Our King" because it has the same tune as "My Country 'Tis of Thee."

R18   SILVER THEATRE
December 8, 1940. "The Great Adventure" from the novel *Buried Alive* by Arnold Bennett. Host: Conrad Nagel. CBS. 30 minutes. See R70.

Cast: Ronald Colman (Priam Farll), Paula Winslowe (Alice Farll). Other cast names unavailable.

Renowned artist Priam Farll assumes the identity of his dead valet so he can live a life of quiet anonymity with his newfound wife while continuing his painting. This splendid cultural satire was made into movies starring Roland Young (1932) and Monty Woolley (1943).

R19   SALVATION ARMY SHOW
December 14, 1940. Host: Mary Pickford. Music: San Francisco College A Capella Choir and Don Lee Concert Orchestra. KHJ Hollywood for Mutual. 5 p.m. PST, CTC, 30 minutes. See D11.

Program includes a 6-minute sketch, "The Nativity", about the birth of Christ, with Colman as Joseph and Pickford as Mary. Colman enunciates well while Pickford is stilted in the extreme, both hobbled by a horrible, almost self-parodying script that presents Joseph and Mary as fully prescient about the impact their child will have on the world.

R20 GULF SCREEN GUILD THEATER
December 22, 1940. "The Juggler of Notre Dame" from "Our Lady's Juggler" by Anatole France, adapted by John Nesbitt. CBS, sus. 30 minutes. See R29, R42, R85.

Cast: Ronald Colman (Narrator and Barnaby) and Nelson Eddy (Singing Monk).

Colman reads France's charming religious fantasy about a juggling simpleton named Barnaby who performs his act before a statue of the Virgin Mary at a monastery in the Middle Ages, rewritten to take place on Christmas Eve. Songs: "God Rest Ye Merry Gentlemen," "The Longest Journey," "Ave Maria," and "The Lord's Prayer." A dull show overall—flatly read by Colman, with insufficient background music and sound effects, and tiresome singing by Eddy—it was nevertheless repeated live by popular demand with Colman and Eddy in 1941 and 1942.

R21 HOLLYWOOD'S NEW YEAR'S WITH A HEART
January 1, 1941. Produced under the auspices of Bundles for Britain. Director: Arch Oboler. Announcers: Harlow Wilcox, Ben Alexander. Writers: Don Quinn (Joe J. Public segments), Oboler ("Mr. Pip" and "The Laughing Man"), Bill Morrow, Ed Beloin (Benny sketch), Milton Krims (Cagney half of dualogue), Irv Brecker, Leonard L. Levinson. Music director: Gordon Jenkins. KFI and KECA Hollywood for NBC Red and Blue. 60 minutes. Broadcast from Hollywood Palladium ballroom at 7 p.m. PST, CTC. Rebroadcast by transcription that night on Mutual. See R16, R30, page for other Oboler-directed shows. See also B70.

Joe J. Public (Elliott Lewis) is escorted by Adolphe Menjou to what he thinks is a star gala, only to have Menjou and Merle Oberon show him several other stars contributing their time to the Bundles for Britain campaign. The stars perform in exchange for badly needed equipment and supplies.

Program: Tony Martin ("Home on the Range"); Walter Brennan and 7-year-old Raymond Severn ("Mr. Pip," introductory narration by **Colman**); The Merry Macs ("Comin' Through the Rye"); Jack Benny and Georgie Stoll ("Alter Ego Rides Again) Myrna Loy (appeal); Judy Garland ("I Hear a Rhapsody"); Charles Boyer and Lou Merrill ("The Laughing Man"); Mickey Rooney, Myrna Loy, Merle Oberon, Adolphe Menjou, Brian Donlevy ("The Screen Kids Quizzeroo," *Quiz Kids* parody); The Merry Macs ("Oh, Suzanna"); **Ronald Colman** and James Cagney (reading respectively "Letter from an English Father to an American Father," a British newspaper letter by Malcolm Saville, and "Letter from an American Father to an English Father" by Milton Krims for this show, with background music from Dvorak's *New World Symphony*); Claudette Colbert (final plea); Garland ("Auld Lang Syne").

R22 LUX RADIO THEATER
January 13, 1941. "Libel," from the play by Edward Wooll. CBS. 60 minutes. See R44.

Cast: Ronald Colman (Sir Mark Lodden), Frances Robinson (Enid Lodden), Otto Kruger (Mr. Foxley), Frederic Worlock (Sir Wilfrid), Alec Hartford (Buckinham), George Surrell (Flourdon), Eric Snowden (the Judge), Norman Field, Claire Vedera, Thomas Mills, and Fred Mackaye.

Former WWI POW and current Member of Parliament Sir Mark Lodden must prove his identity in court after suing a London newspaper for libel when it accuses him of taking Lodden's name and life as his own.

Sharply written, potent play about the difficulty of proving one's identity and the defensive mechanism of self-induced amnesia that's used to forget a nightmarish past, in this case the horror of war. One of Colman's best and strongest radio roles, which he repeated even more strongly on *Lux* in 1943. This was such an ideal drama for him that you have to wonder why he didn't do it as a movie. Otto Kruger is also superb as the incisively sardonic defense lawyer.

Dirk Bogarde starred in the 1959 movie version.

R23 LUX RADIO THEATER

February 3, 1941. "Rebecca," from the 1940 Selznick movie directed by Alfred Hitchcock, based on the novel by Daphne du Maurier. CBS. 60 minutes.

Cast: Ronald Colman (Maxim de Winter), Ida Lupino (The Woman Whose Name We Do Not Know), Judith Anderson (Mrs. Danvers), Dennis Green (Jack Favell), Hans Conried (the Doctor).

This show's chief historical interest is the chance to hear Colman playing a movie role he turned down: The mysterious aristocrat Maxim de Winter, who is haunted by memories of his first wife, Rebecca. Colman is only fair in the role (you get the impression he was reluctant to play it, acceding because of popular audience demand for a return visit to *Lux* so soon after "Libel"), Lupino is miscast as wife number two, Anderson is impeccably chilling as Danvers (repeating her screen role), Green tries to imitate George Sanders from the movie, and Conried does a good, crisp job as the doctor. David O. Selznick appears after the play to receive a movie magazine award for cinematic excellence.

R24 AMERICA CALLING: GREEK WAR RELIEF

February 8, 1941. Coordinator: Samuel Goldwyn, Chairman of the Motion Picture Permanent Charities Committee. Writers: Carey Wilson (Hardy family sketches); Dory Schary (Taylor-Stanwyck-Douglas sketch); Dick Mann (Marx-Carroll sketch); Robert Reilly Crutcher (Gable-Oberon playlet); Bill Morrow and Ed Bulloin (Benny material). Co-hosts: Jack Benny and Bob Hope. Announcers: Don Wilson and Knox Manning. Music conducted by Meredith Willson. CBS, NBC Blue, Mutual, Warner's independent stations, Radio Normandy for England, CBC, and Greek stations. Broadcast from Grauman's Chinese Theater in Hollywood at 8:15 p.m. PST, CTC, sus. 90 minutes. KFWB Hollywood aired a 15-minute on-stage pre-show locally only at 8 p.m. See R39, R67-68.

Program: Tyrone Power (Keynote address); Meredith Willson (conducting his "America Calling" march with chorus); Mickey Rooney, Lewis Stone, Ann Rutherford, Fay Holden (Hardy family sketch); Connee Boswell ("That Sunrise Serenade"); Robert Taylor, Barbara Stanwyck, Melvyn Douglas (comedy sketch); Shirley Temple (banter with Benny and Hope and war relief pitch); Charles Laughton (reads cable to Sam Goldwyn from Albert Alexander Koretsis, the Greek Premier); Madeleine Carroll, Groucho Marx (comedy sketch); second Hardy family sketch; The Merry Macs ("The Old Bucket"); Clark Gable, Merle Oberon (romantic comedy sketch); Reginald Owen, introducing songs from *The Mikado* by Gilbert & Sullivan, performed by Frank Morgan ("I've Got a Little List"), Dick Powell ("A Wandering Minstrel, I"), and Hope, Benny and Groucho ("Three Little Maids from School"); **Ronald Colman** ("The Jervis Bay Goes Down" by Gene Fowler with original score by Willson); Myrna Loy, Mary Martin, Benny and Hope (comedy sketch); entire cast sings "My Country 'Tis of Thee"; Laughton reads cable to Goldwyn about pledge from AHEPA, a Greek-American organization.

This program was broadcast before a capacity audience of 2000 at $10 per ticket. Shots of stars arriving are included in a Hearst Metrotone Newsreel segment on file at UCLA, though none show Colman.

Colman magnificently performs Gene Fowler's maritime poem (11-minute segment), about the sinking in battle of an Australian freighter (pronounced Jarvis). The poem became so popular because of this broadcast that Fowler published it in book form and Colman performed it once more in 1944.

R25 LET'S MEET THE STARS
Recorded February 14, 1941. Scripted interview done as a glorified commercial for Ronson cigarette lighters. CBS(?) 15 minutes. See R115, R124-25, R377, R404.

R26 UNITED CHINA RELIEF
June 6, 1941. Host: Tyrone Power. Announcer: Bud Hiestand. Music: Gordon Jenkins. KFI Hollywood for NBC Red. 6:30 p.m., PST, CTC. 30 minutes.

   Cast: Lionel Barrymore, Claudette Colbert, **Ronald Colman**, John Garfield, Kathryn Grayson, Alan Marshall, Anna May Wong.

   Colman narrates "Burma Road," a dramatic testimony to the importance of the Burma Road as a lifeline to China during WWII. Music by Jenkins.

R27 LUX RADIO THEATER (Season Premiere)
September 15, 1941. "Lost Horizon" by James Hilton. CBS. 60 minutes. See F45, R27, R54, R110, R173, D3, D10, D15.

   Cast: Ronald Colman (Hugh Conway), Dennis Green (Charles Mallinson), Cy Kendall (Chang), Donald Crisp (High Lama), Dennis Hoey (Rutherford), Jill Esmond (Lo-Tsen), Dick Elliot and Peter Leeds.

   Fair version of the novel. Author Hilton was set to make his acting debut on this show as Rutherford, but backed out due to pressure of work.

R28 RUSSIAN WAR RELIEF
October 25, 1941. With Robert A. Millikin, Alexis Kall, Ronald Colman, Edward G. Robinson, Mischa Auer and others. KECA Hollywood for NBC Blue, 8:05 p.m. PST, CTC. 25 minutes.

R29 GULF SCREEN GUILD THEATER
December 21, 1941. "The Juggler of Notre Dame." Live restaging of the 1940 show. CBS. 30 minutes. See R20, R42, R85.

R30 AMERICAN RED CROSS PROGRAM
December 24, 1941. MC: Eddie Cantor. Music: Edgar Fairchild's Orchestra. KFI Hollywood for NBC Red. 6 p.m. PST, CTC. 60 minutes.

   Cast: Dinah Shore, Bert "The Mad Russian" Gordon, Harry Von Zell (Cantor regulars), Jim and Marian Jordan (Fibber McGee and Molly), Loretta Young, Deanna Durbin, Dennis Day, Don Wilson, Red Skelton, *Aldrich Family* sketch with Ezra Stone (by Clifford Goldsmith), **Ronald Colman** (reads "Their Finest Hour" by Gene Fowler, music composed and conducted by Gordon Jenkins), Irving Berlin and New York City Mayor Fiorello H. La Guardia.

   Note: Program mostly taken from a newspaper clipping.

R31 MESSAGE TO AUSTRALIA
Sometime in early 1940s. Introduction by Herbert Marshall. Colman talks about slogans. Second guest is poet Archibald Macliesh. Syndicated, company unknown. 15 minutes.

R32 LUX RADIO THEATER
January 12, 1942. "A Tale of Two Cities" by Charles Dickens. Host/Narrator: Cecil B.

DeMille. CBS. 60 minutes. See F43, R5, R6, R32, R102, R186, D5, D9.

Cast: Ronald Colman (Sydney Carton), Edna Best (Lucie Manette), Halliwell Hobbes Jarvis Lorry), Norman Field (Dr. Manette), Dennis Green (Charles Darnay), Verna Felton (Madame Defarge), Griff Barnett (Stryver), Alec Hartford (Barsad), Arthur Q. Bryan (Jerry Cruncher, Tribunal Juror), Eric Snowden (Judge), Kathleen Fitz, Victor Rodman, Ed Max, Boyd Davis, Jeff Corey, Thomas Mills, Ferdinand Munier, Don Thompson, Jane Morgan, and Charles Seals.

Colman gives his accustomed fine performance replaying his favorite screen role, but Verna Felton is the surprise of this show, full of fire and thunder as the murderously vengeful Madame Defarge.

The direction, pacing, casting and acting for this *Lux* version are superior to those for the second version Colman did in 1946 (R102), using the same script.

R33 MARCH OF DIMES ON THE AIR
January 24, 1942. Producer/Director/Sketch Writer: Arch Oboler. Music: Gordon Jenkins, conducting a 60-piece orchestra and 16-voice chorus. KFI Hollywood for NBC Red. 6 p.m. PST, CTC. 60 minutes.

Program: Marlene Dietrich, Tyrone Power and Kay Kyser in "a streamlined musical"; Maureen O'Sullivan, James Cagney and Thomas Mitchell in "Marriage—1942"; Claudette Colbert, Humphrey Bogart, Janet Beecher, Mary Lansing and Frank Graham in "Pay the Piper"; Irene Dunne, Spencer Tracy (appeals); Bing Crosby, Jim and Marian Jordan (Fibber McGee & Molly), Edgar Bergen & Charlie McCarthy, Bob Hope, Deanna Durbin, the Merry Macs and Dennis Day (comedy and songs); **Ronald Colman**, monologue called "Letter at Midnight" about Pearl Harbor, with a score by Meredith Willson.

Note: Program mostly taken from a newspaper column.

R34 THE NEW NETWORK OF THE AMERICAS (LA CADENA DE LAS AMERI-CAS)
May 19, 1942. Production, writing and directing credits not announced. Spanish and English-speaking announcers not identified. MC: Melvyn Douglas. Music: Leith Stevens Orchestra, The Shadoweo Trio (sic?), Howard Barlow in New York conducting the Columbia Symphony Orchestra, Alfredo Antonini in Latin America conducting Orquesta Panamerica. KNX Hollywood and WABC New York for all 121 CBS stations, plus a Latin American network of 76 stations in 20 republics south of the Rio Grande, and 3 CBS shortwave stations. 6:30 p.m. PST, CTC. 90 minutes.

Guests: (Hollywood) **Ronald Colman** ("Tribute to South America"), Jinx Falkenburg (swimming champion turned actress), Rita Hayworth, Dick Powell, Rosita Moreno, Edward G. Robinson (speaking fluent Spanish). (New York) Lauritz Melchior and Meduse Marial (sic?) (Metropolitan Opera stars), CBS President William S. Paley. (Washington, D.C.) Nelson A. Rockefeller, Vice-President Henry A. Wallace, Under-Secretary of State Sumner Welles and Latin American dignitaries. (Latin America) President Anastasio Somoza (Nicaragua), President Manuel Prado (Peru), Eva Garza, Juan Alabiso (sic?), Olga Coelho.

Special inter-American program inaugurating CBS's Latin America network. Colman's accustomed cadence gives a fine work of prose a soothingly poetic ring.

R35 TOWARD THE CENTURY OF THE COMMON MAN
June 14, 1942. United Nations Flag Day broadcast. Script by Stephen Vincent Benét and George Faulkner. Music by Robert Armbruster and Kurt Weill. KFI Hollywood for NBC Red, 2 p.m. PST, CTC, sus. 60 minutes. See R379, R380.

Cast: Thomas Mitchell (Narrator), Charles Boyer, Ray Collins, Ronald Colman, Melville Cooper, Paul Henreid, Peter Lorre,.Nazimova, Maria Ouspenskaya. Concluding 8-minute address by President Roosevelt via NBC Blue.

Note: Rebroadcast on KFI and KMPC Hollywood on August 15, 1942 at 11 p.m. and 11:15 p.m. respectively.

R36 UNLIMITED HORIZONS
August 15, 1942. "Blood for a Hero," an original play written and directed by Arnold Marquis. Produced in association with the Hollywood Victory Committee and the American Red Cross. Music composed and conducted by Charles Dant. KFI Hollywood for NBC Red. 6:30 p.m., PST, CTC, sus. 30 minutes. See R30.

Cast: Ronald Colman (Narrator), Donald Crisp (Dr. Max Stroumeir [sic?]), Martha Scott (Anna Trimble), Hans Conried (several voices), and other actors not announced.

Series about medical and scientific discoveries. This episode is an excellent play about the development of plasma and how it was saving thousands of soldiers' lives during WWII. Colman's narration is affectingly humane, while the use of sound effects and vocal montages showcases radio's power to convey emotions and propaganda for a good cause, in this case blood to make plasma for soldiers. The unique central idea is to personify the blood of a female donor (Scott) as it passes from her body to become plasma en route to the body of a dying gunner pilot, personalizing a dull technical process. One of radio's finest and most powerful half-hours.

The one, inexplicable, historical fault is that the doctor who invented plasma was changed from a black American named Charles Drew to a fictitious white Italian. Crisp appears at show's end to make a personal plea for blood donors to create millions more gallons of plasma for the war effort.

R37 HOUR OF THE VICTORY CORPS
December 1, 1942. NBC Blue. 30 minutes.

Series for high school students aimed at mobilizing them for the war effort, transcribed to be heard during school hours.

Program: Victory Corps Pledge; talk by George V. Denny of Indianapolis, IN; analysis of the Tunisian campaign by news commentator William Hillman; interviews with Colu Roscoe Turner and CAA students at Bolling Fields; music by the Air Force band; address by **Colman** titled "History Will Record."

R38 GREEK WAR RELIEF PROGRAM
December 7, 1942. Host: Dr. Homer Davis, President of Athens College and President of Greek War Relief. CBS. 30 minutes. See R25.

Program: Dr. Davis, discussing current conditions in Greece; Westminster Choir, under Dr. Williamson; **Ronald Colman**, speaking on behalf of Greek War Relief; Greek opera singer Nicholas Mascomas singing Greek folk songs, with piano accompaniment by Constantine Kallinikos.

R39 OVER HERE
December 12, 1942. Variety show. Announcer: Jimmy Wallington. Music: Joe Reichman's and David Broekman's Orchestras. Sponsor: Treasury Dept. NBC Blue, sus. 60 minutes.

Cast: Milton Berle, Bob Burns, **Ronald Colman**, Linda Darnell, Rep. Robert L. Doughton (Chairman, House Ways & Means Committee), Jane Froman, Igor Gorin, Treasury Secretary Henry V. Morgenthau, Maxine Sullivan, and John Vandercook.

R40 RADIO READER'S DIGEST
December 13, 1942. Director: Robert Nolan. Host: Conrad Nagel, Music: Lyn Murray. Sponsor: Hallmark Cards. CBS. 30 minutes.

Program includes Colman in "The Man Who Won the War," a playlet about a WW1 officer who fooled the Germans.

R41 OVER HERE
December 19, 1942. NBC Blue, sus. 60 minutes.

Cast: Ronald Colman, Ilka Chase, Jane Froman, Igor Gorin, Susan Hayward, Peggy Lee, Betty Lou, George Murphy, Tommy Riggs.

R42 SCREEN GUILD PLAYERS
December 21, 1942. "The Juggler of Notre Dame." CBS. 30 minutes. Second and final encore with Colman and Eddy. See R20, R29, R85.

R43 CEILING UNLIMITED
February 8, 1943. "Dive Bomber" by Harry Kronman. Producer: Thomas Freebairn-Smith. Guest star: Ronald Colman. Music: Lud Gluskin. CBS. 15 minutes.

New format for series formerly hosted by Orson Welles: top stars in dramatizations of aviation stories. On season opener, Colman acts as observer in plane, describing the emotions of a diving pilot.

R44 LUX RADIO THEATER
March 15, 1943. "Libel" by Edward Wooll. CBS. 60 minutes. See R22. Excellent repeat of the script from 1941, if not better. Same cast as before except for Edna Best replacing Frances Robinson.

R45 THE CHASE & SANBORN HOUR STARRING EDGAR BERGEN & CHAR-LIE MCCARTHY
April 18, 1943. Announcer: Buddy Tevis. Sponsor: Chase & Sanborn Coffee. Music Director: Ray Noble. With Dale Evans, Billy Gaxton, Victor Moore and the Sportsmen Quartet. NBC Red. 60 minutes.

Colman makes a speech exhorting listeners to volunteer spending their summer vacations working in food processing plants to ensure supplies for soldiers and to replace farm workers away at war. He also makes a pitch on behalf of the Civilian Food Corps and banters with McCarthy about *Random Harvest*. Moore and Gaxton do a draft board sketch, Evans sings "As Time Goes By." See F55.

R46 ANZAC DAY
April 24, 1943. Commemoration of the 28th anniversary of the landing of ANZAC (Australia/New Zealand Air Corps) in Gallipoli. NBC Red. 30 minutes.

Guest speakers: Ronald Colman (message from author James Hilton), Marjorie Lawrence, John Brownlee, Nola Luxford.

R47 LUX RADIO THEATER
May 17, 1943. "The Talk of the Town" by Irwin Shaw and Sidney Buchman from a story by Sidney Harmon. CBS. 60 minutes. See F53, R106, R252, R394.

Cast: Ronald Colman (Prof. Michael Lightcap), Cary Grant (Leopold Dilg), Jean Arthur (Nora Shelley), Lynne Whitney (Regina), Leo Cleary (Sam Yates), Norman Field

(Senator Boyd), Ken Christy (Judge Grunstadt), Horace Willard (Tilney), Charles Kelbert, Robert Harris, Warren Ash, Charles Seal, Fred Mackaye, Stanley Farrar, and Julia Warren.

The stars replay their roles from the picture, each narrating one of the three acts. With the screenplay streamlined, the movie's theme of ideal vs. everyday law is in sharper relief. Splendidly acted and fast-paced show.

R48 LUX RADIO THEATER
June 21, 1943. "In Which We Serve", from the screenplay by Noel Coward. CBS. 60 minutes.

Cast: Ronald Colman (Captain Terrance Kinross), Edna Best (Mrs. Kinross), Pat O'Malley (Walter Hardy), Charlie Lung (Shorty), Claire Vadera (Kat), Gloria Gordon (Mrs. Leemon), Esta Mason (Frieda), Frederic Worlock, Dennis Green, Eric Snowden, Robert Regent, Norbert Muller, Mary Lou Harrington, Fred Mackaye, Vernon Steele, Alec Hartford, Douglas Grant, Anthony Marsh, Roland Drew, Virginia Gordon, and Raymond Lawrence.

Saga of the men who served aboard the battleship H.M.S. Torrin during WWII. Sincerely played but dull adaptation of the 1942 movie starring Noel Coward and Celia Johnson.

R49 THIRD WAR LOAN DRIVE
September 8, 1943. War bond variety show. Producer/director: George Zachary. Music: Gordon Jenkins Orchestra. All networks. 6 p.m. PST, CTC. 69 minutes.

Cast: George Burns & Gracie Allen, Edgar Bergen and Charlie McCarthy, Charles Boyer, James Cagney, **Ronald Colman**, (role in play about the last days of the African campaign), Bing Crosby, Jimmy Durante, Dinah Shore, Akim Tamiroff, Robert Young, Secretary of the Treasury Henry Morgenthau Jr., President Franklin D. Roosevelt (6:51-7:07).

R50 COMMAND PERFORMANCE
September 25, 1943. Program #85. Director: Vick Knight. MC: Ronald Colman. Announcer: Ken Carpenter. Music: 43rd Army Air Force Band of Gardener Field. Theme song: "Over There" by George M. Cohan. AFRS. 30 minutes.

Colman does a GI mail call throughout the show, honoring requests for entertainers and sounds from home (including Walter Tetley hawking a newspaper in front of Radio City), and introduces his guest stars: Lena Horne ("St. Louis Blues" and "You're So Indifferent"), opera star Risé Stevens ("Because You Come to Me"), Robert Benchley (comically answering listener questions), and Jascha Heifetz, with pianist Emmanuel Bay ("Intermezzo" and "Flight of the Bumblebee").

Weekly variety show on which nearly every movie, radio and musical star performed without charge as a GI morale booster. Rarely heard in the states, it was recorded in Hollywood at CBS and NBC. On a few occasions—such as VJ Day, R92—it was broadcast live to capture a moment in history.

EVERYTHING FOR THE BOYS (January 18-June 13, 1944; 21 shows)
Produced, written and directed by Arch Oboler. Associate producer: Barbara Smitten (later Merlin). Story advisor: Jerome Lawrence. Special additional material: Jerome Lawrence and Milton Merlin. Announcer: Frank Martin. Pitchman: James Bannon. Musical director: Gordon Jenkins. Sponsor: Electric Auto-Lite. NBC. Broadcast day and times: Tuesday at 7:30 p.m. EST, 9 p.m. PST. 30 minutes. See R16, R21, R30 for other Oboler-directed shows.

In June of 1943, the ad agency of Ruthrauff and Ryan, which handled the Electric Auto-Lite account, teamed Colman with star radio dramatist Arch Oboler for a half-hour morale-boosting series aimed at a stateside audience hungry for assurance that their sons in the military were safe.

The series idea originated with Auto-Lite's owner, a man named Armstrong. He was in awe of Colman as the ultimate British gentleman and thought it would be a great idea for him to host a show written by Oboler, whose work he also admired.

Each week, Colman would act in an 18-minute playlet (average timing) with a major female co-star (there were exceptions), using mostly scripts by Oboler which he either adapted from famous plays and novels or which he wrote as occasional originals. These were preceded or followed by dramatic vignettes supplied by Jerome Lawrence and Milton Merlin, what Merlin calls Colman's "champagne and caviar." The climax was a four to five-minute shortwave talk with allied servicemen at an unidentified base in another country, with Colman and his co-star giving these servicemen the news from home. These talks were also written by Oboler (to prevent freeze-ups), but still they did provide a much-needed stateside connection with the war's progress. Today, these talks are historically valuable for individualizing the soldiers fighting and winning that war.

However, the on-air cordiality belied what was going on week after week behind the scenes. Before the first show aired, according to the Merlins, Ronnie and Arch had become mutually cold and antagonistic. They had worked together before, but those shows were individual programs as opposed to a series.

In an interview with me in 1977, Oboler said that after working in close quarters with Colman for six months to get the series on the air, "I saw Ronnie as a stuffy martinet while he thought of me as a disheveled vulgarian. We hated each other's guts. I was constantly fighting to do original plays, while he insisted on sticking with proven material. I wanted to open the series with my original play 'This Living Book', which had won some radio awards when it was first broadcast a few years earlier, but Ronnie wanted to go with 'The Petrified Forest' because he saw himself imitating Leslie Howard. It went on like this for months, though I did finally get to write some originals and produce "This Living Book" as an Easter special."[1]

Barbara Merlin, the show's associate producer, well remembers the Colman-Oboler feud, saying that "Arch and Ronnie hated each other from the start, but Arch wasn't without blame. He would often get the script to us the day of the broadcast, and one time I recognized a script as a story I had heard on the air just the week before, though I don't now remember what it was. It wasn't conscious plagiarism on his part—he would unconsciously rewrite shows he had heard—but I did call him on it."[2]

The end result, beginning with "The Petrified Forest," was mainly a series of stilted and unbelievable, often sermonizing abridgements in which Colman was miscast, indifferent, or homogenous, lacking flair and color. A few well-written scripts spread throughout the short run showed how good the series could be when Oboler wasn't himself indifferent to the whole enterprise as it is clear he was when these shows are heard today. However, those few scripts were not worth all of the hostility between the two men. Radio dramatist Jerome Lawrence was called in after two months to seek and suggest stories for adaptation, but it was too little, too late.

The series' main problem was that it was a bastardized form of radio variety in too short a time slot. Eighteen to 20 minutes is an absurd length for adapting a novel or full-length play. No matter how splendid the writing and acting (the supporting actors were always first-rate and usually better than Colman), the story is too condensed for believability. By the time the listener is involved with the story, it's over. Furthermore,

Colman kept casting himself in roles made famous on screen by other actors, like Robert Donat and Tyrone Power, but for which he was manifestly unsuited by voice and temperament.

The show was preempted once for D-Day, but by then it was in its final throes. Contracted for an initial six-month run, the dramatic format was canceled for low ratings and on-set hostilities after 21 shows, to everyone's relief. Colman and Oboler were each paid for the remaining unproduced shows. Colman's paycheck was $5000 per show, part of which he donated to war relief. In any case, this first version of the series was an expensive fiasco.

Starting June 20, 1944, it became a more popular musical variety show hosted by singers Dick Haymes and Helen Forrest, running until October 2, 1945.

R51 EVERYTHING FOR THE BOYS

January 18, 1944. "The Petrified Forest", from the play by Robert E. Sherwood. See also R87. Colman opens the premiere show with a pitch for war bonds. Guest Ginger Rogers joins shortwave talk with Staff Sgts. Cassidy and Badman at an allied flying base in England.

Cast: Ronald Colman (Alan Squier) and Ginger Rogers (Gabrielle). Supporting cast not announced.

Review: Rose, *Weekly Variety*, January 26: "Lacking sufficient time to fully develop both the atmosphere and the characters, the audience was left in a maze with the principals lacking either clarity or reality. It was no fault of Colman's or Miss Rogers, both of whom turned in able performances...Admitting the human interest and good will generated by the direct contact with fighting men, the entertainment quotient is low so far as the general listening public is concerned."

Oboler changed the period and locale of the original play to a wartime bomber base in England. Otherwise, it's a plodding, maudlin truncation that asks the listener to believe Colman and Rogers (who is miscast) falling in love in five minutes. The 1936 movie stars Leslie Howard, Humphrey Bogart and Bette Davis.

R52 EVERYTHING FOR THE BOYS

January 25, 1944. "Knuckles", from the story by Jack London. With Irene Dunne. Shortwave talk with two marines based in the South Pacific. No other details available.

R53 LUX RADIO THEATER

January 31, 1944. "Random Harvest" by James Hilton. CBS. 60 minutes. See F55, R121, A5.

Cast: Ronald Colman (Smithy/Charles Rainier), Greer Garson (Paula Ridgeway), Joan Loring (Kitty), Norman Field (Chemist), Ramsay Hill (Psychiatrist), Ray Lawrence, Ed Harvey, Gloria Gordon, Eric Snowden, Frederic Worlock, Charles Lung, Joe Gilbert, Byron Steele, Dennis Green, Charles Steele, Richard Nugent, Alec Hartford, and Thomas Mills.

Okay version of the movie with the two stars re-playing their popular screen roles.

R54 EVERYTHING FOR THE BOYS

February 1, 1944. "Lost Horizon" by James Hilton. Actress Janet Blair joins shortwave talk with Sgt. Gannon and Pvt. Maloney stationed in Algiers, South Africa. See F45, R27, R110, R173, D3, D10, D15.

Cast: Ronald Colman (Hugh Conway), Hans Conried (Charles Mallinson), Mercedes McCambridge (Lo-Tsen), Norman Field (the High Lama).

Poor writing combined with equally poor performances (the cast got the script just hours before the show, so it was under-rehearsed) results in an insufferable dramatization.

R55 NBC WAR BOND PARADE

February 6-7, 1944. Producer/Director: George Zachary. MC: John W. Vandercook. Writers: Ranald MacDougall, Glenn Wheaton, Manny Manheim, Harry Bailey and the team of Lipscott & Davie. Music: Gordon Jenkins. WEAF New York and KFI Hollywood for NBC Red. 12 a.m. EST February 7; 11:45 p.m. PST February 6 by transcription. 60 minutes.

Cast: Edgar Bergen & Charlie McCarthy, Charles Boyer, George Burns & Gracie Allen, **Ronald Colman** (monologue on "Enemy Smugness"), Bing Crosby, Kay Kyser, Dinah Shore, Red Skelton, Nora Sterling, Akim Tamiroff, Loretta Young.

Note: Program from newspaper column and LC printout.

R56 EVERYTHING FOR THE BOYS

February 8, 1944. "Berkeley Square," from "The Sense of the Past" by Henry James and the 1934 film of same based on John L. Balderston's 1929 play. Colman speaks of a photo in Time, Collier's and Saturday Evening Post showing a 2-year-old girl longing for her daddy in the army. Guest Greer Garson joins shortwave talk with Pvt. James Springer and Technical Sgt. John Thompson stationed in Australia. See R84, R260.

Cast: Ronald Colman (Peter Standish), Greer Garson (Helen Pettigrew), Gloria Gordon (Lady Anne Pettigrew), Joe Kearns (Tom Pettigrew).

Dull wartime update of James's time travel fantasy, poorly acted by the stars. See R84 for story details and far superior *Lux* version. The 1934 film stars Leslie Howard, the 1952 version stars Tyrone Power.

R57 EVERYTHING FOR THE BOYS

February 15, 1944. "A Man to Remember," from the 1938 movie based on the novel *Failure* by Katharine Haviland-Taylor. With guest Bob Burns. Burns was an Arkansian Will Rogers who was famous for his "Bazooka," a long, pipe-like instrument he invented, after which American soldiers named their WWII anti-tank gun. Shortwave talk with Sgt. Joseph J. Cleves, stationed in England. Ronnie also reads the famous short poem "High Flight" by John Gillespie McGee, Jr. McGee was a Royal Canadian Air Force pilot who died in action in 1941 at age 19.

Cast: Ronald Colman (Narrator) and Bob Burns (Dr. John Abbott). Supporting cast not announced.

Warmly performed *Goodbye Mr. Chips*-like saga of a country doctor whose material legacy is a few minor mementos, but whose spiritual legacy is incalculable. One of the best shows in the series because Oboler adapted it with feeling.

R58 EVERYTHING FOR THE BOYS

February 22, 1944. "The Women Stayed at Home," an original play by Oboler. Ronnie recites the poem "The White Magnolia Tree" by Helen Deutsch. Guest Mercedes McCambridge joins shortwave talk with Sgt. Wellman and Pvt. Peter Siletos in Port Morsby, New Guinea, joined by a Mrs. Gamill, whose son is stationed in the South Pacific.

Cast: Ronald Colman (John), Mercedes McCambridge (Celia), Hans Conried (Helmer Olafson).

Melodrama set in Norway about a young woman (McCambridge) and the two men she loved. One a fisherman (Conried) who dies at sea, the other an RAF pilot (Colman) who dies in battle. Dreadful overacting by McCambridge of a soggy script and the use of *Tristan and Isolde* excerpts make this sketch embarrassing to hear.

R59 EVERYTHING FOR THE BOYS

February 29, 1944. "Rogue Male," from the story by Geoffrey Household about a man who tries to assassinate Hitler. With Merle Oberon. No other details available. Filmed in 1941 with Walter Pidgeon as *Man Hunt* and 1975 with Peter O'Toole as *Rogue Male*.

R60 EVERYTHING FOR THE BOYS

March 7, 1944. "Of Human Bondage," from the 1934 movie of the novel by Somerset Maugham. Guest Bette Davis recreates her movie role. Shortwave transmission to Reykjavik, Iceland fails, so Ronnie and Bette have to make do with messages from home to the men with whom they would have spoken—Pvt. Ben Cohen and Sgt. Jimmy Jones.

    Cast: Ronald Colman (Priest narrator), Bette Davis (Mildred Rogers), Hans Conried (Philip Carey), Lou Merrill (Harry Griffith).

    Masterly reading by Conried as a masochistic cripple who falls for a slovenly cockney waitress. Otherwise, Davis's overdone performance, combined with Colman's half-hearted narration, make an already absurd story alternately dull and laughable. The 1964 film stars Kim Novak and Laurence Harvey.

R61 EVERYTHING FOR THE BOYS

March 14, 1944. "The Ghost Goes West," from the movie script by Eric Keowne and Robert E. Sherwood. Guest Anne Baxter joins shortwave talk with Sgt. Bill Sarr (sic?) and Sgt. Charles Blair, based in Chungking, China.

    Cast: Ronald Colman (Murdoch Glowery and Donald Glowery), Anne Baxter (Peggy Porgy), Joseph Kearns (George Porgy).

    The story is too compressed, but Colman is clearly having fun as a Scotsman and his ghostly ancestor, using a brogue for the latter. Even better is Joe Kearns as the bumptious chain store magnate. Enjoyable show, but this one-act misses by a light year the fantasy high of the 1936 René Clair movie starring Robert Donat.

R62 EVERYTHING FOR THE BOYS

March 21, 1944. "Girl in the Road," an original play by Oboler. Ronnie reads a "Letter to Gen. Montgomery from Gen. Nye." Guest Martha Scott joins shortwave talk with squad leader Burt Hewell (sic?) and Pvt. Rod McKenzie, Canadians stationed in Naples, Italy.

    Cast: Ronald Colman (Jim Dornan) and Martha Scott (Mary Stevens). Supporting cast not announced.

    An army training manual writer (Colman) picks up and befriends a young female hitchhiker (Scott), whose husband is in the war and who has become cynical and aimless because of the separation. Good script and good straight performance by Colman as a man whose compassion, sympathy and understanding shake the woman (equally good work by Scott) out of her war-induced torpor.

R63 EVERYTHING FOR THE BOYS

March 28, 1944. "Ostrich in Bed," an original by Oboler. Colman reads "Letter to a Soldier's Wife from India." Guest Joan Bennett joins shortwave talk with Lt. Bill Larsen (sp?) and Sgt. Frank Stella, stationed somewhere in the South Pacific.

    Cast: Ronald Colman (Bart Reynolds), Joan Bennett (Jean Reynolds), Hans Conried (Mr. Talbot).

    Comedy about a businessman (Colman) who comes home one day to find an ostrich in his bed. He and his wife (Bennett) are perplexed about what to do with it. Meanwhile, the ostrich makes a shambles of their meeting with a pompous potential client (Conried).

Delightful bit of farcical fluff, but you do wonder how Barbara Stanwyck, originally announced the previous week, would have played the Bennett role.

R64 EVERYTHING FOR THE BOYS
April 4, 1944. "This Living Book," an Oboler original built around quotations from the Bible. Commercial-free Easter special. Guest Dennis Day joins shortwave talk to Cpl. Jim Bastian and Pvt. Bob Gross in Fairbanks, Alaska. Transmission fails, so Colman and Day send messages from home. Day sings "Back Home in Indiana" and "I'll Take You Home Again, Kathleen."

Colman narrates this spiritual mosaic of mankind, which includes excerpts from *Song of Songs*, and "The Lord's Prayer." Featuring Mercedes McCambridge (the Girl) and Robert Bailey (the Boy).

Originally broadcast on *Arch Oboler's Plays*, "This Living Book" won critical acclaim for its connection of biblical passages to contemporary life. Heard today, it sounds pretentious, heavy-handed and sappy, lacking Norman Corwin's wit, bite and poetry with the same sort of material. Though Oboler claimed he had wanted to open the series with this show, beginning an expensive series like this with a commercial-free program would not have been financially feasible.

R65 EVERYTHING FOR THE BOYS
April 11, 1944. "The Citadel" by A.J. Cronin. Colman recites Elizabeth Barrett Browning's "How Do I Love Thee." Shortwave transmission to Sgt. Wally Reed and Sgt. Joe Sudano in Cairo fails, so Ronnie and guest Ida Lupino read messages to them from home. Ronnie also pays tribute to the women behind the home front contributing to the war effort.

Cast: Ronald Colman (Andrew Manson), Ida Lupino (Christine Manson), Joseph Kearns (Narrator).

A research scientist forsakes his medical ideals for material success. The stars walk through a sketchy script. The best part is Kearns's nimble narration. Robert Donat and Rosalind Russell starred in the excellent 1938 MGM movie, directed by King Vidor.

R66 EVERYTHING FOR THE BOYS
April 18, 1944. "The Jervis Bay Goes Down," prose poem by Gene Fowler, with additional dialogue by Oboler and original music by Meredith Willson. See R24, R67.

Guest Ella Logan sings "I Have a Date with a Ranger," a swing version of "My Bonnie Lies Over the Ocean," and the now classic "I'll Be Seeing You" by Irving Kahall and Sammy Fain. She joins Ronnie for shortwave talk with radioman first class Orville Edward van Horn and chief radioman Ralph Woodward, stationed in Nouméa, New Caledonia.

Ideal blend of dramatic monologue, songs and shortwave talk, though I think Colman's first reading of the poem (R24) is superior. Logan's definitive rendition of "I'll Be Seeing You" is easily the best musical segment in the series. Colman ends the show by paying tribute to Red Cross worker Esther Richards, who died on the front line in battle.

R67 NAVY SPOTLIGHT
Late April or early May 1944. "The Jervis Bay Goes Down." Announcer: Frank Martin. AFRS, 15 minutes. See R24, R66.

Repackaging of R66 with wraparound by Martin and Colman, as "a tribute to the navy women in blue." Show ends with Colman praising the work being done by navy women.

R68   EVERYTHING FOR THE BOYS

April 25, 1944. "Death Takes a Holiday," from the Italian play by Alberto Casella as adapted for the screen by Walter Ferris. Guest Ingrid Bergman joins shortwave talk with Commander Joe Caron (sic?) and Chief Yeoman Gordon Nelson of the U.S. Coast Guard in Naples, and sings "As Time Goes By."

Cast: Ronald Colman (Death), Ingrid Bergman (Grazzia), Hans Conried (Corrado), Luis Van Rooten (Duke Lamberto), Norman Field (Opening narrator).

Fairly good performance by Colman as Death on holiday, discovering the meaning of love with Bergman, though this play was an oddly morbid choice for a war morale series. Worse, the short format renders the love story unbelievable, though Bergman is her usual passionate self. Fredric March starred in the 1934 movie.

R69   SILVER THEATRE

April 30, 1944. "The Snow Goose" by Paul Gallico. Director/Host: John Loder. Music: Felix Mills. Guest star: Ronald Colman. Other cast names unavailable. CBS. 30 minutes.

A crippled man and a girl find love while rescuing a wounded bird during the British evacuation from Dunkirk. In 1971, this story became a one-hour TV movie with Richard Harris and Jenny Agutter for *Hallmark Hall of Fame*.

R70   EVERYTHING FOR THE BOYS

May 2, 1944. "Buried Alive," from the novel by Arnold Bennett. Guests Ruth Chatterton and jive singer Ella Mae Morse join shortwave talk with Sgt. Michael Stallone and PFC Dick Dickie, somewhere in the South Pacific. Morse sings "Milkman, Keep Those Bottles Quiet." See R19.

Cast: Ronald Colman (Priam Farll), Ruth Chatterton (Alice Farll), Dennis Hoey (Doctor), Lou Merrill (Mr. Oxford), Joe Kearns (Trial attorney), Claud Allister (Duncan Farll).

Fun try, but no match for the hilarious 1943 movie version, *Holy Matrimony*, with Monty Wooley and Gracie Fields.

R71   SCREEN GUILD PLAYERS

May 8, 1944. "The Dark Angel," from the play by H.B. Trevelyan. Director: Bill Lawrence. Host: Truman Bradley. Music: Wilbur Hatch. CBS. 30 minutes. See F21.

Colman co-stars with Merle Oberon as they replay their roles from the 1925 and 1935 movie versions respectively.

R72   EVERYTHING FOR THE BOYS

May 9, 1944. "This Above All" by Eric Knight, film script adaptation by Harry Kronman. Guest Olivia de Havilland joins shortwave talk with Petty Officer George Caswell and Pvt. Earl Crosher of the Royal Canadian Navy at a base in England.

Cast: Ronald Colman (Clive), Olivia de Havilland (Prudence Cathaway), Joseph Kearns (British soldier).

A British army deserter falls in love with the young woman he's been dating. Fair truncation of the 1942 movie with Tyrone Power.

R73   EVERYTHING FOR THE BOYS

May 16, 1944. "Blithe Spirit," from the play by Noel Coward. Guests Loretta Young and Edna Best join shortwave talk with Pvt. Roy Little and PFC Edgar "Nebraska" Draper at a base in New Guinea.

Cast: Ronald Colman (Charles Kent), Loretta Young (Gladys Kent), Edna Best (Dolores Kent), Mercedes McCambridge (Madame Arcati).

Charming fantasy about a best selling author (Charles Condomine in the original) who is bedevilled by the ghosts of his two wives. This was the first radio version of the play, nicely adapted by Oboler. Makes you wish Colman had done the 1945 David Lean movie as well instead of Rex Harrison.

R74 EVERYTHING FOR THE BOYS
May 23, 1944. "Quality Street" by Sir James M. Barrie. Guest: Maureen O'Sullivan joins shortwave talk with Cpl. Thomas Richard St. George and Sgt. Anthony Petrocelli at a base in Australia. See R262.

Cast: Ronald Colman (Valentine Brown), Maureen O'Sullivan (Phoebe Throssel), Agnes Moorehead (Susan Throssel), and Gloria Gordon.

Terrible truncation of Barrie's love story set at the time of the Napoleonic Wars. Colman gives an incredibly stilted performance as a dashing young soldier. The dialogue is wooden and he is clearly trying to be done with it. Filmed in 1927 with Marion Davies and 1937 with Katharine Hepburn and Franchot Tone.

R75 EVERYTHING FOR THE BOYS
May 30, 1944. "The House I Live In", an Oboler original suggested by the song by Earl Robinson and Louis Allen, unrelated to the Oscar-winning Frank Sinatra short. Colman opens show with Stephen Vincent Benét poem, "We Shall Maintain It, It Shall Be Sustained." Guest Dinah Shore joins shortwave talk with marine and sailor in the Pacific (names spoken too fast to decipher), singing "It Had to Be You" and "I Had a Man" during talk. José Iturbi and Jimmy Durante are announced as next week's guests, but were canceled when that show was preempted by D-Day.

Cast: Ronald Colman (Narrator), Joseph Kearns (John Rogers), Bea Benadaret (Neighbor), Dinah Shore (Ann), Lillian Randolph (sings title song).

Well-acted (especially by Kearns) but thinly written wartime sketch about the residents of Elm Street, USA.

R76 A POEM AND PRAYER FOR AN INVADING ARMY
June 6, 1944. NBC, 4:30 p.m. PST, CTC. 15 minutes. See D2.

Colman premiered this D-Day poem by Edna St. Vincent Millay, which was commissioned by NBC for whenever D-Day took place. The reading takes 9 minutes, preceded by news and followed by organ music. Colman then recorded it for RCA.

Millay was busy revising her poem up till a half-hour or so before airtime and it shows. One can hear the internal struggle she was having over its wording as she tried to please two masters: NBC and her own anti-war conscience. She is pleading for an end to the war while urging on the soldiers who are fighting it, rationalizing their killing in the names of God and democracy. Colman's reading of Millay's more inspired imagery is affecting, but it's mostly a walkthrough. Though not a memorable poem, it did deserve better than this placid reading.

R77 EVERYTHING FOR THE BOYS
June 13, 1944. "Reunion in Vienna", from the play by Robert E. Sherwood. With Claudette Colbert. Dick Haymes is announced as the new host starting next week.

R78 FIFTH WAR LOAN DRIVE: ONE FOR THE MONEY
June 13, 1944. Director: Howard Wiley. Writer: Don Quinn. Music: Major Meredith Willson and the Armed Forces Orchestra. NBC, 8:30 p.m. PST, CTC. 90 minutes.

Cast: Abbott and Costello, Jack Benny, Bob Burns, **Ronald Colman** (monologue titled "One For the Money"), Bing Crosby, Joan Davis, Freeman Gosden and Charles Correll (Amos 'n Andy), Jack Haley, Bob Hope, Jim and Marian Jordan (Fibber McGee and Molly), Kay Kyser, Frances Langford, Frank Morgan, Hal Peary, Ginny Simms, John Charles Thomas, Yvette (complete name).

Note: Cast taken from newspaper clipping and LC data.

R79 COMMAND PERFORMANCE #128
August 6, 1944. Host: Claudette Colbert. Announcer: Ken Carpenter. Guests: Jimmy Durante, Ronald Colman, Dale Evans, Alan Hale, and Betty Hutton. AFRS. 30 minutes.

Colbert and Durante take a comic tour of New York City. They encounter Colman as a panhandling amnesiac (shades of *Random Harvest*) claiming to be Ronald Colman; Evans (GI mail call, "Amour, Amour"); Hale at Jack Dempsey's Beer Parlor (PFC Paul Kaye of the Fort Marines asked to hear him "drinking a large mug of Eastern draft beer and eating a mess of pretzels"); run into Colman again, who does impressions of Charles Laughton, Edward G. Robinson and Lassie; Hutton (mail call and unidentifiable song); and Colbert, Durante, Colman, Hutton sing "I'm Gonna Hang My Hat on a Tree that Grows in Brooklyn." Colman's singing voice is off-key but fun to hear nevertheless.

R80 COMMAND PERFORMANCE #130
August 20, 1944. Host: Ronald Colman. Guests: Ginny Simms, C. Aubrey Smith, Dame May Whitty, Cary Grant, Ida Lupino, Reginald Gardiner. AFRS. 30 minutes. See F31, F39.

Simms ("The Man I Love"); Whitty and Smith (banter with Colman); Grant (banter, sings British ditties—"Goodbye Mother," "Watching the Trains Come In"); Lupino (duet with Colman of "I've Got Sixpence"); Gardiner et al. (except Simms) join Colman for a *Bulldog Drummond* spoof; Simms ("Lili Marlene"), Smith, Whitty (final jokes). Fun show.

R81 ATLANTIC SPOTLIGHT
September 16, 1944. "The Battle of Britain." NBC. 30 minutes. Broadcast on KFI Hollywood at 1 p.m. PST. Broadcast on the BBC's *General Forces Programme* at 6:30 that night.

Cast: C. Aubrey Smith, Ronald Colman, Basil Rathbone, Herbert Marshall, John Brownlee, and Merle Oberon.

Marking the fourth anniversary of the sky battle between Royal Air Force (RAF) bomber fleets and the German Luftwaffe. Combines drama with documentary recordings of news and speeches. Trans-Atlantic hook-up to allied forces in the field in France and Italy.

R82 STAGE DOOR CANTEEN
November 3, 1944. Guest turn along with Mary Boland and singer Hildegarde. CBS. 30 minutes.

R83 PHILCO RADIO HALL OF FAME
November 6, 1944. Guest host: Ronald Colman. With Paul Whiteman and his Orchestra, Rudolph Friml, Henny Youngman and pianist Dorothy Donnegan. CBS. 60 minutes.

Colman introduces Youngman as one of his favorite comedians, then acts in a misfired 12-minute playlet titled "Lord Byron in Greece." The writing is weak; Colman is too old, vocally miscast and gives a half-hearted performance; and the story sounds like the third act of a mediocre *Lux*, with no explanation as to why Byron was involved in a foreign revolution, giving his life for it.

R84 LUX RADIO THEATER
December 18, 1944. "Berkeley Square." CBS. 60 minutes. See R56, R260.

Cast: Ronald Colman (Peter Standish), Maureen O'Sullivan (Helen Pettigrew), Eric Snowden (Mr. Thrussel), Dorothy Lovett, Charles Seal, Gloria Gordon, Leslie Dennison, Jacqueline DeWitt, Norman Field and Colin Campbell.

Time travel fantasy about a romanticist (Colman) who literally steps into the past as his ancestor, falling in love with the very woman (O'Sullivan) as his forbear in 18th century London. In so doing, he discovers a past steeped in filth, disease, pollution and ignorance. Fine script and direction, with Colman giving one of his strongest radio performances: Impulsively romantic, intellectually curious, sardonically witty and candidly appalled by a gritty period in time and place that has been romanticized.

R85 THE JUGGLER OF OUR LADY
December 25, 1944. From the story "Our Lady's Juggler" by Anatole France. Scripted, produced and directed by Jerome Lawrence and Robert E. Lee. Performed by Ronald Colman and John Charles Thomas, with a song by Gladys Swarthout. AFRS. 30 minutes. See R20, R29, R42.

Fourth and best version of this story with Colman. Program opens with opera star Swarthout singing "I Wonder as I Wander." Colman then beautifully tells the story of a juggling simpleton and the miracle he invokes with his routine. Thomas powerfully sings "God Rest Ye, Merry Gentlemen," "Good King Wenceslas," "Ave Maria," and "A Mighty Fortress is Our God." Except for the dull opening song, a Christmas classic.

R86 MEMORIAL TRIBUTE TO PRESIDENT ROOSEVELT
April 15, 1945. All-star tribute to President Roosevelt three days after his death. Announcers: Don Wilson, Harlow Wilcox, Ken Carpenter. Except for two sketches, writing credits are unavailable. NBC, 4 p.m. PST, CTC. Two hours.

Program: Ronald Colman (specially written tone-setting prose poem, backed by a choir); Chaplain Lynn H. Brown, U.S. Army Air Corps (Benediction); John Charles Thomas ("Battle Hymn of the Republic" and "Home on the Range," the latter Roosevelt's favorite song); Jim and Marian Jordan (in character as Fibber McGee and Molly); Kay Kyser; Harry von Zell; Major Meredith Willson with the U.S. Armed Forces Orchestra ("San Juan Baptista" movement from Willson's *Missions of California* symphony); Ed "Archie" Gardner; Ginny Simms (war psalm, "Taps"); Dick Powell ("Anchors Aweigh"); violinist Joseph Szigeti/pianist Harry Kaufman ("Largo" by Veracini; James Cagney ("The Common Man," agit prop prose poem about laborers); The Charioteers (black choir, "Swing Low, Sweet Chariot"); Eddie Cantor; Freeman Gosden and Charles Correll (Amos n' Andy); Will H. Hays (head of the movie censorship office); Shirley Ross ("Flow Gently, Sweet Afton"), Robert Young and Bette Davis (Carlton E. Morse playlet, "Paean to Youth"); Jack Benny (reading a letter from a soldier to his son); Hal Peary (*The Great Gildersleeve*); Edgar Bergen; Charles Laughton; Bing Crosby and Bob Hope; **Colman** (*Lamentations* excerpts, revised by Morse); Ingrid Bergman (war prayer by Roosevelt, first read 11-6-44); "The Star Spangled Banner" (Everyone); address by President Harry S Truman.

In addition to the movie stars and other celebrities, the cast comprised all of NBC's comedy and musical stars, all appearing as themselves (except for the Jordans) to speak their sentiments about Roosevelt and the war he left behind from well-written heartfelt scripts. However, Colman's reading of *Lamentations* would have worked better without the usual overdone musical backdrop. For the most part, a fine memorial tribute.

R87 LUX RADIO THEATER
April 23, 1945. "The Petrified Forest", from Robert E. Sherwood's play. Host: Thomas Mitchell. CBS. 60 minutes. See R46.

Cast: Ronald Colman (Alan Squier), Susan Hayward (Gabriella), Lawrence Tierney (Duke Mantee). See R51.

You would think Colman would be ideally cast as Sherwood's vagabond fatalist intellectual, but he merely walks through the part. Good script, dull show. After the play, Ronnie speaks of his 9-month-old daughter, Juliet, and his visits to 7000 men in Army-Navy hospitals.

R88 MEMORIAL DAY BOND APPEAL FOR THE 7TH WAR LOAN DRIVE
May 30, 1945. MC: Jack Benny. Keynote address: John Nesbitt. Music: Ken Darby Chorus, Spike Jones and His City Slickers, Victor Young's Orchestra. NBC, 6:30 PST, CTC. 60 minutes.

Cast in Alphabetical Order: Eddie "Rochester" Anderson, Billie Burke, Bob Burns, Judy Canova, **Ronald Colman** (pays tribute to American soldiers), Joan Davis, Phil Harris, Dick Haymes, Art Linkletter (conducts audience quiz), Mary Livingstone, Hal Peary, Dinah Shore, John Charles Thomas.

Note: Program from newspaper clipping and LC data.

R89 SUSPENSE
May 31, 1945. "August Heat", adapted by Mel Dinelli from the W.F. Harvey story. Producer/Director: William Spier. Announcer: Joseph Kearns. Sponsor: Roma Wines. CBS. 30 minutes. See R258.

Cast: Ronald Colman (James Clarence Withencroft) and Dennis Hoey (Charles Atkinson).

Macabre story about a sketch artist (Colman) meeting a tombstone maker (Hoey) who has just carved a headstone with the artist's name and that very day as his deathdate. Fascinating story, with sultry music evoking a humidly hot August day in London, though the pacing is a bit slow for maximum effect. Colman gives a fairly good performance on his first *Suspense* show, and reads an excerpt from Kahlil Gibran's *The Prophet* ("On Death") not in the original story. He also makes an after-show plea on behalf of the 7th War Loan Drive.

R90 THE DOCTOR FIGHTS
July 3, 1945. "The Magic Drug" by Arthur Miller. Producer/Director: Fletcher Markle. Announcer: Arthur Harris. Music: Leith Stevens. Sponsor: Schenley Laboratories. CBS. 30 minutes.

Cast: Ronald Colman (Dr. Alexander Fleming), John Beal, William Conrad, Peter Leeds, Lurene Tuttle and others.

Story of the discovery and development of penicillin by Dr. Fleming. Fleming is interviewed after the story from South Bridge, MA by announcer Harris. Colman does a fine job in this well-produced show with outstanding sound effects.

R91 COLUMBIA PRESENTS CORWIN
July 10, 1945. "Daybreak". Written, produced and directed by Norman Corwin. Music: Lyn Murray. CBS, sus. 30 minutes.

Cast: Ronald Colman (The Pilot), Corrinha Murra (Singer), and other actors not announced.

Remake of acclaimed Corwin play in which Colman narrates a day in the life as though following the Earth around the sun. His narration is often poetic and better than some of the interpolated corny sketches. It is certainly a fascinating concept. Murra was an acclaimed singer at the time. Corwin previously did this show on CBS on June 22, 1941 with announcer Frank Gallup as The Pilot. He got Colman to do the show as a result of being a dinner guest at Ronnie's San Ysidro Ranch.

R92 COMMAND PERFORMANCE: VICTORY EXTRA
Recorded August 15, 1945 for immediate shipment to allied bases throughout the world. Produced by Pat Weaver and True Boardman. Serious segments (opening prayer etc.) written or revised and directed by Jerome Lawrence and Robert E. Lee. Comedy segments from the best of *Command Performance* by Bill Morrow, Sherwood Schwartz and others. Host: Bing Crosby. Announcer: Ken Carpenter. Music: Major Meredith Willson conducting the Armed Forces Orchestra. AFRS. 100 minutes.

Program: Ronald Colman (opening 50-second prayer slightly revised from the Hebrew Union Prayer book by Jerome Lawrence); Risé Stevens ("Ave Maria"); Dinah Shore ("I'll Walk Alone"); Bette Davis, Jimmy Durante, José Iturbi in skit; Lionel Barrymore announcing Iturbi playing Chopin's "Polonaise in A Flat"; Marlene Dietrich; Burgess Meredith (reading from war correspondence of Ernie Pyle); Ginny Simms ("You'd Be So Nice to Come Home To" by Cole Porter); Frank Sinatra ("The House I Live In"); Rita Hayworth, Pvt. Desi Arnaz, Ernie "Bubbles" Whitman, Ida Lupino, Ginger Rogers, Ruth Hussey, Claire Trevor, Don Wilson, newspaper cartoonist Bill Mauldin, Cpl. George Montgomery, Pvt. John Conte, Jinx Falkenburg, Diana Lewis, **Ronald Colman** (all giving personal victory greetings); Janet Blair ("What is This Thing Called Love"); William Powell (introducing Crosby singing "San Fernando Valley"); Harry Von Zell and Lucille Ball (brief bit in which Von Zell gets kissed by Lucy); the King Sisters ("Shoo Shoo, Baby"); Cary Grant; Robert Montgomery (reads from a speech by President Roosevelt); William Conrad (intermission announcer); Loretta Young; Lena Horne ("The Man I Love"); Col. Thomas H.A. Lewis, Commandant of AFRS; G.I. Jill; Johnny Mercer ("G.I. Jive"); Edward G. Robinson; Orson Welles (reads from written remarks of Generals Douglas MacArthur and Dwight Eisenhower and Adm. Chester W. Nimitz); Lina Romay ("Chiu Chiu"); Danny Kaye (novelty number, "Manic Depressive Pictures Presents"); Marilyn Maxwell ("I Got Rhythm"); Herbert Marshall (reading John Gillespie McGee, Jr.'s poem "High Flight", see R61); Carmen Miranda ("Tico Tico"); Claudette Colbert and Ed "Archie" Gardner (skit about acting together); Greer Garson (introduces Crosby singing "White Christmas"); Orson Welles (prayer by Yeoman William Welch); playing of "The Star Spangled Banner."

Special edition featuring 50 movie, radio and musical stars celebrating the American victory over the Japanese and the end of World War II on August 14. One-of-a-kind show that perfectly captures the mood of the country after nearly four years at war. The tone ranges from prayerful thanksgiving to exhilarated relief that the war is finally over, while the songs are a good overview of popular music during the war. Colman's reading of the opening prayer is especially moving. Jerome Lawrence recalls that "Ronnie was impressed that the 'star' receiving the most applause during the victory greeting parade wasn't a movie name, but Bill Mauldin!" Chicago newspaper cartoonist Mauldin was reknowned with

American soldiers for his G.I. characters, Willie and Joe.

R93 REQUEST PERFORMANCE (Premiere show)
October 7, 1945. Produced under the aegis of the Masquers' Club of Hollywood. Director: William N. Robson. Writers: Jerome Lawrence and Robert E. Lee. Music: Leith Stevens. Hosts: Ronald Colman and Frances Langford. Guests: Arthur Treacher, Marlin "Beulah" Hurt; Charlie Cantor (Finnegan from *Duffy's Tavern*); and Mel Blanc (the Postman from *Burns and Allen*). Commercial pitchman: Del Sharbut. Sponsor: Campbell Soup Company. CBS. 30 minutes.

One-season variety show written by Lawrence and Lee, intended as the civilian equivalent of *Command Performance*. Colman and Langford take an audio tour of New Orleans (asked for by Mrs. William Bell, Wausean, OH) ; Colman and Treacher reverse roles as butler and master (E.J. Newman, Tucson, AZ); Langford sings "I Wish I Knew" (the Sidney Holmeses of Glendale, CA); the servants and postman from three sitcoms perform a fantasy skit (Mrs. S.L. Follien, Boston); and Colman reads from Kahlil Gibran's *The Prophet* (Ruth Insell, Forest Hills, Long Island).

The 7-minute New Orleans tour is enjoyably offbeat, the only time Colman ever did narration to a jazz backdrop. Jerry Lawrence says that "Ronnie delighted in doing that kind of offbeat material."

R94 THEATER OF ROMANCE
October 16, 1945. "Reverie" by Jean Holloway. Producer/Director: Charles Vanda. Music: Lud Gluskin Orchestra. Sponsors: Colgate Tooth Powder and Halo Shampoo. CBS. 25 minutes.

Cast: Ronald Colman (Claude Debussy), Lurene Tuttle (Gabrielle), Gerald Mohr (Opening narrator).

Overwrought melodrama about Debussy's love life. A miscast Colman walks through the part, pushing his voice at times for believability, while Tuttle is floridly over-the-top.

R95 SUSPENSE
November 1, 1945. "The Dunwich Horror" by H.P. Lovecraft. CBS. 30 minutes.

Cast: Ronald Colman (Prof. Henry Armitage), Elliott Lewis (Wilbur Wately), Joseph Kearns ("Wizard" Wately), William Johnstone (Dr. Ken Houton).

Dull radio version of a story by horror master Lovecraft. Though faithful to the story's details, the show is contrived as an emergency midnight broadcast from Dunwich, MA, during which Prof. Armitage recounts the strange goings-on there. Furthermore, a somber Armitage was called for instead of Colman's unflappable urbanity. Lewis alters his voice into an unreal rumble, making it unrecognizable as his till almost the end. A 1970 film version stars Dean Stockwell.

R96 LUX RADIO THEATER
November 19, 1945. "The Keys of the Kingdom", from the movie of the novel by A.J. Cronin. Host: William Keighley. CBS. 60 minutes.

Cast: Ronald Colman (Father Francis Chisholm), Ann Harding (Mother Maria-Veronica), Joseph Kearns (Monseigneur Tarron, Narrator), Colin Campbell (Father/Bishop McNab), Eric Snowden (Willy Tullock), Ramsay Hill (Monseigneur Angus Neeley), Charles Seel (Dr. Fiske), Alan Napier (Joseph), Duane Thompson (Sister Martha, Mrs. Fiske), Anne Stone (Sister Clothilde), Barbara Jean Wong ((Thilomena), Charles Lung (Mr. Chin, Captain), Lal Chand Mehra (Mr. Poo), H.T. Tsang (Hosannah), Peter Chong (Major).

Scottish village priest Chisholm is assigned to missionary work in China for 40 years because of his unorthodox views and methods and his friendship with an atheist (Snowden). He also befriends an arrogant nun (Harding). Colman is so pleasant as Chisholm you wonder how such a charming priest could be undervalued by his superiors. Gregory Peck starred in the 1945 movie.

R97   DRUMBEATS AND DRUMSTICKS
November 22, 1945. KNX Hollywood for CBS. 30 minutes.

Thanksgiving variety victory show from the Beverly Hills Hotel with Colman as one of the guests.

THE JACK BENNY PROGRAM (1945-1951, 21 shows)
Producer: Hilliard Marks. Director: Bob Ballin. Musical director: Mahlon Merrick. Writers: George Balzer, Milt Josefsberg, Sam Perrin, John Tackaberry, Al Goldman, Hal Gordon (the latter two from 1950 on). Announcer: Don Wilson.

Regulars: Eddie "Rochester" Anderson, Mary Livingstone (Mrs. Benny), singer Larry Stevens (until March 10, 1946), singer Dennis Day (from March 17, 1946 on, after returning from war service) Phil Harris, Mel Blanc, Frank Nelson, Sheldon Leonard, Sara Berner (Mabel Flapsaddle, Gladys Zabisco), Bea Benadaret (Gertrude Gearshift), Artie Auerbach (Mr. Kitzel), the Sportsmen Quartet. Sponsor: American Tobacco Company.

Broadcast day and times: NBC. Sundays at 4 p.m. PST, CTC. until June 13, 1948. Sundays at 7 p.m. EST, 5 p.m. PST from October 3, 1948 to December 26, 1948. Then Sundays at 4 p.m. PST, CTC on CBS starting January 2, 1949. 30 minutes.

See B21, B56, B112, B433.

Using friendly persistence, Jack Benny coaxed Colman into appearing with his wife, Benita as themselves, playing comically long-suffering next-door neighbors of his tightwad character in Beverly Hills. (In reality, they lived eight blocks from Benny.) They were such a huge audience hit on a December Sunday in 1945 that Benny asked them back two weeks later for his Christmas show, causing an even bigger sensation. The result was that for the first time in his career, Colman found himself signing a contract with his wife for the two of them to play "themselves" a minimum of three times per season, in the process spoofing the Colman screen image as the perfect gentleman.

The exceptions to the three-per-season rule were the first season they were on—five shows—and the 1947-48 season—again five—because of Colman's Oscar win. In fact, it was their comic rapport and timing as husband-and-wife on the Benny show that led to their being signed for their own series, *The Halls of Ivy* (see pages 179-182). Benny returned the favor with a guest shot during the second season of *Ivy*, see R304.

What made the Benny/Colman pairing work so hilariously well was the contrast between Benny's vulgarian stinginess—forever borrowing from and imposing on his famous neighbors—and Colman's established image of elegant urbanity. The writers took this contrast even further by having Ronnie play against that image, giving him an interest in things like the Dick Tracy comic strip, pulp murder mysteries and popular novelty songs like "Open the Door, Richard," showing him to be in tune with popular as well as high culture. They also portrayed him as a star who was always concerned that one of his movies was playing somewhere, thereby displaying a comic vanity. Giving Ronnie a common touch beneath the sophisticated veneer made him seem to be more of a regular guy, though still infinitely more worldly than the unintellectual Benny.

In short, the Colmans became Benny's upper-class stooges, making the most of generally first-rate comedy scripts. Indeed, Benny's writers had a knack for tailoring comic material to them *and* to the many other stars who appeared on the show. Just as important, their teaming on Benny gave the mass radio audience a rare chance to know something of the private Ronnie and Benita, or rather the private couple the writers concocted. With impeccable comic material, they came across as a loving, witty and radiantly warm couple who enjoyed playing off each other. It was a delightful audio chemistry *and* a hugely popular one.

For all their on-air comedic chemistry, Ronnie and Benita were professional rather than personal friends of Jack's, to which Benny's daughter, Joan, attests. "I frankly don't recall that I ever met him except to say 'Hello' and 'Goodbye' at a radio broadcast," she says. "Nor do I remember them ever being in our home."[3]

The Benny shows were broadcast on NBC until the end of 1948, when Benny switched to CBS, along with most of NBC's other comedy stars, whom CBS President William S. Paley had lured away with more money and respect than they were getting from NBC president David Sarnoff.

R98 JACK BENNY
December 9, 1945. "The Mistaken Dinner Invitation." See R384, TV46. NBC. 30 minutes.

On this first show, Benny mistakenly thinks he has been invited to the Colmans' home for dinner. Ronnie, meanwhile, is working on his entry for the "I Can't Stand Jack Benny Because" contest. The contest's entry screening judges were Peter Lorre and Goodman Ace, the latter of the radio series *Easy Aces*. Fred Allen was final judge of the best entries. Eric Snowden plays the Colmans' good friend, Jack Wellington.

R99 THE GINNY SIMMS SHOW
December 21, 1945. Music: Frank De Vol. CBS. 30 minutes.

Colman tells Heywood Broun's story of the shepherd Amos; St. Luke's Choristers (60 boys and young men) sing carols with Ginny; Simms does some solos and presents a discharged serviceman on her "Give a Discharged Veteran a Job" segment.

R100 JACK BENNY
December 23, 1945. "The English Butler." NBC. 30 minutes.

Jack reciprocates by inviting the Colmans to *his* house for dinner. He hires an English butler (Mel Blanc) for the evening who turns out to have an incomprehensible accent. Snowden again plays Jack Wellington, but on subsequent shows, he plays the Colmans' valet, Sherwood.

R101 JACK BENNY
February 3, 1946. "The Isaac Stern Concert." NBC. 30 minutes.

Jack and Mary attend an Isaac Stern concert, where they run into the Colmans. Stern (who was 25) plays the 12-minute first movement of Mendelssohn's *Concerto in E Minor for Violin and Orchestra*, edited and double-timed to a little over 5 minutes. This makes his playing come off ragged. He is accompanied by pianist Alexander Zakin. Ronnie reads the winning entry in the "I Can't Stand Jack Benny Because" contest. The winner was Carroll P. Craig, Sr. of Pacific Palisades, CA, who wrote his entry as a rhyme:

I can't stand Jack Benny because/he fills the air with boasts and brags/and obsolete, obnoxious gags. The way he plays his violin/is music's most obnoxious sin. His cowardice alone, indeed/is matched by his obnoxious greed./And all the things that he portrays/show up my own obnoxious ways.

R102 LUX RADIO THEATER
March 18, 1946. "A Tale of Two Cities" by Charles Dickens. Host: William Keighley. CBS. 60 minutes. See F43, R5-6, R32, R186, D5, D9. Also aired on AFRS Radio Theater in 1946.

Cast: Ronald Colman (Sydney Carton), Joe Kearns (Charles Darnay), Heather Angel (Lucie Manette), Dennis Green (Stryver), Janet Scott (Madame Defarge).

Remake of 1942 script, which was also used for a 1945 Orson Welles performance as Carton. Colman again shines as Carton, but this time the pacing is surprisingly sluggish and two supporting roles are oddly cast. Crusty character actor Kearns plays the romantic lead, while Green plays the pompously foolish Stryver, a casting switch that doesn't work.

R103 JACK BENNY
April 14, 1946. "The Violin Lesson." NBC. 30 minutes.

With Mel Blanc as Prof. LeBlanc, Benny's perpetually exasperated violin teacher. Ronnie tries to rehearse for an upcoming radio version of *If I Were King* (R105), but Jack's screechy violin playing keeps interrupting him.

R104 JACK BENNY
May 5, 1946. "Jack Goes to Chicago." NBC. 30 minutes.

The Colmans appear for just a minute toward the end to see Jack off at the train station with a huge sigh of relief that they're rid of him for awhile.

R105 ACADEMY AWARD
May 11, 1946. "If I Were King," adapted from the Preston Sturges screenplay by Frank Wilson. Producer/Director: Dee Engelbach. Music: Leith Stevens. Announcer: Hugh Brundage. Sponsor: The House of Squibb. CBS. 30 minutes. See F48, R147.

Cast: Ronald Colman (François Villon), Gerald Mohr (King Louis XI), Lurene Tuttle (Katherine de Voucelles), Virginia Gregg (Huguette), Harry Lang (Prisoner), Gloria Blondell (Tavern Wench), Stanley Farrar (General), Ted von Eltz (Opening narrator), and Ed Max.

One-season series featuring stars who had either been nominated for an Oscar or who had been in an Oscar-nominated movie. Very good show, giving full rein to Colman's talent for romantic idealism, repeating his film role, with Mohr in fine support. Frank Wilson's script improves on the Sturges original by giving the story a solid romantic climax.

R106 SCREEN GUILD THEATER
May 13, 1946. "The Talk of the Town," adapted by Bill Hampton and Harry Kronman from the screenplay by Irwin Shaw and Sidney Buchman. Producer/Director: Bill Lawrence. Music: Wilbur Hatch. CBS. 30 minutes. See F53, R47, R106, R252, R394.

Cast: Ronald Colman (Michael Lightcap) and Virginia Bruce (Nora Shelley). Other cast names unavailable.

R107 ENCORE THEATER
June 18, 1946. "Yellow Jack," adapted by Jean Holloway from the play by Sidney Howard. Producer/Director: Bill Lawrence. Announcer: Frank Graham. Sponsor: Schenley Laboratories. CBS. 30 minutes.

Cast: Ronald Colman (Narrator), Frank Nelson (Major Dr. Walter Reed), Ed Max (Agramonte), Norman Field (Dr. Finley), Vic Perrin (Dr. Jesse Lazeire), Ken Christy (Dr. Carroll), Jerry Hausner (Pvt. Brinkerhof).

In the summer of 1900, four research scientists in Havana determine that mosquitoes cause malaria, called Yellow Jack. Excellent program. Holloway's script is a compelling one, his opening narration in particular a model of prose poetry, abetted by Colman's rich voice. However, the format is an odd one: When Colman is speaking, he is backed by somewhat melodramatic music, but the play itself has no distracting score. Otherwise, the show is faultlessly produced. Colman ends the show with Maimonides' "The Physician's Prayer."

Robert Montgomery starred in the 1938 movie version.

R108 THEATER GUILD ON THE AIR

October 20, 1946. "The Green Goddess," from the play by William Archer. Producer/Host: Roger Pryor. Sponsor: United States Steel. Classical excerpt: "The Funeral March of a Marionette" by Gounod, better known as the Alfred Hitchcock show theme. CBS. 60 minutes. See S21.

Cast: Ronald Colman (Raja of Rukh), Walter Abel (Major Antony Crespin), Anita Louise (Lucilla Crespin), E.G. Marshall (Dr. Basil Traherne), Alfred Shirley (Watkins), Anthony Ross (Lt. Denis Cardew).

Nearly 26 years after being fired from the original stage cast, Colman did the show before a national radio audience as the villain. He performs with menacingly urbane relish, using a halting quasi-Indian accent, making you believe he really *is* a wily heathen beneath the cultured veneer. He also makes you wish he had played this role or an equally villainous one at least once in a sound movie.

R109 JACK BENNY

November 17, 1946. "Leo Durocher Visits the Wrong House." Brooklyn Dodgers manager Durocher calls at the Colmans' house by mistake, looking for Jack, but is invited in when he mentions that he "loved" Ronnie in *Lost Horizon*. NBC. 30 minutes.

R110 ACADEMY AWARD

November 27, 1946. "Lost Horizon," edited by Frank Wilson from George Wells's Decca record script from the James Hilton novel. CBS. 30 minutes. See F45, R27, R54, R173, D3, D10, D15.

Cast: Ronald Colman (Hugh Conway), Dennis Green (Mallinson), Howard McNear (Chang), Lurene Tuttle (Lo-Tsen), Norman Field (the High Lama), Gerald Mohr (Opening narrator).

R111 JACK BENNY

February 16, 1947. "Jack Benny's Birthday." The Colmans and Isaac Stern meet at Jack's house for Jack's birthday dinner, getting more than they bargained for. Funny show about Jack trying to get a sumptuous dinner for nothing and having it backfire on him. Stern plays a 1:54 excerpt from Wieniawski's *Violin Concerto #2*, accompanied by pianist Alexander Zakin. NBC. 30 minutes.

R112 JACK BENNY

April 27, 1947. "Going to See the Benny Show." When the Colmans reluctantly accept a ride in Jack's beloved but broken down Maxwell to a broadcast of his show, they try to avoid being recognized along the way. They happily leave the car to see Ronnie's new movie, *The Late George Apley* (F57) when they find themselves parked in front of Grauman's Chinese Theater. NBC. 30 minutes.

R113 HOLLYWOOD STAR PREVIEW (Premiere show)

September 28, 1947. "Star Light, Star Bright," an original play by True Boardman. Producer/ Director: Nat Wolff. Guest host: Ronald Colman. Music: Bernard Katz. Announcer: Ken Peters. Sponsor: American Home Products. NBC. 30 minutes.

Cast: Vanessa Brown (Kathleen Gray), William Conrad (Arnold Thorson), Herb Vigran (Mike Nichols, Thorson's Agent), Elliott Reid (Steve Marshall), Ted von Eltz (D.J. Bear).

Would-be actress Gray goes to Hollywood, where she prevails upon her vain and egocentric movie star father, Thorson, to get her a screen test. Fun, witty, insightful show, with a good, fearless performance by Brown.

Colman's first of five programs as host on this showcase for new movie talent, in this case Vanessa Brown, his co-star from *The Late George Apley*. Brown had been a regular on *Quiz Kids* as Cmylla Brind, her real name. From its second season on, this series was called *Anacin Hollywood Star Preview* because Anacin was made by American Home Products.

R114 JACK BENNY

November 9, 1947. "The Fake Invitation." Phil Harris has Dennis Day imitate Ronnie's voice on the phone to Jack, inviting Benny to a fictitious party at the Colmans. Jack and his date, Mabel Flapsaddle (Sara Berner), go to the "party" dressed in western costumes. NBC. 30 minutes.

R115 THE LOUELLA PARSONS SHOW

January 4, 1948. Producer: Richard Diggs. Announcer: Marvin Miller. KECA Hollywood for ABC. 15 minutes. See F58-9, R116, R119, R124-25, R377, R404, B35, A7, A8.

Louella "interviews" Ronnie to plug *A Double Life* which was playing at one Hollywood theater and which Parsons was raving about as an Oscar contender. Scripted interview runs four minutes, with some corny humor. However, Ronnie does get to reflect on his hospital visits with soldiers during the war, telling Parsons that the two movies of his soldiers mentioned most were *Lost Horizon* and *The Prisoner of Zenda*.

R116 JACK BENNY

February 1, 1948. "Special Screening of A Double Life." NBC. 30 minutes. Jack and Mary attend a preview of Ronnie's new movie. See F58-59, R116, R119, R124-25, A7, A8.

R117 HOLLYWOOD STAR PREVIEW

February 15, 1948. "It's Tough to Be a Lady." Program details unavailable. Guest host: Ronald Colman. NBC. 30 minutes.

As a further promotional push for *A Double Life* (F58), Colman presents his co-star, Shelley Winters.

R118 SCREEN GUILD THEATER

March 8, 1948. "The Late George Apley," based on the movie from the John P. Marquand novel. Producer/Host: Roger Pryor. CBS. 30 minutes. See F57, R113.

Cast: Ronald Colman (George Apley), Edna Best (Catherine Apley), Peggy Cummins (Eleanor Apley), Vanessa Brown (Agnes Willing), Richard Haydn (Horatio Willing).

R119 THE 20TH ANNUAL ACADEMY AWARDS

March 20, 1948. MC: Jean Hersholt. Opening narrator for Best Songs montage: Ken Carpenter. KECA Hollywood for ABC. Three hours, sus. 7 p.m. PST, CTC. See F58, R116,

R117, R120, R122-R125.

Oscars for 1947 movies. Show includes over an hour of song and film clip montages celebrating 20 years of Oscar. Colman accepts his Oscar for Best Actor in *A Double Life* from Olivia de Havilland and makes a 1-minute acceptance speech. Segment 95 minutes in.

R120 JACK BENNY
March 28, 1948. "The Stolen Oscar." When Jack offers Ronnie and Benita the chance to be in his new western movie (they affect western drawls to read from an awful B western script), he also asks to borrow Ronnie's Oscar to show it to Rochester, only to have it stolen right away by a mugger. NBC. 30 minutes. See F58-59, R116, R119-20, R122-125, A8.

Second in an eight-show sequence. Benny or his writers were certain that Colman would win the Academy Award, so a series of scripts was conjured in which Jack would be set up for several falls by being robbed of the borrowed Oscar, then trying to borrow other Oscars to replace it. The other Oscars belonged to Bing Crosby, Paul Lukas, Samuel Goldwyn and Frank Sinatra.

R121 LUX RADIO THEATER
April 19, 1948. "Random Harvest," from the movie of the James Hilton novel. Host: William Keighley. CBS. 60 minutes. See F55, R53. Colman and Garson play their movies roles again.

R122 JACK BENNY
April 25, 1948. "Charley's Aunt Disguise." Jack disguises himself in his Charley's aunt costume (from the 1941 movie) to avoid facing Ronnie about the borrowed Oscar. Ronnie appears without Benita for 2 ½ minutes. Opera star Dorothy Kirsten also guests. NBC. 30 minutes. See F58, R116, R119-20, R123, A7.

R123 JACK BENNY
May 9, 1948. "The Stolen Oscar Returns." The end of the running gag. The secret of the stolen Oscar is revealed as Ronnie and Benita pack for a trip to England for the British premiere of *A Double Life*. NBC. 30 minutes. See F58, R116, R119-20, R123, A7.

R124 WOMAN'S HOUR
May 21, 1948. (Recorded May 20). Producer: Miss D.E. Gibbs. Interviewer: Douglas Willis. BBC. 60 minutes. Colman segment: 4 minutes, 45 seconds. See F58, R116-17, R119-20, R122-23, R125, A7, A8.

Unscripted interview with Colman at the London premiere of *A Double Life* in the foyer of the Leicester Square Theatre. The disc recording does not survive. According to BBC archivist Jeff Walden, "this was due to the cost of processing discs for permanent retention....The late 1940s was a period of particular financial austerity in this country. For the day in question, for example, not a single item of BBC output was retained in recorded form."

Woman's Hour was a weekday afternoon talk show with a summer break. It began in 1946 and is still on the air.

R125 IN TOWN TONIGHT
May 22, 1948. Producer: Peter Duncan. Interviewer: John Ellison. BBC. 30 minutes. Colman segment: 3 minutes. See F58, R116-17, R119-20, R122-24, A7, A8.

Live broadcast of a scripted interview promoting *A Double Life*. No recording was made and the script is lost. In a British newspaper item dated June 20, 1948, Peter Duncan states that Colman was one of the most cooperative guests he has had on the show. "'He rehearsed four-and-a-half hours for a three-minute shot,' Duncan says with awed amazement."

In Town Tonight was a Saturday night talk show (off summers) running from 1933 to 1960. "Again, it was rarely recorded," says Jeff Walden, "and indeed, made a virtue of being 'live.' It was classed as a variety production, although it was mostly talk."

R126 FAVORITE STORY (Third season premiere)
September 14, 1948. "The Country of the Blind," from the H.G. Wells story "Strange Valley." Show #92 in the series. Script and direction by Jerome Lawrence and Robert E. Lee. Chosen by opera star Gladys Swarthout. KFI Hollywood. 30 minutes. See R128, R212, B86.

 Cast: Ronald Colman (Juan Francisco Nunez), Joan Banks (Medina), Herb Butterfield (Father), Wilms Herbert, Jeff Corey and Naomi Robison.

 Colman performed just once on the live version of this series during its three-season run on Los Angeles radio. His work as host-actor for the syndicated version is detailed on pages 164-65. In this show, he plays a Spanish mountain guide who stumbles into a mythical valley where all the inhabitants are naturally blind. Though he gives a technically okay performance, Colman is miscast. His urbanity makes him unconvincing as a Spanish peasant, thus rendering the production unbelievable as an allegorical fantasy about superstitious conformity and being blinded to reality.

 A color videotaped TV version titled "The Richest Man in Bogota" was broadcast on NBC's *Dupont Show of the Month* on August 5, 1962, starring Lee Marvin as a uranium prospector named Juan de Nunez. A B&W kinescope of that show is at UCLA.

R127 HALLMARK RADIO THEATER
September 16, 1948. "Goodbye Mr. Chips," adapted from the James Hilton novel by Jean Holloway. Producer/Director: Dee Engelbach. Host: James Hilton. Music: Lyn Murray.

 Cast: Ronald Colman (Mr. Chips), Eric Snowden (Carter, Headmaster). Other cast names not available. CBS. 30 minutes.

 Fair show but Colman is miscast and weak as Chips, while the script emphasizes his short-lived marriage over his role as a schoolteacher, which is the book's main thrust. And the pacing is slow, making the show an utter bore. It's amazing that host Hilton allowed this treatment of his story. The classic 1939 movie stars Robert Donat.

FAVORITE STORY (Frederic W. Ziv Productions, 118 episodes. Syndicated from the fall of 1948 on.) See R128, B86.
Half-hour versions of classic short stories and novels (and some originals) produced, directed and written by Jerome Lawrence and Robert E. Lee, except where noted. Host and occasional lead actor/narrator: Ronald Colman. Story editor: George Palmer Putnam. Sound effects: Jack Hayes. Musical director: Claude Sweeten. First heard as a live weekly show on KFI Hollywood from June 18, 1946 to March 25, 1949 for a total of 119 episodes.

 Of the 115 scripts broadcast on KFI (four shows were live repeats by popular demand), 105 were chosen for the syndicated version, with another 13 stories added for original production. In all, 118 programs were recorded between April of 1947 and November 17, 1949. Syndication broadcasts began nationwide in the fall of 1948, except for Los Angeles.

 The reason for the syndication blackout in Los Angeles, explains Lawrence, was that

"When we first made a deal with Bullock's at the beginning of 1946, we offered them the exclusive live run of the show in Los Angeles. When syndication sales began less than a year after the show started airing, we were in our second season, so no other Los Angeles station *could* air it. Once the live run was over, the show was so identified with KFI and Bullock's that no other Los Angeles station or sponsor would buy it."[4]

Even without the Los Angeles market, the show made a lot of money for its creators and host.

Colman was paid $5000 for each 12 shows as host, plus $3500 for each 13th show as host and actor and another $3500 for the lead in the holiday bonus of *A Christmas Carol* for a total of $80,000. He was also paid a 10% "contingent compensation" (legalistic doubletalk for royalty) from the sale of transcriptions up to $7500 for each group of 13 shows for a potential sum total of $147,500. (How much royalty he was paid for *A Christmas Carol* I couldn't find.) However, he only kept about 15% after taxes, agent's fee and alimony. He also narrated 11 shows, 8 of them for the final season of 39 recordings. His host wraparounds were consistently inviting, while his work as a lead actor and narrator was variable.

The repertory cast comprised scores of first-rate actors. Appearing five or more times were: William Conrad (37), Byron Kane (24), Herb Butterfield (21), Janet Waldo (17, Mrs. Robert E. Lee), Gloria Gordon (15), Edmund MacDonald, (15), Hans Conried (14), Norman Field (14), Ed Max (12), John Beal (11), Lurene Tuttle (11), Raymond Burr (9), Eric Snowden (9), Henry Blair, Arthur Q. Bryan, Jeff Corey, Joseph Kearns, Berry Kroeger, Naomi Robison, Earle Ross, Luis Van Rooten (8 each), Jerry Farber, Virginia Gregg (7 each), Rolfe Sedan, Jeanne Bates, True Boardman, Howard Duff, David Ellis, Thomas Freebairn-Smith (6 each), Edna Best, Helen Craig (Mrs. John Beal), Betty Lou Gerson, William Johnstone, Peter Leeds, Frank Lovejoy, Tom McKee, Janet Scott, Irene Tedrow, Peggy Webber, John William (5 each).

Good as these actors were, they were sometimes miscast (though not deliberately) when Lawrence and Lee couldn't get who they really wanted. For example, William Conrad was cast in three British romantic leads, roles for which he was manifestly unsuited by virtue of his gruffly American voice, however modulated. Lawrence says he really wanted Orson Welles, but that Welles was tied up with other series and movie work. By the same token, Howard Duff, though classically trained, doesn't sound right as D'Artagnan or Ishmael.

These occasional drawbacks aside, the series was praised by critics and educators, says Lawrence, for its many exceptional scripts, production values and acting. Listening to the series today, the ratio of good to excellent shows to mediocre or awful ones is about 40/60. Many of the lesser shows are truncations of novels. As other half-hour drama anthologies had shown, an average of 22 minutes after commercials, theme music and host wraparound is a terrible format for condensing books. Which Lawrence today says he is the first to admit.

"Halfway through the KFI series," he recalls, "Bob and I stopped trying to condense novels and focused on short stories, which were more easily dramatized. Also, several celebrities chose historical figures or incidents for us to write about rather than published stories. That was often easier than dramatizing well-known works because we could fit the story to the time limit.

"We were able to sign Ronnie because we shared the same agent, Nat Wolff, and we felt he was the ideal host. He was also a fan of the KFI series. At the same time, he was more than just the host. With our scripts, he put the stories in context, acting as a genially well-read man who was sharing his library with the audience. The series continued in syndication till he died."[5]

The commercial hook for the series was that famous people from the arts, show business, journalism, literature, music and sports chose each week's favorite story, though it was rarely hinted why. Presumably, the story itself provided that insight and thereby an insight into the celebrity. One thing is clear, though: nearly half the celebrities polled chose science fiction, fantasy and horror stories as the ones they most loved as children.

The best of these programs hold up as potent examples of radio drama without the hindrance of networks or corporate sponsors. Indeed, several shows pungently dramatize controversial social and historical themes with actors known for their incisive versatility. Recurring themes are conscience, injustice, moral irony, greed, disillusionment, spirituality, materialism, and the theater. The authors most frequently adapted were Robert Louis Stevenson (6 shows), Charles Dickens (5), Mark Twain, Henry James (4 each), Anton Chekhov, Maurice Level, Rudyard Kipling, Guy de Maupassant, H.G. Wells and Leonard Merrick (3 each).

The broadcasts of *Favorite Story* from January of 1950 to June of 1952 meant that Ronald Colman could be heard two or three times a week (he did several shows in between *Halls of Ivy* episodes) in millions of homes during the simultaneous series run of *The Halls of Ivy*. What he lost in movie stardom during this period he made up for with a loyal radio following in the tens of millions.

The following is a detailed list of the 118 syndicated shows in order of release (with the exception of "A Christmas Carol"), with an asterisk denoting the shows starring or narrated by Colman. Title and author are followed by the person who chose the story and the cast members. All episodes with Colman as actor or narrator are annotated, as are what I think are the superior episodes without him of the 75 I have heard.

R128 "The Bishop's Candlesticks" from *Les Miserables* by Victor Hugo. Chosen by: Artist Rockwell Kent. **Cast:** Edmund MacDonald (Jean Valjean), Norman Field (the Bishop), Ruth Perrott, Naomi Robison, Herbert Ratner, Bill Bissell, Herman Waldman and Stanley Waxman.

R129 "The Diamond Lens" by Fitz-James O'Brien. Chosen by: Composer George Antheil. **Cast:** William Conrad (Professor Linley), Gloria Gordon, Ed Max, Byron Kane, Jack Edwards and Dick Clayton.

Brilliant virtual monologue by Conrad as a scientist who makes the ultimate microscope lens and discovers living beings in a drop of water. This was the syndication audition show. It was broadcast live twice on KFI because it won an award—deservedly so—for excellence in radio drama. It's an exceptional metaphoric story about the spiritual price to be paid for obsessive tampering with the hidden worlds of nature.

R130 "Little Women" by Louisa May Alcott. Chosen by: Actress Shirley Temple. **Cast:** Adele Longmire (Jo), Betsy Kelly née Blair (Amy), Jean Gillespie (Meg), Naomi Robison (Beth), Jane Morgan (Marmee), Myra Marsh (Aunt Marsh).

R131 "Wuthering Heights" by Emily Bronte. Chosen by: Author-editor Bennett Cerf. **Cast:** Janet Waldo (Cathy), William Conrad (Heathcliff), Jane Morgan (Nelly), Gil Stewart (Edgar), Peggy Webber (Isabella).

R132 "A Connecticut Yankee in King Arthur's Court" by Mark Twain. Chosen by: Radio comedian Ed "Archie" Gardner. **Cast:** Ben Alexander (the Yankee), Byron Kane (Sir Sagamore), Sidney Miller (Clarence), Joseph Kearns (Merlin), Murray Wagner (the Sportscaster), Joel Davis (the Newsboy).

R133* "Cyrano de Bergerac" by Edmund Rostand. Chosen by: Actor-host Ronald Colman. **Cast:** Ronald Colman (Cyrano), Janet Waldo (Roxanne), David Ellis (Christian), Joseph Kearns (Le Bret).

Considering this was Colman's favorite story, it's a very disappointing show. The script is patchy and his lead performance is surprisingly wan for such a famously aggressive character. Film versions include: 1906 (France, synchronized sound one-reeler with Coquelin), 1922 (Italy, with Pierre Magnier), 1950 (USA, with José Ferrer), and 1990 (France, with Gerard Depardieu).

R134 "David Copperfield" by Charles Dickens. Chosen by: Pianist-humorist Alec Templeton. **Cast:** Jerry Farber (David Copperfield), Gloria Gordon (Peggotty), Janet Waldo (Mrs. Copperfield), John William (Mr. Murdstone), Dick Ryan (Mr. Micawber).

R135 "The Queen of Spades" by Alexander Pushkin. Chosen by: Explorer Vihljalmur Stefannson. **Cast:** Edmund MacDonald (the German), Byron Kane (Tomsky, the other gambler), Gloria Gordon (the Countess), Jeff Corey (the Banker).

R136 "Huckleberry Finn" by Mark Twain. Chosen by: Big band leader Artie Shaw. **Cast:** Jimmy Lydon (Huck Finn), Horace Willard (Jim), Peter Rankin (Tom Sawyer).

R137 "The Arabian Nights", original script by True Boardman from legendary sources. Music: Themes from *Scheherezade* by Rimsky-Korsakov. Chosen by: Newsman-lecturer-explorer Lowell Thomas. **Cast:** Paula Winslowe (Scheherezade), William Conrad (Shahrayar the King), Betty Arnold (Zumurrud), True Boardman (Alisher), Ed Max (Vizier Hassan), Edmund MacDonald, Barbara Eiler, Ken Christy, Naomi Robison and Thelma Hubbard.

R138 "Jane Eyre" by Charlotte Bronte. Chosen by: Broadway producer Brock Pemberton. **Cast:** Peggy Webber (Jane Eyre), William Conrad (Rochester), Thomas Ames (Mason), Gloria Gordon (Mrs. Fairfax), Colin Campbell (the Clergyman), Helen Geddes (Blanche), Eric Snowden (Briggs).

R139 "Vanity Fair" by William Makepeace Thackeray. Chosen by: Author Sinclair Lewis. **Cast:** Joan Loring (Becky Sharp), Barbara Eiler (Amelia Cedley), Herb Butterfield (Sir Joseph Cedley), Raymond Lawrence (Sir George Osmond), Edmund MacDonald (Sir Pitt), Howard Duff (Rorden Crawley), Wilms Herbert (Lord Stain), William Conrad (William Makepeace Thackeray, Narrator).

R140 "Joan of Arc", original script by Lawrence and Lee from historical sources. Chosen by: Actress Jennifer Jones. **Cast:** Joan Loring (Joan of Arc), John William (the Inquisitor), Jeff Corey (Tremonillie), Howard Duff (La Hire), Frank Graham (the Dauphin), Norman Field (the Uncle), Naomi Robison (St. Catherine).

R141 "Frankenstein" by Mary Shelley. Chosen by: Comedian Fred Allen. **Cast:** Edmund MacDonald (Dr. Frankenstein), Ed Max (the Monster), Joe Worthy (Clerval), Dorothy Scott (Elizabeth).

R142 "20,000 Leagues Under the Sea" by Jules Verne. Chosen by: Actor-director Orson Welles. **Cast:** Edmund MacDonald (Captain Nemo), Jeff Corey (Professor Pierre Aranax),

Thomas Ames (Ned Land), Bill Bissell (Commodore Farragut).

R143 "The Importance of Being Earnest" by Oscar Wilde. Chosen by: Stage director Margaret Webster. **Cast:** Tom Collins (Jack/ Ernest Worthing); Thomas Freebairn-Smith (Algernon), Lurene Tuttle (Gwendolyn), Janet Waldo (Cecily), Gloria Gordon (Aunt Augusta), Ruth Perrott (Miss Prism).

R144 "Dr. Jekyll and Mr. Hyde" by Robert Louis Stevenson. Chosen by: Producer-director Alfred Hitchcock. **Cast:** William Conrad (Jekyll and Hyde), Eric Snowden (Utterson), Carl Harbaugh (Lanyon) Paul Theodore (Poole), Sheila Jameson (the Maid).

R145 "The Man Who Sold His Shadow to the Devil" by Adelbert von Chamisso. Chosen by: Poet Robert Frost. **Cast:** Sam Edwards (Peter), True Boardman (the Stranger), Barbara Eiler (Mina), Cy Kendall (Mr. Jones), Dink Trout (Benchel), William Conrad (the Father).

R146[*] "A Lodging for the Night" by Robert Louis Stevenson. Chosen by: Newsman Frank Sullivan. **Cast:** Ronald Colman (François Villon), Janet Waldo (Ysabeau), William Conrad (Prefect of Police), Byron Kane (Mautaint). See F48, R105.
　　　French poet-vagabond Villon thinks he's being accused of a murder he didn't commit. Punchy script overhauled from the original story, with three new characters and a strong lead performance helped by Colman's identification with the role of Villon in the movie *If I Were King*.

R147 "Alice in Wonderland" by Lewis Carroll. Chosen by: Songwriter Irving Berlin. **Cast:** Dawn Bender (Alice), Jerry Hausner (White Rabbit), Herb Vigran (Mad Hatter), Arthur Q. Bryan (Mock Turtle), Buddy Duncan (March Hare), June Foray (Duchess), Dick Ryan (Cheshire Cat), Earle Ross (King of Hearts), Lurene Tuttle (Queen of Hearts).

R148 "Rappaccini's Daughter" by Nathaniel Hawthorne. Chosen by: Actor Sydney Greenstreet. **Cast:** Howard Duff (Giovanni), Janet Waldo (Beatrice), True Boardman (the Professor), Irene Tedrow (Lisabette), Byron Kane (Rappaccini).

R149 "Moby Dick" by Herman Melville. Chosen by: Playwright Howard Lindsay. **Cast:** Howard Duff (Ishmael), William Conrad (Ahab), Frank Lovejoy (Starbuck), Ed Max (Tashtego), Earle Ross (the Blacksmith).

R150 "Great Expectations" by Charles Dickens. Chosen by: Actor Walter Hampden. **Cast:** Joel Davis (Pip), Peggy Webber (Estella), True Boardman (Joe), Gloria Gordon (Miss Havisham), Edmund MacDonald (Abel Magwitch), Eric Snowden (Mr. Jaggers).

R151 "The Phantom Rickshaw" by Rudyard Kipling. Chosen by: Music critic-composer Deems Taylor. Original score by Bob Mitchell. **Cast:** William Conrad (Pansay), Eric Snowden (Heatherlegh), Edmund MacDonald (Gem Merchant), Lois Corbett (Agnes), Jean Vander Pyl (Kitty), Guy Kingsford (The Commissioner), Ramsay Hill (Sadhu). See R8.

R152 "Sire de Maletroit's Door" by Robert Louis Stevenson. Chosen by: Author-critic Henry Seidel Canby. **Cast:** Howard Duff (Denis), Janet Waldo (Blanche), True Boardman (Sire de Maletroit), Eric Snowden (Sentry), William Johnstone (Voice of the Camera).

R153 "God Sees the Truth but Waits" by Leo Tolstoy. Chosen by: Actor Eddie Dowling. **Cast:** Edmund MacDonald (Ivan Oxyanov), David Ellis (Sergei), William Conrad (Makar), Sarah Selby (Anna), Ed Max (Prison Official), Joe Duval (Court Official).

A merchant named Ivan is falsely accused of murdering another merchant, spending 26 years in Siberia for his "crime." Devastating study of crime and conscience finely ground.

R154 "The Debt Collector" by Maurice Level. Chosen by: Actor Van Johnson. **Cast:** Tom Tully (Narrator), Tony Barrett (Maley), Ed Max, Virginia Gregg (Night Club Singer), Lou Krugman, Joe Granby and Adrienne Marden.

Superbly ironic story about a collection agency messenger (Barret) who absconds with a bank deposit, then can't remember under what name he banked it after he has served a prison term for theft. The script's genius is adding a sardonic Narrator/Conscience.

R155 "Gulliver's Travels" by Jonathan Swift. Chosen by: Actor Ray Milland. **Cast:** Carl Harbaugh (Gulliver), Walter Tetley (Gen. Glumbuck), Sidney Miller (King of Lilliput), June Foray (Captain of Lilliput army), Dink Trout, Walter Craig and Buddy Duncan.

R156 "Mayerling" by Lawrence and Lee from historical sources. Chosen by: Actor Gregory Peck. **Cast:** William Conrad (Rudolph of Hapsburg), Lurene Tuttle (Maria Vetsera), Earle Ross (Franz Joseph), Herman Waldman (Tokar), Rolfe Sedan (Dr. Widerhofer).

R157 "Mr. Shakespeare", an original play by Lawrence and Lee, previously broadcast on AFRS. Chosen by: Actor Spencer Tracy. **Cast:** Vincent Price (William Shakespeare), William Conrad (Arthur Green), Peggy Webber (Mrs. Tidball), Betsy Blair (Ann), Elliott Reid (Jimmy O'Neil), Peter Leeds (Bill Mosier), Hugh Thomas, John William, Harry Lang, and Bill Chelios, Headwaiter of the Brown Derby, as Himself.

Hilarious play about what might happen if Shakespeare came back to life to write screenplays for a movie studio. Hollywood jokes pepper a script that has reincarnated Will delighting in the comforts of Beverly Hills while finding that sonnets aren't box office. Delicious comic performance by an ideally cast Price.

R158 "Casey at the Bat" by Ernest Lawrence Thayer. Chosen by: Baseball player Tris Speaker. **Cast:** Lionel Stander (Casey), Sports commentator Hal Berger (Manager Hal Nickerson), Anne Stone (Mrs. Casey), Tommy Bernard (Timmy), Al Hill, Jr. (the Umpire).

R159* "The Light That Failed" by Rudyard Kipling. Chosen by: Publisher-Favorite Story story editor George Palmer Putnam, who introduces the play himself. **Cast:** Ronald Colman (Dick Heldar), Ben Wright (Torpenhow, narrator), Heather Angel (Bessie Broke). See F49.

Colman replays his movie role as the arrogant painter, giving a fair, somewhat mechanical performance, not nearly as strongly affecting as on *Good News of 1940*, R15. Wright outacts him with a more natural reading. Script taken from the movie. Okay show.

R160 "The Man Without a Country" by Edward Everett Hale. Chosen by: Theatre Guild Producer Theresa Helburn. **Cast:** John Beal (Philip Nolan), William Conrad (Lt. Masterson), John William (Capt. of the Intrepid), Byron Kane, Louise Arthur (Mrs. Graff), and Jay Michael.

R161 "Mary, Queen of Scots" by Lawrence and Lee from historical sources. Chosen by: Singer-actor Bing Crosby. **Cast:** Edna Best (Mary, Queen of Scots), Benita Hume (Queen

Elizabeth), Ben Wright (Bothwell), Whit Bissell (Maitland), John William (Seton), Norman Field (John Knox), Adrienne Marden (Maid-in-waiting).

R162 "Dr. Heidegger's Experiment" by Nathaniel Hawthorne. Chosen by: Actor Robert Walker. **Cast:** John McIntire (Dr. Heidegger), Lurene Tuttle (Widow Wycherly), Norman Field (Mr. Melbourne), Arthur Q. Bryan (Col. Killigrew), Earle Ross (Mr. Gascoigne).

R163 "Oliver Twist" by Charles Dickens. Chosen by: Father Edward Flanagan of Boys Town. **Cast:** Henry Blair (Oliver Twist), Arthur Q. Bryan (Mr. Bumble), Gloria Gordon (Mrs. Corney), Edmund MacDonald (Fagin), Peter Rankin (Artful Dodger), Herb Butterfield (Mr. Brownlow), Virginia Gregg (the Old Woman).

R164 "The Legend of Sleepy Hollow" by Washington Irving. Chosen by: Actor Walter Huston. **Cast:** Sidney Miller (Ichabod Crane), Arthur Q. Bryan (Van Ripper), Ted Reid (Brom Bones), Margaret Brayton (Katrina), Dick Ryan (Van Tassel), True Boardman (Brower), Joel Davis, Norman Wilner and William Conrad.

R165 "The Three Musketeers" by Alexander Dumas. Script by E. Jack Newman. Chosen by: Boxer Gene Tunney. **Cast:** Howard Duff (D'Artagnan), Bernice Barrett (Constance), Ed Max (Porthos), Tom McKee (Athos), Anne Stone (Milady de Winter), Ben Alexander (Aramis), Cy Kendall (Treville), Jack Carrington (the Executioner), Byron Kane (the Citizen).

R166 "The Mystery of Room 323", based on legend. Chosen by: Comedians George Burns and Gracie Allen. **Cast:** Janet Waldo (Ellen), Hans Conried, Luis Van Rooten, Ruth Perrott, Rolfe Sedan and Barton Yarborough.

R167 "Tom Sawyer" by Mark Twain. Chosen by: Actress Ruth Gordon. **Cast:** Skip Homeier (Tom Sawyer), Jimmy Lydon (Huck Finn), Ann Todd (Becky Thatcher), Peter Rankin (Ben), Byron Kane (Judge Thatcher), Ed Max (Injun Joe), Hans Conried (Muff Potter).

R168 "Peter Ibbetson" by George DuMaurier. Chosen by: Actress Merle Oberon. Theremin music: Dr. Samuel Hoffman. **Cast:** John Beal (Peter Ibbetson), Helen Craig (the Duchess of Towers), Lou Merrill, Dawn Bender, Henry Blair.
    Note: An unreal sounding electronic musical hand instrument, the theremin was invented in 1927 by Russian engineer Lev Theremin. Hoffman used it to score *Spellbound* (1945).

R169 "The Necklace" by Guy de Maupassant. Chosen by: Actress Greer Garson. **Cast:** Heather Angel, Hans Conried, Irene Tedrow, Byron Kane and Rolfe Sedan.

R170 "Jamie Freel", based on an Irish folk legend. Chosen by: Actor Barry Fitzgerald. **Cast:** Sean McClory (Jamie), Arthur Q. Bryan (the Elf), Gloria Gordon, Dorothy Scott and Edmund MacDonald.

R171 "The Strange Mr. Bartleby" by Herman Melville. Chosen by: Actor Robert Montgomery. **Cast:** William Conrad (the Attorney), Hans Conried (Bartleby), Jeff Corey (Nippers), Herb Butterfield (the Old Man).

R172* "Lost Horizon" by James Hilton. Abridged from George Wells's script for the Decca record, D6. Chosen by: Actress Mary Pickford. **Cast:** Ronald Colman (Hugh Conway), Norman Field (High Lama), Jeanne Bates (Lo-Tsen), Joseph Kearns (Chang), Dennis Green (Mallinson). See F45, R27, R54, R110, D3, D10, D15.

The best of the Colman radio versions of this story. Colman's poetic affinity for his role makes the listener overlook Hilton's story holes, which are transferred intact. The major flaws are that sensitive Lo-Tsen would fall for hot head Mallinson and that Mallinson can so easily talk Conway into leaving Shangri-La; faults Hilton reportedly acknowledged when the movie was being made in 1936.

R173 "The Lady of the Lamp" by Lawrence and Lee from historical sources. Chosen by: Actor Robert Young. **Cast:** Edna Best (Florence Nightingale), Tony Ellis, Joseph Kearns, Peggy Webber, Gloria Gordon, Herbert Rawlinson and Eric Snowden.

R174 "The Moonstone" by Wilkie Collins. Chosen by: Playwright Russel Crouse. **Cast:** Thomas Freebairn-Smith (Franklin Blake), Colleen Collins (Rachel Verinder), Marvin Miller (Sgt. Cuff), Ramsay Hill and Naomi Robison.

R175 "Pride and Prejudice" by Jane Austen. Chosen by: Painter and scenic designer Oliver Smith. **Cast:** Verna Felton (Mrs. Bennett), Helen Craig (Elizabeth Bennett), William Conrad (Darcy), Thomas Freebairn-Smith (Bingley), Janet Waldo (Lydia Bennett.

R176 "The Bottle Imp" by Robert Louis Stevenson. Chosen by: Comedian Ed Wynn. **Cast:** Jeff Corey (Keawe), Mary Jane Croft (Kokua), Earle Ross, Edmund MacDonald, David Ellis, Lou Krugman and Herb Butterfield.

An enchanted bottle curses its owner with unhappiness after granting wishes. It must then be sold for a lesser amount each it changes hands. Fascinating tale of the supernatural on themes of desire and greed. The acting varies from naturalistic to melodramatic but the story is so compelling in itself that one can overlook the uneven direction.

R177 "Cashel Byron's Profession" by George Bernard Shaw. Chosen by: Actor Danny Kaye. **Cast:** Dan O'Herlihy (Cashel Byron), Joan Banks (Lydia), Verna Felton (Mrs. Byron), Hans Conried (Dr. Moncrief), Wally Maher (Mellish), Tom Collins (Lucian), Jack Edwards, Jr. (Hibbs).

R178 "Ben-Hur" by General Lew Wallace. Chosen by: Big game hunter Clyde Beatty. **Cast:** John Beal (Ben-Hur), Marvin Miller (Messala), Janet Scott (Mother), Henry Blair (David), Jeanne Bates (Tirzah), Herb Butterfield (Baltasar the Wise Man).

R179 "Mutineers of the Bounty" by Lawrence and Lee from the eyewitness account of James Morrison, officer of HMS Bounty. Chosen by: Movie producer Walter Wanger. **Cast:** Frank Lovejoy (Fletcher Christian), William Conrad (Captain Bligh), Lon McCallister (Peter Haywood), Georgia Backus (Mrs. Haywood), Earl Lee and Kirk Ragan.

R180 "The Golden Ingot" by Fitz-James O'Brien. Chosen by: Opera star Lauritz Melchior. **Cast:** Frank Albertson (Dr. Luxor), Morris Carnovsky (William Blakelock), Jeanne Bates (Marian).

R181 "Washington Square" by Henry James. Chosen by: Actress Susan Hayward. **Cast:**

Vanessa Brown (Catherine Sloper), William Conrad (Dr. Sloper), Lois Corbett (Aunt Lavinia), Donald Curtis (Morris Townsend).

R182 "The Casting Away of Mrs. Alecks and Mrs. Aleshire" by Frank Stockton. Chosen by: Actor Ozzie Nelson. **Cast:** Ben Alexander (Mr. Craig), Lurene Tuttle (Mrs. Aleshire), Jane Morgan (Mrs. Alecks), Byron Kane (Mr. Dusante).

R183 "The Travels of Marco Polo" by Lawrence and Lee from historical sources. Chosen by: Actress Eva Le Gallienne. **Cast:** Rolland Morris (Marco Polo), John Dehner (Nicolo Polo), Herb Butterfield (Matthew Polo), Virginia Gregg (Vang Cha), Byron Kane (Vang Chu), Norman Field (Kublai Khan).

R184 "The Man From Yesterday" by Maurice Level. Chosen by: Singer Frank Sinatra. **Cast:** Joan Banks (Lorraine), Hans Conried (the Art Dealer), Eric Snowden (the Jeweler), Marie Windsor and Henry Blair.

R185* "A Tale of Two Cities" by Charles Dickens. Chosen by: Movie director Cecil B. DeMille. **Cast:** Ronald Colman (Sydney Carton), Joan Banks (Lucie Manette), Ben Wright (Charles Darnay), Norman Field (Dr. Manette), Janet Scott (Madame Defarge), Herb Butterfield (Jarvis Lorry), Barbara Eiler (Lisette, the Seamstress), Ed Max (Barsad), Byron Kane (Judge). See F43, R5, R6, R32, R102, D5, D9.
    Unavailable for listening. Transferred to Decca records with a few of the same cast and five minutes more script.

R186* "Aladdin's Lamp" by Lawrence and Lee from the Arabian Nights. Directed by True Boardman. Music from Rimsky-Korsakov's *Scheherezade*. Chosen by: Baseball star Rogers Hornsby. **Cast:** Virginia Gregg (Scheherezade, Aladdin's Mother), ? (Aladdin), Earle Ross (Majrabi), Ed Max (Genie, Fruit Vendor), Luis Van Rooten (Magician, Sultan Al Rashid, King of Bagdad), ? (Princess Bazrah Vadour), Marvin Miller (Visier), Ronald Colman (Scene setter).

R187 "The Suicide Club" by Robert Louis Stevenson. Chosen by: Humorist S.J. Perelman. **Cast:** Raymond Burr (Prince Florizel of Bohemia), William Conrad (A Colonel of Bohemia), Peter Leeds (Man with the Cream Tarts), Herb Butterfield (Suicide Club President), Rolfe Sedan (Bartholomew Malthus).

R188 "Inside a Kid's Head", an original radio play by Lawrence and Lee, previously broadcast on a different series. Chosen by: Actor Douglas Fairbanks, Jr. **Cast:** Jerry Farber (Richie Price, age 10), Hans Conried (Mr. Price), Irene Tedrow (Mrs. Price), Arthur Q. Bryan (J. B. Winkler), Edmund MacDonald (Mac), Peter Leeds (Tour Guide), Paul McVey and Diane Johnson (Tourists inside Richie's Head).
    Fantasy tour inside a young boy's brain as he flits in and out of various daydreams while coping with school, classmates and his parents. Lawrence and Lee perfectly capture what it's like to be a boy whose daydreams are his best friends. Splendid show.

R189 "A Doll's House" by Henrik Ibsen. Chosen by: Conductor Alfred Wallenstein. **Cast:** Janet Waldo (Nora Helmer), John Beal (Torvald Helmer), William Conrad (Krogstad).

R190 "The Crime of Sylvestre Bonnard" by Anatole France. Chosen by: Opera star Risé Stevens. **Cast:** Sam Jaffe (Sylvestre Bonnard), Luis Van Rooten (Gabry), Mary Lou Harrington (Jeanne), Rolfe Sedan (Mouch), Gloria Gordon (Madame Prefere).

R191 "Looking Backward" by Edward Bellamy. Chosen by: Poet-humorist Louis Untermeyer. **Cast:** John Beal (Julian West), Helen Craig (Edith, his fiancée and Edith Leet in the year 2000), Herb Butterfield (Dr. Leet), and other cast members not announced.

An insomniac (Beal) awakens in the year 2000 after being in a suspended animation hypnotic trance since 1887. Excerpt from a long novel makes predictions about a more cultured and civilized late 20th century, almost all of them wrong but touchingly optimistic. Passionately well-acted romance about striving for a better future.

R192 "The Telltale Heart" by Edgar Allan Poe. Chosen by: Actor Cary Grant. **Cast:** William Conrad (the Young Man), Herb Butterfield (the Old Man and the Homicide Detective).

R193 "The Brownings", an original play by Lawrence and Lee. Chosen by: Playwright Garson Kanin. **Cast:** Berry Kroeger (Robert Browning), Betty Lou Gerson (Elizabeth Barrett), William Conrad (Edward), Jeanne Bates (Miss Norris), Naomi Robison (Henrietta) and Moulton Barrett.

R194 "The Window" by Anton Chekhov. Chosen by: Comedian Eddie Cantor. **Cast:** Ludwig Donath (Fedor), Hans Conried (Ivan), William Conrad (Valentin), Betty Lou Gerson (Katia).

R195 "The Glass Eye" by John Kier Cross. Chosen by: Choreographer Jerome Robbins. **Cast:** Lurene Tuttle (Julia), Byron Kane (Max Collodi), Herb Butterfield, Dick Ryan, Wilms Herbert, Jerry Farber, Frank Lovejoy (Narrator).

Intense story of a 42-year-old woman's obsession with a ventriloquist. Tuttle is magnificent as the woman who ends up traumatically disillusioned, with only a glass eye as a keepsake. The chilling finale stands the demented ventriloquist premise on its head. A knockout production.

R196 "The Sunken City" by Frederick Gerstacker. Chosen by: Actress Jane Cowl. **Cast:** Donald Buka (Arnold), Bernice Barrett (Gerta), Herb Butterfield, Arthur Q. Bryan, Byron Kane.

R197 "The Aspern Papers" by Henry James. Chosen by: Actress Joan Fontaine. **Cast:** Cathy Lewis (Tina), Lurene Tuttle (Juliana), Jeff Chandler (the Man), Irene Tedrow (Mrs. Prest.)

R198[*] "The Man Who Married a Dumb Wife" by Anatole France. Chosen by: Actress Elizabeth Bergner. **Cast:** Ronald Colman (Judge Botal), Bea Benadaret (Katherine), Hans Conried (Adam Fumée), Luis Van Rooten (the Doctor), Hugh Thomas (Giles).

Splendid change of pace for Colman in this charming farce about a corrupt judge whose beautiful wife is mute. When she is cured with a pill, she makes him so miserable with her incessant talking, he wants to be deaf. Colman is delightful in a role showing his comic versatility, with a witty script by Lawrence and Lee.

R199 "The Young Years" by Lawrence and Lee from historical sources. Chosen by: Actress

Ethel Barrymore. **Cast:** Jimmy Lydon (Tom), William Johnstone (George Washington), William Conrad (Cresswell), Kirk Ragan (Hobe), Mary Lou Harrington (Patsy Custis).

Compelling tale of George Washington as a patriotic man of unassailable integrity, focusing on the bitter winter at Valley Forge.

R200 "Green Mansions" by W.H. Hudson. Chosen by: Singer Dinah Shore. **Cast:** Berry Kroeger (Abel), Janet Waldo (Rima), Herb Butterfield (Nuflo), Norman Field (Runi), and special vocal effects by Loulie-Jean Norman.

Haunting tale of a political fugitive (Kroeger) who falls in love with an ethereal beauty named Rima, but who loses her to an insensitive real world. Kroeger is unexpectedly lyrical in a role you would expect Colman to play, which is clearly why he was cast against type. Kroeger's voice has a different rhapsodic ring, drawing the listener into Hudson's language and metaphoric subtleties. Ethereal performance by Waldo is her best in the series. An exquisite show.

R201* "The Vendetta" by Guy de Maupassant. Chosen by: Trumpet player/band leader Harry James. **Cast:** Gloria Gordon (Widow Savareni), Edmund MacDonald (Nicholas Ravalati), Everett Sloane (Town Butcher), Ronald Colman (Narrator).

The Widow Savareni in the town of Bonifacio avenges the murder of her son, Antoine, by the merchant Ravalati by having her vicious dog, Semilanti, tear Ravalati to pieces. It isn't long before the townspeople, who hated Ravalati, have forgotten him. Engrossingly grim tale.

R202* "The Son's Veto" by Thomas Hardy. Chosen by: Actor Fred MacMurray. **Cast:** Edna Best (Sophy), Tom Collins (Rev. Twicott), William Conrad (Sam Hobson), William Roy (Randolph, the Son), Ronald Colman (Narrator).

R203 "Rhythm" by Ring Lardner. Chosen by: Cartoonist Rube Goldberg. **Cast:** Johnny Mercer (Harry Hart), Alan Reed (Benny), Joseph Kearns (Spencer Deal).

Songwriter Mercer plays a songwriter whose forté is jazzy pop songs taken from the classics. He aspires to more "serious" music when he has a hit song. In the end, he reverts to what he does best, turning out Tin Pan Alley hits with his partner. Delightful comedy about musical pretensions on the theme of "Don't try to be something you're not."

R204* "The Bet" by Anton Chekhov. Chosen by: Actor Charles Boyer. Theremin music: Dr. Samuel Hoffman. **Cast:** John Beal (Semyon), William Conrad (Stokovich), Rye Billsbury, Ronald Colman (Narrator).

A young man (Beal) rashly bets a rich businessman (Conrad) that he can stay put in a small house for 20 years without leaving once in return for a large sum of money. A good and well-played tale on the theme of material vs. spiritual wealth that would have been better if Beal hadn't overacted in a few scenes and without the theremin music, which adds an annoyingly out-of-place surreal touch.

R205 "The Valiant" by Robert Middlemas and Halworthy Hall. Chosen by: Comedian Bob Hope. **Cast:** Frank Lovejoy (James Dyke/Joseph Paris), Janet Waldo (Josephine Paris), William Conrad (Warden Holt), Norman Field (Father Daley).

As a convict (Lovejoy) awaits execution, a woman claiming to be his sister (Waldo) pays a last visit. Heart-rending self-sacrifice vignette with a typically tough-but-sensitive performance by Lovejoy and a poignant one by Waldo.

R206 "The Maniac" by Maurice Level. Chosen by: Singer-actor Al Jolson. **Cast:** John Huston (the Maniac), Jeff Corey (the Cyclist), William Conrad, Tom McKee, Anne Whitfield and Jerry Farber.
     Electrifyingly offbeat horror tale of a self-possessed psychotic seeking to live out a recurring nightmare in real life. Huston's matter-of-fact performance as the Maniac makes the story and its gruesome finale all the more absorbingly weird. Creative use of sound effects.

R207 "Youth" by Joseph Conrad. Chosen by: Journalist-critic H.L. Mencken. **Cast:** William Conrad (Marlow), Norman Field (Captain Beard), Janet Scott (Mrs. Beard), Luis Van Rooten (Matheson), Ted von Eltz (Sir Robert).
     A 62-year-old seaman (Conrad) recalls his early years at sea. Passionately well-done production with good sound effects. Major drawback: Conrad sounds the same at 20 and 62.

R208 "The Blue Danube", an original play by Lawrence and Lee based on the life and works of Johann Strauss. Chosen by: Singer-actress Jeanette MacDonald. **Cast:** Berry Kroeger (Johann Strauss the Elder), Bob Cole (Johann Strauss the Younger), Virginia Gregg (Mrs. Strauss), David Ellis, Earle Ross and Rye Billsbury.

R209 "The Jest of Hahalaba" by Lord Dunsany. Chosen by: Movie director Frank Capra: **Cast:** Joseph Kearns (Sir Arthur), Herb Butterfield (the Alchemist), Raymond Burr (Hahalaba), Eric Snowden (Snags, the Butler).
     A greedy British businessman (Kearns) uses black magic to conjure a spirit to grant him a birthday wish: all of the next year's London Times so he can make a fortune on stocks, headlines and the Derby. Gripping blackly comic fantasy that keeps you wondering what's next. Fine acting by all, but Burr is surprisingly devilish as the laughing demon.

R210 "A Piece of String" by Guy de Maupassant. Chosen by: Actor Jean Hersholt. **Cast:** Herb Butterfield (Mr. Hauchecorne) John Beal (Narrator), Jeanne Bates (Seraphine), David Ellis (Leveque) Earle Ross (Malandain), Rolfe Sedan (the Mayor), Byron Kane (the Town Crier).

R211* "The Country of the Blind" by H.G. Wells. See R126.

R212 "Work of Art" by Anton Chekhov. Chosen by: Opera star Dorothy Kirsten. **Cast:** Berry Kroeger, Jeff Corey, Lurene Tuttle, William Conrad, Hans Conried, Noreen Gamill and Henry Blair.

R213 "All My Children", an original play by Lawrence and Lee. Chosen by: Car maker Henry Ford II. **Cast:** Helen Craig (Jane Adams), Adrienne Marden, Harry Bartel, Anne Whitfield, Henry Blair, Tommy Bernard and Naomi Robison.

R214 "The Assignation" by Edgar Allan Poe. Chosen by: Radio pioneer Dr. Lee De Forest. **Cast:** William Conrad (Poe), Raymond Burr (the Man in Black), Jeanne Bates (the Marquesa), Gloria Gordon (the Duena), Bill Shirley (the Gondolier).

R215 "Long Ago", adapted from *Marjorie Daw* by Thomas Bailey Aldrich. Chosen by:

Actor-dancer Gene Kelly. **Cast:** John Beal (Jack), Richard Denning (Ned), Margaret Brayton, Sammi Hill, Will Wright and Bill Shirley.

R216* "The Time Machine" by H. G. Wells. Chosen by: Bandleader Kay Kyser. **Cast:** William Johnstone (the Time Traveler), Thomas Freebairn-Smith, Naomi Robison, Byron Kane and Ronald Colman (Narrator).

Dull abridgement of Wells's time travel fantasy, with pallid narration. The classic 1960 movie stars Rod Taylor.

R217 "The Monkey's Paw" by W.W. Jacobs. Chosen by: Playwright Oscar Hammerstein II. **Cast:** Jeanette Nolan (Mrs. White), Norman Field (Mr. White), William Conrad (Sgt. Major Norris), Gene Reynolds (Herbert), Herb Butterfield (the Solicitor).

R218 "The Copper Penny" by Arthur Wister Mays. Chosen by: Movie director Michael Curtiz. **Cast:** Jack Webb (the Reporter), Herb Butterfield (Ben Carter), Ed Begley, David Wolfe, Shelby Newhouse, Tom McKee and Jerry Farber.

R219 "Roll Call of the Reef" by Sir A.T. Quiller-Couch. Chosen by: Author MacKinlay Kantor. **Cast:** Ed Begley (the Quarryman), Billy Roy (Drummer Boy), Ed Max, Irene Tedrow, Byron Kane and Luis Van Rooten.

R220 "The Gambler" by Fyodor Dostoevsky. Chosen by: Broadway producer-director George Abbott. **Cast:** Jeanette Nolan (Granny), Tony Barrett (Alexy), Janet Waldo (Polina), Thomas Freebairn-Smith, Herb Butterfield and Peter Leeds.

R221 "Francesca da Rimini", an original play by Lawrence and Lee. Chosen by: Actor Dana Andrews. **Cast:** Berry Kroeger (Gianciotto), Betty Lou Gerson (Francesca), David Ellis (Paolo), Gloria Gordon (Bianca), Raymond Burr (the Cardinal). Music based on themes from Tchaikovsky.

R222 "The Judgment of Paris" by Leonard Merrick. Chosen by: Actress Cornelia Otis Skinner. **Cast:** Alan Reed (Robichon), Hans Conried (Quinquart), Mary Ship (Suzanne), Luis Van Rooten and Wilms Herbert (Jacques Roux).

Two ham actors (Reed and Conried) vie to marry the same woman (Ship), so she challenges them to an acting contest, letting the Parisian public decide who is the better thespian. Hilarious anecdote about the love-hate friendships between actors with a comic twist ending.

R223 "The Flying Dutchman" by Lawrence and Lee based on legend. Chosen by: Actress Loretta Young. **Cast:** Raymond Burr (the Flying Dutchman), Virginia Gregg, Sam Edwards and Tom McKee.

R224* "Around the World in 80 Days" by Jules Verne. Chosen by: Aviator Eddie Rickenbacker. Announcer: Joseph Kearns. **Cast:** Ronald Colman (Phileas Fogg), Joseph Kearns (Passepartout, Reform Club Member), Lurene Tuttle (Princess Aouda), Ramsay Hill (Detective Fix), Ben Wright (Reform Club member, Train Engineer). See F68, R378.

Briskly enthusiastic Colman performance in contrast to his stiff-upper-lip one for the *Hallmark* version, which is actually more in keeping with Fogg's character.

R225 "The Dynamiter" by Robert Louis Stevenson. Chosen by: Comedian Jack Benny. **Cast:** Janet Waldo (Clara), William Conrad (Zero), Jeff Chandler (Paul).

R226 "The Magic Shop" by H.G. Wells. Chosen by: Actress Joan Leslie. **Cast:** Joan Banks (Amelia Denning), Paul Dubov (Roger Denning), Jeffrey Silver (Jip Denning), Hans Conried (Proprietor of the Genuine Magic Shop), Peter Leeds (Dr. Curtis).

The real magic of this show is Hans Conried, whose unfailing vocal sorcery happily steals an otherwise trite domestic update of the Wells original.

R227 "Enoch Soames" by Sir Max Beerbohm. Chosen by: Author-screenwriter Donald Ogden Stewart. **Cast:** Hans Conried (Enoch Soames), Berry Kroeger (Max Beerbohm), Paul Frees (the Devil), Herb Butterfield (Rothenstein).

R228 "How Much Land Does a Man Need?" by Leo Tolstoy. Chosen by: Scientist Albert Einstein. **Cast:** John Beal (Pahom), Earl Lee (the Father), Gloria Gordon (the Mother), Paul Frees (Bashkier chief), Byron Kane and Janet Scott.

R229 "When the Door Opened" by Sarah Grand. Chosen by: Conductor André Kostelanetz. **Cast:** Mercedes McCambridge, Raymond Burr, Miriam Wolfe, Byron Kane and Thomas Freebairn-Smith.

R230 "Change of Face" by Leonard Merrick. Chosen by: Opera star Lily Pons. **Cast:** Bea Benadaret (Madame de Val Fleury), Nina Klowden (Berthe), Joseph Kearns (the Doctor), Whitfield Conner, Lucille Meredith and Robert Cole.

R231 "The Young Man Who Stroked Cats" by Morley Roberts. Chosen by: Actress Dorothy Lamour. **Cast:** Lon McCallister (Tom), Carol Smith (the Girl), Ruth Perrott (the Mother), Berry Kroeger (Narrator).

R232* "The Turn of the Screw" by Henry James. Chosen by: Ventriloquist Edgar Bergen. **Cast:** Edna Best (Miss D, the Governess), Tom Collins (Mr. Douglas), Ronald Colman (Narrator), and others not announced. Dull production.

R233 "The Man Who Corrupted Hadleyburg" by Mark Twain. Chosen by: Singer Dennis Day. **Cast:** Frank Lovejoy (The Man), Norman Field (Edward Richards, Banker), Virginia Gregg (Mrs. Richards), Ed Begley (Newspaper publisher Cox, Lawyer Wilson), Byron Kane (Rev. Burgess), Lou Krugman (Mr. Bilson).

Lovejoy is ideally cast as a successful but cynical man who shows up the residents of Hadleyburg for the greedy hypocrites they really are. Sardonically witty moral anecdote.

R234* "Pacific Crossing" by E.W. Hornung. Chosen by: Bandleader Paul Whiteman. **Cast:** William Conrad (Captain Breen and Porter), Stanley Waxman (Charles Callatin), Janet Waldo (Marie Callatin), Ronald Colman (Narrator).

An embezzler and his wife murder the employer they've stolen from while on a train trip, then flee to Australia from Canada by cargo ship. In the end, they are tripped up by their respective guilty consciences. Well-done tale on the theme of crime and conscience.

R235* "The Substitute" by François Corpais. Chosen by: Actor James Mason. **Cast:**

William Johnstone (Charles François Le Turk), Lurene Tuttle (Christine), Jerry Farber (Charles as a boy/Jean François Le Turk, his son), Edmund MacDonald (Magistrate), Ronald Colman (Narrator).

A Frenchman (Johnstone) substitutes himself at trial for a petty theft committed by his son so that his child will not be twisted by the corrupt penal system as he was. Heart-rending tale about the ways in which a justice system can promote the very injustices it is supposed to prevent. Colman's even-tempered narration allows the listener to come to his own angry conclusion.

R236 "Billy the Kid" by Lawrence and Lee from historical sources. Chosen by: Actor Mickey Rooney. **Cast:** Leo Penn (Billy the Kid), William Conrad (Pat Garrett), Janet Scott, Raymond Burr, Herb Butterfield and Byron Kane.

R237* "The Gift of Laughter" by Lawrence and Lee from theatrical history. Chosen by: Pianist Arthur Rubinstein. **Cast:** Ronald Colman (Charles Deburau), Betty Lou Gerson (Angelique), Herb Butterfield (the Doctor), Tom McKee (the Father), Henry Blair (Charles the Boy), Rolland Morris (Charles the Young Man).

For a tragi-comic change of pace, Colman plays the French mime Deburau, whose tragedy was being able to make other men laugh while his son could not because he didn't discipline his son as his father had with him. Hans Conried played the part on the live KFI version. The Colman version was not available to hear. This is the same Deburau on which the classic 1945 French movie *Children of Paradise* is based.

R238 "Passing of the Third Floor Back" by Jerome K. Jerome. Chosen by: Radio comedians Jim and Marian Jordan, better known as Fibber McGee and Molly. **Cast:** Edna Best (Mrs. Pennycherry), John Beal (the Stranger), Helen Craig (Vivian), Janet Waldo (Stasia), Lurene Tuttle (Mrs. Tompkins), William Conrad (Major Tompkins), Jeanette Nolan (Miss Kite), Gloria Gordon (Mrs. De Hooley), Berry Kroeger (Narrator).

Allegory of a Christ-like stranger (Beal) who changes the lives of the tenants at a boardinghouse where he lives for a short while. Uplifting drama about love and charity.

R239 "Lifeline", from the story "A.V. Laider" by Max Beerbohm. Chosen by: Actor John Garfield. **Cast:** Raymond Burr (Max Beerbohm), Hans Conried (A.V. Laider) and others not announced.

Palmist Laider tells Beerbohm a hair-raising tale of the time he read the palms of a group of socialites during a train trip, but could not bring himself to tell them that their lifelines would all end in death by accident at the end of the trip. Engrossingly acted deadpan con job, climaxing with Conried's fever-pitched histrionics.

R240* "The Magnificent Lie" by Lawrence and Lee from historical sources. Chosen by: Actor Charles Laughton. **Cast:** William Conrad (Galileo Galilei, "Il Tescano"), Raymond Burr (Medici Prince), Ronald Colman (Narrator).

Excellent production about the life and tragedy of Galileo, who challenged scientific dogma about the Earth in relation to the sun and the shape of our planet, and who paid for his "heresy" through forced public recantation in old age. Conrad is magnificent as a visionary who saw the world as it literally was and paid for his "crime". Laughton chose this story because Galileo was one of his heroes. In the 1950s, he tried to stage a production of Bertolt Brecht's play about him.

R241* "The Brushwood Boy" by Rudyard Kipling. Chosen by: Actor Humphrey Bogart. **Cast:** Elliott Reid (George Carter), Virginia Weidler (Mary Lacey/Annie Ann Louise), Gloria Gordon (Nurse Harper), Tommy Bernard (Young George), Ronald Colman (Narrator).

A young man (Reid) has a recurring dream from childhood on about tending to a comforting brushwood fire with the aid of a pretty young girl named Annie Ann Louise. When he grows up, he finally meets the woman (Weidler) who has shared the dream and they become soulmates. Movingly ethereal romance that reveals the romantic side of Bogart for choosing it.

R242* "In the Time of the Terror" by Honoré de Balzac. Chosen by: Boxer Jack Dempsey. **Cast:** Ed Max (Executioner), William Johnstone (Priest), Bea Benadaret (Sister Agatha), Ronald Colman (Narrator), Byron Kane and Bill Nugent.

In 1793 Paris, two nuns and a priest gather in secret to hold a funeral service for their beheaded king at the behest of a stranger. This ritual is repeated once a year until 1795, when the reign of terror ends and the stranger's identity is revealed. Slow but movingly ironic drama aided by Colman's even-tempered narration.

R243 "The Doll in the Pink Silk Dress" by Leonard Merrick. Chosen by: Radio personality Art Linkletter. **Cast:** Betty Lou Gerson (Jeanne Laronne), Hal March (Paul de Varenne), Norman Field (Secretary), Will Wright and Shepard Menken.

An amateur actress (Gerson) aspires to stage stardom by her second role, aided by a gifted young playwright (March). Terrific show on a triple theme: Career vs. marriage, love vs. the theater, and happiness vs. fame.

R244* "The Little Minister" by Sir James M. Barrie. Chosen by: Actor James Stewart. **Cast:** Hurd Hatfield (Gavin Dischart, the Little Minister), Janet Waldo (Babbie, Gypsy woman), Ed Begley (Thomas Waymond), Norman Field (Ogilvy, the Schoolmaster), Gloria Gordon (Margaret), Luis Van Rooten (Thomas), Byron Kane (the Captain), Ronald Colman (Narrator).

Splendidly narrated, affecting story about the love between a short man who is a minister and a gypsy woman in the bigoted town of Thrums.

R245* "A Christmas Carol" by Charles Dickens. Chosen as The World's Favorite Christmas Story. Announcer: Joseph Kearns. **Cast:** Ronald Colman (Ebenezer Scrooge), Eric Snowden (Bob Cratchit), Jimmy Lydon (Fred the Nephew), Arthur Q. Bryan (Mr. Portley), Earl Lee (Marley), John Beal (Ghost of Christmas Past), Lurene Tuttle (Belle the Sweetheart, Mrs. Cratchit), Cyrus Kendall (Ghost of Christmas Present), Henry Blair (Tiny Tim), Joe Kearns (Ghost of Christmas Future), Jerry Farber (Boy in the Street). With the Robert Mitchell Boy Choir. See R403.

Fairly good production with Colman repeating his Scrooge performance from the Decca record (D1), but with a slightly sharper edge. The one other difference is that the Men in the Street bit was cut for time. This was the only *Favorite Story* episode with two specific original airdates: Christmas Eve and Christmas Day 1949, depending on the station airing it.

Movies of this story are too numerous too list. The best of them is the 1951 British version starring Alastair Sim as Scrooge. The best animated version is the 1962 NBC musical special *Mr. Magoo's Christmas Carol.*

R246 SEALTEST VARIETY THEATER
October 7, 1948. Host: Dorothy Lamour. Sponsor: Sealtest Inc. Guest appearance. NBC. 30 minutes.

R247 ANACIN HOLLYWOOD STAR THEATER
October 9, 1948. "Before I Die." Writer and story details unavailable. Host: Ronald Colman, presenting newcomer Colleen Townsend. NBC. 30 minutes. See B356.

R248 JACK BENNY
October 24, 1948. "Dinner with the Colmans." Ronnie and Benita are desperate to get out of their dinner date with Jack. Mel Blanc plays Polly the parrot and a grocery delivery man. Last NBC show with the Colmans. 30 minutes.

R249 SCREEN GUILD PLAYERS
December 9, 1948. "Michael and Mary," from the play by A.A. Milne. NBC. 30 minutes.
    Cast: Ronald Colman (Michael Rowe), Edna Best (Mary Rowe). Other cast names not available.

R250 BURNS AND ALLEN
December 16, 1948. CBS. 30 minutes.
    Ronnie and Benita are dinner guests of George and Gracie, who are staying at Jack Benny's house while Jack is out of town.

R251 JACK BENNY SHOW PROMOTIONAL SPOT
December 25-31, 1948. The Colmans recorded a comic 15-second skit to tell listeners that as of January 2, 1949, Jack Benny would be heard on CBS on Sunday nights.

R252 FORD THEATER
January 7, 1949. "The Talk of the Town," adapted by David Shaw from the Sidney Buchman/Irwin Shaw screenplay. Producer/Director/Host: Fletcher Markle. Music: Cy Feuer. Sponsor: Ford Motor Co. CBS. 60 minutes. See F53, R47, R106, R394.
    Cast: Ronald Colman (Michael Lightcap), Jean Arthur (Nora Shelley), Elliott Lewis (Leopold Dilg), Myron McCormick (Sam Yates), Mercedes McCambridge (Regina), Lou Merrill (Senator Boyd), Miriam Wolfe (Mrs. Shelley), Hans Conried, Joseph Granby and Byron Kane.
    The physical attraction between Lightcap and Shelley is emphasized (with a new scene set at a lake), while Dilg's role is diminished so that the story is more romantic comedy than social comedy. The movie is both.

R253 JACK BENNY
January 16, 1949. "Ronald Colman Dreams He is Jack Benny." Ronnie and Jack dream they have switched places, though Colman is better at mimicking Benny than vice versa. Ronnie as Jack does a Lucky Strike commercial as Shakespeare might have written it. First Colman show on CBS. 30 minutes.

R254 THE NBC THEATER PRESENTS THE SCREEN DIRECTORS GUILD
February 20, 1949. "The Prisoner of Zenda," from the Selznick movie of the Anthony Hope

novel. Introduced by the movie's director, John Cromwell. 30 minutes. See F47, R12.

Cast: Ronald Colman (Rudolf Rassendyll), Benita Hume (Princess Flavia), Thomas Freebairn-Smith (Col. Zapt), Lou Krugman (Black Michael), Carl Harbaugh (Rupert of Hentzau), John Dehner (King Rudolf).

Mostly mechanical abridgement in which Rassendyll kills Hentzau. Midway into its first season, the series' title was changed to *Screen Director's Playhouse*.

R255 JACK BENNY
March 6, 1949. "At the Races." Jack annoys Ronnie and Benita at Santa Anita Race Track. CBS. 30 minutes. See R381.

R256 THE 21ST ANNUAL ACADEMY AWARDS
March 24, 1949. MC: Robert Montgomery. ABC. 90 minutes. See F60.

Since he had won the previous year's Oscar for Best Actor, Colman was called upon to present this year's award for Best Actress. It was Jane Wyman for *Johnny Belinda*.

R257 SUSPENSE
April 7, 1949. "Noose of Coincidence," an original play by William Fifield. Adapted by Herb Meadow. Producer/Director: Anton M. Leader. Music: Lucien Morawek (Composer), Lud Gluskin (Conductor). Announcer: Paul Frees. Pitchman: Harlow Wilcox. Sponsor: Electric Auto-Lite. CBS. 30 minutes.

Cast: Ronald Colman (Christopher Swan), Hans Conried (Christopher Swan), Bea Benadaret (Margaret), ? (Anne Stevens), Ben Wright (Constable Smithers).

A London bookseller (Colman) has his marriage and death foretold by a man with the same name as his, only the other man is not what he seems. Very good romantic suspense story with a grisly twist ending and Conried outacting Colman for style and vigor.

R258 PHILIP MORRIS PLAYHOUSE
April 22, 1949. "August Heat," adapted by Mel Dinelli from the W.F. Harvey story. Producer/Director: William Spier. CBS. 30 minutes. See R89 for story details. Name of second actor is unavailable.

R259 ANACIN HOLLYWOOD STAR THEATER
August 27, 1949. "Sacrificial Lamb," an original play by Walter Brown Newman. Host: Ronald Colman. NBC. 30 minutes.

Cast: Jeanne Bates (Hallie Hughes), William Johnstone (Oliver Shore), Janet Scott (Mother Shore), Paul McVey (Fireman).

Seemingly affluent Oliver Shore hires out-of-work actress Hallie Hughes to impersonate his dead sister, ostensibly to please his blind mother, but it's really a scheme to murder Hughes for insurance money. Chillingly well-done story, but with a reference by Shore to having done it before, which would surely tip off the insurance company.

Curiously, Bates is presented by Colman as a newcomer, though she makes it clear in their after-show banter that she is a widely experienced performer.

R260 FAMILY HOUR OF STARS
October 9, 1949. "Berkeley Square" by Jean Holloway from the John L. Balderston play based on the novel **The Sense of the Past** by Henry James. Producer: Murray Bolen. Music director: Carmen Dragon. Announcer: Frank Goss. Sponsor: Prudential Life Insurance. Other cast names unavailable. CBS. 30 minutes. See R56, R84, B132.

R261 COMMUNITY CHEST DRIVE SHOW
October 17, 1949. Host: Bob Hope. Colman is one of several guest stars. NBC. 30 minutes.

R262 FAMILY HOUR OF STARS
November 6, 1949. "Quality Street," adapted by Charles Tazewell from the novel by Sir James M. Barrie. Cast list unavailable. CBS. 30 minutes. See R74.

R263 JACK BENNY
November 13, 1949. "Studio Visit." When Jack visits the set of *Champagne for Caesar*, he makes a nuisance of himself with Ronnie and director Richard Whorf as the final scene is being shot. CBS. 30 minutes. See F62.

R264 LOS ANGELES SALUTES THE NATION
December 17, 1949. KFI Hollywood for NBC. 30 minutes.
    Christmas pageant. Colman narrates a musical segment.

R265 FAMILY HOUR OF STARS
December 25, 1949. "The Small One," an original radio play by Charles Tazewell. CBS. 30 minutes.
    Colman narrates the story of the donkey that carried Joseph and Mary to Bethlehem. Other credits and cast names unavailable.

THE HALLS OF IVY (NBC, January 6, 1950 to June 25, 1952, 108 original episodes, two restaged repeats.) See R389, B103, B237, B245, B296, B357, B413.
    Creator: Don Quinn. Producers: Archie Scott for NBC, Sam Fuller for Young & Rubicam, ad agency for the sponsor (the latter for first two weeks of first season), Charles Henry for Y&R (third week on). Director: Nat Wolff (first two seasons, except for R324, Charles Henry), Milton Merlin (third season). Main writers: Don Quinn, Barbara and Milton Merlin, Walter Brown Newman, David Robison, Arthur Ross. Announcer/Scene setter: Ken Carpenter (except for R280, Hy Averback). Music: Composed and conducted by Henry Russell. Chorus: Thurl Ravenscroft Quartet (1-23-52 on). Theme song: "The Halls of Ivy" by Henry Russell (Music) and Vick Knight (Lyrics). Sound effects: Wayne Kenworthy. Sponsor: Joseph Schlitz Brewing Company of Milwaukee, Wisconsin. WNBC New York for NBC, but originating in Hollywood. 30 minutes.
    Broadcast live the first season except for R292-93, live and tape the second season, all tape the third.
    Broadcast days and times: First season: Friday at 8 EST, 8:30 PST till May 5, 1950. Then Wednesday at 8 EST, 6 PST starting May 10, 1950.
    Second season: Wednesday at 8 EST, 6:30 PST.
    Third season: Wednesday at 8 EST, 7 PST. Time change to 6:30 PST starting February 6, 1952.
    Cast: Ronald Colman (Dr. William Todhunter Hall, called Toddy by his wife), Benita Colman (Victoria Cromwell Hall), Herb Butterfield (Clarence Wellman, Ivy alumnus and Chairman, Ivy Board of Governors), Willard Waterman (John Merriweather, member Ivy Board of Governors, first season only), Gale Gordon (John or Charles Merriweather, one episode first season, semi-regular last two seasons), Arthur Q. Bryan (Prof. Joseph Warren, occasional), Alan Reed (Prof. Heaslip, occasional), Gloria Gordon (Penny, the cockney maid, 11 of first 13 episodes), Elizabeth Patterson (Louisa Tate, the rural-sounding maid, 7 episodes third season).

Notes: I was unable to obtain copies of 29 shows from the second and third seasons, so I had to get information on 11 of them from copies of Schlitz index cards provided by LC librarian Edwin Matthias. Program Information Unavailable is cited for missing shows. A question mark is used for actors I could not identify from Voice of America copies, on most of which credits are deleted.

Episodes for which I learned the script title (though titles were never announced) are marked by *. Other titles are mine from the plots. Regulars for each episode are cited by name only, not character played. Guests are cited by full name and character played. For most episodes, players are listed in order of appearance.

Theme Song Lyrics

Oh, we love the halls of Ivy/that surround us here today/and we will not forget/though we be far, far away.

To the hallowed halls of Ivy/every voice will bid farewell/and shimmer off in twilight/like the old vesper bell.

One day our hearts will fall/the footsteps of us all/will echo down the hall and disappear.

But as we sadly start/our journeys far apart/a part of every heart will linger here/in the sacred halls of Ivy/where we've lived and learned to know/that through the years we'll see you/in the sweet afterglow.

After 15 years of writing for his first series creation, *Fibber McGee & Molly* (begun in 1934), Don Quinn felt unfulfilled. He wanted to write a series for which he would be remembered, that had substance as well as comedy. So, he took the template of *Fibber McGee* and came up with *The Halls of Ivy*. The formats of the two shows are similar except that *Ivy* is sophisticated, with a warmly erudite, witty couple at its center.

Quinn's audition script, "Reappointment," was recorded on June 23, 1949, with Gale Gordon and Edna Best as Dr. and Mrs. Hall. Good script, but the audition misfired because the stars were miscast and had no chemistry. Gordon, especially, was out of place playing a charmingly learned college president since he was best known for playing pompous bureaucrats on *Fibber McGee, Our Miss Brooks, My Favorite Husband* and other shows.

But, the audition's misfire was not what caused it to be recast. Best took an offer to perform on Broadway in *The Browning Version*, which subsequently flopped. Furthermore, *Ivy* writer the late Walter Brown Newman told me, the heads of Young & Rubicam, ad agency for the sponsor, Schlitz Beer, wanted a couple with proven star appeal. So that axed Gordon, who was well known on radio but did not have star quality. That's where Ronnie came in. He had been a movie star for more than 25 years and he and his wife, Benita, were a comedy smash on the Jack Benny show. So, Nat Wolff, who produced and directed the audition, suggested his friends and clients. They were approached and signed.

Once it caught on in the first season, *Ivy* was a hit with the mass audience for the comfortable warmth of the Colmans, for the way they unabashedly sparked and played off each other with literate and affectionate love. Millions tuned in every week to spend time with the Colmans for their heart, humor and humanity. This enabled the show to deal with hard topics like racism, sexism, ageism, destructive gossip, freedom of speech, political blackmail, the value of a rounded education, students following their dreams instead of their parents' footsteps, etc. No other show on radio at the time, drama or comedy, went near these subjects.

Another part of the show's appeal was its structure: An opening four to five minutes of witty repartée between the Halls, the problem of the week, romantic flashback to Toddy courting Vicky in England to fill in the background of their relationship, resolution of problem.

After 17 episodes, the Halls' background had been established, so the flashbacks were dropped in favor of more plotting; Newman left after 13 shows because he was offered a fortune to write a screenplay; and other writers were hired, including and especially Barbara and Milton Merlin, who had worked with Ronnie on *Everything for the Boys*. The Merlins leavened Hall's stuffy verbosity (for all his charm, Toddy in the first season is often annoyingly pedantic) by inserting comic routines, patter and banter that played with the English language, making the show in general funnier and more affectingly humane.

Just as important, the Korean War flavored some scripts and became the backdrop for others, usually written by Don Quinn.

For his part, Quinn had a penchant for sermonizing messages in shows like "The Chinese Student" (R272), "Minister's Son" (R344) and "Student Vandalism and the Draft" (R323, 327). But he also wrote scripts that let the messages speak for themselves as movingly provocative drama; "The Leslie Hoff Painting" (R296) and "Medal of Honor" (R353) are two of these. Indeed, *The Halls of Ivy* was often as much drama as sitcom, which is why it won awards for drama.

Whether being comic or serious, all the writers seem to have had the most fun dreaming up ways for Toddy to get the upper hand of Clarence Wellman, the pompous and reactionary Chairman of Ivy's Board of Governors, who is obsessed with endowment money and his own overblown sense of personal and scholastic dignity. Herb Butterfield played Wellman to such flustered comic perfection as the resident straw man villain that he seemed to *be* the character. He naturally repeated the role for the TV version.

For his part, Colman was so at ease with the role of Dr. Hall that he wrote two scripts: "The Goya Bequest" (R313) and "Halloween" (R342).

Everyone associated with the show recalls it as one big happy crew. Charles Henry, Willard Waterman, Les Tremayne, Gladys Holland and others I have interviewed all spoke glowingly of the Colmans as being a joy to work with. Waterman especially enjoyed the contrast between his rambunctious Merriweather and the more sedate Toddy. And everyone fell in love with Benita for her vivacious humor and sparkle.

(Waterman left the show after one season to replace Hal Peary as *The Great Gildersleeve*. In preparation for this, Merriweather's twin brother, Charles (Gale Gordon), was introduced on May 10, 1950 (R284) so that there would always be a Merriweather to banter with Toddy. While Gordon did a good, droll job with the part, I much prefer Waterman's genially plainspoken earthiness.)

Ivy was also an influential show, earning nine awards for that influence, including one for Benita (R329). It encouraged learning and scholastic achievement for their own sake; it boosted the image of the American college system, making millions of students want to go to a college like Ivy, with a president like Ronald Colman; and it resolved complex human problems in a humane manner. It also had college presidents vainly trying to emulate Colman without the advantage of his writers. In reality, college presidents are administrators who rarely, if ever, meet students, let alone handle their personal problems. In that regard, *Ivy* took wholesale dramatic license, to its audience's delight.

Heard today, *The Halls of Ivy* remains for the most part a unique gem in American radio's golden age. Its faults are that it is often overly smitten with *Bartlett's Familiar Quotations*, it sometimes takes half the show to get to the story, it is sometimes preachy and pretentious, and it is often more mildly amusing than hilarious. Yet it has a world of class and elegance unlike any other series, presuming the education and intelligence of its audience. For most episodes, *Ivy* makes listeners feel good, smart and ennobled for spending time with it.

Though the Colmans wanted to continue *Ivy* for a fourth season, it ended after three. For all the beer sold, prestige accrued and awards won, Schlitz chose a wholesale move into television sponsorship, yet they didn't take *Ivy* with them. Nor did the Colmans seek a new sponsor. When *Ivy* did make the switch to television in 1954, with new sponsors, the charm and warmth of the radio version were lost in the transition.

R266* January 6, 1950. "Reappointment" by Don Quinn. **Cast:** Herbert Rawlinson (Member, Board of Governors), Herb Butterfield, Willard Waterman, Lee Millar ("Pushy" Morgan, a student), Gloria Gordon. Song: "The Sidewalks of New York." See TV6.

Toddy anxiously awaits news of his reappointment to a second term as Ivy's President. Meanwhile, Vicky unknowingly befriends Merriweather's nephew, "Pushy" Morgan, teaching him a dancing routine for the Junior Follies. Charmingly warm and literate, if slight, premiere that sets the tone for the series.

Review: Rose, *Weekly Variety*, January 13: "'Ivy' is tailored to the Colman Mr. & Mrs. touch; so much so that it's possible to imagine that Quinn conceived the whole idea with the Colmans in mind...show permits for the kind of restrained situation comedy that's strictly geared to the Colman manner...The comedy was never forced or dragged in, but stemmed, in its own dignified way, out of the situations themselves."

R267 January 13, 1950. "Student Editorial" by Walter Brown Newman. **Cast:** Gloria Gordon, Rolland Morris (Jared Buckley), Herb Butterfield.

Enraged over an Ivy Bulletin article criticizing the Board of Governors, Wellman demands the expulsion of the Bulletin's editor, Jared Buckley. In this episode, Wellman is from the Ivy class of 1907. See R357 for a different year.

R268 January 20, 1950. "Gangster's Son" by Don Quinn. **Cast:** Gloria Gordon, William Conrad (Mike Mallotte), Gil Stratton, Jr. (Eddie Gray), Ted Osborne (Irish New York cop), Willard Waterman, Herb Butterfield. See TV32.

A gangster (Conrad) wants to buy his son, Eddie (Stratton) "a square deal" at Ivy by donating $250,000 for a new gym, but Hall refuses the money. The Halls, meanwhile, advise Eddie to dress like the other students and drive a run-down car instead of a new model to be one of them.

R269 January 27, 1950. "Wellman's Nose/Charter Day Ceremonies" by Walter Brown Newman. **Cast:** Gloria Gordon, Herb Butterfield, Peter Leeds (Luther Bland, photographer), Henry Blair (Merton Savada).

Clarence's's nose swells in proportion to his fear of giving his Charter Day speech, while Toddy is upstaged for Charter Day photos of him in cap and gown by a photographer enamored of Vicky since she performed for the troops at Anzio. Thirteen-year-old prodigy Merton Savada begins the ceremony. Splendid show about regaining one's self-confidence. See R274 for a suddenly older Savada.

R270 February 3, 1950. "Dr. Bromley, Shakespeare Expert" by Walter Brown Newman and Don Quinn. **Cast:** Gloria Gordon, Willard Waterman, William Johnstone (Dr. Chester Bromley).

Merriweather calls on Hall to persuade Dr. Bromley, a noted Shakespeare scholar, to join the Ivy faculty.

R271* February 10, 1950. "The Snowman" by Walter Brown Newman and Don Quinn. **Cast:** Gloria Gordon, Arthur Q. Bryan, Alan Reed. See R350.

Toddy worries that he may have lost touch with and the affection of Ivy students because they have built snowmen in front of all the faculty houses but his, the snowmen being a symbol of student affection. Charmingly affecting episode. Pitch for the Heart Fund. Bryan is best known as the voice of Elmer Fudd in all those Bugs Bunny cartoons. Reed is best known as the first voice of Fred Flintstone.

R272 February 17, 1950. "The Chinese Student" by Don Quinn. **Cast:** Gloria Gordon, Barbara Jean Wong (Margaret Lee), Herb Butterfield, Willard Waterman. See TV19.

Chinese student Margaret Lee withdraws from the campus election and leaves Ivy because of student body racism toward her. Hall addresses the students about this racism at chapel. Show in honor of National Brotherhood Week.

R273 February 24, 1950. "Student Thief" by Nat Wolff and Don Quinn. **Cast:** Gloria Gordon, Earle Ross (Doc Fish, barber), Gil Stratton, Jr. (Eddie Gray), Ben Wright (Paul Hunter).

Believing that Eddie Gray has been stealing magic tricks from the campus bookstore because Eddie's father is a gangster, Doc Fish, the local barber, starts spreading his opinion as gospel. Good show on judging a man by his character, not by association.

R274 March 3, 1950. "Merton Savada's Crush" by Walter Brown Newman. **Cast:** Gloria Gordon, Barney Phillips (Brooks), Henry Blair (Merton Savada). See R269.

Fifteen-year-old physics prodigy Savada thinks he has fallen in love with Vicky. Newman based Savada on a boy he knew at summer camp named Morty Savada.

R275 March 10, 1950. "Victoria's New Revue" by Walter Brown Newman and Don Quinn. **Cast:** Gloria Gordon, Joseph Kearns (Artie Pinero), Janet Waldo (Sally Keating).

Vicky's former stage partner, Artie Pinero, visits Ivy to get her to go back to the stage in a new revue. Toddy recites Shakespeare sonnet 29: "When in disgrace with fortune and men's eyes."

R276* March 17, 1950. "Dirty Politics" by Walter Brown Newman and Don Quinn. **Cast:** Eleanor Audley (Political science Prof. Pauline Larson), Ed Max (Petey Grainger), Herb Butterfield.

Machine politico Petey Grainger tries to blackmail Dr. Hall into endorsing Grainger's candidate for governor.

R277 March 24, 1950. "Professor Gerhardt's Secret" by Walter Brown Newman and Don Quinn. **Cast:** Florence Walcott (Mrs. Gerhardt, Mrs. Reed), Dick LeGrand (Street Cop), Hans Conried (Prof. Hans Gerhardt, Egyptologist), Anne Whitfield (Christine Leslie).

Mrs. Gerhardt suspects her husband of infidelity, so Dr. Hall goes to the home of the woman in question to find out what's going on. There he finds a charming crippled girl named Christine whom Gerhardt wants to adopt as a surprise for his wife since she cannot bear children. Moving show on behalf of the National Society for Crippled Children and Adults in Chicago.

R278* March 31, 1950. "The Ivy Chamber Music and Knockwurst Society" by Walter

Brown Newman and Don Quinn. **Cast:** Gloria Gordon, Cliff Arquette (Officer Grogan), Frank Martin (Prof. Quincannon). See R390.

Fippleflute in hand, Toddy anxiously waits for a call from Quincannon to join the above-titled club, meeting at Quincannon's house across the street from the Halls, but the call doesn't come in the usual way.

R279 April 7, 1950. "Toddy Plays Hookey" by Walter Brown Newman and Don Quinn. **Cast:** Gil Stratton, Jr. (Eddie Gray), Frank Martin (Prof. Quincannon).

Toddy wants to play hookey from a faculty meeting for a picnic with Vicky, but two of his professors make it difficult for him to leave his house. Amusing show with a cute twist ending.

R280 April 14, 1950. "Mrs. Foster's Lost Dog" by Walter Brown Newman and Don Quinn. **Cast:** Jack Kruschen (Policeman, Kirby the Butler), Herb Vigran (Cab Driver, Apt. Tenant), Jane Morgan (Apt. Tenant), Jerry Hausner (Apt. Tenant), Janet Scott (Millicent Foster), Herb Butterfield.

The Halls are delayed for a donor dinner by a lost dog. Warm, charming, witty show. Kruschen is outstanding as a well-read, grammar purist beat cop.

R281* April 21, 1950. "Traffic and Cocoanuts" by Nat Wolff and Don Quinn. Song: "I've Got a Lovely Bunch of Cocoanuts" by Fred Heatherton (1944). **Cast:** Willard Waterman, Eric Snowden (Ian). See TV18.

While Vicky is out buying a thermometer for an ill Toddy, Merriweather visits him to share a secret recording he made of Vicky singing for the student follies. When Vicky returns late, she confesses that she received four tickets for traffic violation. Carpenter announces the release of *Champagne for Caesar* the following week.

Fun show (which Benita later said in a magazine interview, B183, was based on a real life incident with her), with the added treat of Benita singing the above song twice, with a cockney accent. The first time it's done live. The second time we're listening to a recording as she sings with herself. Ronnie joins in for a few seconds, in fine voice, with a slight cockney accent.

R282* April 28, 1950. "The Scofield Prize" by the Merlins. **Cast:** Bea Benadaret (Alice the maid), Willard Waterman, Jerry Hausner (Crane, Ivy News reporter), Rolland Morris (Jared Buckley). See TV21.

Toddy thinks he has won the Scofield Prize of $20,000 for his biography of scientist Jonathan Gillie. Beautifully written, moving paean to teachers. Release of *Champagne for Caesar* is plugged. Announcement that *Ivy* is moving to Wednesdays on May 10.

R283 May 5, 1950. "Student Actress" by Nat Wolff and Don Quinn. **Cast:** Bea Benadaret (Alice, the Maid), Lucille Norman (Betty Garnett), Herb Butterfield, Lois Corbett (Mrs. Garnett).

When Vicky writes the mother of student Betty Garnett about her daughter's acting talent, Betty runs away with a burlesque company. Vicky gets the blame and Wellman is furious because Betty is his niece. Soprano Norman sings the Ivy theme song in its entirety, backed by a 16-voice choir. See also R375 for entire theme song.

Alice was dropped after the above two episodes because she was a loud-mouthed former WAC who terrified the Halls; you wonder why they hired her in the first place.

R284* May 10, 1950. "Mrs. Whitney's Statue" by Don Quinn and Hector Chevigny. **Cast:** Jerry Hausner (Crane, Ivy News reporter), Gale Gordon, (Charles Merriweather, John's twin brother), Herb Butterfield, Paula Winslowe (Genevieve Whitney), Raymond Laurence (Yeoman Porter), Harry Martin (Palace Guard). See TV10.

Genevieve Whitney, an Ivy alumna and renowned sculptor of awful-looking avant garde statues, offers to pay for the building of a new gym provided they put her new statue in it.

R285* May 17, 1950. "Dr. Abel" by Nat Wolff and Don Quinn. Song: "Drink, Drink, Drink" by Henry Russell (music) and Vick Knight (lyrics). **Cast:** Sam Edwards (Mike Candor), Sam Hearn (Abel Candor).

Music student Mike Candor, who has become rich at Ivy writing popular songs, wants to enroll his father as a student in proud gratitude for encouraging his education.

R286* May 24, 1950. "The Fighting Med Student" by Don Quinn. **Cast:** Stacy Harris (Terry Ryan), Sheldon Leonard (Beans Phillips), Ken Christy (Jeff Packard). See TV14, B90.

Medical student Terry Ryan is torn between becoming a doctor and a more profitable career as a boxer. The *Ivy* version of the Clifford Odets play *Golden Boy*.

R287 May 31, 1950. "The Sexton Award" by Cameron Blake and Don Quinn. **Cast:** Willard Waterman, Jean Vander Pyl (Hospital Nurse), Herb Vigran (Mr. Brown, a Hospital Orderly), Charles Seal (Tobias Sexton), Herb Butterfield, Johnnie McGovern, Jeffrey Silver (Prof. Quincannon's children).

Complications of babysitting for Mrs. Quincannon while she is giving birth at the hospital prevent Toddy from showing up for a meeting to accept a $250,000 check from Tobias Sexton for medical research. Good show with a warmly humane twist ending.

R288* June 7, 1950. "D-Day" by the Merlins. **Cast:** Bill Thompson (Mr. Weatherby), Conrad Binyon (Philip Weatherby).

Weatherby is determined that his son, Philip, will be a lawyer and not a farmer like him, even though that is what Philip really wants.

The title refers to Toddy planting his dahlias, but is also a metaphor for Decision Day. Good show on the theme of following your heart's desire and a rare chance for *Fibber McGee and Molly* fans to hear Bill Thompson's real voice. He played Wallace Wimple and The Old Timer on that show.

R289* June 14, 1950. "Stolen First Edition" by the Merlins. **Cast:** Willard Waterman, William Tracy (Tucker Mills), Herb Butterfield, Rolfe Sedan (Mr. Empson), Sidney Miller (Mr. Maypole, Ivy librarian). See TV27.

Vicky buys a rare first edition of John Donne poems for Toddy, not knowing it was mistakenly brought to the campus bookstore from the Ivy library as a discard. Carpenter announces *Look* magazine cover story about the Colmans on *The Halls of Ivy*. See B237.

R290 June 21, 1950. "The Bentheimers and the Census" by Leonard St. Clair and Don Quinn. **Cast:** Virginia Gregg (Miss Gregg, Census taker), Herb Butterfield, Jeffrey Silver (Tommy Bentheimer), Bob Sweeney (Walt Bentheimer).

Clarence is upset that a family of welfare vagabonds is temporarily living on campus, demanding that Hall get rid of them. Toddy has a better idea that ties in with the census.

R291* June 28, 1950. "Faculty Raffle" by Cameron Blake and Don Quinn. **Cast:** Herb Butterfield, Arthur Q. Bryan, Peter Leeds (Bill Davis, a student), Sheldon Leonard (Norman, livery stable owner).

The annual student prom and faculty raffle are marred by the revelation that beloved Prof. Warren, who instituted the raffle, is going blind. Poignant show with a heart-tugging finale. Warren is over 70 on this show, but 65 in R314.

R292* July 5, 1950. "Poetry Reading" by Dean Stone and Jack Robinson. **Cast:** Robert Easton (Philip Karns), Alan Reed (Prof. Heaslip), Gloria McMillan (Dolores Whitaker), Lois Corbett (Poetry reading hostess and Helen).

Football player Philip "The Moose" Karns is having problems with his girlfriend, Dolores, so he asks Dr. Hall for advice on dealing with them. Hall then goes to his annual poetry reading at the Women's Civic Reform League.

R293* July 12, 1950. "The Education of Annie Bell" by the Merlins and Don Quinn. **Cast:** Earle Ross (Ira Bell, City Councilman), Barbara Whiting ? (Annie Bell), Ted von Eltz (City Council Chairman), Herb Butterfield, Willard Waterman.

Illiterate and pig-headed city councilman Ira Bell is opposed to his daughter, Annie, getting a college education and to Dr. Hall's dog being in the city park. Incisively witty script with delightful toying with language, typical of the Merlins. Colman signs off for the season by quoting "Our revels now are ended" speech from Shakespeare's *The Tempest*. See R375.

R294 September 13, 1950. "Ivy vs. the United Nations." Writer and cast names unavailable.

When Ivy Bulletin editors and writers criticize the United Nations for being "idealistic," Hall tells them that any attempt at world peace is better than none. He then uses a campus feud between two fraternities as a parallel between Ivy and world affairs as considered by the U.N.

R295 September 20, 1950. Program information unavailable.

R296* September 27, 1950. "The Leslie Hoff Painting" by Cameron Blake and Don Quinn. **Cast:** Jerry Hausner (Crane, Ivy News reporter), Herb Butterfield, Lois Corbett (Mrs. Wilma Marshall), James Edwards (Leslie Hoff).

Wilma Marshall offers Ivy a $500,000 donation because an award-winning painting by Ivy student Leslie Hoff is of her late son, Gene. However, she is a bigot, stipulating that the money not be given to "certain races and creeds," meaning blacks and Jews. She then meets Hoff, who is black.

One of the best shows and the most wrenching in the series. Comic first act banter with Hausner sets up straight, serious second act drama that rips your heart out. In 1949, Edwards, who is splendid, was acclaimed for his performance in the anti-racist war movie *Home of the Brave*. Announcement that the U.S. army has accepted Schlitz's offer to ship 600,000 free cans of beer to soldiers in Korea.

R297 October 4, 1950. "The New English Teacher" by Jerome Lawrence and Robert E. Lee and Don Quinn. **Cast:** Ken Peters (Prof. Bentley-Brook), Sandra Gould (Louise Turner), Helen Crutchfield and Murray Alden.

When Vicky becomes a student in Prof. Bentley-Brook's new English class, she thinks he has developed a crush on her, but it's really a blonde bombshell (Gould) with whom he is smitten. Cheeky show about mistaken signals that asks the cosmic question: Why do erudite men fall for dumb blondes?

R298 October 11, 1950. "Phone Problems" by the Merlins. **Cast:** Robert Easton (Phone man).

When a phone repairman visits the Halls, he does everything *but* repair the phone. Salute to members of the First Rifle Team, Texas Legionnaires, currently attending the American Legion Convention in Los Angeles.

R299* October 18, 1950. "Scandal" by the Merlins. **Cast:** Barbara Whiting (Linda Matthews), ? (Prof. Rousseau), Herb Butterfield. See TV31.

English student Linda Matthews spreads a rumor that her English teacher, Prof. Rousseau, who is a bachelor, is in love with her.

R300 October 25, 1950. See A10. Program information unavailable.

R301 November 1, 1950. Program information unavailable.

R302 November 8, 1950. Program information unavailable.

R303 November 15, 1950. Program information unavailable.

R304* November 22, 1950. "Jack Benny Visits Ivy." Script by ? **Cast:** Jim Backus (Milton Morton, Benny's advance man), Herb Butterfield, Jack Benny (Himself).

At Vicky's behest, Benny visits Ivy to appear in the annual Charity Benefit Show. He also sends his advance man to clean up on concessions, infuriating a greedy Wellman. Funny show with several jokes poking good-natured fun at Benny and Ronald Colman, movie star.

R305 November 29, 1950. Program information unavailable.

R306 December 6, 1950. Program information unavailable.

R307 December 13, 1950. Program information unavailable.

R308 December 20, 1950. "The Gangster and the Christmas Tree." Script by ? Cast names unavailable.

While decorating their Christmas tree with the help of students, the Halls learn that one of the students is being hunted by a gangster.

R309 December 27, 1950. Program information unavailable.

R310 January 3, 1951. "Professor Barrett's Play" by Robert Sinclair and Walter Brown Newman. **Cast:** Elliott Lewis (Harry Nolan), Norman Field (Prof. Barrett). See TV11.

Toddy's former class and roommate, Harry Nolan, offers $150,000 for the TV rights to Ivy's football games and additional money to Toddy to host a TV series on the world's great plays. Meanwhile, Prof. Barrett, Ivy's foremost drama teacher, wants the Halls' opinion of a play he once wrote that he needs to produce to pay his wife's medical bills.

R311   January 10, 1951. Program information unavailable.

R312   January 17, 1951. Program information unavailable.

R313[*]   January 24, 1951. "The Goya Bequest" by Ronald Colman. **Cast:** Herb Butterfield, Ken Peters (Mr. Benson).

There is some doubt that a Goya painting bequeathed to Ivy by an alumna is genuine. Colman's first of two scripts for *Ivy* is typical of many other scripts: charming but verbose and pedantic, and with a reverie flashback. Cut in half and without the daydream, this would be a five-minute sketch.

R314[*]   January 31, 1951. "Professor Warren's Retirement" by the Merlins. **Cast:** Arthur Q. Bryan, Sidney Miller (Joe Warren), Verna Felton (Miss Burgess, Prof. Warren's housekeeper). See TV26.

Ivy policy mandates that Prof. Warren must retire at 65, but Toddy adores Joe both personally and professionally, so he devises a scheme to keep the veteran history teacher on faculty. Warren is over 70 in R291.

R315   February 7, 1951. By Jerome Lawrence and Robert E. Lee and Don Quinn: **Cast:** Griff Barnett (Dr. Stebbins). See A11. Synopsis and other cast names unavailable.

R316   February 14, 1951. "Dr. Hall Resigns?" by Cameron Blake and Don Quinn. **Cast:** Herb Butterfield.

The Halls think that the Board of Governors think Toddy is going to resign because of a rumor that State University wants him as *its* President.

R317[*]   February 21, 1951. "Calhoun Gaddy" by the Merlins. **Cast:** Barton Yarborough (Calhoun Gaddy), Katie Lee (Glory Golightly), Gale Gordon.

Gaddy is a southern farmer turned Ivy student who raises chickens and sells eggs to pay his tuition. Yarborough is best known as Doc Long on *I Love a Mystery.*

R318[*]   February 28, 1951. "The French Scholarship" by the Merlins. **Cast:** John McIntire (Alexander Simmons), Ramsay Hill (Prof. Duvoir), Charles Smith ("Whizzer" Larkin). See TV34.

Duvoir of the Sorbonne and Simmons of the LeGrande Foundation visit Ivy to determine if the college should be given a scholarship to support foreign exchange students. They arrive during the traditional fraternity hazing period known as Hell Week.

R319   March 7, 1951. "Eddie Gray's Wedding" by the Merlins. **Cast:** Gil Stratton, Jr. (Eddie Gray), Sammi Hill (Mary), Earle Ross (Doc Fish). See A12.

Eddie and his fiancée, Mary, decide to make a business of their impending marriage instead of going with their feelings for each other.

R320 March 14, 1951. Program information unavailable.

R321 March 21, 1951. Program information unavailable.

R322 March 28, 1951. "Night Club Singer" by the Merlins. **Cast:** Lucille Norman (Julie Crane). Other cast names unavailable.
    Night club singer Julie Crane is an Ivy student by day, a benefit singer by night to raise funds in the name of her dead crippled baby to help other crippled children.

R323 April 4, 1951. "Student Vandalism and the Draft" by Don Quinn. Cast names unavailable. See R327 and TV42.
    Fear of the Korean War draft causes two students, "Rif" Dorsey and "Potsy" Clayton to vandalize the local movie theater. When they are given a talking to by ex-boxer Champ Waterford about facing up to their patriotic duty and taking life's sometimes bitter medicine like men, the students learn their lesson.

R324 April 11, 1951. Script by the Merlins. See A13. Synopsis and cast unavailable.

R325* April 18, 1951. "Romiette and Julio" by Fay Wray Riskin and Don Quinn. **Cast:** ? (Roger), ? (Hazel), Vic Perrin (Jimmy), Herb Butterfield. See A14.
    The Ivy dramatic society, The Atheneum Club, decides to stage an original play modernizing *Romeo and Juliet*. Wellman, naturally, objects, and so do the Halls, at first.

R326* April 25, 1951. "Note the Quote" by Jerome Lawrence and Robert E. Lee. Cast names unavailable. See TV23.
    Toddy competes for a radio quiz jackpot on the show "Note the Quote."

R327 May 2, 1951. "Student Vandalism and the Draft" by Don Quinn. **Cast:** ? ("Champ" Waterford), Bob Hastings ("Rif" Dorsey), ? ("Potsy" Clayton). See R323, TV42, A15, A16.
    Preachy, santimonious and evasive (Quinn dodges the Korean War issue he raises) "Face up to your patriotic duty" type of show. Yet it was because of these qualities in a right-wing era that there were scores of requests for the script, resulting in this live restaging from Washington, D.C. just four weeks after the original broadcast.

R327a May 2, 1951. "After Show." Recording of speeches immediately following the broadcast. Ronnie speaks ad lib for a little over 4 minutes, Don Quinn speaks from a script for 3 minutes, Benita just says thank you very much, and Ken Carpenter does likewise. Timing: 10 minutes, 10 seconds.
    A rare instance of Colman giving what amounts to an after-dinner speech before a D.C. Chamber of Commerce audience. First broadcast by John and Larry Gassman, at my behest, on their KPCC Pasadena show on February 3, 1991 in honor of Colman's 100th birthday the following week. They played it after the "Student Vandalism" show itself.

R328 May 9, 1951. Program information unavailable.

R329* May 16, 1951. "The Eleventh Commandment" by Decla Dunning. **Cast:** Joan Banks (Ann Garrick), Herb Vigran (Bullock, Ivy News reporter), Herb Butterfield. See TV13.
    Ivy architectural graduate Garrick causes a controversy when she has the words "The

Eleventh Commandment" carved into the front door of the new Theological Building she designed. But, what *is* "The Eleventh Commandment?" It is from the Gospel of St. John, 13:34: "A new commandment I give unto you—that ye love one another."

Special guest: Maxine Blake, President of Alpha Delta Phi, the world's oldest college sorority, founded May 15, 1851 at the first chartered college for women: Wesleyan College in Macon, Georgia. Blake presents Benita with an award and scroll naming her an Honorary Member of ADP, citing her for "her true-to-life portrayal of the first lady of the Campus at Ivy College (and) for bringing recognition to the wife who stands so understandingly at the side of the president in these institutions of higher learning."

R330 May 23, 1951. Program information unavailable.

R331* May 30, 1951. "Finals Day Award" by Arthur Ross and Don Quinn. **Cast:** Herb Butterfield, Eddie Firestone (Richard Alden), Jeanne Bates (Beth Lansing).

Brilliant science student Alden doesn't see why he should be denied graduation and the prestigious Nobling Dale Award simply because he has refused to take courses other than scientific ones. He also doesn't see that his girlfriend, Beth, wants love and a sense of humor as much as financial security. Outstanding show that gets to the heart of the need for human knowledge and understanding.

Quoth Dr. Hall: "Like so many impetuous people, he has no understanding whatsoever of the pertinence of accumulated knowledge in fields other than his own. He has never understood that wise men have recorded their yesterdays to help fools meet their tomorrows."

R332 June 6, 1951. "Vicky and the New Professor's Wife" by ? **Cast:** Les Tremayne and Alice Reinheart.

When a new professor comes to Ivy, his wife discovers she knew Vicky when Vicky was an actress.

R333* June 13, 1951. "Finals Season" by the Merlins. **Cast:** Hy Averback (Ray Adams), Barbara Eiler (Penny Sherman), Arthur Q. Bryan, Herb Butterfield.

With his desk cleared for the year and students engrossed in finals, Toddy is beside himself with nothing to do. The climax is especially funny when Toddy calls Wellman to create a problem where none exists and knee-jerk Clarence takes him up on it.

R334* June 20, 1951. "Pork Barrel Politics" by Cameron Blake and Don Quinn. **Cast:** Herb Butterfield, Bill Minn (Jim Jeffries), Jim Backus (Mayor Frank Baker).

Mayor Baker wants to pay for an unnecessary addition to Ivy city hall as a tribute to himself by taxing Ivy students under an 1885 law.

R335* June 27, 1951. "Commencement." Writer, synopsis and cast names unavailable.

R336 September 26, 1951. Program information unavailable.

R337 October 3, 1951. "Adoption" by Ted Rosnach and Quinn. **Cast:** Lou Merrill (Prof. Valdec), Vic Perrin (Bradford B. Bradford).

New England blueblood Bradford is upset to learn that he was adopted.

R338 October 10, 1951. "Editorial in the Ivy Bull" by Arthur Ross and Don Quinn. **Cast:** Herb Butterfield, Hy Averback (Thomas Finley).

Finley's editorial in the Ivy Bulletin (known as the Ivy Bull) causes Wellman to demand his expulsion because it is sharply critical of Hall, the Board of Governors and the Ivy administration in general.

R339 * October 17, 1951. "Student Council Election" by Arthur Ross and Don Quinn. **Cast:** Virginia Gregg (Deborah Jameson), Herb Butterfield, Sidney Miller (Elihu Potter).

Student councilman Potter objects to Deborah Jameson running for student council president because she's a woman.

Good, witty show with an anti-sexist theme and a great dirty joke that went right past the NBC censor. Aristophanes' play *Lysistrata* is invoked to resolve the conflict. In *Lysistrata*, Grecian women refuse to make love to their soldier husbands until they put an end to war. Vicky puts it differently, saying that Greek women refuse to go back to their soldier boyfriends etc., which is not the same thing. Community Chest appeal as part of story.

R340 * October 24, 1951. "Mrs. Why?" by the Merlins. **Cast:** Joseph Kearns (Addison Yates), Jane Morgan (Felicia Yates), Norman Field (Prof. Castle), Herb Butterfield. See TV15.

Addison Yates wants Hall to expel his mother, Felicia, from Ivy, because he fears that her age—she's in her 70s—will hold him up to public ridicule. Meanwhile, she is one of the most challenging students Ivy has had in years. Running gag question: What was Plato's first name? Answer: Aristocles.

R341 * October 31, 1951. "The Football Coach" by (?) **Cast:** Ken Christy (Coach Delavan), Alan Reed (Andy, sweet shop owner.)

On a visit to the local sweet shop, the Halls learn that Coach Delavan is in trouble for having a losing season.

R342 * November 7, 1951. "Halloween" by Ronald Colman. **Cast:** Charles Smith (John Smith, Jr.), Hanley Stafford (John Smith, Sr.). See TV17.

A Halloween prankster has drawn a moustache on the bust of Clarence's grandfather at Wellman Hall and excavated a big hole in front of Clarence's house. Like Colman's first *Ivy* script, this one is 80% longwinded verbosity, 20% plot.

R343 November 14, 1951. "The Late Student" by the Merlins. **Cast:** Vic Perrin (Jeff Kimball), Paul Frees and Jerry Hausner.

Jeff Kimball, who has hitchhiked from Oregon to Ivy College, has arrived too late to enroll, so he educates himself at the Ivy College library. He encounters the Halls when their car breaks down during a joy ride.

R344 * November 21, 1951. "Minister's Son" by Don Quinn and Audrey Call. Song: "I Just Telephone Upstairs" by Audrey Call, first violinist in the Henry Russell Orchestra. A song about religious faith, this show was its debut. **Cast:** Rye Billsbury (Rev. Dr. Jarvis), Ted Osborne (Ben Jarvis), Eric Snowden (George Wilson, Vicar in flashback). Quartet: Les Baxter, Gil Mershon, Bernie Parks and Thurl Ravenscroft (singing voice of Ben Jarvis).

Rev. Jarvis wants his son, Ben, to follow him into the ministry, but Ben yearns for a career as a song writer. Another of Quinn's pious message dramas. Ravenscroft is best known as the voice of Tony the Tiger for the Kellogg's Sugar Frosted Flakes commercials.

R345   November 28, 1951. "Professor Warren's Romantic Folly" by the Merlins. **Cast:** Arthur Q. Bryan (Prof. Warren), Sarah Selby (Fern Winthrop). See TV16.
Warren falls in love with the wrong woman, but the Halls decide to let him realize it for himself.

R346   December 5, 1951. "Calhoun Gaddy's Agricultural Project" by the Merlins. **Cast:** Elizabeth Patterson (First show as Louisa Tate), Barton Yarborough (Calhoun Gaddy), Herb Butterfield.
Calhoun Gaddy starts a farm for other students on land that happens to be owned by Wellman. Funny show, especially Yarborough, who died shortly after it was taped.

R347*   December 12, 1951. "Prof. Royce Returns" by the Merlins. **Cast:** Alan Reed, William Johnstone (Prof. Lucien Royce). See TV36.
After 15 years of retirement, Ivy's pre-eminent English professor emeritus, Lucien Royce, returns to Ivy out of boredom and nostalgia. Pompous and insecure Heaslip wants to put him in an old folks home, but Toddy has a better idea for making use of Royce's sweet demeanor and knowledge.

R348*   December 19, 1951. "The Snowman". Restaged rerun and one of the shows responsible for the program winning a Peabody Award. Chorus sings "Joy to the World." **Cast:** Arthur Q. Bryan (Prof. Warren), Alan Reed (Prof. Heaslip). See R277.

R349*   December 26, 1951. "Sweet Sorrow" by Nat Wolff and Don Quinn. **Cast:** Joyce McCluskey (Ellen Kirby), Glenn Vernon ("Spider" Kane).
The Ivy Dramatic Club is staging a British play called "Sweet Sorrow", made famous by Vicky years earlier, so Ellen Kirby, head of the club, wants Vicky to judge an audition for her old role.

R350*   January 2, 1952. "Hell Week" by Gene O"Brien and Don Quinn. **Cast:** John McIntire (Police Chief Bentley), Lee Millar (Larry Rogers), Herb Butterfield.
A hazing accident puts a student in the hospital for shock, causing a near-scandal at Ivy.

R351   January 9, 1952. "Nelson Carter's Son" by Clyde W. Park, Prof. of English, Emeritus, University of Cincinnati. Final draft by the Merlins and Don Quinn. **Cast:** Elizabeth Patterson, Rye Billsbury (Jerry Carter), Lou Merrill (Nelson Carter). See TV38.
Jerry Carter wants to change economics teachers because Prof. Hamlin is giving him a hard time. Prof. Park sent Ronnie a script in lieu of a fan letter. He was so pleased with it that he passed it to Quinn and the Merlins for purchase and polishing.

R352*   January 16, 1952. "Art Exhibit" by Arthur Ross and Don Quinn. **Cast:** Paul Frees (Alfred Chermondy), Stanley Farrar (Charles Neivers), Herb Butterfield.
Toddy turns down his traditional role as judge of the Ivy art exhibit because the

abstract artist in charge, Alfred Chermondy, prefers theory to feeling in his art. Instead, he gets wallpaper maker and art expert Neivers to judge the show. Keenly written jab at the pretensions of abstract art, with a good straight performance by Frees, best known as an announcer and cartoon voice.

R353* January 23, 1952. "Medal of Honor" by Don Quinn and John DeGrazio. With Thurl Ravenscroft Quartet. **Cast:** Gale Gordon, Curt Martell (Capt. Dawson Ferber, Ivy ROTC), Alice Backes (Penny Sherman), Jess Kirkpatrick (Fred Sherman).
　　Dawson Ferber is smitten with Penny Sherman, but is perturbed that she is ashamed of her father, Fred, a Congressional Medal of Honor winner, because he runs the campus hot dog concession, called A la Cart. Good show about pride of accomplishment with a movingly patriotic finale. Appeal for Blood Bank donations.

R354* January 30, 1952. "Track Star" by the Merlins. **Cast:** William Tracy (Wally Lovett), Herb Butterfield, Ken Peters (Coach Simmons), Vic Perrin (Bruce Dillon). See TV20.
　　Ivy's top track star Bruce Dillon decides not to compete in the annual competition against a rival college because he considers his grades more important. March of Dimes appeal.

R355* February 6, 1952. "Glee Club Donation". Script by Henry Russell and Don Quinn. Song: "Fair Weather Friends" by Russell, Hy Lewman and Leroy Pritchett. **Cast:** Arthur Q. Bryan (Prof. Warren), Sam Edwards (Tommy Thornhill), Herb Butterfield, with Ken Johnson Octette.
　　Wellman secretly donates $2500 to the Ivy Glee Club.
　　First act ends with a few seconds of honky tonk piano played by Toddy. Wellman says he was an Ivy student in 1914, yet in R271, he was an Ivy student in 1907.

R355a After show, not recorded. Virginia Witmer of Santa Ana, Moonlight Girl for the 71 chapters of the Phi Sigma Kappa Fraternity, presents the Colmans and the series with awards. See A17.

R356* February 13, 1952. "Dean Huxley" by the Merlins and Don Quinn. **Cast:** Elizabeth Patterson, Alan Reed, Paula Winslowe (Dean Agnes Huxley). See TV43.
　　Pompous and pretentious Heaslip tries to put Dean Huxley (Dean of Women) in a bad light by twisting a remark she made about Hall to make him question their professional relationship. Starting with this episode, Colman opens occasional shows by dedicating them to a college or university president. First up is Dr. Lynn Townsend White, Jr., President of Mills College, Oakland, California.

R357* February 20, 1952. "Voice of the Ivy Vine" by the Merlins and Don Quinn. **Cast:** Charles Wolf (Jack Hatter), Marian Richmond (Betty Gibson), Gale Gordon. See TV39.
　　Radio station KIVY's new 10 p.m. gossip segment becomes the talk of the town, outdrawing the commercial station. Delightful script with deliciously witty patter routines for the Colmans.

R358* February 27, 1952. "Budget Problems" by the Merlins and Don Quinn. **Cast:** Eric Snowden (Mr. Lundquist, Ivy librarian), James Gleason (Officer Frances Xavier Grogan),

Herb Butterfield.

The Board of Governors won't allocate $2000 to the college library, so Toddy has to find the money elsewhere. Very funny show with a welcome first appearance by veteran character actor Gleason.

R359* March 5, 1952. "Astronomy Exam" by the Merlins and Don Quinn. **Cast:** Bruce Payne (Prof. Maxwell), Elizabeth Patterson, Herb Butterfield, Herb Ellis (Leslie Gifford). See TV12.

Astronomy student Gifford causes a commotion when he refuses to take Prof. Maxwell's exam on the ground that "it's too easy". Announcement that Ivy has been named best radio show of 1951 by the National Association for Better Radio and Television.

R360 March 12, 1952. "The Lame Girl and the Hypochondriac" by Don Quinn. **Cast:** Mary McGovern (Sheila Quincannon), John Brown (Prof. Harmon).

When Prof. Harmon tells Hall he is resigning from Ivy because he feels vaguely ill, though nothing he can put his finger on, Toddy introduces him to Sheila Quincannon, a lovely and charming crippled girl wearing braces, to show him the grace and self-determination of a child who has a real physical disability. Easter Seal appeal. Show dedicated to Dr. Horace Mann Bond, President of Lincoln University, Chester County, Pennsylvania.

R361* March 19, 1952. "The Oldest Living Graduate" by David Robison and Don Quinn. **Cast:** Gale Gordon, William Johnstone (Silas Livingstone), Herb Butterfield. See TV30.

Wellman invites Livingstone, Ivy's oldest living graduate—Class of 1880, age 91—to the annual Founders Day celebration in hope of getting a cash gift from him, but he gives Ivy a more valuable gift instead. Highlight: Toddy calling a square dance. In real life, Colman was a square dance buff. Fun, wise show about being young in spirit. However, Livingstone would have to have been 19 when he graduated.

R362* March 26, 1952. "Stolen Money" by the Merlins and Don Quinn. **Cast:** James Gleason (Officer Grogan), Sammi Hill (Eleanor Joyce), Elizabeth Patterson.

Eleanor Joyce, an Ivy student who heads the Student Judiciary Committee, believes her roommate stole $25 from another student. Good show about jumping to conclusions before the facts are in. Hilarious first act exchange between Toddy and Grogan about the psychology of sign-stealing. Toddy invokes the absurd titles of books by Drs. Von Schmickelburg and Dipfelmeyer, using gibberish German, the comic inspiration of Milton Merlin.

R363* April 2, 1952. "Professor Grimes" by the Merlins and Don Quinn. **Cast:** Herb Butterfield, Larry Dobkin (Prof. Hugh Grimes). See TV35.

Clarence wants history teacher Grimes fired for not publishing a book in five years until Grimes discovers while researching Wellman's genealogy that Clarence may be related to King Charles II. Guest audience was 300 female professors, in Los Angeles for a meeting of the National Association of Deans of Women.

R364* April 9, 1952. "Faculty Marriage" by David Robison and Don Quinn. **Cast:** John Dehner (Prof. John Gardner), ? (Prof. Lucy Otis Gardner), Herb Butterfield. See TV44.

Ivy professors Gardner and Otis are married to each other in violation of an Ivy college regulation against inter-faculty marriages, so they ask Hall to intercede for them with Wellman, who wrote the bylaw in the first place for fear of upsetting the food chain of teacher salaries. Wickedly clever script puts Toddy in top form manipulating Clarence so that an absurd principle is overruled in favor of human happiness.

R365* April 16, 1952. "French Exchange Student" by the Merlins and Benita Colman. **Cast:** Gladys Holland (Mme. Heloise Genét), Herb Butterfield, Dennis Frasier (Flower Vendor). See TV28.

Encouraged by Toddy, Heloise Genét publishes an article in the Ivy Bulletin from an outsider's perspective that is critical of the way the college is run. Clarence is naturally outraged.

R366* April 23, 1952. "Professor Walden's Son" by David Robison and Don Quinn. **Cast:** Lee Patrick (Miss Goodson, Hall's secretary), Vic Perrin (Matthew Walden), Paul McVey (Prof. Jeremy Walden).

As a student in his father's English literature class, Matthew Walden feels his father is far stricter with him than the other students because he is his father's son.

R367* April 30, 1952. "Faculty Follies, Part 1" by Don Quinn and Charles Henry from an idea by Henry. **Cast:** Sidney Miller (Sidney Mullins), Herb Butterfield, James Gleason. See TV24.

Clarence opposes the annual faculty follies as a fund-raiser for theatricals on the ground that they are frivolous. Show dedicated to Tufts College, Bedford, MA, founded in 1852 and celebrating its 100th anniversary. Tufts President, Leon Carmichael, is saluted by Colman.

R368* May 7, 1952. "Faculty Follies, Part 2" by Don Quinn and Charles Henry from an idea by Henry. Song: "Alice's House." Kipling patter routine by Quinn. **Cast:** Sidney Miller, Herb Butterfield, James Gleason. See TV25.

Follies director Sidney Mullins strokes Clarence's ego by making him MC of the show. Vicky sings "Alice's House" backed by a chorus, and Toddy recites "Three Blind Mice as Kipling Might Have Written It." Delightful show with Miller a stand-out and wonderful song and patter.

R369 May 14, 1952. "Student Singer" by David Robison and Don Quinn. **Cast:** Lee Childs (Marion Coulter), Ben Wright (Prof. Zeller), Gale Gordon.

Gifted music student and opera singer Marion Coulter inexplicably wants to leave Ivy.

R370* May 21, 1952. "Dr. Spatzen" by the Merlins and Don Quinn. **Cast:** Herb Butterfield, Fritz Feld (Dr. Oscar Spatzen). See TV41.

Clarence is smitten with hiring Dr. Spatzen for the psychology department, not knowing he's a fraud.

R371* May 28, 1952. "Mummynapper" by the Merlins and Don Quinn. **Cast:** Joseph Carbo (Tommy Spencer), Sammi Hill (Lynn Gordon). See TV22.

Reserved student Tommy Spencer suddenly vents his pent-up need for attention by stealing a mummy from the Egyptology department. Psychologically insightful script.

R372* June 4, 1952. "Pregnant Student" by the Merlins and Don Quinn. **Cast:** James Gleason, Janet Warren, Jeanne Tatum (Nurses). See TV8.

Hall goes over Heaslip's head to postpone a final exam until one of his students, Caroline Swanson, can deliver her baby.

R373* June 11, 1952. "The Wellmans Come to Dinner" by the Merlins and Don Quinn. **Cast:** Elizabeth Patterson, Gale Gordon, Herb Butterfield, Sarah Selby (Bertha Wellman). See TV9.

By mistake, the Wellmans come to the Hall's for dinner a week early, but the mistake allows Merriweather to get a large check from a donor without Clarence's bumbling interference.

Okay show with a potentially gripping climax. Act two builds to a long overdue moment of truth between Hall and Wellman, a scene in which Toddy *must* drop his roundabout diplomacy to be matter-of-factly direct with Clarence, but robs us of it by stopping at the moment of confrontation. The standard opening scene could easily have been trimmed to play the final scene to its logical and necessary conclusion.

R374 June 18, 1952. "Math Professor" by Philip Nelson and Don Quinn. **Cast:** Virginia Gregg (Prof. David Upshaw), Herb Butterfield, Elizabeth Patterson, William Erwin (Prof. Kent).

Newly hired math department head, Professor David Upshaw, stuns everyone by being a woman. Gregg stands out for her warm intelligence and sexy aplomb.

R375 June 25, 1952. "Summer Vacation" by Don Quinn. **Cast:** Lee Patrick (Miss Goodson), Gil Stratton, Jr. (Jimmy).

Toddy ties up loose administrative ends at year's end, then heads off for vacation with Vicky. Show ends with Toddy quoting Prospero from *The Tempest* to end the season and the series. Splendid, touching finale. Second and last time entire theme song is sung. See R283.

R376 HALLMARK PLAYHOUSE
January 19, 1950. "Around the World in 80 Days" by Jules Verne. Host: James Hilton. Producer/Director: Bill Gay. Music director: Lyn Murray. Announcer: Frank Martin. CBS. 30 minutes. See F68, R225.

Cast: Ronald Colman (Phileas Fogg), Hans Conried (Passepartout, Reform Club Member), Ramsay Hill (Detective Fix) Bernice Barrett (Princess Aouda), Ben Wright (Reform Club Member), Edgar Barrier (Indian native).

Entertaining synopsis with a crisp, clipped performance by Colman. A different approach from his *Favorite Story* performance.

R377 GISELE OF CANADA
Ca. March 1950. Starring Gisele MacKenzie. Producer/Director/Writer/Announcer/Interviewer: Rupert Lucas. Guest: Ronald Colman. CBC. 14 minutes. See R25, R115, R124-25, R404.

Transcribed weekly one-season series trading on the popularity of singer MacKenzie's other CBC show, *Meet Gisele*. Lucas recorded all the guest star "interviews" at their homes in Los Angeles (whether on tape or disc MacKenzie doesn't recall), then decided which star would be on which show.

On this episode, MacKenzie accompanies herself on piano for five songs, in between which is a scripted 2 ½-minute chat with Colman, who makes some general remarks on the U.S. and Canada as North American neighbors, with his customary humor.

R378 ANACIN HOLLYWOOD STAR THEATER
April 1, 1950. NBC. 30 minutes. Details unavailable.

R379 DOCUMENT A-777
April 17, 1950. (BBC broadcast on January 27, 1951.) Written, produced and directed by Norman Corwin. Music composed and conducted by Lyn Murray. Mutual, sus. 60 minutes. See R35, R380.

Narrator: Van Heflin. Speaker for the United Nations: Herbert Evatt, President of the United Nations General Assembly. Guest speaker by shortwave: Sidney G. Holland, Prime Minister of New Zealand. **Cast:** Richard Basehart (Trelawney), Ed Begley (Ivan the Terrible, Voice of the Portfolio, and Banquet Member), Charles Boyer (Emile Zola), Herb Butterfield (Rev. Smith), Lee J. Cobb (Swedish officer), **Ronald Colman** (Lord Byron), William Conrad (Anatole France, Parish, and Voice of the New England Palladium), Joan Crawford (Eliza Lynch), Maurice Evans (Capulet), José Ferrer (Francisco Solano Lopez, Dictator of Paraguay), Reginald Gardiner (Baron de Mandeville), Virginia Gregg (Bookstore clerk, Marriage bureau registrar), Jean Hersholt (Swedish peasant), Lena Horne (sings "Let My People Go"), Marsha Hunt (Juliet), William Johnstone (Thomas Jefferson, Napoleon), Byron Kane (Chinese scholar, William Smith), Alexander Knox (Contact Man), Charles Laughton (Walt Whitman), Elliott Lewis (Tupac Amaru, Voice of Bible excerpt and history of African slave trade), Laurence Olivier (Preamble), Vincent Price (Ordinances of Indian Law), Edward G. Robinson (Chinese officer), Elliott Reid (Alexander the Great, Man in Marriage bureau), Robert Ryan (Opening Voice), Hilda Vaughan (Lady Capulet), Emlyn Williams (Spanish officer), Ben Wright (Minister in Suthington, CT), Robert Young (The Document).

Rivetingly creative and incisive, nearly perfect program dramatizing human rights abuses through the centuries. A roll call of the United Nations at the Pallais de Chaillot on December 10, 1948 for their 1949 Human Rights Charter is the backdrop for the vignettes. Show starts with a spy thriller gimmick to grab attention. Weak segments: Colman as Lord Byron addressing the House of Lords on a death penalty bill for jobless workers who destroy machinery lacks scorn. And the *Romeo and Juliet* scene is both out of place and badly acted by Maurice Evans. Otherwise, a bitingly sharp hour that ranks among radio's best.

R380 THE BIRTHDAY STORY
Recorded July 1950 at NBC in Hollywood for United Nations Radio. Written, produced and directed by Jerome Lawrence and Robert E. Lee for the fourth anniversary of the United Nations in San Francisco. Internationally syndicated to 500 stations. 60 minutes. See R35, R379.

Narrator: Ronald Colman. Transcribed cut-ins by Eleanor Roosevelt, Eddie Rickenbacker, U.N. Secretary General Trygive Lie and others, plus news clips, forming a documentary montage.

R381 THE MIRACLE OF AMERICA
August 20, 1950. Presented by the Advertising Council of America (ACA). Produced and transcribed in Hollywood by Sterling Tracy. Host: Robert Young. Music: Leith Stevens.

Unidentified chorus. CBS. 60 minutes. See R255.

Cast in order of appearance: Bob Crosby, Jo Stafford, Jack Benny, Mary Livingstone, **Ronald and Benita Colman**, Maurice J. Tobin (Secretary of Labor), Frank Sinatra, Jack Smith, Dinah Shore, Dick Haymes, Lucille Norman, Charles Laughton, Bing Crosby, Gary Crosby, California Governor Earl Warren, Sam Gale (Chairman of the Board of ACA).

Right wing-flavored propaganda show comprising original skits and in-studio singers plus an 8-minute segment lifted bodily from the Jack Benny show "At the Races," featuring the Colmans (R255). What this had to do with the show's theme is a mystery.

The program was designed to motivate listeners to send for a booklet called "The Miracle of America," prepared by the ACA. Though the booklet's contents are never specified except to say that they are about the freedoms we take for granted, the insistent and sappy nationalism of the script and chorus (singing the insipid theme song ad nauseam) make it clear that the booklet was equally insistent propaganda, with an "America, love it or leave it" undertone. In the era of Communist witch hunting, shows like this had insidiously conformist implications.

R382 RED FEATHER ROUNDUP
September 29, 1950. The Colmans are guests. NBC. 30 minutes. Details unavailable.

R383 SCREEN GUILD PLAYERS
October 5, 1950. "Champagne for Caesar," adapted from the screenplay by Harry Kronman. Director: Bill Lawrence. Music: Basil Adlam. KECA Hollywood for ABC, sus. 60 minutes. See F62.

Cast: Ronald Colman (Beauregard Bottomley), Audrey Totter (Flame O'Neil), Vincent Price (Burnbridge Waters), Barbara Britton (Gwen Bottomley), Art Linkletter ("Happy" Hogan), Joseph Kearns (Jeffers, aide de camp to Waters).

Delightful abridgement outdoes the movie in many ways: Brisker pacing for the second half, romantic dead weight dropped, funnier lines for a few scenes, and a sexy performance by Audrey Totter that outshines Celeste Holm's in the picture. During its last season, this series was an hour show. Performers donated their fees to the Motion Picture Country Home in Calabasas, CA.

R384 JACK BENNY
October 29, 1950. "How Jack Met the Colmans." CBS. 30 minutes. Or how to recycle a script. Revision of R98, minus the contest. See also TV45.

R385 HEDDA HOPPER'S HOLLYWOOD
November 19, 1950. An FMB Production. Director: Gil Faust. Music: Frank Worth. Announcer: Harlow Wilcox. NBC. 30 minutes.

Program includes a "behind-the-scenes" look at *The Halls of Ivy* with Ronnie and Benita and *Ivy* director Nat Wolff. This 7-minute sequence is a rehearsal for a *Romeo and Juliet* flashback written for R277. It is mainly notable for a rare radio appearance by Wolff, who has a charming personality and gravelley voice. Barbara Merlin, who once dated him in the late 1930s, recalls that "He was a charming con man and everyone who worked with and knew him knew this, and we adored him for it."

R386 JACK BENNY
February 18, 1951. "The Colmans' TV Set." When Jack's TV set breaks down, he goes next

door to the Colmans' to watch his own movie, *To Be or Not to Be* on their set. Mel Blanc plays Benny's violin teacher, Prof. LeBlanc. CBS. 30 minutes.

R387 SUSPENSE
March 8, 1951. "A Vision of Death," by Walter Brown Newman from an original story by Jerry Hausner. Producer/Director: Elliott Lewis. Music: Lucien Moraweck. Conductor: Lud Gluskin. Announcers: Harlow Wilcox, Joseph Kearns. Sponsor: Electric Auto-Lite. CBS. 30 minutes. See R398.

Cast: Ronald Colman (Judd Stone), Cathy Lewis (Aurora Stone), Larry Dobkin (Harry Arnold), Joseph Kearns (Stanford, Nightclub Manager), Florida Edwards (Phone Operator), Charles Calvert (Western Union Man, Bartender).

The female half (Lewis) of a phony nightclub mentalist act conspires with their agent (Dobkin) to drive her husband (Colman) mad as part of a plot to murder him. Not as sharply compelling, taut and believable as the 1953 remake.

R388 JACK BENNY
April 15, 1951. "The Tax Agents." Two IRS agents (Joseph Kearns and Will Wright)) show up at Ronnie's doorstep to find out why Jack deducted so little for entertainment in 1950. Flashback to a restaurant scene with Jack, Mary, the Colmans and waiter Frank Nelson. CBS. 30 minutes.

R389 THE GEORGE FOSTER PEABODY AWARDS
April 26, 1951. WJZ New York for NBC. See A15. Not heard in Los Angeles. 15 minutes of recorded highlights from afternoon ceremony that day. Colman makes a few thank you remarks.

R390 DOUBLE OR NOTHING
May 22, 1951. Guest on afternoon game show. Host: Walter O'Keefe. Sponsor: Campbell Soup Co. NBC. 30 minutes.

R391 JACK BENNY
October 28, 1951. "Jack Benny's Song." The Colmans discover an awful song written by Jack in their Sunday newspaper. CBS. 30 minutes.

R392 JACK BENNY'S 20TH ANNIVERSARY SHOW
November 9, 1951. The Colmans are among several guests, including CBS President William S. Paley, paying tribute to Benny's 20th anniversary in radio. (Actually two months into his 20th year.) Ronnie and Benita do a skit about minding Jack's parrot while he's away accepting the honor. Their last radio show with Benny. CBS. 30 minutes.

R393 LOS ANGELES SALUTES THE NATION
December 22, 1951. Christmas pageant. Narrates segment titled "Song of Christmas," accompanied by chorus and orchestra. NBC. 30 minutes. See R264.

R394 PHILIP MORRIS PLAYHOUSE ON BROADWAY
January 13, 1952. "The Talk of the Town." CBS. 30 minutes. See F53, R47, R106, R252.

Twelfth in a series of 16 shows featuring the collegiate winners of the Philip Morris International Acting Competition, all of whom played opposite movie stars. On this show, Minrose Lucas of St. Louis University plays Nora Shelley to Colman's Michael Lightcap.

Lucas received a guest fee of $250, membership in AFTRA and an all-expenses-paid round trip to New York City. Other credits are unavailable.

R395 THE 24TH ANNUAL ACADEMY AWARDS
March 20, 1952. MC: Danny Kaye. Radio announcer: Paul Douglas. Colman presents the Best Actress Oscar to Vivien Leigh for *A Streetcar Named Desire*, accepted by Greer Garson. ABC, sus. 90 minutes.

This broadcast is preserved on 16mm color film because the Academy's then Board of Governors wanted a color keepsake. However, the photography is not that good because everyone looks orangish.

Archival Source: 16mm print at AMPAS main office building in Beverly Hills.

R396 LUX RADIO THEATER
December 22, 1952. "Les Miserables" (1865) by Victor Hugo. Host: Irving Cummings. Announcer: Ken Carpenter. **Cast:** Ronald Colman (Jean Valjean), Robert Newton (Javert), Debra Paget (Cosette), Ted von Eltz (Robert the Narrator), Lamont Johnson (Marius), Paul Frees (Prison Ship Clerk, Coshpai), Herb Butterfield (Bishop), Victor Rodham (Judge), William Johnstone (Montieux), Yvonne Peattie (Fantine), Ruth Perrott (Housekeeper), ? (John Mathieux), Herb Rawlinson, Hal Gerard, Bob Griffin, George Baxter, Tim Graham, Eddie Marr. CBS. 60 minutes.

Good show. Colman makes a fine and forceful Jean Valjean, matched by an equally fine cast, except for Paget, who is a bland ingenue. The 1952 movie, on which the script is based, stars Michael Rennie, Newton and Paget. A 1918 Fox film version starred William Farnum, Jewell Carmen and Hardee Kirkland. The masterful 1935 version starring Fredric March and Charles Laughton is the best of all.

R397 THE 25TH ANNUAL ACADEMY AWARDS
March 19, 1953. Presents Best Actress award to Shirley Booth for *Come Back, Little Sheba*. NBC television and radio simulcast. Two hours. See TV2.

R398 SUSPENSE
June 1, 1953. "A Vision of Death." CBS. 30 minutes. See R387.

Cast: Ronald Colman (Judd Stone), Mary Jane Croft (Aurora Stone), Hy Averback (Harry Arnold), Benny Rubin (Western Union man, Night Club manager), Julie Bennett (Phone operator), Charles Calvert (Bartender).

Rare villainous part for Colman and one of his best radio roles period. Sharply conniving and cynical performance and story. This excellent remake (despite a major plot hole about audience "plants") was a last-minute substitute for the previously announced "The Voyages of Sinbad the Sailor" by Antony Ellis.

R399 LUX RADIO THEATER
November 23, 1953. "The Browning Version" from Terence Rattigan's 1948 play. Host: Irving Cummings. **Cast:** Ronald Colman (Andrew Crocker-Harris), Benita Colman (Millie Crocker-Harris), Robert Douglas (Frank Hunter), Dick Beymer (Taplow), Ben Wright (Gilbert), Herb Butterfield (Headmaster Frobisher), Martha Wentworth (Mrs. Frobisher), Michael Tate (Fletcher), Michael Miller, Michael Edwards. CBS. 60 minutes.

Goodbye Mr. Chips in reverse. A stiff and stodgy Greek professor learns that he is hated by all of his students except one. Meanwhile, his wife is having an affair with a chemistry teacher (Douglas).

Good acting by all except Colman, who walks through his part with none of the shadings and nuances of Michael Redgrave in the excellent 1951 Anthony Asquith movie. Benita especially shines in a bitchy role as the love-starved wife. The 1994 remake stars Albert Finney, Greta Scacchi and Matthew Modine.

R400 SUSPENSE

December 7, 1953. "Trent's Last Case" by E.C. Bentley, adapted by Oliver Gard. CBS: 30 minutes.

Cast: Ronald Colman (Philip Trent), Joseph Kearns (Mr. Cupples), Ellen Morgan (Mabel Manderson), Richard Peal (Inspector Murch), Gloria Ann Simpson (Western Union clerk), William Johnstone (John Marlowe).

Noted criminologist Philip Trent thinks he has solved the murder of an American tycoon who was hated by all who knew him. Dull bit of tongue-in-cheek mystery with a walk-through performance by Colman.

R401 HANDEL'S MESSIAH

December 24, 1953. (Taped rerun December 24, 1954). Presented by the Southern California Oratorio Society, Norwalk Parks and Recreation District. Frederick Davis, Conductor. Producer: Winton Burn. Direction and Editorial Supervision: Milton Merlin. **Narrator: Ronald Colman**. With 50-piece orchestra and 150-member chorus. Soloists: Phyllis Moffatt (Soprano), Marjorie McKaye (Alto), William Ovis (Tenor), Don Hubler (Bass). Special guest: Kenneth Hahn, Los Angeles County Supervisor, 2nd District. Announcer: Lee Zimmer. Produced and transcribed by KABC Hollywood for the ABC network. 60 minutes.

Program: "Hallelujah" excerpt (Colman with Chorus, *Revelations* 19:6, 11:15, 19:16); "Comfort ye" (Colman, *Isaiah* 40:1-3); "Every valley" (Ovis, *Isaiah* 40:4); "And the glory of the Lord" (Chorus, *Isaiah* 40:5); "Thus saith the Lord" (Colman, *Haggai* 2:6-7, *Malachi* 3:1); "But who may abide" (Hubler, *Malachi* 3:2); "And He shall purify" (Chorus, *Malachi* 3:3); "Behold, a virgin shall conceive" (Colman, *Isaiah* 7: 14); "O, thou that tellest" (McKaye and Chorus, *Isaiah* 40: 9, 60:1); "For, behold" and "The people that walked in darkness" (Colman, *Isaiah* 60:2-3, 9:2); "For unto us a Child is born" (Chorus, *Isaiah* 9:6); "And lo!," "And the angel," "And suddenly" (Colman, *Luke* 2:9-11, 13); "Glory to God" (Chorus, *Luke* 2:14); "Rejoice greatly" (Moffatt, *Zechariah* 9:9-10); "Then shall the eyes" (Colman, *Isaiah* 35:5-6); "He shall feed his flock" (McKaye, *Isaiah* 40:11); "His yoke is easy" (Chorus, *Matthew* 11:30); "Lift up your heads" (Colman, *Psalms* 24:7-10); "Hallelujah" entire (Chorus); "Blessing and honor" (Colman, *Revelations* 5:13).

The numbers selected are the so-called Christmas sections of *Messiah*. After the 1954 rerun, this program was not heard again until I played a 15-minute excerpt on KPCC Pasadena, December 24, 1989, as part of a Christmas marathon.

R402 MUTUAL MEETING ROOM OF THE AIR

October 18, 1955. Ronald and Benita Colman with Gladys Seymour, director of the Santa Barbara Volunteer Bureau. 8:15 p.m. KTMS Santa Barbara. 15 minutes. See R261, B366.

The Colmans make an appeal on behalf of the 1955 Santa Barbara Community Chest Drive. They lived in Santa Barbara at San Ysidro Ranch, which Ronnie co-owned with his friend Alvin Weingand. KTMS was owned by Thomas Moore Storke, who also owned the *Santa Barbara News-Press*.

R403 MONITOR

December 23, 1956. (Recorded December 5, 1956.) Solo reading of *A Christmas Carol* by

Charles Dickens. NBC. 30 minutes. See R25, R115, R245, D1.

Taking a break from filming his role in *The Story of Mankind* (F69), Colman flew to New York to record an abridged reading of *A Christmas Carol* for NBC's weekend cultural show, *Monitor*.

R404 MONITOR

Recorded December 5, 1956. He was also interviewed by an unidentified NBC staffer for a five-minute segment to air when *The Story of Mankind* was released in New York; the release was 11 months later. There is no evidence that it did air.

Copies of the uncut 7-minute interview tape (on which Colman verbally fumbles during the first minute) are held by collectors. This version was first aired by me on KPCC Pasadena on December 24, 1989 as part of a 2½-hour Ronald Colman tribute within a 12-hour Christmas Eve marathon.

This interview's importance is that it was one of only two such with Colman on radio that weren't scripted, the other being on *Woman's Hour*, R125. He describes the premise of his new picture, then answers questions about star over-exposure, his favorites of his own movies, his hobbies, what he is doing now professionally, and his future plans. There is no real depth in such a short interview, but because it *is* ad lib, the listener gets a sense of the private man, especially since Colman uses his straight voice as opposed to the cadenced one he perfected for acting.

NOTES

1. Author interview with Arch Oboler in 1977.
2. Author interview with Barbara Merlin in 1979.
3. From letter to author by Joan Benny, January 1992.
4. Author interview with Jerome Lawrence in 1993.
5. Author interview with Lawrence in 1990.

RADIO SHOW SOURCES
ARCHIVAL

Jerome Lawrence & Robert E. Lee Theatre Research Institute at Ohio State University. 1430 Lincoln Tower, 1800 Cannon Dr., Columbus, OH 43214. Nena Couch, Curator. 614-292-6614. Fax: 614-292-3222. Open Monday, Thursday, Friday 8-5, Tuesday 8-1, Wednesday 1-7.

Collection includes scripts and transcription discs for the Ziv run of *Favorite Story*.

Museum of Broadcast Communications at Chicago Cultural Center. Michigan at Washington. (312) 629-6024. Cary O'dell, Acting Archives Director. Mon-Sat 10-4:30, Sun Noon-5.

Scores of Colman shows in their huge radio collection that are accessible for listening.

Museum of Television and Radio. 25 W. 52 St., New York, NY 10019. 212-621-6600. Tues-Sun: Noon-6; till 8 p.m. on Thursdays.

Scores of Colman shows in their huge radio collection that are accessible for listening.

Pacific Pioneer Broadcasters. Broadcasting club founded in 1965 by veteran radio and TV people. Basement of the Home Savings building at 1500 Vine St. in Hollywood, the former site of NBC. Homy clubhouse warehousing thousands of discs and reel tape transfers of same, plus a splendid library which includes rare newspaper clipping scrapbooks. Listening equipment is one Sony reel machine. Collection includes *Favorite Story* (KFI and Ziv versions), *The Halls of Ivy*, *Jack Benny*, and *Lux Radio Theater*.

Open Mondays 1-4:30 p.m. Call Ron Wolf at (213) 462-9606 for appointments. Mailing address: POB 4866, N. Hollywood, CA 91607.

Society to Preserve and Encourage Radio Drama, Variety and Comedy (SPERDVAC). Membership and Radiogram subscriptions: Carrolyn Rawski, 7430 Gaviota Ave., Van Nuys, CA 91406. Information and Official Business: (310) 947-9800.

Catalog of 16,000 shows, either on reels or cassettes, that are loaned to members for a small lending library fee. Thus, a cheaper source for collecting shows than any of the mail order companies. Colman shows include *The Halls of Ivy*, *Favorite Story*, *Jack Benny*, *Suspense*, *Lux*, *Screen Guild*, *Everything for the Boys*, and many more.

COMMERCIAL, MOSTLY CASSETTES

BWP Radio, Inc. 1105 N. Main St. #9E, Gainsville, FL 32601.
Favorite Story, 13 episodes; *Hallmark Radio Theater*: "Goodbye Mr. Chips," R127; *Suspense*: "The Dunwich Horror."

The Can Corner. POB 1173, Linwood, PA 19061.
Jack Benny, *Suspense* and *Lux*.

Hello Again, Radio. POB 6176, Cincinnati, OH 45206.
The Halls of Ivy, 2 episodes; *Jack Benny*, 2; *Lux*: "The Prisoner of Zenda," R12.

Radio Showcase. POB 4357, Santa Rosa, CA 95402. Steve Kelez, Owner.
Academy Award: "If I Were King," R105; *Arch Oboler's Plays*: "The Most Dangerous

Game," R16; *Favorite Story*, 4 episodes; *The Halls of Ivy*, 30; *Jack Benny*, 9; *Lux*, 4: *Screen Guild Theater*: "Champagne for Caesar"; *Suspense*, 4; *The Circle*, R9.

Radio Yesteryear. Box C, Sandy Hook, CT 06452. 800-243-0987 for cassette and reel prices and catalog cost. Scores of Colman shows for sale.

TELEVISION SHOWS

Ronald Colman's television work was minor in output, but he did do a few good shows, including episodes of *The Halls of Ivy* (1954-55) and a *General Electric Theater* (1956). He also did a final guest shot on *Jack Benny* (1956) and tried producing a series of his own, for which see TV5.

His television debut was to have been a live *Jack Benny* show in 1951, but it never happened. For details, see TV46.

I am also including three TV shows about him, one of them a BBC documentary that aired in England in 1978, but which has never been seen in the U.S. I was able to see it at the producer's office when I visited London in October of 1982.

TV1 FOUR STAR PLAYHOUSE (First season, third show). Discount Video Tapes #359. October 23, 1952. "The Lost Silk Hat" by Lord Dunsany, adapted by Ronald Colman and Milton Merlin. Producer: Ronald Colman. Executive Producer: Don W. Sharpe (Colman's agent). Director: Robert Florey. Production Supervisor: Ruby Rosenberg. Director of Photography: Les White, ASC. Assistant Director: Nate Barragar. Art Director: Ralph Berger. Editor: Samuel E. Beetley, ACE. Music: Mozart's "Sonata in C Major" and "The Blue Danube" by Strauss. Sponsor: Singer sewing machines. CBS. 30 minutes.

Cast: Ronald Colman (Gentleman Caller), Richard Whorf (Poet), Jay Novello (Clerk), Tudor Owen (Laborer), Leo Britt (Policeman).

Synopsis: In this offbeat comedy of manners, a tuxedoed gentleman attempts to retrieve his silk hat, which he has accidentally left inside his ex-fiancée's house.

Review: Kap, *Daily Variety*, 10-24-52: "Ronald Colman earns a three-way credit in this Singer 4 Star Playhouse production. He has produced with taste, collaborated with Milt Merlin in a deft teleplay and delivered, in the key role, a slickly shaded portrayal."

Commentary: After agreeing to help friend David Niven get *Four Star* off the ground in the ratings, Colman bought the rights to this story on the advice of *Halls of Ivy* writer Milton Merlin, who then worked with Colman to conjure a viable teleplay. They crafted a comedy of manners, giving Colman a chance to be glibly debonair in his television debut at 61.

Following a delightful opening half-minute of pantomime, that's all this show amounts to: a lot of glib banter about retrieving a silk hat because a 60ish gentleman is afraid to be seen in public without it and doesn't want to admit he was wrong to have had a fight with his fiancée. The second half is a battle of wits between the melodramatically superficial gentleman and a pseudo-romantic poet, played with hammy self-indulgence by Whorf. When the gentleman goes back into the house after all and makes amends with the woman, the viewer can only feel glad that a meaningless talky half-hour is over.

Archival Source: UCLA. 16mm print from the syndicated run of *Four Star* shows called *Star Performance*. (PVA7948).

TV2 THE 25TH ANNUAL ACADEMY AWARDS
March 19, 1953. MCs: Bob Hope (Hollywood), Conrad Nagel (New York). NBC radio and TV simulcast from the Pantages Theatre in Hollywood with cut-ins from NBC's International Theatre at Columbus Circle in New York City. Two hours. See F61 and R399.

Colman's *only* live TV appearance was as a presenter on the first television broadcast of the Academy Awards. He presented the Oscar for Best Actress to Shirley Booth for *Come Back, Little Sheba*. Booth was seen accepting from the International Theatre on a huge TV screen mounted back of the Pantages stage. She was then playing at the Empire Theatre in *Time of the Cuckoo*.

A kinescope of this show is on file at the AMPAS building at 8949 Wilshire Blvd. in Beverly Hills.

TV3 FOUR STAR PLAYHOUSE
March 26, 1953. "The Man Who Walked Out on Himself," an original screenplay by Milton Merlin. Producer: Ronald Colman. Executive Producer: Don W. Sharpe. Director: Robert Florey. Assistant Director: John Pommer. Production Supervisor: Ruby Rosenberg. Director of Photography: George E. Diskant, ASC. John Pommer. Art Director: Ralph Berger. Editor: Frank Doyle, ACE. Camera Effects: Clarence Slifer. CBS. 30 minutes.

Cast: Ronald Colman (John Cameron), Francis Pierlot (Edward, Men's Club valet).

Synopsis: A wealthy clubman is about to marry a younger woman—after separating from his wife—when his mirror image walks out on him in disgust. A virtual one-man show comprising mostly one-way telephone conversations and the man talking to himself out loud or in voice-overs.

Review: Helm, *Daily Variety*, 3-30-53: "Suave and polished in all his movements and mannerisms, Colman embellishes the role with consummate artistry and conviction despite the difficulty of playing it alone and, for the most part, to himself."

Commentary: The mirror image is a metaphor for Cameron seeing himself as he really is, a glibly charming but selfish and empty man who rationalizes his selfishness. His wife, who knows him all too well, fends off a gift of his summer home as a self-serving gesture because the place is run down. Even his intended fiancée, Lenore, sees through him, putting off their impending marriage and a lunch date. But, even though Cameron comes to his senses in the end, he has no more depth than at the beginning. Merlin's intent, clearly, was to use Colman's patented surface charm to point up the shallowness of such charm. He also gave the actor nothing to show below that surface except for a clichéd change of heart and nothing to do except indulge his matinée idol mannerisms. The only human moments are when Pierlot shows up for two scenes, upstaging Colman with his unassumingly gracious warmth.

Archival Source: UCLA. 16mm print under *Star Performance* banner, PVA7948.

TV4 FOUR STAR PLAYHOUSE
May 21, 1953. "Ladies on His Mind," an original screenplay by Milton Merlin. Producer: Ronald Colman. Executive Producer: Don W. Sharpe. Director: Robert Florey. Assistant

Director: John Pommer. Production Supervisor: Ruby Rosenberg. Director of Photography: George E. Diskant, ASC. Art Director: Ralph Berger. Pantomime Choreography of Daydream Scenes: Ronald Colman. Editor: Samuel E. Beetley, ACE. Makeup: Karl Herlinger. Furs: A.Z. Arnold. CBS. 30 minutes. See B423.

Cast: Ronald Colman (Dr. Matthew Bosanquent), Benita Hume (Deborah Bosanquent), Patricia Morison (Charlotte Kirby), Elizabeth Fraser (Diana Shore), Hillary Brooke (Miriam Newsom), Alix Talton (Nurse Kimble).

Synopsis: A debonair psychiatrist deals with the anxieties and egos of three of his female patients (Morison, Fraser and Brooke). Hume appears at the beginning and end as the psychiatrist's wife. Each of the three psychiatric vignettes features a pantomimic daydream of the psychiatrist.

Review: Daku, *Daily Variety*, 5-26-53: "It's a too-talky, too-static, tiresome half-hour of Ronald Colman being whimsical. Veteran radio scripter Milton Merlin...failed to readjust his typewriter for TV."

Commentary: Merlin's idea was to satirize psychiatry, a profession he feels is pretentious and fatuous. So, he wrote Colman a role as a fatuously charming psychiatrist who claims that all he does is listen. Well, if all a "shrink" does is listen, why does he need an M.D.? It's how he interprets what he hears that makes the difference, as anyone should know.

The problem with the premise is that Merlin deals with psychiatry and real emotional problems in a glibly dismissive manner. And yet, there is gold here. Morison steals the show as an actress who acts love but cannot feel it, giving off a sexual glow as Colman, trying to hog the camera by not looking at her, explains her defensive mechanism in order to cure her neurosis.

The main problem with these three *Four Star* shows is that Merlin, who told me this in an interview, saw Colman as a charming but limited actor with an equally limited vocal range. So he wrote and co-wrote scripts that pandered to Colman's limitations rather than playing to his strengths; flattering his star vanity, but giving him no chance to convey the emotional solidity beneath the charm and vocal cadence that made him a star in the first place. For "The Lost Silk Hat", of course, Colman was equally to blame.

Archival Source: UCLA. 16mm print under *Star Performance* banner, PVA7948.

TV5 FOUR STAR PLAYHOUSE
January 21, 1954. "A String of Beads" by W. Somerset Maugham. Rhino Video #2953.

An Everest Production. Executive Producer: Don W. Sharpe. Production supervisor: Ronald Colman. Producer: William Frye. Adaptation by Don Ettlinger. Designer/Director: William Cameron Menzies. Editorial Supervisor: Bernard Burton. Director of Photography: George E. Diskant, ASC. Art Director: Duncan Cramer. Editor: Samuel E. Beetley, ACE. Fashions: Helfts. Pearl necklace: Kenneth Brown. Assistant Director: Bruce Fowler. Associate Producer: Ann Marlowe (Credit by contract since she owned the story rights). CBS. 30 minutes.

Cast: Ronald Colman (Somerset Maugham), Angela Lansbury (Joan Robinson), George Macready (Count Borselli), Brenda Forbes (Edythe Livingstone), Ron Randell (Peter Jeffries), Nigel Bruce (Colonel Mournay), Sean McClory (Robert Upton), Sarah Selby (Delia Charlton), Ben Wright (the Jeweler), Dorothy Green (Laura).

Synopsis: An unemployed young woman (Lansbury) becomes governess for an upper-class British household when a count (Macready) appraises her string of paste beads as a valuable pearl necklace, making her appear to be the equal of the socialite who hires her. She is romanced by a fortune hunter (Randell), but ends up marrying the count, who began the hoax to see what would happen.

Review: Daku, *Daily Variety*, 1-26-54: "...a worthy entry which...shows fine prospects for a series...Colman is on briefly, and suavely essays the storyteller role."

Background and commentary: Colman produced this show in 1953 as the pilot for a Somerset Maugham series, with the working title of *Ronald Colman TV*. That is the show title on the print from which these credits are taken. Colman comes on at the end in formal dress to pitch the series to prospective sponsors. There had been an earlier Maugham anthology on CBS and NBC from 1950-51.

Colman bought the rights to "A String of Beads", but it was an anecdotal bit of nothing, so Ettlinger had to overhaul it. He mostly threw it out altogether, doing a good job of transforming it into a real story with real characters. His script combined with Menzies' direction and a first-rate cast resulted in a show that is a polished, well-acted, and smoothly entertaining but forgettable trifle.

However, Colman's performance is flawed by his star ego. For example, in the restaurant scenes that bookend the story, he never makes eye contact with actress Dorothy Green.

A few weeks after this show aired on *Four Star*, attempts to sell the series were dropped when CBS offered Colman and his wife, Benita, the lead roles in a TV version of *The Halls of Ivy* after first they, then other husband-and-wife teams, including Rex Harrison and Lilli Palmer, had turned it down. A sad footnote is that this was Nigel Bruce's only television performance. He died on October 18, 1953, shortly after his two days' work on this show.

Archival Source: UCLA. 35mm and 16mm prints. PVA1428 for the latter.

THE HALLS OF IVY (CBS, 1954-55, 39 episodes) See B74, B90, B183, B198, B210, B397.

Edward Small Productions. Created by Don Quinn. Producer: William Frye. Co-producer: Leon Fromkess. Directed in rotation by Norman Z. McLeod (pronounced McCloud, 16 shows), William Cameron Menzies (16) and William D. Russell (7). Most scripts mostly verbatim from episodes of the radio series by Barbara Merlin and other writers as noted. Announcer: Ken Carpenter. Theme song: Henry Russell and Vick Knight. Director of Photography: Al Gilks, ASC. Camera operator: Al Lane. Assistant cameramen: Roger Hager and Hugo Brandon. Art director: Perry Ferguson. Film editor: Otto Meyer, ACE. Sound editor: Jack Hunsaker. Sound mixer: Dean Thomas. Sound lab: Glenn Glenn. Make-up: Lee Greenway. Wardrobe: Bob Richards. Assistant director: Bruce Fowler, Jr. Script supervisor: Mary Gibson. Casting director: Betty Pagel. Rotating sponsors: International Harvester and Nabisco.

Broadcast day and time: Tuesday nights at 8:30 until July 14, 1955, when it switched to Thursdays at 10:30. CBS. 30 minutes.

Broadcast History: CBS premiere: October 19, 1954 for a one-season run of 39 episodes, 20 of them without a laugh track as a commercial compromise. The final episode, a rerun, aired October 13, 1955. The series was briefly syndicated in the late 1950s and late 1960s. In Los Angeles, it aired on KWHY Channel 22 from 1966-67.

Cast: Ronald Colman (Dr. William Todhunter Hall), Benita Colman (Victoria Cromwell Hall), Herb Butterfield (Clarence Wellman, 32 shows), Mary Wickes (Alice, the Maid), James Todd (John Merriweather, 4 shows), Ray Collins (John Merriweather, 2 shows), Arthur Q. Bryan (Prof. Warren, 8 shows).

Note: Todd dropped out as Merriweather after four episodes, but because the shows were not aired in the order they were filmed, Todd was seen in TV21 after Collins was in

TV18.

Syndication source: ITC, Domestic Sales Dept., 12711 Ventura Blvd., Studio City, CA 91604. 818-760-2110.

Because no TV station in the U.S. has asked to lease this series since 1967, the prints on hand have not been transferred to tape. They are strewn over several ITC warehouses in London, according to Valerie Bisson-Goldberg of ITC.

Background and Commentary: The literate qualities that made *The Halls of Ivy* click on radio worked against it on television. On radio, the Colmans could get away with endless literary quips, epigrams and bon mots because the series was tailored to that medium. Their timing also depended on playing to a studio audience. Television was a different matter. Without quick pacing, visual humor now and then, and music—what was funny on radio fell flat on the small screen. All that many episodes amounted to were static shots of Ronnie and Benita endlessly talking to each other or that week's cast.

Another problem was that Ronnie seldom looked straight at Benita, but to one side of her so that attention was focused on him. He was again being the consummate camera thief.

Radio script revisions were more extensive than Don Quinn admitted to *TV-Radio Life* (B198.) Dialogue had to be written for Mary Wickes since the Hall's maid did not appear in most of the radio originals; two episodes, "Football Fix" and "F. Canis Minor", were TV originals; and romantic flashbacks were limited to a few episodes, naming a few changes.

Shooting started Friday June 5, 1954, with a budget of $50,000 per episode, the highest budget of any half-hour show to that time. Episodes were shot two at a time back-to-back over seven days with a three-day break between each shoot.

As the series wore on, Colman's health deteriorated. In poor shape at 63, he didn't have the stamina required for the long days of TV production, and he was still smoking a good deal, aggravating his long-time lung fibrosis. Moreover, he would not go for a checkup because he didn't trust doctors. And yet despite being rundown, when the last of 39 episodes was finished on March 9, 1955, Colman wanted to continue for a second season.

Ivy producer William Frye recalls that "Ronnie would have gone on despite his ill health because he loved the work, but CBS canceled the series because it had poor ratings. It was an erudite show that was ahead of its time and it lacked physical action. It didn't fit in with other sitcoms like *I Love Lucy* and *Make Room For Daddy*, which were made on the same RKO lot."

Los Angeles Mirror columnist Hal Humphrey told a different story in his December 28, 1956 column (B210) when the show was in syndication. He stated that the sponsors had dropped the series and that Colman was continuously disgruntled by their continual interference during production. Asked about this column today, Frye says that "Humphrey was a nice guy, but I don't recall any sponsor or ad agency interference. It was smooth sailing all the way. It simply didn't generate the numbers it needed for a second season."

For whatever reason the series was canceled, it was just as well because it wasn't right for television.

Ironically, though *The Halls of Ivy* was not a hit series, it *was* Colman's major contribution to television, earning him a posthumous star for his TV work on the Hollywood Walk of Fame (A20), rather than for his far more prolific and qualitative radio work.

Notes: Since all but two episodes were remakes of the radio versions, rather than repeat every synopsis from that chapter, I am giving the number for each episode based on a radio script (except for TV7, 29, 37 and 40 for lack of radio dates for them) and providing a synopsis where the storyline was revised or updated or wholly new for television. Because most scripts were verbatim from the Merlin's radio originals, only Barbara Merlin received credit. Quinn's credit was mostly due to contractual agreement, as it was on radio.

Finally, where I give two titles, the left one is the script title, the right one is the TV syndication title.

TV6 October 19, 1954. "Reappointment," by Barbara Merlin from Quinn's radio script. Director: McLeod. **Cast:** Herb Butterfield, James Todd, John Hamilton, Charles Evans, Lonnie Sherman, Gloria Gordon (Penny the Maid in flashback scene). Includes opening voice-over narration by Colman, a device used only for this episode. See R266.

> **Review:** Chan, *Weekly Variety*, 10-27-54: "There's a class of radio properties which have lost much of their charm on being translated into television. 'Halls of Ivy,' to judge from the first filmed episode, unfortunately appears to fall into this category. The addition of sight to the dulcet Ronald Colman & Co. tones appears to rob the show of much of its comfortable warmth, and that, above everything else, was the quality that made the show a hit on radio.
> "Not that the Colmans...don't dress up a tv screen....But the zing is missing. First episode...was a rambling and rather dull affair, with nary a flash of humor throughout the proceedings. The dialog, another ingredient that made the ayemer successful, was flat though still high-flown. Use of a million-dollar vocabulary without endowing it with meaning or wit is purposeless, and that's just another of the faults of the first show.
> "On the face of it, the new vid-pixer defies classification—and appears to lack purpose. It's not a situation comedy, because there was little comedy. It's certainly not a dramatic entry. It might be classified as a 'family' show, but that doesn't mean anything. Producer Frye, directors Norman McLeod and William Cameron Menzies and writer Quinn, all of them topflight filmmaking-broadcasting pros, need to give 'Halls of Ivy' much more direction, pace and humor before it can even begin to compare to its radio counterpart."

Comment: The dancing lesson from the radio original was dropped for new dialogue about Mother Goose, but Merlin and Quinn also removed the charm and wit of the original. McLeod, the sole director, substituted laborious pacing for sparkle, just as Chan observed.

TV7 October 26, 1954. (Rerun August 25, 1955.) "Heart of Passion/Warren's Novel," by Barbara Merlin from the Merlins' radio script. Director: Menzies. **Cast:** Herb Butterfield, Arthur Q. Bryan, Verna Felton (Miss Burgess, Warren's housekeeper).

TV8 November 2, 1954. (Rerun August 18, 1955.) "Pregnant Student/Dr. Hall's Baby," by Barbara Merlin from the Merlins' radio script. Director: Menzies. **Cast:** Joseph Sawyer (Officer Grogan), Howard Freeman (Prof. Heaslip), Connie Marshall (Caroline Swanson), Cecil Weston (Floor nurse), Jeanne Bates (Nurse #1), Dorothy Bruce (Nurse #2), Lee Millar (Prospective Father in Waiting Room). See R372.

When Heaslip refuses to let pregnant Caroline Swanson take a late examination regardless of doctor's orders confining her to bed at home, Hall gives her the exam himself, only to learn she is giving birth immediately.

Note: Preempted in California and other states for election returns. First seen in those states when it was rerun on the above date.

TV9 November 9, 1954. (Rerun August 11, 1955.) "The Wellmans Come to Dinner," by Barbara Merlin from the Merlins' radio script. Director: McLeod. **Cast:** James Todd, Herb Butterfield, Sarah Selby (Bertha Wellman). See R373.

TV10 November 16, 1954. "Mrs. Whitney's Statue," by Barbara Merlin from the radio script by Hector Chevigny and Quinn. Director: McLeod. **Cast:** Elliott Reid (Crane, Ivy News reporter), James Todd, Herb Butterfield, Paula Winslowe (Mrs. Whitney). See R284.

TV11 November 23, 1954. (Rerun August 4, 1955.) "Professor Barrett's Play," by Jerry Davis from the radio script by Robert Sinclair, Walter Brown Newman and Quinn. Director: Menzies. **Cast:** Henry Hull (Prof. Barrett), John Litel (Harry Nolan). See R310.

TV12 November 30, 1954. "Astronomy Exam/The Astronomer," by Barbara Merlin from the Merlins' radio script. Director: Menzies. **Cast:** Herb Butterfield, Jay Novello (Prof. Maxwell), Douglas Dick (Leslie Gifford). See R359.

TV13 December 7, 1954. "The Eleventh Commandment," by Decla Dunning from her radio script. Director: Menzies. **Cast:** Herb Butterfield, Joanne Davis (Ann Garrick), Herb Vigran (Bullock, Ivy News reporter. See R329.

TV14 December 14, 1954. "The Fighting Med Student/The Prizefighter," by Barbara Merlin from the Merlins' radio script. Director: McLeod. **Cast:** Arthur Q. Bryan, Leonard Freeman (Beans Phillips), Ken Christy (Jeff Packard). See R286, B72.

TV15 December 21, 1954. "Mrs. Why?," by Barbara Merlin from the Merlins' radio script. Director: McLeod. **Cast:** Herb Butterfield, Arthur Q. Bryan, Charlotte Knight (Felicia Yates), Olan Soulé (Addison Yates). See R340.

TV16 December 28, 1954. (Rerun September 1, 1955.) "Professor Warren's Romance," by Barbara Merlin from the Merlins' radio script. Director: Menzies. **Cast:** Herb Butterfield, Arthur Q. Bryan, Gladys Hurlbut (Fern Winthrop). See R345.

TV17 January 4, 1955. "Halloween/Pinkerton Day," by Barbara Merlin from the radio script by Ronald Colman. Director: McLeod. **Cast:** Herb Butterfield, Ken Christy (Mr. Barnaby), Charles Smith (John Smith, Sr.), Tom Powers (John Smith, Jr.) See R342.

TV18 January 11, 1955. "Traffic and Cocoanuts/Cocoanuts," by Barbara Merlin from the radio script by Nat Wolff and Quinn. Song: "I've Got a Lovely Bunch of Cocoanuts" by Fred Heatherton (1944). Director: McLeod. **Cast:** Herb Butterfield, Ray Collins, Bill Thompson (Mr. Conkle, the druggist), Joe Hamilton, Gene Puerling and Clark Burroughs (trio performing with Benita.) See R281. Colman doesn't sing at the end as he did on radio.

TV19 January 18, 1955. "The Chinese Student," by Barbara Merlin from Quinn's radio script. Director: McLeod. **Cast:** Herb Butterfield, Barbara Jean Wong (Margaret Lee), Ralph Moody. See R272.

TV20 January 25, 1955. "The Track Star," by Barbara Merlin from the Merlins' radio script. Director: McLeod. **Cast:** Herb Butterfield, William Tracy (Wally Lovett), James Milligan and Larry Garr. See R354.

TV21 February 1, 1955. (Rerun July 28, 1955.) "The Scofield Prize/Dr. Hall's Book" by Barbara Merlin from the Merlins' radio script. Director: Menzies. **Cast:** James Todd, John Lupton (Jared Buckley), Herb Vigran (Bullock, reporter), Shirley O'Hara (newspaper secretary). See R282.

TV22   February 8, 1955. "Mummynapper," by Barbara Merlin from the Merlins' radio script. Director: McLeod. **Cast:** Herb Butterfield, James Hayes (Tommy Spencer), Mollie McCart (Lynne Gordon). See R371.

TV23   February 15, 1955. (Rerun July 21, 1955.) "Note the Quote," by Barbara Merlins from the radio script by Jerome Lawrence and Robert E. Lee. Director: Menzies. **Cast:** Herb Butterfield, Willard Waterman ("Chuckles" Harrison), Robert Nichols (Bradley B. Bradley), John Smith, Fran Bennett, Tom Irish and Fred Grimes (Students in malt shop). See R326.

TV24   February 22, 1955. "Faculty Follies, Part 1," by Barbara Merlin from the radio script by Don Quinn and Charles Henry. Director: Menzies. **Cast:** Paul Smith (Danny Flannagan), Arthur Q. Bryan, Herb Butterfield. See R367.

TV25   March 1, 1955. "Faculty Follies, Part 2," by Barbara Merlin from the radio script by Don Quinn and Charles Henry. Song: "Alice's House." Kipling patter routine by Quinn. Director: Menzies. **Cast:** Paul Smith (Danny Flannagan), Frank Yenks, Herb Butterfield, and Rex Evans. See R368.

TV26   March 8, 1955. "Warren's Retirement," by Barbara Merlin from their radio script. Director: Menzies. **Cast:** Herb Butterfield, Arthur Q. Bryan. See R314.

TV27   March 15, 1955. "Stolen First Edition," by Barbara Merlin from the Merlins' radio script. Director: Menzies. **Cast:** Herb Butterfield, Moroni Olsen (Henry Vanderlip), Rolfe Sedan (Mr. Empson), Henry Blair (Tucker Mills), Thom Conroy. See R289.

TV28   March 22, 1955. "The French Student/The French Exchange Student," by Barbara Merlin from the Merlins' radio script co-written with Benita Colman. Director: McLeod. **Cast:** Herb Butterfield, Gladys Holland (Heloise Genét). See R365.

TV29   March 29, 1955. (Rerun September 8, 1955.) "Calhoun Gaddy," by Barbara Merlins from the Merlins' radio script. Director: Russell. **Cast:** Herb Butterfield, Jimmy Weldon (Calhoun Gaddy).
   Weldon's Southern-fried exuberance makes this episode a comic pleasure. He was also a great TV kid show host.

TV30   April 5, 1955. (Rerun September 15, 1955.) "The Oldest Living Graduate/The Oldest Alumnus," by Barbara Merlin from the radio script by David Robison and Quinn. Director: Russell. **Cast:** Herb Butterfield, Erville Alderson (Silas Livingstone). See R361.
   At the finale, Livingstone makes a public confession that dismays some while cheering others.

TV31   April 12, 1955. (Rerun September 22, 1955.) "Professor Rousseau/Scandal," by Barbara Merlins from the Merlins' radio script. Director: Russell. **Cast:** Herb Butterfield, Maurice Marsac (Prof. Rousseau), Tamar Cooper (Linda Matthews), Melinda Markey and Byron Foulger. See R299.

TV32   April 19, 1955. (Rerun September 29, 1955.) "Football Fix," an original by Barbara and Milton Merlin using the basic idea of "Gangster's Son" (R268) by Nat Wolff and Don Quinn. Director: Russell. **Cast:** Ted DeCorsia (Mike "Kid Gloves" Coster), Adam Williams

(Johnny Adams, Coster's nephew), Jack Elam (Percy, Coster's bodyguard), Herb Butterfield.

Except for a few lines lifted from the radio script, an original. Mike Mallotte is now Mike "Kid Gloves" Coster, an unabashed gangster with a rising football star nephew named Johnny. Only nephew Johnny is barred from the Ivy football team for flunking his "bonehead English" exam, so Coster offers to donate a building to Ivy in exchange for a re-exam for Johnny six weeks sooner than allowed...or else.

First-rate dramatic episode with a few laughs. It's sharply written and directed, smartly paced, and makes good, creative use of ominous music at the beginning. DeCorsia's polished, insinuating menace is beautifully matched by Colman's steely integrity; there is a crackling tension in their scenes. All of these qualities make one wish *all* the episodes were this good.

TV33 April 26, 1955. (Rerun October 6, 1955.) "F. Canis Minor," an original script by Frederick Brady. Director: Russell. **Cast:** Richard Tyler (Phipps Lassiter), Jerry Paris (Steve Henry), Bob Sands (Michael), and Hal Lytton.

A group of pranksters enroll the Ivy mascot, a dog named Fritz, under the name of F. Canis Minor to impress board chairman Wellman with the problem of large classes and too few teachers. Thick-headed Clarence misses the connotation, so Hall steps in to drive the point home, with comic results.

TV34 May 3, 1955. (Rerun October 13, 1955.) "The French Scholarship/Fountaine Foundation," by Barbara Merlin from the Merlins' radio script. Director: Russell. **Cast:** Herb Butterfield, John Hoyt (Prof. Duvoir), John Litel (Alexander Simmons), Barry Truex (Whitmore Larkin). See R318, on which it was the Le Grande Foundation.

TV35 May 10, 1955. "Professor Grimes," by Barbara Merlins from the radio script by Kenneth Brown and Quinn. Director: McLeod. **Cast:** John Bryant (Prof. Grimes), Herb Butterfield, Sarah Selby (Bertha Wellman). See R363.

TV36 May 17, 1955. "Professor Royce/Old Professor Forgot His Umbrella," by Barbara Merlin from the Merlins' radio script. Director: Menzies. **Cast:** Herb Butterfield, Francis Pierlot (Royce). See R347.

TV37 May 24, 1955. "The Honor Student," by Barbara Merlin from the Merlins' radio script. Director: Menzies. **Cast:** Arthur Q. Bryan, Carol Brannon (Dale Anderson), Howard McNear.

TV38 May 31, 1955. "Nelson Carter's Son/Changing Professors," by Barbara Merlin from the radio script by Clyde W. Park. Director: Russell. **Cast:** Martin Milner (Jerry Carter), Nelson Leigh (Nelson Carter). See R351.

TV39 June 7, 1955. "Voice of the Ivy Vine," by Barbara Merlin from the Merlins' radio script. Director: Menzies. **Cast:** Herb Butterfield, Ray Collins. Karen Steele (Betty Gibson, the Voice), Grandon Rhodes, Eddie Ryder and Fred Grimes. See R357.

TV40 June 14, 1955 "Maxwell's Comet," by Barbara Merlin from the Merlins' radio script. Director: McLeod. **Cast:** Herb Butterfield, Jay Novello (Prof. Maxwell).

TV41 June 21, 1955. "Dr. Spatzen," by Barbara Merlin from the Merlins' radio script. Director: McLeod. **Cast:** Herb Butterfield, Sig Ruman (Dr. Spatzen). See R370.

TV42 June 28, 1955. "Student Vandalism and the Draft/Hoodlumism," by Barbara Merlin from Don Quinn's radio script. Director: Menzies. **Cast:** Paul Smith (Danny Flannagan), Dick Kaiser (Thomas Clayton), James Flavin and Jeff York (Policemen). See R323 and R327.
Unlike the original, the Korean War is not at issue since it had ended in 1953.

TV43 July 5, 1955. "Dean Huxley," by Barbara Merlin from the Merlins' radio script. Director: McLeod. **Cast:** Arthur Q. Bryan, Howard McNear (Grosvenor), Jeanette Nolan (Dean Huxley). See R356.

TV44 July 14, 1955. "Faculty Marriage," by Barbara Merlin from the Merlins' radio script. Director: McLeod. **Cast:** Whit Bissell (Prof. John Gardner), ? (Prof. Lucy Otis Gardner), Herb Butterfield. See R364.

TV45 STUDIO 57 (Syndicated, shown in Los Angeles on KABC) October 11, 1956. (Rerun June 27, 1957.) "Perfect Likeness" by David P. Harmon from a story by Richard Lewis and Harmon. Revue Productions for Heinz Food Co. Producer: Richard Lewis. Director: Don Weis. Director of Photography: John McBurnie, ASC. Editor: Michael R. McAdam, ACE. Art director: Martin Obzina. Music supervision: Stanley Wilson.
     Cast: Ronald Colman (Painter), Kim Hunter, Steve Brodie, Philip Pine, Peggy Maley, Charles Tannen, Gloria Marshall, George Keymas, Than Weyenn, Bert Holland, Stanley Adams.
     Synopsis: The owner (Brodie) of a Saroyan-like bar peopled by offbeat characters is in love with his waitress (Hunter), who in turn is fixated on a heel (Pine). An itinerant artist (Colman) sets things right with an idealized portrait of the waitress for a quick $10.
     Review: Kove, *Daily Variety*, October 15: "Colman essays this stint lightly, but his lines, which are skillfully delivered, add up to little...Director Don Weis does a good job of establishing mood, but can't quite make the weak story come to life."

TV46 JACK BENNY
November 4, 1956. "The Mistaken Dinner Invitation." CBS. 30 minutes. See R98, R384.
     J&M Productions, Inc. Executive Producer/Director: Ralph Levy. Producer: Hilliard Marks. Associate Producer: Richard Fisher. Writers: Sam Perrin, George Balzer, Al Gordon, Hal Goldman. Musical Director: Mahlon Merrick. Director of Photography: John McBurnie, ASC. Art director: John Meehan. Set decorator: James Redd. Editorial supervisor: Richard G. Wray, ACE. Film editor: Daniel A. Nathan, ACE. Sound: Earl Crain, Jr. Assistant director: Jack Corrick. Wardrobe supervisor: Vincent Dee. Makeup: Leo Lotito, Jr. Cigarette pitchman in final commercial: André Baruch. Sponsor: American Tobacco.
     Cast: Jack Benny, Ronald and Benita Colman, Eddie Anderson, Mary Livingstone, Don Wilson, John Sutton (Jack Wellington), Eric Snowden (Sherwood, the butler), Lois Corbett (second woman at bridge game).
     Background and Comments: In 1951, Ronnie and Benita were set to make their TV debuts on the live version of the Benny show, but backed out after their appearance was announced when Ronnie had second thoughts. Though he had done hundreds of live radio shows, live television was a daunting prospect because he would have been appearing in a live stage performance for the first time in nearly 29 years. In the end, the Colmans made

only one filmed appearance on the Benny TV show, a revision of their first Benny radio show from 1945.

It's a fair show with a few laughs (the gimmick is a flashback to August 15, 1945—see R96—the day after WWII ended), but not as good as the radio version because watching the Colmans and Benny being awkward with each other makes the viewer feel uncomfortable. It's not as funny as hearing it.

Print Source: UCLA, PVA7468.

TV47 GENERAL ELECTRIC THEATER

December 16, 1956. (Rerun July 21, 1957.) "The Chess Game", adapted by Bernard Schoenfeld and Robert Howard from a story by Edmund Rice. Revue Productions for General Electric. Producer: William Frye. Director: Herschel Daugherty. Host: Ronald Reagan. Photographer: Herbert Kirkpatrick, ASC. Film editor: Edward Haire, ACE. CBS. 30 minutes.

Cast: Ronald Colman (Mr. Graham), Clifford Tatum, Adam Williams, Russ Conway, Maxine Cooper, Sarah Selby.

Synopsis: A 15-year-old boy (Tatum) escaping the police after stoning a woman to death takes refuge for three months as the nephew of a cynical and alcoholic though intellectual gentleman named Graham who believes the boy can be redeemed. The divinity student (Williams) who lives in the apartment below Graham and plays chess with him knows what Graham is doing but does not go to the police about it.

Review: Helm, *Daily Variety*, December 19: "As an intellectual with a thick coating of cynicism and a philosophy veined with irony, he seemed happily encased in the role... Colman disported with all the gay abandon of an actor doing what he likes to do."

Comment: Colman's role sounds like Sydney Carton grown old.

TV48 HOLLYWOOD HIST-O-RAMA (1961)

Jayark Films Corp. A Julieart Production. Produced and directed by Joseph R. Juliano. Created by Raymond R. Stuart. Unidentified narrator. 4 minutes.

One of a series of hastily assembled pseudo-tributes to movie stars produced as filler for five-minute slots on local stations. Greta Garbo, Humphrey Bogart and Robert Montgomery were some of the other stars. The one on Colman is typical, comprising a poorly assembled procession of 36 stills, accompanied by a high-pitched, breathlessly nasal, inane narration that jumbles the chronology of Colman's movies because the writer-whoever he was—didn't bother to get his facts straight. At one point, the narrator says that *Clive of India* (1935) was followed by Colman's own production of *Arrowsmith* (1931), for which he won the Oscar as Best Actor, followed by *A Tale of Two Cities* (1935). The script also mistakes *Kismet* stills for photos from *If I Were King*. For the final segment (there are two commercial breaks), you can hear the narrator turning his script page.

Print Source: UCLA, PVA7467.

TV49 THE HOLLYWOOD GREATS (BBC-1, Program 2 in a series) August 10, 1978.

8:10-9 p.m. Producer: Barry Brown. Writer/ host: Barry Norman. Research: Sue Mallinson, Barbara Paskin. Director: Margaret Sharp. Photography: Nigel Walters, Ken MacMillan, Reg Pope. Rostrum camera: John Clement. Graphic designer: Clive Piercy. Sound: Maurice Everitt, Basil Harris. Film editor: Victor Jamison. dubbing Mixer: Alan Dykes. Production assistant: Judy Lindsay. Film clips courtesy of: Columbia Television, EMI-Pathé,

Filmfinders, Johnar Film Productions, MGM, Visnews, Juliet Colman. Photographs courtesy of: Juliet Colman, Culver Pictures Inc., the Kobal Collection, Mander & Mitchenson, National Film Archive.

People Interviewed (In order of appearance): Bessie Love, Henry King, Celeste Holm, David Niven, Juliet Colman, Lillian Gish, Milton Merlin, Alvin Weingand, John Cromwell, Joseph L. Mankiewicz, Barbara Merlin, George Cukor, Shelley Winters.

Commentary: A dryly personal overview of Colman's life and career with an amateur feel to the production. There's little depth and a predictable selection of clips, but rare color home movie footage of the Colmans aboard their yacht and a clip from a 1948 British newsreel. Strictly for Colman fans rather than movie buffs in general. Producer Brown told me in October of 1982, when I was at his London office to see this show on tape, that the *Hollywood Greats* series could never be shown in the U.S. because of clearance rights for clips. Which may mean that Brown didn't have the money for those rights.

TV50 STAR CLIPS
1987. Host: Tom McCorkle. Nostalgia Channel. 7 minutes, 20 seconds.

Filler Colman tribute showing lengthy clips from *Raffles*, *Arrowsmith* and *Clive of India*, interspersed with standard publicity stills, but no clips from his best work of the mid to late 1930s. Whoever wrote the script also got a few facts wrong. Still, a welcome if inadequate primer.

Discount Video Tapes: (818) 843-3366. "The Lost Silk Hat." Paired with another *Four Star Playhouse* show, "Welcome Home", starring Dick Powell.

Rhino Video: (800) 432-0020. "A String of Beads." EP tape as part of a 2-cassette Angela Lansbury set. Other show is "The Indiscreet Mrs. Jarvis" from Fireside Theater. Picture quality at 6-hour speed is inferior.

DISCOGRAPHY

Ronald Colman made seven commercial recordings, four of which—1,3,5,7—are on audio cassette. Commercial releases of his radio shows are also listed, along with recordings of music from his movies. The commercial records are listed first, followed by the radio shows and movie scores, the latter two in chronology of air dates and film release years.

D1 A CHRISTMAS CAROL (1941)
Decca DA-290. 29M Personality series. Three-record 12" 78 rpm set. Catalog numbers 29108-110. This series comprised records featuring movie stars. Reissued on LP as DL-9022 with *Mr. Pickwick's Christmas* on side two, narrated by Charles Laughton. Timing: 22 minutes, 45 seconds.
Recorded September 17, 1941 in Hollywood. Released late November of 1941. See R245, R403.
Adapted from the Charles Dickens novel and directed by George Wells. Musical director: Victor Young. Vocal director: Ken Darby.
Cast: Ronald Colman (Ebenezer Scrooge), Eric Snowden (Bob Cratchit), Barbara Jean Wong (Tiny Tim), Lou Merrill (Jacob Marley), Hans Conried (Ghost of Christmas Past, Man in the Street), Cy Kendall (Ghost of Christmas Present), Gale Gordon (Ghost of Christmas Future), Heather Thatcher (Mrs. Cratchit), Fred Mackaye (Fred the Nephew, Man in the Street), Stephen Muller (Boy in the Street on Christmas Day), Duane Thompson (Belle the Sweetheart), Ferdinand Munier (Mr. Portley, the Charity Solicitor).
Comments: In a change of pace from his usual roles, Colman gives a fairly good performance in this workmanlike truncation of the famous story. Because of the brief running time, this record could only present the highlights of the Dickens story, so it lacks the depth and dimension of the hour-long version performed on radio for nearly 20 years with Lionel Barrymore as Scrooge. Ironically, Barrymore's half-hour version on his series, *Mayor of the Town*, was also released on 78s in the early 1940s so that for several years, he and Colman were competing Scrooges.

D2 A POEM AND PRAYER FOR AN INVADING ARMY (1944)
RCA ND-4-MC-5606. One 12" 78 rpm record. Released August(?) 1944. Timing: 9 minutes. See R76.

Commemorative recording of Colman's reading of Edna St. Vincent Millay's poem, originally read live on D-Day. Profits went to war relief.

D3 LOST HORIZON (1946)
Decca DA-402. 29M Personality Series. Three-record 12" 78 rpm set. Catalog numbers 29188-90. Reissued on 12" LP with "A Tale of Two Cities" as Decca DL-9059 (D5). Timing: 27 minutes, 43 seconds.

Recorded September 15 and 16, 1944 in Hollywood. See D10, D15, D16, F44, R27, R54, R110, R173.

Adapted from the James Hilton novel, produced and directed by George Wells. Music composed and conducted by Victor Young.

Cast: Ronald Colman (Hugh Conway), Dennis Green (Mallinson), ? (Chang), Lurene Tuttle (Lo-Tsen), Norman Field (the High Lama).

Comments: Of all the audio abridgments of the Hilton story—none of which are based on the movie—this is by far the best for all of the usual qualities and its lingering mood, though Hilton's story flaws are immediately apparent. This script was later used twice on *Favorite Story*: once for the live KFI broadcast with Raymond Burr as Conway, the second time for the syndicated version starring Colman.

D4 TALES OF THE OLYMPIAN GODS (1946)
Decca DA-475. Three-record 10" 78 rpm set. Catalog numbers 40013-15. A fourth record was made but not issued. Timing: 20 minutes.

Recorded January 21 and 22, 1946 in Hollywood.

Based on Bullfinch's *The Age of Fable*. Adapted by Louis Untermeyer and Nat Wolff. Direction and music by Victor Young. Cast names unavailable.

Colman narrates dramatized Greek myths on this recording made for children. The Gods are Apollo, Daphne, Clytie, Hyacinth, Diana, Echo, Narcissus and Phaeton.

Comment: Blandly narrated, dull and stiffly acted truncation of these myths.

D5 A TALE OF TWO CITIES (1948)
Decca DA-696. Three-record 12" 78 rpm set. Catalog numbers 29253-55. Reissued on 12" LP with *Lost Horizon* as Decca DL-9059 (D3). Timing: 27 minutes, 35 seconds.

Recorded December 31, 1947 in Hollywood. Just under the wire because the next day the music union went on strike. See D9, F42, R5, R6, R32, R102, R186.

Adapted from the Charles Dickens novel by Jerome Lawrence and Robert E. Lee. Director: George Wells. Musical Director: Claude Sweeten. Liner notes by Louis Untermeyer and brief bio notes on Colman, Lawrence and Lee.

Cast: Ronald Colman (Sydney Carton), Lurene Tuttle (Lucie Manette), Dennis Green (Charles Darnay), William Johnstone (Jarvis Lorry), Norman Field (Dr. Manette), Janet Scott (Madame De Farge), Alec Hartford (John Barsad), Barbara Eiler (Seamstress), Griff Barnett (Jailer), Byron Kane (Judge).

Comment: Mechanical production but fine performance by Colman. Too much story in too little time. A shorter version of this script with some of the same cast was originally performed both live and syndicated on *Favorite Story*.

D6 READINGS FROM THE BIBLE (1951)
RCA Red Seal LM-124. 10" LP. Catalog numbers EI-LRB-3191 to 3195. Recorded March 12, 1951 in Hollywood. Released December 1951. See R64, R86, R92, R401 for other biblical readings.

Side 1, Band 1: *II Samuel* 1:12-27. *Job* 28:12-28. B2: *Psalms* 8, 19. B3: *Psalms* 23, 121. *Ecclesiastes* 11. Timing: 9:58.

Side 2, Band 1: From *Proverbs*. B2: *Song of Solomon* (*Song of Songs*), 2:8-14. *First Corinthians* 13. B3: *Revelations* 21: 1-7. *Psalm* 24. Timing: 10:22.

Simultaneously released as a 45 RPM set, WDM-1573:

EI-RC-2400 and 01. Side 1: *Samuel* and *Job*. S2: *Psalms* 8, 19. EI-RC-2402 and 03. Side 1: *Psalms* 23, 121. *Ecclesiastes*. S2: *Proverbs*. EI-RC-2220 and 21. Side 1: *Solomon, Corinthians*. S2: *Revelations, Psalm* 24.

D7 THE COMPLETE SONNETS OF WILLIAM SHAKESPEARE (1956)
Audio Books 607. Three-record set of 7" 16 rpm discs. In the 1970s, a select group of these sonnets was reissued, with background music, on a single 12" LP by Living Literature. Currently available on two cassettes, 21-7534, from Time-Life through Book-of-the-Month Club. Timing: 3 hours.

Comments: As a labor of love, Colman recorded the 154 sonnets at his home in Santa Barbara, but you can't hear any love in his monotonously plain reading, which focuses on iambic pentameter at the expense of emotion and meaning. Rarely varying his singsong cadence and inflection, he never brings the sonnets to life as he did with his story readings on radio. What should have been a masterful performance of great poetry by one of the world's most famous poetic voices is shockingly devoid of feeling.

D8 AUGUST HEAT (*Suspense*)
Pelican 108. Flip side is "Murder by the Book" with Gloria Swanson. See R89.

D9 A TALE OF TWO CITIES (*Lux Radio Theater*)
Pelican 127. I don't know if it's the 1942 or 1946 version.

D10 LOST HORIZON (*Lux Radio Theater*)
Pelican 140. See R173.

All of these Pelican releases of radio shows were made in the early to mid-1970s.

D11 THE NATIVITY
Mark 56 record titled *America's Sweetheart*. Compilation of radio shows and excerpts featuring Mary Pickford. Timing: 6½ minutes, including organ wraparound. See R19.

D12 ACADEMY AWARD
Nostalgia Lane NLR-1501. 12" LP (1978). 29 minutes each side. See R105, R110.

"If I Were King" and "Lost Horizon," with excellent liner notes capturing the essence of Colman's star quality. Mint sound.

D13 JACK BENNY
Nostalgia Lane NLR-1003. 12" LP (1978). 29 minutes each side. See R122.

One of the two Benny shows on this record is the "Charley's Aunt Disguise" episode. Mint sound.

D14 COMMAND PERFORMANCE VICTORY EXTRA
Radiola MR-1100. 12" LP; CMR-1100, cassette; and CDMR-1100, CD. One-hour (1979). See R92.

Abridgement of the 100-minute special program, but including Colman's opening prayer. Excellent sound.

D15 LOST HORIZON (*Lux Radio Theater*)
Radiola MR-1200. 12" LP. Also CMR-1148, cassette. One-hour (1987). See R27.

D16 LOST HORIZON: THE FILM SCORES OF DIMITRI TIOMKIN (1976)
RCA ARL1-1669. See F45, D17. Produced by George Korngold. National Philharmonic Orchestra conducted by Charles Gerhardt. Side one is a 23-minute suite of themes from *Lost Horizon*. The LP comes with a four-page brochure of liner notes and photos. Available on cassette and CD.
   Comment: Excellent recording of Tiomkin's score, but with too much time spent on the Funeral Procession for the High Lama. However, the score as heard in the movie has a warmer tone. Side two comprises lesser movie themes.

D17 CINEMA CAMEOS: HOLLYWOOD'S GREATEST ROMANTIC THEMES
(1977) Corinthian Records COR-107. CBS Inc. See D16. Paul Weston and His Orchestra play love themes from ten movies, including *Lost Horizon*.

D18 THE PRISONER OF ZENDA (1975)
United Artists Records. UA-LA374-G. See F47. Orchestrations: Paul Swain. Conductor: LeRoy Holmes. Liner notes: Tony Newman, son of the score's composer, Alfred Newman. Timing: 33 minutes.
   Comment: A great score is ruined by tinny orchestration and lumbering conducting, especially in comparison with Newman's original as heard in the movie. The best thing about this album is the full-color reissue poster on the cover.

D19 THE FILM WORLD OF MIKLÓS RÓZSA (1974)
Sound Stage Recordings 2308. See D20, F58, A13. Produced by William Stout, comprising Rózsa scores for several movies, most of them taken from 78 rpm records. Side 2 features a 12-minute suite from *A Double Life*, taken from a recording of a live radio broadcast (probably KFAC Hollywood) from the Hollywood Bowl in 1948, orchestra conducted by Rózsa.

D20 MIKLÓS RÓZSA CONDUCTS HIS GREAT FILM MUSIC (1975)
Polydor 2383327. See D19, F58, A13. Rózsa Conducts the Royal Philharmonic Orchestra. Includes the opening credits music from *A Double Life*. Timing: 2 minutes, 15 seconds.

D21 HOLLYWOOD: THE POST-WAR YEARS 1946-1949 (1980)
American Entertainment Industries, Inc. AEI 3104. Music written for motion pictures by Hugo Friedhofer, Miklós Rózsa and David Raksin. Includes *A Double Life* suite from D19. Color poster from movie on cover.

D22 AROUND THE WORLD IN 80 DAYS (1956, Original soundtrack)
Decca DL-79046. MCA CD 31134. See F68. Never-out-of-print stereo recording of Victor Young's score. Has gone through several front cover permutations through the years, but the liner notes are the same as when this record was first released, mentioning Colman in the cast. Fine symphonic recording.

AWARDS, HONORS,
AND NOMINATIONS

For all the fine movies he made, Ronald Colman was only honored for that work three times with prestigious awards. Nor did any of his Oscar-nominated movies win for Best Picture. Of the two awards he most coveted, the Academy Award and British knighthood, he only received the former. He also won awards for his still-life paintings and photography, but I wasn't able to get information on those.

The following is a list of mostly performance-related honors and nominations accorded Colman over a span of 45 years, including two posthumous honors. For other Oscar nominations, the reader is referred to the Filmography.

1915

A1 Mons Bar. Awarded for distinguished service as a soldier upon his discharge from World War One service in May.

1927

A2 Photoplay Gold Medal: Seventh annual reader poll award for Best Movie for the 1926 production of *Beau Geste*. Awarded in the December issue. See F25, B330.

1929-1930

A3 Academy Award nominations for Best Actor for *Bulldog Drummond* and *Condemned*, both 1929. He lost to George Arliss for *Disraeli*. The ceremony honored movies released between July 1929 and June 1930. *Bulldog Drummond* wasn't released in Los Angeles until mid-August of 1929, thereby qualifying it for the following year's awards. See F32 and F33.

1934

A4 *Every Week* magazine. Named by 50 leading movie actresses-including Benita Hume, Loretta Young, Irene Dunne, Barbara Stanwyck and Bette Davis—as their favorite male star.

Colman won with 22 votes, followed by 7 for Fredric March, 6 for Clark Gable and 15 for Nils Asther, Joel McCrea, Francis Lederer, James Cagney, Richard Arlen and Randolph Scott. See B411.

1942

A5 Academy Award nomination for Best Actor for *Random Harvest*. Lost to James Cagney for *Yankee Doodle Dandy*.

1948

A6 January 27. Members of the University of California sorority Alpha Gamma Delta voted Ronald Colman "the most handsome man in the United States. See B241. Sorority president June Hill stated that "Our selection should be an inspiration to all handsome college men because these men we selected have brains as well as good looks and all are successful." As the poll winner, Colman was also invited to a special luncheon at the AGD chapter home in February. The irony of the poll is that he never went to college.

Runners-up were former U.S. Secretary of State Edward R. Stettinius, Gen. Dwight D. Eisenhower, University of Michigan quarterback Bob Chappuis, and Ford Motor Co. president Henry Ford III.

A7 March 10. Golden Globe award for Best Actor for *A Double Life*. See F58, B200.

A8 March 20. Academy Award for Best Actor for *A Double Life*. See F58, F59, R119, B372.

1950

A9 *Daily Variety* poll of the movie industry for "Best Actor of the Half Century." Charlie Chaplin came in first, with Ronald Colman and Laurence Olivier tieing for second place.

A10 October 25 on *The Halls of Ivy*. Dr. Frederick L. Hovde, President of Purdue University and member of the Phi Delta Theta national fraternity, presented Colman with a scroll from the fraternity in recognition of service rendered by the series to college students and college faculty members, including college presidents. See R300.

1951

A11 February 7 on *The Halls of Ivy*. See A17, R315. Pat Hogan, President, Radio Editors of Southern California, presented Colman with the *Fame* magazine award for "The Film Personality Most Effective in Radio."

A12 March 7 on *The Halls of Ivy*. Presented with a certificate reading "Motion Picture Daily has the honor to present to Ronald Colman, Selected by the Radio Editors of the United States and Canada as the Film Personality Most Effective in Radio in Fame's Annual Radio Poll." See R319, B296.

A13 April 11 on *The Halls of Ivy*. *Radio and Television Mirror* chose *Ivy* as "Best in Evening Dramatic Radio Programs." See R324.

A14 April 18 on *The Halls of Ivy*. California Teacher's Association Award "in recognition of meritorious service to public education and thereby to American youth." Presented by Dr. Lionel DaSilva of the CTA, Southern Section. Colman was also named Radio Chairman for Public Schools Week from April 23-28, otherwise known as Open House Week. See R325.

A15 April 26. George Foster Peabody Award for Best Dramatic Radio Program of 1950-51 to *The Halls of Ivy*. See R389.

A16 May 2 on *The Halls of Ivy*. Harry A. Bullis, Vice-President, U.S. Chamber of Commerce and Chairman of the Board of General Mills presented a Citation for Merit for *Ivy*'s contribution to the educational standards of the American people, giving special congratulations to Don Quinn, series creator and writer. The Colmans accepted the citation on behalf of the cast, sponsor and production and writing staffs. See R327.

1952

A17 February 6 on *The Halls of Ivy*. See A11, R355. For the second consecutive year, Ronald Colman won the *Fame* magazine award "for his portrayal of a typical college president with sympathy and humor." Also, all 71 chapters of the Phi Sigma Kappa Fraternity rated *Ivy* as the "Radio program series best typifying American college life." After the show, Virginia Witmer of Santa Ana, CA, the "Moonlight Girl" of Phi Sigma, presented scrolls to the Colmans for the program and to Henry Russell and Vick Knight for their theme song.

1955

A18 December 7. George Eastman House reunion of silent movie stars. See B158, B231. Colman was one of the winners of a silent film pioneers poll, flying to Rochester, New York for the ceremony and reunion.

1958

A19 August 15: Hollywood Walk of Fame. See B244.
One of the first six stars to be inducted into this world famous walkway on Hollywood Blvd. The other five were Olive Borden, Preston Foster (the only one unveiling his own star that day), Burt Lancaster, Edward Sedgwick and Joanne Woodward, all picked by lottery. Located at 6801 Hollywood Blvd. (Hollywood and Highland) in front of Hollywood Sporting Goods, originally the site of the Hollywood Hotel.

1960

A20 February 9: Hollywood Walk of Fame. Colman's was one of 1538 additional stars unveiled all at once in a ground breaking ceremony on what would have been his 69th birthday. This second star, for his TV work on *The Halls of Ivy*, is just a few yards north of the Doolittle Theater at 1615 Vine St.

OTHER OSCAR NOMINATIONS: F32, F37, F43, F45, F47, F48, F53, F55, F58, F68.

ANNOTATED BIBLIOGRAPHY

This chapter is in four sections: 1) Books about Ronald Colman and books with chapters about him; 2) books discussing him; 3) magazine and newspaper articles; 4) program notes for film and radio revivals.

Several movie star anthologies and film reference books mentioning or discussing Colman are excluded because they rehash the same biographical details and use the same stills over and over. Ephraim Katz's **The Film Encyclopedia** is included because it is the reference book most widely used.

A few items are given in between "a" numbers because they were included after indexing was completed.

Cross referencing is limited to the Filmography, Radiography etc. and similar types of material, such as historical essays and movie cast anecdotes. Everything else is in the index.

There are several instances in the book section where I am critical of an author's research. This is because historians often borrow each other's facts without double-checking documentary records for themselves. These critiques are meant to set the record straight after decades of inadvertent misinformation.

Many of the newspaper items are wire service reports and syndicated articles. There were hundreds of other reports and articles on Colman in these and other papers, but they are either standard stuff or paraphrases/verbatim printings of press releases.

I have limited the newspaper items to what I think is informative, pertinent, biographically valuable and give an excellent overview of what was written about Ronald Colman in newspapers about his career and attempts to get divorced. Taken altogether, they paint a fascinating picture of both the private and public man.

I have excluded all but a few of the hundreds of portrait pages of Colman in scores of movie magazines since they add nothing of substance on the man. Exceptions include color magazine covers and color portraits for their rarity. I have included a few movie premiere ads as examples of publicity hype and evidence of opening night appearances by Colman.

For articles without a byline—standard practice for movie magazines and newspapers of the 1920s through 1940s—the publication itself is listed as the "author."

BOOKS ABOUT RONALD COLMAN
AND BOOKS WITH CHAPTERS ABOUT HIM

B1 Brundige, Harry T. **Twinkle, Twinkle, Movie Star!** New York: E.P. Dutton, 1930. pp. 168-175.

Interview. Four pages of uninterrupted Colman quotes about his life and early career. However, the details of his American stage work are so utterly inaccurate that the reader has to ask whether Brundige actually interviewed Colman. Not recommended.

B2 Carpozi, George Jr. **That's Hollywood: Volume 5**. New York: Manor Books, 1979. pp. 201-223.

Biographical chapter recounting all the facts, but in an irritatingly pulpy style. Not recommended.

B3 Colman, Juliet Benita. **Ronald Colman: A Very Private Person**. New York: William Morrow, 1975. 294 pages with photos. British edition: 1975, W.H. Allen, with color cover.

The first and only biography of Ronald Colman, written by his daughter. Her work is thoughtful and well-intended, but not nearly as thorough, insightful, factual and definitive as it should have been. Some chapters are inspired and illuminating, while others are matter-of-fact and perfunctory. The best parts are the vivid stories about Colman's WWI army service, anecdotes about home life with Daddy, and the recollections of those who worked with him and were his friends. In these sections, the reader gets to know Colman as a man, artist and friend.

What Miss Colman apparently didn't do was challenge the people she spoke to by questioning their memories. She seemingly took them all at face value without interviewing other people who had worked on the same films and shows, and without checking historical records such as playbills, newspapers, trade papers, and radio and TV shows.

Example: Edith Lester Jones of the London cast of *Damaged Goods* recalls Reginald Bach—whom she disliked—being fired in favor of Colman, yet Bach was back in the cast when Colman went on tour with the play, though Colman replaced him again after a month.

Example: She says that her father joined the 1921-22 road company tour of *East is West* a month after it began, when in fact he was with it from the start in September of 1921, as a quote from the *Minneapolis Journal* (S21) attests.

Example: She questioned Milton and Barbara Merlin about the radio shows *Everything for the Boys* and *The Halls of Ivy*, but didn't question Arch Oboler for the former or Don Quinn and Nat Wolff for the latter. She also didn't interview one of her father's best friends, William Powell, though he was perfectly healthy in the late 1960s when she was talking to other people. These are just a few of the many unexplained interview omissions.

Her reading of magazine, newspaper and trade paper articles also appears to have been scattershot. The results include missing the story of her father's first romance in 1914 (B189); giving the wrong year for his marriage to Thelma Raye (it was 1919, not 1920); getting much of the story about his 1932 lawsuit against Goldwyn dead wrong by placing it during the making of *The Masquerader* instead of *Cynara*; and placing the making of *A Tale of Two Cities* three years after *Clive of India* when they were made six months apart.

This book is entertaining for its colorful if often biased or embellished stories, but unreliable as a complete and accurate chronicle of Colman's career. What it's really about is a well-educated woman discovering and paying heartfelt tribute to her famous father, who died when she was 14.

B4 Current Biography for 1943. New York: H.W. Wilson Co., 1944. pp. 139-141.

Useful for a basic biographical rundown and information about his early stage career not found elsewhere, but there are several errors such as a 1929 date for 1925 and 1926 films, so please check that essay against the rest of this book for accuracy.

B5 Minney, R.J. **Hollywood by Starlight**. London: Chapman & Hall Ltd., 1935. pp. 114-119. See F41.

In chapter 15, titled "At Ronald Colman's," screenwriter Minney tells a charming tale of being a guest at Colman's home one day, along with author Hugh Walpole. Minney quotes a brief discussion on whether to shave or not shave the famous Colman moustache for the role of Clive of India. He also mentions that the star's ancestral link to English dramatist George Colman the Elder was made by his, Ronnie's, Aunt Constance.

B6 Niven, David. **Bring on the Empty Horses**. New York: Putnam, 1975. pp. 167-185. See F46, B18, B117.

Niven details his friendship with Colman and tells some hilarious, if invented, anecdotes about the making of *The Prisoner of Zenda*. Niven emphasizes Colman's obsession with privacy and general absence from typical Hollywood parties and social gatherings.

B7 Norman, Barry. **The Hollywood Greats**. London: Hodder & Stoughton/BBC, 1979. Franklin Watts: New York, 1980. pp. 167-187, with five photos. Based on the 1978 BBC TV series. See TV49.

Chapter on Colman expanded from the TV script, but based largely on Juliet Colman's book (B3), which is to say that Norman takes her often inaccurate chronicling at face value, erring on several details. And yet, while Juliet claims her father walked out on his first wife, Thelma, after she slapped him at a dance party in Italy, Norman has him walking out on her after she slapped him in their box during an opera in Italy. Norman also mentions a celebrity golf tournament at which Bing Crosby, Frank Sinatra and other stars did not recognize him. For all that, Norman, whose hallmark is a drily ironic British wit, cannot be faulted for his personal admiration for the man and his work:

"...he was, without doubt, magical—incomparably the best, most glamorous and most popular movie star Britain ever gave to the cinema."

B8 Parish, James Robert. **The Great Love Teams**. New York: Arlington House, 1974. pp. 23-40. See F21, F26-29.

Chapter on the five Colman-Banky movies for Goldwyn. Included are credits and plot synopsis for each movie and filmographies for each star. Not included is a critical evaluation of any of the four surviving films.

B9 Parish, James R. and Don E. Stanke. **The Swashbucklers**. New York: Arlington House, 1976. pp. 101-182.

Since Colman only starred in six swashbucklers (F25, 28, 29, 44, 47, 48) out of 55 features, he hardly qualifies as a star of that genre. This chapter would have been more appropriate in the subsequent Parish volume, *The Debonairs*. That caveat aside, this chapter is an engrossingly informative rundown of Colman's career (though Parish feels his performance in *Lost Horizon* is more polished than inspired), with lots of valuable details, but a fair amount of inadvertent misinformation as well, corrected in this volume.

B10   Peary, Danny. **Close-ups: Intimate Profiles of Movie Stars by Their Co-Stars, Directors, Screenwriters and Friends.** New York: Workman Publishing, 1978. pp. 379-81. See F45, B88.

Chapter on Colman ghostwritten for Jane Wyatt (she claims she knew nothing about it), providing a conventional rundown of his life and career, but with an excellent evaluation of his magic as a movie star. Even better is a charmingly personal sidebar on her experience with him making *Lost Horizon*, pieced together, Wyatt recalls, from an interview.

B11   Quirk, Laurence J. **The Films of Ronald Colman**. Secaucus, NJ: Citadel Press, 1977. 255 pages with 340 photos.

Long overdue chronicle that is flawed. Quirk captures some of the essence of Colman's poetically debonair screen persona, but mars his work with several inaccurate release dates, incorrect running times, a faulty British film chronology, incorrect name spellings, and inaccurate details of Colman's radio and TV work.

Examples: He states that prior to *The Halls of Ivy*, "Colman had made occasional forays into radio over the years." Colman did 265 shows before *Ivy*. See the Radiography. He imprecisely states that the TV version of *Ivy* "lasted a number of weeks on television in the mid-1950s, then folded." It lasted one season of 39 episodes. See TV6. He gives New York release dates for all of the American films when some of them premiered in Los Angeles and elsewhere. He names the lead character in *Around the World in 80 Days* as Phineas Fogg when it is Phileas Fogg.

An above-average **Films of** entry, this book nevertheless falls short of being a definitive filmography of Colman's legacy as a cultured movie star.

B12   Smith, R. Dixon. **Ronald Colman, Gentleman of the Cinema: A Biography and Filmography**. Jefferson, N.C.: McFarland, 1991. 322 pages with 67 photos.

Polished and well-intended but hagiographical filmography that parrots other writings on Colman and has even more inaccuracies than the Quirk book, especially the sections on *Lost Horizon* and Colman's radio career. Smith seems to have taken three primary sources—Juliet Colman, Julian Fox and Laurence J. Quirk—at face value instead of double-checking everything. Several times he quotes Quirk, who is quoting from Juliet Colman, who is quoting from Gladys Hall, making the Quirk quote three sources removed.

Nor did he double check casts, credits, release dates and timings. And he lists *$20 a Week*, *Handcuffs or Kisses?*, *The Magic Flame* and *The Rescue* as lost films when the last three have been archivally accessible for more than a decade, and the first was recovered by the Library of Congress in 1987.

For much of the book, Smith makes short stories of plot synopses, with lots of verbatim dialogue (invaluable for researchers), interjecting his own critical thoughts and extensively lifting without attribution from articles, programs (e.g., the one for *Beau Geste*) and other books for his text. He also freely paraphrases from Quirk's biographical text.

However, Smith gets so caught up at times in synopsis stories that he leaves room for just a paragraph of happy puffery on movies like *Lucky Partners*, while dodging specifics on others. These include *Champagne for Caesar*, saying of it only that "it would have been more successful had the script been carefully pruned and tightened." By the same token, he often devotes more space to technical achievements than to analyses of Colman's performances. Nor does he ever fault a Colman performance. He also mostly aligns his opinions with contemporary concensus reviews, rarely venturing a contrary opinion. And for a book about a star, the main thrust is the themes and backgrounds of the man's movies rather than what made him extraordinary in them and their cultural context.

Only in his final chapter does Smith attempt to define Colman's stardom and why it is that he has been passed over for retrospectives and the shelf of biographies routinely accorded other romantic male stars of that era. But it's only five pages, a good part of it quotes. This is a handsomely produced work, but overall lacking the scope, depth, originality, excitement and flair its audience had every right to expect.

B13 Tashman, George. **I Love You Clark Gable, Etc.: Male Sex Symbols of the Silver Screen**. Richmond, CA: Brombacker Books, 1976. pp. 37-42.

Brief biographies of movie stars from Valentino to Redford. The Colman bio is full of inaccuracies about his early stage career, his army stint, his first released movie, his first contract with Goldwyn, his first movie with Vilma Banky and so on. Not recommended.

B14 Wild, Roland. Ronald Colman. Entry in the **Popular Lives** series. London; Rich & Cowan, 1933. 127 pages.

A dreadful, horribly padded and clearly hastily written "biography" that blithely reinvents Colman's life and career. As Wild tells it, Colman was an only child who was delighted to work as a stool polisher when his father died prematurely; saw his first movie as a teenager after his father died; quit his office job to become a full-time soldier from 1909-1913; enjoyed the thrill of World War I until he was blown up by a shell; as a mature actor became a popular and moustachioed leading man in British movies; and married his first wife, Thelma Raye, three weeks after they met. And so on, mixing a lot of fiction with little fact.

This book's importance is that it was the only one written about Colman while he lived and just before the start of his classic period in sound movies, which was 1934 on.

BOOKS DISCUSSING HIM

B15 Affron, Charles. **Cinema and Sentiment**. Chicago and London; University of Chicago Press, 1982. pp. 146-149. See F58.

Academic study of the affective power of cinematic imagery. Affron analyses *A Double Life* for its ironic mirroring of stage craft versus film acting, pointing to Colman as an actor who mastered the latter, then virtually ended his movie career by using his film technique to play a stage star.

B16 Aherne, Brian. **A Dreadful Man**. New York: Simon & Schuster, 1979. pp. 32-37, 39, 62, 67-71. See F43, F45.

Ostensibly a book about his good friend, George Sanders, it is more about Aherne himself and his relationships with Sanders and the Colmans. Two of his stories are about how he, Aherne, nearly got the lead roles in *A Tale of Two Cities* and *Lost Horizon*. These anecdotes ring false since Selznick knew Colman coveted the lead in the former and Capra states in his autobiography that Colman was his first and only choice for the latter.

The best material on Colman is in Benita's letters to Aherne about Ronnie, depicting him in the late 1950s as increasingly depressed and hermit-like in his travels outside the U.S., especially to London. No matter where they traveled, Ronnie felt ill and blue, his illness finally being diagnosed as emphysema, leading to his death from pneumonia.

B17 Allvine, Glendon. Screenplay edition of **Beau Geste** by P.C. Wren, with an article on the making of the movie by Allvine and stills from the picture. New York: Grosset & Dunlap, 1926. See F25, B40, 330.

B18 Astor, Mary. **A Life on Film**. New York: Delacorte Press, 1971. See F47, B6, B117. pp. 127-30.

Astor recalls making *The Prisoner of Zenda*.

B19 Behlmer, Rudy, editor. **Memo from David O. Selznick**. New York: Viking Press, 1972. pp. 84, 86, 110-11, 123, 139-40, 252, 416. See F43, F47, B50, B94.

Several memos regarding Colman's starring roles in the Selznick productions of *A Tale of Two Cities* and *The Prisoner of Zenda*. They show that the two men had long talks about these movies, especially the latter. Colman liked the screenplay for *Zenda*, but balked at playing a dual role because of his unpleasant experience three years earlier filming *The Masquerader* for Goldwyn. Other memos show that he was offered the leads in *Intermezzo* and *Rebecca*, turning them down after exasperating Selznick by taking months to make up his mind. In short, he is shown to be quixotic in his choice of roles.

B20 Behlmer, Rudy. **America's Favorite Movies**. New York: Ungar, 1984. pp. 22-39. See F45, B65, B172, B175.

Chapter on *Lost Horizon*. Behlmer's sources include the faulty and self-serving Capra and Aherne books (B16, B31). Otherwise an impeccable and entertainingly concise recounting of the production with an astute summing up of Colman's star qualities.

B20a Behlmer, Rudy, editor. **Inside Warner Bros. (1935-1951)**. New York; Viking, 1985. pp. 21, 339-40.

Memo on page 21 from production supervisor Harry Joe Brown to executive producer Hal Wallis suggesting Colman for the title role in *Captain Blood* if they cannot get Leslie Howard or Clark Gable. Fredric March had just turned it down after the first choice actor, Robert Donat, said no.

August 1930 deposition on pages 339-40 from screenwriter John Monk Saunders about Howard Hawks wanting to sell Saunders' story for *The Dawn Patrol* to Goldwyn as a vehicle for Colman. Saunders also states that he told the story to Goldwyn "in the presence of Mr. (Sidney) Howard, Ronald Colman and Arthur Hornblow." *The Dawn Patrol* was made by Warner Bros. in 1930 as a vehicle for Richard Barthelmess, then was remade by them in 1938 as a vehicle for Errol Flynn.

B21 Benny, Jack and His Daughter Joan. **Sunday Nights at Seven: The Jack Benny Story**. New York: Warner Books, 1990. pp. 137-41. See B56, TV46.

In his unfinished autobiography, Benny relates how the Colmans came to be a running gag on his show, but misremembers how many times they were on. He counts nearly 50 shows, but it was actually 22, including the 20th anniversary show in 1951. He also says the Colmans lived down the block from him when they were actually a mile away.

B22 Berg, A. Scott. **Goldwyn: A Biography**. New York: Knopf, 1988. pp. 116, 127, 130, 138, 147, 149-52, 155-6, 160-2, 167, 169, 174-77, 181-83, 185-86, 191-93, 197, 205-6, 217-25, 235, 256, 317, 323, 334. See F13, 16, 18, 21, 22, 26-29, 31-39.

Devotes more space to Colman's sound films for Goldwyn than his silents, while emphasizing Banky in the five silents they made. Assessing the talkies, Berg accurately observes that after the triumph of *Bulldog Drummond*, Goldwyn petrified Colman's career by casting him in outmoded and stodgy stage vehicles such as *Cynara* and *The Masquerader,* or miscasting him for prestige in *Arrowsmith*. Overall, a more in-depth examination of the Colman-Goldwyn relationship than can be found in the other Goldwyn biographies, which is why they are not included.

However, Berg is amiss when discussing the Sidney Skolsky column (B393) that triggered Colman's lawsuit against Goldwyn. He doesn't give the item's date, name the paper in which it appeared, or quote further than the drinking allegation. Had he done all of this, quoted Rosalind Shaffer's interview with Colman about the lawsuit (B379), and tracked production dates and trade paper reports, Berg would have been able to write a more accurately detailed and precise sequence of events leading to the lawsuit and how and why it ended.

B23 Blum, Daniel. **A Pictorial History of the Silent Screen**. New York: Putnam, 1953. pp. 242, 258, 259, 273, 276, 287, 295, 311, 320.

The first book of its type. A year-by-year photo history of Hollywood movies, both the well-known and the forgotten. Colman's silent movies are generously pictured.

B24 Blum, Daniel. **A Pictorial History of the Talkies**. New York: Putnam, 1958. pp. 7, 29, 53, 73, 79, 85, 88, 93, 97, 105, 115, 144, 174, 185, 186, 203.

Stills from most of Colman's sound movies are included. Starting with the 1973 edition, publicity stills for *A Tale of Two Cities* on page 73 (including a portrait shot of Colman as Carton) and a full-page portrait on page 85 were deleted.

B25 Bodeen, DeWitt. Magill's Survey of Cinema: **English Language Films, Volume 3**. Englewood Cliffs, NJ: Salem Press, 1980.

Essay on *The Prisoner of Zenda*. pp. 1375-78. See F47, B81, B83, B130.

B26 *Ibid*. Volume 4.

Essay on *A Tale of Two Cities*. pp. 1667-70. See F43.

B27 Bowers, Ronald. **Magill's Survey of Cinema: Silent Films: Volume 2**. Englewood Cliffs, NJ: Salem Press, 1982.

Essay on *Her Sister From Paris*. pp. 546-49. See F20.

B28 *Ibid*. Volume 3.

Essay on *Stella Dallas*. pp. 1049-52. See F22, B43.

B29 Brownlow, Kevin. **The Parade's Gone By**. New York: Bonanza Books, 1968. pp. 114-17. See F26.

Choice anecdote about the making of *The Winning of Barbara Worth*, but it's about a scene with Colman and Gary Cooper that was deleted from the final print.

B30 Brownlow, Kevin. **Behind the Mask of Innocence**. New York; Knopf, 1992. Pages 58-60. See S10.

In this examination of silent movies with a social conscience, Brownlow discusses the American and British films of *Damaged Goods*: how they differed in putting the play on film, and how the lost American version not only remained true to the stage original, but took viewers into an actual hospital ward to examine real syphilitic patients up close.

Brownlow mentions Colman as the juvenile lead in the British stage production (erroneously stating that it opened with him), but doesn't say why he was passed over for the 1919 British film. It could have been a footnote.

B31 Capra, Frank. **The Name Above the Title: An Autobiography**. New York: Macmillan, 1971. pp. 190-202, 224-26. See F45, B65, B172, B175.

The chapter titled "Burn the First Two Reels" is an account of the making of *Lost Horizon* in 1936. Capra states why he chose Colman for the lead role of Robert Conway, and recounts the various joys and technical tribulations involved in the production. He also tells his legendary, and now discredited, tale about burning the first two reels to make the movie more commercially acceptable. It is one of several stories about the making of this movie that are self-serving fiction, as Joseph McBride's Capra biography (B65) makes abundantly clear.

B32 Cody, Iron Eyes. **My Life as a Hollywood Indian**. New York: Everest House, 1982. pp. 60, 115.

Cody recalls the time he rode to San Simeon castle with Ronnie, pointing out buffalo on the castle's acreage. They were riding in a Rolls Royce driven by their mutual friend, Tim McCoy.

B33 De Cordova, Fred. **Johnny Came Lately**. New York: Simon & Schuster, 1988. pp. 225-27.

Autobiography of the director of *The Tonight Show* includes a charming anecdote about the time he met Ronnie at a dinner party given by the Colmans in the early 1950s.

B34 Dietrich, Marlene. **Marlene Dietrich**. New York: Grove Press, 1989. Dietrich briefly recalls the making of *Kismet*. Page 192. See also B84.

B35 Duncan, Peter. **In Town Tonight**. London; Wemer Laurie, 1951. Page 62. See R122.

Duncan recalls the time Colman was interviewed on his Saturday night show, *In Town Tonight*, as publicity for the London premiere of *A Double Life*.

B36 Everson, William K. **The Detective in Film**. Secaucus, NJ: Citadel Press, 1972. pp. 62-66. See F32, F40, R40.

Delightful book with an excellent chapter on the *Bulldog Drummond* series in which Everson singles out Colman's two movies in the title role as the definitive ones. His descriptions of Colman's performances in *Bulldog Drummond* and *Bulldog Drummond Strikes Back* are enthusiastically specific models of passionately informed scholarship. Everson makes the reader want to see both movies, especially the rarely seen second one.

B37 Fairbanks, Douglas, Jr. **The Salad Days**. New York: Doubleday, 1988. pp. 269-276, 343. See F46, B6, B18.

Fairbanks recounts his work in *The Prisoner of Zenda*.

B38 Frank, Sam. **Magill's Survey of Cinema: English Language Films, First Series, Volume 2**. Englewood Cliffs, NJ: Salem Press, 1981. pp. 363-66. See F32.

Essay on *Bulldog Drummond*.

B39 Frank, Sam. **Magill's Survey of Cinema: Silent Films, Volume 3**. Englewood Cliffs, NJ: Salem Press, 1982. pp. 357-60. See F21.

Essay on *The Dark Angel*.

B40 Franklin, Joe. **Classics of the Silent Screen**. New York: Bramhall House, 1959.

Bought and permanently reissued in the 1970s by Citadel Press. pp. 80-81, 104, 148-49. See F22, F25, B43.

Included in Franklin's personal selection are *Beau Geste* and *Stella Dallas*, both of which he lovingly evokes. He also includes Colman in a series of affectionate tributes to 75 silent stars. It's a beautifully written personal essay, specifying the qualities that make Colman special to Franklin.

B41 Gish, Lillian. **Dorothy and Lillian Gish**. New York: Scribner's, 1973. pp. 116-120, 130-131. See F10, F14, B77.

Sections on *The White Sister* and *Romola*, with photos of Colman in both.

B42 Gish, Lillian with Ann Pinchot. **The Movies, Mr. Griffith and Me**. Englewood Cliffs, NJ: Prentice-Hall, 1969. pp. 253, 156, 262. See F10.

Mentions of making *The White Sister*.

B43 Griffith, Richard. **Goldwyn: The Producer and His Films**. Museum of Modern Art illustrated monograph. New York: Simon & Schuster, 1956. Pages 16-22. See F22, F26, F32, F37, F38.

Griffith reflects on the dramatic, cinematic and thematic qualities of *Stella Dallas*, *The Winning of Barbara Worth*, *Bulldog Drummond*, *Arrowsmith* and *Cynara*, stressing that Goldwyn and his directors/technicians labored to produce commercial movies that were also satisfying as dramatic art.

B44 Griffith, Richard. **The Movie Stars**. New York: Doubleday, 1970. Pages 98-99, 128.

A brief recap of Goldwyn's obsession with Colman as his "beau ideal of an actor," and a ranking of the "Greatest Movie Stars of All Time" in order of longevity. Griffith lists Colman ninth at 33 years from 1920-1953 when it was actually 27 years from 1923-1950.

B45 Halliwell, Leslie. **Halliwell's Hundred**. New York: Scribner's Sons, 1982. pp. 180-183, 282-286. See F45, F47, B81, B83, B130.

Affectionate but critical essays on the author's hundred favorite movies, including *Lost Horizon* and *The Prisoner of Zenda*.

B46 Halliwell, Leslie. **The Filmgoer's Book of Quotes**. New York: Signet, 1975. Page 171. See B47, F67.

When asked a by a woman at a dinner party if he had indeed received a Cadillac for half a day's work on *Around the World in 80 Days*, Colman replied: "No madam, for the work of a lifetime." He borrowed this riposte from painter James McNeill Whistler.

B47 Hardwicke, Sir Cedric, as told to James Brough. **A Victorian in Orbit**. New York: Doubleday, 1961. pp. 211-212.

Hardwicke briefly recalls his friendship with Colman, noting ironically Colman's professed nostalgic love of the theater versus the reality of his stage career in England. This book is also the source for the anecdote in B46.

B48 Harrison, Rex. **An Autobiography**. New York: William Morrow, 1975. pp. 85-6, 95, 98.

Harrison mentions his acquaintanceship with Colman and talks about the star-status implication of being ordered to grow a Colman moustache for *The Foxes of Harrow*.

B49 Harrison, Rex. **A Damned Serious Business: My Life in Comedy**. New York: Bantam, 1991. pp. 83, 85, 87.

In his second autobiography, Harrison misspells Colman's name as Coleman in his mentions of the star. He also complains that the Colman moustache Zanuck ordered him to grow for *The Foxes of Harrow* did nothing to further his career, though Harrison did star in other movies wearing a moustache.

B50 Haver, Ronald. **David O. Selznick's Hollywood**. New York: Knopf, 1979. pp. 168-71, 207-13. See F43, F46, B19.

Production details about *A Tale of Two Cities* and *The Prisoner of Zenda*. However, Haver is mistaken about Colman's seeming reluctance to play Sydney Carton in the former. In fact, the star had been telling interviewers for ten years before he played Carton that it was a role he coveted. The visual treats of these sections are the publicity stills, the rarest of which are three color shots from *Zenda*, showing how the picture might have looked had it been filmed in Technicolor as originally planned.

B51 Hepworth, Cecil. **Came the Dawn**. London: Phoenix House, 1951. pp. 170, 173. See F4.

British silent film producer Hepworth recalls working with Colman.

B52 Higham, Charles and Roy Moseley. **Cary Grant: The Lonely Heart**. New York: Harcourt Brace Jovanovich, 1989. pp. 102, 120, 128, 133, 141. See F52-3.

Includes item about money Grant and Colman had raised for British War Relief being stolen by a publicist, but that the matter never went to court. Authors also claim that Grant was nervous about working with Colman on *The Talk of the Town* for fear that his co-star would outact him as a light comedian.

B53 Holland, Larry Lee. **Magill's Survey of Cinema: Silent Films, Volume 2**. Englewood Cliffs, NJ: Salem Press, 1982. pp. 641-43. See F23, B352.

Essay on *Lady Windermere's Fan* that is mostly synopsis with a bit of visual analysis.

B54 Johnson, Timothy W. **Magill's Survey of Cinema: English Language Films, Second Series, Volume 1**. Englewood Cliffs, NJ: Salem Press, 1980. pp. 320-22. See F62.

Essay on *Champagne for Caesar* that is mostly synopsis with a bit of flippant historical background and critique.

B55 ———— *Ibid*., Volume 4.

Essay on *The Talk of the Town*. pp. 1671-74. See F53.

B56 Josefsberg, Milt. **The Jack Benny Show**. New York: Arlington House, 1977. pp. 65, 69, 140-41, 214-16, 317, 329-32, 391-92, 455, 473-74, 476-79. See pp. B12, TV46.

Wonderful biography by a veteran Benny writer that contains a wealth of information and anecdotes about the Colmans' numerous appearances on the Benny show. Includes several segments of scripts that were tailor-made for the Colmans, giving the reader enjoyable insight into how the Benny show was written and how his writers crafted scripts to the personalities of the Colmans.

B57 Kanin, Garson. **Hollywood**. New York: Viking, 1974. Pages 85-86.

A profoundly ironic August 1928 letter from Colman to Samuel Goldwyn regarding the advent of talking pictures is reprinted. In this letter, Colman expresses his disdain for "this sound business" and his feeling that the use of sound is a step backward in the art of movie making.

B58 Kath, Laura. **San Ysidro Ranch: A Century of Legendary Hospitality**. Santa Barbara, CA: Legacy Publishing, 1993. Pages 33-36, 42-43, 45-47. See B384.

Elegantly written, gorgeously illustrated history with a delightfully informative section on the Colman-Weingand years of ownership (1935-1958), when the ranch became a celebrity hideaway. Lovely full-page photo on page 47 of the Colmans with daughter Juliet, mistakenly typed as Julia.

B58a Katz, Ephraim. **The Film Encyclopedia**. New York, Harper Perennial Library, 1979 and 1995 editions.

Since this is one of the most frequently used film references, Katz's factual errors about Colman must be pointed out. He says that Colman was orphaned at 16 in 1907 when in fact his mother, Marjory, lived till late 1929. That Colman played bits in "some short British films, then turned to features in 1918." In fact, Colman's only British short was *The Live Wire*, shown once only at a sneak preview in 1917. That Lillian Gish discovered him for stardom in 1923 when she and Henry King both discovered him when they saw him in a stage play in October of 1922. And Katz gives the wrong release years for *The Light That Failed* (1939) and *A Double Life* (1947). These are the correct dates.

B59 Kobal, John, compiler/editor. **The Movie Poster Book**. New York: Bounty Books. 1975. See F19, F44, F45, F56.

Oversized book includes full-color poster and lobby card facsimiles for *The Sporting Venus*, *Under Two Flags*, *Lost Horizon* and *Kismet*, in chronology.

B60 Kotsilibas, James and Myrna Loy. **Myrna Loy**. New York: Knopf, 1987. pp. 62, 66, 164. See F35 and F37.

Mentions of making *The Devil to Pay* and *Arrowsmith* and of a Coconut Grove benefit in 1940 raising $15,000 for Franco-British Relief. At this benefit, Colman was part of an all-star chorus singing "The Man on the Flying Trapeze."

B61 Lambert, Gavin. **On Cukor**. New York: Putnam, 1972. pp. 7, 197-200. See F58, B15, B62, B67, B76, B98.

Cukor discusses the making of *A Double Life* and evaluates Colman's performance in it.

B62 Lucas, Blake. **Magill's Survey of Cinema, English Language Films: Second Series, Volume 2**. Englewood Cliffs, NJ: Salem Press, 1981. pp. 664-66. See F58, B15, B61, B67, B76, B98. Essay on *A Double Life*.

B63 Marion, Frances. **Off With Their Heads**. New York: Macmillan, 1972. pp. 95, 121-126. See F16, F18, F21, F26.

Marion talks about the screenplays she wrote for Goldwyn as vehicles for Colman, stating that neither Colman nor co-star Vilma Banky felt suited for their roles in *The Winning of Barbara Worth*. Includes a two-page insert of stills from the Colman movies she wrote.

B64 Marx, Groucho with Richard Anobile. **The Grouchophile**. New York: Bobbs-Merrill, 1976. Page 175. See R8-11.

Brief mention of radio series *The Circle* and publicity still showing the cast, including Colman.

B65 McBride, Joseph. **Frank Capra: The Catastrophe of Success**. New York: Simon & Schuster, 1992. Pages 77, 241, 328, 331, 351-74, 429, 430, 600-1. See F45, B19, B31, B172, B176.

In the chapter on *Lost Horizon*, "In the Dog House," McBride expresses intense dislike of the movie, seeing nearly every aspect of its production as proof that it was and remains a monument to Capra's self-indulgent ego. He makes it look as though this is not only one of the worst films ever made—losing millions for Columbia—but that it was a wretched professional experience for its crew. When I interviewed most of the same people, they gave me a completely opposite perspective. Sound man Ed Bernds, assistant cameraman Al Keller, and mike man Buster Libbott spent several hours with me in 1979 recalling how much fun they had making this film. Bernds also gave me a copy of his daily diary for the shoot, as he did McBride.

Though the Bernds diary is filled with notations of personal and professional admiration for Capra's work on this movie, McBride does not quote them, which misleads the reader by their omission. McBride's thesis is that the movie mirrors what he sees as Capra's reactionary political views, though the plot is from James Hilton's novel and the screenplay is largely the work of liberal screenwriter Robert Riskin.

Lost Horizon was revived numerous times during the 1940s, was restored to nearly its original length and condition in the 1980s, voted one of the classic films to be preserved at the Library of Congress, and aired on TNT in October of 1993 as parts of its *Favorite Movies* series, yet McBride calls it a commercial and artistic disaster that put a jinx on the rest of Capra's career. He then contradicts himself by documenting Capra's string of successes that followed it, such as *You Can't Take it With You, Mr. Smith Goes to Washington, Meet John Doe*, and *It's a Wonderful Life* (which lost money on its first release, but went on to become a nationally popular TV favorite at Christmastime).

McBride further states that the longterm net profits for *Lost Horizon* through October 1985 were $1,048,337, of which Capra received $262,084, nearly half of which was for the commercial and cable TV sales of *Lost Horizon*, and nearly $70,000 of that for cable sales in 1984. If this movie was a commercial loser for most of 48 years, why did Columbia keep rereleasing it, and where did more than half of Capra's profits from it come from by the early 1950s?

B66 McCoy, Tim with Ronald McCoy. **Tim McCoy Remembers the West**. New York: Doubleday, 1977. pp. 239-41, 248.

McCoy affectionately recalls his friendship with Colman.

B67 McGilligan, Patrick. **George Cukor: A Double Life**. A Biography of the Gentleman Director. New York: St. Martin's Press, 1991. pp. 139, 194-97. See F58, B15, B61, B62, B76, B98.

Section on the making of *A Double Life* and the campaign by Cukor and the Kanins to win Colman his Oscar. Details here on the production that cannot be found elsewhere.

B68 Medved, Harry with Randy Dreyfuss. **The 50 Worst Films of All Time (and how they got that way)**. New York: Popular Library, 1978. pp. 224-228. Chapter on *The Story* *of Mankind.*

B69 Meyerson, Harold. **Magill's Survey of Cinema, English Language Films: First Series, Volume 3**. Englewood Cliffs, NJ: Salem Press, 1980. pp. 1006-8. See F45.
Essay on *Lost Horizon*. Like McBride, Meyerson sees this movie as an artistic and thematic abomination.

B70 Minnelli, Vincente with Hector Arce. **I Remember It Well**. New York: Doubleday, 1974. p. 198.
Minnelli recounts how he persuaded Colman to come to then wife Judy Garland's 23rd birthday party in 1946 gift-wrapped in cellophane because she had never met him, and that Garland was taken by Colman's whimsical humor. In fact, she had previously met him on January 1, 1941 (R21).

B71 Morley, Sheridan. **The Other Side of the Moon**. New York: Harper & Row, 1985. pp. 45, 52-3, 57, 60-1, 63, 66, 67-8, 69, 79-81, 91, 95, 111, 119, 168. See B6.
Morley depicts Niven as a lightly talented actor who spent most of his career trying to emulate or imitate Colman (especially in a remake of *Raffles*, F33), but almost always ending up as a pale carbon copy rather than as a distinctive screen personality in his own right. Morley asserts that Niven finally established his professional pedigree when he acted in his own *Four Star Playhouse* television shows, and the 1964-65 NBC TV series, *The Rogues*.

B72 Morsberger, Robert E. **Magill's Survey of Cinema: English Language Films, First Series, Volume 3**. Englewood Cliffs, NJ: Salem Press, 1981. See F47. pp. 1107-12.
Essay on *If I Were King*.

B73 —————. **Magill's Survey of Cinema: Silent Films, Volume 3**. Englewood Cliffs, NJ: Salem Press, 1982. pp. 1235-37, 1254-56. See F10, F26.
Essays on *The White Sister* and *The Winning of Barbara Worth*.

B74 Moseley, Roy with Philip and Martin Masheter. **Rex Harrison: The First Biography**. New York: St. Martin's Press, 1987. pp. 88, 137, 139, 141, 147. See B48-49, TV6.
Several mentions of Ronnie and Benita's close friendship with Harrison and his wife Lilli Palmer (closer than Harrison lets on in his own books), and an anecdote about the Harrisons turning down the TV version of *The Halls of Ivy* because they could only see the Colmans doing it.

B75 Olivier, Laurence. **On Acting**. New York: Simon & Schuster, 1980. pp. 252-3. See F58, B15, B61-2, B67, B75, B79, B98.
Olivier praises Colman's artistry with screen close-ups, and his performance in *A Double Life*.

B76 Osborne, Robert. **A Pictorial History of the Academy Awards**. La Habra: Ernest E. Schwork, 1966. pp. 148-49. See B15, B61-2, B67, B75, B79, B98, F58.
Two-page section on Colman for his role in *A Double Life*.

B77 Paine, Albert Bigelow. **Life and Lillian Gish**. New York: Macmillan, 1932. pp. 178-192 and 194-204. See F10 and F14.

Chapters on the making of *The White Sister* and *Romola*. A lot of good, detailed material here. Discusses the intensive rehearsals during the sea trip to Italy for *White Sister* so that the drama was well in place by the time shooting started in January after two months of pre-production hassles such as location scouting, casting, talks with church officials about the script, and weather delays. Similar problems also arose with *Romola*.

B78   Palmer, Lilli. **Change Lobsters and Dance: An Autobiography**. New York: Macmillan, 1975. pp. 153-55.

Anecdote about the slump in Colman's career after World War Two. One of the few good scripts he received had too many rainy scenes to suit him. Otherwise, he would have done it if only to relieve his boredom.

B79   Peary, Danny. **Alternative Oscars**. New York: Delta, 1993. Page 91. See F58, B15, B61-2, B75-6, B98.

Peary states that although he was initially impressed with Colman's performance in *A Double Life*, he now feels that it is undeserving of the Oscar Colman won for it. He also asserts that Colman "wasn't a particularly good actor."

B80   Place, Janey. **Magill's Survey of Cinema, English Language Films: Second Series, Volume 1**. Englewood Cliff, NJ: Salem Press, 1981. pp. 110-12.

Essay on *Arrowsmith*.

B81   Quirk, Laurence J. **50 Great Romantic Films**. Secaucus, NJ: Citadel Press, 1979. pp. 52-55, 105-7. See B25, B45, B69, B88, B130, F39, F43.

Chapters on *The Prisoner of Zenda* and *Random Harvest*.

B82   Rathbone, Basil. **In and Out of Character**. New York: Doubleday, 1962. Page 145. Reissued by Limelight Editions in 1989. See B100.

Rathbone recalls a dinner party at which Colman was unresponsive to Rathbone's wife, Ouida, prompting her to tell Colman she was so put off by his behavior that she'd like to be on hand when he got his head chopped off for the final scene in *A Tale of Two Cities*. Properly and amusedly chastened, Colman invited her to the set for the shooting. Charming anecdote, but no such scene was filmed.

B83   Richards, Jeffrey. **Swordsmen of the Screen: From Douglas Fairbanks to Michael York**. London: Routledge & Kegan Paul, 1980. pp. See B25, B45, B72, B130, F39.

The entire book is a beautifully written Valentine to a vanished era of classic adventure movies, but Richards especially shines when he enthusiastically discusses what makes the Colman version of *The Prisoner of Zenda* one of the greatest adventure movies of all time and far superior to any other film version. Richards's flair in capturing the celluloid magic of one of his favorite movies makes the reader want to revel in the movie once more right away, as much to appreciate a vintage cinematic wine as to lament that the Hollywood studios are no longer capable of this kind of gleamingly literate storytelling.

The other pages discuss Colman's performance in *If I Were King* (F48) in comparison to others who have played François Villon.

B84   Riva, Maria. **Marlene Dietrich**. New York: Knopf, 1993. pp. 352-354, 536. See B34.

Riva recalls her mother's affair with Colman in 1934, in particular a dinner at which Dietrich plied Colman with lobsters, which he did not enjoy. She also reprints a letter in which Dietrich regrets that Colman was so shaken by his bad first marriage that he was impotent with her. Since Colman had no sexual problems with Benita Hume, whom he met a few months later, one can conclude that Dietrich's cosmopolitan sexuality overwhelmed and scared him. There is also a bit on Colmans's sudden and ill-timed moment of passion with Dietrich on the set of *Kismet* while she was wearing itchy gold paint.

B85 Rogers, Ginger. **My Story**. New York: Harper Collins, 1991. pp. 215-16, 240. See F49.

Rogers recounts the making of *Lucky Partners* and how much she enjoyed working with Colman even though the movie was mediocre.

B86 Rouse, Morleen Getz. **A History of the F.W. Ziv Radio and Television Syndication Companies: 1930-1960**. University of Michigan, Ph.D. dissertation, 1976. Ann Arbor, MI: Xerox University Microfilms. Pages 92-97. See R129-247.

Subsection of this engrossing study recounts the syndication history of *Favorite Story*, giving contract dates for Lawrence and Lee and Colman, telling how much all three were paid up front and in profits, over how long a period the 118 shows were recorded, how Ziv got hundreds of stations to sign on, and other fascinating details.

However, Rouse erroneously states that before Ziv signed Lawrence and Lee, they had been producing the show as a limited run 32-episode series for Bullock's department stores in Los Angeles. Although that many episodes had been broadcast by the time of the Ziv deal, the series kept going for another 87 shows.

B87 Russell, Rosalind. **Life Is a Banquet**. New York: Random House, 1977. pp. 61-2, 93, 217. See F44.

Russell recalls the making of *Under Two Flags*, telling a story about a kissing scene that isn't credible because it impugns Colman's and director Lloyd's sensitivity toward her and their professionalism in general. She also recalls a fund-raiser for British War Relief at which Colman, David Niven, Errol Flynn and several other male stars performed in a chorus line. "You never saw a line-up of so many good-looking men in your life," she says.

B88 Scherle, Victor and William Turner Levy. **The Films of Frank Capra**. Secaucus, NJ: Citadel Press, 1978. pp. 142-155. See B10, B45, B69, F45.

In this welcome departure from the usual *Films of* format, the authors quote many of the people who worked with Capra and actors whose lives were profoundly affected by Capra movies, making this a more personal book in that sense than others in the series. In the chapter on *Lost Horizon*, the authors print a letter to them from Jane Wyatt recalling her pleasurable experience working with Capra and Colman.

B89 Schickel, Richard. **The Men Who Made the Movies**. New York: Atheneum, 1975. pp. 221-3. See F49.

William Wellman recalls the personality clash between himself and Colman when making *The Light That Failed*, some of which had to do with casting Ida Lupino as the prostitute because Colman preferred Vivien Leigh. However, Wellman's tale of threatening to punch Colman for ruining two takes of his first scene with Lupino is not credible. Had Wellman made such a threat, Colman would surely have complained to Paramount head Adolph Zukor at once. Also, as producer, Wellman had a share of the gross, so he was certainly not going to do anything to jeopardize it. Wellman told other interviewers variant versions of this story.

B90 Settel, Irving, ed. **Best Television Humor of the Year**. New York: A.A. Wyn, Inc., 1956. pp. 283-315. See TV23.

Anthology of scripts from TV sitcoms of the 1954-55 season includes a *Halls of Ivy* script by Milton and Barbara Merlin and Don Quinn. It was first broadcast December 14, 1954 (but not rerun as Settel notes) and is listed in the TV chapter as "The Fighting Med Student." The script is preceded by a 1 ½-page capsule biography of Colman.

B91 Spoto, Donald. **Laurence Olivier: A Biography**. New York: Harper Collins, 1992. pp. 33, 48-9, 62, 64, 65, 75, 137, 139, 141, 142, 154, 227. See B75.

More than any other Olivier biographer, Spoto writes of Olivier's self-conscious attempts in the 1920s and 30s—on stage and screen and in private life at the Hollywood cricket club—to emulate Colman in looks (the pencil moustache), personality and acting style. He also writes of their warm friendship and reveals that RKO signed Olivier in the early 30s as their answer to Goldwyn's Colman. The other Olivier biographies mostly mention Colman in passing, which is why they are not included.

B92 Taylor, John Russell. **Strangers in Paradise: The Hollywood Emigrés, 1933-1950**. New York: Holt, Rinehart & Winston, 1983. pp. 30, 88, 92, 93, 94-5, 97-8, 102, 132.

Taylor writes about British and European emigrants who found work and a home in Hollywood and how doing so affected their beliefs, views, values and choices of friends. Discussing images versus realities, he makes the point that the British gentleman stereotype was usually far removed from the real lives of individual stars:

"The stereotype was always going to be more potent than the exception...True, Ronald Colman had one of the most extensive libraries in Hollywood as well as his abiding passion for sports—and true also that at certain times in his life...he was quite a ladies' man. But the dreamy idealist stereotype...always seems to have taken precedence even for those who knew him well."

B93 Thomas, Bob. **King Cohn**. New York: Putnam, 1967. pp. 122, 178, 266-7, 285. See B31, B65, F45, F52.

Most of the Colman mentions are about *Lost Horizon*. There is also an anecdote on pages 266-7 about Cohn's crude behavior toward Colman when *The Talk of the Town* was being previewed on the studio lot.

B94 Thomson, David. **Showman: The Life of David O. Selznick**. New York: Knopf, 1992. pp. 90, 188, 212-13, 308.

The important Colman mentions have to do with *Gone With the Wind* and *Rebecca*. The *GWTW* material is evidence that Colman was Selznick's second choice for the role if he couldn't get Clark Gable. A May 28, 1936 memo to Selznick's secretary, Kay Brown, is quoted, mentioning Colman for Rhett Butler "if Metro deal falls thru." Also quoted is an August 1936 letter from Colman to Selznick in which Colman says the story "is tremendous and I'd like to play Rhett...If you think I could, and should, play Rhett, I'd do it like a shot, subject to the character not being too much emasculated for picture purposes, and conditional on a chat with you as to Scarlett." Colman proposed Katharine Hepburn for Scarlett.

Regarding *Rebecca*, the reader learns that "Hitchcock had wanted Ronald Colman to play Maxim de Winter, but had been unable to persuade him." Regarding *The Prisoner of Zenda*, Thomson says it cost $1.25 million to make, earning a profit of $182,000. See F47 for different figures.

B95 Vidal, Gore. **Screening History**. Cambridge: Harvard University Press. 1992. Page 40.

Discussing Hollywood movies of the late 1930s, Vidal claims that "Unknown to us at the time, Colman was British Intelligence's man in Hollywood, in place to make sure that England would look its best on the screen." Interesting, but what's his source?

B96 Wiley, Mason and Damien Bona. **Inside Oscar: The Unofficial History of the Academy Awards**. New York: Ballantine, 1986. pp. 20, 68, 69, 123, 173, 175, 177, 180, 230. See B76, B79, R123.

Page 69 cites Colman as one of 50 judges for the 1936 race, making recommendations for acting nominations. The 1947 chapter documents his lobbying for the Best Actor Oscar, but inaccurately quotes part of his short acceptance speech.

B97 Wilson, Marilynn. **Magill's Survey of Cinema: Silent Films, Volume 1**. Englewood Cliffs, NJ: Salem Press, 1982. pp. 187-90.

Essay on *Beau Geste*.

B98 Winters, Shelley. **Shelley, also known as Shirley**. New York: Putnam, 1980. pp. 184-94. See F58, B15, B61, B62, B67.

Chapter on the making of *A Double Life*. Winters recounts how she got the role of Pat, the waitress doomed to be murdered by her actor lover, and her experience making the movie. Everything mentioned in other books on Colman and Cukor about Winters's part in this movie are taken from this book.

Winters also recalls that Colman told her a story over lunch about his American stage career: a time when there was no Actor's Equity, he acted with Florence Eldridge in several plays, and replaced a star on Broadway opening night when the man fell ill, etc. All of it false, but presumably told to make Winters relax after 60 "blown" takes her first day filming because she was frozen in awe of Colman.

B99 Yeck, Joanne L. **Magill's Survey of Cinema: English Language Films, Second Series, Volume 5**. Englewood Cliffs, NJ: Salem Press, 1981. pp. 1979-82. See B81, F55.

In her *Random Harvest* essay, Yeck accurately pinpoints the movie's audience appeal in its time despite its many holes and overall implausibility, though she underestimates its perennial appeal to contemporary audiences.

B100 Yurka, Blanche. **Bohemian Girl: Blanche Yurka's Theatrical Life**. Athens, OH; Ohio University Press, 1970. pp. 223-25. See B82, F43.

Yurka recalls studying her fellow actors and Colman in particular while making her screen debut as Mme. Defarge in *A Tale of Two Cities*.

MAGAZINE AND NEWSPAPER ARTICLES

Numbers after newspaper dates are section, page and column or page and column.

B101 Adams, Evangeline. "Written in the Stars." *New Movie*. February 1931.

B102 Albert, Katherine. "Exposing Ronald." *Photoplay*. February 1930. pp. 62-63, 96.

In a gushingly starstruck manner, Arnold discusses how Colman acquired a reputation for aloofness by not playing the Hollywood publicity game. She "exposes" him as a nice guy who values his privacy and lets the gossip columnists say what they wish.

B103 Ames, Walter. "Halls of Ivy Time Changed." *Los Angeles Times*. February 6, 1952. 1-24-1. See R355 and A18.
Because the Bing Crosby show and *Ivy* are competing with each other and losing listeners, NBC is switching *Ivy* to a different west coast time slot: 7 p.m. on KFI Hollywood. On tonight's show, Virginia Witmer will honor the Colmans and the series with awards on behalf of all 71 chapters of the Phi Sigma Kappa fraternity.

B104 Archerd, Army. "Just for Variety" column. *Daily Variety*. February 1, 1971. 2-2. See B398, F26.
After attending a private screening of *The Winning of Barbara Worth* at the home of one Richard Simmonton in Toluca Lake (with Gaylord Carter at the former Paramount Theater organ), Archerd enthuses about its roadshow re-release by Goldwyn.

B105 Arnold, Hank. "Ronald Colman's Tragedy of Success." *Movie Mirror*. June 1932. pp. 58, 88.
The "tragedy," as revealed by Goldwyn publicist Arnold, is that Colman has created an idealized screen persona so finished, he has nowhere to go with it, so he might stop making movies after filming "The Brothers Karamazov" for Goldwyn. Also "revealed" is Colman's poor estimation of himself as a stage actor; his reluctance to film intense love scenes for fear of showing emotion; that he shaves his moustache when leaving Los Angeles on a trip so that people won't recognize him. Facts: That he draws a yearly $250,000 salary and that his net worth is now estimated at more than $2 million.

B106 Babcock, Muriel. "Colman Voice a Reality." *Los Angeles Times*. August 18, 1929. 3-16-4. See F32.
Opens with enthused comments about Colman's performance in *Bulldog Drummond*, then segues to interview with him, full of laconically reserved answers. He reveals his enthusiasm for seeing stage plays when he can and states his preference for playing comedy versus melodrama. He also says that the story he most wants to film is **A Tale of Two Cities**.

B107 ————. *Los Angeles Times*. October 16, 1932. 2-1-6.
About Hollywood's "male Garbos," actors who dislike publicity and interviews, Ronald Colman being first among them. Babcock notes that he lives alone atop a high hill, seldom goes out, has laconic conversations, and has a wife in England from whom he is separated but not divorced.

B108 Badder, David J. *Film Dope*. April 1975. p. 45.
Number 310 in a series of filmographies of golden age stars in this homemade British magazine. Badder crisply defines Colman's star qualities while stating that "In comparison with the other great male stars of his era, Colman's current standing is inexplicably low...The day must arrive soon when Colman's performances regain the recognition they deserve."

B109 Bahn, Chester. "Ronald Colman." *Cinema Digest*. October statements. Includes quote from Colman's lawyer. Press agent 31, 1932. p. 15. See B393, B416.
Item about Colman libel suit over Goldwyn press release. Goldwyn publicist Lynn Farnol takes responsibility for the statement. Bahn says that trade papers were reporting

Colman and Farnol contracts were expiring, yet Farnol was retained by Goldwyn. Bahn erroneously reports that Goldwyn has exercised Colman's contract option for another five years.

B110 Bartlett, Maxine. "Dimout Fails to Dim Out Glamour at Gay Preview." *Los Angeles Times.* August 31, 1942. 1-8-5. See F53.

Report on benefit premiere of *The Talk of the Town* (F53) on August 27 at the Four Star Theater to raise money to start the Hollywood Canteen. Dimout was absence of searchlights and arc lights during wartime. Enough money was raised to open the canteen "by no later than Oct. 1." (It opened in November.) The picture's stars—Colman, Arthur, Grant—saw to it that several servicemen were given tickets for the movie and the party afterward at Ciro's. Also lists dozens of other celebrities who attended, including Ronald and Benita Colman.

B111 Baskette, Kirtley. "The Star Nobody Knows." *Movie Mirror.* May 1936. pp. 25, 77-80.

Angle is trying to analyze Colman from what other stars say about him. Puff piece cobbled together from other puff pieces and press releases, apparently because Colman would not give the writer an interview.

B112 Berg, Louis. "Mr. Benny's Neighbor." *Los Angeles Times.* March 21, 1948. *This Week Magazine.* pp. 22-23.

Puff piece about Colman's career timed to appear the day of the 20th annual Academy Awards since Sunday papers are also sold on Saturday. Nothing new except for anecdotal paragraphs about the men with whom he played poker at his home, including Clark Gable and director Walter Lang.

B113 *Beverly Hills Citizen.* "Wife of Film Actor Colman Given Decree." July 31, 1934.

B114 Bird, R. Steven. "Ronald Colman: Forgotten Legend." *Hollywood Studio Magazine.* September 1990. pp. 7-11. See B165.

Loving though too short tribute to Colman intended for the 29th anniversary of his death, but clearly shelved for more than three years until the editors had space to fill. The writing is not as polished or substantial as one would like, but at least this magazine was willing to allot space to Colman at a time when all other movie magazines running articles about Golden Age stars weren't even mentioning him. Illustrated with five gleaming stills and a poster for *The Prisoner of Zenda.*

B115 Camp, Dan. "The Original Clam of Hollywood." *Motion Picture.* October 1938. pp. 32, 60-61.

About Colman's hatred of publicity and interviews, and his habit of answering questions by saying a lot of nothing. Mentions that he and Benita live in adjoining houses on Benedict Canyon Road (sic, Summit Drive); that he owns a ranch in Big Sur; took six weeks to grow a beard for *If I Were King;* was the second top earner in movies for 1937 with $362,500 before taxes; is loyal to England; and showed up in raggedy clothes on the *If I Were King* set so that no one would recognize him. For all of Camp's gushy, overawed style, a factually informative article.

B116 Carlisle, Helen. "Too Temperamental—That's Why Ronald and Vilma Are Parting." *Motion Picture*. April 1928.

B117 Carroll, Madeleine. "The Role I Liked Best." *Saturday Evening Post*. April 24, 1948. See B6, B18, F47.
    Carroll chooses Princess Flavia in *The Prisoner of Zenda* as her favorite, explaining why and telling an anecdote about filming the coronation sequence with Colman. Still from movie accompanies text.

B118 Carson, James. "I'm No Male Garbo." *Modern Screen*. July 1941.
    Typical interview in which Colman inventories his hobbies, friends, likes and dislikes etc. He misremembers *Tarnish* as his first American movie. Best bit of information: Photo caption saying he has paid $15,000 for the film rights to Alice Duer Miller's poem, "The White Cliffs of Dover," in which he will star, profits to go to British War Relief.

B119 Castle, Molly. "And Then There Were Three." *Photoplay*. July 1938. pp. 18, 19, 77.
    Anecdotes about the Three Musketeers clique of Colman, William Powell, Warner Baxter, Richard Barthelmess and Clive Brook. Charming portrait of intimates who happen to be stars.

B120 Churchill, Douglas W. "Picture of the Month: If I Were King." *Redbook*. February 1939.

B121 Close, Roy M. "In Xanadu, a stately Colman is reviewed." *Minneapolis Star*. June 26, 1975. C-2. See B364.
    Mundane article written as a tie-in to the summer-long Colman film festival organized by R. Dixon Smith and held at the Xanadu Theater in Minneapolis. Its chief value is providing dates and titles for most of the Saturday evening series.

B122 Colman, Ronald. "The Way I See It." *Photoplay*. September 1931. pp. 65, 94-95.
    Colman talks about his experiences with poverty and success. He recounts several instances in which he tried, often without success, to secure a niche for himself, both professionally and financially.

B123 ————. "My Own Story." *Film Pictorial Annual 1935*. Published in early 1935. pp. 134 to 141.
    Well-written article in which Colman recounts his boyhood and the struggles he endured to achieve success and fame as a movie star. He relates his early stage and film careers, with anecdotes about his work, his family and his quest for privacy. Despite a few misremembered details—such as when he first went to work as a clerk—an engrossingly stylish job that leaves the reader feeling Colman has been candid and forthright, though diplomatic to a fault by omitting criticism of his poorer movies like *The Unholy Garden,* and any mention of his conflicts with and libel suit against Samuel Goldwyn.
    It appears that this article is actually a string of autobiographical chapters Colman wrote at Goldwyn's behest for the Goldwyn publicity department from the late 1920s through early 1930s, published here for the first time as one smoothly flowing narrative.

B124 ————. "The New Loretta Young." *Film Weekly*. March 22, 1935. See F41.
    Fan letter to Young in the guise of an article after co-starring with her in three movies,

noting her evolution as an actress and movie star, focusing on *Clive of India.*

B125 ————. "What the Oscar Means to Me." *Motion Picture.* July 1948. Page 40. See F58, R119.
   The 1947 Oscar winners for acting reflect on winning.

B126 Connor, Edward. "Revisiting Lost Horizon." *Screen Facts.* Volume 1 #2, 1963. pp. 50-60.
   Article about the constant re-editing of the movie from a roadshow event to a 95-minute piece of TV filler. Well-written essay by a man who loves the movie and has a justifiable axe to grind with the people at Columbia who butchered it.

B127 Cottom, J.V. Biographical article. *Cine Revue.* April 4, 1974. pp. 20-23.

B128 Crow, James Frances. "Garson and Colman win film favor." *Hollywood Citizen-News.* January 1, 1943.
   Report on opening of *Random Harvest* at four Los Angeles theaters on December 31, 1942, in time to be eligible for Oscar nominations, and a synopsis of most of the plot. "... for sincerity and versatility the performances by Colman and Miss Carson (sic) may indeed be worthy of Academy consideration."

B129 *Cue.* Promotional layout for *Champagne for Caesar* with three stills. March 19, 1950. Page 18. See B230, B294, F62.

B130 Cutts, John. "The Finest Zenda of Them All." *Films and Filming.* March 1971. pp. 40-42. See B25, B45, B83.
   Lovingly written tribute to Cutts's favorite movie. This at a time when *The Prisoner of Zenda* had become a nearly forgotten classic.

B131 *Daily Variety.* "Colman Will Make 52 Pix for Televish." June 8, 1948. 1-2 and 6-4.
   Television producer Ben Finney has signed Ronald Colman to act in and narrate a series of 26 27-minute programs and is negotiating with him to narrate an additional 26 shows. The first 26 will be 13 each from stories by Robert Louis Stevenson and Charles Dickens. The second 26 will all be O. Henry stories with Colman doing narration only. "Production will start on the first 26 around August 1 when Colman returns from European vacation....No sponsor has been set for the Finney-Colman films, but several offers are under consideration."

B132 ————. "New Faces Characterize Prudential's Family." September 21, 1949. 7-1. See R260, R262, R265.
   Announcing a new roster of rotating stars for the new season of *Family Hour of Stars,* sponsored by Prudential Life Insurance. The lineup comprises Ronald Colman, Loretta Young, Irene Dunne, Dana Andrews, Jane Wyman and Kirk Douglas.

B133 ————. "Colman 'Champagne' coin got corked up too soon, suit says." October 27, 1952. 15-4. See F62.
   Report that Colman sold his suit against Yoland Prod. and Cardinal Pictures (owned by Harry Popkin) for money owed him for his performance in *Champagne for Caesar* to one C. Fanning for an undisclosed amount. "Suit alleges that Colman was to receive 7% of the

first $2,500,000 grossed and 10% of everything thereafter. The contract called for a minimum of $100,000. He received $25,000 but did not receive any payment of the deferred portion of his salary, the action adds."

B134 D'Arne, Wilson. "The Lover with the Armour-Plated Heart. Part 1." *Picturegoer Weekly* September 3, 1932. pp. 8-9.

B135 ————. "Part 2: Woman Hater or Idealist?" *Ibid.* September 10, 1932. Pages 8-9.

B136 ————. "Part 3: Skating on the Thin Ice of Life." *Ibid.* September 17, 1932. Pages 12-13.

B137 ————. "Part 4: Ronald Colman's New Love." *Ibid.* September 24, 1932. Pages 9-10.
     Biographical series derived from numerous sources, including Colman's British stage and screen co-stars. D'Arne provides useful biographical details, but is misinformed on or has faulty recall of others. In part 3, he says that Colman's British stage work was "meager"—it wasn't—and erroneously states that Colman nearly starved to death in New York for 18 months before getting a substantial stage role. It was more like six weeks.

B138 Darrow, Isabel. "A Soldier and a Gentleman—Otherwise Ronald Colman, Silent and Reserved Briton." *Movie Classic.* December 1925.

B139 Deitz, Edith. "Hollywood Storms the Bastille." *News Telegram.* November 15, 1935. See F43, B82, B100.
     Article about the making of *A Tale of Two Cities.*

B140 Dorn, Norman K. "Colman's Touch in Classic Roles." *San Francisco Chronicle.* January 25, 1981. p. 24. See B364.
     Wistfully appreciative run-down on Colman's career as a tie-in to screenings of his early talkies at the Gateway Theater and Pacific Film Archive in the Bay area. Nothing new but much needed at the time.

B141 Everson, William K. "Rediscovery: The Devil to Pay." *Films in Review.* May, 1978. pp. 233-236. See F35.
     Everson evaluates this movie on its own terms as art and entertainment, in the context of other early talkies, and in comparison of direction, acting and camera technique to *All Quiet on the Western Front.* An important, thorough, enthusiastic essay—typical of Everson—which itself is a model of how to write such an essay.

B142 Fairbanks, Douglas Jr. "An Appreciation." *Vanity Fair.* October 1932.
     Affectionate tribute by a friend and colleague.

B143 Fender, Robert. Interview. *Movie Classic.* March 1935.

B144 ————. "He Forgot He Was Ronald Colman." *Motion Picture Classic.* August 1930.
     Fender deftly sketches a portrait of Colman as a man who zealously kept his private life separate from his public one. Above all, he is revealed as an unpretentious,

down-to-earth man who would rather talk about the world at large than talk shop.

B145 *Film Pictorial.* Cover and "Souvenir in Story and Pictures" of *Under Two Flags.* October 31, 1936. See B59, F44.

B146 *Film Weekly.* Interview. May 27, 1929.

B147 ——————. Interview. November 18, 1929.

B148 ——————. Benita Hume interview. December 9, 1929.
Hume challenges the interviewer's belief that audiences are to be pitied for buying manufactured movie romances, and that as a performer in those movies she cannot possibly take romantic male stars seriously. She refutes this theory by saying that when she first saw Colman at a West End restaurant in London, she found him glamorously attractive indeed.

B149 ——————. Interview. May 1931.

B150 ——————. Interview with Benita Hume as part of "Love and Marriage by the Stars" series. March 22, 1932.
Hume reflects on how Colman's effectiveness as a screen idol to millions of women might be affected if he were happily married.

B151 ——————. September 22, 1933. Pages 8-9.

B152 ——————. January 25, 1935. Interview. pp. 7-9.

B153 ——————. "Colman's Far, Far Better." April 11, 1936. Publicity for *A Tale of Two Cities.* See F43.

B154 ——————. Interview with Elizabeth Allan about *A Tale of Two Cities* and working with Colman. April 18, 1936. pp. 7-8. See B82, B100, F43.

B155 ——————. October 17, 1936. Pages 7-9.

B156 ——————. "Two Colmans?" July 1938.

B157 ——————. "Life with Benita Hume." August 12, 1939.

B158 Fox, Fred W. "Silent Film Stars Receive Awards." *Los Angeles Mirror-News.* December 8, 1955. See B231, A18.
Report on the George Eastman House ceremony honoring 19 living actors, directors and cameramen of the 1915-1925 era for their contributions to the art of silent movies. All were awarded medallions nicknamed "Georges." Colman was honored for his work, along with Richard Barthelmess, Buster Keaton and Harold Lloyd.

B159 Fox, Julian. "Ronald Colman: Part One." *Films and Filming.* March 1972. pp. 26-32.

B160 ——————. "Ronald Colman: Part Two." *Ibid.* April 1972. pp. 34-39.
Poorly written career rundown that blends an inaccurate biography with articulate

assessments of individual movies and analyses of Colman's maturation as a gentleman hero in each phase of his career. Fox is at his most eloquent when assessing Colman's work from 1935 to 1939, stating his hope that Colman's style of acting and heroic type may once more come into favor when the Bogart and Eastwood cults have run their course.

B161 Franchey, John R. "He's Got Life Licked." *Movies*. July 1941.

B162 Frank, Sam. Review of "Ronald Colman: A Very Private Person" by Juliet Benita Colman. *Los Angeles Times*. August 17, 1975. See B3, B187.

B163 ————. "Lost Footage of Lost Horizon." *Los Angeles Times*. February 25, 1977. 4-13-1. See B65, B166, B168-76, B273.
Article on the movie's missing scenes and Colman as a forgotten star using a Columbia Pictures retrospective as the tie-in.

B164 ————. "'Ronald Colman' fills gap in movie history." Review of "The Films of Ronald Colman" by Laurence J. Quirk. *Los Angeles Times Book Review*. January 8, 1978. See B11, B164, B399.

B165 ————. "Ronald Colman: The Screen's Greatest Romantic Hero." *Nostalgia Monthly*. June 1978.
This article was supposed to coincide with the 20th anniversary of Colman's death, but was published a month later. It was an attempt to make him better known by recounting his life and putting his career into perspective. It could have been better written, with better researched facts, but the worst thing about it is the numerous typos by the editor and typesetter.

B166 ————. "Lost Horizon Found." *Hollywood Press*. September 14, 1979. See B163, B168-75, B273.
Article about the upcoming Best Remaining Seats series presentation of the restored movie.

B167 ————. Essay on *The Light That Failed* as a tie-in to a LACMA screening of the movie. *Santa Monica Free Weekly*. June 24, 1983.

B168 ————. "Lost Horizon: Reconstructing a Capra Classic, one frame at a time." *Chicago Tribune*. August 19, 1984. 13-10. See B175, B273.

B169 ————. "A Restoration of Capra's 'Lost' Classic is on the Horizon." *San Francisco Chronicle*. August 26, 1984. Datebook, pages 17 and 22. More complete version of above article. See B175, B273.

B170 ————. "Lost Horizon Finds Shangri-La...Finally." *Los Angeles Reader*. July 26, 1985. See B175, B273.

B171 ————. "Born-Again Classic." *Los Angeles Reader*. June 27, 1986. See B175, and B273.

B172 —————. "Lost Horizon—A Timeless Journey." *American Cinematographer.* April 1986. pp. 30-39. See B175.

B173 —————. "On Location with Lost Horizon." *The Californians.* November/December 1986. See B175, B273.

B174 —————. "On Location with Lost Horizon." *California Living.* Sunday supplement to the *Los Angeles Herald Examiner.* March 1, 1987. (An edited reprint of the *Californians* piece.) See B175.

B175 —————. "Lost Horizon Losses Restored." *American Cinematographer.* July 1987. pp. 46-48, 50, 52, 54. See B273.

The above eight articles were written to take advantage of the publicity surrounding the restoration revival of *Lost Horizon.* They either tell the story of the movie's production or discuss the history of its serial butchery, setting the record straight on what was cut, when and why. However, I have since learned that my recounting of the production for B156 and my recounting of the butchery for this article were flawed by taking Capra's accounting of both at face value.

B176 —————. "Ronald Colman on Home Video." *Entertainment Today.* February 9, 1990. Page 4. See BB45, B69, B88.

Published on Colman's 99th birthday. I used the release on tape of *The Prisoner of Zenda* as an excuse to extol Colman's virtues as a star and to cite the best of his movies then in video release.

B177 Friedman, Favius. "Lux Radio Theatre Presents Hollywood." *Radio & Television Best.* September 1948. pp. 12-16. See R12.

Fascinating, delightfully written and generously illustrated behind-the-scenes article about the *Lux* series and its durability as the Rolls Royce of radio drama anthologies. Among the details are that *Lux* reached an average weekly audience of 22,000,000 in the late 1940s and that the stars were paid $5000 per show. The biggest revelation is the names of seemingly poised stars who got nervous at air time, including Colman. "Even Ronald Colman, the epitome of suavity, finds broadcasting a bit shattering."

B178 Gammie, John and Herbert Thompson. "What Stardom Means: Editorial." *Film Weekly.* August 1, 1936.

B179 Garson, Greer. "The Role I Liked Best." *Saturday Evening Post.* August 16, 1947. See F55.

Garson chooses her role in *Random Harvest* as her favorite. Includes still of Colman and Garson in the movie.

B180 Gish, Dorothy. "Ronald Colman Minus His Greasepaint." *Movie Weekly.* March 14, 1925.

B181 *Glamour.* "We Call on the Ronald Colmans." March 1940.

Photographs at home by Alexander Paal, including a color shot of Colman reclining in a lawn chair, impeccably dressed in a brown plaid suit.

Caption: "Ronald Colman, polished as to personality, perfect as to performance, is every woman's idea of 'The kind of man I should have married.' His latest triumph is 'The Light That Failed.'"

B182 Glyn, Elinor. "Would You Like to Be Mrs. Ronald Colman?" *Picturegoer*. May 1932. pp. 12-13. See B258.
    Imagine being married to your favorite movie star, like Colman, John Gilbert, Adolphe Menjou and others. Would he be at home as he is on screen?

B183 Goode, Bud. "The Colmans of Ivy." *TV-Radio Mirror*. August 1955. pp. 46, 47, 68, 69. See B183, B198, B210, TV46.
    Charming peek at the Colmans' home life from Benita's perspective, and written on the assumption that *The Halls of Ivy* would be renewed for a second season. The most revealing aspect is about their daughter, Juliet, who wanted to go on the show as their child mainly so she could see her parents more often. She would complain to them, "I don't see *why* you haven't got a child." Goode reveals Benita as a vivaciously witty woman. Page 47 is a full-page, full-color portrait of the Colmans.

B184 Gordon, Shirley. "The Colmans of Beverly Hills." *Radio-Television Life*. November 17, 1950. pp. 4, 5, 38. Flopped color cover of Ronnie and Benita, meaning it was printed in reverse.
    A visit with the Colmans at their British style home. Text less valuable than 7 shots of Ronnie and Benita in and outdoors of their home and one shot of the house by itself. Asked about the architectural scheme of the house, Benita says, "Oh, I wouldn't call it formal at all. It's more of a rambling house with a hodgepodge of a garden. I don't believe in a house being just *so*. Our home isn't *precisely* anything. A home, I think, should be an extension of the personalities in it—not a decorator's triumph."

B185 Grant, Jack. "The Three Musketeers of Hollywood." *News Telegram*. February 1931.

B186 Green, Alice. "Colman's Clean Shave." *Film Weekly*. September 6, 1935. Page 27. F41.
    Recounting of Colman's star career by way of commenting on how shaving his moustache for *Clive of India* (released in England the following week) makes his performance as Clive all the more dimensional. "It is now possible to see, by the firm yet sensitive mouth, the straightforward yet thoughtful gaze of his handsome eyes, that nearly all his previous films have allowed him to show only one side of his paradoxical personality."

B187 Haber, Joyce. "Ronnie: Round Peg in a Hollywood Square. *Los Angeles Times*. September 21, 1975. Calendar, page 29. See B3, B162, B399. Interview with Juliet Colman to promote her biography of her father.

B188 Hall, Gladys. "Woman Waiter." *Motion Picture Classic*. April 1930.
    Colman reveals his seemingly male chauvinist attitude toward women, explaining why he has generally preferred the company of men to that of women. What he doesn't reveal is why he formed this attitude.

B189 —————. "Ronald Colman's Secret Romance." *Movie Mirror*. May 1934. pp. 25-27, 66.

Colman tells Hall about the great romance of his life, a woman he calls Alice, whom he met as a young man in England. They loved each other deeply, but couldn't marry because he was determined to be an actor and she couldn't see herself being an actor's wife. He tells of meeting her by chance in Venice in 1927, then again in 1933 in Colombo on vacation, the latter time meeting her husband and two sons.

This enchantingly romantic tale, a major gap in the Colman story, isn't mentioned by Juliet Colman in her book because she didn't read it. There is no other source for it, but it isn't made up because Hall was Colman's favorite interviewer at that time. He revealed things to her he wouldn't tell any other journalist because he knew she would not sensationalize them.

B190 —————. "Ronald Colman Gives the Lowdown on Himself." *Motion Picture*. June 1937. pp. 30-31, 70-71.

Colman talks freely about what is important to him: His feelings about privacy, solitude, freedom from the public eye, how keeping to himself makes the columnists livid because he doesn't make good copy, his interest in the role of Rhett Butler, but only for a stage version of *Gone With the Wind*, his personal Shangri-La etc. Anecdote about jumping into a carful of women from Michigan, he thinking it was David Selznick coming to pick him up, they thinking he was Colman's gardener.

About 80% is quotes so that the reader gets a substantial sense of a man who is a star but dislikes promoting himself.

B191 —————. "Romantic Recluse: The Private Life of a Public Hero: Part One." *Photoplay*. January 1939. pp. 12-13, 84-85.

B192 —————. *Ibid*. Part Two. February 1939. pp. 66-67, 77-78.

The most revealing of all the magazine interviews. More than any other journalist, Hall established a rapport with Colman that prompted him to speak candidly and with self-effacing humor about his life and career. For the first time in this two-part series, he speaks extensively about his childhood and adolescence, how and why he became an actor, how and why he came to be a naturally reticent person, and how he came to hold his particular views on fame, stardom, Hollywood and friendship. There is more genuine insight into Colman and his screen image in these two articles than in almost all the other articles published on him while he was alive combined. The reader comes away knowing him as a reserved yet warmly humane man. Though there are a few factual errors, this is *the* research starting point for anyone writing about Colman or wanting to know the real man. See B404 for Joseph Henry Steele article that takes up where these two leave off.

B193 Hall, Ruth. (Pseudonym for Gladys Hall.) "His Greatest Secret." *Picturegoer*. March 11, 1933.

The secret is Colman's belief in reincarnation, encouraged by his conviction that he himself was reincarnated from his playwright/actor ancestor, George Colman the Elder.

B194 Hartley, Katherine. "Ronald Colman's Lost Horizon." *Movie Classic*. July 1936.

B195 —————. "The Ronald Colman You Have Never Met." *Movie Classic*. November 1936.

B196 —————. "Play Truth and Consequences with Ronald Colman." *Photoplay*. March

1940. pp. 16, 17, 79.

Delightful game of questions and answers in which Colman reveals that he is as witty as the men who wrote scripts for him. When he declines to answer certain personal questions, he takes the whimsical consequences, shown in photos. The most candid remark is in answer to this question:

Why do columnists and interviewers refer to you as The Man in the Iron Mask?

Answer: "Possibly because I dislike talking too much about myself. Interesting things are often unpublishable and the publishable things are so dull."

B197   Haymes, Dick. "My Favorite Movie Scene." *Saturday Evening Post*. December 4, 1944. See F45.

Singer Haymes describes scene of Colman looking out a porthole deciding whether to leave the ship to return to Shangri-La in *Lost Horizon*. Scene was only in the sneak preview version shown in Santa Barbara on November 2, 1936.

B198   Holland, Jack. Cover title is "The Deal that the Colmans Couldn't Turn Down." Article title is "TV Goes to College." *TV-Radio Life*. November 5, 1954. pp. 4, 5, 38. Beautiful color cover of Ronnie and Benita. See B183, B210.

Background story of how *The Halls of Ivy* shifted from radio to television for the 1954-55 season. Don Quinn says he created the series as "something to be remembered by" and that all 39 scripts are from the radio show (actually, two were originals), making the transition an easy one, that the stories "fit very neatly into TV with practically no re-writing necessary." For further details, see pages 209-10.

B199   *Hollywood Citizen-News*. "Colman Suffers Severe Infection, but Doing Nicely." September 9, 1946.

Two weeks after finishing work on *The Late George Apley*, Colman is rushed to St. John's Hospital in Santa Barbara for a head infection, with a temperature of 105. A few days later, his private doctor, Robert J. Kositchek, reports that his patient is "coming along very nicely."

B200 —————. "'Agreement' Gets Vote of Foreign Film Writers." March 11, 1948. See A7.

Report on the Fifth Golden Globe Award winners for 1947 movies, including Colman as Best Actor for *A Double Life*.

B201   *Hollywood Reporter*. "Goldwyn Borrows Howard Estabrook." September 22, 1932. 3-3. See B202.

Report that William Anthony McGuire, who was adapting *The Masquerader* for Goldwyn, suffered an appendicitis attack on September 19 and will be confined to his home for several weeks. For that reason, Goldwyn has borrowed RKO's Howard Estabrook to write the adaptation.

B202 —————. "Estabrook's Record on 'The Masquerader.'" October 25, 1932. 7-2. See B201.

Report that Howard Estabrook completed the adaptation of *The Masquerader* in a record two days and that he and Bayard Veiller (not credited on screen) will complete both script and dialogue today, "eight days after they started."

B203 —————. "'Caesar' Preem in Gotham to Benefit Heart Fund." January 9, 1950. 4-2. See F62.

Harry M. Popkin's new production, *Champagne for Caesar* will be given a special preview February 5 at the Mark Hellinger Theatre in New York City for the New York Heart Fund Campaign. Event called Mark Hellinger Memorial Night. Movie will be preceded by an all-star show staged by Ed Sullivan.

B204 Hopper, Hedda. "Corner of Veil Lifted to Afford Glimpse Into Private Life of Ronald Colman." *Los Angeles Times.* Sometime in 1940.

Teaser title for a well-written, fun piece about Colman's home life and friends and the things he does for fun and amusement: entertaining guests with card tricks, playing poker with Warner Baxter, Richard Barthelmess and others; being the fourth in a barbershop quartet with Frank Capra, William Powell and Harold Lloyd; photographing Benita at 5 in the morning after waiting for days "for the right light" and so on. There is also Colman's serious side: attending to his bills and mail, and disliking phone talks because he made mistakes as a child answering his father's business calls.

In short, a well-rounded glimpse into Hollywood's most private male star, yet one of its warmest and most grandly humorous once you got to know him.

B205 —————. "Acting for, Not to, Camera Basis of Colman Success." *Los Angeles Times.* March 7, 1948. 3-1-1 and 3-3-1. See B125, F48.

Colman talks about the challenge he faced in playing the schizophrenic actor in *A Double Life* and his initial trepidation about the part because he didn't think he could do it. Hopper thinks he should win the Oscar for his performance and suggests to Colman that he "could do justice to the stormy, introspective character of the monomaniac Captain Ahab in a screen version of 'Moby Dick.'" In fact, in the mid-1950s, John Huston approached him about playing Ahab in Huston's film of the novel, but Colman said no.

B206 *Horoscope Screen Album.* June 1931. Page 26.

Analysis of Colman's horoscope.

B207 Hosic, Richard. "Exploding the Colman Myths." *Screen Book.* December 1938. Color cover of Colman and Frances Dee in *If I Were King.* pp. 40-41, 79, 82.

Hosic reveals the truth behind the legends that Colman is a miser, woman-hater, nearly friendless hermit, a star who is indifferent to stardom and publicity, and an all-work-no-play sort. Opening anecdote tells of a newspaper managing editor trying to confirm Colman's marriage to Benita Hume, but unable to find anyone who knows how to contact him at home because of his mania for privacy. Material separating fiction from fact taken from articles by other fan magazine writers. The one fault is Hosic's mistaken claim that Colman was romantically involved with Vilma Banky and Loretta Young when he worked with them.

B208 Hughes, Elinor. "Ronald Colman Eulogized." *Hollywood Cinema Digest.* February 3, 1936. Page 2.

Hughes "eulogizes" Colman before the fact, praising him for the personality, manners and professional restraint that have kept him a star for so long. On the other hand, she had sometimes felt that Colman was substituting personal charm and British reticence for acting. But, with the release of *A Tale of Two Cities,* and his "display of feeling, vivid humor and sympathy," she feels reassured about this acting talent.

B209 Hume, Benita. Letter. *Films in Review.* May 1958. Page 281. See B213.

Mrs. Colman took offense at what she saw as writer Jack Jacobs's suggestion in the April 1958 issue that her husband was wistfully longing for the parts he used to play and for which he was now too old. She denied this, saying in part that "Ronald Colman is not and never will be the less magical for being mortal."

B210 Humphrey, Hal. "The Colmans Have Had It." *Los Angeles Mirror.* December 28, 1956. See B183, B198.

Column about the reported sponsor hassles involved in filming the TV version of *The Halls of Ivy* and why Colman was glad to be done with the series after filming 39 episodes. Both sponsors (not named, but they were Nabisco and International Harvester) reportedly dropped the show due to low ratings. Colman says he prefers to stick to one-shot programs from now on.

B211 *Illustrated Daily News.* "Colman, Screen Star, Glad Wife Granted Divorce." August 1, 1934.

B212 *International Photographer.* May 1937. *Prisoner of Zenda* color cover. See B225, F47.

B213 Jacobs, Jack. Biographical sketch including filmography. *Films in Review.* April 1958. pp. 175-89. See B209.

After a few opening paragraphs touching on Colman's star qualities, a perfunctory review of his life and career. What made Benita Colman take offense was the following statement:

"Today at 67, Colman is still good-looking and debonair, and still interested in screen acting. But there aren't many parts suitable for the Colman personality aged 67."

Benita overreacted, but Jacobs was right because Colman's debonair persona was mostly out of fashion in 1958.

B214 Kellog-Van Rheeden, Marjorie. "Modern day Sherlock Holmes tracks down late movie star's daughter." *Los Altos Town Crier.* February 27, 1991, page 25.

Recounting of how David Packard tracked down Juliet Colman for guest appearances at a two-month Ronald Colman film festival he was staging at the Stanford Theater in Palo Alto in celebration of Colman's 100th birthday. Plus an interview with and background on Juliet, who was delighted to make the trek from her castle in Spain to honor her father's career.

B215 Kingsley, Grace. "Flashes" column. *Los Angeles Times.* October 25, 1924. 2-9-2. See F16.

Director George Fitzmaurice and the company of "A Thief in Paradise," including Ronald Colman, will leave tomorrow to begin location filming in Del Monte and San Francisco. Locales used will include San Francisco Bay, Chinatown and the Pebble Beach home of U.S. Senator Charles W. Clark.

B216 ————. *Los Angeles Times.* "Ronald Colman is Hurt." January 9, 1925. 2-7-2. See B249, F18.

Colman is reported injured by a falling door during the filming of a mob scene for *His Supreme Moment* and was judged unable to work for several days because of the injury, "according to Dr. C.E. Galloway, who was summoned to attend the injured player."

B217 —————. *Los Angeles Times*. "Goldwyn and Wife Go East." November 24, 1926. 2-8-3. See F26.

Report that the Goldwyns are leaving their six-month-old son, Sam Jr., to go East for the New York opening of *The Winning of Barbara Worth*; that Colman will be heading for Honolulu for a month's vacation once he gets over "a slight attack of flu"; and that Vilma Banky is on a touring vacation of the East, with stops in Kansas City for a short radio talk and Thanksgiving dinner as a guest of the Kansas City Star, and Chicago for the midwest premiere of *Worth*. From there to New York City for the New York premiere of the movie.

B218 —————. "Ronald Colman's First." *Los Angeles Times*. May 2, 1928. 2-8-6.

Goldwyn plans to star Colman as Sydney Carton in a silent production of *A Tale of Two Cities*, his first solo star vehicle after five movies with Vilma Banky. His leading lady will be Lily Damita and the director will be Herbert Brenon.

B219 Klumph, Helen. "The Paradoxical Mr. Colman." *Picture Play*. February 1926.

B220 Landry, Bob. "'Parlor Tricks and Banter' Formula of the $28,000 All-Star Kellogg Circle." *Weekly Variety*. January 18, 1939. 36-1. See R8-11.

Review and commercial analysis of the premiere episode, with a listing of star and personnel salaries.

B221 Lang, Harry. "The Private Life of Ronald Colman Revealed." *Motion Picture*. July 1936. pp. 32, 70-71. See B260.

Article taken from news stories and other articles. Part one tells of the three times Colman escaped death: at a bull ranch in Madrid, while filming a pier scene for *Condemned*, and during a knife throwing scene for *Under Two Flags*. Part two is speculation about his remarrying and his social life with his friends. Part three is anecdotes about his travels.

B222 Lawson, Robb. "Ronald Colman, the Elusive." *Film Pictorial*. April 18, 1936. pp. 16, 17, 23.

Lawson expounds on Colman's hatred of publicity by recounting his introduction to the actor. In March of 1928 when Colman visited England to quietly see his mother only to be mobbed by the press and thousands of fans when he arrived at Southampton for a train to Waterloo, Lawson was his guide by default through the chaos. Though Colman shyly answered reporters' questions, he would just as soon have avoided them. Lawson states that Colman's Goldwyn contract gave him immunity from fan mail and did not require personal appearances. One quote in particular sums up his feeling about publicity: "Why all this fuss about a harmless unnecessary actor?"

B223 Leslie, Jane. "Are Actors People?" *Motion Picture*. April 1927. pp. 60-61, 100. See F27.

Leslie interviewed Colman on the set of *The Night of Love*, where he expounded his view on the press telling the public more than it needs and has a right to know about its stars and matinée idols.

"When there is no more to know about any person or any thing," he says, "we aren't interested. You may create a false interest by tricks and shams—resulting in *this* state of affairs—but you can't do it forever. Actors aren't goldfish, they are people, and they are entitled to a certain amount of privacy."

B224 *Life*. "$2,000,000 Worth of Scenes from Lost Horizon." December 14, 1936. pp. 31-33. See F45.
First movie to be spotlighted in *Life* features double-page spread of reflecting pool still with Colman and Wyatt not in the final film. Text touts January 1937 release.

B225 *Life*. "Movie of the Week: The Prisoner of Zenda." September 13, 1937. Page 94. See F47.

B226 —————. "Movie of the Week: The Light That Failed. Paramount is faithful to Kipling." December 18, 1939. pp. 53-56. See F49. Twelve-still text/caption storyboard.

B227 —————. "Movie of the Week: The Talk of the Town. Grant, Arthur and Colman mix love and law." September 7, 1942. pp. 68-70, 73. See F53. Ten-still text/caption storyboard.

B228 —————. "Movie of the Week: Random Harvest. Greer Garson shows her pretty legs and dances." December 14, 1942. pp. 61-64, 66. See F55. Ten-still text/caption storyboard.

B229 —————. "Movie of the Week: The Late George Apley. The movie is ingratiating but far less biting than the book or play." April 21, 1947. See B236, F57. Seven-still promotional layout with dialogue excerpts from several key scenes.

B230 —————. "Champagne for Caesar." April 10, 1950. pp. 119-122. See B129, F62. Seven-still promotional layout with plot synopsis.
These layouts are included to show the consistent high regard in which *Life's* editors held Colman's movies.

B231 —————. "Film Pioneers Roll of Their Living Immortals." January 23, 1956. See A18, B158.
Pictorial spread of silent movie stars chosen for a George Eastman House (GEH) retrospective on December 7, 1955. GEH asked more than 300 silent movie pioneers "to choose among themselves the 20 stars, directors and cameramen who made the most distinctive contribution to the American cinema within the historic period from 1915-1925." The winners all had to be living.
The stars chosen included Mary Pickford, Gloria Swanson, Harold Lloyd, Buster Keaton, Ronald Colman, Lillian Gish and Charlie Chaplin. The writer fails to mention that Chaplin was dropped from the list of winners at the ceremony, probably because he was barred from returning to the U.S. All are shown at the height of their silent movie fame and as they are today.

B232 —————. "Departure of a Debonair Star." June 2, 1958.
Memorial tribute with five small portrait shots of Colman in some of his best-known roles, a large photo of him taken two years before at his San Ysidro Ranch home, and a photo showing Benita, Juliet and William Powell at the funeral.

B233 *Lions Review*. British magazine. "The Colman Tradition." December 1944.

B234 *London Daily Telegram.* "Romantic Hero Who Remained English." Obituary. May 20, 1958.

Standard obituary until the last four paragraphs, when the writer gives a mixed verdict on Colman's talent, yet conceding that "Though there have been many actors more powerful and much more profound, few won so much affection and admiration as a man. Sorrow at his death will be all the greater because he has no successor."

B235 *London Times.* "A Gentleman of the Cinema." Obituary. May 20, 1958. Page 13.

Also a standard obituary until the final paragraphs, when the writer agrees with his colleague above, saying that "His acting range was perhaps not great, but he was capable of revealing a sincere and moving emotion...to those of the pre-war period, he will always be thought of with affection as the most complete gentleman of the cinema."

B236 *Look.* "Look's New Movie Review. The Late George Apley." April 29, 1947. pp. 72-73. B229. Ten-still layout.

B237 ————. "Ronald Colman Becomes a College President." July 1950. Picture and text layout on *The Halls of Ivy.* See B245, B357, R289.

B238 *Los Angeles Daily News.* "Benita Hume and Ronald Colman Married in Secret." October 1, 1938. 1-8-6.

B239 *Los Angeles Evening Herald and Express.* "Ronald Colman Sues Goldwyn for Millions." September 13, 1932.

Front page banner headline story detailing Colman's lawsuit over a press release and subsequent newspaper items claiming he would get drunk to film his love scenes.

B240 ————. "Ronald Colman Divorced by London Actress Wife." July 31, 1934. B-1-2 and 3.

The reporter inaccurately states that Colman married Thelma Raye shortly after he was discharged from the British army in 1915 when they didn't meet till more than three years later; and that he followed in the footsteps of his actor parents. Otherwise, the divorce details are accurate.

B241 ————. (Berkeley) "Ronald Colman Elected Handsomest by U.C. Sorority" from International News Service. January 27, 1948. B-1-6. See A6.

B242 *Los Angeles Examiner.* "Colman Sails in 'Answer' to Wife's Action." June 17, 1934.

B243 ————. "Ronald Colman's Wife Wins Divorce Decree in London." August 1, 1934. 1-4-8.

B244 ————. "Fame Walk Ceremonies Honor Stars." August 16, 1958. 1-6-2. See A19.

Preston Foster's is the first star to be unveiled on the new Walk of Fame. His star was placed at Hollywood and Highland, to be followed at the same spot by five others, including Ronald Colman.

B245 *Los Angeles Mirror.* "Colmans Get Own Program." December 12, 1949. 1-22-1. See

B237, B357, R266-375.

Announcement that Ronald and Benita Colman will co-star on their own NBC radio show called *The Halls of Ivy* beginning Friday January 6 on KFI Hollywood at 8:30 p.m.

B246 *Los Angeles Record.* "'Kiki' breaks records for N.Y. attendance." May 13, 1926. 12-3. See F24.

Report that *Kiki* was seen by 183,000 people during its two-week run at the Capitol Theater in New York City, a world's record for moviegoing. Frank L. Newman, managing director of the Publix theaters in Los Angeles, believes that *Kiki* may set a similar record when it opens at the Million Dollar Theater on May 20.

B247 *Los Angeles Post Record.* "Colman's Wife Given Decree." July 31, 1934. Divorce decree for Thelma Raye Colman.

B248 *Los Angeles Times.* "Star's Wife Refuses to Quash Suit." April 2, 1925. 2-8-5.

After the previous day's negotiations between attorneys for an out-of-court settlement, Thelma refuses to budge.

B249 —————. "Ronald Colman Recovers from Minor Injuries." Tuesday June 16, 1925. 2-11-4. See B216.

Item reporting that Colman has recovered from a door falling on him and knocking him out during the making of *His Supreme Moment*, which is now playing at Loew's State Theater.

B250 —————. "Plan Premiere of 'Dark Angel' at Loew's State." September 25, 1925. 2-9-5. See F21.

Item on special late night world premiere of *The Dark Angel*, with Colman and Banky attending. Upper left column of page has large, eye-grabbing, gimmick-loaded ad for premiere.

B251 —————. February 7, 1928. 2-10-5.

Leaves for New York today to sail from there to England to visit his mother Marjory for the first time in five years. See B253.

B252 —————. "Two Tie as Favorites of London Film Fans." April 3, 1929. 1-12-3.

A poll of 250,000 British film fans reveals that Ronald Colman is their favorite male star while Dolores Del Rio and Betty Balfour tie for favorite female star. Colman was also tops in 1928 poll.

B253 —————. "Colman's Tragedy Arouses Sympathy." (Sydney, Australia) September 13, 1929. 1-6-5. See B251.

Colman's mother, Marjory, is reported dead on September 12 of a heart attack suffered while watching her son's first talking picture, *Bulldog Drummond*. "Mrs. Colman passed away in Sydney, N.S.W. from the shock of hearing from the screen his voice for the first time in eight years (sic)." Colman's Hollywood peers are deeply sympathetic to his grief.

B254 —————. *Condemned* premiere ad touting personal appearance by Colman. December 5, 1929. See F33, R2.

B255 —————. "Colman Waxes Talkative." February 23, 1930. 3-11-7 and 3-12-4.
Colman states that sound films have finally established him "as he has always wanted to be known, a light comedian. The voice with a sense of humor did it." He also says that just once "He would like to rave and rant and saw the air with all the gusto of classic days." But that, he feels, would shock his public.

B256 —————. "Ronald Colman in Court; Out Past 10." (Shanghai) International News Service. February 9, 1932. 1-3-2.
Colman is arrested by Shanghai police for staying out past curfew, but is released when he promises to do his sight-seeing during the day. He is there to visit his uncle, Bercy Colman. He is also given a tour of the marine base by Captain C.B. Yates.

B257 —————. "Ronald Colman Files Huge Suit." September 14, 1932. 2-2-3.

B258 —————. "Libel Suit Reply Made by Goldwyn." November 11, 1932. 2-1-6.
The law firm of Loeb, Walker and Loeb answers Colman's lawsuit of September 12, denying that the Goldwyn company issued a statement depicting the actor as "moderately dissipated" when performing his love scenes, while affirming that such a statement was indeed made. This was their way of saying that someone within the company did indeed make an unauthorized statement regarding Colman's professionalism, for which, of course, the company cannot be held liable.

B259 —————. "Colman May Quit Films for Awhile." March 21, 1933. 2-2-6.
While he is en route to England by ship, it is reported that Colman might sit out the last two years of his Goldwyn contract so that he can become a freelance movie star.

B260 —————. "Colman-Brent Bullfight in Spain Succeeds." (Madrid) Associated Press. April 22, 1933. 1-1-4. See B221.
On April 21, while visiting Spain, Colman and actor George Brent happily played at being bullfighters at the Duke de Tovar bull farm 15 miles south of Madrid. "They received the applause of several score witnesses."

B261 —————. "Ronald Colman to Face Divorce Trial in London." June 16, 1934. 1-1-6.

B262 —————. "Wife's Suit Approved by Colman." August 1, 1934. 2-2-6. Thelma Colman is granted divorce from Ronald Colman in a British court on July 31.

B263 —————. "Studio Change Easy Task for Ronald Colman." September 22, 1934. 1-7-3. Item about Colman now being a star for Twentieth Century Pictures.

B264 —————. "Colman Divorce Made Absolute." February 19, 1935. 1-5-2.

B265 —————. Display ads for the Los Angeles premiere of *Lost Horizon* that make it sound like the cinematic equivalent of the Second Coming because Columbia executives were afraid of losing their $2.6 million investment. These ads appeared March 9-11, 1937. The final ad announces a 10-minute audience ovation after the screening even though the ad was placed the day before. See F45.

B266 —————. "Ronald Colman Weds Actress." October 1, 1938. 1-1-4.
   Report on "surprise" wedding of Ronnie and Benita on September 30 at the home of the Alvin Weingands at San Ysidro Ranch in Montecito. A surprise because the couple gave no advance notice except to their guests. Judge Frederick T. Marsh performed the ceremony. Guests included the Weingands, actress Heather Thatcher, William Hawks (Colman's business manager), and Col. Tim McCoy.

B267 —————. "Ronald Colman Seriously Ill But Improving." September 9, 1946. 1-2-8.
   Colman is recovering from an attack of pneumonitis.

B268 —————. Display ad for *A Double Life* trumpeting Colman's Oscar win two days earlier. Ad lists 19 theaters now showing the movie and 20 more in Southern California and Nevada by that Friday. March 22, 1948. 2-5. See F58, R119.

B269 —————. Display ad for *Champagne for Caesar* paid for by Westinghouse and trumpeting their new model, 619T62, seen in the movie. April 26, 1950. 1-14. See F62.

B270 —————. "Actor Ronald Colman Gains After Illness." March 14, 1957. 3-1-4.
   Colman has been a patient at St. John's Hospital in Santa Barbara for two weeks after entering the hospital for a bad cold that turned out to be pneumonitis, a lung inflammation. He is getting stronger and should return to his Santa Barbara ranch by next week. Same day article by Louella Parsons (B326) says he had been at St. John's for three weeks.

B271 —————. "Colman's Estate Set at Million." May 26, 1959. 1-1-5.
   Colman's estate is appraised at $1,088,234 in an inventory and appraisement filed in Los Angeles Superior Court. Trust funds were set up for widow Benita and daughter Juliet, bequests were left to his surviving sisters and brother—Gladys, Edith and Eric—and his valet, Thomas Turner. Benita, now Mrs. George Sanders, was left his personal property and stock in the San Ysidro Ranch Corp.

B272 Ludlam, Helen. "Ronald Colman Confesses!" *Screenland*. September 1930.

B273 McCarthy, Todd. "AFI Screens Results—So Far—of Search for 'Lost Horizon' Scenes." *Daily Variety*. October 22, 1979. 4-1 and 9-4. See B166.
   Report on Chinese Theater screening of the work-in-progress archival print of the movie and efforts by Robert Gitt and Lawrence Karr to restore every missing scene.

B274 Mack, Grace. "Ronald Colman's Private Life." *Motion Pictures*. November 1935. pp. 38, 56, 58.
   Opens with a story about a London woman who accosted Colman on a movie set during a studio tour. He handled the fannish verbal assault with his usual cordial aplomb. Story illustrates his gentlemanliness at all times and under trying circumstances. Mack then enumerates Colman's personal habits, hats, social life, wanderlust and clothes to fill space because she couldn't get anything deeper from him.

B275 Manners, Dorothy. "Are They the Real Heartbreakers?" *Motion Picture*. April 1928.

B276 —————. "Five Big Stars are Retiring in 1933." *Motion Picture*. May 1933.

Colman pages are 28 and 81.

The stars are Colman, Clive Brook, Ramon Navarro, Constance Bennett and Ruth Chatterton. When asked about *his* so-called retirement, Colman says about his two year "breather" that he wants a rest and perhaps a return to the stage. Manners points to his lawsuit against Goldwyn as the real reason for his not making movies right now.

B277 Mannock, P.L. "Ronald Colman Strums a Banjo." *Picturegoer*. February 18, 1950. See B136, S6.

Theater critic Mannock recalls first meeting Colman when the latter was a light comedian with George Denby's pierrot troupe. From then on, Mannock, says, he not only followed Colman's career, but was a friend.

B278 Marsh, Paul. "In the Colman Manner." *Screenland*. February (?) 1947.

B279 Maxwell, V. "Colman Sees the War in China." *Motion Picture*. June 1932.

B280 Mayer, Mary. "Colman Modestly Mute. *Los Angeles Times*. February 8, 1931. 3-9-4. See F21, F35.

Interview with Colman, whom Mayer says "occupies a throne a little apart in Hollywood's 'Royal Filmly.'" Latest movie, *The Devil to Pay*, is his third light comedy talkie. Colman says his return to romantic drama depends on progress of sound technique in coming months, but that audiences won't accept the type of love scenes in talkies they did in silents. Would like to remake *The Dark Angel* with sound and has adopted the terrier used in *The Devil to Pay*.

B281 M.D.P. "Colman as World's Greatest Lover." *Picturegoer*. February 4, 1939.

The writer marvels at Colman's longevity as a star, while puzzling over the seeming contradiction between his swashbuckling movie roles and his reclusive private life. "Give him a sword and put him in front of a camera and he drops his off-screen shyness like a cloak and hurls himself into the fairy-tale fray or love-making with almost boyish delight."

B282 Merrick, Mollie. "Beauty Cast with Colman." *Los Angeles Times*. August 11, 1932.

Announcement that Colman's next movie after *Cynara* will be a submarine film with Anna Sten. Also that he might do a play in New York after that.

B283 Merton, Arline. "Could You Love, Honor and Obey These Men?" *Photoplay*. January 1935. pp. 30-32, 121. See B168.

Female readers are asked to imagine being married to several male stars, including Colman. Merton says Colman prefers English women, likes the British idea of male superiority, and prefers feminine women who play tennis. English women in Hollywood who know him "will tell you, in strict secrecy, that he is the most gay and charming companion imaginable."

B284 Millier, Arthur. "Colman the Free-lancer Ends Two-Year Silence." *Los Angeles Times*. June 30, 1946. 3-1-2, 3-2-6. See B288, F57, D4.

Interview with Colman about his first movie in two years, *The Late George Apley*. "'To tell you the truth,' he says, 'I almost hate to make a picture. I am very loath to sign. It's really terrible work, you know. Yesterday, I went to the studio for tests. I positively creaked. Radio is so much easier." An assertion that producer Fred Kohlmar disputes, saying that all young movie actors should watch that test.

Also mentioned are Colman's baby daughter, Juliet Benita; his various hobbies, including painting, in which he is coached by artist Richard Kitchin; and his new record album of Greek mythology for which he says he wrote the script. He didn't.

B285 Milton, Mark. "Ronald Colman De-Bunked." *Picturegoer*. April 2, 1932. Page 9. See F37.

Portrait of Colman as an affable, courtly man who doesn't reveal anything of himself in interviews; is entirely businesslike in his dealings with Goldwyn; has thoughts of returning to the stage so can be forgotten by the world as a whole; prefers good books of a few years back to trendy best sellers; and reportedly adjusted his natural accent to sound more American in the title role of *Arrowsmith* (he didn't). In short, a thoroughly nice chap, but also a thoroughly elusive and reclusive one.

B286 *Modern Screen*. "Stars Correspond." July 1931.

Photostat of an undated letter from William Powell to his friend Ronald Colman. Powell addresses him as "Dear Ronny." The letter invites Ronny to a farewell dinner at Bill's home before he, Bill, leaves for a trip to Havana.

B287 —————. "Ah There, Ronnie!" April 1934. Page 74. See B136, B191, S6, F7.

A look-back at Colman's pre-stardom career. Still from *A Son of David*, and a still of him in Pierrot costume for a British revue called The Scallywags. The same shot appears in B192, in which Gladys Hall identifies it as publicity for Denby's Pierrot Troupe.

B288 Monroe, Keith. "Top Man on the Totem Pole." *Motion Picture*. April 1947. pp. 40, 41, 108, 109. See B284, F57.

Monroe asks why Colman has stayed a star for 25 years (actually 23 years). Because he's a handsome, debonair, polished actor? No. Monroe says it is because Colman did as he was told for his first eight years in Hollywood, then freelanced. Colman advises young actors to obey their studios for seven to ten years, learning what's best for them, *then* freelance. He omits mention of the lawsuit that ended his Goldwyn contract. Rest of piece recounts recent recording and radio work and plugs new movie, *The Late George Apley*.

B289 Moore, Viola. "Come and Visit the Ronald Colmans." *Radio-Television Mirror*. April 1951.

B290 Mooring, W.H. "Stars Are Overrated Says Ronald Colman." *Film Weekly*. January 25, 1935.

Colman credits the creative teamwork of movie-making for at least half of his success as a star, discussing the script writing, craft and technical expertise that surround an actor, but which are taken for granted by the audience.

B291 —————. "Hollywood Once-Over." *Picturegoer*. June 1, 1940.

B292 —————. "Ronald Colman." *Picturegoer Weekly*. July 2, 1949. Pages 12-13. See B58.

Mostly about San Ysidro Ranch and Colman's discreet ownership of same by way of illustrating his low-key lifestyle.

B292a Morrison, Patt. "'Caesar' Played The Game Before 'Quiz.'" *Los Angeles Times*. Sunday Calendar section. October 16, 1994. Pages 27-28.
Morrison calls delighted attention to *Champagne for Caesar* as a TV quiz show satire predating and predicting the quiz show scandals dramatized in *Quiz Show* (1994). She notes the plot similarities, gives *Caesar's* plot in detail, and speculates on the reasons for its commercial failure. Four letters in response from *Caesar* buffs were printed in the Sunday Calendar letters section two weeks later.

B293 *Motion Picture*. "Screen Loves of Ronald Colman." Double page photo spread. February (?) 1932.

B294 ——————. "Movie of the Month: Champagne for Caesar." June 1950. Page 54. See B230. Promotional puffery. Four stills.

B295 *Motion Picture Classic*. "The Next Romeo." July 1925.

B296 *Motion Picture Daily*. Award for "Film Personality Most Effective on Radio." March 8, 1951. See R319 and A12.

B297 *Motion Picture Herald*. "A Plea for Mr. Colman." June 20, 1931. Page 7. See B355, B431.
In potpourri column, George Shaffer of the Chicago Tribune is quoted. He says that Colman bragged to listeners on the United Artists lot, where he is filming *The Unholy Garden*, that whenever he is invited to a dinner or social function in Hollywood, he asks to see the guest list to make sure no press people will be there. Column's writer then sarcastically says "This editorial is a plea to the American press to be fully considerate of Mr. Colman's desires and delicately retiring position."

B298 ——————. "Magazines Present Amazing 'Readers' for 'Random Harvest.'" December 19, 1942. See F55.
New York ad and publicity man Howard Deitz has come up with a novel magazine ad campaign for *Random Harvest*, executed by ad agents Ly Donahue & Coe. Idea is that the top 13 national magazines are running phony editorials about the movie, each article written by a famous journalist with art by a famous illustrator. In 6-point type in the corner of each article is a disclaimer marking the work as "Adv."
"Typical of the campaign is the Saturday Evening Post treatment, with a piece by Clarence Buddington Kelland, ace writer of serials for these many years, illustrated by Symeon Shimin." The other 12 magazines are *Ladies' Home Journal, Collier's, Woman's Home Companion, McCall's, Cosmopolitan, American, Redbook, Good Housekeeping, Liberty, True Story, Life*, and *Look*.

B299 *Motion Picture*. Autobiographical sketch. March 1925.

B300 *Movie Classic*. "From a Land Afar—An Adventure in Beauty." February 1937. Promotional piece for *Lost Horizon*.

B301 *Movie Magazine*. "He Wants to Play Cyrano de Bergerac and Cover His Perfect Nose." January 1926.

B302 *Movie-Radio Guide.* "The Movie Front." September 19, 1942. Page 7. See F54.
    Ronald Colman, Greer Garson, Irene Dunne and Hedy Lamarr are pictured en route to Washington, D.C. to sell war bonds as part of the Stars Over America campaign.

B303 *Movies.* Tinted portrait. December 1946.

B304 Mulvey, K. Sketch. *Woman's Home.* March 1940.

B305 Newspaper story, paper unidentified. "Abandoned in Italy is Wife's Divorce Claim." February 25, 1925.
    Thelma Raye Colman claims desertion while Ronald Colman was making a movie in Italy in March of 1924, so she is suing him for separate maintenance, asking for $1000 a month and half of their community property, worth $25,000. Item also states that Colman is under contract to Goldwyn with a starting salary of $1250 a week, rising to $4000 a week in 1928.

B306 ——————-. "Star May Face Wife Today." April 1, 1925.
    Ronald and Thelma Raye Colman are scheduled to meet for a conference through their lawyers "as a prelude to Mrs. Colman's suit for separate maintenance, the preliminary hearing of which comes up April 6." Mr. Colman's lawyer is Edwin J. Loeb. A few nights earlier, the story says, Ronnie met Thelma for the first time since he left her when the two of them showed up with friends at a local playhouse, but left immediately when he recognized Thelma, leaving her feeling humiliated, she said.

B307 ——————. February 8, 1928.
    In an item about Colman visiting his family in England, the reporter states that British film companies "would give nearly anything they can to get him for a picture," but can't because he is under contract to Goldwyn.

B308 ——————. "Great Britain in Film Race, Says Star." April 7, 1928.
    Arriving home from England by train in Pasadena, Ronald Colman comments on England's drive to become a major force in world-wide film production.

B309 ——————. "Ronald Colman at Nice to Consult Divorce Lawyers." October 31, 1931.

B310 ——————. "Ronald Colman in Europe Maps Plans for Divorce." November 2, 1931.

B311 ——————. "Goldwyn Calls Them Off." May 26, 1932.
    Goldwyn cancels production of two planned Colman vehicles, *The Way of the Lancer* and *The Brothers Karamazov.* The former reportedly "because it is politically partisan," the latter because "it may clash with the German 'Karamazov', lately produced but not yet released in England, where Colman is a tremendous favorite."

B312 ——————. "Denies Charge in $2,000,000 Coleman (sic) Suit." November 11, 1932. See B258.
    Acting for Samuel Goldwyn, the law firm of Loeb, Walker and Loeb, denies that Goldwyn pictures characterized Ronald Colman as being "moderately dissipated" when

filming his love scenes, but does affirm that the statement was made.

B313 —————. "Extremely Reticent." December 11, 1932.
Colman says that after finishing *The Masquerader*, he hopes to return to the stage. Those close to him in Hollywood say they feel he will leave for England once shooting is done.

B314 —————. December 30, 1932.
Report about Colman giving a farewell Christmas dinner party for his friends before packing for England. Also that he is determined to take his suit against Goldwyn to court.

B315 —————. "Actor Who Schooled Ronald Colman Dies." December 30, 1932. See F7.
Bob Vallis, formerly a renowned British character actor, dies of starvation in a Brighton tenement. Years earlier, he had coached Colman for the stage and screen.

B316 —————. "Ronald Colman May Quit Films." April 29, 1933.
While visiting Madrid, Colman tells a reporter that he may never make another movie. "He has reached the time, he explained, when happiness in life is the most important and that henceforth he expects to follow his personal desires."

B317 —————. "Mrs. Ronald Colman Held Seriously Ill." May 9, 1933. Thelma Colman is reported "to be seriously ill in a hospital in Nice, France.

B318 —————. Untitled. August 22, 1933.
Report that Colman may have changed his mind about completing his contract with Goldwyn.

B319 *New York Times*. "Ronald Colman Sues Firm for $2,000, 000." From Associated Press. September 14, 1932. 1-26-3. See B239, B257.

B320 —————. "The New Production Set-Up at Fox." November 24, 1940. 9-5-7.
Article announcing that agent Charles Feldman and his clients Ronald Colman, Charles Boyer, Irene Dunne, Lewis Milestone and Anatole Litvak have formed Group Productions in association with 20th Century-Fox. This independent company plans to make movies at Fox using Fox money, star fees being deferred in favor of profit-sharing.

B321 The Nomad. "Ronald Colman Pawned His Coat to Get Food." *Film Pictorial*. December 22, 1934. See F41.
Promotional piece for *Clive of India* with title anecdote.

B322 Parsons, Harriet. *Los Angeles Examiner*. September 22, 1932. 1-11-2. See B200, B201.
Report that Sam Goldwyn has borrowed screenwriter Howard Estabrook from RKO to adapt *The Masquerader*, replacing a hospital bound William Anthony McGuire. (McGuire was recovering from appendix surgery.) Parsons speculates that Colman will drop his lawsuit against Goldwyn. She also finds it curious, in view of the suit, that his role in this new movie "will be a sort of Jekyll-and-Hyde," and that he would take a legal action at all against Goldwyn given his hatred of publicity.

B323 Parsons, Louella O. "Colman-Goldwyn Row Settled by Mutual Consent; Century to Get Actor." *Los Angeles Examiner*. October 17, 1933. 1-13-1. Banner headline story.

The Colman-Goldwyn contract "is to be abrogated by mutual consent...making it possible for Twentieth Century to immediately sign the English actor for a series of screen productions....Undoubtedly, with the new Twentieth Century contract, the lawsuit will be dropped."

B324 —————. "Colman Weds Benita Hume at Montecito." *Los Angeles Examiner*. October 1, 1938. 1-1-4.

B325 —————. Citation for Best Performance of the Month for *A Double Life*. *Cosmopolitan*. March 1948. See F58.

B326 —————. "Ronald Colman Fights Lung Ailment." *Los Angeles Examiner*. March 14, 1957. 1-5-4. See B270.

Colman is reported to be improving from his bout with pneumonitis after three weeks at St. John's Hospital in Santa Barbara under the care of his personal physician, Dr. William Bethea. He is expected to return home in a week. Same day item in Los Angeles Times (B224) states that he had been at St. John's for two weeks, not three.

B327 —————. "Death Takes Ronald Colman" and "Ronald Colman's Death Mourned," obituary titles in morning and evening editions respectively. *Los Angeles Examiner*. May 20, 1958. Front page, page 3 (photos only) and page 6, 1-3. Banner headlines above newspaper title: "Ronald Colman Dies of Pneumonia" (Morning) and "Ronald Colman Death of Pneumonia" (Evening).

First person obituary recapping Colman's career and Parsons' professional relationship with him.

B328 Payne, Norman. "Ronald Colman." *Picturegoer*. November 5, 1938.

B329 *Philadelphia Inquirer*. *Picture Parade* section for October 30, 1938. See B348, F48.

Cover story on *If I Were King*, including full-color cover shot of Colman and Frances Dee in their beautiful Edith Head-designed costumes.

B330 *Photoplay*. "'Beau Geste' Wins Seventh Photoplay Medal of Honor." December 1927. pp. 36-37. See F25, A2.

B331 —————. Color portrait promoting *Random Harvest*. June 1943. Page 46. See F55.

B332 *Picturegoer*. Interview. March 1925. Page 42.

B333 —————. November 1927. Page 30.

B334 —————. Interview. April 1928. Page 10.

B335 —————. July 1930. Page 17.

B336 —————. March 1931. Page 34.

B337 —————. August 1931. Page 8.

B338 —————. Interview. February 8, 1936. Page 16.

B339 —————. February 29, 1936. Page 8.

B340 —————. August 8, 1936. Page 8.

B341 *Picturegoer Weekly*. February 6, 1943. See B331, F55.
Cover story on *Random Harvest*. Cover photo of Colman and Greer Garson.

B342 *Picturegoer: Weekly Supplement*. "Ronald Colman Speaks About Sydney Carton."
September 6, 1935. See F43.
Colman talks about the fulfillment of his pent-up yearning to play Carton, explaining why the character has such a grip on him.

B343 —————. "The Evolution of Colman." Two-page photo spread of 14 photos showing his film roles since 1920. Promotion for *Lost Horizon*, opening in England the next day. April 18, 1937.

B344 *Picture Play*. June (?) 1929. *Bulldog Drummond* promotion.

B345 *Picture Show*. Art supplement. Full-page photo from *The White Sister*, with inserted poem, "Fireside Reverie." January 5, 1924. See F10.

B346 —————. Art supplement. Double-page photo from *The White Sister* titled "The Dawn of Love." June 14, 1924. See F10.

B347 —————. February 10, 1934. Cover story and cover photo of Colman and Elissa Landi in *The Masquerader*. See F39.

B348 —————. *If I Were King* cover showing Colman and Frances Dee. February 11, 1939. See B329, F48.

B349 *Picture Show Annual for 1928*. "Ronald Colman—And Some Lucky Ladies to Whom He Made Love."

B350 *Picture Show Annual for 1929*. "The Perfect Screen Lovers—Ronald Colman and Vilma Banky in scenes from their Five Photoplays." See F21, F26-29.

B351 *Picture Show Annual for 1930*. "The Real Ronald Colman."

B352 Pinkerton, Robert N. "Lady Windermere's Fan." *Classic Images*. July 1992. pp. 20, 22. See B53, F23.
Essay points out Lubitsch's visual touches in support of classic status, spending only two sentences on Colman.

B353 Proctor, Kay. "Why Colman Changed His Mind." *Hollywood*. January 1939.

B354 Pryor, Nancy. "It Looks Like Divorce for Ronald Colman." *Motion Picture*. February 1932. pp. 48-49, 85.
About his marriage to Thelma Raye, his various attempts at divorcing her, and speculation that he might marry actress Thelma Todd, whom he has been dating.

B355 Quirk, James R. "Close-Ups and Long-Shots." *Photoplay*. October 1931. Page 25. See B297, B431.
Quirk apologizes for taking at face value a story fed him by a newspaper writer that "Ronald always insisted on a list of the guests before he accepted a dinner engagement lest some magazine or newspaper writer be there." Calls to eight people who knew Colman well confirmed that he was given a false story. He then called Colman to apologize, which Ronnie took in stride, no hard feelings.

B356 *Radio-Television Life*. "Seen on the Radio Scene" photo section. January 9, 1949. Page 39. See R247.
Photo of Colman with actress Colleen Townsend. Caption: "Distinguished sponsor of Colleen Townsend on NBC's 'Hollywood Star Theater' was Ronald Colman, as handsome and charming as ever—an auspicious radio introduction for the young starlet."

B357 —————. Color cover of Ronald and Benita Colman and feature story titled "Halls of Ivy are Decked with Laughter." Color photo by Elmer Holloway. January 27, 1950. pp. 4-5. See R266-375.
Radio-Television Life was a weekly Southern California magazine similar to and predating *TV Guide* by several years, and which was retitled *TV-Radio Life* in 1951. Ronnie and Benita appeared 3 times on the cover in color, twice during the series' run on radio, once when it switched to television in the fall of 1954.
This unsigned article appeared three weeks after the series' premiere, telling the official story behind the series' creation and how the Colmans were cast. For the real story on the series' genesis and evolution, see pages 180-182.
Otherwise the text is sprightly fun, ending with a capsule list of Colman's career. Also several photos of the Colmans, Don Quinn and director Nat Wolff at work preparing an episode, plus photos of the Colmans and the Quinns in front of their respective homes.

B358 —————. "How Not to Spoil Juliet." July 27, 1951. Pages 3 and 34.
Fluff piece on 7-year-old Juliet and her life as the daughter of famous parents. Discusses her pets, her playtime and reveals that her favorite TV show is *Time for Beany*. Features three photos, two with her mother, Benita, one with both Ronnie and Benita as delighted parents.

B359 *Radio Times*. British magazine. October 20, 1990. Page 40.

B360 Ramsey, Walter. "There Is Privacy in Hollywood!" *Movie Mirror*. April 1935. pp. 33, 86-87.
Colman tells a variety of tales about his recent world travels, in almost all of which he was hounded by rabid, often obnoxious fans. Upon returning to Hollywood, he discovered, ironically, that here, where he was best known, he was able to maintain the privacy that was so dear to him. This was because the film colony was home, where everyone knew him and respected his wishes. Overseas, where he didn't have a home, his privacy was invaded because his movie star presence caused a sensation wherever he went.

B361 Richards, Jeffrey. "Ronald Colman and the Cinema of Empire." *Focus on Film.* September/October 1970. pp. 42-55.

Straightforward biography mixed with an eloquent analysis of Colman's screen character and speculation as to why he became a forgotten star when cult stars like Bogart and Gable were all the rage. He also theorizes about why other film historians haven't given Colman his due as a golden age star. One of his theories is that Colman represented the cinema of empire, that is, his characters were emblematic of British imperialism. This theory is debatable in that Colman made only one movie specifically about British imperialism, *Clive of India.* Otherwise, Richards has a keen and incisive grasp of Colman's art and technique.

B362 Roosevelt, Eleanor. "My Day" syndicated newspaper column in 1937. Mrs. Roosevelt discusses watching *Lost Horizon* at the White House with her husband, the President, and their sons, James and Elliot. See F45.

B363 St. Johns, Adela Rogers. "Ronald Colman—The Hollywood Huntresses' Despair." *Liberty.* February, 1, 1930.

B364 Sanden, Laura J. "Ronald Colman." *Minnesota Daily.* May 30, 1975. pp. 21 and 26. See B116.

Affectingly written article as a tie-in to the Xanadu Theater Ronald Colman film festival that summer, beginning with an eloquent lament for the good old movies that were shown on local Minnesota television in the late 1950s. Rest of piece is nicely done run-down of Colman's career and a look at the movies being shown at the festival.

B365 *Santa Barbara News-Press.* "Colman Heads Group Seeking Television Channel." April 11, 1952.

Announcement that actor Ronald Colman "and a group of local residents are incorporating as the Santa Barbara Broadcasting and Television Corp to apply for a Santa Barbara television channel." Colman will be chairman of the board and Colin Selph, radio station owner, will be president. Others in the plan are Alvin C. Weingand as secretary, Cecil Smith as treasurer, C.H. Jackson and Arthur Marquette as directors.

Two television channels are being allotted to Santa Barbara. The Colman group is applying for one while Harry C. Butcher, radio station owner, is applying for the other.

B366 —————. "Colmans Plan Radio Chest Appeal Tonight." October 18, 1955. See R402.

The Colmans will appear on KTMS Santa Barbara tonight, along with Gladys Seymour, director of the Volunteer Bureau, to make an appeal on behalf of this year's Community Chest drive.

B367 Schaaf, Miv. "The Dethroning of Ronald Colman." *Los Angeles Times.* September 6, 1978. 4-3-1.

Schaaf relates her fantasy of marrying Colman when she was 9, and how other stars paled in comparison. She decided against marrying him because "he had almost a monopoly on sensitivity, would there be any left over for me?" Very nice personal column that probably speaks for the millions of women who grew up swooning over Ronald Colman.

B368 Schallert, Edwin. "Glamour Still High Requisite." *Los Angeles Times.* September 7,

1931. 2-9-6.

Column about stars who have glamour and actors who don't, comparing the screen styles of Garbo, Colman and Dietrich. Schallert compares Colman's serious but charming roles in silent movies with his new lightness in sound films, a quality formerly associated with John Gilbert. "Colman has speeded ahead of Gilbert by becoming a gayer and less restrained type."

B369 —————. "Ronald Colman Lining Up With Twentieth Century." *Los Angeles Times.* October 17, 1933. 2-9-1.

Report that "It's practically as good as set that Ronald Colman will be a Twentieth Century Pictures star...(Goldwyn) is agreeable to the deal, which has been rumored in the last day or two. Colman is expected to return within about a month or six weeks." Money is not mentioned as part of the deal.

B370 —————. Banner headline: "Ronald Colman and Leslie Howard Candidates for 'Lloyd's of London." *Los Angeles Times.* January 9, 1936. 1-9-1.

Writing about Fox's forthcoming production of *Lloyd's of London*, Schallert says that "it is very probable that Ronald Colman will be seen as Lord Nelson, although one also hears the name of Leslie Howard mentioned." The role was finally played by C. Aubrey Smith.

B371 —————. "Meet one contented thespian. Ronald Colman admits career yields happiness." *Los Angeles Times.* September 17, 1944. 3-1-7 and 3-2-4. See F56.

With the release of *Kismet*, Colman discusses his self-contentment while looking back over the 22 years since he made *The White Sister*. He quashes a rumor that he doesn't make more movies for fear of a higher tax bracket and dismisses a report that he wants to become a producer. When it comes to choosing scripts to film, he says, "I am guided entirely by the character of the stories which come to me from the studios." Although he makes fewer movies than ever, he doesn't worry about it and is, in fact, as in-demand as ever for romantic roles. He attributes his longevity to his years with Goldwyn, without mentioning the producer by name.

B372 —————. "Ronald Colman Honored; Oscar for Loretta Young." *Los Angeles Times.* Front page and page two of morning edition for March 21, 1948. Plus group photo with banner headline: "Four Top Winners Pose With Their Oscars." See B125, B391, R119, A8.

Front page and page three of final edition, headlined "Best Actor' Film Oscar Goes to Ronald Colman." Plus photo of Mr. and Mrs. Colman arriving for the ceremony.

Two differently written articles conveying the same information about the previous night's Oscar show.

B373 —————. "Film Pioneers Given Eastman 'George' Honor." *Los Angeles Times.* December 8, 1955. See B158, A18.

Report on George Eastman House tribute to silent movie pioneers of the period 1915-1925.

B374 Schallert, Elza. (Edwin's wife.) "Will Ronald Colman Marry Again?" *Movie Classic.* June 1934.

Frank and sympathetic piece about Colman's unhappy marriage to former actress

Thelma Raye and the divorce she finally granted him in 1934. That divorce, plus the end of his contract with Goldwyn, made him more receptive than usual to an in-depth interview and therefore more open personally .

B375 Schatz, George Evans. "Tribute to a Gentleman." *Classic Film Collector*. Winter 1970.
Passionately personal article by a man to whom Colman has been a spiritual and emotional inspiration since 1937, when he first saw *Lost Horizon*. Schatz provides more insight to the phenomenon of Colman's uniquely mystical romanticism and timeless heroic appeal than most professional film historians.

B376 —————. "The Professional Career of Ronald Colman in All Media. Part One." *Classic Images #132*. June 1986. pp. 58-61.

B377 —————. Ibid, part 2. *Classic Images #133*. July 1986. pp. 22-25.
Elegantly written analysis of Colman's stardom and the timeless emotional impact of that stardom, taking up where his article in *Classic Film Collector* (B375) left off.

B378 Scheuer, Philip K. *Los Angeles Times*. September 2, 1928. 3-9-7 and 3-10-8.
Samuel Goldwyn says that Ronald Colman and Vilma Banky have been separated as a team for their own good, each to be given a chance to develop as a real screen artist. Lots of talk by Goldwyn about the value of Colman and Banky as artists. He also tells Colman-Banky fans that if the right vehicle can be found for them, he would cast them in it.

B379 —————. "Friends Pay High Tribute to Colman." *Los Angeles Times*. May 20, 1958. 1-15-1.
Scheuer quotes Colman's publicist, Joseph Henry Steele, William Powell, Jack Benny, Herbert Marshall and Samuel Goldwyn, and paraphrases Gary Cooper, on the death of their friend, co-star and colleague.

B380 *Screen Book*. Two-page story on Colman as promotion for *The Light That Failed*. February 1940. See F49.

B381 *Screen Guide*. "Murder with a Kiss." April 1948.
Photo spread for *A Double Life*. See F58.

B382 *Screen Romances*. September 1940. Story behind *Lucky Partners*. See B355, F50.

B383 *Script*. November 12, 1938. Cover shot of Colman in armor for *If I Were King*. See F48.

B384 Senate, Richard. "Does the ghost of Ronald Colman haunt Santa Barbara?" *Ventura County & Coast Reporter*. March 11, 1993. Page 20.
Senate tells his readers that Colman once owned the San Ysidro Ranch in Santa Barbara and that his ghost may still haunt its grounds. He also tells of a woman named Barbara who visited Colman's tombstone at Santa Barbara cemetery with its inscription from *The Tempest*. She had a dream that night of meeting and talking with him, waking "with a complete feeling of peace." The ghost stuff is nonsense, but the dream's effect on the woman

perfectly expresses Colman's legacy of personal serenity after watching his best movies.

B385 Service, Faith. (Pseudonym for Gladys Hall.) "I Hope to Marry Again." *Movie Classic*. November 1931.
Debunking of Colman's "Man of Mystery" image. Colman assesses himself as a "cross between a business man and an actor—rather evenly balanced," saying that he does publicity for his movies but hates it. "I have been called a Man of Mystery...I'm passive about it. I certainly do not *feel* like a man of mystery." He also states his belief that marriage is "out-of-date...But until some substitute is found, it must go on—and should go on." Service's point is that the Man of Mystery "doesn't exist. A much more satisfactory person does. Much more *real*."

B386 ————. "Fame is a Thief." *Modern Screen*. February 1935. pp. 44-45, 95-98.
Colman complains vehemently to Service of all the things he has lost personally because he became a famous actor: Friends and privacy and being able to travel without being mobbed by fans, naming a few.

B387 Shaffer, George. *New York Daily News*. August 2, 1932. 30-1; *Chicago Tribune*, August 2, page 13. See F38.
Item on Goldwyn's production of *Cynara* that "they have orders to retain a bit of dialogue in which Miss (Dorothy) Hale, as Clemency Warlock, is supposed to tell her husband, Jim Warlock (Colman): "I don't like too much of that Adolphe Menjou-Ronald Colman kind of thing."

B388 Shaffer, Rosalind. "His Married Life." *Motion Picture*. February 1931.

B389 ————. "Ronald Colman Protests. *Motion Picture*. December 1932. See B393.
Interview with Colman about his libel suit against Goldwyn and why he filed it. He says he was surprised by the publicity given the suit in the media, but that he felt he had to go through with it to protest the libelous things said about him in the Sidney Skolsky column, though he holds Skolsky free from blame.

B390 Sheridan, Michael. "Expectant Father." *Motion Picture*. August 1944. pp. 38-39, 129. See F56.
Perfunctory review of Colman's life and career with the added attraction of news about the upcoming birth of his child. A gimmick to promote his latest movie, *Kismet*.

B391 *Silver Screen*. "We Point With Pride to Ronald Colman." June 1948. Tribute to his Oscar win for *A Double Life*. See B372, R119, F58.

B392 *The Sketch*. Untitled promotional blurb. September 12, 1917. See S8.
The first individual notice given Colman was this cameo item in a British theater magazine noting his role as "The Patient" in *Damaged Goods* at St. Martin's Theatre and recounting his war background. Writer states that Colman is in his early 20s when he was 26. Oval photograph by Carbonora.

B393 Skolsky, Sidney. Tintypes column. *New York Daily News*. Hollywood dateline. August 17, 1932. Page 36. See B416.
The basis for Colman's lawsuit against Goldwyn is this snide hatchet job, written after

Skolsky made Colman nervous watching him play a scene for *I Have Been Faithful* (production title for *Cynara*). Skolsky puts a negative spin on Colman's working habits and quotes a press release claiming that Colman drinks liquor to do his love scenes. He also claims that Colman kicked *Rescue* leading lady Lily Damita in the pants when she "got a bit gay," to which "Miss Damita retaliated by socking him in the jaw." Colman did not want to be interviewed by Skolsky or have him on the set, so this column was clearly Skolsky's revenge, using material given him by Goldwyn publicist Lynn Farnol and his own distortive observations to defame the actor.

B394 Sloan, Lloyd L. "Colman Discusses Effect of Roles on an Actor." *Hollywood Citizen News*. March 11, 1948. See F58.
Colman talks about his performance in *A Double Life* and the problems some actors have living their roles off screen. Colman tells a story on himself about carrying his blind man portrayal in *The Dark Angel* to his performance in *Stella Dallas* until director Henry King called it to his attention.

B395 Smalley, Jack. "Mutiny of the Talayha." *Photoplay*. November 1934. pp. 37, 114-115.
Whimsical article with photos. Smalley purportedly relates from the log of Colman's sloop, the Talayha, a series of mishaps and misadventures (including an abortive attempt at mutiny by first mate, William Powell) that occurred during a yachting cruise headed by "Captain" Colman. Others on the cruise were Warner Baxter and Richard Barthelmess.

B396 —————. "Through India with Colman and Camera." *Hollywood*. April 1935. pp. 42, 73. See F41.
Tongue-in-cheekish report on the filming of the Battle of Plassey sequence for *Clive of India*, starting with elephants being unloaded by trucks in the middle of Santa Monica Boulevard in Hollywood.

B397 Smith, Cecil. "Prize-Winning Radio Show, Halls of Ivy, in Television Debut." *Los Angeles Times*. October 19, 1954. 1-26-1. See TV6.
Column about TV premiere of series, with background on the radio version. Ad for show in bottom middle of page.

B398 Smith, Jack. "'Barbara Worth' still a winner." *Los Angeles Times*. February 3, 1971. 4-1-1. See F26.
Colman fan Smith relates the pleasurable experience of a screening of *The Winning of Barbara Worth* at the Wiltern Theater in Hollywood with Gaylord Carter at the organ.

B399 Smith, R. Dixon. "Colman book recaps career of the 'Perfect Gentleman.'" *St. Paul Dispatch*. January 12, 1978. See B11, B164.
Less a review of Quirk's book on Colman than a reflection on what made Colman unique as a gentlemanly movie star. Smith also cites failings in the book—not writing sufficiently in depth about Colman's unique star magic—that he carried over to his own book in 1991. Except for the three paragraphs devoted to the book, this nicely written essay was reused verbatim in Smith's own book on Colman.

B400 Spensley, Dorothy. "The Rival Nordic Lovers." *Photoplay*. October 1925. pp. 28-29.
Comparison of the backgrounds and screen styles of Colman and John Gilbert.

B401 —————. "Countenancing Mr. Colman. Ronald Is Asked How He Got That Way." *Motion Picture*. February 1929. pp. 50, 109. See F31.

Mainly a puff piece for *The Rescue*. Spensley spends much of it exclaiming over Colman's serious expression. "...why the brooding eyes, the sometime-fretted brow, the eloquent eyebrows, the quizzical, ironic mouth? What soul-cataclysms have wrought that Colman countenance?" Responding to her attempt at insight, Colman spins a rhetorical philosophical ring around her regarding literature and art.

B402 —————. "Exploring Ronald Colman's Unseen Home in Hollywood." *Screen Secrets*. October 1929.

B403 Steele, Joseph Henry. Sketch. *Movie Classic*. February 1937.

B404 —————. "This Is Ronald Colman." *Movieland*. February 1943. pp. 38-42.

Steele accompanied Colman on a bond-selling tour for the Treasury Department, getting to know him very well. The result was this article, a treasure trove of anecdotes and details about Ronald Colman the man: his wit, humor, warmth, generosity, humanity and lack of pretension and affectation. Also mentioned are recordings and films he made on behalf of British War Relief, and a U.S. government-sponsored series of radio shows, none of which I was able to document. Also 11 photos from movies, at home with Benita, and the war bond tour, one of which shows him tending bar at the Crystal Chandelier Bar in Virginia City, Nevada. Steele became Colman's publicist because of this story.

B405 —————. "Portrait of a Casual Sophisticate." *Photoplay*. January 1943. pp. 30-31.

Cumulative portrait of Colman through a recitation of facts, idiosyncracies, likes, dislikes, values, beliefs and ideals gleaned from Steele talking to him for the above article. In fact, much of the material in B404 is reused here. On one point Steele is inaccurate. He says Colman has no hobbies when he had several, including painting, photography, astronomy, gardening and collecting first editions of classic novels.

B406 Strauss, Theodore. "A Rolling Milestone." *New York Times*. December 8, 1940. 10-9-3.

Director Lewis Milestone discusses the formation of Group Productions in league with 20th Century-Fox. Colman is credited with the concept, the idea being to give him and his colleagues creative control of their movies while using Fox's studio and money.

B407 Sullivan, Kay. "Twenty-five Years of Stardom." *Parade*. February 1, 1948. See F58.

Sunday supplement puff piece as a tie-in to the national release of *A Double Life* on February 19.

B408 Taviner, Reginald. "Prince Charming—In Spite of Himself." *Modern Screen*. October 1940. pp. 32-33, 64.

Portrayed as a reticent man who became a movie star in spite of himself when director Henry King drew a moustache on him during a screen test; who initially preferred only the company of his Hollywood Musketeer friends; who became more socially outgoing thanks to wife Benita's gregarious nature; and who has a whimsical side, photographing her in bed at 5 a.m. when the light was just right. Point is that "Ronald Colman, like all creative artists, is a human complexity who responds to just the proper touch."

B409 *Thames Valley Times.* May 21, 1958.
Obituary with anecdote about Colman's father, Charles, as member of the Thames Valley Shakespeare Society, quoting Charles on Ronnie tagging along to rehearsals for *Twelfth Night* in 1903 (it was actually *Much Ado About Nothing*): "The kid's mad on acting."

B410 —————. January 10, 1959.
Report that Colman's British estate is valued at £10,436.

B411 Thomas, Dan. "Handsomest Man in Hollywood." *Every Week.* June 1934. See A4.

B411a Thomas, Tony. The Great Adventure Films. Secaucus, NJ; Citadel Press, 1976. pp. 68-73.
Pictorial essay on *The Prisoner of Zenda.*

B412 *Time.* Review of *A Double Life* and biographical sketch with Colman interview quote for this issue. February 23, 1948. pp. 99-101. See F58.

B413 *Time.* "Kilocycle Prexy." November 6, 1950. See B357.
Article about *The Halls of Ivy.*

B414 Torring, Rex. "Ronald's Painted Moustache." *Photoplay.* August, 1933. pp. 51, 92-93.
The story of how director Henry King "discovered" Colman for the male lead in *The White Sister* despite Ronnie's insistence that he was not photogenic. Torring doesn't say it was famed New York photographer James Abbé who told King to catch Colman's stage performance in *La Tendresse.*

B415 Tully, Jim. "The Luck of the Game." *Picturegoer.* February 29, 1936.

B416 *Variety.* "Skolsky's Yarn Is Cause of Colman's Goldwyn Lawsuit." September 20, 1932. See B393.
Report on the lawsuit, the making of *Cynara*, and the upcoming production of *The Masquerader*. Also reference to Helen Hayes magazine interview (no title or date) in which the actress recalled Colman drinking on the set of *Arrowsmith*. Also says that Goldwyn publicist Lynn Farnol admitted telling Skolsky about Colman drinking and giving him a press release, but that Skolsky distorted the release and that he, Farnol, had apologized to Colman for the slip-up.

B417 Waterbury, Ruth. "Ronald Talks at Last." *Photoplay.* January 1926. pp. 29-30, 121.
Colman talks matter-of-factly about his modest ambitions as an actor and private person, revealing a much deeper emotional and intellectual sensibility than he was able to convey in even his best movies. He comes across as a comfortable man to be with, though not an easy one to know well.

B418 —————. "His Double Life." *Photoplay.* June 1948. pp. 46-47, 113-115. See F58.
Two generations later, Waterbury interviewed Colman a second time. The years between made a profound difference: his life and career could be seen in retrospect, and he was a happily married man in his late 50s with a daughter he adored. This story is about his home life, the making of *A Double Life*, and remaining a British national. Opens with anecdote about Juliet pumping Daddy about his appearances on *Jack Benny*. Charming and

revealing.

B419 *Weekly Variety.* "Star-Load Already, Show Adds Colman." December 28, 1938. 22-3. Announcement that Colman will join Cary Grant and Carole Lombard on the new Kellogg talk-variety show, *The Circle.* See R8-11.

B420 —————. "Tibbett Practically Unrehearsed Kellogg." January 18, 1939. See R8.
    Three-part report. 1) Metropolitan opera star Lawrence Tibbett almost missed being on first episode of *The Circle* because of a snowstorm in Manhattan, and would appear on January 29 show pending flight arrangements. 2) José Iturbi and possibly Noël Coward will guest on the 29th and Tibbett will start appearing on a regular basis starting February 5. 3) Ad agency J. Walter Thompson "is dickering" with Mrs. Franklin D. Roosevelt for the fourth broadcast on February 5.

B421 —————. "Reber Exercises Tongue and Temper; Now Kellogg's 'Circle' Has No Prez." February 15, 1939. 27-1. See R8. Detailed behind-the-scenes report on what made Colman leave *The Circle* after only 4 shows of a 12-show commitment.

B422 —————. "Circle Deflating." February 15, 1939. 27-2.
    Report that Cary Grant and Carole Lombard are threatening to walk off *The Circle* if they don't get better scripts. The Marx Brothers have their own independently hired writers, so they have no complaints.

B423 —————. "Colman, Karloff on OF Agenda." June 17, 1953. See TV5. 36-5.
    Ronald Colman and Boris Karloff will host and act in a series of half-hour shows to be produced by Official Films, which distributes *Four Star Playhouse.* These films will use the staff of Four Star Productions. The Colman series has not been titled.

B424 Whitaker, Alma. "Ronald is Still Discreet." *Los Angeles Times.* December 30, 1928. 3-1-6 and 3-17-6. See F31.
    Promotional interview for *The Rescue.*

B425 —————. "Colman and Chaplin Most Independent Englishmen." *Los Angeles Times.* December 8, 1935. 3-1-6 and 3-3-4.
    Interview with Colman about his career to date, his upcoming movies, his relationship with Goldwyn and his marriage to Thelma. Regarding Goldwyn, he says "I got along with Mr. Goldwyn very well, but I'm happier freelancing." Chaplin is mentioned because he and Colman have in common their zeal for personal and professional independence.

B426 Whitchel, J.A. "Yo Ho! For a Six-Month Vacation." *Silver Screen.* January (?) 1932.

B427 Wood, Edward. "The Brighter Side of the Star Shortage." *Picture Show.* December 1944.

B428 Wood, Thomas. "'Story of Mankind' filmed as a trial." *New York Herald Tribune.* March 10, 1957. 4-4-1. See F69.
    Wood previews a three-hour cut of the movie, detailing the various vignettes and sketches that comprise the story, and mentioning the stars Irwin Allen has cast in the leads and cameo roles. Wood also states that "The guest stars all get $2,500 for their

work—usually, it lasts only one day."

B429 Wooldridge, A.L. "Is Ronald in Love?" *Photoplay*. April, 1932. pp. 20-21, 68.
Gossip about Colman's marriage to and impending divorce from Thelma and speculation on whom he might marry next.

B430 Worth, Sheila. "At Last! Ronnie Talks About Romance." *Movie Mirror*. October 1936. pp. 31, 84-88.
Long article that boils down to gossip interest in his romance with Benita Hume and his disinterest in remarrying. The rest is empty verbiage to fill space.

B431 Zeitlin, Ida. "Rough Sketch of a Gentleman." *Photoplay*. December 1937. pp. 28, 72. See B297, B355.
Fascinating portrait of the private Colman drawn from several other stories. Lot of good material here, but one item sets the record straight on the *Motion Picture Herald* story of 1931 that Colman asked to see a guest list before attending a dinner party. In fact, it was a made-up gossip column item that appears to have been picked up by *Motion Picture Herald* and further embellished. Story ends with anecdote about Colman's largesse with a married couple hitchhiking to San Francisco. He picked them up in Los Angeles, took them to the Santa Barbara train station and paid for their train tickets to San Francisco.

PROGRAM NOTES

B432 Frank, Sam. Program notes for LACMA screening of *Around the World in 80 Days*. Summer of 1977. See F68.

B433 *Nostalgia Digest and Radio Guide*. Benny-Colman cover. February-March 1991. pp. 18-19. Local bi-monthly magazine for the Chicago area. This issue features a February program guide for Chuck Shaden's Saturday radio nostalgia show on WNIB-WNIZ FM 97. He was celebrating Colman's 100th birthday and Benny's 97th birthday. Special guest on February 9, Colman's birthday, was R. Dixon Smith. See page 156 for Benny show background.

B434 Shipman, David. Program notes for a four-day, seven-film Colman tribute at the National Film Theatre in London on December 12, 13, 15 and 16, 1975.

INDEX

This index is keyed to all sections of the book except the Acknowledgments and Chronology. Except for subtopics, numbering is keyed to chapter order. Numbers alone are page numbers for the Introduction, Biography, The Art and Influence of Ronald Colman, A Bibliographical Essay, and cast and credit regulars for *The Circle, Everything for the Boys, Jack Benny, Favorite Story* and *The Halls of Ivy.* Numbers after that are S=Stage Work, F=Filmography, R=Radiography, TV=Television Shows, D=Discography, A=Awards, Honors, and Nominations and B=Annotated Bibliography.

About the Author

SAM FRANK is a film critic, film and television historian, and freelance writer in Los Angeles. He is the author of *Sex in the Movies* (1986) and co-author of *Your Guide to Children's Videotapes & Discs* (1985). His articles, essays, and reviews have appeared in *Magill's Survey of Cinema*, *Magill's Literary Annual*, *The Dictionary of Literary Biography*, *American Cinematographer*, *Twilight Zone*, *Los Angeles*, *Californians*, *Movie Collector's World*, the *New York Times Book Review*, the *Los Angeles Times*, the *Los Angeles Herald Examiner*, the *San Francisco Chronicle*, and many other publications. He is now writing a biography of Ronald Colman and a guidebook to televison shows on home video.

Titles in
Bio-Bibliographies in the Performing Arts

Milos Forman: A Bio-Bibliography
Thomas J. Slater

Kate Smith: A Bio-Bibliography
Michael R. Pitts

Patty Duke: A Bio-Bibliography
Stephen L. Eberly

Carole Lombard: A Bio-Bibliography
Robert D. Matzen

Eva Le Gallienne: A Bio-Bibliography
Robert A. Schanke

Julie Andrews: A Bio-Bibliography
Les Spindle

Richard Widmark: A Bio-Bibliography
Kim Holston

Orson Welles: A Bio-Bibliography
Bret Wood

Ann Sothern: A Bio-Bibliography
Margie Schultz

Alice Faye: A Bio-Bibliography
Barry Rivadue

Jennifer Jones: A Bio-Bibliography
Jeffrey L. Carrier

Cary Grant: A Bio-Bibliography
Beverley Bare Buehrer

Maureen O'Sullivan: A Bio-Bibliography
Connie J. Billips

Ava Gardner: A Bio-Bibliography
Karin J. Fowler

Jean Arthur: A Bio-Bibliography
Arthur Pierce and Douglas Swarthout

Donna Reed: A Bio-Bibliography
Brenda Scott Royce

Gordon MacRae: A Bio-Bibliography
Bruce R. Leiby

Mary Martin: A Bio-Bibliography
Barry Rivadue

Irene Dunne: A Bio-Bibliography
Margie Schultz

Anne Baxter: A Bio-Bibliography
Karin J. Fowler

Tallulah Bankhead: A Bio-Bibliography
Jeffrey L. Carrier

Jessica Tandy: A Bio-Bibliography
Milly S. Barranger

Janet Gaynor: A Bio-Bibliography
Connie Billips

James Stewart: A Bio-Bibliography
Gerard Molyneaux

Joseph Papp: A Bio-Bibliography
Barbara Lee Horn

Henry Fonda: A Bio-Bibliography
Kevin Sweeney

Edwin Booth: A Bio-Bibliography
L. Terry Oggel

Ethel Merman: A Bio-Bibliography
George B. Bryan

Lauren Bacall: A Bio-Bibliography
Brenda Scott Royce

Joseph Chaikin: A Bio-Bibliography
Alex Gildzen and Dimitris Karageorgiou

Richard Burton: A Bio-Bibliography
Tyrone Steverson

Maureen Stapleton: A Bio-Bibliography
Jeannie M. Woods

David Merrick: A Bio-Bibliography
Barbara Lee Horn

Vivien Leigh: A Bio-Bibliography
Cynthia Marylee Molt

Robert Mitchum: A Bio-Bibliography
Jerry Roberts

Agnes Moorehead: A Bio-Bibliography
Lynn Kear

Colleen Dewhurst: A Bio-Bibliography
Barbara Lee Horn

Helen Hayes: A Bio-Bibliography
Donn B. Murphy and Stephen Moore

ISBN 0-313-26433-3

90000>

EAN

9 780313 264337

HARDCOVER BAR CODE